SHOCK TROOPS OF THE CONFEDERACY

The Sharpshooters were the elite troops of the South. Whether screening Stonewall Jackson's flank march at Chancellorsville or leading the last desperate assault at Fort Stedman, they led the Army of Northern Virginia in the advance, protected it at rest, and covered its retreat.

Although little has been written about them (the last book, written by a former sharpshooter, appeared in 1899), they played an important and sometimes pivotal role in many of the battles and campaigns of 1864 and 1865. By the end of the war the sharpshooters were experimenting with tactics that would become standard practice fifty years later. As such they were the predecessors of the special operations soldiers of today.

At the beginning of the Civil War the Army of the Potomac had a marked advantage in sharpshooting and light infantry, something that came as a rude shock to the Confederates during the 1862 Peninsular campaign and at battles like South Mountain. In response the Confederates organized their own corps of specialized light infantry, the Sharpshooters. Building on the ideas of an obscure Alabama colonel, Bristor Gayle, General Robert Rodes organized the first battalion of sharpshooters in his brigade in early 1863, and later in each brigade of his division. Drawn from across the brigade, only the best men were accepted, and any who failed to meet their high standards were sent back to their regiments. All sharpshooters underwent rigorous training in marksmanship and skirmish drill.

In early 1864 General Lee adopted the concept for the entire Army of Northern Virginia, directing each infantry brigade to field a sharpshooter battalion. Rodes then combined these battalions into a "demi-brigade" for his division. These units found ready employment in the Overland campaign, in the trenches of Petersburg, and in the fast-moving Shenandoah campaign of 1864. Commanders at Petersburg used them to scout and capture prisoners, and the sharpshooters did much of the fighting in the endless skirmishes of Jubal Early's Valley campaign. As the numbers and quality of the Confederate infantry continued to decline late in the war, the burden of combat fell more and more on the elite sharpshooter battalions.

Although most people think of Berdan's two regiments when the subject of Civil War sharpshooters comes up, the Confederate sharpshooter battalions had a far greater effect on the outcome of the conflict. Later in the war, in response to the Confederate dominance of the skirmish line, the Federals began to organize their own sharpshooter units at division level, though they never adopted an army-wide system.

Making extensive use of unpublished source material, *Shock Troops of the Confederacy* tells the story of the development of the Army of Northern Virginia's sharpshooter battalions, the weapons they used, how they trained with them, and their tactical use on the battlefield. It also tells the human story of the sharpshooters themselves, who describe in their own words what it was like to be in the thick of battle, on the skirmish line, and at their lonely picket posts.

Shock Troops
of the Confederacy

the sharpshooter battalions
of the Army of Northern Virginia

FRED L. RAY

CFS Press

FIRST EDITION

ISBN-13: 978-0-9649585-9-3
ISBN-10: 0-9649585-9-3

LCCN: 2005910213

Cover painting: "Skirmishing" by Keith Rocco, Tradition Studios.

Back cover photograph: "Sharp Shooter's Badge" (worn by Henry A. Wise,
Second Maryland Infantry, Archer's brigade, Army of Northern Virginia)
Dean Nelson/Maryland Historical Society.

All maps not otherwise credited by Fred Ray.
Book and cover design by Randal Pride.
Book typefaces: Berkeley and Myriad.

Publisher's Cataloging-in-Publication Data

Ray, Fred L.

Shock troops of the Confederacy : the sharpshooter battalions of the
Army of Northern Virginia / Fred L. Ray.—1st ed.—Asheville, NC :
CFS Press, c2006.

    p. ; cm.

    ISBN-13: 978-0-9649585-9-3

    ISBN-10: 0-9649585-9-3

    Includes bibliographical references and index.

    1. Confederate States of America. Army—History.
2. United States—History—Civil War, 1861-1865—Regimental
histories. 3. Shooters of firearms—United States History
4. Virginia—History—Civil War, 1861-1865—Regimental histories.
5. Sharpshooting (Military science)—History. I. Title.

E581.4 .R39 2006   2005910213

973.7/455--dc22   0601

To

Lieutenant Jason O. Patton,

Sharpshooter

"After twenty-five years of peace, many of the important engagements of the late war are but vaguely understood by the general reader. The historian collects the facts of battles as best he can from the reports of commanding officers; but those reports convey but little of the details of the real fighting, and the importance of movements or the general results of campaigns."

– A veteran of the 122nd New York, 1890

CONTENTS

List of Illustrations   viii

Foreword by Robert K. Krick   x

Preface   xiv

Prologue   xviii

1   **Antecedents**   1
"When opposed to riflemen, it is the bravest who fall"

2   **American Riflemen**   6
"The wickedest corps in the Army"

3   **Zouaves**   14
"The bayonet will always be the queen of weapons"

4   **Beginning**   21
"It was the province of the sharp shooter to shoot some body"

5   **Seven Pines, Gaines's Mill and South Mountain**   32
"We skedadle & halt, fight & then skedadle again"

6   **Winter at Fredericksburg**   42
"We are always in the front of the brigade"

7   **Chancellorsville**   52
"It is a post of honor, not one of ease"

8   **Gettysburg**   62
"The mere raising of my hand would be the signal for a dozen Yankees to fire at me"

9   **Manassas Gap**   73
"Every shot took effect"

10   **Winter 1863-64**   80
"They were good soldiers, whoever they were"

11   **Preparing for 1864**   93
"The best men in the company"

12   **The Wilderness**   99
       "For God's sake go up and stop them"

13   **Spotsylvania**   108
       "The hottest place I was ever in"

14   **The North Anna and Cold Harbor**   127
       "Honor is nothing more than a puff of wind"

15   **Monocacy and Fort Stevens**   149
       "A pretty stiff picket line"

16   **Charles Town, Winchester, and Fisher's Hill**   172
       "Take charge of the boys, do the best you can and give the yanks Hell"

17   **Cedar Creek**   193
       "It must be confessed that we bought our victory at a dear rate"

18   **Petersburg**   207
       "They done the thing up brown and deserve credit for it"

19   **Assault on Hare's Hill**   224
       "Knock down and drag out"

20   **Fort Stedman**   241
       "It was better to attack than be attacked"

21   **Decision at Petersburg**   252
       "These men will fight"

22   **Weapons and Uniforms**   270

23   **Confederate Sharpshooters in the West**   286

24   **The Opposition**   294
       Skirmishers and Sharpshooters of the Army of the Potomac

25   **The Open Order**   315
       The Boer War to WWI

26   **Evaluating the Sharpshooters**   328

       Appendixes   334
          A. Testing the Sharpshooters' Weapons
          B. Orders Issued by the Confederates Pertaining to the Sharpshooters
          C. The Assault on Fort Stedman: Numbers and organization

       Bibliography   353
       Abbreviations   367
       Notes   368
       Index   397

LIST OF ILLUSTRATIONS

Eighteenth century brigade formation	2	Map of the Mine Run campaign	85
American rifleman, 1st Virginia 1775	7	A Union column passes through Locust Grove	87
Rifleman of the 1st US Rifle Regiment, 1814	9	Map of the action at Robertson's Tavern	88
French *Chasseur* and *Zouave*, 1853	16	The Confederate defenses at Mine Run	90
William Hardee, Henry Heth, and Cadmus Wilcox	17	Rifle training from Hardee's *Tactics*	94
Infantry brigade in line of battle	22	Map of The Wilderness	103
Skirmishers in open order	23	Map of Laurel Hill	109
Picket duty	24	Confederate defenses at Laurel Hill	111
Action on the skirmish line	27	A rifle pit as described by Berry Benson	114
Union sharpshooter	28	Confederate sharpshooter	117
Confederate riflemen early in the war	29	Major General John Sedgwick	118
Robert E. Rodes	30	Fighting at the Bloody Angle	121
Map of the vicinity of Boonsboro and Sharpsburg	35	Map of Spotsylvania Court House	122
Map of Boonsboro or South Mountain	36	Map of the North Anna	129
Map of Sharpsburg or Antietam	41	Confederate entrenchments at Chesterfield bridge	133
Map of Northern Virginia	44	Map of Chesterfield bridge	135
Judging distance drill	47	Map of Doswell House	137
Map of Jackson's flank march at Chancellorsville	53	Skirmish line	140
General Thomas J. "Stonewall" Jackson	54	Union Coehorn mortars in action	142
The Union XI Corps struggles to repel Jackson's attack	55	Map of Stone bridge	151
Map of Gettysburg and vicinity	63	Map of Monocacy	153
Map of the action at Oak Ridge	64	Map of the defenses of Washington, 1864	156
Rebel sharpshooters in the houses of Gettysburg	69	Confederate assault on Ft. Stevens, July 11, 1864	158
Map of Manassas Gap	75	Map of the action at Fort Stevens, July 11, 1864	159
Skirmishing in Virginia	78	A heavy Parrot rifle at Ft. Stevens	160
Union cavalry pickets	82	President Lincoln at Fort Stevens	163
Map of Bristoe Station	83	Map of the action at Fort Stevens, July 12, 1864	166

Scene of the fighting near Fort Stevens 169

Jubal Early and Philip Sheridan 173

Map of Charles Town 175

Map of Third Winchester 183

Rickett's division advances on Rodes's position 186

Map of the Union breakthrough at Winchester 187

Cavalry charge at Winchester 188

Map of Fisher's Hill 190

The Federals struggle to resist Gordon's attack 194

Map of Gordon's attack at Cedar Creek 195

Map of Confederate assaults on Cemetery Hill 196

Map of Sheridan's counterattack 199

General Stephen Dodson Ramseur 200

The Confederate line of battle 205

Map of Petersburg 1864-65 208-209

Union sharpshooters at Petersburg 211

Map of Major Wooten's "seine hauling" 213

The Confederate assault on the Crater 215

Map of Captain Dunlop's picket line raid 217

Trading during a lull at Petersburg 220

Map of Fort Stedman, 4 a.m. March 25, 1865 225

General John B. Gordon 227

Map of the fight for Fort Stedman 233

Map of the fight for Battery IX 238

Map of the Confederate penetration 239

Map of Hartranft's first counterattack 242

General John F. Hartranft 243

Map of the attack on Fort Haskell 244

Map of the final Union attack on Fort Stedman 247

Map of the action at McIlwaine's Hill 255

Map of VI Corps deployment for attack 257

Map of VI Corps breakthrough, April 2, 1865 260

Map of Sutherland's Station 265

Delvigne and Thouvenin systems 271

Minié projectiles 271

Springfield 1861 Rifle-musket 273

Davidson rifle telescope 275

Whitworth ammunition 276

Sharps rifle and ammunition 279

Spencer rifle 281

Target rifle and bullet starter 283

General Patrick Cleburne 286

Longstreet's sharpshooters attacking a wagon train 288

General Earl Van Dorn 292

Berdan's Sharpshooters at practice 296

Soldiers after a truce 301

Pennsylvania Bucktails 307

148th Pennsylvania assaults a Rebel fort 312

Post of Honor: A Sharpshooters Gallery facing page 206

PHOTOGRAPHS

page 1 – Eugene Blackford, Robert Rodes, Ben Powell, William S. Dunlop.

page 2 – Marion Hill Fitzpatrick, Berry Benson, Lewis and James Branscomb

page 3 – Hamilton Brown, Thomas Boone, Edwin Osborne, William E. Stitt

page 4 – Alexander Beattie, Aldace Walker, Samuel Carroll, Jerry Brown

page 5 – Hiram Berdan, John Sedgwick, Homer Stoughton, Napoleon McLaughlen

page 6 – Fort Stevens, fraises at Fort Sedgwick, Zouaves

page 7 – Enfield, Whitworth, Sharps, and Morgan target rifles; sharpshooter badge

page 8 – Interior of Fort Stedman, John Gordon, advanced picket post at Petersburg, Confederate chevaux-de-frise

FOREWORD

The American war of the 1860s often has been called the last of the old wars, and the first of the new. This first modern war employed railroads, ironclad warships, primitive aerial reconnaissance, telegraphic communications to the front, battlefield photography, universal conscription, and rifled muskets—most especially rifled muskets.

The pervasive revolution in military operations effected by the availability of rifled muskets during the American Civil War wrought fundamental changes in the way soldiers functioned on battlefields. Men had been firing rifled long arms at foes for a century before that war. Their weapons, however, had required slow and methodical loading of small-caliber bullets, and otherwise had proved inapt for most battlefield settings. The popular concept of sturdy American yeomen revolutionaries using rifles against foolish British musketeers in the 1770s bears little relation to actual combat events.

The advent of rapid muzzle-loading shoulder arms that fired large-caliber projectiles, thanks to a bullet that expanded at the base to pick up the rifling grooves, turned every Civil War soldier into a rifleman, once ordnance supply caught up with demand. Adapting to that profound change in battlefield circumstances challenged leaders on both sides. Before the war's end, Northern soldiers had access to arms of yet another technological generation: repeating weapons, some of them breechloading.

Military sluggishness in reacting to change is almost axiomatic—indeed humans in all endeavors tend to adapt only slowly. "Changes in tactics have...taken place after changes in weapons," wrote renowned military theorist Alfred Thayer Mahan (1840-1914), "but the interval between such changes has been unduly long. An improvement of weapons is due to the energy of one or two men, while changes in tactics have to overcome the inertia of a conservative class."

How did the leaders of American armies respond to the sea change in weaponry? Conventional wisdom long has held that they ignored it, clinging to beloved Napoleonic tenets and generating needless bloodbaths in consequence. In fact, as this book demonstrates in detail, effective tactical innovations in reaction to rifled arms began early in the war and continued steadily through to the end.

Fred Ray focuses in this important study on the Army of Northern Virginia, though his grasp extends across the lines and both backward and forward in historical time. Lee's readiness to reconfigure his units by the addition of light-infantry battalions has received virtually no attention heretofore. The army commander's widely quoted hesitance about indiscriminate infantry fire seems to suggest a leader loath to adjust to technological verities. "What we want is a fire-arm that cannot be loaded without a certain loss of time," Lee said, "so that a man learns to appreciate the importance of his fire, and never fires without being sure of obtaining a result." That caveat, evidently aimed at repeating weapons rather than rifled muskets, surely was driven in part by concern for the always precarious question of Confederate ammunition supply.

The need for adept skirmishers, always requisite in land warfare, multiplied manifold when rifles extended defenders' reach by hundreds of yards. Early war fiascoes proved the point emphatically. Federal General Julius Stahel butchered a New York regiment at Cross Keys in June 1862 when he sent it forward into a murderous deadfall without benefit of any advance guard whatsoever. Confederate General Alfred Iverson, despite the evidence afforded by two years of war, did the same thing on a larger scale at Gettysburg, with dire consequences for hundreds of North Carolina infantrymen unfortunate enough to fall under his maladroit control. On the opposite face of the adaptive curve, Lee himself deftly used a swarm of skirmishers at Chancellorsville on May 2, 1863, to bewilder the enemy opposite him while General Thomas J. "Stonewall" Jackson clandestinely marched a dozen miles to get behind the Federal army.

To a modern reader, a "sharpshooter" sounds like a sniper, firing from covert at specific, long-range targets. In the lexicon of the Civil War era, as Ray makes abundantly clear, "sharpshooters" were light infantrymen designated and trained for duty as advance guards, pickets, scouts, and skirmishers. Accurate marksmanship certainly constituted a useful element of such a fellow's arsenal, but beyond that attribute, the modern implication bears little resemblance to the 19th-century usage. Sir Garnet Wolseley (1833-1913), who visited North America and met both Lee and Jackson in the winter after Fredericksburg, understood the concept: "The most arduous, while at the same time the most important duties that devolve upon soldiers in the field are those of outposts."

The universal hunger of military commanders for information on enemy positions and intentions suffered in the face of rifle fire. Approaching an enemy for reconnaissance suddenly became dramatically more difficult, and less accurate, than it had been in the smoothbore era. The oft-cited oracle Jomini, in his seminal *Precis de l'Art de la Guerre* (1838), wondered aptly "How can any man say what he should do himself if he is ignorant what his adversary is about?" More prosaically (and more famously) Arthur Wellesley (the Duke of Wellington), grumbled: "I have been passing my life in guessing what I might meet with beyond the next hill, or round the next corner." The sharpshooter battalions of the Army of Northern Virginia attempted to answer that need for information as part of their job description.

Fred Ray adroitly tells the story of those battalions here for the first time, based on a very strong range of primary material. The sources include some thirty manuscript collections, scores of arcane articles and narratives, and numerous obscure contemporary Southern newspapers.

A quarter-century ago, in describing a fine old book about late-war sharpshooter battalions, written by a veteran of one of them, I innocently wrote of the battalions' organization before the Wilderness Campaign as an innovation in response to the hard experience of three years in the laboratory of war. In truth, the evidence shows that by that date some such battalions had been in operation for nearly two years.

At the same time that light-infantry battalions came into their own, rifled muskets dictated another result: they drove defenders behind fortifications of earth and wood. Men scornful of digging dirt in 1862 were scurrying to throw up earthworks every time they halted on the march by 1864. Shelter for infantry evolved relentlessly, to the point that a World War I officer said accurately if resignedly, "When all is said and done, the war was mainly a matter of holes and ditches." The pendulum that swung toward defensive power made light-infantry detachments steadily more important.

Ray ably sets the stage for the sharpshooter battalions by charting the roots of the function back into the 18th century, and even earlier, in his opening chapters. He also traces, in one chapter apiece, the parallel efforts across the lines in the Union establishment, and in the Confederacy's other armies. Finally, in a brief but well-crafted chapter, Ray carries the story through Boer country and to the era of breakthroughs by armored, mechanized tanks at Cambrai in the fall of 1917.

The men who made up Fred Ray's sharpshooter battalions really did become the *Shock Troops of the Confederacy*. In his *Maxims of War*, Napoleon insisted that "an advance guard should consist of picked troops, and…should be selected for their respective capabilities and knowledge." Ray describes the attempts of Army of Northern Virginia officers to pick such troops, train them, and employ them to best effect on battlefields raked by long-range infantry weapons.

Shock Troops unveils the story, as its subtitle suggests, of all of ...*The Sharpshooter Battalions of the Army of Northern Virginia*. An uncommonly important and useful source, though, steers author Ray toward special attention concentrated on one of the battalions. Major Eugene Blackford, a native of Fredericksburg, Virginia, but an officer in the 5th Alabama Infantry, led a sharpshooter battalion in the sterling division commanded by General Robert E. Rodes. I have suggested (in *The Smoothbore Volley that Doomed the Confederacy* [LSU Press, 2002]) that Rodes deserves consideration as perhaps the best division commander in Lee's Army. The light-infantry force formed by Blackford in Rodes's division reflects that quality, and makes a fitting study as a prototype. Blackford's rich primary source supplies invaluable detail on the subject.

In his Preface, author Ray acknowledges the shrinking range of important but unexplored Civil War subjects—the difficulty of finding "something really new on the Civil War." In this work on the evolution of sharpshooter battalions, he has achieved precisely that result.

Robert K. Krick
Fredericksburg, Virginia
September 2004

PREFACE

This book began as a family history project. When my research got back to the Civil War era I found that one of my great-grandfathers, Lieutenant Jason Patton, had commanded a Confederate sharpshooter company. This, in turn, led to an investigation of the sharpshooters themselves. I found little about them in tactical studies and only a few references scattered in unit histories. Yet it was undeniable that they had played an important, sometimes pivotal, role in many campaigns. Indeed the Confederates had, as in so many areas, moved the military art far forward, and were trying things that would become standard tactical practice fifty years later. The War Between the States has been aptly called the first modern war, and nowhere was this more true in the creation and use of the sharpshooter battalions. Although most people think of Berdan's Sharpshooters when the subject comes up (a circumstance that would no doubt greatly please the shade of Hiram Berdan), the Confederate sharpshooter battalions had a far greater effect on the outcome of the war. Unfortunately this Southern *corps d'elite* has received only a passing mention from historians—certainly nothing like the credit they deserve.

Several documents have surfaced in the last few years that materially helped my inquiries into the initial organization of the sharpshooters, but by far the most useful by far was Eugene Blackford's diary/memoir, which had been languishing in a boy's school where he taught after the war until Butch Maisel rescued it from oblivion. Blackford began the diary before the war, stopped shortly after it began, then started work on it again after the war and evidently toyed with the idea of publishing it. Unfortunately, he abandoned the project half-finished, and the narrative ends in early 1864. Still, Blackford covers the founding and initial training of the sharpshooters in considerable detail, and definitively credits Robert Rodes with the idea.

Historian Robert K. Krick rates Rodes as Lee's best division commander, and based on this new evidence he rates highly as a tactical innovator as well.

This book is not an exhaustive history of all sharpshooter units or their actions, and it deals primarily with the Army of Northern Virginia. Although the Army of Tennessee did field some very effective sharpshooter units (especially those of Cleburne's division) they were never organized army-wide as they were in Virginia. Still, in order to fully understand the historical context of the sharpshooter battalions, I needed to begin with the first use of light infantry in Europe in the 1750s, look at the use of riflemen in the Napoleonic Wars, then research obscure American units like the U.S. Rifle Regiment and the Regiment of U.S. Voltigeurs and Foot Riflemen. After the Civil War I continued to follow the thread of light infantry and the open order to the Boer War and finally into the trenches of World War I. Here the Germans independently adopted tactics very similar to those pioneered by the Confederates half a century earlier that led in turn to the blitzkriegs of WWII.

Yet for all their effectiveness, the sharpshooters were virtually forgotten after the war. Men tended to write about famous individuals, their own regiments, or the great battles rather than about composite units. Thus when ex-Confederate major W.S. Dunlop finally did write a book about the sharpshooters in 1899 he aptly subtitled it "a story of Southern valor that has never been told." The same can be said for modern historians, who tend to think of sharpshooters either as snipers in the modern sense or as skirmishers.

To understand the Southern sharpshooters one needs to know something about their opponents also, hence the chapter on Union sharpshooters. While researching it I also found some Federal sharpshooter units that had almost escaped the historical record. Evidently formed in response to the Confederate battalions, they played an important part in several late war battles.

Thanks to Robert K. and Robert E. L. Krick (*Père et Fils*), Rob Wynstra, Scott Sherlock, Scott Patchan, Lee Sherrill; Joe Bilby and Bill Adams, who generously shared their vast knowledge of nineteenth century firearms and equipment; Chris Calkins and Bill Wyrick at Petersburg National Battlefield, Jeffry Wert, Dr. Frank Cooling for his help in understanding what went on around Fort Stevens; Wally Owen from the Fort Ward Museum and Historic Park; Gloria Swift and Gail Stevens at Monocacy National Battlefield for making available their research at the Huntington Library; Art Bergeron, Gary Yee, and especially Butch Maisel, who was willing to share Eugene Blackford's diary/memoir with me. Thanks also to the patient staffs of the Maryland Historical Society in Baltimore, the Alabama and Georgia archives, and the US Army Military History Institute at Carlisle, PA, who provided access to Eugene Blackford's letters and other papers, as well as the reference librarians at the Pack Library here in Asheville, who responded to numerous requests for obscure books about the Civil War.

Neither the book or its accompanying web site (www.cssharpshooters. com) would be complete without photographs, especially of the sharpshooters themselves. Thanks to John Everett for providing the photo of Ben Powell, Marion Hodges for the likeness of Marion Hill Fitzpatrick, and Sam Hodges and Jeffry C. Lowe for transcribing and publishing his letters. Howard McManus generously allowed me to use Robert Rodes's *carte de visite* photo, and Frank Chappell contributed photos of sharpshooters James and Lewis Branscomb.

As for equipment, Dean Nelson supplied a photo of the sharpshooter's badge at the Maryland Historical Society, and Les Jensen of the United States Military Academy museum sent photos of several period rifles. Special thanks to artist and historian Jack Coggins for permission to use illustrations from his classic *Arms and Equipment of the Civil War*.

Thanks also to Sylvia Frank Rodrigue for her patient editing, but I should emphasize that the responsibility for all mistakes is mine.

It's worthwhile to say a word about other sources also.

Confederate administrative records were never that good even when regularly kept, and many were lost during the war or scattered after it. Thus they tend to be fragmentary at best, and so this invariably requires a certain amount of speculation on the part of historians. Readers should keep this in mind throughout the book, as I will not constantly belabor the point (and bore the reader) by repeating "that while sources are fragmentary and often contradictory, I think that … ." One should also keep in mind that although the Confederacy, like any military system, established general rules and organizations, these were Southerners and so there were *always* exceptions. An example is that a regiment have ten companies. This was certainly true in a general sense, yet one can readily cite examples of regiments like the Sixth Alabama and Palmetto Sharpshooters that had twelve.

Since I have by design concentrated on the sharpshooters and their activities, it may seem when reading this that they won battles all by themselves. The continued emphasis on the sharpshooters does not mean that other troops were inactive—indeed, the decisive fighting (as at Monocacy) often took place on other parts of the field. I have assumed that the reader has some familiarity with these battles, and recommend consulting the general works referred to herein in case of doubt.

One final caveat to those already mentioned is the wide usage of the word sharpshooter in the 19th Century, a term derived from the German *scharfshutzen* that considerably predates the first rifle by American arms maker Christian Sharps in 1850. Today we distinguish between a sniper, a soldier armed with a long-range rifle who shoots from a concealed position, and a light infantryman, who performs the missions of scouting, skirmishing, and infiltrating enemy positions. The soldiers of the day observed no such distinction and used the term sharpshooter for both. To further muddy the waters, many used sharpshooter and skirmisher interchangeably. As with the records, I have tried to sift through these terms as best I can and describe them in as accurate a way as possible.

PROLOGUE

Assault at Cedar Creek

Yankee captain James McKnight's regular army battery had already been over-run once that foggy October morning at Cedar Creek, losing a gun and several men. Now, as part of General George Getty's division, they waited on a low hill outside Middletown, Virginia, as another Rebel attack materialized out of the mist. The gunners gaped at the Confederate skirmishers loping wolf-like up the hill, howling their trademark yell. "I could not believe they were actually going to close with us," said one, "until the men on the remaining gun of the left section abandoned it and retreated toward the old graveyard wall. Their front line was not in order, but there was an officer leading them, and I distinctly heard him shout: 'Rally on the Battery! Rally on the Battery!'" The Yankee gunners managed to fire off a last shot of double canister, but "as the Rebel veterans understood this kind of business they 'opened out' so that the charge did not hit any of them." In a moment the Southerners fell in amongst the gunners, as one recalled, "amid smoke, fog, wreck, yells, clash and confusion … man to man, hand to hand, with bayonet and musket butt on their side and revolvers, ram-mers, and hand spikes on ours!"

The gunners' confusion is understandable. Skirmishers were simply not sup-posed to close with a strongly defended enemy position, much less assault it. They did not know that they faced Ramseur's Division's elite Corps of Sharp-shooters—the shock troops of the Confederacy. They were, as one former member put it, "the spike-head of Toledo steel" that led both the advance and retreat of the army. The sharpshooters served not only as skirmishers in the usual sense, but instead as powerful combat units in their own right. As a tacti-cal innovation, the Confederate sharpshooters were years ahead of their time, presaging both the "open order" of the late-nineteenth century and the German Stosstruppen of World War I.

1

Antecedents

"When opposed to riflemen, it is the bravest who fall"

For two thousand years European infantry, from the Greek phalanx to the linear formations of the nineteenth century, fought virtually shoulder to shoulder in potent but rather ponderous formations that had to move slowly in order to maintain their alignment. This remained true even after the introduction of firearms, and for the period this book covers—roughly the years 1740-1918—the "line of battle" continued to dominate land warfare.

European armies also fielded light troops since ancient times. Unlike the infantry of the line, these soldiers fought in a more open order. Their duties, generally, were similar to those of the cavalry: to warn, protect and screen the main body, while at the same time scouting and harassing the other side's movements. Along with the light cavalry they also fought the *petite guerre*—the secondary but vital war of outposts, pickets, ambushes and raids. They could be thrown out quickly for skirmishing and flank protection and were especially effective in broken or wooded terrain, which tended to disorder a line of battle. The light troops had their own vulnerabilities, however. An open order meant reduced firepower, which in turn meant that they could not stand against a line of battle in open country and were susceptible to being ridden down by cavalry.

Although light troops fell out of favor in the seventeenth century, commanders rediscovered them in the eighteenth. The Austro-Hungarians introduced light semi-regular Croat and Pandour *grenzer* (borderers) units from their Balkan borderlands to their wars with Frederick the Great. Although the Prussian king professed to despise them as bandits and cutthroats (which they certainly were), he had to change his mind after they were instrumental in costing him the battle of Kolin in 1757. To oppose them he raised his own light regiments, and since he recruited those soldiers from woodsmen, gamekeepers, and the like, they were called *jägers* (hunters). These men, chosen for their initiative and self-reliance, carried the short, heavy rifles that had been developed for hunting in the dense forests of central Europe. The *jägers* proved so successful that both the Austrians and Russians copied the concept, and, as the idea spread, nearly all European armies began to field substantial bodies of light infantry.

The French, as always, addressed the concept somewhat differently. In pre-Revolutionary times the royal army had employed units of light infantry and cavalry *chasseurs* (hunters), and during the Republican period the army supplemented them with regiments of *infanterie légér* (light infantry). There was also a long tradition in France and the low counties of the *franc-tireur* (free shooter), a guerilla fighter similar to the Balkan *grenzer* or the American Minuteman, who harassed regular formations from the bush. After the revolution the new French Republic suddenly found itself without a professional army and under attack by surrounding royalist powers. French leaders responded with the first universal conscription, the *levée en masse*, in which all able-bodied male citizens were drafted into the military. A large but untrained army resulted from the draft, and French generals tried to compensate for their troops' lack of drill by employing these hastily raised fighters in dense swarms. The *tirailleurs* (often translated as sharpshooters, even though they used smoothbore muskets) simply swamped the linear formations of their opponents. Quite effective in the broken terrain of the low countries but rather vulnerable on open ground, the *tirailleurs* kept the royalists at bay until the army could be organized on a more regular basis.

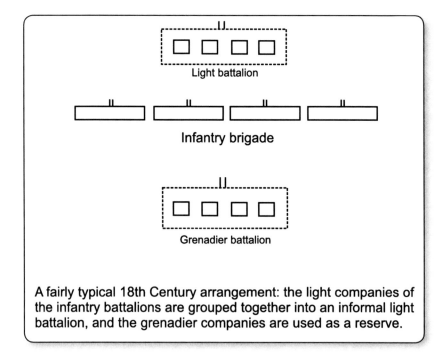

Light battalion

Infantry brigade

Grenadier battalion

A fairly typical 18th Century arrangement: the light companies of the infantry battalions are grouped together into an informal light battalion, and the grenadier companies are used as a reserve.

By Napoleon's time the basic tactical field unit for most European armies was the eight- to ten-company battalion. The regiment, by contrast, was primarily an administrative unit. The right flank company, which occupied the so-called post of honor, was composed of picked men who usually bore an honorific title like grenadiers. The left flank company, the designated light company, received special training as skirmishers. In the French Army these elite light troops, called *voltigeurs* (springers or leapers) wore distinctive yellow uniform facings and epaulettes. Commanders often combined the light companies of brigades and even divisions into larger units to sweep away enemy skirmishers in preparation for an assault by a heavy column of line infantry. Grenadiers and light troops were often grouped together into elite semi-permanent battalions. Since French tactical doctrine emphasized the offensive, their commanders did not envision using *voltigeurs* as marksmen. Instead, they issued them smoothbore muskets on the theory that fast-moving assault troops did not have time for aimed fire.

The British began using light troops about the same time as other European armies, but they generally followed the practices of the Germans, with whom they were allied against the French for most of the eighteenth century. During the Revolutionary War the British had a distinctly unpleasant experience with American riflemen, who operated in a manner similar to the continental *tirailleur*. As with the French, each British battalion had a light infantry company, and commanders often grouped the light infantry together with others from the brigade into an informal light battalion. For instance, when Lord Howe began his campaign at New York in 1776, he combined his grenadier companies (the right-flank company of each battalion) into a grenadier battalion, and the light companies (the left-flank companies) into a light infantry corps under the command of Lieutenant Colonel Thomas Musgrave. These light infantrymen were armed not with rifles but with smoothbore muskets, which put them at a disadvantage at longer ranges against American riflemen. The British light infantry generally bested the Yankees in close fights, however, since American rifles had a slow rate of fire and could not take a bayonet. To answer to the American riflemen the British added Hessian *jägers* to their forces, issued German rifles to some of their own men, and employed a small corps of riflemen under Captain Patrick Ferguson, using his advanced breech-loading rifle. As a result of its experiences in North America, in 1797 the British Army raised its first all-rifle unit, the Fifth Battalion, 60th Royal Americans. Most of its initial members were former German *jägers*.[1]

Integrating rifles and muskets was not easy. Although the rifle was more accurate and had an effective range roughly twice that of a musket, it was more delicate and had a considerably slower rate of fire. One of the major reasons for this was the buildup of residue from the black powder. To make the round grip the rifling tightly, the rifleman had to place a greased cloth or leather patch around the ball. This snug fit made for slower loading, even in the best of circumstances, and as the fouling worsened it became progressively more difficult to force the ball down the barrel. Some armies actually provided a small mallet for the rifleman to tap it down. In contrast, a smoothbore musket ball could be made considerably smaller than the bore (e.g. a .69 caliber musket might have a .65-inch ball). This made loading quick and easy, even after prolonged firing, although muzzle velocity and accuracy suffered greatly from all that rattling around in the bore. Hence a good musketeer could get three shots off in about a minute, which was about the time it took to for a rifleman to load and fire once. This put the latter at a grave disadvantage in a standup fight on the line of battle.

Riflemen excelled, however, at picking off officers and gun crews, and generally at harassing a line of battle from cover. Further, they exercised a powerful psychological effect. As a British officer in a rifle regiment observed:

> When opposed to riflemen, it is the bravest who fall, for it is the bravest who expose themselves most, and thus become most conspicuous. The Officers of our own army in Holland obtained this experience, and in several instances found it necessary to change their hats, and assimilate themselves to the private men. That powerful influence on the mind also, which prevails in a variety of ways in an army, has its full effect in that by which this species of force is employed, as well as that against which it is directed. It has been readily confessed to the writer by old soldiers, that when they understood they were opposed by riflemen, they felt a degree of terror never inspired by general action, for the idea that a rifleman always singled out an individual, who was almost certain of being killed or wounded; and this individual every man with ordinary self-love expected to be himself. How much more must this influence operate, where individual danger is incurred in heroic actions, the success of which must be rendered almost impossible, while the individual conceives himself the particular object of perhaps numerous riflemen. Destroy the mind, and bodily strength will avail but little in that courage required in the field of battle.[2]

The mix of rifles and smoothbores varied. Some armies, such as those of Austria and Russia, fielded *jäger* regiments armed mostly with smoothbores, but included a certain number of men (usually about ten percent) armed with rifles. Others, like the Prussians and Hessians, armed whole regiments with rifles but spread them in company-sized units along the line of battle, where they acted as sharpshooters. Although the British intended to employ the 5/60th as a *jäger* outfit in the German fashion, in Ireland and the

Caribbean they used it as a unit rather than parceling out companies to the line battalions. As such it performed so well that Whitehall raised two more battalions of German riflemen for the regiment in addition to giving each of the regiment's four line battalions a rifle company similarly trained and organized. The British army lacked a suitable domestic rifle, so the authorities temporized by buying some short, heavy-barreled German *jäger* rifles. Eventually they replaced the German rifles with the British-made Baker, which the army used through the Napoleonic wars. The nine-pound Baker looked a lot like the *jäger* rifle it replaced, and it sported a 24-inch sword bayonet to top off its 30-inch barrel. The rifleman used a primitive rear blade sight to aim the .625 caliber ball (considerably smaller than that of the standard .75 caliber Brown Bess). Although in one celebrated case a British marksman in Spain picked off a French general and his bugler at more than three hundred yards, the Baker was usually good for about half that.[3]

In 1800 the Duke of York set up a training camp for a new unit, The Experimental Corps of Riflemen. Initially, he included only a small detachment of rifle-armed sharpshooters for each line infantry battalion, and ordered each one stationed in England to send a company of thirty-five men and two officers (one a captain) for training. By April he had assembled ten such detachments and began instruction. Most eventually went back to their regiments, but part of the Experimental Corps remained. Supplemented with volunteers, it was officially designated the Corps of Riflemen later that year. Lieutenant Colonel William Stewart took over the 400-man outfit and began to build it into an elite unit. The riflemen borrowed much of their drill from the Germans, along with their green uniforms. Stewart expected his riflemen to be adept in the tactics of both skirmish and line, and encouraged both unit camaraderie and individual initiative by enlisted men (something unheard of at the time). He trained his riflemen to operate in files of two men so that one could keep his weapon loaded at all times, and to maneuver in open order by the sounds of the bugle and their officer's whistles. Soldiers trained extensively in the critical skill of range estimation and practiced on man-sized targets at ranges up to three hundred yards. The army recognized four classes of marksman and allowed first class shots to wear a green silk cockade in their caps.[4]

In 1803 the British Army designated Stewart's outfit as the 95th or Rifle Regiment. The British also converted several line regiments into light infantry and combined them into larger units. Eventually, during the Napoleonic wars, they fielded both a light brigade and a light division. The 95th Rifles went on to fame in Peninsular campaign under the Duke of Wellington, proving itself to be a singularly flexible formation capable of employment as sharpshooters, skirmishers, or even line infantry in a pinch. On the battlefield they regularly bested their formidable rivals, the French *voltigeurs*.

2

American Riflemen

"The wickedest corps in the Army"

The Americans had long recognized the usefulness of the rifle as a sharp-shooter's weapon. The Kentucky rifle was, after all, an American invention, and during the American Revolution it proved quite effective against the British. Early in the war George Washington raised a special five-hundred-man Corps of Rangers consisting entirely of riflemen, and the corps played a prominent part in the Saratoga campaign under the command of Colonel Daniel Morgan. With their long range sharpshooting Morgan's men mastered the British light troops and their Indian allies, harassed their line of battle, and rendered a good part of their artillery ineffective. At Bemis Heights one of Morgan's soldiers, Timothy Murphy, shot down British general Simon Fraser at a range estimated to be between two hundred and three hundred yards, substantially aiding the American cause. The American rifleman—that "unerring marksmen ... in forest warfare a much more formidable foe than the Imperial Guard of France"—made a great impression on his adversaries, enough so that the British sought to emulate him with the 5/60th Royal Americans and 95th Rifles.[1]

Still, the Kentucky rifle had definite limitations. Essentially a sporting weapon, it was rather delicate compared to a service musket and lacked a bayonet. Thus General Washington issued standing orders that riflemen be employed only when they could be protected by line troops at close quarters. Line infantry and light troops armed with smoothbore muskets like those of their British opponents comprised the bulk of the American army, and the proportion of riflemen declined as the war progressed. Although they have attained a nearly mythic status, firearms expert Joseph Bilby observed that "the overall role of the early American rifleman has often been grossly exaggerated."[2]

An American rifleman of the 1st Virginia, 1775. *NA*

At the start of the war Americans lacked any sort of light infantry, but in summer 1777 General Washington levied each infantry brigade for 108 men and nine officers to form a Corps of Light Infantry. As in the British army, the specially trained skirmishers used regulation infantry muskets. These temporary outfits disbanded at the end of the campaigning season, but Washington eventually convinced Congress to authorize a permanent company of light infantry for each battalion, bringing to nine the total number of companies in the organization. "Like the British Grenadiers," wrote one army historian, "the American Corps of Light Infantry became the elite body of the Army," and as such attracted the best and most daring men. Among their specialties was the night bayonet attack, and it was the Light Corps—light companies grouped together in the Continental fashion—that launched audacious nocturnal assaults at Stony Point and Yorktown.[3]

The U.S. army abolished its rifle units after the war in 1783, but the idea lived on. Rifle units raised in 1794 took part in the battle of Fallen Timbers as part of General Anthony Wayne's "Legion," but they were disbanded again two years later. During the 1798 "Quasi-War" with France Congress authorized the army to form a battalion of riflemen at George Washington's behest, but it was never raised. Nevertheless, in 1803 Secretary of War Henry Dearborn ordered the Harpers Ferry Arsenal to design a new infantry "short rifle" based on European *jäger* designs. The result was an elegant nine-pound .54 caliber rifle that was superior to the British Baker in range and accuracy, as well as being somewhat lighter. Unlike the Kentucky rifle, the new weapon was field rugged though not equipped with a bayonet. As tensions again ran high with Britain, the U.S. army formed the Regiment of Riflemen in 1808 and issued them these new rifles. This unit, in an ironic reversal, looked much like the British 5/60th and the 95th Rifles, down to their distinctive green uniforms and reliance on British manuals and tactical doctrine.[4]

The Regiment of Riflemen saw its first action in General William Henry Harrison's 1811 Indian campaign, fighting with smoothbore muskets in the Battle of Tippecanoe, and it participated in the comic-opera intervention in Spanish East Florida the following year. When the War of 1812 broke out, however, the Rifle Regiment went to Canada, where its members found many opportunities to exercise their skills. One of the regiment's most effective commanders—as well as its most colorful character—was North Carolinian Benjamin Forsyth. Historian John Fredriksen described Forsyth as "a consummate light-infantry officer whose reckless hauteur became legendary. Equally disconcerting for superiors was his appetite for plunder, which was rapacious and permeated his entire command." The Tarheel captain "fulfilled his role as a partisan raider brilliantly and was equally revered or reviled for it," wrote Fredriksen. "But, in an army destitute of military leadership, he proved too valuable an asset to dispense with."[5]

The vast reaches of the Northeast frontier provided an ideal venue for the rifle regiment, and Forsyth was quick to take advantage of it. Shortly after reaching northern New York Captain Forsyth led his rifle company on a raid into Canada, during which he netted a number of prisoners and a haul of plunder. The exploit won him a promotion to major. In February 1813 he struck again, this time capturing most of the garrison of Elizabethville (now Brockville, Canada) while liberating a number of American prisoners. Though these exploits had little overall effect on the war, they provided a much-needed bright spot in the generally gloomy American military picture. As a reward Forsyth received a brevet to lieutenant colonel, despite criticism that he and his men "shoot the officers and as soon as they fall they do not stop to load again before they run up and plunder his epaulettes, watch, etc.....Forsyth is a perfect savage himself, he, it is said, encourages it. He is as brave as any brute in the woods."[6]

Rifleman of the 1st U.S. Rifle Regiment, 1814. Jan AtLee from the original
by Alan Archambault, Old Fort Niagara Association, NY

Forsyth met his match in Lieutenant Colonel "Red George" MacDonnell, who after an exchange of insults led the Glengarry Light Infantry Fencibles in a raid on the American base at Ogdensburg, whipping the Yankee riflemen after a hard fight and taking, among other trophies, Forsyth's sword. Undaunted, the American commander and his riflemen spearheaded a raid the next April on York (now Toronto), defeating a grenadier company sent to block them (one of whom admitted that he had "never experienced such sharpshooting") and leading the American column into the town. Although Forsyth and his men were praised for their "coolness and bravery," they helped themselves to public and private property alike once the battle was over. A month later they settled up with the Glengarries, who lost seventy-five men at the storming of Fort George, and cemented their reputation after the battle as "the wickedest corps in the army." A fellow American observed that "one was never safe with them on the field of battle, friend or foe." The regiment's most memorable victory came under the leadership of Captain Daniel Appling, a Georgian. In late May 1814 Appling and his riflemen laid a devastating ambush of a larger British and Indian force at Big Sandy Creek, killing or capturing almost two hundred while losing only two of their men. Forsyth and Appling served as prototypes for the Confederate sharpshooters who were to follow.[7]

Forsyth and his little corps could not, of course, make up for the generally miserable American generalship in the conflict, but the riflemen continued their outstanding service—sterling on the battlefield and scurrilous off it—even after their roguish commander's death in battle on June 28, 1814. Encouraged by their example, Congress authorized three more rifle regiments in that year, and these soon joined in the fighting in both larger engagements like Conjockta Creek, where the riflemen under Major Ludowick Morgan of Maryland distinguished themselves by repulsing a superior British force, and in the seemingly endless war of outposts on the northern frontier. Morgan fell in one of these minor exchanges in August, shortly before another conspicuous performance by the 4th Rifles at Fort Erie and the 1st Rifles, now under Lieutenant Colonel Appling, at Plattsburg.[8]

The Americans' opponents in the War of 1812 generally followed European practices for light infantry, arming their troops mostly with smoothbore muskets. Despite their respect for the "unerring" American rifleman, the British did not send any of their specialized rifle units to Canada. The Regiment of Fencible Infantry, raised in 1808, was a typical formation, composed of a grenadier company, a light company, and eight line companies. Though the unit's paper strength was more than one thousand men, only about seven hundred were available at the war's outbreak. In June 1812 the flank companies were detached and formed into an elite unit, the Flank Battalion. The light companies were grouped into an ad hoc unit under Major Charles Plenderleath, allowing them opportunities for specialized skirmish drill. The next spring the Flank Battalion was "disembodied" and its companies returned to their parent regiments. Nevertheless, "the practice of grouping flank companies was continued throughout the war whenever possible; especially with embodied militia flank companies." To meet the American advance on Montreal, for example, the British fielded a force of "the Canadian Fencible light company, two Voltigeur companies, and the light company of 3rd Battalion of Embodied Militia" to feel out the enemy. The Americans withdrew after an indecisive engagement at the river Chateauguay. Throughout the war both Canadian and British light infantry continued to spar with the Americans. Although their smoothbore weapons put them at a disadvantage against the American rifle units, they generally acquitted themselves quite respectably.[9]

One semi-mythical incident in the region illustrates the outer limits of rifle performance in the early nineteenth century. In April 1813 a British and Indian force besieged Fort Meigs on the Maumee River in Ohio. The Americans, who had to send daily details to the river to fetch water, began to draw fire from an Indian sharpshooter in an elm tree some six hundred yards away. At first they joked about him, but the laughter stopped when after a few days' practice he found the range and wounded three soldiers. A Kentuckian, Elijah Kirk, received permission to return fire, so he set his rifle on a rest and waited for the Indian to shoot again. Kirk soon saw a puff of smoke, used it to gauge the windage, and let fly with a round of his own. "Then, a long rifle dropped and was soon followed by the Indian marksman himself." Intrigued by the story, which had been handed down orally, modern rifleman Walter Cline decided to test whether such a long shot was possible. Using a re-bored period rifle and modern powder, Cline hit a man-sized target four times out of ten at six hundred yards and reported his misses to be near ones, thus showing that while this feat would have been pushing the limits of the period's technology, it was possible.[10]

In January 1815 American riflemen got in some final shots at the Battle of New Orleans, fought after the peace treaty's signing. Major General Sir Edward Pakenham's eleven thousand British veterans considerably outnumbered the polyglot citizen army of four thousand men under General Andrew Jackson. The American general had, however, selected a strong position behind a canal and had improved it with a ditch and breastworks constructed from cotton bales. Because it consisted largely of militia units, many from the frontier areas of Mississippi and Tennessee, the American army contained an unusually large proportion of riflemen. More than half its men carried rifles of one sort or another—many of them the highly accurate Kentucky long rifles—and the frontiersmen who wielded them, though perhaps lacking in formal drill and discipline, were crack shots. The British riflemen, the 3rd battalion of the famed 95th Rifles, numbered only about 550 men and were split up among the attacking columns. Thus, in this singular contest between the Baker and Kentucky rifles, the Americans held all the advantages: they had four rifles for every one in British hands, a clear field of fire at long range (more than four hundred yards), and protection for themselves. The results were what might have been expected.

The British advance on the morning of January 8 was a confused affair. The fog meant to cover the attack lifted suddenly, exposing their three advancing columns to merciless fire. American artillery ripped holes in the British formations at long range, and, as the attackers closed to within 400 yards, their rifles began to exact a heavy toll as well. A British soldier commented that "the American riflemen are very slow, though most excellent shots." One of them, a Kentucky officer named Ephraim Brank, was particularly effective, dropping a man with every shot. "The cannon and thousands of musket balls playing upon our ranks, we cared not for; for there was a chance of escaping them," wrote one of the British officers. "Most of us had walked as coolly upon batteries more destructive, without quailing, but to know that every time that rifle was leveled toward us, and its bullet sprang from the barrel, one of us must surely fall…was awful." Brank's "unfailing aim" so unnerved the advancing Redcoats that they began to see him as an almost supernatural figure, a veritable angel of death. The British compounded their problems by stopping to return fire about eighty yards short of the breastworks, throwing themselves into further disorder. The lead battalion broke, taking the rest of the column with it. General Pakenham was mortally wounded in an attempt to rally his men. "We lost the battle," conceded an anonymous British officer, "and to my mind, the Kentucky Rifleman contributed more to our defeat, than anything else…we were in utter confusion, and unable to restore order sufficient to make any successful attack" Similar scenes played out along the line, and the heavy losses among the British officers played a major role in the assault's failure. Overall, the British lost more than two thousand men. The outnumbered Americans, protected by their palisade of cotton bales, lost only 71.[11]

Following the 1815 peace treaty the U.S. Army consolidated its four rifle regiments into one and sent it west. The regiment remained there until 1821, when it merged with regular infantry regiments. After 1825 regular regiments, at least in theory, followed European practice and designated the left company as light infantry company and the right one as grenadier company. "The truth is," noted an army historian, "that conditions in America did not favor the specialization of particular companies. Indian wars had to be fought by whatever troops were available; there was no time to await the arrival of elite corps, whether called grenadiers or something else. Nor did fights with Indians give much opportunity for infantry to assume the formal line of battle with light units out front. Finally, the scattering of the companies of Regular regiments made specialized training impossible." The War Department briefly converted the 2nd Dragoons to a foot rifle unit in 1843, mostly as an economy measure, but remounted them a year later.[12]

    To increase unit mobility in the vast western frontier the Army experimented with mounted rifle units, which were mounted infantry rather than cavalry. This resulted in one of the most unusual Army units ever fielded, the Regiment of U.S. Voltigeurs and Foot Riflemen. Raised in 1847, it was a mixture of horsemen and foot infantry. The idea was that the ground pounders would hop up behind their mounted counterparts and quickly deploy around the battlefield. The regiment served in the Mexican War, where it fought as a line infantry regiment, but was disbanded after just a year and the concept dropped.

The Regiment of Mounted Riflemen, organized in 1846, was a more successful unit. "It was," wrote a regimental historian, "armed with the hunting rifle, persistently called the 'yawger' [probably a mispronunciation of *jäger*]. The barrel was too large for the shank of the bayonet furnished, and the latter was used for a time with a wooden plug that fitted into the bore, another source of chaff for army wags. Company blacksmiths eventually overcame this difficulty by swelling the shanks." The regiment rendered distinguished service in the Mexican War, in which all but two companies fought on foot, later trekked northwest to serve in the Oregon Territory, and in 1861 was redesignated the 3rd U.S. Cavalry Regiment.[13]

Overall, the American experience in the Mexican War seemed to confirm the notion that light troops were of secondary importance. Local volunteer outfits such as the Texas Rangers had performed many of their traditional scouting and screening functions, and regular units had simply designated groups of line companies to act as skirmishers when needed. "Composite battalions of this sort," wrote an army historian, "usually did not do as well in battle as established ones, in which men and officers understood each other and regimental pride was an active stimulant. There was, however, more distinction between flank and line in volunteer regiments. Two companies out of ten were specifically organized as light and allowed to choose between rifles and muskets. The flank rifle companies which resulted were often detached from their regiments and used together for special sharpshooting assignments." The place of the "rifle regiment" had in part been filled by volunteer units like Colonel Jefferson Davis's First Mississippi Rifles, which their commander had contrived to arm with the state-of-the-art percussion rifle (most of the army was still using flintlocks) that would forever bear their name. The individual sharpshooter, too, had fallen out of favor. Nineteenth century attitudes of gallantry, which emphasized honorable combat between equals in the open, led men to despise a foe who skulked behind rocks and trees. One British soldier sneered that "the American rifleman ... conveys the idea of an assassin waiting for his victim." Finally, the Indians, the Army's chief opponents for most of the century, did not field armies with such high-value targets as officers, buglers, and artillerymen. These were the lessons that the junior officers of the army took with them, and upon which they would later rely when commanding troops in the bloodiest war in American history.[14]

3

Zouaves

"The bayonet … will always be the queen of weapons"

As the Americans fought Indians on the frontier and campaigned in Mexico, the French contended with a colonial counterinsurgency in Algeria (1830-47). The French Army, which had previously rejected the rifle because of its slow rate of fire, abruptly rediscovered its virtues the hard way. Algerian natives, primarily the Berber Kabyles, initially conducted a highly successful hit-and-run war against the French. Their old-fashioned snaphaunce (and even matchlock) guns, long obsolete in Europe, proved quite effective against French infantry armed only with smoothbore muskets. The Kabyles typically fought in a loose skirmish line, concealing themselves behind any available cover. From there they picked off the French soldiers, who were quite unable to hit back, with their old long-barreled pieces. If the French skirmishers charged them, the Kabyles would simply melt away, and the Europeans, now dispersed, ran a serious risk of being ridden down by native irregular cavalry lurking behind the line with lance and shield.

The French eventually won in Algeria, though it took them seventeen years. However, the improvements in both arms and tactics meant that this relatively minor colonial war would eventually have a far-reaching effect on Western military practices, including those of the United States. The French army's first order of business was to replace the smoothbore musket. Fortunately Captain Gustave Delvigne had invented just such a weapon, a rifle that could be loaded as fast as a smoothbore. During loading the powder fell into a secondary chamber smaller than the bore. The soldier would rap the soft lead ball three or four times with a heavy ramrod, deforming it enough to grip the rifling without crushing the powder grains. The French army began issuing these short *jäger*-style rifles to its light troops and soon heard stories of Algerians picked off at 400 yards. In 1846 they began using the improved *carabine à tige*, which used a conical bullet that the soldier expanded by tapping it down on a small post (*tige*) in the bottom of the bore. Both these designs had serious shortcomings in the field, but they represented a major improvement over the patch-and-ball system and worked well enough to tip the military balance in Algeria back to the French. Even though they had roughly triple the effective range of the old smoothbores, the new rifles by themselves were not enough to ensure victory.[1]

As their infantry struggled in Algeria, the French Ministry of War investigated forming light companies armed with the new Delvigne carbines, and in 1837 the Duc d'Orléans raised a single company of *tirailleurs* to test his theories of light fighting. Breaking with traditional European practice, he emphasized physical fitness, a more practical uniform, extensive field exercises, and "scientific" individual marksmanship training. The core of the marksmanship program was range estimation, but it also included training in the use of cover, firing from kneeling or prone positions, and repelling cavalry. In short, it was the first course of light infantry instruction that could be considered truly modern. These new light troops moved at a trot (the gymnastic pace) and used battle formations that emphasized speed and flexibility rather than parade-ground precision. The next year the company expanded into a full battalion of ten companies, took the name 1st Battalion *Chasseurs à Pied*, and deployed to Algeria. Their battlefield successes prompted the Ministry of War to form nine more battalions. All performed well, and in Algeria the French followed the practice of brigading them with native Kabyle and Arab soldiers called *Zouaves*, which led to a mutually beneficial interchange of practices. Over time the Zouave battalions changed from a mix of Europeans and Algerians to become all French. Due to the particularly Gallic combination of hard fighting and astute publicity, exotic uniforms (baggy red pants, tassled fez, short collarless jacket and vest, all modeled on native Algerian dress), and innovative tactics, the Zouaves became one of the most famous military units in the world, especially after their highly visible service in the Crimea (1854-55) and Italy (1859).[2]

The new French light infantry system emphasized small-unit tactics and individual initiative, both revolutionary concepts in nineteenth-century Europe but an absolute necessity in an irregular war. The French extended the British practice of training skirmishers to fire by files by grouping two files into a four-man section called *comrades de bataille*, or comrades of battle, who were also encouraged to form strong bonds of friendship and mutual reliance. It also allowed the soldiers, especially those armed with those new rifles, to maintain a steady fire while always keeping at least one weapon loaded. To control their lengthy skirmish lines the *chasseurs* used the bugle, and they added more than twenty calls to their repertoire. In 1845 they codified these new tactics in a manual, and ten years later American lieutenant colonel (and future Confederate general) William J. Hardee translated the manual into English at the behest of then-Secretary of War Jefferson Davis to replace the volume written by General Winfield Scott. The War Department adopted Hardee's *Rifle and Light Infantry Tactics* (later simply *Tactics*) in March 1855. This drill book, essentially a word-for-word translation of the French manual, would be the standard tactical reference for both sides during the Civil War.[3]

French Chasseur (l) and Zouave (r), Algeria, 1853. LC

The French continued to refine their "scientific method" of riflery with a demanding four-month instruction course at Vincennes. Their influential manual on the subject, *Instruction sur le tir,* or "Instructions on Firing," was translated in 1858 by U.S. Army captain (and future Confederate general) Henry Heth as *A System of Target Practice.* The British, not to be outdone, established their own School of Musketry at Hythe in 1853, where they taught a similar two-and-a-half month course. The Spanish, Dutch, Swedes, and Russians followed suit. In addition to their instructional duties, school staffs were expected to develop doctrine and follow technical advances in riflery.[4]

The mid-nineteenth century was a period a great technological innovation and consequently of tactical flux. The weapons and tactics of the day did not develop in isolation; rather, they fed off a lively exchange of ideas. Some pundits, such as the Prussian Captain Wittich, believed the new long-range rifles spelled the end of the massed columns of the Napo-leonic era, and recommended a thicker, semi-independent skirmish line of riflemen to cover the line of battle. A Belgian officer, Captain Gilluim, went even further, prophesying the end of the line of battle altogether and its replacement by an open order skirmish line of riflemen. Both men expected battles to occur at much longer ranges than were then usual, perhaps up to a thousand yards. Indeed, British tests at Hythe with their new Enfields showed that riflemen could effectively suppress artillery batteries at more than eight hundred yards, and they made practical application of long-range sharpshooting in India during the Great Mutiny of 1857.[5]

Though the United States was a military backwater and its army small, its officers kept abreast of these developments through professional jour-nals and books and by periodically sending some of their number abroad on inspection tours. One such was a West Point instructor, Lieutenant Cadmus M. Wilcox, who spent two years in Europe at his own expense studying the various schools of musketry, especially those at Vincennes and Hythe. After his tour Wilcox published in 1859 an influential book on the subject, *Rifles and Rifle Practice*, in which he echoed much that Wittich and Gilluim had said about the importance of long-range firepower. Another American, "R. E. C.," expressed similar sentiments in an essay entitled "Modern Tactics."[6]

William J. Hardee, Henry Heth, and Cadmus Wilcox, as Confederate generals. *B&L*

In Europe, Wilcox wrote, "the smooth-bored musket and round ball have been entirely superceded by the rifle and the elongated or cylindro-conic ball." Most European nations used a form of the *tige* rifle. Arrange-ments varied, but many European armies issued rifled carbines to their skirmishers with sights graduated to longer ranges, while the line infantry generally had rifles with shorter ranges on the sights or no backsight at all. Thus, the French progressively reduced the backsight range for their line infantry from six hundred to four hundred yards, and issued the longer-range *carabine à tige* without an elevating backsight at all. A soldier was expected to use his thumb for the purpose. French generals rejected the backsight (except for special units like *chasseurs*), as they once had the rifle, as being too slow and cumbersome for the average soldier to set on a fast-moving battlefield. The Austrians, on the other hand, issued short rifles sighted to up to a thousand yards to their third-rank soldiers, who acted as skirmishers, as well as to their NCOs and selected riflemen. The line infantry, however, received a rifle-musket with a sight graduated to only 245 yards. Most countries fielded both special light battalions (e.g. *chasseurs, jägers*) and a number of men per infantry company (for example, ten men per company in Baden and Wurtemburg) who carried long-range short rifles for sharpshooting.[7]

"With the improved rifle," wrote Wilcox, "the infantry fire is fourfold more destructive than formerly; hence the necessity … to have a thorough system of instruction in target practice; every infantry soldier should be so instructed before he enters his battalion." He cited 1851 tests the British army had conducted showing that, because shooters had time to aim and pick their targets, skirmish fire was about twice as effective as volley fire. Thus "50 skirmishers would produce the same effect … as 100 men firing by company." The British had also compared muskets to rifles and found that at 164 yards there was no difference in effect of the two, but that at 218 yards the rifle was 1½ times more effective in accuracy and penetrating power. At 437 yards it was six times as effective. "Beyond 437 yards the musket had neither *accuracy* nor *penetration*, but the rifle still had considerable efficacy." Wilcox warned that although in the past armies could approach to within three hundred yards of each other with little loss, the situation would be different in the next war. "Now this fire is destructive at 1000 or 1200 yards, and well directed at 600 yards, becomes irresistible."[8]

Though much of Wilcox's book consisted of translations or adaptations of various school materials, he included some cogent observations of his own. Most significantly, he recommended that a regiment be organized into four battalions, and "as some men will excel others in the use of the rifle, and have greater aptitude for the duties of light troops, the fourth battalion of each regiment should be formed of such soldiers. *These battalions, although excelling at target practice, are not to be employed exclusively as skirmishers, but to be organized at times into special corps, to be launched at critical periods of battle in mass, moving with the accelerated pace against the almost victorious adversary.*" (emphasis added)[9]

Unlike the Europeans, the Americans never established a formal school of musketry, but in 1855 they put the idea into practice with the newly formed 10th Infantry at Carlisle, Pennsylvania. Although the regiment was never formally designated "light," its soldiers adopted some uniform items from the *chasseurs à pied*, used bugles rather than drums, and became the first unit to train using Colonel Hardee's tactical manual. In keeping with the new French theories, all companies were to take skirmish training, and thus the specialized flank companies disappeared from American regiments. Captain Heth transferred to the regiment and began teaching his new course of rifle instruction in 1856.[10]

As an army historian recorded:

> It was impressed on the soldiers that their duties as "Light Infantrymen" required of them a complete knowledge of the use of the rifle, and especially deliberation and calmness in firing, that each shot might be effective. The ranges for target practice were two, three, four, five, six and seven hundred yards. Five shots were allowed at 200 yards, seven at 300, nine at 400, nine at 500, and ten each at 600 and 700 yards. The target used was a piece of white cotton, seven feet long and four feet wide, stretched on an iron frame. The bull's-eye was a circle eight inches in diameter, four feet from the ground and equidistant from the sides, painted black, with the exception of a small spot in the centre left unpainted to determine the centre accurately. Outside the bull's-eye were two black rings concentric with it, with radii of six and nine inches respectively. All shots were recorded and the men classified according to ability. Squads and individuals were practised, and the percentage of hits to misses governed the score, record in the cases of individuals being kept of bull's-eye hits.[11]

Following British practice, the Army recognized four classes of marksman and awarded the best shot in each company a brass stadia (a primitive range finder) as evidence of his superiority; the best shot in the regiment got a silver one, and the best in the Army got an inscribed silver medal to wear around his neck.[12]

In typical American fashion, however, the regiment was soon split up and deployed to the upper Midwest on Indian-fighting duty. Though the officers tried to keep up a semblance of light infantry training, the results can well be imagined. On one winter campaign, for instance, a battalion under Captain Barnard Bee (yet another future Confederate general) marched fifteen to eighteen miles a day breaking trail through the snow, and "in addition to the severe strain this labor imposed upon the men, they were, after reaching camp, drilled in skirmishing, as many of them were recruits who had never been instructed in this drill." The regiment then marched to Utah to help subdue the Mormons. By 1860 they were in New Mexico campaigning against the Navajo.[13]

In the 1850s the French unquestionably held sway in matters of military theory. The journal *Scientific American* gushed in 1861 that Napoleon III was the "most shrewd and far-sighted ruler of men now living." He was considered a martial oracle of sorts, especially after his victories in Italy. Yet the emperor, who had done so much for the adoption of the long-range rifle and light infantry tactics, abruptly changed his tactical emphasis after his Italian campaign. Even though the Zouaves had played a prominent part, the lessons from the campaign all seemed to point toward the primacy of the bayonet. In fact, it was the Zouaves who had used bayonet charges instead of long-range fire to carry Austrian positions with spectacular élan (and heavy casualties). This sent the military pundits into a tizzy, and the conventional wisdom abruptly shifted. "Many people supposed that the long range of muskets and rifles would do away with the bayonet charge," opined one, "but ... it [the bayonet] has become the king of the battles." Another conceded that though the rifle was useful for skirmishing and sharpshooting, "the bayonet ... will always be the queen of weapons." Rifles might be necessary to deal with bedsheeted skulkers in the desert, but civilized men preferred to settle their differences face to face with cold steel. Thoroughly seduced by the mystique of the bayonet, few military analysts of the day noted the number of French officers lost to Austrian sharpshooters in Italy. At the 1859 battle of Montebello, for instance, sharpshooters had killed half the French brigadiers and killed or wounded three-quarters of the colonels, a disquieting circumstance that led the French Emperor to ban epaulettes and ostentatious uniforms from the battlefield.[14]

Meanwhile, the rifle continued to improve. French captain Claude Minié devised a base-expanding, self-sealing conical bullet that proved a quantum leap in military technology. Here at last was a simple, trouble-free system that allowed a rifle to be loaded and fired as fast as a musket. The British used it in their new .577 caliber P53 Enfield, which the Americans quickly copied as the .58 caliber Springfield. Still, the smoothbore musket remained in service. "Buck and ball,"—adding three or more buckshot to the single round ball—produced a shotgun-like effect that gave the larger-caliber smoothbore musket superior firepower at one hundred yards or less. The conservatism of the field commanders, most of whom still thought in terms of opposing lines of battle shooting it out at whites-of-the-eyes range to soften up the enemy for a bayonet charge, enhanced this effect.

These were the arms and the theories with which the armies would begin the American Civil War.

4

Beginnings

"It was the province of the sharp shooter to shoot some body"

When the Civil War began, the Union and the new Confederacy stumbled into the conflict woefully unprepared. In 1860 the regular army numbered only 1,080 officers (roughly a third of whom resigned to join the Confederacy) and 15,000 enlisted men in ten regiments strung out on the frontier from Canada to Mexico. As a result the vast majority of men who would serve in the upcoming conflict would be volunteers—ordinary citizens who had no experience with drill, discipline, or soldiering.[1]

The rapid expansion of the armies in 1861 meant not nearly enough modern rifles would be available for some time, even for Union forces, and initially both sides carried mainly smoothbore weapons. Confederates marched to war with whatever they could scrounge, including old flintlocks, civilian sporting pieces, and even pikes. As the war progressed, the combatants began to replace smoothbore muskets with rifles, the Union by manufacture and the Confederacy by capture on the battlefield and purchase overseas. Even at mid-war, however, most units still fielded a mixture of the two types of firearms. Not until after the 1863 battle of Chancellorsville could the Army of Northern Virginia, for example, boast that the majority of its soldiers fought with rifled arms.

Nor could it be said, despite predictions of prewar visionaries, that the new infantry weapons wrought an immediate change in battlefield tactics. Both scenarios prophesied by the pundits—close-in bayonet charges and long-range fire fights—remained rare. Nevertheless, the debate between long-range fire and a close assault continued, and for the first two years of the war the French-inspired idea of the bayonet attack remained strong. Some officers continued to prefer old-fashioned arms. In early 1864 one journalist interviewed an officer of Battle's Alabama brigade "who disagreed entirely with me in regard to the utility of long-range muskets ... . In practice [he said], these long-range weapons had been found of little or no use, inferior in every way to the Mississippi or Harper's Ferry rifle, especially in warfare against the Yankees, who had been whipped by Lee's army always by bold charges and by firing at close quarters—never by shots from long taw." Nevertheless, both armies equipped themselves with Minié rifles for all ranks as soon as possible. Even with the increased range, however, the rifles' slow rate of fire meant that the calculus of battle remained relatively simple: to mass fire, one must mass men. Thus a Civil War line of battle remained much as it had in Europe during the Napoleonic wars. Soldiers stood elbow to elbow in a solid formation of two ranks, one behind the other, and fired by volleys. Though a thousand men (the nominal strength of a regiment) standing in a double line could produce tremendous firepower to their front, maneuvering such a linear formation was difficult, especially in wooded or broken terrain, and it was extremely vulnerable to flank attack. Men standing close together in the open also made a compact, convenient target for the new weapons, as both sides would soon find out.[2]

An infantry brigade in line of battle. Officers and NCOs ("file closers") stood behind to keep the men in place. *B&L*

Mass formations did, however, have the advantage of being relatively easy to police. The physical closeness of the men helped the less courageous hold their places, and company officers and NCOs ("file closers") could easily spot anyone who wavered. Much more so than today, the drills and formations were intended to turn each soldier into part of a functioning machine that operated more or less automatically, and to consider himself a part of his unit rather than an individual. As the war progressed and ranks began to fill with men who did not want to be there, battlefield discipline became harder to maintain. In mid-1863 a Confederate sergeant wrote his family that "conscripts as a general thing are, I believe, worthless and unreliable in the hour of battle, but when advancing on an enemy we have a line of file closers behind the line of battle with orders to shoot down the first one that falters. In this way we get some right good fighting out of the scamps."[3]

On the skirmish line, by contrast, soldiers stood in an open formation, usually in a single line three or four paces apart, and fired individually. "There is nothing in this world that is more exciting, more nerve stirring to a soldier," claimed one Southerner, "than to participate in a battle line of skirmishers, when you have a fair field and open fight. There it takes nerve and pluck, however, it is allowed each skirmisher to take whatever protection he can in the way of tree or stump. Then on the advance you do not know when to expect an enemy to spring from behind a tree, stump, or bush, take aim and fire. It resembles somewhat the order of Indian warfare, for on a skirmish line 'all is fair in war.'" Similarly, a Union soldier writing in 1864 claimed that skirmishing had been "reduced to a science." It depended, he said, "on two general rules: every man must keep concealed as much as possible behind trees, logs, fences, buildings, or what not, and each party must run upon the approach of its opponent with anything like determination. If a skirmisher should show himself unnecessarily he stood a great chance of getting hit, and if he waited until the enemy came within forty or fifty yards, it was exceedingly dangerous either getting away or staying. The skirmish line was conducted on principles that looked to personal safety in a great degree, and was the favorite position of the experienced soldier."[4]

In his sketch "Feeling the enemy," artist Winslow Homer accurately portrayed skirmishers in open order. *B&L*

Skirmish lines depended on the temperament of individuals rather than on the machine-like obedience required of soldiers in mass formations. No file closers policed the skirmish line, and keeping track of a strung-out line of riflemen, especially in wooded terrain, presented quite a challenge. Here a slacker could lie down and hide, or even leave the battle. Drill-manual authors had failed to realize that some men (and commanders) were better suited to this type of warfare, which put a high premium on individual marksmanship and initiative, than others. Commanders could issue all the rifles to flank companies, but this did not mean that the men wielding them were good shots, nor ensure that they could maneuver effectively in an open order. Skirmish drill differed considerably from that of the line, adding yet another training requirement for an army of amateurs. Further, the actual practice of controlling a skirmish line, especially in the densely wooded American terrain, was a difficult proposition, far more so than it had been in Mexico. The Civil War armies were larger than any yet fielded in North America, and they required very long skirmish lines. A brigade commander would find himself trying to give orders through his regimental commanders, who in turn had to pass along the orders to their company commanders, who would not necessarily know what the unit next to them on the skirmish line was doing.

Many of the same problems applied to the picket line, an institution vital for the army's security. In the early days of the war, said one Confederate officer, "picket and outpost duty of all kind was performed by details drawn hap-hazard from the various companies of the regiments constituting a brigade; a single regiment or even company being rarely sent as a body on this kind of service. The promiscuous details were usually placed under officers with whom they were as utterly unacquainted as each man was with his right and left file. As a natural consequence, the details failed to act in the presence of the enemy as a compact, confident body." As with the skirmishers, picket-line soldiers needed initiative, and one Federal officer thought that "picket duty is, of all others, that which requires most individual intelligence in the soldiers.[5]

Picket duty was a lonely, dangerous job. *B&L*

That same officer, Lieutenant Colonel Theodore Lyman, left an excellent description of a picket line's operation:

> A picket line is always one of the most picturesque sights in an army, when it runs through woods and fields. You know it consists of a string of 'posts,' each of half a dozen men, or so, and, in front of these, a chain of sentries who are constantly on the alert. The squads of men make to themselves a gipsy bough-house in front of which they make a fire in cool weather. They must always have their belts on and be ready to fight at a moment's notice. In the woods, you follow along from one rustic shelter to another, and see the sentries, out in front, each standing behind a good tree and keeping a sharp lookout for Rebel scouts, bushwhackers and cavalry. A short distance in the rear you from time to time come on a 'reserve,' which is a large body, perhaps of fifty or a hundred, who are concealed and who are ready to come to the assistance of the posts, if they are attacked .... A picket line, judiciously posted, in woods or swamps, will oppose a formidable resistance, even to a line of battle. There was careful Mr. Corps, officer of the day, with his crimson scarf across his shoulder, inspecting his outposts and reserves; each one falling in as he came along and standing at a shoulder.[6]

Although in many ways the volunteers were equally matched in their inexperience, the Southerners did have a big advantage in one area. Early on, a Federal officer admitted, "it became painfully apparent that, however inferior the rank and file of the Confederate armies were in point of education and general intelligence to the men who composed the armies of the Union, however imperfect and rude their equipment and material, man for man they were the superiors of their northern antagonists in the use of arms. Recruited mainly from the rural districts ... their armies were composed mainly of men who had been trained to the skillful use of the rifle in that most perfect school, the field and forest." He compared them to their northern counterparts, "whose life-long occupations had been such as to debar them from those pursuits in which the men of the South had gained their skill. Indeed, there were in many regiments in the northern armies men who had never even fired a gun of any description at the time of their enlistment." The North did, however, have "scattered throughout the loyal states, a great number of men who had made rifle shooting a study, and who, by practice on the target ground and at the country shooting matches, had gained a skill equal to that of the men of the South in any kind of shooting, and in long range practice a much greater degree of excellency." The Union army gathered these experts into a specialist sharpshooter regiment led by a flamboyant organizer, Hiram Berdan, who would garner considerable publicity for his efforts.[7]

The Confederates, meanwhile, tried to organize their skirmishers and pickets into a more regular establishment. On April 2, 1862, Major General Richard Ewell, then commanding an infantry division in the Confederate Army of the Potomac, ordered each brigade to form "a battalion of which will more than the other troops be instructed in the duties of Light Infantry." This battalion, to be commanded by a field officer, was to consist of two companies per regiment, each of which was to be armed with "as far as possible, rifled arms, either Minnie Muskets or Mississippi Rifles." This, in theory, would have been a force of eight hundred to a thousand men per brigade. Ewell was never able to implement this order, because shortly thereafter his division joined Stonewall Jackson for his Shenandoah Valley Campaign, leaving little time for organizing or training such a force.[8]

April 1862 also saw the complete reorganization of the Confederate army. Most volunteers had joined for twelve months a year before, and as an inducement to reenlist the government allowed the soldiers to elect officers and, in some cases join new units. One such new unit was the Palmetto Sharpshooters, which included men from the Fourth, Fifth, and Ninth South Carolina infantry regiments. Commanded by Colonel Micah Jenkins, it fielded twelve companies instead of the usual ten and was originally intended to be a specialized sharpshooter regiment like those organized by Hiram Berdan for the Union. As desirable as this sort of unit might have been, the perennial shortage of Confederate manpower militated against it, and the Palmetto Sharpshooters ended up serving as a line unit. Every available soldier was needed on the line of battle, making specialist sharpshooter units a luxury too difficult to justify.[9]

There were practical problems as well: "it was well nigh impossible to find such an organization in any division as combined all the qualities found necessary for single and determined picket fighting. Besides, at this time, it was considered a duty not only extra dangerous, but otherwise specially onerous and distasteful; and regimental commanders were inclined to stand on their rights of only acting in their regular routine on the brigade roster."[10]

When Major General George McClellan and his Union army began moving up the Yorktown peninsula in spring 1862, he found the Confederates ill prepared. Caught off guard by the Federal move, the outnumbered defenders under Major General John Magruder scrambled to slow McClellan's advance until reinforcements could arrive from the Potomac front, and for a time they could put up little more than a bold front. To hold the critical right end of his line on the Warwick river, Magruder deployed Gracie's Special Battalion, an outfit composed of a company each from the five regiments of Wilcox's Alabama brigade. Given the relatively high strength of the infantry regiments in the war's early days, the battalion probably numbered between four and five hundred men. Commanded by Major (later brigadier general) Archibald Gracie, the battalion served as a screening force of light infantry. The companies were assigned "by chance" and although Gracie drilled the men rigorously "they were not especially qualified as sharpshooters, armed as they were with old smoothbore muskets." Still, the battalion performed well, helping "Prince John" Magruder sustain the illusion of having a much larger force than he actually did. When the Confederates fell back to Williamsburg, Gracie's battalion formed the rear guard. It was not actively engaged at the battle there, and it disbanded when Gracie was promoted and reassigned May 7, 1862.[11]

Actions on the skirmish line severely tested small unit leadership. *B&L*

The two armies continued to spar as McClellan moved toward Richmond, and the Rebels soon encountered Yankee target rifles. Unlike the Confederates, the Federals had organized, trained, and equipped specialized sharpshooter units (including Berdan's two sharpshooter regiments). One Alabama soldier, Murrie Rudulph, wrote that "these nasty sharpshooters killed one of our company the other day. ... They were shooting at some of the Artillery men and he put his head over the breastworks and a ball broke his neck. It must have been over 700 yards. I wish I had one of those long range guns here." His commander, Brigadier General Robert Rodes, agreed. "The sharp shooters are annoying us dreadfully from behind pits and rail piles in the peach orchard," he wrote, adding that he had dodged "half a dozen balls" while observing the action. The Confederates sent out two infantry companies to drive them off, but the fear remained. "Every time I heard anybody blow his nose, I would dodge," wrote Rudulph.[12]

In response Magruder collected what rifles he had and issued them to a few selected units. On April 28 he wrote his superiors that "of twelve regiments now at Dam No. 1 there are four companies, armed with long-range guns, and constitute the only corps of sharpshooters." They had, he said, been on continuous duty, and he requested that "any ... regiment armed with long-range guns, be detailed to constitute, with the four already there, a corps of sharpshooters to act against the enemy at that point." Deeming this "essential," he closed by saying that "as it is, the enemy has vastly the advantage of us, and shoot at every man and horse they see exposed."[13]

Union sharpshooters armed with precision target rifles came as a shock to the Confederates during the Peninsular campaign. Winslow Homer immortalized them in *Harper's Weekly*, but confided to a friend that he found it "as near murder as anything I ever could think of in connection with the army & I always had a horror of that branch of the service." *Harper's Weekly*

A Vermont captain in Berdan's Sharpshooters described his company's routine:

> ...daily details for picket duty were made, and always where the danger was the greatest; for, as it was the province of the sharp shooter to shoot some body, it was necessary that he should be placed where there was some one to shoot. In a case of this kind, however, one cannot expect to give blows without receiving them in return, hence it came about that the sharp shooters were

constantly in the most dangerous places on the picket line. At some point in the Union front, perhaps miles away, it would be found that a few rebel sharp shooters had planted themselves in a position from which they gave serious annoyance to the working parties and sometimes inflicted serious loss, and from which they could not readily be dislodged by the imperfect weapons of the infantry. In such cases calls would be made for a detail of sharp shooters, who would be gone sometimes for several days before returning to camp, always, however, being successful in removing the trouble.[14]

Kentucky Rifle Brigade.   Tennessee Sharp-shooters.

Confederate riflemen early in the war. Not until 1862 did their government get around to formally organizing sharpshooter units. *Harper's Weekly*

In early May 1862 the Confederate Congress formally authorized special sharpshooter units, approving the discretionary formation of "a battalion of sharp-shooters for each brigade, consisting of not less than three nor more than six companies, to be composed of men selected from the brigade, or otherwise, and armed with long-range muskets or rifles." The order was rather vague about exactly how this was to be done. Adding to the confusion many Confederate (and some Union) units, large and small, used the title *sharpshooter* as an honorific much like the Europeans used such terms as *grenadier*, but they did not train or fight as specialists. Though various commanders tried to form sharpshooter units early that summer, their efforts were soon subsumed into the bloody campaigns of 1862.[15]

One of the first Confederate sharpshooter units was formed later in May. The Twenty-first North Carolina regiment (Trimble's brigade), which had twelve companies, formed an independent sharpshooter battalion by splitting off the two "extra" companies. The resulting outfit, the First North Carolina Battalion (Sharpshooters), spent the rest of the war as a line infantry unit. Like the Palmetto Sharpshooters, it accumulated a distinguished combat record but never served in its intended role. A week later a private in the Forty-fourth Georgia, then stationed on the Carolina coast, wrote that "we are getting up a company of sharp-shooters from our regiment. ... A battalion will be organized from the brigade." However, they soon moved to Virginia and nothing more seems to have come of it.[16]

The next month Major General Earl Van Dorn, who had recently transferred from the Virginia front to Mississippi, attempted to form a composite sharpshooter battalion of 750 men for each brigade, to be armed with rifles. Although he never completed the project, one sharpshooter battalion, Rapley's Sharpshooters (officially the Twelfth Arkansas Sharpshooter Battalion) was formed on June 30, 1862, with four companies totaling two hundred men.[17]

Robert E. Rodes. *B&L*

An interesting coincidence in the formation of Confederate sharpshooter units is that many of the men responsible for organizing them had served together early in the war. Richard Ewell briefly led a brigade under Van

Dorn in Virginia while the latter commanded what later became D. H. Hill's division, and among Ewell's subordinates were Robert Rodes, Eugene Blackford, and Bristor Gayle. Both Gayle and Blackford played major roles, but Rodes deserves most of the credit for untangling this knotty tactical dilemma.[18]

A native of Lynchburg, Rodes graduated from the Virginia Military Institute in 1848, making him one of the few non-West Pointers with a formal military education. A trim man, over six feet tall, with blue eyes, sandy blond hair and huge tawny mustache that drooped below his chin, the thirty-three-year-old Rodes cut an impressive figure in a gray uniform. After a stint instructing at VMI he moved to Tuscaloosa, Alabama, where he married and worked as a civil engineer. When the war broke out, Rodes took part in early actions at Mobile and Pensacola as captain of the "Warrior Guards," a volunteer company he had raised in Tuscaloosa. He was elected colonel of the Fifth Alabama after his company had been incorporated into that regiment. Assigned to Richard Ewell's brigade, Colonel Rodes quickly became the unit's drillmaster. At First Manassas Ewell's brigade had been on the army's right flank and had seen little action, but Rodes's handling of his regiment there and at a skirmish near Fairfax Court House had garnered him a mention in General P. G. T. Beauregard's dispatches. From then on Rodes was regarded as a man on the way up. When Ewell was promoted to division command, Rodes took over his brigade as brigadier general in October 1862. One of his junior officers, Robert Park, described Rodes as "a precise and somewhat stern military man, of resolute expression and soldierly bearing."[19]

5

Seven Pines, Gaines's Mill, and South Mountain

"We skedadle & halt, fight & then skedadle again"

Robert Rodes led his brigade to its baptism of fire on May 31, 1862, at Seven Pines. As part of Major General D. H. Hill's division, Rodes and his men drew the task of assaulting Brigadier General Silas Casey's formidable work, Casey's Redoubt, on the Williamsburg road. Six Federal guns defended the bastion, which also bristled with *abatis*, trees chopped down with sharpened branches pointing toward the enemy. A second defensive line lay behind it. Hill's division was strung out in front of Casey's position, with Rodes's brigade covering the extreme southern end on the Charles City Road. A "dreadful" storm the night before left the already wet roads "deep with mud and water, and the woods and fields held water as high as our ankles, and often went to our knees, and even to our waists."[1]

The Confederate assault went poorly that muddy morning. Rodes' relief did not arrive until nearly noon, and his men had to wade across flooded fields and swamps through waist deep water to get to their attack positions. General Hill, growing impatient, ordered Rodes's brigade into action immediately. Rodes had no choice but to send each regiment forward *en echelon* as it arrived: first the Twelfth Mississippi and the Fourth Virginia Heavy Artillery, fighting as infantry, then the Fifth Alabama, and finally the Twelfth Alabama. Perhaps attempting to put his skirmish line under a single commander, Rodes deployed Colonel John Gordon's Sixth Alabama across the brigade's entire front as skirmishers. Although Gordon's men swept away the few Yankee skirmishers in the swamps, the brigade arrived at the fortifications in a disorganized mass. The Fifth Alabama had been separated in two, and the eager Twelfth Alabama, which had started last, arrived at the breastworks first. Rodes halted his line just short of the redoubt to reform, reconcentrating the Sixth Alabama prior to the final assault. Halting literally under the muzzles of the enemy guns—though certainly a brave act—cost the brigade dearly. "I can never forget the calm resolve with which the men reformed their line," remembered one soldier, "after we had reached the open field, within a hundred feet of the enemy's breastworks. They did not wince nor dodge under the terrible and destructive fire, but, with the utmost coolness and precision, returned it, undisturbed by their trying situation." Finally, as riflemen in the trees picked off the Yankee gunners, Rodes gave the order and brigade went forward, hacking their way through the abatis, mounting the first line of breastworks, and driving Casey's men rearward in panic-stricken flight. Rodes's men swept through the camp, taking six guns that the Virginia artillerists-turned-infantrymen turned against their former owners. After chasing the Federals to their second line, the exultant Rebels were abruptly stopped by heavy fire, as the reinforced bluecoats crouched behind their breastworks and poured out a storm of lead. Rodes's men, unsupported, had to fall back at dark. Tactically, though the battle had cost the brigade nearly half its men, it had changed nothing. Nor had Rodes's skirmishing arrangement worked very well: it was just too cumbersome, and neither he nor anyone else used it again.[2]

One notable casualty at Seven Pines was the Confederate commander, General Joseph Johnston, whom Jefferson Davis soon replaced with his military advisor, General Robert E. Lee. As McClellan's men waited four miles from Richmond, Lee reorganized his army and planned a counteroffensive. Rodes's brigade became an all-Alabama unit, consisting of the Third, Fifth, Sixth, Twelfth, and Twenty-sixth Alabama regiments. The Twelfth Alabama's colonel, Robert Jones, died at Seven Pines, and the lieutenant colonel, Bristor B. Gayle, assumed command of the regiment. While Gayle was not a professional soldier, he did have some prior experience as an instructor at the Virginia Military and Collegiate Institute at Portsmouth, Virginia.

Lee's offensive in the Seven Day's battles began June 26 with an unsuccessful assault at Mechanicsville. During the battle D. H. Hill's division marched from Williamsburg Road past Mechanicsville to join Stonewall Jackson, who had recently arrived from the Shenandoah Valley. Although Lee's attack failed, the Federals nevertheless retreated, gaining for themselves an even stronger position at Gaines's Mill. The Confederates launched another attack the next day. Hill's division made a flank march, much delayed by misdirected units and Union artillery fire, and found itself on the north end of the line. There the division began an uncoordinated advance on the Union right flank, its brigades crowding together while crossing a small creek that Federal pioneers had obstructed with fallen timber. In the confusion the Twelfth Alabama, near the end of the line, began taking artillery fire from a Federal battery on their left. In response Colonel Gayle quickly formed a detachment of riflemen drawn from across the regiment. Each company contributed their four best shots, and Gayle selected a promising young lieutenant, Robert Park, to lead them. "The cannon belched forth fire and smoke, and bursting shells were hurtling among us," Park recalled. "Wounded men were being carried to the rear, while we were saddened by the sight of motionless and lifeless comrades. In obedience to instructions, I hurried forward through the lowland, and before we had gone two hundred yards we captured seven prisoners, and I disarmed and hurried them to the rear." Park and his men "marched as best we could in line till we reached a deep sunken road, near enough to one of the batteries to shoot the artillerymen." As they did the Federal gunners caught sight of them and opened up, showering the riflemen with "the limbs of trees and countless leaves." But the intrepid little company continued to creep forward until they found a suitable position to open fire. "The men were not slow in doing execution, and very soon we silenced the battery in our immediate front," Park recalled. One of his sergeants, Jason Patton, captured a Union courier carrying an enciphered message for General McClellan, and the lieutenant quickly packed the Yankee messenger off to headquarters.[3]

The firing ceased, and Park's sharpshooters cautiously advanced to find "many artillery horses lying dead, and numerous cannoneers by their side, stiff and cold. My little band remained in possession of the large collection of knap-sacks, haversacks, etc., until recalled about night, and every man returned to his company loaded with trophies, many of them of some value, others worthless, except as curiosities." Colonel Gayle's innovation had proved quite successful.[4]

Boonsboro and Sharpsburg

After the Seven Day's battles D. H. Hill's division remained near Richmond to watch the departing Yankees, thereby missing the battle of Second Manassas. On September 2 they rejoined the army and waded across the Potomac into Maryland two days later. Lee then divided his army. As Stonewall Jackson laid siege to Harpers Ferry, Longstreet advanced to Hagerstown. Hill's division, the last to arrive, marched through Frederick and continued fifteen miles west to Boonsboro, where it covered the northern approaches to Harpers Ferry and guarded the army's artillery and trains. McClellan approached cautiously but experienced an incredible stroke of luck when his men found a copy of Lee's campaign orders. Armed with knowledge of his opponent's plans, he moved towards Boonsboro, whose capture would put him in a good position to destroy Lee's army in detail.

Hill and his four thousand men would have to hold two gaps in a rugged, wooded ridge called South Mountain against Little Mac's whole army: the main road, the National Pike, crossed the mountain at Turner's Gap just east of Boonsboro, and a smaller crossing at Fox's Gap lay a mile farther south. The Confederates nervously watched campfires grow and cover the whole plain that evening, and early on September 14 Hill found himself facing two Federal corps. "The vast army of McClellan [was] spread out before me," he recalled. "The marching columns extended back as far as the eye could see in the distance; but many of the troops had already arrived and were in double lines of battle, and those advancing were taking up positions as fast as they arrived. It was a grand and glorious spectacle, and it was impossible to look at it without admiration. I have never seen so tremendous an army before, and I did not see one like it afterward."[5]

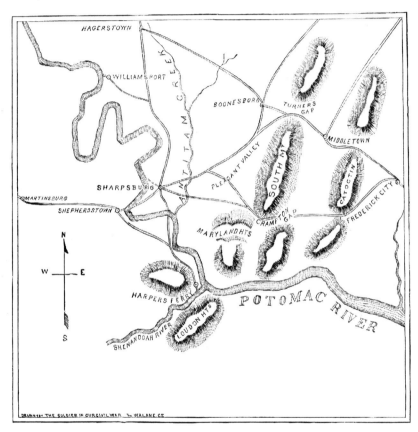

Boonsboro and Sharpsburg. W.A. Lane,
The Soldier in Our Civil War, modified by Fred Ray.

Around noon Rodes's brigade began tramping up to the pass. Hill sent them to hold the northern approaches to Turner's Gap. "We had just reached the scene of action," said Robert Park, "when an order ... directed that skirmishers should be deployed in front, and while our precise adjutant, L. Gayle, was looking over his roster of officers, to detail on one his regular turn, Colonel Gayle hurriedly exclaimed, 'detail Lieutenant Park to command the skirmishers.'" Gayle used the same arrangement as he had at Gaines's Mill. Park took forty men, again the four best shots from each company, with orders to "keep the enemy back as long as possible." The young lieutenant and his little band clambered down through the trees over a series of limestone ledges. "On our way down we could see the enemy, in the valley below, advancing, preceded by their dense line of skirmishers. I concealed my men behind trees, rocks, and bushes, and cautioned them to aim well before firing."[6]

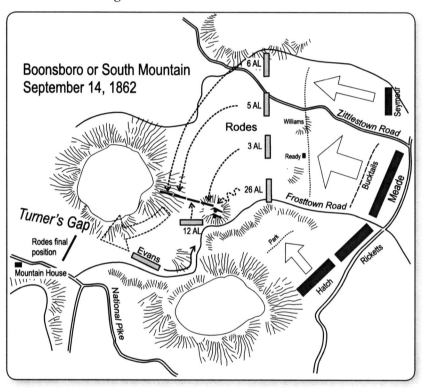

Meanwhile Rodes reconnoitered his position and found that to cover it he had to stretch his brigade so far that there would be large gaps between his regiments and also between him and the Georgia brigade holding the pike. Worse, he discovered another good road that ran all the way around his left flank, which meant he had to push out his brigade even further to cover it. General Hill brought up a couple of guns (whose firing, he noted dryly, "was the worst I ever witnessed") and ordered Rodes to detach the Twelfth Alabama to protect them. The sweating, cursing Alabamians had to climb back through the deep ravine they had just crossed. "Having thrown out skirmishers along the whole front and to the left," wrote Rodes, "they very soon became engaged with the enemy's skirmishers. This was about 3 p.m., and it was perfectly evident then that my force of about 1,200 muskets was opposed to one which outflanked mine on either side by at least half a mile. I thought the enemy's force opposed to my brigade was at least a division."[7]

Rodes's assessment was correct. His opponent was the peppery George Meade and his four-thousand-man division of Pennsylvania Reserves. Many of these men were hunters and lumberjacks from western Pennsylvania, and the rugged forest was a familiar environment to them. One regiment, the 13th Reserves—the famous "Bucktails," whose trademark was a deer's tail hanging from their caps—wielded breech-loading Sharps rifles and boasted special expertise in skirmishing. This formidable group of men, spread out in open order, spearheaded the advance of Meade's division. Rodes, on the other hand, had reverted to the usual practice of letting his regimental commanders post their own skirmish line. Given the length of the front they had to cover, a strong, coordinated skirmish line was essential, but Rodes appointed no overall commander. He placed his smallest regiment, the Twenty-sixth Alabama, on the right, with Colonel Cullen Battle's Third Alabama next to it, followed by the Fifth Alabama. Colonel John Gordon's Sixth Alabama held the vulnerable left flank.[8]

The Pennsylvanians soon pressed the issue. Concealed behind boulders Robert Park and his men "awaited, with beating hearts, the sure and steady approach of the 'Pennsylvania Bucktails.'" On Park's order they let off a volley, driving back the Yankee skirmish line. Now the Federal line of battle started forward, and the Alabamians gave them another taste of lead. "At least thirty men must have been killed or wounded," said Park. "But they continued to advance, their officers cursing loudly, and earnestly exhorting them to 'close up' and 'forward.'" Park tried to keep his little company together as they fell back uphill, dodging from boulder to boulder. "Several of them were wounded, and six or eight or more became completely demoralized by the unbroken front of the rapidly approaching enemy, and, despite my commands, entreaties and threats, left me, and hastily fled to the rear." Park pointed out an officer to Corporal Porter Myers, but as the man raised his rifle to fire he took a Yankee ball in his chest. Stopping to give Myers a drink of water, Park looked up to see "a dozen muskets were pointed at me, and I [was] ordered to surrender." Park and his men had been outflanked after the skirmishers on their left fell back. Captain Edward Ready of the Third Alabama and fifty of his company also went into the bag when the Bucktails overran a nearby house they held. The remorseless Pennsylvanians kept the pressure on, never giving Rodes's men an opportunity to reform.[9]

Farther down the line the Fifth Alabama also strained to hold its ground. Its acting commander, Lieutenant Colonel Edwin Hobson, had assigned three companies that had just rejoined the regiment as rear guard. He told Captain Jonathan Williams, the commander of Company D, to "take the three first companies, halt here and keep them in check as long as possible," then withdraw up the mountain with the rest of the regiment. "I saw some large rocks just in our rear," said Williams, "and I ordered the companies back there to protect themselves as best they could." Williams and his men stopped the Yankee skirmish line, but their line of battle soon approached, "halted and got behind rocks and trees and opened a heavy fire on us. The balls would hit those rocks and it sounded like heavy hail. Soon they had killed three or four of our men, all shot through the head. In a short time they began to fire into us from the rear, and also from above us." Captain Williams, seeing that his position was hopeless, hoisted a white handkerchief on a ramrod and surrendered himself and 150 of his men. A lieutenant of the 5th Pennsylvania Reserves demanded Williams's sword, but he refused to relinquish it to someone of lower rank. Tempers flared, and the two men exchanged "some language that would not sound very nice in Sunday school." Finally a Federal colonel arrived and took Williams's sword.[10]

On the line's far left end Colonel Gordon sent an infantry company from the Sixth Alabama down the mountain to act as skirmishers. "We reached our position just as the enemy's line of skirmishers, a full regiment, extending beyond our right and left, came out of a field of corn," recalled Private Otis Smith. He thought that with their "perfect line ... neat uniform, and glistening bayonets, they were an imposing and beautiful sight." The ragged Alabamians waited until the Pennsylvanians began to cross a fence about a hundred yards away, then let them have it with a volley that "dropped a score or more." The Yanks pulled back into the cornfield, regrouped, and came on again. Smith's company "fell back as rapidly as possible, firing at every opportunity," as the Pennsylvanians' return fire pursued them. The Rebel skirmishers had almost reached their line of battle when Smith and three other men took cover behind two large trees flanked by a couple of huge boulders. "From this vantage point we checked the line in our immediate front, but did not notice that the enemy had passed us on either side." His men wanted to pull back, but it was too late. As they began to retreat "a storm of bullets poured upon us" severely wounding Smith and killing his three companions. "Just then," he said, "the battle began with terrific fury."[11]

After capturing Park and Ready the Pennsylvanians continued to advance uphill against Colonel Edward O'Neal's Twenty-sixth Alabama, holding Rodes's right. Private Henry Miller's experience was typical: his company commander assigned him to sharpshooting duty "with orders to 'get' some of the Yanks who were harassing us on our left." Miller soon went down with a shoulder wound, and although Colonel O'Neal helped him back to the regimental command post, he was forced to abandon the private as the regiment fell back. Shortly thereafter O'Neal was wounded also, and most of his men, "completely demoralized," headed up the road, although a few hardier souls attached themselves to the adjacent Third Alabama. This left Rodes's right flank open, and if the Yankees turned it, they could push up the Frosttown road and cut off his retreat.[12]

It was now near dusk. The westering sun dropped behind the mountain, leaving the battlefield in a deep shadow. The aggressive Reserves took advantage of the gaps between the Confederate regiments, making it extremely difficult for Rodes to keep any line intact. He quickly decided to pull back into the woods near the crest of the mountain, then wheel left to reestablish his line. To the men who traded shots in the gathering twilight, it seemed like Indian fighting. "Now we stop and are almost surrounded," wrote one soldier in the Sixth Alabama. "Our men are falling all around. We skedadle & halt fight & then skedadle again."[13]

The Twelfth Alabama came up and took a position between the Third and Fifth Alabama regiments. Rodes established his line behind a stone wall, but the implacable Pennsylvanians lapped around his flank in the darkening woods. Rodes and Colonel Gayle of the Twelfth saw a line of men approaching them in the woods.

"What troops are those?" asked Rodes.

"I don't know, sir. I'll see," said Gayle. "My God," he gasped as he got close enough to make them out, "it's the Pennsylvania Reserves."[14]

The Yankees called for Gayle's surrender, "but drawing his pistol and firing in their faces, he exclaimed: 'We are flanked, boys, but let's die in our tracks' and continued to fire until he was literally riddled by bullets." The regiment's lieutenant colonel, Samuel Pickens, also fell with a dangerous wound, but Rodes escaped unscathed. A Federal officer described the fight. The Rebels, he said, "having gained an admirable position behind a stone fence … appeared determined to hold on to the last. Here it was they sustained their greatest loss. Colonel Gayle, Twelfth Alabama, fell dead … but in a little while we were over the fence and among them, taking 68 prisoners, killing and wounding quite a number, and causing the remainder to fly precipitately to the top of the mountain." As darkness gathered Rodes finally managed to rally a line with Gordon's Sixth Alabama, the only intact unit left, and the fragments of Cullen Battle's Third Alabama, near the top of the pass at Mountain House. Gordon turned on his pursuers and gave them a withering volley, whereupon the tenacious Pennsylvanians broke contact at last.[15]

Near midnight Hill's exhausted Confederates pulled off the pass and marched to the village of Sharpsburg, where they threw themselves down in the grass in the first light of dawn. It had been a close-run thing. Hill's division, reinforced by Longstreet, had held the passes until Lee's army could be reunited. In his report Rodes claimed that "we did not drive the enemy back or whip him, but with 1,200 men we held his whole division at bay without assistance during four and a half hours' steady fighting, losing in that time not over half a mile of ground." He also lost 422 men, a third of his brigade, of which 61 were dead and 157 wounded. Most of the 204

missing, including Otis Smith, Jonathan Williams, and Robert Park, had
been captured on the skirmish line.[16]

Thus, even given the disparity of numbers and the difficulty of the terrain, the experience of Rodes's skirmishers can be described only as disastrous. The brigade's skirmish line was not effectively coordinated, and the
advancing Pennsylvania Reserves had surrounded and captured almost all
of them. Though Rodes managed to hold his brigade together long enough
for a fighting retreat to Turner's Gap, the experience seems to have made a
permanent impression on him. Colonel Gayle lay among the dead at Boonsboro, but Robert Rodes would not forget his tactical innovations.

For the moment, however, Rodes and his men had little time to sort out
the lessons learned on the slopes of South Mountain. Three days later they
bivouacked in Henry Piper's cornfield, along a low range of hills that ran
behind Antietam creek, "subsisting on green corn mainly and under an
occasional artillery fire." McClellan's army slowly approached, and early on
September 17 the battle of Sharpsburg (Antietam to the Federals) opened
with a furious contest on the left of the Confederate line as Stonewall Jackson
took on two Union corps. Just before nine o'clock McClellan sent in his II
Corps in to reinforce the stalled offensive, but Jackson turned and launched
a devastating attack on the leading division. The corps commander, Major
General Edwin Sumner, sent an aide galloping back to the next division in
the column, commanded by Major General William French, with orders
for him to "press the enemy." Sumner had evidently intended that French
should support the division just then being cut to pieces in the West Woods,
but his largely green outfit had fallen behind. French's division tramped
by the Roulette farm, where they began to draw fire from the farmhouse
and outbuildings. "Old Blinky" French evidently concluded that the noisy
riflemen on the farm were the enemy he had been ordered to press, so his
division angled off southward toward the center of the Confederate line.[17]

Seeing French's approach, Lee moved Rodes's brigade, along with Brigadier General George Anderson's North Carolina brigade, from their camps
into a sunken road near Piper's place that bypassed the town of Sharpsburg
and had, over the years, had been worn down by wagons until in some
places it was several feet deep. The soldiers began piling fence rails as a
makeshift breastwork. Shortly thereafter French's men crested the rise in
front of the road and began their attack. A desperate fight ensued, and although the Yankees drove the Confederates from their positions, forever
after known as the Bloody Lane, the Southerners still managed to hold the
center of their line.[18]

Through the long day Lee held his line, barely, against attacks on his
center and later that afternoon by Major General Ambrose Burnside on his
right. The next night Lee withdrew across the Potomac in good order, but

his invasion of the North was over. McClellan failed to press him, giving the Army of Northern Virginia a short interlude to rest and reorganize after the bloody summer of 1862.

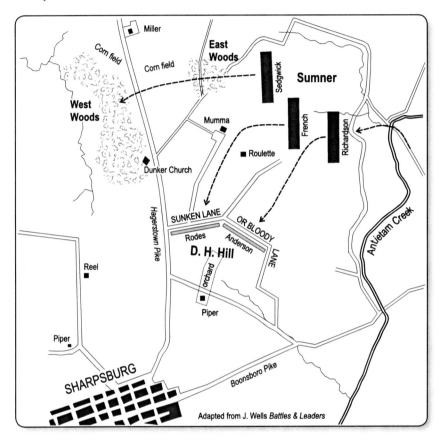

The Federal attack on Lee's center at Sharpsburg, 9:30-10 a.m. September 17, 1862. Sedgwick's division of Sumner's II Corps advances into the West Woods but is surrounded. French's division, distracted by fire from the Roulette farm, angles southwest and attacks Hill's men in the Sunken Lane, followed by Richardson's division.

The riflemen at Roulette's farm—likely detachments from Rodes's and perhaps Anderson's brigades—changed the course of the battle at Antietam, which certainly would have unfolded differently if French had followed Sumner's orders to support his leading division. The Maryland campaign, particularly the fight at Boonsboro, made clear the dangerous weaknesses of the conventional skirmish line. Simply sending a body of men out as skirmishers did not ensure that they could do their jobs effectively, a fact driven home by the number of men now held as prisoners.[19]

6

Winter at Fredericksburg

"We are always in the front of the brigade"

As the Army of Northern Virginia rested after the summer's ordeals, its commanders considered the lessons learned on the battlefield. One man who would be called upon to put them into practice was Major Eugene Blackford of the Fifth Alabama. A rangy twenty-three-year-old ex-teacher, who like Robert Rodes sported a drooping handlebar mustache, Blackford returned to active duty in the Army of Northern Virginia in December after a bout with typhoid fever. In 1861 Blackford had raised a company of infantry, the Barbour Greys, and brought them to Virginia after the Alabama governor declined his services. Attaching himself to Colonel Rodes's Fifth Alabama, which was then just short a company, he had led them through the maelstrom of Seven Pines and the Seven Days Battles, including the ill-fated assaults on Malvern Hill. Blackford survived these battles unscathed in spite of having had, at various times, his haversack and revolver carried away by Yankee fire and his clothes perforated with holes. But his Company K was not so lucky. By the time the smoke cleared at Malvern Hill only thirteen men, including Captain Blackford, still stood. His battlefield performance, coupled with casualties among the regiment's field officers, earned him promotion to major, but the fever laid him low just after the Seven Days.

Rodes and Blackford had quickly established a friendship, at least in part because both hailed from Lynchburg, Virginia. Blackford was somewhat unusual in being part of a staunchly abolitionist family. In 1783, in fact, his maternal grandfather introduced a bill in the Virginia legislature to abolish slavery. His mother, who urged her sons to seek their fortunes in a free state, helped found the Colonization Society and was an avid fan of Harriet Beecher Stowe's *Uncle Tom's Cabin*. Yet like so many other Virginians, when the war came, Blackford and his four brothers drew their swords for the Confederacy.

Although winter was upon them Lee's army still had one more test to face before year's end. On December 11, 1862, the Army of the Potomac, now under General Ambrose Burnside, tried to steal a march by crossing the Rappahannock at Fredericksburg, Virginia. On December 13 Burnside made a series of bloody assaults against the dug-in Confederates at Marye's Heights and Prospect Hill, leaving thousands of Union wounded or dead. Jackson's command held the right of the Confederate line on Prospect Hill, with D. H. Hill's division standing in reserve. Rodes's brigade did not fight that day and suffered only a few casualties from artillery fire. At four the next morning Hill's division moved to the front behind a railway embankment, and in the sun's first rays Blackford could see that "the army of the enemy was drawn up in battle array ... dressed as accurately as if on dress parade. These lines glittering in the light of the rising sun presented a sight which was grand in the extreme. In front of either army were skirmishers lying on the ground, not more than 150 yards apart, the first lines of battle being not more than 500 yards distant from each other. So near were they that the buzz of conversation was distinctly heard."[1]

Burnside's commanders talked him out of renewing the battle that day, and the two sides tried to arrange a truce to recover the Federal wounded. Blackford went forward to command the picket line and supervise the truce negotiations, which were quite lengthy.

> I allowed his ambulance corps to advance to our picquet line, where our men met them bearing their dead and wounded ... I had much pleasant conversation with the Yankee officers, many of whom advanced to the front. Our men came forward in crowds and mingled with the enemy. It was curious to see the difference between them. The Yankees were all nicely dressed but had a cowed look ... whereas our poor dirty fellows went about with uplifted and defiant looks ... . These men would never trouble us much more. Their spirit is broken, and a more dejected set of wretches I have never seen.[2]

The next morning Rodes again sent Blackford forward to investigate, this time with "his whole line of skirmishers," which stretched "nearly a mile flank to flank." As they reached the high ground near the river they saw the last of Burnside's army crossing the pontoon bridges, and the only casualties of the day resulted when one of Blackford's men shot a comrade who had made the mistake of putting on a captured Yankee overcoat. Not all the Federals got the word to withdraw. "In my advance I picked up about two hundred prisoners," wrote Blackford. "In one tent we found a full band of musicians, with their instruments, who asked us *if it was reveille!* They

were aghast when informed they were prisoners." The captured instruments
made a nice addition to the Third Alabama's band.[3]

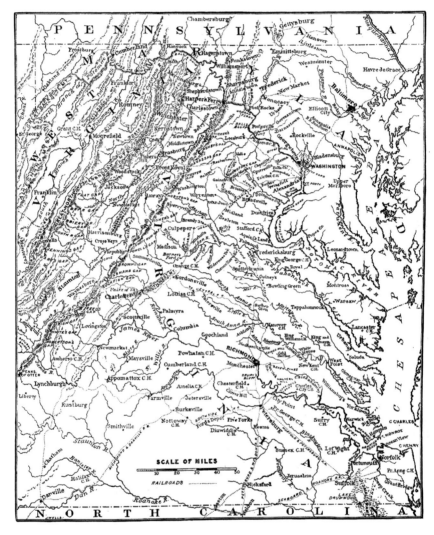

Northern Virginia. *B&L*

Blackford grew up in Fredericksburg, and later he and another officer
got a pass into the town. Appalled at the carnage at Marye's Heights, the
scene of the heaviest fighting, Blackford lamented: "There were thirteen
hundred and fifty dead Yankees in a two-acre field. My horse could not
make his way through. I have seen battlefields, but never anything equal to
this." Even worse, to him, was the wanton vandalism Yankee soldiers had
inflicted on his hometown. "Fredericksburg is completely sacked. Every
house ... without exception, has been broken open and pillaged ... . You
may imagine with what emotion I witnessed the ruins of our old home."

Federal troops had turned the Blackford family's former homestead into a hospital, leaving a gory pile of limbs under a tree as well as six men buried in the yard. Furious at the desecration of his old home, Blackford kicked over the grave markers. Nearby he discovered, much to his satisfaction, a Yankee sharpshooter "shot through the head, and lying just as he was found by the wandering bullets." He was mystified at how the man came to die at that location, since "his post was a mile from our works."[4]

During the lull in operations that followed Fredericksburg, Confederate commanders took some time to make new arrangements for their skirmishers. Just after New Year's the irascible Harvey Hill sent down an order "stating that the last campaign had fully demonstrated to the Maj. Gen. commanding the impossibility of getting on without regularly trained sharpshooters." He therefore placed Rodes (who had probably suggested it) in charge of the project and directed him to appoint an officer of the grade of major or above "conspicuous for gallantry and coolness in action, upon whom he could depend as to judgment." Rodes chose Blackford, but the job came with a price. "Great was the jealousy at me excited by this order against me and the organization which I was to effect." Much of it came from his own lieutenant colonel, Edwin Hobson, and eventually the unrest would lead to an ugly episode indeed.[5]

Rodes explained his plans to Blackford:

> He [Rodes] had felt the absolute need of trained skirmishers always ready to go to the front instead of the miserable system heretofore existing of calling for details from each company hurriedly when approaching the enemy—who arrived at the head of the column in march all breathless, and utterly ignorant of the duty required of them—and besides company officers when called upon in this manner in entering battle, did not wish to lose a good man & so sent the worst they had. Thus the indifferent men in the brigade, indifferently commanded by any detailed officer, who knew not one of his men or any thing of the skirmish drill, were sent to protect the front. The consequences were inevitable—a feeling of insecurity in the main body—the necessity of keeping a second line for protection, the incessant alarms made by the men in the front, who mistook every movement.

Rodes wanted to go far beyond this and make the Corps of Sharpshooters into an elite unit. "The result from our conversation," said Blackford, "was that I was to have one man in every 12 in the Brigade. This man was to be 1st picked by his Capt. and Col. & then subject to my approval after a trial—I was at liberty to send any one back I pleased. They were to be commanded by me absolutely and organize them as I pleased."[6]

Under Rodes's new system, each regiment detailed a sharpshooter company, commanded by a lieutenant, with a sergeant "to act as guide orderly." Eventually a second noncommissioned officer was added to the company. These men marched and bivouacked with their regiment but could be detached at any time for sharpshooting duties. As an extra inducement, they were exempt from routine fatigue details. "This freedom from the irksome and distasteful duties of the camp," said one, "which were always especially detested by the average Confederate soldier—unaccustomed as he was to do any menial labor for himself—made a place in the ranks of the sharpshooters an honor much to be desired." Only the best were accepted. Any man who did not meet the major's strict standards of soldiering, marksmanship, and "fidelity to the Southern cause" was sent back to his unit. "I belong to a corps of sharpshooters which excuses me from guard," one soldier wrote his sister. "We are formed for the purpose of going in advance in the time of battle to shoot officers. We are to be armed with the best of guns." The regimental commanders naturally resisted giving up their best men, but with Rodes's backing, Blackford prevailed. "A great and weary struggle did I have with the Regimental and Company officers," he wrote, "before I succeeded in placing my battalion beyond their efforts."[7]

On January 15, 1863, Blackford wrote to his mother, "I was yesterday assigned to the command of a battalion of Sharpshooters organized in this Brigade. They are all volunteers, and with proper discipline and drill may be made very effective. I am very much interested in it, today I obtained a quantity of ammunition with which to practice at a mark. Tho' there is a great deal of danger in such a position in battle, yet this is a chance for distinction, and as such are too rare in our service to be neglected. I estimated it a great compliment from Gen. Rodes to have received the appointment."[8]

Once his volunteers were in place, Blackford equipped each man with a suitable weapon. Although Blackford states in his diary that his men were "armed with the Springfield long range rifle," it is more likely that they used Enfield rifles, when they could get them. Informal testing had demonstrated that the precision-made Enfield consistently bested all other service rifles for accuracy at extended ranges. According to Captain W. S. Dunlop, "in the target drill, the Minnie rifle, the Enfield, the Austrian, Belgium, Springfield and Mississippi rifles were put to the test. And while each and all of them proved accurate and effective at short range, the superiority of the Enfield rifle for service at long range, from 600 to 900 yards, was clearly demonstrated, both as to force and accuracy of fire. The ulterior range of the Enfields proved reliable and effective to a surprising degree to a distance of 900 yards, while the other rifles named could only be relied on at a distance of 500 yards." The Confederates captured large numbers of Springfield rifles at Fredericksburg, and in late December a soldier in the Fifth Alabama wrote that "our Co. had to exchange their Enfield Musk. for Minié Muskts." Although the term "Minié Musket" could refer to any rifle firing the Minié ball, here it most likely refers to the .58 caliber Springfield service rifle used by the Union forces, and it is equally likely that the exchanged Enfields went to the sharpshooters.[9]

With his new weapons Blackford began an intensive training program. Following established practice he used a bugler to control his strung-out skirmish line, but he quickly realized that one was not enough and increased his "staff" of buglers to three (later to four). The buglers provoked another tussle with regimental commanders, "who from the beginning did all in their power to thwart my designs, being unwilling to give up the men." While the buglers began learning their calls, Blackford tutored the officers in skirmish tactics and drilled the battalion for two-and-a-half hours each morning. At first he had to shout commands, "but very soon the buglers could sound a few notes, and this relieved me very much, as it was a great strain to make myself heard at the great distances required."[10]

Judging distance drill, as recommended in Heth's *A System of Target Practice.*

Before actually firing at targets Blackford trained his men to estimate ranges. Given the low muzzle velocity of black-powder rifles, this was essential, because a fired bullet traveled in a high arc rather than on a flat trajectory. One manual warned that if a riflemen fired an Enfield at a target at 570 yards with the sight set at 600, "the bullet will strike 2.38 feet above it; if at an object 630 yards distant with same elevation, the bullet will strike 2.54 feet below. Thus, at 600 yards range an error in distance ever so slight, over 30 yards, would cause a ball shot at the waist-band to pass over the head or under the feet as the error was over or under." Thus, the manual writer emphasized, *"the greater the distance the greater the necessity of knowing it accurately."*[11]

To drill his company Blackford hid men in front of the battalion at various ranges known only to him, then told his buglers to call up each one with a series of notes. When a man presented himself each rifleman would estimate the range. A grader would write down his estimate, compare it to the actual range, and enter it into a record. "At first their guesses were very wide of the truth," wrote Blackford, "some missing it by 2 or 300 yards, and of course he would have set his sight the same way." After training and practice, "the improvement was astonishing, and soon they became so perfect that I discontinued the lessons."[12]

Blackford devised a unique way to speed up target practice. He set up his range with several targets, and ordered that a four-feet-deep pit be dug in front of each target, with the spoil piled toward the riflemen. In each pit stood a man with a long-handled paddle, black on one side and white on the other. If the shooter made a hit inside the 18" bull's-eye, he saw the black side of the paddle, and if he hit anywhere else on the 2' x 6' white board the observer waved the white side of the paddle. This practice allowed a large number of men to fire at the same target and assess their skills instantly. Each sharpshooter company had its own target, with the men standing twenty paces apart. Each of the five companies would fire by file; that is, a man would fire, then drop back to the end of the line to reload while the next man stepped forward. The major's tight discipline had the desired effect of preventing accidents. Blackford opened and closed the range with the bugle and found it amusing to watch the "markers" scramble for their holes when the first notes sounded. A grader kept a record of each man's progress, marking each shot as hit, center, or miss. With this system Blackford claimed that "the record was kept with perfect accuracy, yet the firing was as rapid as ordinary file firing." Any man who failed to improve went back to his regiment.[13]

Blackford himself was himself a crack shot—he claimed to be the best in the battalion—and even as a company commander had carried a breech-loading Sharps rifle. "I always carry a rifle into the action myself," he said, "and use it faithfully too." He was proud of his men and their rapid progress. "The skill acquired was wonderful—at 500 yards the number of hits far exceeded the misses, and many struck every time. At 800 [yards] 30 per cent of the bullets would strike the target, and all these were offhand." Here Blackford departed from the prevailing orthodoxy, which emphasized using a rest at long ranges.[14]

General Rodes, meanwhile, did not neglect marksmanship training for the regular infantry, many of whom still carried smoothbore muskets, and it is interesting to compare the standards to those of the sharpshooters.

One soldier described how Rodes held a contest for his old regiment, the Fifth Alabama, with the prize being an oyster supper. The regiment shot by companies, the winners being the ones who could put the most shots into a barrel head at a hundred yards. Company D, Captain J. W. Williams's company—the same ones who had been captured at South Mountain—won with nine hits. By comparison the previous four companies had collectively hit the barrel a total of only ten times.[15]

In addition to concentrating on the sharpshooters' riflery, Blackford added new bugle calls and even worked out a system of indicating ranges with them. At the end of January he wrote his mother: "I am very much interested in the instruction of a battalion of Sharpshooters, which has lately been organized in this brigade, and to the command of which I have been assigned. I have lately commenced drilling them by the bugle signals altogether. Tis a beautiful sight to see the line deployed for more than a mile, all controlled by the single sounds of a bugle. I am much in hopes that I shall be able to win some credit in line of battle, this as a general rule Skirmishers have had a poor chance, being brushed off the field early in the action."[16]

While his commanders focused on training, General Hill fell ill in late January and tendered his resignation. Eventually authorities in Richmond worked out a compromise transfer for him to the North Carolina coast. "We are extremely uneasy here just now," wrote Blackford. "There is a report that Hill's division will be ordered to N.C. ... . There is no Brigade in the service which will regard the order with such horror as ours. ... There is no spot on the globe that I had not rather go to than the coast of N. C." In the end Hill went by himself, leaving Robert Rodes as acting division commander. Although considered too junior for permanent division command, Rodes nevertheless continued the sharpshooter program while he awaited Hill's replacement.[17]

On January 28, 1863, he issued an order directing each of the division's five brigades to organize a corps of sharpshooters on the same pattern as had his brigade:

> Each corps will number one-twelfth of the men now present for duty in its Brig. It will be composed of picked men, who may volunteer for the service & [be] armed with long range pieces. An officer not below the rank of Captain selected for his gallantry & experience will be detailed by the Brigade commander to command the corps & each regimental detail will be commanded by a Subaltern volunteering for the duty.
>
> The corps of Sharpshooters thus formed will be constantly drilled as Skirmishers by its commander but is not to be considered a separate command except in the immediate presence of the enemy when it will cover the front of the brigade. At all other

times the officers and men belonging to it will remain & do duty
with their respective Regts.[18]

Thus in spring 1863 Rodes's sharpshooter battalions numbered between
100 and 125 strong, a small group to cover the brigade's front, and only
slightly larger than a full-strength infantry company. When not training,
they often practiced their new specialty, picket duty. Blackford wrote his
mother on March 1, "We were on picket six days in all that bad weather,
but no one is the worse for it that I know of, save a cold contracted by
me, while making the guard's rounds through the swamps which line the
river bank, as I was required to do twice during the night, once before &
once after 12 o'clock. While on duty there we decoyed two Yankees who
consented to come over into our lines with all their accouterments." He
commented on the low morale of the Yankees across the river, who "excited
the compassion of our men by their forlorn appearance on post without fire
in the bitter cold, while our men baked around large piles of burning logs,
and amused themselves cooking biscuits, laughing all the while at the poor
shivering wretches just opposite, who said they had not tasted hot bread
for 18 months. Without exception they all expressed their determination to
desert as soon as their wages were paid to them."[19]

On off-duty days Blackford's soldiers often engaged "at some kind of
game, mostly at ball, which is a great treat to them after the late hardships
on picket. I always do all that I can to encourage the men in athletic games,
three days thus employed reduces the sick list 75 per cent; so does anything
that interests the men. During a long rainy spell, when there is no duty to
do, and no attraction out of doors, the sick list increases wonderfully, but
three or four days of pleasant weather with moderate drills soon brings it
down again." Blackford was also savvy enough to know that physical exercise conditioned the men for the strenuous duties of the skirmish line.[20]

"My battalion of SharpShooters progresses finely," he added. "I drill
them altogether by the bugle, and the merry clear notes of the bugles may
be heard at almost any hour in good weather. I have now declared them fit
for service, and have spoken for the first job that comes up." Esprit de corps
blossomed—"I never saw anything like it in my military life"—and to add
to their pride Blackford allowed the men to wear "a little red trefoil shaped
piece of flannel" to mark them as being in an elite unit. He boasted that
"a more effective corps never existed in any army since warfare has been
practiced; and this was acknowledged by all ere long."[21]

A day seldom passed without at least one general officer visiting Blackford's unit. One of them may have been newly promoted Brigadier General
William T. Wofford, who formed his own sharpshooter battalion that spring
in his Georgia brigade. It numbered about twice as many as Blackford's and
presumably had similar equipment and training. One of Wofford's soldiers,

William Montgomery, wrote home that "Gen. Wofford had 50 men from each Regt. in the Brigade (5) to form a battalion of Sharp Shooters. ... We are in camp to ourselves and are known as the 1st Geo. 'sharpshooters.'" Someone remembered that there were already two Georgia sharpshooter battalions in the Army of Tennessee, so Wofford's battalion was redesignated the Third Georgia Battalion, Sharpshooters. "Perhaps you don't know what our duty is," Montgomery asked his wife. "We are always in the front of the brigade, about 300 to 400 yards, to clear out the way and I tell you we done it too, to perfection."[22]

Several other brigade commanders also formed sharpshooter battalions around the same time as Blackford's. Captain William Haskell organized a sharpshooter battalion in McGowan's South Carolina brigade in January, 1863, and there was an attempt that spring to form a sharpshooter battalion in Hood's Texas brigade, but it was broken up shortly after the campaign against Suffolk in May following the death of its commander.[23]

7

Chancellorsville

"It is a post of honor, not one of ease"

Eugene Blackford and his corps of sharpshooters did not have to wait long for a chance to fight. In late April the new Union commander, Major General Joseph Hooker, marched the revived Army of the Potomac across the Rappahannock and provoked the battle of Chancellorsville. On April 29 Rodes's division marched toward Fredericksburg, where Hooker was reportedly advancing. Blackford, ill with a fever, had been enjoying the bountiful hospitality of the Gordon family at nearby Santee plantation. He returned to Guiney Station but neglected to have his horse sent there, leaving him to walk seven miles to his regiment's camp only to find that the men had departed. After another five miles on shank's mare he finally caught up with them near Fredericksburg.

General Rodes sent Blackford's sharpshooters out to cover Hamilton's Crossing on the Rappahannock, above which they could see several Yankee balloons "looking like huge oranges." The men were anxious for action. "With a yell they began to deploy and very soon at a single note of the bugle the line was formed in the exact position required, as accurately dressed as if on parade," he wrote. Moving forward, they bumped into a Yankee picket line across the river, "but neither side seemed desirous of firing." For the rest of the day the two sides regarded each other warily, with the only incident being a fox that broke cover and found itself trapped between the lines, rushing frantically back and forth until it found its way out. The men bedded down for a watchful night. Blackford, who had spent the previous night in a feather bed, "found the bivouac out in the wet clover very unpleasant."[1]

At dawn the next morning the sharpshooters followed their division, which had continued on, catching up with it about 10 a.m. There, near Zoan Church, Stonewall Jackson faced down Hooker, who abruptly stopped his advance and began to dig in. Blackford put his new battalion on line in advance of the division in the scrub oak and pines of the Wilderness. It was not a pleasant experience. "I then went out with my sharpshooters and deployed them by the bugle within 400 yards of the enemy. Here I spent Wednesday night in a drenching rain without fire or blankets ... and the whole of Thursday until 2 AM of Friday [May 1] when I received an order to retire to the works, as the Brig. was about to march."[2]

That night Lee and Jackson planned their famous flank march, and the next morning Jackson's Second Corps set off around the Federal right. Blackford's sharpshooters provided flank security to the column, "marching their laborious way thru swamps & pine thickets." Blackford used his bugles frequently to create the illusion that he led cavalry rather than infantry. "I frequently passed in sight of the enemy troops, but they took no notice of us ... as we took good care to keep under cover of the undergrowth."[3]

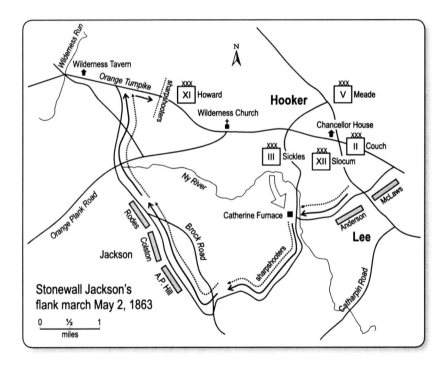

Stonewall Jackson's flank march May 2, 1863

In late afternoon, having reached his assembly position on Hooker's flank, Blackford found Rodes with Stonewall Jackson. Old Jack ordered Blackford to scout in front while the rest of the corps filed up and deployed. Blackford took a dozen men and advanced three hundred yards in front of the Confederate position, where they caught three Yankees out foraging. "They took us for their own men & walked up to us boldly—I never saw such amazement as when I told them they were prisoners." The three prisoners were Germans, "Dutchmen" from the Union XI Corps. They confirmed that the Federals were cooking dinner and that "none of them had any idea we were nearer than Fredericksburg."[4]

By 5:15 Jackson was ready, his Second Corps poised like a giant battering ram on the Federal flank. He sat on his horse, Little Sorrel, "visor low over his eyes, lips compressed, and with his watch in his hand." Finally he gave Rodes the signal to advance "with several gestures of his hand," saying "'just push them, General, push them, all is well.'" Rodes ordered Blackford to take his position three hundred yards in front of the main line and keep it until he made contact with the Yankees. Bugles echoed up and down the line and the sharpshooters melted into the forest. There was an embarrassing delay as Rodes's old brigade, now commanded by Colonel Edward O'Neal, overran some of its sharpshooters who had evidently not gotten the word to move. After a short delay the advance began again.[5]

General Thomas J. "Stonewall" Jackson. *B&L*

Blackford's men moved forward silently for a quarter of a mile. Then, as Blackford wrote his family:

> Presently one of the men near me put up his gun and taking aim, fired, and instantly reloaded. I told him I would break his head if he fired again without seeing the enemy, he called me to him and pointed out the Yankee line of battle not 50 yds off lying

down in a well worn road. I had not sounded more than a note or two of the "Commence Firing" when the whole line opened up with a terrible yell, which was too much for the Dutchmen of Sigel's (11th) Corps, and they ran off in confusion taken utterly by surprise. Our main line then came up and soon ran in the other lines of battle which the enemy had, and the rout became general. We pursued until it was too dark to see how to shoot and then rested for the night. Our loss was perfectly trifling; hardly a man killed, and booty in abundance. As we had had nothing to eat for two days (not a mouthful for me) you can imagine how I enjoyed the fine 8 days rations with which the Yankees were supplied. [6]

Although the Confederates completely routed the Union XI Corps, the tangled thickets of the Wilderness scattered and disorganized both sides by the time darkness closed over the field. In the dim light disaster struck the Confederates. Some nervous North Carolina troops fired a volley that hit Stonewall Jackson, and minutes later a shell burst wounded the next senior man, Major General A. P. Hill. Robert Rodes temporarily took command of Second Corps, but yielded it shortly afterward to cavalry Major General Jeb Stuart.

The Union XI Corps struggles to repel Jackson's flank attack. *B&L*

On the morning of May 3 the Rebel infantry advanced against a thoroughly alerted enemy who had had all night to set up log barricades and move his artillery forward. Rodes's division, having carried the burden of the attack the previous day, formed the third line. "Before sunrise we moved in, my sharpshooters [acting] as a separate Battalion but in the regular line as infantry," wrote Blackford. Initially the attack went poorly. "For some reason, Colston's division laid down, and Gen. Rodes coming up ordered us to step over them, which we did, and thus reached the works simultaneously with the leading Division." A storm of musket and artillery fire awaited them at the Yankee works, which were situated on the low rise of Chancellor's Hill. "I never in all my career have ever seen such a storm of bullets & grape as we encountered in this attack," Blackford continued, "and it is almost incredible that our men were enabled to capture such a position."[7]

Yet capture it they did. "Just when it seemed as if men could not stand such a fire," said Blackford, "they were falling like grass before the blade, a few men only were with each color, too feeble, it seemed, to drive the enemy out of their strong entrenchments. Still one last effort, one last wave of the colors, and with a fearful yell this heroic band washed up the hill and entered the works shooting down the retreating foe." But the battle was not over. A Yankee counterattack drove back Rodes's division, capturing half of the Fifth Alabama, its flag, and much of the Twenty-sixth Alabama. The Stonewall brigade and Ramseur's North Carolina brigade followed, retaking the heights again in fighting "of a most desperate character." Ramseur's men freed many captured Alabamians but were forced to relinquish the heights by another Federal counterattack. Finally the Confederate artillery, situated *en enfilade* at the nearby Hazel Grove clearing, provided the key by literally blasting the Unionists out of their barricades, allowing the exhausted Southern infantry to occupy the stronghold. The taking of the high ground around Fair View clinched the victory, allowing the two wings of Lee's army to unite. As Marse Robert rode into the clearing near the Chancellor House, he received a thunderous cheer from the parched throats of his men. Hooker's men retreated into a strong semicircular position, their flanks protected by the river. Victory belonged to the Confederates, but the cost was high. Casualties in the assaulting brigades approached fifty percent.[8]

Meanwhile, Wofford's Georgia sharpshooters had also been busy. As part of McLaws's division, Wofford's brigade had remained in front of Hooker's army during Jackson's flank march. William Montgomery described in a letter home how on the evening of May 2 his "little battalion" had assaulted the Federal works three times only to be driven back. The next day they tried again. "We charged under the most deadly fire," he wrote. "Got within a few feet of the works, but it was fixed with brush [abatis] that we could not climb." The Georgians again fell back, but when the men of Second Corps began pressing toward them about noon, "we thought it a good time to charge again. So at them we went like so many wild Indians. Fired only two or three rounds when they showed a white flag." Unbeknownst to Montgomery, Brigadier General Paul Semmes's Georgia brigade, also part of McLaws's division, had moved behind the Yankees and cut off their retreat.

So although Montgomery claimed that "800 or 900 men" had surrendered to his "small Batt. of Sharp Shooters," the real number was around 350. The men of the 27th Connecticut and 145th Pennsylvania had in fact surrendered to Semmes.[9]

The fighting had been intense, and Montgomery acknowledged that "our loss was quite heavy." His battalion, like Blackford's, was composed of five companies, and he noted the loss in his own company as one officer and one enlisted man killed as well as eight severely wounded. "Other companies," he wrote, "lost in proportion," which would make the aggregate loss somewhere around ten killed and forty wounded, or twenty to thirty percent of the battalion.[10]

Next McLaws's men had to face about to handle a Union force advancing on their rear from Fredericksburg. They met the Yankees at Salem Church where, according to Montgomery, they "held them in check" while other units flanked them. The Yankees fought stubbornly at first but soon "made tracks for the river" at Bank's Ford. As they withdrew across the river the next night, the sharpshooters led the pursuit "pressing them at every point until 1 o'clock at night, capturing many prisoners. Sharp Shooters made a charge in a pine thicket, dark as Egypt, fired a volley & you ought to have heard the Yanks beg for quarter. Took a Lt. Col. & about half a Reg." Montgomery's performance earned him a recommendation for promotion from sergeant to first lieutenant in the sharpshooters.[11]

The fighting may have been over for Montgomery and his battalion, but Blackford's sharpshooters had not yet seen the end of their work at Chancellorsville. They had been the first to engage the Yankees and they would be the last. Hooker's army, which still substantially outnumbered the Confederates, occupied a entrenched position in the bend of the Rappahannock. During May 4, while the rest of Lee's army was dealing with Sedgwick's detached VI Corps at Bank's Ford, Jeb Stuart tried aggressively to distract Hooker with his cavalry and the exhausted Second Corps, which totaled no more than 21,000 men, considerably less than half of what Hooker could muster inside his perimeter. Stuart held the roads in force and trusted to his sharpshooters and dismounted cavalry to screen the wilderness in between. The riflemen in butternut brown pressed close to the Federal lines, "making it," as one man put it, "as much as life is worth to walk along our lines." They fought off a couple probes, tangled with Berdan's Yankee sharpshooters in a series of hotly contested picket actions, and picked off Brigadier General Amiel Whipple as he was deploying them. Stuart's troops had brought down another of III Corps's division commanders, Brigadier General Hiram Berry, the day before, and only narrowly missed adding the commander of the Union XII Corps, Major General Henry Slocum, to their trophy bag.[12]

Hooker stayed put, and Rodes's riflemen waited on the picket line. "Monday night it rained," remembered John Bone, one of Ramseur's sharpshooters. "We were expecting an attack that night, so there was a strong line put in front and another just in our rear. I was in the front line." Unfortunately, as was so often the case when so many armed men were in close proximity, there was an outburst of nervous firing, and the second line of sharpshooters began firing into the first line. Their commander, thinking quickly, "ordered the front line to fall back to the rear line which we did in quick order without much damage. Our officer being a profane man, the rear line understood his meaning." The men waited out the rest of the night listening to the whippoorwills and shivering through periodic rain showers. On May 5, "very wet, sleepy, cold and hungry," they stood at their posts hoping for a move to the rear, "where our chances would be better for a little refreshment, [of] which we were very much in need."[13]

Lee, however, was contemplating an attack and wanted to know more about Hooker's defenses. He gave the mission to Rodes, who sent for Blackford "and directed me to make an armed reconnaissance of the enemy's works. This I did with my battalion of Sharpshooters, and driving in their skirmishers, advanced to within a few hundred yards of their works, and made a fair plan of their position. This drew upon us a murderous fire of grape, canister, and musketry, from which I withdrew my men as speedily as possible, tho not without considerable loss, and with the narrowest escapes I have yet made. The general seemed much pleased with my report, and I returned fully satisfied that the enemy was there in *force*." The worst part of it, thought Blackford, "was that there were no trees to shelter us, for it is lawful for a skirmisher to use these." The lack of cover led to the loss of some of his best men.[14]

Ramseur's men went with them, and John Bone left a detailed description of the action:

> Both lines were now thrown together, making a very strong line and we advanced forward. As we started off, the enemy opened their artillery on us, being loaded with grape-shot and canister shells, which was not very pleasant to face, but we went until we drove the enemy's line and they fired from their breast-works, and also from their batteries. We were just in the edge of a woods, taking in the situation of their lines, from the view it seemed as though a great many of our men would be killed and a great number were killed. I remember a man who was lying very near to me, and all at once a cannon ball or shell struck his head and knocked it from his body. After locating their condition we fell back to our former line and had grape-shots and canister shells thrown among them, but they made it so very hot for us that we retreated.

Bone and his men fell back and manned a picket line until evening, when "greatly exhausted for want of sleep and refreshment," they were finally relieved. "At this time," said Bone, "I felt about as despondent as I had in any part of my life, after realizing things as they were; my relatives, tent mates, school mates and nearest comrades were gone."[15]

Wednesday morning, May 6, Blackford and his sharpshooters prepared for another probe of the Yankee works, but instead of the expected storm of shot and shell they found the Federal works empty. "Pursuing them to the river, my men took many prisoners and acquired much plunder," he said. One of their prizes was a tiny jackass, "not more than four feet tall," that one of the sharpshooters captured. The rifleman, "after hearing something in the bushes," waited patiently for his shot, only to see the pathetic little animal, loaded with ammunition, crashing through the underbrush. Blackford renamed the diminutive beast "Johnny Hooker" and took him to carry his baggage.[16]

Although it was a pleasant surprise to find a pack animal, many of the battlefield scenes appeared downright hellish. "All the Yankee wounded were burnt to death by the burning leaves which the shells set afire," wrote Blackford after reaching the river. "The sight was perfectly horrible—enough to make one's hair turn gray. The whole atmosphere was impregnated with the odor of burning flesh." After the battle the sharpshooters' trials continued. As soon as the battalion returned they were ordered to march back to camp—a distance of eighteen miles—in a driving hailstorm. Much later Blackford fumed about the "shameful" way the men were treated after battle. The generals moved out early, leaving the regimental officers to take the men back to the camps. When Blackford finally arrived at camp, with no more than twenty men following the colors, he found that his personal quarters had been demolished. Hypothermic, (he was, after all, still recuperating from a serious illness) he made it to Santee Plantation with his last remaining strength, where the Gordon family once more took him in and nursed him back to health. "I never saw or experienced such misery," he said. Jim Branscomb, a sharpshooter with the Third Alabama, agreed, writing his sister after the battle that they were "the worst used up set of men I have ever seen."[17]

At Chancellorsville Blackford had proved the worth of his sharpshooters to everyone's satisfaction. Rodes's five sharpshooter battalions had showed exemplary flexibility, as well as expertise in scouting, screening and the ability to fight as heavy infantry when needed. Rodes's sterling performance earned him the wreath of a major general and permanent command of D. H. Hill's old division (now Rodes's division). Still, Rodes thought the sharpshooter's organization needed some tweaking. A one-hundred-man battalion was simply not strong enough to perform the missions Rodes had in mind. In particular, although a battalion could picket the brigade front, no extra men were available for relief. In late May, therefore, Rodes ordered the formation of a second corps of sharpshooters, the same size as the first.

Shepherd G. Pryor, a captain in Doles's Georgia brigade, described the change in a letter to his wife:

> I've been put on another duty that I don't like much, but my motto is to do the best I can under any and all circumstances: go ahead and do my duty. I am now in command of the First Battalion of Sharpshooters composed of the detail from the 12th and 4th [Georgia] Reg., about 70 men. It is a post of honor, not one of ease. There is another battalion in the brigade compo[sed] of the detail from the 21st & 44th [Georgia], that is the 2nd [Battalion]. The duties are whenever in line of battle we are in front [and] go ahead to feel the way & find out when and where the enemy is in force. Whenever a general engag[ement] takes place, then we fall bac[k] to the main line. The cause of there being two battalions [is] for the purpose of relieving each other. My company is very m[uch] dissatisfied at it, or at least so express themselves to me: much rather I'd command them and be with them when a fight comes off.[18]

The only extant order regarding the second corps's formation is from Brigadier Alfred Iverson's brigade, specifying on May 25, 1863, that "a second battalion of sharpshooters will at once be organized in this Brigade containing the same number of men as the first—one twelfth (1/12) of the whole number of men present for duty in each of Regts." This brought the total number of sharpshooters to one-sixth of the brigade's strength, or about two hundred men, and this is the figure Blackford gives for the strength of his battalion in his memoir, which skips over the second corps's formation. Iverson's order also specified that one battalion would drill on the first three days of the week ("Mondays, Tuesdays & Wednesdays"), while the second drilled on the next three days ("Thursdays, Fridays and Saturdays"). The brigade commander was to confirm each corps/battalion commander.[19]

Lee reorganized his army after Chancellorsville. Rodes's division exchanged Alfred Colquitt's Georgia brigade, which went to the coast, with Junius Daniel's excellent Tarheel brigade. One of Daniel's soldiers, Private Louis Leon, noted in his diary that "when we got to the Army of Northern Virginia, we were told that each company must furnish one skirmisher out of every six men, and there was a call for volunteers for that service. So I left the colors and went as a skirmisher, whose duty it is in time of battle to go in front of the line and reconnoitre and engage the enemy until a general engagement, then we fall in line with balance of the army." He makes no mention of the number of companies in his battalion. In addition to Daniel's men, Rodes's division now consisted of his old Alabama brigade, now under Colonel Edward O'Neal of the Twenty-sixth Alabama; Doles's Georgia brigade; and Iverson's and Ramseur's North Carolina brigades.[20]

In Wofford's brigade Sergeant William Montgomery wrote his sister on June 11 that "our Batt. of Sharpshooters has been called out again & I think this time will permanently organize & I will be first Lieut." He was right. He received his promotion, and on August 18 he addressed a letter as being from the Third Georgia Battalion Sharpshooters.[21]

Around the same time the men of Brigadier General Alfred Scales's North Carolina brigade (part of Major General Dorsey Pender's division) faced their opponents at Hamilton's Crossing on the Rappahannock. The Federals, who held the road to Fredericksburg, had thrown up "a considerable barricade" across it, protected by a strong skirmish line. To keep them in check the Confederates established "a battalion composed of a company from each of the five regiments, and commanded by a field officer," which picketed the area for a tour of twenty-four hours before relief, "covering a front equal to that of a brigade." Soon the arrangement became permanent, and the rest of the brigades in the division—McGowan's South Carolina brigade (then under Colonel Abner Perrin), Thomas's Georgia brigade, and Lane's North Carolina brigade—formed sharpshooter battalions on the pattern established by Rodes and Blackford. They were, said the chronicler of McGowan's brigade, "picked men ... young, active, and good shots—amounting to a hundred and twenty or more." Captain William T. Haskell commanded the three-company battalion: "They were designed for skirmish and picket duty, or for special service in a general engagement. They always marched at the head of the brigade."[22]

8

Gettysburg

*"The mere raising of my hand would be the signal for
a dozen Yankees to fire at me."*

After his victory at Chancellorsville Lee moved north again, crossing the Potomac in late June and marching into Pennsylvania. Blackford wrote his father that June 22 was "the proudest day of my life ... when Confederate infantry would invade this state. As we approached the line the band prepared to play, and just as the head of the column reached it, they struck up Bonnie Blue Flag most cheerily." Rodes's division soon reached Carlisle, only twenty miles southwest of Harrisburg, Pennsylvania. "We spent 3 days there very pleasantly, some of our Brigades being in the Barracks, and one in the College grounds within the City limits," wrote Blackford. "I never saw a more beautiful place than this." He was taken aback by the behavior of some Pennsylvania women, who would "rush out screaming" when Confederate soldiers knocked at their doors and asked to buy food. Imagine, he wrote his mother, "a great Dutch woman ... begging you not to murder the child she has at her breast, and actually, in her gratification, refusing to take any compensation for the butter and eggs!"[1]

On July 1 some of Major General Henry Heth's infantry tangled with dismounted Union cavalry just outside the little town of Gettysburg, thirty-seven miles south of Harrisburg, and the fight soon escalated into a major battle as reinforcements from both armies converged there. When the fighting began Rodes's division was at Heidlersburg, seven miles north of Gettysburg. With the two other divisions of Second Corps strung out several miles behind him, Rodes headed south toward the sound of the guns. As it happened, his fortuitous appearance from the north placed him on the flank of the defending Union I Corps, which was just then slugging it out with Heth's division of A. P. Hill's new Third Corps. The Confederates now had an opportunity to hammer their opponents before the trailing Union XI and III Corps could arrive. Rodes led his division south in a column of brigades down a long wooded rise called Oak Ridge, his sharpshooters driving off the screening Yankee cavalry as they went. "They repeatedly charged," wrote Blackford, "but my men rallying coolly & promptly sent them back every time with more empty saddles."[2]

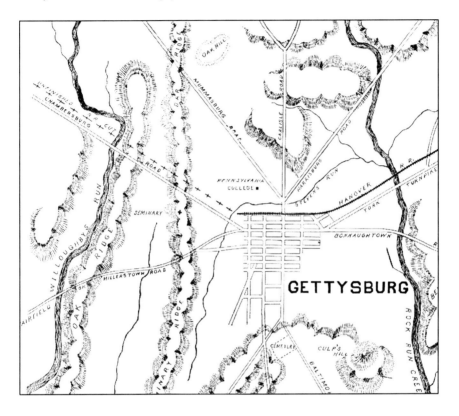

Gettysburg. Walter A. Lane, *The Soldier in Our Civil War.*

Major General John Reynolds, the Union I Corps commander, conducted a stout defense of McPherson's ridge against Heth's men. But a Confederate sharpshooter's bullet ended his life, and his successor, Major General Abner Doubleday, scrambled to cover his flank against Rodes's impending attack. To this end Doubleday placed Brigadier General Henry Baxter's tough 1,500-man New York and Pennsylvania brigade at the edge of a plateau that fell away steeply near the town. With strong Federal reinforcements making their way toward Gettysburg, Rodes needed to whip Baxter before his own left flank was compromised.

Baxter held a precarious position. Lacking enough men to tie in his flanks, he instead had to adopt a V-shaped position with the sharp end facing the Confederates. Rodes planned to overwhelm him with three brigades:

Alfred Iverson's and Edward O'Neal's brigades would attack the sides of the V, overlapping Baxter's flanks, while Junius Daniel's brigade would swing past his left rear. As Rodes deployed his division near Oak Hill, however, the Federal XI Corps—their old opponents from Chancellorsville—arrived on the field and began massing on his left. To hold them off the Confederate general stationed Doles's Georgia brigade on the low ground to face the XI Corps, which by now had two of its divisions advancing on him, then assigned Blackford and his sharpshooters the difficult task of connecting Doles's brigade to the rest of the division on Oak Hill. Rodes stationed the Fifth Alabama in reserve just behind them and placed an artillery battery on the hill for support.[3]

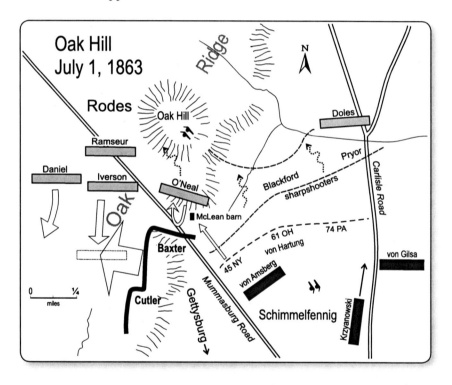

"I was directed to deploy my corps across the valley to our left," wrote Blackford, "and do my best to make the enemy believe that we had heavy infantry supports, whereas there was not a man." He and his men exchanged fire with four companies of skirmishers from the mostly-German 45th New York, led by Captain Francis Irsch. The New Yorkers initially pushed the Alabamians back, but soon wilted under their withering fire. Next the rest of the 45th New York moved forward in skirmish formation, and two artillery batteries dueled fiercely with the Confederate pieces on the hill. As the 3rd division of the XI Corps arrived on the battlefield, two more regiments, the 61st Ohio and the 74th Pennsylvania, moved up to reinforce the Union skirmish line. These Federal regiments were considerably understrength, but with some 425 men all together they substantially outnumbered Blackford's sharpshooters.[4]

The sharpshooters' winter training paid off in the fight. For most of the afternoon Blackford's thin line of riflemen "made so determined a front that the Yankees were persuaded that we were heavily supported." It was dangerous work, especially for an officer on the skirmish line. "The mere raising of my hand would be the signal for a dozen Yankees to fire at me," wrote Blackford. "The men would constantly urge me to take care, but there was no help for it." Fortunately for the Confederates, the Yankees' aim was not as good as that of the superbly trained Alabamians. "Thus did we fight it out until the sun was well nigh down, and I almost exhausted by running up & down the line exhorting the men, and making a target of myself. My loss was considerable, mostly however in wounded." Union losses also ran high. Confederate bullets wounded the skirmish-line commander, Colonel Adolph von Hartung, and killed or wounded ninety-six of his men. "If I did not kill a yankey this time I don't think I ever will," wrote sharpshooter Jim Branscomb. "I guess I shot 75 or a hundred rounds at them and some of them very close shots."[5]

Meanwhile, Rodes's attack on Baxter had gone disastrously wrong. Colonel Edward O'Neal, commander of Rodes's old brigade, was a politician-turned-soldier who entirely lacked the tactical ability to carry out Rodes's scheme of maneuver. Instead of attacking in concert with Iverson, O'Neal made a hasty head-on assault on Baxter's position with only three of the four regiments available to him—rather than overlapping his flank as Rodes had ordered—and was quickly repulsed with loss. In addition to heavy musketry from Baxter's men, who occupied an excellent position behind a stone wall, O'Neal's Alabamians also had to dodge vigorous artillery shelling from the Union batteries posted on the low ground and a peppering long-range fire from the XI Corps skirmish line. Blackford, who had been driven out of the McLean farmstead near the base of Oak Hill, had not been entirely successful in keeping the Yankees back, and Rodes had to commit a company of the Fifth Alabama to cover O'Neal's flank. These men went in near the barn on the McLean farm under a hail of bullets, and one of them, Sam Pickens, found "some N.C. sharp-shooters there who had shot away all their cartridges." These men were undoubtedly from Iverson's brigade, but it is unclear why they were so far from their parent unit. Their absence would have severe consequences. Pickens and his men, who were not trained sharpshooters, "kept up pretty brisk firing at the Yankees, but it seemed as if we could do very little execution as they were so far off & behind a fence in the woods, though they made the bullets whistle over us."[6]

Hard on the heels of O'Neal's failure, Iverson's brigade suffered an even worse fate. Evidently distracted by another Federal brigade to their front, Iverson's Tarheels missed Baxter's position altogether and advanced "with arms at right shoulder…in splendid array, keeping step with an almost perfect line" at a right angle to it. The Yankees, hidden behind a stone fence, rose and poured a overwhelming fire into their flank, then followed with a strong counterattack, killing or capturing most of the brigade. Iverson's sharpshooters should have screened his front and reported Baxter's location, but they were out of position. Iverson did not accompany his brigade in the attack, and he made a bad situation worse by accusing his men of misconduct in surrendering.[7]

Rodes hurriedly rallied his old brigade, added the Fifth Alabama, and flung the soldiers into another assault. In the rear he found Colonel O'Neal, who had remained there, with the Fifth Alabama. The second disorganized attack fared as badly as the first, although some of O'Neal's men managed to cross Mummasburg road and fire at the Yankees who were finishing off Iverson's men. "I never saw [our] troops so scattered & in such confusion," wrote Pickens. "We were under a heavy fire from the front & a cross fire from the left & pretty soon had to fall back to a fence where the Brig. was rallied by Col. O'Neal & Gen'l Rodes." During the disordered retreat Irsch's men pressed forward to McLean's barn, where they captured a number of Rebels who had taken refuge inside. The Confederates now faced defeat in what had began as a promising flank attack.[8]

Still, help was at hand. Rodes brought up his last unengaged brigade, that of North Carolinian Dodson Ramseur. It was one of the army's best, and the young, aggressive Ramseur—a military professional—was full of fight. Ramseur took the remnants of Iverson's brigade and the Third Alabama, a stray regiment of O'Neal's the Alabama colonel had inexplicably ignored, and organized them for an attack on the Federal position. Meanwhile Baxter, who was running low on ammunition, had pulled back to a supporting position, with Brigadier General Gabriel Paul's fresh brigade replacing him at the top of the "fishhook." Junius Daniel's Tarheel brigade, which had been repulsed in an attack on the nearby railroad cut, now swung back towards Paul's flank, as Rodes had originally intended.

On Rodes's left Blackford and his men could not hold out much longer. As more of the XI Corps deployed in front of the town, the pressure increased, bowing back the end of Blackford's line, forcing his men up the steep rise to the plateau.

> About 6 o'clock the enemy advanced a triple line on my left. I rushed up there and did my best, but it was useless to do more than give them what we had, and then run for it. So we kept up a terrible popping until they came within 200 yards, the Yankees

not firing again, expecting to meet a heavy force of rebels over the hill. Then sounding the retreat away we went at our best speed. I was much concerned, but could do nothing against that mass. We had not gone more than 100 or so yards, when "Halt, Halt" was heard, and just in front of me to my infinite delight could be seen a long line of skirmishers of Early's Division sweeping on to the front. Soon afterwards we met his dusty columns hurrying up. I knew then that all was safe.[9]

Until then the pugnacious Yankees fought Rodes's men to a standstill, but Jubal Early's arrival changed the situation entirely. Ramseur, with Daniel supporting his flank, launched a devastating attack on Paul's position, carrying it at a single bound. O'Neal's Alabamians, who "had assembled without order on the hill, rushed forward, still without order, but with all their usual courage, into the charge." The Federals collapsed, and almost the entire 16th Maine, Paul's rear guard, was captured. Meanwhile Daniel slammed into Baxter's men, driving them from the woods with heavy casualties. At the same time Early's men, aided by Doles's aggressive Georgians, began to systematically dismantle the poorly placed XI Corps.[10]

Soon the Rebels swept the field, driving the Union I and XI Corps in disorder through Gettysburg. Blackford's sharpshooters reversed course to assist John Gordon's Georgia brigade of Early's division, then fell in with Ramseur's brigade of their own division. As Blackford recalled:

We overtook them as they were entering the town and my men took their own share in the plundering that went on. I employed myself with the aid of such men as I had with me in destroying whiskey, of which there was an enormous quantity in the town. [In] half an hour many men were dead drunk, and others were wild with excitement. It was truly a wild scene, rushing through the town capturing prisoners by hundreds; a squad of us would run down a street and come to a corner just as a whole mass of frightened Yanks were rushing up another. A few shots made the whole surrender, and so on until we caught them all.[11]

It was a euphoric moment after the day's trials. The number of prisoners captured topped 2,500. One was the redoubtable Captain Irsch who had given Blackford so much trouble that day.[12]

Despite the heady victory, the Confederates, who were in considerable disarray themselves, failed to capture the dominating terrain of Cemetery Hill just outside Gettysburg, a tactical lapse that would have dire consequences. Unhappy with the day's fighting, Blackford complained in a letter that Rodes had "attacked at once, without the smallest concert of action with the other Division Commanders." That night he and his exhausted men slept in a barn near the town.[13]

The first day's fighting at Gettysburg illustrates the failures and successes of Confederate sharpshooters there. With Iverson's brigade in the lead, Rodes advanced down Oak Ridge. As the Yankee cavalry became more than Iverson's sharpshooters could handle, Rodes deployed Blackford's battalion to sweep them away, a task they successfully accomplished. When Rodes sent Doles and Blackford to cover his left flank, for an unknown reason some of Iverson's sharpshooters ended up there as well. Federal accounts clearly state that Iverson's brigade went forward without scouts or skirmishers, which led directly to its disastrous deadfall. O'Neal, also deprived of his sharpshooter battalion, returned to the old system, designating some of his companies to cover his line. Thus his attack, though unsuccessful, at least avoided the deadly surprise Iverson's soldiers encountered. Although O'Neal's riflemen were able to harass Baxter's men as they scooped up Iverson's men in Forney's field, their lack of sharpshooter training limited their effectiveness.[14]

Blackford's battalion performed its mission quite well. His handful of sharpshooters held off von Hartung's men and aided materially in keeping the XI Corps away from Rodes's flank. Nevertheless, Irsch got close enough to harass O'Neal, forcing Rodes to commit part of his Fifth Alabama reserve to protect his flank. Overall, however, Blackford skillfully employed his men, making effective use of terrain and pulling back before any of his companies could be surrounded. As for marksmanship, the Federal casualties on their skirmish line—almost 25 percent—told the tale. The Yankees employed a conventional skirmish line, which had been considerably less effective. Although they lacked nothing in valor and aggressiveness, and the skirmish line was rightly placed under a single commander, the Union command had thrown together three regiments from two different divisions, who had never worked in concert before. Despite a considerable numerical superiority the Yankees signally failed to sweep away the Rebel skirmishers as they had at South Mountain.

On July 2 the sharpshooters, along with the rest of Rodes's division, lay in the hot sun under a tremendous artillery duel. Once again the Confederate commanders seemed incapable of coordinating their attacks. Although some of Jubal Early's division reached the top of Cemetery Hill on the second day of the battle, they had no support and were unable to hold it. Finally, at dusk, Rodes's men were ordered to form for an assault on Cemetery Hill. The news caused considerable consternation in the ranks. "I well remember," Blackford recalled later, "what feelings I had as I fastened my saber knot tightly around my wrist. I knew well that I had seen my last day on earth. … It was to be a bayonet affair, the guns were all inspected to see that none were loaded. Then we lay silently waiting the word to advance, when to my relief I must say, I saw the dark masses of men wheeling to the rear—the idea had been abandoned."[15]

Rebel sharpshooters in the houses at Gettysburg. Alfred Waud, LC.

Shortly afterward Rodes instructed Blackford "to draw a skirmish line as closely across the enemy's works as I possibly could, and when daylight came annoy them within all my power." This assignment was more to the major's liking, and he stationed his men in the houses in Gettysburg facing Cemetery Hill. To prepare for the next day's fighting, Blackford's men expended "a great deal of labor" breaking passages between the adjoining houses and "thro' every thing else we met."[16]

At first light Blackford's sharpshooters unleashed a furious fusillade at the Union positions "without regard to ammunition." Many of his riflemen scaled the roofs and took posts behind the chimneys, putting them at the same level as the Yankees on Cemetery Hill, who were "as thick as bees." Their first target was a battery of six guns drawn up about four hundred yards away, "standing as if on parade." Not for long: "One signal from my bugle," boasted Blackford, "and that battery was utterly destroyed." To keep his men supplied, Blackford employed soldiers in a baker's cart to pick up abandoned cartridge boxes in the town's streets. As the day wore on his riflemen began to complain of "having their arms & shoulders very much bruised by the continual kicking of the muskets." Blackford estimated he had personally fired eighty rounds that day and thought the number closer to two hundred for most of his men.[17]

Although the Federals hesitated to level the town with their artillery—which they could easily have done—they sent their own sharpshooters to engage the Southerners, "who killed so many of our artillerymen that it became almost impossible to work our guns." Some were the same men that they had tangled with at Oak Hill, such as a volunteer detachment of "ten good shots" from the 45th New York under Sergeant Charles Link. One such Yankee sharpshooter put a ball near Blackford that ricocheted across his knees, giving him a painful but superficial wound.[18]

Later that day Blackford's elder brother William, one of Jeb Stuart's staff officers, paid him an impromptu visit. He described the incongruous sight of his brother's men "stripped to the waist and blackened with powder" in the elegant surroundings, the scene further marred by the pools of blood on the floor where the Yankee riflemen had exacted their own toll. Blackford admitted "a good many casualties," but insisted that "it was a mere trifle compared to with the enormous damage they inflicted." Indeed, the battle was costly for both sides. For example, in the 45th New York's sharpshooter detachment, "every one of these ten brave men was killed or wounded."[19]

The sharpshooters fared well in Gettysburg that day, helping themselves to the rich larders in the houses from which they fired. Blackford wrote his family that...

> I have never lived so high since I have been in the Army as we did those two days. My buglers, 4 in number, are all good cooks and, being perfectly devoted to me, you can imagine how I fared. They had nothing to do so I made them keep under cover, thus giving them ample time to prepare all manner of edibles: we have some five or six meals a day. If my conscience had been tender on this point it might have been quieted by the reflection that it was absolutely necessary, as no rations could reach us from the rear, there being nothing to protect the bearer from the fire of the enemy.[20]

As senior officer Blackford also took command of some Louisiana sharpshooters from Hayes's brigade who had set up headquarters in one house's parlor. There they were playing the piano, which, he noted, "sounded sadly out of harmony with the roar of musketry." On a nearby table sat "a doz. brands of wines and liquors of which all partook freely." The fun-loving Louisianans were greatly put out when Blackford insisted that they rejoin the fight.[21]

The battle's climax approached as the day wore on. From his elevated perch Blackford could see Pickett's men "charge, then waver, when almost in the works, and finally fall back. How my heart ached when I saw the fearful fire with which they were received." In a futile attempt to help, he redoubled his sharpshooters' fire into the Federal position. "I fired 84 rounds with careful aim into their midst, one gun cooling while the other was in use. My shoulder pad became so sore that I was obliged to rest."[22]

It was all in vain. With the failure of Pickett's charge, Lee had to admit defeat. At dawn on July 4, in a pouring rain, Blackford and his men "sullenly drew slowly out of the town, returning the sour looks of the citizens with others equally as stern." A group of Federal skirmishers moved through the town and deployed in front of him. "They used the bugle, the first I had seen with them. Their signals sounded clear & [distant], thro' the damp air." When Blackford moved against them, they retreated after a minor skirmish. The Yankees, in fact, seemed to be as exhausted as the Confederates. Seeing this, Blackford put a subordinate in charge and tried to grab some sleep. The next morning the Army of Northern Virginia, burdened by an immense train of wounded, began its long retreat south.[23]

That night Rodes gave Blackford command of all the division's sharpshooter battalions, which he formed into a makeshift "demi-brigade" nearly a thousand strong to act as the army's rear guard—another improvisation that would soon become permanent. "I was to keep my line until day or longer if I saw fit, and then follow keeping a half mile or more in the rear, and acting as rear guard. Accordingly by 11 p.m. the troops all disappeared on the prescribed route and I was left in sole command at Gettysburg. It was the first time I had ever commanded more than one battalion and now I had five. My only embarrassment was in not knowing the officers but this I soon remedied, and got on quite well."[24]

The Yankee pursuit was tepid, but on the afternoon of July 6 Federal cavalry appeared, brought up a field piece, and deployed for a fight. Blackford formed his men into two long skirmish lines, one behind the other. "All the front rank men kept their ground & fired away, the rear rank men meanwhile retired to some good positions in the rear. I then formed a new line leaving vacancies for those of the first. I here would seize a favorable occasion after the new line was formed, and retreat at a run, suddenly disappearing before the enemy. These would then come in quickly thinking our men had been routed, they would be checked by the fire of the new line, snugly posted behind trees, stone fences &c … by this arrangement I [avoided] all difficulties." The major, a student of military history, had read of the French marshall Soult using this tactic in the Peninsular War.[25]

In contrast to their plush digs in the town of Gettysburg, the sharpshooters often went hungry on the retreat. With the Confederate supply system in its usual disarray and the main body of the army cleaning out everything before them, the pickings were slim indeed. Yet at one point the famished battalion passed an untouched cottage with "countless fowls" around it. "My hungry fellows looked eloquently to me for leave," recalled Blackford. "I told the bugler to sound the 'disperse,' and then shouted 'one minute.'" The riflemen quickly put their shooting skills to practical use. "When the 'Assembly' sounded two minutes afterwards, every man had one, two or more chickens slung over his gun, and the march was resumed with out delay."[26]

Even though the Gettysburg campaign had turned out badly for the Confederates, Robert Rodes had reason to be pleased with his sharpshooter battalions. They had done everything he had asked of them: cleared the way for the division's columns advancing down Oak Ridge, kept the bulk of a Federal division off his flank for most of the afternoon, used their marksmanship skills to telling effect the next day, and acted as rear guard on the retreat. They had come a long way from South Mountain.

9

Manassas Gap

"Every shot took effect"

During the long, painful retreat to Virginia, Blackford and his men frequently sparred with pursuing Yankees, who did not press their attacks. The Federal cavalry struck them a stinging, though indirect blow, however. The bad luck that had shadowed Rodes' men all through the Pennsylvania campaign seemed to culminate when, "half starved," they reached Hagerstown. There Blackford's servant met him with "the appalling news...that our private wagon had been captured and burned by the enemy." All of his personal gear and purchases in Pennsylvania were gone, and "our mess, from being one of the most elegantly equipped in the Division, is now reduced to one tin cup." The men in blue had also captured most of the brigade's wagons, including the one carrying their payroll, to the tune of $11,235.[1]

For Blackford, more personal humiliations followed. In Hagerstown the Federals looked up Dr. MacGill, a family friend of the Blackfords. The Yankee officer who called wore Blackford's pants carried his field glasses. "Perhaps you would like to hear what he says of you?" he asked. Lounging insolently in the family's parlor rocker, the officer read aloud from Blackford's captured diary, which detailed the MacGill's pro-Southern sympathies, then informed them that they were expelled from their home to the Confederacy. Incidents like this, coupled with news of Vicksburg's surrender on July 4, sent morale plummeting. "My blind confidence in Gen. Lee is utterly gone," Blackford confided to his mother. "I keep up my spirits where the men are ... but may as well confess that I am utterly miserable."[2]

Nevertheless, Blackford kept his men at their position as rear guard as the army started to cross the Potomac. From his advanced position he could hear the Yankees singing and shouting as they entered Hagerstown. Near sundown on July 6 he was told to scout a stone fence line behind a hill about six hundred yards in front of him. General Jubal Early, whose division held the sector near Rodes, had reported that a Yankee column was

massing behind the hill for an attack. Certain that the information was
false, Blackford had no choice but to proceed once he received a written
order to conduct a reconnaissance in force. He regarded this as a fool's errand, since a few scouts could have done the job just as well. Near the crest
Yankee sharpshooters waited behind a fence. "Still, I had to go, so causing
the forward to be sounded, and then a wheel till we were parallel with the
fence, away we dashed at them. The bullets came like hail, and the corn
stalks fell all around us," wrote Blackford. The veteran Yankee marksmen
directed much of their fire toward the sound of the bugle, "where they knew
the officer was." Blackford and his men could not stop to fire, and they managed to get close enough to see that no troops were behind the hill. They
hustled back. This "miserable affair" cost the sharpshooters six wounded,
some of whom had to remain on the field until after dark before they could
be evacuated. This was typical of the many nasty little fights during the
retreat—real enough for those involved, but not big enough to be described
in any official reports. Nor did it endear Jubal Early to Blackford and the
sharpshooters.[3]

On the rainy night of July 14 Rodes's division crossed the Potomac at
Williamsport. The operation, wrote Rodes, "was a perilous one." Soldiers
stumbled down the slippery banks in the dark, many losing their shoes in
the process. The "cold, deep, and rising," water rose to the armpits of an average man, and smaller men needed help to cross. In spite of the danger and
hardships, the division made it over without losing a man, and "be it said
to the everlasting honor of these brave fellows, they encountered it not only
promptly, but actually with cheers and laughter." The bedraggled soldiers
marched a little ways further to a camp, and according to Rodes, "there
ended the Pennsylvania campaign, so far as this division was concerned."[4]

Blackford, however, remained on the other side of the river. About 3 a.m.
the sharpshooters were relieved by a group of badly disciplined cavalrymen,
who declined to provide them a guide to the rear. By then the rain had stopped
and the night had cleared somewhat, and Blackford and his men tried to feel
their way toward the ford. "After floundering around for some hours" they
struck the Williamsport Pike, which brought them to the river about dawn.
A sentry at the ford stopped Blackford and refused to let him pass until some
of the sharpshooters, exasperated by the man's obstinacy, "threatened to
make daylight through him." Even then Blackford found his way blocked
by another division whose officers refused to make space for him. Since an
aqueduct blocked their way, going around was impractical. He finally solved
the problem by having his men slip into the ranks of the passing units one
by one. Even though it was now daylight, the crossing was anything but
easy. "I never saw anything like the mud," wrote Blackford, who claimed he
saw a man fall off his horse near the water's edge and go completely out of
sight. When he was sure that all his men had reached the other side, he had

"assembly" sounded, "whereupon the whole command promptly formed and moved off." They caught up with the division a few hours later.[5]

Having failed to catch Lee and his beaten army north of the Potomac, General Meade made another attempt to cut off his retreat at Manassas Gap, near Front Royal, Virginia. Brigadier General John Buford's Union cavalry seized the gap, and from his position he could see long lines of men and wagons retreating before him. It was one of the best opportunities the Federals would get to cut off a portion of Lee's army, or at least a substantial part of his trains. Buford called for reinforcements, and early on July 23 Major General William French's Union III Corps, followed by the V Corps, began to push through the gap. French fielded some six thousand men in three divisions, a force the Confederates could for the moment oppose only with the 600 men of Wright's Georgia brigade,[*] part of Anderson's division of Longstreet's corps. Watching the mass of bluecoats pouring through the gap, the Georgians called for help. General Ewell dispatched Rodes's division, which had bivouacked outside Winchester the night before, hustling toward the gap to support them.

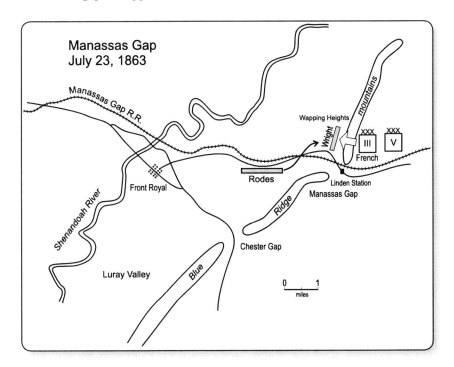

---

* Wright's Georgia brigade, under the command of Colonel E. J. Walker, consisted of the Third, Twenty-second, and Forty-eighth Georgia as well as the Second Georgia Battalion (not to be confused with the Second Georgia Sharpshooter Battalion).

By Rodes's arrival at mid-morning, French had begun his attack, sending a division against the Georgians on Wapping Heights. Fortunately for the outnumbered Confederates, French and his subordinates seemed incapable of mounting a vigorous attack. The corps had been thoroughly roughed up at Gettysburg, losing its popular commander, Dan Sickles, and many of its other leaders. "Old Blinky" French ("a perfect old soaker" according to one of his men) had only been in command for two weeks, as had Brigadier General Hobart Ward, the acting commander of the leading division. Ward had performed credibly at Gettysburg, but his fondness for the bottle, which may have contributed to his lack of celerity that day, would soon get him kicked out of the army. In any case, even though most of his men had arrived the night before, Ward spent the entire morning sending out scouts and a battalion of skirmishers to develop the situation. Not until 2 p.m. did he follow them with a line of battle, "steadily but surely driving the enemy from his positions until all the hills were in our possession." To judge from his report, he scattered much of his division about the battlefield as pickets and artillery guards. French's corps included both the 1st and 2nd U.S. Sharpshooter regiments, and this would have been an ideal place to have employed them as an advance guard brigade, as Sickles had done at Chancellorsville.[6]

Ward's men pushed the Georgians, who were trying to hold a line nearly two miles long, off the heights "into a gentle cow trot," but they reformed in the muddy bottom below. By now Rodes's division had begun arriving on the field, and he sent word to the Georgians that they would have to hold until he could deploy. Rodes directed his old Alabama brigade, still under Colonel O'Neal, to deploy in skirmish formation about three hundred yards behind the embattled Georgians, and sent "all my sharpshooters (about 250 men) ... to strengthen Wright's line." In his report Rodes does not specify whether this number included all of his division sharpshooters or just those from the leading brigades. Since he mentions that one of the officers killed was from Ramseur's brigade, it seems likely that these were Ramseur's and O'Neal's sharpshooter battalions, which, after the rigors of the Gettysburg campaign, might have been expected to constitute some 250 men.[7]

Meanwhile the Yankee advance stalled as the Union chiefs tried to decide what do next. "The Rebel object was not to fight, but to escape; ours seemed to be the same," quipped one of Ward's soldiers, Private John Haley of the 17th Maine. "What were our generals doing? Napping, simply napping." Meanwhile Haley and his brigade lay in an very exposed position on the ridge, "heels up, heads down," as two pieces of Rodes's artillery arrived and began lobbing shells at them as the bullets of Blackford's men whizzed past. The Yankees' dark uniforms stood out against the faded grass, making them easy targets. "Thus we were left to artillery and sharpshooters without the least likelihood that they would err on the side of mercy," said Haley.

Ward reformed his men and began his glacial advance again, but French countermanded the order. Instead, he directed a brigade from the following division, five New York regiments under Brigadier General Francis Spinola, to attack through a ravine and flank the Rebel position on the right.[8]

A desperate fight broke out in the swampy bottom. Unlike Ward, Spinola pressed his attack and fell seriously wounded while leading it. "We resisted them to the utmost of human capacity," wrote the commander of the Georgians, who averred that some of the fighting took place "at the distance of 15 paces." Blackford's men went forward and worked their way around the Union left flank behind some limestone ledges. "So near were we that every shot took effect," wrote Blackford, "and having perfect protection ourselves, we enjoyed the fun highly—losing only three men." Together the Georgians and the sharpshooters repulsed three separate attacks. When at last the New Yorkers split their thin line, the Georgians retreated to the cover of Rodes's main position some six hundred yards behind them. Blackford rallied his men "on a commanding bluff to the left of the road, some quarter of a mile to the rear, whence they annoyed the advancing columns of the enemy very seriously, firing until it was too dark to see."[9]

"These troops," wrote General Ewell, "in full view, showed great gallantry, and though intended merely to make a show, held the enemy back so long and inflicted such loss that they were satisfied not to come within reach of O'Neal, but remained at a safe distance, where they were leisurely shelled by Carter's artillery." Rodes thought little of his opponents, who, considering their overwhelming numbers, had signally failed to press their advantage. "His officers acted generally with great gallantry," he sniffed, "but the men behaved in a most cowardly manner. A few shots from Carter's artillery and the skirmishers' fire halted them, broke them, and put a stop to the engagement."[10]

Overall losses in this sharp little fight had been about equal. The Georgians reported losing 102 men killed and wounded, plus 65 missing and probably captured; to this one killed and perhaps half a dozen wounded of Rodes's sharpshooters must be added. Union losses totaled 103, of which 75 were from Spinola's brigade, showing clearly who had done the fighting. Both regiments of Federal sharpshooters were present, and according to one man, they "opened the engagement and, indeed, bore the brunt of it." Be that as it may, neither Ward nor French mentioned them in his report. Blackford's men may have traded some shots with them, and as before they seem to have been scattered out in small groups as scouts and skirmishers. Nevertheless the 1st U.S.S.S. had a busy day. Its riflemen fired off all their ammunition—sixty rounds per man—and in the process lost two men killed and six wounded. The 2nd U.S.S.S., which was deployed "on the right," lost no one.[11]

Skirmishing Between the Pickets of the Two Armies in Virginia.
The Soldier in Our Civil War

Once again Blackford's sharpshooters had proven their worth. Rodes was beginning to use them as an independent fighting force that could be sent out as an advance guard to engage or harass an enemy while he deployed the division. As before he used the combined battalions of his brigades as a division-level force under a single commander, a concept he would further refine in the coming months. For the Federals Manassas Gap was yet another lost opportunity. With one corps up and another close behind, the Federals vastly outnumbered their foe. Had French used his sharpshooters aggressively and followed them with a coordinated infantry assault, he might have dealt Lee a serious blow. "When we found what fools the Rebs had made of us," groused Private Haley, "we were so mad our teeth hung out. While we fooled around they made tracks for Richmond."[12]

Still, the incident was not quite over for the Alabamians, and that night some poor staff work almost got them all captured. Rodes left the sharpshooters at the gap as pickets that evening while the rest of the army withdrew to Chester Gap. However, finding this pass held by enemy infantry, they detoured south through the Luray Valley. Colonel O'Neal sent one of his staff officers, "a miserable apology for a soldier," to inform Blackford of the change of route. Rather than going as far as Blackford's position, the officer decided to wait for him at the crossroads, where he fell asleep. The sharpshooters pulled back around midnight and passed the man in the darkness without awakening him. Blackford's suspicions were aroused when he failed to see any stragglers on the road. He began to move silently, stopping every hundred yards or so to check his surroundings. After going about half a mile further, he saw "clearly defined against the sky the figure of a Yankee vidette, in an attitude of listening." Blackford could see that the picket wore a kepi, "an article entirely eschewed by the Confederate soldier." As quietly as they could, the sharpshooters retraced their steps back down the mountain until they were safe. Meanwhile, "this booby of a staff officer" woke up, realized that he must have missed the sharpshooters, then hustled back to the brigade with news that they had all been captured. Blackford and his men, "completely mystified" as to what was going on, wandered for the rest of the night and into the next day before finding a friendly civilian who directed them to Rodes's column, which they rejoined to loud hurrahs. But for this fortunate escape the sharpshooter experiment might have ended then and there.[13]

Rodes's division returned to its old camps near Orange Court House, which made for a pleasant change of pace after the rigors of the failed campaign. The sharpshooters moved into "a beautiful camp in the woods, and kept it exquisitely policed." In addition to the usual drills Blackford resumed a social schedule with the "intensely hospitable" local families that included balls, picnics, and dancing. For a time, the war seemed in abeyance.[14]

10

Winter 1863-64

"They were good soldiers, whoever they were."

The sharpshooters' rest was not to last long. It ended with a show of confidence in them and their leader: for the first time Blackford's men were ordered to undertake an entirely independent mission. In early October 1863 the division left its camps at Orange Court House and marched to Morton's Ford, where General Rodes had the sharpshooters form a skirmish line with the division entrenched a mile behind. "The enemy," wrote Blackford, "were in force on the opposite bank" and appeared to be contemplating a crossing. The flat, open terrain at Morton's Ford made a poor site for the Confederates to defend. The line of sharpshooters followed the ford's curve for a half mile, and Blackford worried about saving his men in the face of a sudden Federal advance. To provide an escape route, he had a trench cut that connected their breastworks to a long ravine running obliquely into the hills. "The whole bottom was covered with ripe corn," he remembered, "on which my horse got fat as a seal. Of its stalks I made a very snug little hut, and established my Head Quarters with some pomp. One sentinel & a bugler were constantly on duty there." The post at Morton's Ford provided a quiet break from the drills and drudgery of camp. "By tacit agreement" neither side marred the informal truce by firing. Instead, "each side performed their military duties in full view of one another."[1]

Still, the existing guard system allowed little time for the soldiers to rest or sleep. Since the entire burden of vigilance fell on the sharpshooters for long periods without relief, it was only natural that their alertness and efficiency would eventually suffer. Blackford set for himself the task of inventing a better system. "At nightfall," he wrote, "the 'Assembly by Fours' is sounded by my quarters & echoed by each bugler." This signal formed the entire battalion into groups of four men twenty paces apart. Each set of four became a guard group, with one man walking his post "in the manner of camp sentinels." The other three slept, keeping their arms and accouterments nearby. The men rotated in this way, thereby reducing their guard duty to a manageable length: "but once in four hours." Each company appointed an officer to make the rounds every half hour, ensuring that the sentries remained alert. Blackford kept a few men on watch at his headquarters. The officer of the guard gave a whistle blast every hour, at which point the companies would wake up the next man. Blackford himself checked the guards twice a night. "This duty does not injure or fatigue the men," he wrote, and "they can stand it indefinitely." The rotation had the added advantage of virtually eliminating false alarms, which had plagued the picket line since the war began. Suspecting something might be brewing across the Rapidan, Blackford kept watch in the predawn hours, then slept from sunrise till mid-morning.[2]

Rodes had initially given Blackford two sharpshooter battalions to hold the ford, but he later added a third from Junius Daniel's brigade. This North Carolina outfit, which had been on coastal duty, joined the division after Chancellorsville and formed its own sharpshooter outfit after the pattern of Blackford's battalion. When the North Carolinians arrived at the ford, Blackford found them to be indifferently trained and lacking in morale. Most of Daniel's men had come to detest sharpshooter service because they had to stay awake all night on picket. Blackford inducted them into his new guard system, raising the newcomers' spirits considerably, and began working to solve some of their other problems. A few days after Daniel's men arrived, Blackford was awakened by an argument between one of his sentries, who had orders not to disturb him except in an emergency, and a visitor. Unable to sleep with all the shouting, Blackford stumbled out of his corn stalk shack "in the gray dawn in no good humor." The newcomer, "a burly person with a huge saber," demanded to know why not all the men of the battalion were on guard, and peremptorily ordered Blackford to put them on right away. Choking back his anger, Blackford asked the fellow if he was the division officer of the day. No, the man replied, but he was Brigadier General Junius Daniel and those were his men. This was too much for Blackford, who told Daniel that he had no business interfering with his command, and actually threatened to arrest him "if he did not clear out instantly." Daniel rode straight to Rodes's headquarters and demanded satisfaction for this act of rank insubordination, but the division commander simply told him to leave Blackford alone and mind his own business. "This affair," said Blackford, "made me much talked about."[3]

In October Lee tried to turn the tables on Meade and catch part of his army near Bristoe Station, Virginia. Rodes withdrew his division at night, and the sharpshooters followed at daylight. The command of Rodes's old brigade had passed from Colonel Edward O'Neal to Brigadier General Cullen Battle, formerly of the Third Alabama. The Alabamians marched swiftly toward the

Rappahannock river, with Blackford and his men hustling forward to regain their position at the brigade's front. "It soon became evident," he noted, "that General Lee was on one of his flanking expeditions. ... We would frequently pass behind a screen of pine brush, constructed to conceal us from the view of the enemy." That night they camped near Rappahannock Court House, where Blackford drew the job of surrounding the division with a picket line. Since it was now pitch dark and they were in unfamiliar territory, this was no simple task. Blackford solved the problem in his typically original fashion, marching his men around the camp in a narrow column. He dropped off pickets along the way, who each built a small fire and lighted a brand to mark his position. Blackford managed to complete his difficult task in the remarkably short time of one hour, but only "after having stumbled into more ditches than I thought existed in the world."[4]

Union cavalry pickets. *The Soldier in Our Civil War*

On October 12 Rodes's men caught the Federals at the little village of Jeffersonton, just shy of the Rappahannock. General Battle attempted to surround the Yankee cavalry in the town, sending three of his regiments around one side and two around the other. Blackford took his first corps of sharpshooters on a wider flanking movement east of town. While the infantry took care to conceal their movements, Blackford advertised his, "stopping every where it was thought that we could be seen above the bushes, so we went for a mile, I leading a long line, and giving my orders by a handkerchief, as they had been trained for such occasions." Meanwhile the second corps of sharpshooters, spread out six paces apart, moved directly toward Jeffersonton, touching off a noisy and distracting fire fight as they came within range.[5]

Blackford came upon a mounted sentry, whom he decided to take out. Borrowing a rifle, he crawled forward a hundred yards or so and took aim, but the rifle went off prematurely as he touched the trigger, its owner having neglected to mention that he had filed it down to fire at the slightest pressure. The sentry galloped off to raise the alarm, but the sharpshooters already stood between the town and the river, giving the retreating cavalrymen "the best we had" as they passed by. Battle's men pressed in from the other side, and Blackford claimed a dozen Yankees killed and twenty captured.[6]

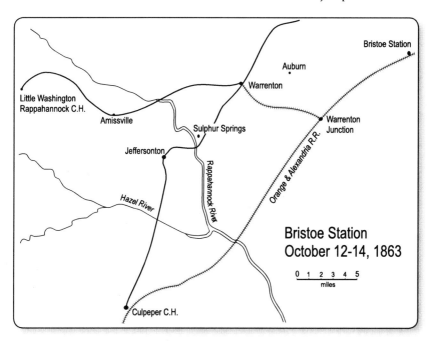

Bristoe Station
October 12-14, 1863

0 1 2 3 4 5
miles

On the Union side all was death and confusion. "The enemy's numerous skirmishers," wrote one Yankee commander, "with heavy supports press-ing upon both flanks and rear, compelled me to fall back hastily, suffering severe loss in men and horses." The Federal brigade commander, Colonel J. Irvin Gregg, described how "they charged impetuously in front and on both flanks ... and we were driven into the woods, where for half an hour the fight raged furiously. At this juncture information was brought to me that the enemy had possession of the road in my rear, and that we were sur-rounded. This information having found its way to the men created some confusion, and it became impossible to reform the command, and I was compelled to retire in some confusion."[7]

The Yankee horsemen scrambled across the Rappahannock, dismounted, and started peppering the ford with bullets. In response the Confederates brought up twenty guns and began pounding the other bank, driving
most of the bluecoats away. Enough of them stayed, however, to make the
crossing a hot one for Blackford and his men. The sharpshooters drove the
Yankees out of the buildings at the sulfur springs near the river and, backed
by Battle's and Doles's brigades, pushed them past the town of Warrenton.
Stuart's cavalry passed them and, after a sharp skirmish outside the town,
drove the bluecoats further down the road.

The next day the sharpshooters pulled back just outside of Warrenton. They
spent the entire day waiting for orders, then moved into a nearby camp.
About 4 a.m. a courier arrived and informed them that Stuart's cavalry had
been cut off behind the Yankee lines. The Confederate horsemen, it seemed,
had gotten themselves sandwiched between two retreating Federal columns
and were laying low in a patch of woods near the village of Auburn, hoping to
avoid discovery. The sharpshooters stumbled forward in the darkness, their
path further impeded by a thick ground fog. Around dawn they reached the
vicinity of the road the Federals had taken but could see nothing in the mist.
Then, to their amazement, artillery shells began landing in their midst. No
one could understand how the Yankees could see to fire, until finally they realized that it was Stuart's horse artillery shooting at them. Finding the Union
columns straggling and disorganized, the Bold Cavalier had decided to cut
his way out. Blackford's men dodged the shells, pushed forward to a position
near the road, and waited for the fog to lift. Soon tired of waiting, Blackford
"undertook to move by the flank, down a road hard by, and put myself at the
head of the line having a bugler and one man by me, and the others all following at the distance of five paces apart." Thus deployed, the sharpshooters
crept closer to the enemy. Blackford descended a steep bank in the half light
and found himself on a road running through a narrow cut, packed with
Yankees "hurrying along with all their might, evidently much exhausted by
their night's march." Blackford's bugler, "a faithful fellow," moved in front of
him and cocked his carbine just as a figure appeared out of the mist. When
asked who he was, Blackford claimed to be a Federal officer. Evidently his
answer raised no alarm, because the Yankees continued on their way. Blackford slowly backed up the embankment and, once on the other side, quickly
dispatched a messenger to General Rodes, asking for help.[8]
    When it became apparent that no one was coming, the sharpshooters,
too weak to take on the entire column, hung off the flanks and scooped up
stragglers, who "were much surprised to see Rebels so close to their line of
march." Despite "constantly sending squads of prisoners to the rear," some
of whom actually reported to him, thinking he was one of their officers,
Blackford was disappointed, since "with 500 men I could have cut off a large

part of the enemy's rear." The sharpshooters continued to sneak around the retreating Federals, once coming within fifty yards of an artillery park.[9]

Finally the Yankees passed. General Rodes appeared, leading his division, and the sharpshooters pressed the Union rear guard. A hot firefight with a detachment of cavalry soon developed. "Here," wrote Blackford, "I had to make a run for it under fire for more than 100 yards" before reaching, "to my great relief," the safety of the woods. He soon pushed the blue-coated horse soldiers against a ford, "and surrounding them while they were crossing we played the deuce with them. I fired a hatful of cartridges into the squadron, and revenged myself for the scare they had given me."[10]

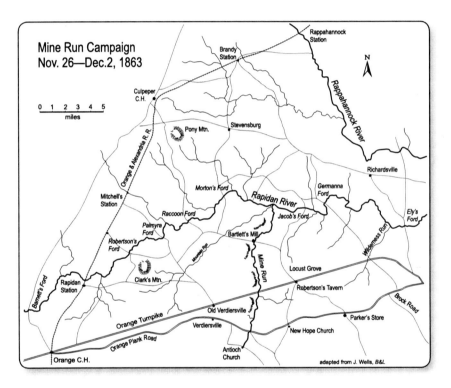

Mine Run Campaign
Nov. 26—Dec.2, 1863

adapted from J. Wells, B&L

Meanwhile, on another part of the battlefield, the Confederates were not doing as well. A. P. Hill's Corps caught up with two retreating Federal corps near Bristoe Station, rashly attacked them, and suffered a sharp repulse. This effectively ended Lee's hopes of cutting off a part of the Federal army, and Meade continued his withdrawal north to Centreville unmolested. Lee contented himself with advancing across the Rappahannock and tearing up the railroad tracks from Bristoe Station south. Along with their comrades, the sharpshooters spent two "unutterably miserable," rain-soaked days engaged in the task before marching south of the Rappahannock again to build winter quarters near Kelly's Ford. On October 15 Blackford boasted in a letter to his mother that he had "made quite a reputation by driving in their rear-guard constantly with my well trained little corps."[11]

The lull did not last. On November 7 the Yankees attacked at Rappahannock Station, capturing a large number of prisoners and unhinging the Confederate line. Lee fell back to the Rapidan, and the sharpshooters ended up at Raccoon Ford, very close to their old picket line at Morton's Ford. Blackford, who suffered severe swelling in his leg from varicose veins, the result of his earlier bout with typhoid fever, took a furlough home.

There would be little rest for either army that winter, however. On November 27 Meade, prodded by Lincoln, attempted a sudden move through the Wilderness to turn Lee's flank. Divining the Federals' intention, the Confederates moved to intercept them. The weather deteriorated steadily, with frequent wintry rains and muddy roads slowing both sides' movements. The Union plan was to quickly cross the Rapidan and concentrate at Robertson's Tavern, located at a crossroads near the village of Locust Grove. Federal cavalry reached the junction early the next day, pushing past the tavern and a cluster of houses into the woods beyond. Behind them Lieutenant Thomas Galwey, an Irishman commanding a company of the 8th Ohio, waited near one of the houses with his men. Galwey's company was one of two in his regiment particularly accomplished in skirmish drill. In fact, open-order fighting was something of a regimental specialty. Suspecting that the enemy was not far away, the 8th Ohio's brigade commander, Colonel Samuel Carroll, sent a detachment of light infantry sharpshooters—ten men from each of the four regiments in his brigade—down the pike to find them, backed by a company of the 4th Ohio. Galwey and a companion company advanced on the right side of the pike, while a company of the 7th West Virginia battalion covered the left side. The rest of the brigade followed not far behind in line of battle. Along with the 14th Indiana, all were part of the 1st brigade of Brigadier General Alexander Hays's 3rd Division, II Corps.

Soon a booming volley echoed from the thickets. The Union veterans recognized the sound as infantry muskets, not cavalry carbines, and in a few moments the Yankee horsemen galloped back in a panic shouting "good God, they've let the infantry out on us." Galwey and his men advanced cautiously beyond the houses in skirmish order, "for the wood was thick and we could not see far ahead." Very soon they met the men in gray. "They must have been glad to see us," quipped Galway, "for they gave us a warm reception." Bullets began to fly, beginning "one of the most desperate skirmishes I had ever seen." Galwey never found out the identity of the Southerners, but he readily conceded that "certainly they were good soldiers, whoever they were."[12]

A Union column from Warren's II Corps passes through Locust Grove
past Robertson's Tavern. Alfred Waud, *Harper's Weekly.*

The hospitable Rebels were Tarheels—the sharpshooters of Daniel's brigade, which led Rodes's division up the Orange turnpike. Rodes was with
them, seeking to concentrate his men at Locust Grove. Seeing the Yankees
already there "in heavy force," he ordered Daniel's sharpshooters to cover the
pike while the rest of the division arrived. Battle's brigade swung into line
on Daniel's right and was followed by Ramseur's brigade. Brigadier General
Robert D. Johnston's North Carolina brigade (formerly Iverson's brigade)
moved up on Daniel's left. Each brigade sent out their sharpshooters to
screen their front as they dug in about a thousand yards back. As they did
so, a soldier from the Fourth North Carolina, Nat Raymer, observed that the
Yankees were "none of your peaceable sort either, for no sooner were they
apprised of our whereabouts than they began pitching minnie balls into
the trees around us and sending *quartermaster hunters* (shells) away over
us." One corps of Ramseur's sharpshooters joined Daniel's men, and "were
soon hotly engaged and called for reinforcements." Rodes sent up Ramseur's
second corps of sharpshooters and Battle's first (who, in Blackford's absence,
fell under Captain Watkins Phelan) to back them. A fierce firefight erupted
all along the line.[13]

While the sharpshooters were thus engaged, the rest of his division "was
busily employed throwing up breastworks of poles and earth, the latter dug
up with picks made of sharpened oak poles and bayonets, and thrown on
the logs and brush with tin plates and cups, and bare hands." Meanwhile
Major General Edward Johnson's division bumped into the Federal III
Corps at Payne's farm just north of them, touching off the sharpest fighting
of the day.[14]

About 1 p.m. Carroll's men pushed forward "on a run," driving the Tar-heel sharpshooters out of the woods and to the foot of a small rise, where the Rebels dug in their heels. "Here," said Galwey, "the skirmishing was re-ally interesting. Our lines were within speaking distance of one another but little was displayed except heads and muskets and an occasional officer's sword." One of his men, a Dutchman named Peter Meermans, wandered in among the Rebels and escaped amid a hail of bullets yelling "they've shot me in der frying pan!" When his comrades calmed him down, they found that the newly-purchased skillet in his knapsack had indeed taken the bul-let, leaving its owner a whole skin.[15]

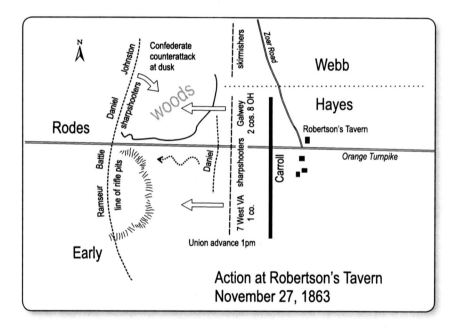

Action at Robertson's Tavern
November 27, 1863

One of Battle's sharpshooters, Jim Branscomb of the Third Alabama, wrote his sister about the "heavy skirmishing" they'd had. "At one time," he said, "a heavy line of the enemy advanced on our battalion of sharpshoot-ers. We had to make tracks to the line of battle. They got so close to me at one time that I did not know whether to run or be taken prisoner. But the thought of Fort Delaware made me sift through a heavy shower of balls. Four of the [sharpshooter] company were wounded."[16]

Toward dusk the Confederates counterattacked, pushing through the gap between the Federal divisions of Hays and Webb. This exposed the 8th Ohio, the rightmost unit of Hays's division, "taking us in the right flank and rear, so that we had to face about and fight our way back through the wood." To further confuse matters, many of the Southerners wore captured Union overcoats, making it difficult to distinguish friend from foe. The Buckeyes fell back, regrouped, and drove the Rebels back to the edge of the wood, "where the skirmishing became severe." By now it was getting too dark to see. The fighting continued, although it was now "one more of mouth than of arms." Each side hurled "the bitterest and most insulting invective" though the dark woods at each other, yet Galwey had to admit that "there was more or less humor mixed with the abuse." An invitation to "come over here, you Grayback s—s of b—s; here's another wagon train for you to take" would provoke a pungent reference to a Yankee defeat, "spiced of course with curses and imprecations." Eventually fresh troops relieved the exhausted Ohioans, allowing them to rest in a hollow at the rear.[17]

Before dawn the Confederates fell back across Mine Run and began to throw up earthworks in a cold heavy rain. The Federals appeared just after sunrise, sending their best skirmishers, the elite 1st and 2nd Sharpshooters, across the low swampy ground to scout the Confederate position. "We were in an open field and the enemy in the woods at a distance of two hundred yards," wrote Jerry Tate, a sharpshooter with the Fifth Alabama who lay just across the creek in a makeshift rifle pit of rocks and fence rails, well in advance of the main line.[18]

By noon the rain stopped. Then, said a North Carolinian, "the clouds broke, partially cleared away, leaving the air chill and frosty so that our frozen garments rattled like dry raw hides." A piercing north wind nipped everyone, but especially the sharpshooters, who, crouched in their rifle pits, could not warm themselves by lighting a fire or exercising. For the Federal riflemen, crossing the mire "through the partly frozen mud, in many places mid-leg deep," nature was a far worse foe than the enemy. What they saw was not encouraging. The frowning Rebel defenses, located on the heights behind the stream, reminded them of Fredericksburg. That night the temperature plunged to near zero as the wind raked the bare hills. Those who were there would never forget the "long and dismal night; the men getting such comfort as they could from rubbing and chaffing their benumbed and frost-bitten limbs."[19]

All the last day of November they lay there under an artillery duel, "picking off a rebel now and then" and losing a few of their own. The Yankees' sorest loss was Lieutenant Colonel Caspar Trepp, the Swiss-born commander of the 1st U.S.S.S., shot through the red diamond on his cap by a Rebel marksman.[20]

The Southerners, though equally cold and more poorly clad, did have the advantage of higher and somewhat drier ground. Jerry Tate was sure that he had "never past sutch a day in my life. I never et nor drank any thing for about thirty hours, twelve hours of the time was lying prostrate on the ground and it was raining about six hours of the time and very cold. About dusk I rose to my feet but could not stand for some minutes."[21]

The Confederate defenses at Mine Run reminded many veterans of Fredericksburg.
The Soldier in Our Civil War

Ramseur's men were relieved just after dark.

> Our boys who came in were well nigh frozen, ("gone up the
> spout" they said) and crouching round the pitiful fires related
> some amusing incidents. The pickets were so near each other
> that they could converse with all ease, and an incessant jawing
> was the consequence. "An faith to you, Reb," said an old Yankee,
> "wouldn't you like to have a hot cup of coffee this cold morn-
> ing?"—with a peculiar Irish brogue. "Got plenty Confederate
> coffee," said Reb in reply, "wouldn't you like to have a chew of
> tobacco?" "Don't care if I do," said Yank. "Well, here are some of
> old Jeff's pills in advance"—and away would go a volley of balls
> that made the Yank dig in his nails into the ground trying to
> lie close. Both parties were lying flat in an old field—rather an
> uncomfortable position in a pelting rain of five or six hours, but
> the slightest move was sure to draw a dozen bullets, hence it was
> to the interest of each that he should keep perfectly still.[22]

During the day some sheep made the mistake of wandering into the skirmish line, and few minutes later one of them walked squarely into a Minié ball. "Don't you want to go halves on some mutton?" shouted the Federal picket who had dropped it. His opposite in gray readily agreed, and the two rose to begin "a good, jolly time" butchering the sheep. "Meanwhile the pickets on each side were peppering away at each other, careful, however, not to disturb the butchers who were working with might, chattering good-humoredly and as much unconcerned as though there were neither abolitionists nor Negroes in America, and when done they divided the meat fairly and honestly; each taking his half and bidding the other good-bye, with much good luck, returned to his respective 'boil' and spent the evening amusing themselves with their Enfields."[23]

The following day, December 1, having considered the strength of Lee's defenses and realizing that his own men were reaching the limits of their endurance, Meade decided to call off his offensive. Realizing this, the pickets quickly "made friends" and began trading. That evening the played-out Federal sharpshooters returned to their lines, but since III Corps was last to leave they ended up as the army's rear guard. "The march," said one, "was simply terrible." The numbed men stumbled through the night, with so many lying down to sleep wherever they could that "at day break there were not guns enough in some of the companies to stack arms with." One Gettysburg veteran called the retreat from Mine Run "the most severe experience" of the war. On the Southern side things looked a bit cheerier that morning, as Jerry Tate savored the real coffee, with cream and sugar, that he had traded a twist of tobacco for the day before.[24]

Rodes's men followed the retreating Yankees, capturing 260. More than half of the total, or 137 men, were scooped up "after a very slight resistance" by eighteen Georgia sharpshooters from Doles's brigade led by Private Charles Grace. Overall casualties were light, as was typical for this sort of battle. Rodes lost 45 men from his division during the campaign, almost all sharpshooters. Daniel's sharpshooters, the most heavily engaged, lost 17 men (3 killed), and Battle's Alabamians admitted to 10 wounded. On another part of the line Captain William Montgomery of the Third Georgia Sharpshooters took a serious wound in the thigh that put him out of action for the rest of the war. On the Union side Galwey's 8th Ohio lost only 1 killed and 8 wounded, while its sister Buckeye regiment tallied 22 (2 killed), and Carroll's brigade lost 64 killed and wounded. The Federal sharpshooter regiments lost more heavily in the actions at Mine Run, with the 2nd U.S.S.S. posting a loss of 11 men and the 1st U.S.S.S losing a striking 47 men, including their commander, Lieutenant Colonel Trepp.[25]

The campaigns in the winter of 1863-64 make for an interesting comparison of the sharpshooters of the two armies. Despite their late start the sharpshooters of Rodes's division were now fully the equal of their Union counterparts, the 1st and 2nd U.S.S.S. This period marked the apogee of the Federal sharpshooter experiment, which had started with such publicity and promise, and the beginning of its decline. Berdan's two regiments, styled the Brigade of Sharpshooters, had performed in exemplary fashion at Chancellorsville but had been split up at Gettysburg, with each regiment assigned to a different brigade. Nevertheless Major General David Birney, one of the few Union generals with an appreciation of the sharpshooters' capabilities, deployed them separately but as regiments at Mine Run. Overall they had suffered from the consistently mediocre leadership of Generals French and Ward, and of Berdan himself, whose tactical abilities were nil. Caspar Trepp, an excellent soldier, took over after Berdan's departure but was killed only two months later, leaving a void of experienced senior officers that would never be filled.

Union colonel Sam Carroll, nicknamed "Old Brick Top," was a West Pointer and tactical innovator who formed his own brigade sharpshooters and ensured that his 8th Ohio was well trained in skirmish drill. "It is certainly no credit to the promotional machinery of the Army of the Potomac," observed a modern historian, "that a man of Carroll's qualifications was still a colonel in ... 1863 when inferior men were wearing stars." The Union did not lack light infantry leaders, but it did lack the means to effectively utilize them. One wonders what might have been accomplished if Carroll or someone like him had been placed in command of the Brigade of Sharpshooters. In any case his innovations seem to have gone no further than his brigade, and there is no other mention of his sharpshooters after Mine Run.[26]

From the Confederate perspective, however, Rodes's experiment worked to perfection. Blackford and his men had done all he had asked and more. Drawing the men from their brigades had proven to be a flexible way of deploying trained sharpshooters that required no extra men. Certainly, they had more than proven their value in the fluid battles during the retreat from Gettysburg and the winter campaigns between the Rappahannock and the Rapidan. At Mine Run, for example, Rodes felt confident enough in his sharpshooters to leave them a thousand yards in front of his line while he dug in. They repaid his trust not only holding by off the better part of Hays's division but also by counterattacking his skirmish line and driving it back. Their performance had not gone unnoticed, and from this point they would assume an increasingly prominent role in the Army of Northern Virginia.

11

Preparing for 1864

"The best men in the company"

In their first year Robert Rodes's sharpshooter battalions performed so well that in early 1864 General Lee issued an order directing all infantry brigades in the Army of Northern Virginia to organize their own battalion of sharpshooters. After the war General Cadmus Wilcox modestly took credit for the whole idea, which he had apparently backed and which fit with the ideas he had advanced in his prewar book. Rodes, however, had implemented the idea a full year earlier. Several other sharpshooter battalions had been organized around the same time as Blackford's, but many of these fell into disuse late in the year. For instance, Captain William Haskell's sharpshooter battalion fought at Gettysburg with McGowan's brigade, where Haskell was killed. Disbanded in early fall, the battalion reformed in March 1864 under the command of Captain William S. Dunlop, who left a detailed account of its organization and training.[1]

Dunlop's new battalion "was composed of three companies of about sixty men each, rank and file; with one commissioned and three non-commissioned officers to the company. A draft was levied upon the regiments of the brigade for three or four men from each company ... to be selected from the best men in the company, with due regard to the peculiar and hazardous service for which they were designed." The companies were designated from right to left as First, Second, and Third. Like Blackford, Dunlop sought volunteers of "intelligence, sound judgment, accuracy of marksmanship, fidelity to the Southern cause, and unfaltering courage." He claimed to have chosen well: "a few men failed in drill ... only one failed in battle." Also like Blackford, Dunlop emphasized range estimation "until every man could tell, almost to a mathematical certainty, the distance to any given point. ... A few, however, were naturally and hopelessly deficient in their powers of estimating distance, and hence were exchanged for others." For marksmanship practice he started with a pine plank target "about the size of a man"

(2 x 6 feet) a hundred yards away, with a five inch bull's-eye inside an inner circle of 14 inches and outer circle of 24 inches. At 500 yards he increased the size of the target to 4 x 6 feet, and at 900 yards to 6 x 6 feet, with a corresponding increase in the size of the bull's-eye. The riflemen used a tripod "constructed of convenient height, with a sandbag lodged in its fork" to steady their weapons. Dunlop and his men used the flagging system worked out by Blackford to score their hits, and continued practicing "until the results achieved in estimating distance and rifle training were as amazing to the brigade commander as they were gratifying to the officers and men of the battalion."[2]

Heth's *A System of Target Practice* advised using a tripod for longer shots. Copied directly from the French manual on the subject, these men are uniformed as *chasseurs*.

Cadmus Wilcox, now a major general commanding A. P. Hill's old light division, began a similar program. "We have established a regular sharp shooting or skirmishing Battalion," wrote Marion Fitzpatrick, a sergeant with the Forty-fifth Georgia, part of Thomas's brigade. "They took two to four men from each Company," he said, adding that he had joined since they needed an NCO. "We drill to ourselves and do the skirmishing when there is a fight. ... Skirmishing is a ticklish business at times, but I like to do it."[3]

Wilcox sent down a printed order on April 2 "for instruction of the Corps of Sharp Shooters," reiterating the importance of correctly judging distances, requiring regular progress reports, and specifying that no ammunition was to be issued "until some proficiency is made" in range estimation. On April 19 target practice began. Each soldier got 22 rounds and was allowed to fire from a rest (probably a tripod like the one Dunlop described). Of these he shot 3 rounds at 100 yards on the first day, then 5 at 300 on the two succeeding days. Over the next three days he fired 10 rounds at 600 yards, and then spent two days firing the remainder at 900 yards, showing the emphasis on long-range shooting. Wilcox ordered the names of the five best riflemen, "in the order of their merit," sent to his headquarters. They got off to a slow start. "Out of 98 shots, only five hit the board," wrote Fitzpatrick about the first go-round at 600 yards. Still, he observed "a considerable improvement" over the next few days. "A good number of shots struck the board," he wrote on the 29th. "We shot 600 yards, the same as yesterday."[d]

Meanwhile, the sharpshooters of Rodes's old brigade (now Battle's brigade) continued to hone their skills. Jim Branscomb of the Third Alabama wrote home that he and his mates "are engaging in target shooting now, and some shoot to 500 yards." A soldier in the Fifth Alabama, Jerry Tate, described "target shooting [at] six hundred yards, the closest shot was [with]in two and a half inches of the center, the other shots varies from six inches to twenty yards. The major commanding [Blackford] gives us praise, or at least some, for our marksmanship."[5]

Although several writers mention Lee's sharpshooter order, no copy has yet come to light. In any case, the army's sharpshooter battalion's organization varied somewhat from brigade to brigade—like everything else in the Confederate army. While all fielded a battalion of 170 to 200 men and used a draft of about one man in six across the brigade, the number of companies varied. This may have been as much a reflection of the chronic shortage of officers as anything else. Blackford's sharpshooter battalion stuck with its five companies, one company per regiment arrangement throughout the war, as did some others (e.g. Mahone's brigade), while some other battalions (e.g. McGowan's and Lane's brigades) used an arrangement of three companies, and still others (e.g. Scales's brigade) fielded four. There were also permanent organizations like the Third Georgia Sharpshooter Battalion of Wofford's brigade, consisting of five companies, that continued to serve until the end of the war. Some brigade commanders used existing units, such as the Third South Carolina Infantry battalion of Joseph Kershaw's brigade. This seven-company battalion was converted to a sharpshooter battalion by adding hand-picked men from across the brigade.[6]

Captain John Young stated that his battalion in Scales's brigade was composed of "one commandant, eight commissioned officers, ten non-commissioned officers, one hundred and sixty privates, four scouts and two buglers," and that its four companies "were subdivided into groups of fours, something like the *comrades de battaille* of the French army. These groups messed and slept together, and were never separated in action save by casualties of disability and death." Although most of the brigade sharpshooter battalions ended up being commanded by captains (or, late in the war, by lieutenants), Lee preferred a field officer if one were available. For example, Mahone's sharpshooters were commanded by Lieutenant Colonel E. M. Field, who even had his own adjutant to keep track of personnel matters. His battalion was identical to Young's, except that it also included two men per company "for ambulance corps duty." All, like Blackford, used the bugle for communication and command.[7]

In the field, however, the sharpshooter battalions continued to be divided into two "corps" for both tactical employment and picketing. As Jerry Tate explained: "Some times we are on post twenty four to forty eight hours with out being relieved, tho it is not so hard now [that] we have two regular organized corps ... when one corps is on duty the other is restin." He added that there was "one consilation, that is I will not have any other duty to do as the sharp shooters are exempt from all details except Pickett and Drills." Tate also describes several instances of Blackford's battalion deploying the first and second corps separately, as they had at Jeffersonton, as well as functioning as a provost guard, strung across the brigade's rear after the fight began "to keep the men from remaining out of the fight."[8]

Since both sides used essentially the same manuals, drill was virtually identical for Johnny Reb and Billy Yank. In fact, the best account of the sharpshooters' tactical training comes from a Yankee, Sergeant Wyman White of the 2nd U.S.S.S. His description clearly shows how the four-man squad formed the basis of skirmish tactics, and why some little training was necessary:

> Skirmish drill is an open order drill. Men form line in two ranks, then at the order deploy by fours, two files off both ranks would take distances twenty feet apart. Then at the order deploy in line, each man on the left of the four would take distance five paces to the left of Number one in the front rank, he standing fast. Number one in the rear rank standing five paces to the left of the Number one in the front rank. Number two in the front rank being five paces to the left of Number one in the rear rank, and Number two in the rear rank taking distance five paces to the left of Number one in the front rank. The squads of fours taking distance still further to the left and deploying to the distance of five paces apart until the whole company or regiment was in a single line five paces space between each man.
>
> Thus deployed, three hundred fifty men would make a line about a mile long. We took our orders from the call of the bugle as no man's voice could reach the length of the line. We had calls to advance, to commence firing, cease firing, by the right flank,

by the left flank, lay down, rise, halt and retreat and finally every movement necessary to move the command. ... There were also movements and bugle calls to rally by sections, rally by platoon, and rally by company and regiment.[9]

White also describes "a very pretty movement"—how the unit would "rally by fours" in case of cavalry attack:

Each man knew his place: Number one of the front rank stood fast, the other three faced to the right and double quick their step, Number one of the rear rank taking his place in the rear of Number one in the front rank and facing the rear, Number two of the front rank taking his place on the left of Number one of the front rank and Number two of the rear rank taking his place to the left of Number two of the rear rank. All face out with bayonet fixed; each man bracing his left foot and his left shoulder solid against his comrade on the opposite corner making a solid group of four. And four cool men drilled in bayonet exercise need have no fear of cavalry."[10]

While the men of the new sharpshooter battalions sweated through their drills that spring, Robert Rodes planned the next stage their evolution. At the camp near Orange Court House he revealed his concept during dinner with Eugene Blackford, who, though his leg still pained him, had returned to active duty on April 3. General Rodes wanted a division-level unit composed of all the sharpshooter battalions. As Blackford wrote, "I was to take command of the whole force and train them thoroughly—that he would put any amount of ammunition at my disposal. I accordingly met the officers of the several battalions at his quarters, and appointed hours for drills to begin at once. These lasted all the forenoon, and were very thorough—sometimes I had as many as 1200 men deployed at one time, in a *great* plain at the foot of the Clarke's Mountain." With Blackford in charge, Rodes could be assured of a uniform standard of training, and for the first time the four sharpshooter battalions would be trained to operate together as a demi-brigade under a single commander, rather than as an ad hoc force of separate battalions, as they had been at Gettysburg. "With them I would perform every maneuver, and rally in squares against cavalry until personally I would come in upon the passed reserve where I could myself ride, and enter the square. These drills attracted much attention, and every morning there was a crowd of officers looking on." Following the morning's drill came marksmanship practice, and after several weeks of it Blackford complained that he was "almost deafened by the noise. A thousand or more of them were banging away for hours, until my head would ache from the noise and smell of the saltpetre."[11]

Some historians and pundits have maintained that the average Civil War infantryman received little if any marksmanship training during his term of service. This may have been true of the line infantry, although the diary of Sam Pickens quoted previously suggests that at least in Rodes's division they did, although it was certainly to a lower measure than that of the sharpshooters. Blackford's account, however, makes it clear that the sharpshooters fired to a very high standard for the period, indeed as high as the technology of the weapons would permit. Because of the changes in weapons technology that allowed the rifle to be loaded as fast as the smoothbore musket, the sharpshooters were also able to act as line infantry and assault troops. Thus, since the Army of Northern Virginia typically fielded around thirty-six infantry brigades in 1864, and each brigade had a battalion of 180-200 men, this would have given the Confederates a corps of more than seven thousand men trained in marksmanship and skirmish tactics. "Grant's intention is to siege Richmond this summer," wrote sharpshooter Jerry Tate, who thought that "he will find some obstacles in the way that will be hard for him to remove."[12]

12

The Wilderness

"For God's sake go up and stop them!"

On May 4, 1864, the Army of the Potomac crossed the Rapidan river, initiating the Overland Campaign. The two armies stumbled into each other the next day at Saunders Field, a small clearing in the Wilderness. Two brigades of Confederate Major General Edward Johnson's division began to set up some hasty entrenchments on both sides of the Orange Turnpike, while Rodes's division filed behind them. Soon the Federals appeared in force, and after some skirmishing launched a serious attack about 1 p.m. Brigadier General John Jones's Virginia brigade, holding the right of the pike, was outflanked and collapsed almost immediately. Behind Jones, Blackford and his sharpshooters led Battle's Alabama brigade toward the sound of the guns, thinking they were heading into a supporting position. As they did their excitable old corps commander, Lieutenant General Richard "Baldy" Ewell, galloped up and shouted, "for God's sake go up and stop them!" Blackford and the Alabama brigade marched on the double-quick up a densely forested ridge to the front, but Jones's Virginians streamed out of the woods with the Federals right on their heels, mixing with the two right-hand regiments of Battle's brigade and throwing them into disorder. "Ere I had time to deploy," recalled Blackford, "I found myself right among the Yankees." In the confusion someone shouted "fall back to Mine Run," and the sharpshooters, the Third and Fifth Alabama, and the Virginians hotfooted it backward in a general rout "like a lot of thorough-breds pulling on their bits."[1]

The brigade's three other regiments across the Orange Turnpike were unaffected by the chaos. Battle deftly wheeled the Sixth and the green Sixty-first Alabama round and smashed into the flank of the advancing Federals, driving them back in turn across Saunders Field. Blackford's sharpshooters "suffered heavily" in the action: "We were fighting them for some time, it seemed hours, before the rest of the division had time to form line and advance, it did so and relieved us. It then retired some 100 yards reforming advanced again & occupied the front." This put Blackford on the edge of Saunders Field again, where Jones's brigade had been. It was time to dig in. Blackford established his men "snugly behind logs" and awaited the advance of a Union brigade. "I passed the word to wait the signal, and let them come quite close ere I said a word, then shouting out 'commence firing' the whole line blazed away at 75 yards distant. Every shot told, I believe, and such as did not run into the ditch for shelter, took to their heels as hard as they could go, pursued by the bullets to the last. Those in the ditch our men fired at until the last came out and surrendered."[2]

After the turbulence of the afternoon's bloody seesaw battles, desultory sharpshooter fire, mainly centered around two guns the Yankees had abandoned, was all that could be heard. The guns were stuck in a ditch about halfway across the field, so they could neither be recovered by the Union nor captured by the Confederates. "That night," wrote Blackford, "I was ordered to go down & bring off the guns, an absurd order, as the enemy could not get them, and it could cost many lives for us to bring them in now." Nevertheless he went "and while crawling around in the dark examining the ways & means about the guns I met a Yankee on the same errand; both of us on our hands and knees, and both backed off without a word." Blackford left the guns where they were.[3]

He spent the rest of the night helping the Yankee wounded, "of which there were an inconvenient number lying around." It had been a hellish day for anyone unfortunate enough to have been hit. Many lay between the lines and beyond the reach of their comrades. The sharpshooters continued to make Saunders Field too hot for the Yankees for the rest of the day and the next, when General Ulysses Grant's move to Spotsylvania shifted the battle elsewhere.[4]

Meanwhile, about a mile away through the dense woods, Harry Heth's outnumbered division of A. P. Hill's Third Corps struggled to hold off Major General Winfield Hancock's Union II Corps along the Orange Plank Road. General Cadmus Wilcox's division came to their aid, with Captain Dunlop and the sharpshooters of McGowan's South Carolina brigade "thrown out upon the left of the plank road and deployed. ... The sharpshooters hung like a fringe on the left of the column, to ward off any disposition on the part of the enemy to thrust himself into the interval between Ewell and Hill and thus disturb our march. We were in the woods for the most part, and maintained our distance of from one to two hundred yards to the left of the brigade for some eight or ten miles before the lines were formed for action." When Wilcox met the enemy and formed his division for battle on the left of a plank road across from Heth, he ordered the sharpshooters to "extend intervals to the left, so as to cover as far as possible the gap between Hill's left and Ewell's right."[5]

The battle quickly commenced. "The sharpshooters were thrown in front," remembered Berry Benson, a sergeant with Company A, "and we advanced." The rest of the brigade followed them in line of battle formation, and "the sharpshooters were condensed on the right, in line-of-battle, the right of the Battalion resting on the Plank Road. A fearful fire of musketry from the enemy swept the woods, and many were killed and wounded. Our line was ordered to lie down." Hunkered in a ditch, Benson exchanged shots with a Yankee hiding behind an abandoned caisson. "Four or five times he fired at me, barely missing me, I firing in return." The man proved to be an excellent shot, and his next bullet hit Benson's knapsack and nicked his shoulder. Benson's sharpshooting antagonist may have been one of the 2nd U.S.S.S., which was deployed across the plank road as a skirmishing force for the Union II Corps. Federal sharpshooter Wyman White described running into "a heavy Rebel picket line, driving it back on a heavy support of infantry." The fighting, he said, was "of the most stubborn sort," with the Rebels "only giving ground to save their being shot or taken prisoner."[6]

Benson's duel was interrupted by Yankee cheers from across the road, followed by a line of retreating Confederate infantry. Shortly afterward, Benson wrote, "our line gave way, and in two minutes the Plank Road was jammed with a disorderly, flying mass of Confederates moving in all directions except the front." Even the sharpshooters had been "scattered," admitted Benson, who managed to collect eight men and began hunting for his brigade. Instead his band fell in with Lane's North Carolina brigade and fought with them the rest of the day "in a dense wood … at close quarters, men falling thick and fast all about." At dusk the battle tapered off, and Benson and his five remaining sharpshooters picked their way back toward their own brigade, still near the plank road where they had started out that morning. By the time they reached the area, it was dark. As he wandered through the stygian woods, Benson lost his way. He was fortunate to run into a soldier who sounded like a Southerner. After a number of pointed questions about unit officers and the like, Benson satisfied himself that he was indeed with the right army, and returned to his company. With battle lines only "a biscuit's toss" apart, the exhausted men tried to grab a little rest. Hill's two divisions had managed to fend off five Federal ones that day, but just barely. A third of Lee's army, Lieutenant General James Longstreet's First Corps, was still en route to the battle, and until they arrived, Hill's exhausted veterans would have to hold the line.[7]

The next morning's battle did not go well. McGowan's sharpshooters took a position some two hundred yards in front of the brigade "behind a low range of breastworks." As the woods lightened one of Benson's sharp-eyed men waved him over and pointed into the gloom. As Benson squinted into the dark forest the man impatiently said "Don't you see? It's the Yankee line of battle." In a moment Benson too could see them distinctly. Grant had ordered a general attack at first light. Benson carried word back to Dunlop and McGowan and had just returned to his post when the first shots cracked through the trees.[8]

"Though only a line of skirmishers against a line of battle," Benson wrote, "we fought stubbornly, dropping back slowly, to give the line of battle behind us good time to meet the enemy with a full volley." As he reached the infantry behind him, however, he was horrified to see the entire brigade take off and "run like deer" after firing only a scattering of shots. The South Carolinians continued rearward pell-mell, until they spotted an august figure on horseback—General Lee—who rode up to them and remarked, "I am surprised to see such a gallant regiment running like a flock of geese." His words had an immediate effect: shame overcame panic, and the brigade meekly reformed into a defensive position.[9]

One of the Federals, Sergeant White of the 2nd U.S.S.S., recalled that in the morning "we knew we had them on the run and our troops kept up a continuous cheer. ... Soon after noon their lines were badly broken." But Longstreet's corps finally arrived, and "Old Pete" launched a stunning counterattack that drove back the Federals. White and his men "had gotten quite a distance in advance" of the rest of Ward's division, when Longstreet's men appeared "on our flanks and almost in our rear." They hurriedly pulled back to some old Confederate earthworks and tried to fight off a heavy attack. "Our regiment," he wrote, "with our breech loading Sharps rifles had no trouble holding them back ... although they poured in a terrific infantry fire." White fired mechanically, shoving one round after another into the breech. When he looked around, he saw that only he and one other man remained. Then two bullets hit him in quick succession, one penetrating his knapsack and the other cutting its shoulder strap and tearing open his blouse. Still, White managed to retreat "a half dozen rods to the rear" without serious injury.[10]

The Rebels were soon upon them and planted their colors on the works. The Yankees shot down their color bearer, then a Confederate lieutenant who picked up the flag. "The fight had caught me wild," wrote White, "and I was singing 'On the Road to Boston' as loud as I could shout." A bullet whizzed past him into the head of the man beside him, which "brought me back to my senses." White started over the works for the fallen colors but a Rebel soldier "threw off his hat, pitched his rifle into the brush" and acted like he wanted to surrender. Hands up, the man glided up to where the colors lay, then suddenly snatched them up and legged it back toward his lines. White fired at the Rebel, who was "so near that I expected to blow him through," but the man's incredible luck held and the "hundred bullets sent after him all missed." White readily gave his enemy credit—"No man ever did a braver act." Their offensive spirit spent, the Confederates pulled back, leaving the battlefield relatively quiet for the rest of the evening.[11]

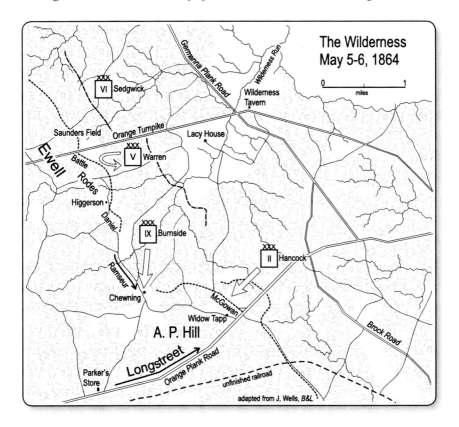

The Wilderness
May 5-6, 1864

adapted from J. Wells, B&L

Though Longstreet had saved Hill and stabilized the situation on the Orange Plank Road, a sizable gap remained between the two wings of the Confederate army. Into the gap blundered Ambrose Burnside's IX Corps, which had been charged by Grant with slicing through the virtually undefended Confederate center. If Burnside could seize the high ground near Chewning Farm, he would outflank both Hill and Ewell, and an advance to Parker's Store, only a mile away, would put him on the Orange Plank Road in Hill's rear. Unfortunately for the Union, Burnside was the man who had led them to disaster at Fredericksburg, and he was not known for his tactical acumen or celerity. After a late start he stopped his command for breakfast, eating up a precious hour just as Hancock's offensive started down the Orange Plank Road. By 7 a.m. Burnside's leading regiments had finally arrived on Ewell's flank. The first Federal brigade to arrive, commanded by Colonel Benjamin Christ, passed through a thick pine forest to the edge of an open field near Chewning Farm.[12]

Christ sent the 1st Michigan Sharpshooters forward to reconnoiter.
Seven companies stepped out in skirmish formation while three remained
in reserve. The rest of the brigade, formed in line of battle behind them, set
up hasty breastworks and waited. Although the 1st Michigan Sharpshooters
had been formed in fall 1862 as a specialized "light" regiment, they had
spent the war so far chasing Morgan's raiders in Ohio and guarding prisoners of war near Chicago. Lacking the political pull of a Hiram Berdan, they
carried ordinary infantry rifles rather than the fancy Sharps, with a few
target rifles available for long-range work. While superbly drilled, especially
in skirmish tactics, they had until now been in only a few minor skirmishes,
and had not yet made the harsh psychological adjustment to the battlefields
of Virginia. A battery of Confederate guns to their left began dropping shells
among them, and the Michigan sharpshooters heard for the first time the
popping of the picket line's rifles followed by the sound of bullets snapping
through the underbrush. "I dared not look at my knees," confessed one
officer, "for I could feel them shaking like a twig in the breeze and I was
afraid the others would notice it."[13]

The 1st Michigan Sharpshooters boasted a company of American Indians who were reputed to be some of the army's best scouts and skirmishers
as well as being crack shots. These men, many of whom listed their occupation as "hunter," also excelled in field camouflage, a rarity in the Civil War.
Realizing that their blue blouses stood out more than the faded butternut
uniforms of their opponents, the Indians "would go out and find a dry spot
of earth and roll in it until their uniform was the complete color of the
ground before going into the skirmish line; and if the day was wet, they
would not hesitate to take mud and rub it over their clothes, for as soon
as it dried a little they would have … the color of the earth. This custom
was adopted by the whole regiment." Some of them went even further, using "twigs and leaves" in their clothing to break up their outline. Sergeant
White met one of these warriors later in the campaign, when he wanted to
cross an exposed field to reach a better position. As White hesitated, the
Indian instructed him to "Make self corn. Do as I do," and he showed White
how to camouflage himself with corn stalks. The ruse worked beautifully:
they drew no fire crossing the field and soon got "a very fine chance on
the rebels." After a successful day sharpshooting they returned after dark,
"never to meet again."[14]

The men from Michigan continued to push forward and feel to the right,
trying to find the flank of their own V Corps in the thickets. Instead they
bumped into enemy pickets and a group of Rebels building breastworks in
a clearing near the Higgerson place. These were probably the sharpshooters
of Daniel's brigade, on flank guard at the end of Rodes's line. A desultory
picket fight broke out. "The sharpshooters of this regiment [the Fifty-third
North Carolina] were much annoyed by one of the Federal sharpshooters,"

related one southerner, "who had a long-range rifle and who had climbed up a tall tree from which he could pick off our men, though sheltered by stump and stones." The Yankee's weapon considerably outranged their Enfields, making direct retaliation impossible. One of Daniel's sharpshooters, Private Louis Leon, "concluded that this thing would have to stop, and taking advantage of every knoll, hollow, and stump, he crawled near enough for his rifle to reach, took a pop at this disturber of the peace, and he came tumbling down." To his surprise Leon found that the Yank was "a Canadian Indian." He dragged him back to his own lines by his scalp lock because, he said, no one would have believed him otherwise.[15]

The Confederates needed to close the gap between their wings to stymie Burnside, but their Second Corps was fully occupied holding off the Federal V and VI Corps. Dodson Ramseur and his North Carolinians, Rodes's remaining brigade, were en route after coming off picket duty on the Rapidan, and Rodes directed them to take a position at the end of Ewell's line. For his part, Burnside cooperated fully by doing nothing the rest of the morning, even though not a single Confederate unit stood directly in front of him. Meanwhile Burnside's other division, led by Brigadier General Robert Potter, engaged in a nasty fight with some of Hill's men near the Widow Tapp's farm. Just when it appeared that Burnside had made up his mind to attack down Parker's Store road, Grant ordered him to move to Orange Plank Road and aid Hancock's men, who were taking a beating from Longstreet.[16]

By now it was early afternoon. Ramseur's men, marching at a double-quick on the dusty paths, had begun to arrive. As the Rebel gunners continued their fire, Ramseur extended his line beyond Christ's and laid a clever trap. Seeing the bluecoats moving toward him across a swampy bottom, he stationed his two corps of sharpshooters behind a hill, telling them that "when the enemy began shooting, they should hold their ground, stand perfectly still, and simultaneously give the Rebel yell until ordered to advance." While Ramseur's men, under Major Edwin Osborne of the Fourth North Carolina, moved into position, Christ received an abrupt order to join Potter's men on the left. He pulled back the line of battle supporting the Michigan sharpshooters, and sent word for them "to withdraw the picket and skirmish line as quickly and quietly as possible."[16]

But Ramseur chose that moment to loose his sharpshooters on Christ's troops, and his unorthodox tactic worked perfectly. As the pickets fired off the first few shots, the unseen sharpshooters began an unearthly howling. "The advance being given, they still yelling, ran pell-mell down the hill" followed by the rest of the brigade. This was too much for the green Yankee skirmishers, who "wildly fled, leaving behind their clothing, knapsacks, etc.; few shots having been fired from the main line of battle." Ramseur's men, "yelling like a pack of fiends," moved so fast that they overtook and captured a number of the white Michigan men. The American Indians reacted differently. "As we drove them back," wrote a man from the Fourteenth North Carolina "one Indian took refuge behind a tree. We saw him and supposed he would surrender." Instead, to their surprise, he shot down the regiment's color bearer—a foolhardy act that immediately cost him his life. "The Indians fought bravely in the wood. When driven into the open they did not fire on us, but ran like deer. We captured not one of them." The exotic booty left to the Tarheels included "a satchel with beautiful figured work" and "copies of the Bible in the Ojibwa language." Shortly after the rout Ramseur made contact with Harris's Mississippi brigade on his left, thus connecting the two wings of the Confederate army. Reinforced by Christ's brigade, Burnside's men continued their attack on Hill's positions, but with scant result.[18]

As for the 1st Michigan Sharpshooters, their first combat experience left them "too much disorganized ... to participate with the rest of the brigade in the remaining operations of the day." Their colonel, ex-newspaperman Charles DeLand, had withdrawn with the rest of the brigade, taking his three reserve companies along. When the Rebels struck he neither returned nor sent back his reserve, leaving his second in command, Major John Piper, to rally what men he could. The soldiers felt, with some justification, that their absence was due to a lack of gallantry on DeLand's part. The events of the day did not help morale, and adding to their discomfiture, a neighboring Union regiment fired into them the next night while they were on picket, killing several of their men.[19]

The fighting at the Wilderness sputtered out on the evening of May 6, leaving Lee's lines intact and too strong to be carried by assault. Although some sharpshooter battalions performed well, such as Blackford's at Saunders Field, the thick woods of the Wilderness offered little opportunity for either long-range rifle fire or skirmishing, limiting the scope of action for the army's new sharpshooter battalions in their first battle. "The Wilderness was a field well adapted by the very nature of the country to the operations of the sharpshooters; but so fierce had been the engagement that no opportunity was afforded them for the display of maneuvers or marksmanship," concluded one sharpshooter commander.[20]

Still, some of the Confederate commanders had used their sharpshooters effectively and had even developed some unique tactics, like "hollerin" the Yankees out of their works without actually attacking. Berry Benson describes an incident two days later in which his division commander, General Cadmus Wilcox, "ordered that the Sharpshooters should move forward and give a loud cheer upon reaching the breastwork." This they did, and when they entered the Yankee position they found "great numbers of knapsacks piled up" and much other equipment of all kinds. "I never saw a field so rich in plunder," said Benson. "It looked as though the enemy had fled in dismay ... we proceeded to help ourselves."[21]

Both sides rested the next day and brought in their wounded, but that night Grant began a sideways move to seize the crossroads at Spotsylvania Court House. Lee sent his army to intercept him.

13

Spotsylvania

"The hottest place I was ever in."

Grant and Lee's race to Spotsylvania on May 8, 1864, came down to a matter of minutes. After a night of hard marching, delayed by the stubborn rear-guard actions of Fitzhugh Lee's cavalry, the bone-tired infantrymen of Major General Gouverneur Warren's Federal V Corps spotted Confederate horse soldiers frantically stacking rails and cutting trees for a stand on the low rise across Sarah Spindle's farm. This modest prominence, soon to be called Laurel Hill, dominated the area. If the Unionists could take it, they would command the vital crossroads at Spotsylvania Court House. Three of Warren's brigades were far enough forward for an immediate attack, and two others were close behind. Around 8:30 a.m. the general waved his weary columns forward, confident they would sweep the high ground. "Never mind cannon! Never mind bullets! Press on and clear this road. It's the only way to get your rations," he shouted, having in mind breakfast at the courthouse.[1]

Not far southwest of the hill, the South Carolinians of Kershaw's brigade, now commanded by Colonel John W. Henagan of the Eighth South Carolina, had stopped to grab a morsel after clearing the smoke and brush fires of the Wilderness battlefield. Like the Yankees, they had marched all night. As bacon began to sizzle in their pans, an agitated civilian—shoeless, hatless, and astride a barebacked horse—rode up and begged General Kershaw (who was now in division command) to "hurry up, Stuart was withdrawing his cavalry." The soldiers kicked out their fires, grabbed a steaming piece of half-cooked meat if they could, and began shuffling toward Laurel Hill. Lee's cavalry chief, Jeb Stuart, directed the South Carolinians into position as they arrived to relieve his hard-pressed troopers.[2]

"We sharpshooters rushed to the front," recalled a soldier with the Third South Carolina battalion, who served as Kershaw's sharpshooters. They quickly fanned out in a skirmish line north of the Spindle house, covering the deployment of the rest of the brigade. The Third South Carolina regiment relieved the horse soldiers in a grove of pines on the right of the road, while the Second South Carolina stopped on the left just a bit behind it. Although the Union force, "two or three columns deep," was barely sixty yards away when the Carolinians reached the rails, they were able to loose a devastating volley on their opponents, driving them back with heavy losses.[3]

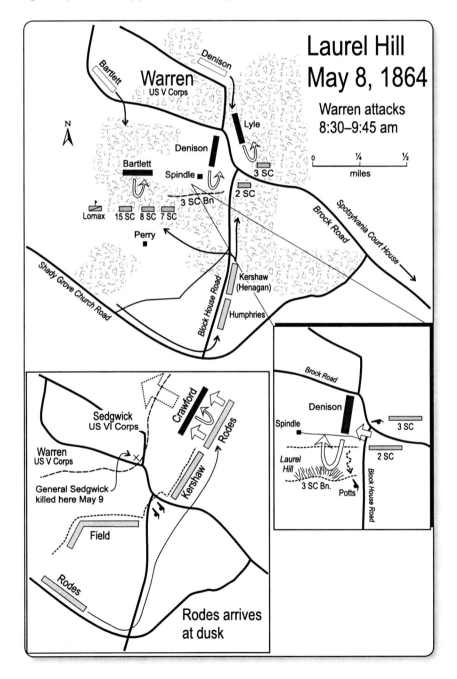

As the rest of Kershaw's brigade continued to file into position and extend their lines, Warren's other two brigades started forward across the
Spindle fields and farmyard west of Brock road. The one nearest the road,
Colonel Andrew Denison's all-Maryland brigade, came on in column without skirmishers. Denison and his division commander, Brigadier General
John Robinson, led the way on horseback, their formation selected more for
speed than fighting. This battering ram of more than seven hundred men
headed directly for the Third South Carolina battalion, whose sharpshooters hastily fell back to their original position, just west of the road. Two
batteries of Rebel guns rolled up, one just to the right of the sharpshooters,
the other further up with the other two regiments. Some of the sharpshooters, in what was to become a favorite Confederate ploy, may have moved off
to the left of the brigade to enfilade the line. The sharpshooters barely made
it to their position, "throwing ourselves behind the rails," as the Yankees
reached the front. The gunners, a North Carolina battery under Captain
John Potts, complained of being protected by "only a line of skirmishers."[4]

Even so, the Southerners fired hotly at their opponents, who instead of
charging the hill made the mistake of halting to return fire. Only a few men
at the column's head had a clear shot, and its momentum pushed forward
the men behind them, transforming their orderly ranks into a disorganized
throng moving slowly up the hill. "Pick that officer off of his horse," shouted
someone, and both Denison and Robinson went down. Colonel Charles Phelps
of the 7th Maryland took over, but he was trapped under his horse when a
shot dropped it just short of the barricades. The attack began to falter.[5]

Still, many Yankees remained—at least three for every Carolinian—and
the bolder ones made it to the works, "completely overlapping our line." The
fighting became hand-to-hand, to the disadvantage of the Southerners, who
"never before needing them" had few bayonets. They swung their clubbed
muskets at the Federals, who poured over the rails and demanded the surrender of the battalion's colors. Sharpshooter Jim Milling snatched the flag
from the badly wounded color bearer and passed it to another man, even as
a point-blank shot burned his face and perforated his bedroll.[6]

Just as it seemed that the whole battalion might be captured, the Confederate guns—especially those of the South Carolina battery posted further
forward on their right—began pumping double canister into the disorganized mass of blue. The Second and Third South Carolina, having repulsed
their attackers, also shifted a number of their men around to fire into the
Yankees. The Marylanders, leaderless and caught in the midst of hellish
firestorm, broke for the rear. "Had not the right of our brigade commenced
driving them back," explained Milling, "they could easily have carried us
off." As it was, the butcher's bill for Denison's unfortunate brigade was 192
men, including Colonel Phelps, who was captured; Denison himself, who
lost an arm; and General Robinson, who lost a leg.[7]

As the Marylanders streamed rearward, a Union brigade under Brigadier General Joseph Bartlett advanced on the other side of the Spindle house. Bartlett had taken the time to form a line of battle and send out skirmishers, at least in part because "while marching in column along the road to the Court-House, our flankers were vigorously attacked by the skirmishers of the enemy." These may have been some of the sharpshooters who had been posted further to the west, or simply an ad hoc group of skirmishers from other regiments. In any case, Bartlett fared no better than his predecessors. Though his men also briefly gained the ramparts, they were driven back with heavy loss. The race to Spotsylvania was over, and the sharpshooters had been instrumental in winning it for the Confederates.[8]

Confederate defenses at Laurel Hill. *B&L*

Loath to accept failure, however, the Federals made several more attacks, accomplishing little except to lengthen their casualty lists. "The ground was literally strewn with dead Yankees, all in front and to the left of where we had fought," recounted Milling, who called it "the hottest place I was ever in." The Confederates fed in reinforcements and continued to dig in, and by noon they had made Laurel Hill virtually impregnable. "The old trained veterans decided that the only way to succeed was to be quick and deliberate, fire with precision, so as to kill as many as possible," wrote one Rebel, "but after a slaughter of thousands in a few days they seemed to multiply like flies that had been poisoned." As the infantrymen continued to improve their positions, the battle settled into a fierce artillery duel. "The rebel sharpshooters opened a very ugly fire on us from ... four hundred yards off," complained the Federal artillery commander, Colonel Charles Wainright, "especially from the wood to the left of the road where they lay thick behind large fallen trees." From there "a dozen or twenty would fire by command at the same object." Wainright sent away his mounted staff, who were drawing fire, and walked behind his own horse, using it as a shield against "the rascals." Nevertheless the Rebels landed "a score of miniés" near him when he ventured out to talk to one of his battery commanders. He readily admitted that the Carolina sharpshooters "hurt us badly."[9]

As Union reinforcements continued to arrive that afternoon, their generals decided to try again. With the Union VI Corps now on the scene they considerably outnumbered the Confederates holding Laurel Hill. This time General Meade would try to fix them with a frontal attack while he sent a flanking column around their right. By the time the Federals were ready it was nearly sunset, but Brigadier General Samuel Crawford's division of V Corps and Eustis's brigade of VI Corps began to move anyway. The two Rebel divisions on the hill were fully occupied with holding their ground, so nothing seemed to stand in the Yankees' way. Once into the gloomy pine forests, so different from the tangled second growth thickets of the Wilderness, however, it was difficult for the men in blue to keep their bearings. The leading division, Crawford's, was George Meade's old outfit, the Pennsylvania Reserves. These men's enlistments would soon be over, a factor that somewhat tempered their earlier enthusiasm for battle. Chance would soon put them up against their old antagonists at South Mountain, and this time the results would be different.[10]

The men of the Confederate Second Corps had had the longest march to Laurel Hill, and they had been in motion all day and most of the night before. Cullen Battle's Alabamians—Rodes's old brigade—led the way. "The sun never shone more warmly," griped one man, "and it would have been impossible to have suffered more than we did." Men threw away their blankets, knapsacks, "even their haversacks, with rations," and finally began to fall out themselves. Another soldier called it "the hardest march of the war ... almost beyond human endurance." Still, "late that evening" the weary Alabama boys heard the order to "close up and dress on center" as the brigade formed in an old field behind Laurel Hill.[11]

Captain J. W. Williams, who had been captured while commanding the Fifth Alabama's skirmishers at South Mountain, watched as his division commander, Robert Rodes, rode up on his fine black mare. Reining in his horse, Rodes said, "Boys, you played hell the other evening; now, when the order is given I want you to run over those Yankees in front." Primed for action, the sharpshooters assembled in front of the brigade. As Williams described it:[12]

> That evening everything was quiet, when our brigadier [Cullen A. Battle] rode up to Major Blackford and gave him orders to move forward. The skirmishers knew that a sound from that old bugle was an order from Blackford, so every man sprang to his place and moved on. When they had advanced about one hundred and fifty yards the division was ordered forward. We had to cross a level field, and we could see the long line of skirmishers ahead of us. Very soon the two skirmish lines began to fight. The order "forward" passed down the line and we were soon in a double quick. When we were about one hundred and fifty yards of the woods in our front, a Yankee line of battle let us have it, but we didn't make a halt; we went over that fence and into the pines after them.[13]

The Alabamians, their blood up, caught the Pennsylvania Reserves flat-footed. After a sharp fight the leading brigade broke, then the supporting one came apart in the dark woods, "so dense that you could scarcely see the sky above you." Joined first by Ramseur's Tarheels and then by Doles's and Daniel's men, the Alabamians pressed on, "through woods, thickets, fields, briar patches, over fences." While one soldier boasted that they "soon made the saucy Yankees 'about face' and hunt a more comfortable position," both sides became "fearfully mixed up" in the darkness and were almost in as much danger of being shot by their own men as by their enemies. Eventually the Confederates ran into a supporting Union line, got a bloody nose, and pulled back. Although they lost the colors of the Sixth Alabama in that last desperate fray, they did have the satisfaction of whipping their old enemies and capturing one of their brigade commanders, Colonel William Talley.[14]

As the balance of the armies arrived on the field, their lines extended eastward. "The movement from the Wilderness to Spotsylvania Court-House was exceedingly arduous to the sharpshooters," recalled Captain John Young, "who were compelled to march to the left flank of the column, deployed as if in regular line." Warfare was changing, and in this more open country the sharpshooters began to come into their own. Heretofore the battles had pitted the armies together in the open for two or three days, after which one side or the other accepted defeat and withdrew. This had been the pattern at Chancellorsville and Gettysburg, the two major eastern theater battles of 1863. Spotsylvania, however, pointed the way to the future: armies would now face each other for extended periods of time, with both sides sheltering themselves behind increasingly elaborate fortifications. Thus when Young and his men arrived, "it failed to afford the expected rest. Almost immediately the command was thrown forward and began what appeared to be an endless picket fight. One day was reflexive of another, though the elements of exposure and excitement prevented their succession from becoming monotonous." [15]

While the line infantry refined their fortifications, Confederate commanders moved their sharpshooter battalions into a rough line of shallow rifle pits forward of their main line. Berry Benson described one of these rifle pits: "There were logs lying about and these we took to make rifle pits. From the general method of constructing protection for sharpshooters by digging a hole in the ground and throwing up earth in front of it as a breastwork, arose the use of the word 'pits' as applied to any construction serving the same purpose. A pile of rails was called a 'rifle pit,' and so with the logs. No hole was dug; the rails were simply arranged in low piles behind which the men lay." [16]

A rifle pit as described by Berry Benson. *The Soldier in Our Civil War*

Captain Young, who commanded the sharpshooters of Scales's brigade, told how his men went about their daily business. "At 3 o'clock, before light, the command would be moved out of the camp inside the main lines, and sent forward to relieve the regimental details who did guard duty at night. Arrived on the picket line, while darkness still reigned, the men were placed in the rifle-pits, and, arranging themselves as comfortably as circumstances permitted, proceeded to make what their rations afforded in the way of breakfast. This was generally light, except when contributions had been levied from some contraband source, or the camp of the enemy had been put into requisition." The historian of Kershaw's brigade described how "sharpshooters were posted in trees in the woods, and kept up a pretty constant fusilade when any head showed itself."[17]

To sustain this pace the sharpshooters discarded most everything except their weapons and haversacks, becoming "the very lightest of light troops." Their main supply source became the Federal commissariat, as they "found it much less burdensome to make a raid for supplies on the line of the enemy than to carry knapsacks." Unfortunately this habitual closeness to the enemy sometimes led to a "rage after plunder," which, said Captain Young, "was fatal to some of our very best men." One Sergeant Warren started it when he dropped a Union vidette who lay close enough for him to relieve of his possessions. To the impoverished Southerner, the dead Yankee seemed to possess a small fortune. "The next morning the men were wild for an attack, beholding in each hostile form the bearer of property, of which they burned to possess themselves." The sharpshooters spent the next day shooting at Yankees and then attempting to keep friend and foe alike away from those they brought down. "The impatience of the sportsmen was too great that night to wait until it was fully dark," said Young. "They stole off in the gray dusk of the evening, and some of them—among whom was Sergeant Warren—returned no more. We passed the next morning their bloated corpses on the very spot where their operations had been so rashly begun." Young issued strict orders forbidding the practice, but no one could say what effect they had.[18]

Tom Paysinger, a scout in Kershaw's brigade, was "a master hand" at this sort of thing, combining his nighttime reconnaissances with a search for "the many crisp five-dollar greenbacks or even hundred-dollar interest-bearing United States bonds [that] could be found in the pockets of the fallen Federal." One night Paysinger relieved a "dead" Yankee of his possessions, then began crawling towards another man. As the South Carolinian left, the first man rose on one elbow, grabbed a nearby musket and fired, yelling "You d—n grave robber, take that." Seriously wounded, Paysinger regained his lines, later claiming that he "would have turned and cut the rascal's throat, but he was afraid he was only 'possuming' and might brain him with the butt of his gun." The commander of Kershaw's sharpshooters, Captain Benjamin Whitener, often shared Paysinger's nocturnal forays and was said to be "the mischief to plunder."[19]

The spirit sometimes infected entire units. Captain Dunlop reported an instance in which his battalion went to check out a Federal position. They found it abandoned but strewn with "the richest field of spoils we had ever seen. The whole face of the earth was literally covered with valuable plunder." This was too much temptation for the South Carolinians, including their commander. He sounded assembly then allowed his battalion to "stack arms, break ranks and help themselves." Things quickly got out of hand, and Dunlop watched in dismay as his "compact body of daring men was converted into a wild and reckless mob, rushing hither and thither in search of plunder." It began to dawn on him that "an organized body of twenty men, if present, could have captured the entire command." Fortunately he managed to get his men under control before any Yankees showed up, and they returned loaded with loot.[20]

Some men were even more specific about getting that they wanted. After the war General Joseph Johnston related a conversation he overheard between two of his sharpshooters during the Atlanta campaign:

> Now, Charley, when you ain't in a fight, but just shootin' so; of course you ought to get a fellow off by himself, before you let fly. Then the next thing is to see what you need most of anything. If it's clothes, why, of course, you choose a fellow of your own size; but if it's shoes you want, you just pick out the very littlest weevil-eaten chap you can find. Your feet would slide 'round in the shoes of a Yankee as big as you are like they was in flat-boats. Why, no longer ago than last evening I had drawed a bead on a fine, great big buck of a fellow, but just as I was about to drop him I looked around and found I didn't have no shoes. So I let him pass, and pretty soon here come along a little cuss of an officer, and—raising his right foot, as the old general did his, by way of vivid recital and illustration—*"there's the boots."*[21]

Still, in spite of the brutality of war, the sharpshooters shared civilized moments. One Southerner claimed that "when it was quiet they became well acquainted with the fellows on the other side, swapping tobacco for coffee, or perhaps the best poker hand would take the pot. Strong friendships were sometimes formed between men on opposing lines," and at times they would even pass letters back and forth.[22]

The Confederate sharpshooters now began to dominate the skirmish line, as they would for the rest of the Overland campaign. According to one Mainer, they "commanded completely the position of our line of battle." A private in the 17th Maine, John Haley, described relieving other troops who held an advanced position: "The Rebel sharpshooters were posted … in such a manner as to cover our approach no matter *how* we came. An enfilading fire caused any of the troops in the line who had the temerity to raise their heads to sink quickly to the ground … we found it conducive to longevity to spread ourselves on the ground as thin as the butter on a slice of boarding-house bread." The Federals tried to push out their own skirmish line as far as possible to reduce their effectiveness, but this gave little respite from the hissing bullets.[23]

Confederate sharpshooter. *B&L*

The Rebels also introduced another unpleasant wrinkle: a small number of men in each sharpshooter battalion now carried the deadly Whitworth rifle, a state-of-the-art weapon that they claimed could bring down a man at twelve hundred yards. Berry Benson described it as "a long, heavy gun of small bore [.45 caliber] made for sharpshooting at long range. This gun carried a small telescope on top of the barrel through which to sight; the hind sight (within the telescope) was a cross of two fine metal threads." Benson's battalion received two: one went to scout Ben Powell and the other to Private Oscar Cheatham. "Both these men were excellent shots," wrote Benson, "and they now became independent sharpshooters, to go where they pleased and carry on war at their own sweet will." In reality, however, the Whitworth sharpshooters were not quite that footloose. They usually reported to brigade or division headquarters, from where they were directed to areas where they might best employ their talents.[24]

Major General John Sedgwick, USA. *B&L*

On May 9 one of these men scored a major prize in the person of Major General John Sedgwick, the commander of the Union VI Corps, who was inspecting his lines near Spindle farm. His chief of staff, Lieutenant Colonel Martin McMahon, had warned him that morning against going near an intersection on Brock Road where a battery of artillery was stationed, as the Rebel sharpshooters had been particularly active there. One in particular was "said to have taken twenty lives," and earlier that day one of Sedgwick's brigade commanders, Brigadier General William Morris, had been shot off his horse and severely wounded. "I beg of you not to go to that angle," implored McMahon. "Every officer who has shown himself there has been hit, both yesterday and to-day." Sedgwick, who was in the process of moving his skirmish line forward to gain some relief from Confederate harassment, sent McMahon to supervise the operation, since it appeared that their newly constructed rifle pits partially obstructed his artillery's field of fire. Shortly afterward he joined McMahon near the guns. As the movement began, "a sprinkling fire" of bullets from Confederate sharpshooters, who were stationed on a low knoll about five hundred yards away, began landing among them. Some of the men, quite naturally, ducked and tried to avoid the whistling rounds.[25]

"What! what! Men, dodging this way for single bullets!" the general admonished them good-naturedly. "What will you do when they open fire along the whole line? I am ashamed of you. They couldn't hit an elephant at this distance." One man hunkered down right in front of General Sedgwick, who prodded him with his boot and said, "Why, my man, I am ashamed of you, dodging that way." He repeated, "they couldn't hit an elephant at this distance." The soldier defended his actions, saying, "General, I dodged a shell once, and if I hadn't, it would have taken my head off. I believe in dodging." Sedgwick, who was in a genial mood, laughed and said, "All right, my man; go to your place."[26]

A moment later a Confederate sharpshooter disputed the general's estimate of his shooting prowess. "For a third time the same shrill whistle, closing with a dull, heavy stroke, interrupted our talk," recalled McMahon, "when, as I was about to resume, the general's face turned slowly to me, the blood spurting from his left cheek under the eye in a steady stream. He fell in my direction; I was so close to him that my effort to support him failed, and I fell with him." Moments later "Uncle John" Sedgwick was dead.[27]

The incensed Yankees sent infantry patrols to find the culprit and killed several Rebel riflemen in retaliation. Eventually they located nine Confederate marksmen in a tree and proceeded to do a little sharpshooting of their own with a rifled artillery piece. "The first shot," chortled a Union soldier, "cut the tree off about 40 feet from the ground & down came Mr. sharp shooter head first. That ended the sharp shooting at this time."[28]

After the war several men claimed the honor of bagging General Sedgwick. One was Ben Powell, who mentioned to Berry Benson on May 9 that "he got a big Yankee officer this morning." He claimed that the shot was "something over half a mile" and that he could tell that the man was a high-ranking officer by the way the others deferred to him. However, Powell described bringing down a mounted man, which would have fit for General Morris but not for Sedgwick, who was on foot. Other candidates included Private Thomas Burgess, another South Carolinian, and Sergeant Charles Grace of the Fourth Georgia, part of Doles's brigade. Given the number of expert marksmen on the line that day, no one will ever know for certain who felled Sedgwick.[29]

Confederate sharpshooters continued to make the day miserable for the Federals, sending a "ceaseless and deadly fire" toward anyone who exposed himself. This led to a number of minor but intense brigade-sized actions in which the Federals tried to drive away their tormentors. When pressed, and after taking a heavy toll, the Confederates would simply fall back, often firing the woods as they did. These efforts culminated with a couple of brigade-sized actions in the late afternoon near Spindle farm. However, in each case the result was the same: having taken the position and driven off the grayback marksmen, the Federals would find that they were too exposed and far from their main line and have to withdraw. The sharpshooter battalions did their job well. "The activity of the litter bearers on the other side," boasted one commander, "testified to the skill of these trained riflemen.[30]

Still, the men in blue, who "displayed an animus of vindictive spite," struck back at the vexatious Southerners when the opportunity offered. "The ground between the lines at this point was for the most part in the woods," wrote Captain Dunlop, "covered with underbrush and seamed with sharp ravines and gullies, which meandered abruptly hither and thither across the interval. These furnished an inviting field and fair protection to the adventurous on both sides to crawl upon the rifle pits of the other side and get in some good shots before their movements and whereabouts could be discovered." In one instance a Yankee marksman killed two men in Young's sharpshooter battalion with a single bullet. Another time two officers of Kershaw's brigade were conversing in a fly tent behind the lines when a Yankee sharpshooter "put a ball through this tent, between the heads of the two." John Bone, a soldier with Ramseur's brigade, described the nonstop action on the line: "during these nights the sharpshooters would fire so heavily at times that we would be certain of an attack, and would arouse from our slumbers to our muskets." Situated near the base of a giant bulge in the Confederate line dubbed "the Mule Shoe," Bone found his outfit "a very bad position as the men stood in danger of being wounded or hit by the enemy, but much to our surprise we found that the trouble was caused by a man up in a tree who was shooting in our midst." The Tarheels finally located the offender's tree and peppered it with musket fire, "but by some means the marksman disappeared."[31]

To deal with the continuous strain of battle, various battalions adopted different schemes for the periodic relief of the sharpshooters. Some, like Dunlop and Young, withdrew the sharpshooters during the night for rest and replaced them with line infantry, sending them back out in the early morning before dawn. Others, like Mahone's brigade, kept their sharpshooters out more or less continuously, but allowed them to come off line one day a week for rest.[32]

On May 10 a Union force under Colonel Emory Upton launched a column attack on the side of the Mule Shoe against Doles's Georgia brigade. Upton first drove in Doles's sharpshooters with his own reinforced skirmish battalion, then ordered his men to cross the ground separating the lines at a run without firing, smothering the defenders under the weight of numbers. Although they killed or captured most of the Georgians, Upton's men were too few to hold their position and were soon driven out by Confederate reinforcements. Foremost in the counterattack was the Fifth Alabama, whose colonel, Josephus Hall, lost an arm, leaving Eugene Blackford in command. Casualties in Battle's brigade were high, and no record remains of who took Blackford's place as commander of the sharpshooters.[33]

The next day was a relatively quiet one. "Our Regt.," noted a Union rifleman with the 2nd U.S.S.S., "engaged the Johnny's S. Shooters, no general engagement by the infantry."[34]

The lull ended in the early morning hours of May 12, when Grant launched a massive repetition of Upton's attack on the tip of the Mule Shoe with the entire Federal II Corps, overrunning and destroying General Edward Johnson's division and nearly splitting Lee's army in two. In the ensuing battle the sharpshooters played their part as both skirmishers and troops of the line. As part of the Confederate response, Ramseur's brigade went forward in a desperate counterattack. "We now passed the line of the sharpshooters," wrote John Bone, "and men were being wounded all along the line. We had orders to charge, and charge we did." Although a bullet punched through one of Bone's lungs, his brigade successfully retook the works that had been lost that morning.[35]

The fighting at Spotsylvania's Bloody Angle was some of the most vicious and sustained of the war. *B&L*

Battle's Alabamians went in on their right, angling further north. They drove the advancing Yankees back, retaking the second line of works in a patch of woods. A substantial gap remained between Ramseur's right and Battle's left, however, and even though Lee threw in both Harris's and Perrin's brigades, they did not entirely close it. The last brigade to arrive was McGowan's South Carolinians, who pushed into the breach, "sharpshooters and all." General McGowan fell with a serious wound, but his men kept going, and for the next twenty hours these four brigades held what would become known as the Bloody Angle. "The ground was literally covered with the dead and dying," recalled Captain Dunlop, "and the water that rippled along the trenches from incessant rain, ran red with the blood of the slain. In the absence of specific orders, the sharpshooters had thrown themselves into the line of the brigade at their proper intervals and fought like tigers throughout the struggle."[36]

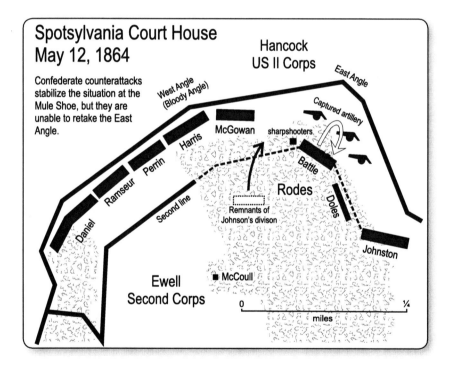

Even then the gap remained, until the few soldiers of Johnson's division who had not been killed or captured that morning stepped up to plug the hole. Among them was John Worsham of the Twenty-first Virginia, who had narrowly escaped capture. Sent to gather in the skirmish line as the Federals attacked, he had led his men around the left of the Mule Shoe to safety. Once in the rear they drew more ammunition and went back into the line. Worsham and his men soon got to the front, where they found the Yankees "in the pens made by our regiment ... as thick as herrings in a barrel." To his surprise Worsham saw only one friendly soldier, "an Alabamian, who was standing behind a large pine tree, loading and firing with as much deliberation as if he were firing at a target. He was keeping the whole of Hancock's force back at this point. He said he was a sharpshooter, and his line was on each side of him." This lone rifleman was most likely from Battle's brigade, which was off to the right, and this would have put him in position as a flank guard. "There certainly was no other Confederate in front of our regiment line," said Worsham, "nor could we see one either on the right or left. We lay down, taking advantage of everything that offered a protection, and opened on the enemy;—musket balls were fairly raining, great limbs of trees were cut off by bullets, as if by an ax." He swore, with pardonable exaggeration, that "this was the heaviest fire the world ever saw at a single point!"[37]

When Lee's counterstrokes stalled his attacks on the tip of the Mule Shoe, Grant switched his focus, ordering Burnside to press the eastern side of the salient with his IX Corps. After a stiff fight two Confederate brigades—Lane's and Weisiger's—stopped the Union advance. Later General Lee complimented Lane on his brigade's performance, but asked his sharpshooters, commanded by Captain William Nicholson of the Thirty-seventh North Carolina, to undertake another hazardous mission. He did not, he said, "have the heart to order them forward again; and yet, he wished them to make an important reconnaissance for him on the Fredericksburg road." When Nicholson assured him that the sharpshooters were game, Lee said "tell them it is a request and not an order." They went anyway, marching past their beloved leader who, "superbly mounted, gracefully bared his head, and uttered not a word, while the troops in the works joined in the cheering as those tired and hungry heroes went to the front."[38]

Across the lines, meanwhile, the Federal sharpshooter regiments were "up against it," and Sergeant Wyman White kept his rifle hot. "Our branch of the service had never been of so much use before in this war," he noted. "The enemy was continually in their earthworks and our troops had formed the habit of putting themselves behind the earth, and this led to a large amount of sharpshooting." During the battle a hot firefight developed over an artillery piece abandoned between the lines, which sharpshooters on both sides effectively kept anyone from recovering. One Southern sharpshooter, whom the Federals could clearly see standing behind a tree, was particularly troublesome: "They fired at him for a long time and he in return sent a bullet as often as one might reload." In spite of intense Union counterfire the man continued to sling lead at them, and no one could figure out how he survived. White at the time was using "a telescope breech loading rifle that weighed thirty pounds" instead of his Sharps. By 1864 these ungainly weapons had been relegated to the baggage train, but in times like this they would be brought forward and given to a trusted marksman like White, who now got a request "to try my rifle on the man they could not hit or silence." Through his telescope White now discovered the macabre truth—"it was the body of a dead rebel lashed up to a tree and a live rebel Sharpshooter was behind the tree doing his best to pick off the Yankees that were sending bullets into his dead comrade hung up beside the tree that covered him." After two days and many attempts a team of Yankee cannoneers dashed out at dusk with a captured limber, hooked up the gun, and returned to their lines "without losing either a man or a horse."[39]

Eventually Lee stabilized his line, although his men could not retake the tip of the Mule Shoe. That night they withdrew to a new, stronger line across its base, where the Confederates easily beat off another assault a few days later. During the lulls his men took what rest they could. In McGowan's brigade casualties among the sharpshooters had been so heavy that their division commander, Cadmus Wilcox, issued an order that they "should not be required to fight in the line of battle, as theretofore, except in cases of extreme necessity, but should confine themselves to their legitimate duties as skirmishers." In the days that followed Berry Benson continued his scouting, often with Ben Powell as his companion. On May 11 Benson and Powell had gone on an extended scout on the Federal right, and Benson had actually been close enough that evening to the Yankee campfires to converse with some of their soldiers in order to learn about their regiment and mission. He also interviewed civilians in the area, some of whom questioned him quite closely before answering, thinking he might be a spy. On his way out of the encampment Benson commandeered a Yankee officer's horse, "a fine black mare, with a colonel's saddle cloth on her back," which facilitated his and Powell's return. The two scouts returned just in time to be caught up in the great attack on the morning of the twelfth, and they spent the day fighting on the western side of the Mule Shoe. After two days and nights without rest Benson actually dozed off during the battle, waking only when the Confederates began pulling back early the next morning.[40]

Georgian Marion Fitzpatrick, who was also in Wilcox's division, wrote his wife that he had been "hard down skirmishing day and night. I have run some pretty narrow risks but not near like being in the regular fighting. They won't let the sharpshooters go into the regular fights but form us in the rear to stop stragglers. We have whipped the yankees badly, but our loss is heavy." A few days later he described his picket routine: "one half the sharpshooters stay on post at a time now and we get a little rest. I was relieved at midnight last night and will stay off till 12 o'clock today and then go on again and stay till midnight tonite."[41]

Benson went out again on May 16. The Yankees were moving, and he was sent to find out where and return in two hours. Taking two men with him, he approached the Federal pickets after dark to listen for moving troops but heard nothing. He went closer to the Northern line, alone, until he was challenged by a sentry. Instead of running he boldly answered the man's questions, saying that he was a Union scout who had come from Hancock's corps further down the line and wanted to take a shortcut back to his unit. Finding Benson quite well informed about the Federal army, the Yankees took him at his word and sent him to their camp without disarming him. They did, however, give him an escort of two men, who conducted him to their brigade commander's tent. From inside the tent the colonel asked which regiment Benson was with. "6th New York," he replied. "You are a Southern soldier." Benson denied this, but it was no use. Yet the Union commander, Colonel Jacob Sweitzer, proved quite affable. Taking Benson into his tent, he asked him what state he was from. When Benson finally admitted that he was from South Carolina, Sweitzer laughed and explained that he had been captured earlier in the war and spent a year at Libby Prison, which had made him quite familiar with Southern voices. The two men chatted amicably awhile as Sweitzer tried to get information from Benson. When the colonel asked about food in the Southern army, Benson assured him there was plenty and offered him a piece of fresh bread from his haversack, which he had just picked up prior to his departure. Finally Sweitzer disarmed him and, after wishing him a speedy exchange, sent him off under guard. Benson briefly broke free of his guards but was soon recaptured. After a narrow escape from being court-martialed and executed as a spy, he was packed off to Point Lookout prison.[42]

As Grant again shifted leftward, Lee sought to strike his right flank and threaten his communications with Fredericksburg. To this end he sent Ewell's badly battered Second Corps marching north on the afternoon of May 19, past the hotly contested Spindle Farm, still strewn with unburied corpses. Rodes's division, sharpshooters at the front, led the way. After crossing the Ni River, where Ewell left his artillery in deference to the muddy roads, the column turned east toward Fredericksburg road. Late in the afternoon Ramseur's sharpshooters ran into Yankee pickets near the Harris Farm. There Dodson Ramseur sustained his aggressive reputation by immediately pitching into the Federal position, which was protected by swampy ground bordering a stream. His opponents were several brigades of Union heavy artillerymen, rousted from their comfortable billets around Washington and pressed into service as infantry. While these men were not new recruits, they had as yet little experience as infantry, and it showed. The Tarheel veterans cut up the green "Heavies" fearfully and pushed them back, but there were more of them than they thought, and though many fell they did not break and run. Ramseur's men soon pulled back to await the rest of the division. More Heavies appeared, and although their awkward performance left much to be desired tactically (they stood when they should have lain down, silhouetted themselves on rises, and sometimes fired into each other), they still managed to stop the rest of Second Corps as it came up, preventing it from seizing Fredericksburg road. Ewell ordered a general attack, which failed, and when the men of General John Gordon's patched-together division stopped to pillage the Federal trains, a Federal counterattack scattered them, nearly collapsing the Confederate line.

As Union reinforcements continued to arrive, Dick Ewell's men found themselves conducting a desperate defense against steadily mounting counterattacks. Outnumbered, far from the rest of the army, and without their artillery, the Second Corps was in real danger of destruction. Fortunately the combination of a violent rainstorm, swampy ground (which now worked to the Confederates' advantage), and the gathering darkness stabilized the situation for the evening. Lee sent the sharpshooters from Jubal Early's division to make contact with Ewell's men. On the whole it was a miserable evening for everyone, but for none more so than the sharpshooters, who shivered out on picket in the swamp. Those who could scraped together mounds of mud and sticks for some protection while stray shots whistled round them.

Ewell tried to withdraw quietly in the "Egyptian" darkness, but the maneuver soon turned into a fiasco as men lost their way in the murky morass. Although most of the corps made it out, it could hardly have been called an organized withdrawal. More than four hundred Rebels were captured, many of them sharpshooters on the skirmish line who did not get the word to retire. All in all, Harris's Farm was a most disheartening experience for the Confederates. Grant continued to sidle southeast, and the two armies soon confronted each other again by the North Anna River.[43]

14

The North Anna and Cold Harbor

"Honor is nothing more than a puff of wind"

Thus far the Confederates had good reason to be pleased with the performance of their new sharpshooter battalions. The Army of the Potomac, however, continued to tolerate a very uneven performance on the skirmish line and in the *petite guerre*. As one historian put it: "Various [Union] corps' headquarters were using different maps of the region. The differences in these maps brought about much confusion. Officers had scant knowledge of roads and terrain. The army as a whole wasted an enormous amount of man-power in the mis-application of reconnaissance techniques. Cavalry and infantry seemed to be at odds in attempting to achieve vague goals. Orders were poorly written and were often ambiguous and erroneous." Yet at the very time the sharpshooters were becoming increasingly important to Lee's army and were being organized at higher and higher levels, the Federals allowed their light infantry to atrophy. They had broken up the Brigade of Sharpshooters (the 1st and 2nd U.S.S.S.) after Gettysburg and assigned each sharpshooter regiment directly to a brigade. Their division commander, General David Birney, who apparently developed an appreciation for the sharpshooters' capabilities, changed this after the battle at Spotsylvania. On May 13 Birney informed the division "that the 1st & 2nd S. S. were to be attached to no Brigade, but were to stop at [his division's] Head Quarters only, when on duty." Still, they had lost many of their experienced officers, most notably Colonel Caspar Trepp, and both regiments grew weaker as the campaign wore on. As for the rest of the Federal army, some brigade commanders habitually designated certain regiments as skirmishers, but on the whole it never seemed to occur to the Army of the Potomac's by-the-book commanders that a sizable light infantry force might be a great help when moving, as they now were, through densely wooded country where they had no reliable maps and few guides. Light infantry would have been especially valuable given the fact that Sheridan's cavalry had been absent much of the time. This would be a critical shortcoming in the Yankees' next big move and subsequent engagement at the North Anna.[1]

After Grant broke off the battle at Spotsylvania the 1st and 2nd U.S.S.S. crept southward seeking the Rebels. "No unusual incident occurred to mark the progress of the sharp shooters," said one, "until the twenty-first, when the [1st] regiment, by a sudden dash, occupied the little village of Bowling Green," where they found and freed "some hundreds of negro slaves" who had been locked up and were due to be sent south. Shortly afterward they fought a skirmish with some green Confederate troops who dropped their knapsacks and ran, leaving their contents to the sharpshooters, which gave them "the opportunity of renewing their own somewhat dilapidated wardrobes." Their luck continued to improve the next day when they stumbled across the county Poor House, where "they proceeded to gratify a soldier's natural curiosity to see what might be found on the premises to eke out their unsatisfactory rations." Much to their delight they found "chickens, mutton, milk and eggs in profusion." If this was how the poor ate in Virginia, said one Yank, they were "greatly to be envied." The next day, however, their easy living ended when they found their way "once again blocked by the rebel army in a strong position behind the North Anna river."[2]

Henagan's Redoubt

Kershaw's South Carolina brigade, now under Colonel John Henagan, occupied an earthen fort—which became known as "Henagan's Redoubt"—on the north side of the river guarding the Telegraph Road bridge. Late on the afternoon of May 23 the men of the Third South Carolina Battalion—Kershaw's sharpshooters—could see three brigades of the Union II Corps forming for an attack. Soon the Union skirmish line, mostly composed of the 1st and 2nd U.S.S.S., began to advance. South Carolinian Jim Milling watched as "one of Longstreet's scouts" drew a bead with his "globe-sighted" Whitworth rifle. The scout fired and knocked a Federal officer off his horse at distance Milling thought "was near a full mile." He and his fellow sharpshooters, having only Enfields, waited until the Yankees came within six hundred yards before they, too, began to fire. "If ever I enjoyed a battle," he wrote later, "it was that one." The sharpshooters would "make it hot" for their Yankee counterparts, who would lie down, then get up and charge. The Federals brought their artillery into the action and knocked down a chimney near the South Carolinians, wounding one of them. Still, Milling and his comrades held their ground until someone yelled, "Look out boys. Look to the left." Henagan's flank had collapsed and "the Yankee colors was almost in our rear." Then it was every man for himself. Milling, who had a horror of being captured, made it back across the bridge, but many of his comrades had to choose between swimming or surrender. In the midst of this confusion Milling's commander, Captain Benjamin Whitener, suddenly remembered that he had left his sword. He ran back into the redoubt to get it, brandishing a huge pistol that Milling waggishly suggested must have weighed as much as one of his soldier's rifles. Whitener rejoined the battalion the next morning with his sword, claiming to have shot down a Yankee officer to get it.[3]

Private William Greene of the 2nd U.S.S.S., one of the men on the skirmish line, claimed that "Our boys stood up manfully under the hot fire of shells, grape shots, and bullets." It had been "a hard fight [but] we compelled them to skedadle." Though "there was considerably many killed & wounded on both sides," the works had been formidable enough, and Greene thought the Confederates should have been able to hold them.[4]

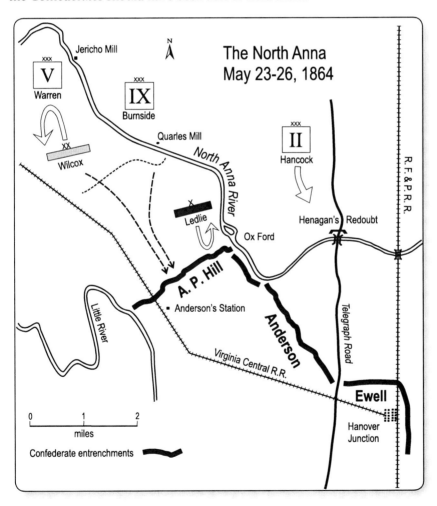

Jericho Mills

During the fracas at Henagan's redoubt General Gouverneur Warren's Union V Corps crossed the North Anna four miles upstream at Jericho Mills and drove off the Confederate cavalry guarding the ford. The horse soldiers took word to General A. P. Hill, whose Third Corps held the area, that the Yankee force was small—only two brigades or so of cavalry. Since holding the line of the river was critical, Hill decided to strike back at once. Cadmus Wilcox's division drew the task, and in mid-afternoon on May 23 he sent a regiment from McGowan's brigade to investigate. The regiment soon came back in disorder, so Colonel J. N. Brown, who now commanded McGowan's brigade, sent in the sharpshooters. Captain Dunlop was absent with dysentery, leaving Captain William Brunson in command of the battalion. The sharpshooter battalion moved forward, and "the feeling process now began." They found more than cavalry at the Jericho Mills ford, but the Federal pickets were napping and they "went crashing through their lines like an Alpine avalanche, dispersing the force and capturing a number of prisoners." The sharpshooters continued until they bumped into "a second and much stronger line," then stopped to await reinforcements. Even though it was obvious that a strong enemy force was in front of them—it was, in fact, three full Union divisions—Wilcox formed his infantry brigades and attacked at about five o'clock.[5]

"We sharpshooters deployed and forwarded ahead of the Brigade through a thick woods," wrote Marion Fitzpatrick of Brigadier General Edward Thomas's Georgia brigade. "We soon ran up with the yankee skirmish line, and fought them hot and heavy, drove them in and fought the line of battle for awhile." Many of the Federals at the ford, oblivious to the repeated probes of the sharpshooters, had stacked their arms and started to cook dinner. Wilcox's surprise assault nearly drove them into the river, but the combination of intense Union artillery fire and a panic by one of his attacking regiments caused the Southern offensive to founder. The Yankees rallied and drove Wilcox's men back with loss but did not press their advantage.[6]

Brunson's sharpshooters stayed near Warren's corps that evening as a combination picket and rear guard, keeping an eye on the Yankees. The rest of Wilcox's division withdrew to dig in at Anderson's Station, which lay about a mile and a half south of Quarles's Ford. "It is useless to tell you how tired and sore I am," Fitzpatrick wrote his wife. "I have not changed clothes or shaved since the fighting commenced."[7]

Lee faced a quandary. He needed to defend the vital rail center at Hanover Junction and continue to engage Grant as far away from Richmond as possible, but the Federals had just convincingly forced the line of the North Anna at minimal cost. The Confederates still held Ox Ford, between Jericho

Mills and Hanover Junction, where high bluffs and rapidly improving fortifications discouraged a direct attack by Burnside's IX Corps. With Warren's V Corps now south of the river on his left, however, Lee's position was effectively turned. Hancock, meanwhile, was preparing to force a crossing with his II Corps on Lee's right at Chesterfield bridge, downstream from Ox Ford.

Lee's response to this point had been so anemic, in fact, that Grant concluded that the Army of Northern Virginia was retreating to Richmond. Grant underestimated his opponent, however, who was about to lay a clever snare. Drawing on his background as a military engineer, Lee devised a unique plan to turn his weakness into strength: by holding the high ground at Ox Ford and drawing back his wings south along the rising ground behind it in an inverted V, he would put his army in a giant and virtually impregnable salient, quickly dubbed the "hog snout." This gave him an interior position from which he could easily reinforce either flank of his army, while his opponent would have to divide his army into three parts once he crossed the North Anna. To reinforce either Yankee wing would require crossing two rivers—a lengthy process—giving Lee an ideal opportunity to strike an isolated part of the Union army. For the trap to work, however, Lee needed to deceive Grant as to the exact nature of his position for as long as possible. The Confederate sharpshooters would play an essential part by screening the location of the army's lines and by giving the Southern army time to dig their entrenchments unmolested.

The first rays of light on May 24 found Captain Brunson and his sharpshooters in an extremely vulnerable position, right under the noses of the Federals and far from their own division. As soon as it was light enough to see, the bluecoats moved on them, but Brunson was ready and fell back "at a run" with the Yankees hot on his heels. When they reached the edge of the nearby woods, the sharpshooters stopped, turned on their pursuers, dropping a number of them. In the woods they fought Indian fashion and "stubbornly contested every inch of the ground back to the station" until nearly noon. The sharpshooters continued to withdraw until they were about four hundred yards in front of Wilcox's new line, just northwest of Anderson's Station, and there the Federals let them stay. Though Wilcox's assault had failed, Brunson's sharpshooters had performed just the sort of mission for which they had been trained. The previous day's major failing had been their inability to accurately scout the strength of the Union position, a fault more likely due to the cavalry's incorrect intelligence and a lack of time.[8]

On a different part of the battlefield, Warren sent the 1st Pennsylvania Reserves downstream to make contact with Hancock's men. The regiment's commander, Lieutenant Colonel Warren Stewart, moved his men single file along the riverbank to avoid detection, but the sharpshooters of Mahone's

Virginia brigade, who had double-quicked some two miles to get there, caught up with at the ford near Quarles's Mill. "We advanced," said one of Mahone's men, "firing as we did so, taking advantage of such protection from the trees as we could until we reached a point where a line could be established." Shortly afterward the sharpshooters of Colonel John Sanders's Alabama brigade arrived. Barely had the Confederates gotten into position and thrown up some fence rails for protection when the blue-coated skirmishers began probing them, and the Pennsylvanians soon followed with a full-scale attack. It failed, leaving Colonel Stewart pinned against the river. He managed to attract the attention of some IX Corps pickets across the river "and succeeded, after some difficulty, in convincing them that he and his regiment were of the National army."[9]

In a postwar account Confederate captain John E. Laughton described how his sharpshooters operated in this action in groups of three. This appears to be a variation of the normal four-man section used in skirmish drill, perhaps because of reduced number of men available in 1864. In any case Laughton specified that "the men in these posts of three each always fired by file, one gun always being loaded." This was fairly standard practice to cover the front during the time needed to recharge a muzzle loader. Tactically this was, of course, completely different from having a line of battle fire by volleys, and using three-man sections ensured that the sharpshooters in their extended line did not get caught with unloaded rifles.[10]

Word of Stewart's plight reached General Warren, and about noon he dispatched General Samuel Crawford's Pennsylvania Reserves division down the bank to their rescue. Even when faced with an entire division, however, the Confederate riflemen gave ground grudgingly. "Such was the coolness of the men and the accuracy of their aim," boasted Laughton, "that this line [of battle] was repulsed with great loss to them. A second and a third charge were made, with stronger lines each time, but they had underestimated the character of the men before them, and were in turn cut down and driven back, some having been killed within thirty feet of our posts." Crawford eventually accepted defeat, after which "the enemy gathered in front and on the flanks of the Reserves in strong force." He formed a perimeter around the ford and awaited reinforcements. "During this time our troops were throwing up a line of entrenchments about half a mile in rear," said Laughton, "and seemed satisfied to leave us to act as a 'reception committee.'"[11]

More Union reinforcements arrived in the form of Major General Thomas Crittenden's division of IX Corps, which sent a brigade across at Quarles's Mill under the protection of the Crawford's Pennsylvanians. Crittenden's division then advanced southeast toward Ox Ford, the last remaining Confederate-held crossing on the North Anna.

Downstream Hancock crossed the river at Chesterfield bridge under the covering fire of his own sharpshooter regiments. The 2nd U.S.S.S. suffered "serious casualties" from Rebel rifle and artillery fire, but by mid-morning the Confederates had pulled back from the bridge, and Hancock's Union II Corps pushed south after them through densely wooded terrain toward Hanover Junction.[12]

Confederate entrenchments near Chesterfield bridge. *B&L*

Ox Ford

Brigadier General James Ledlie's brigade of Crittenden's division led the Federal advance on Ox Ford that afternoon. Ledlie, one of many Union political generals, was rash, tactically inept, and fond of the bottle—qualities that would cost his men dearly that day. He sent out the 35th Massachusetts as skirmishers, and these veterans slowly pushed back Mahone's and Sanders's weary sharpshooters, who occasionally paused long enough to throw a shot back at them. After moving through thick brush for a mile or so they entered a cleared area near Ox Ford and came up against the western face of Lee's defensive line. On the rising ground before them some of the most formidable fortifications of the war stared down at them, covered by a line of rifle pits into which the Confederate sharpshooters had withdrawn. Ledlie, who by all accounts had had a snootful (as did, apparently, most of his staff), recklessly decided to assault the works and take Ox Ford. It was madness, as everyone knew but he. The men of the 35th Massachusetts entered the clearing and started trading shots with the Confederate sharpshooters, then drew back. "Come on to Richmond!" came a taunt from the trenches.[13]

Ledlie formed the green 56th, 57th, and 59th Massachusetts into two lines, stationed them to the right of the reformed 35th, and sent their skirmishers forward to clear the rifle pits. After a nasty and indecisive fight failed to take them, he ordered in his line of battle. Under gathering storm clouds the grayback riflemen started to pick off the newcomers, who lost their formation as they broke into a wild charge. As the Bay Staters neared the earthworks the Confederate batteries opened up, mowing down whole squads with grape and canister. A violent summer thunderstorm boomed into life, soaking Yankee and Confederate alike. In the pandemonium the Massachusetts men tried to form around their colors, but the Confederates shot them down and launched a counterattack, breaking them and capturing 150 men as the rest scrambled back to the ford at Quarles's Mill. The Union command had begun to get an inkling of the sort of defense they faced. As for Ledlie, he not only survived but assumed division command when General Crittenden stepped down two weeks later. In the months ahead he would have one more major role to play.[14]

At the other end of the line Hancock's men bushwhacked through what is even today one of the wilder parts of eastern Virginia. Hidden before them the Confederate fortifications ran southeast from Ox Ford for just over a mile, roughly paralleling the Virginia Central Railroad, turned due east for half a mile to cover the rail center at Hanover Junction, then dog-legged due south past it. Rodes's division held the angle with Cox's and Grimes's Tarheel brigades, while Doles's and Battle's brigades faced east down the leg. Brigadier General Evander Law's Alabama brigade lay across the Richmond, Fredericksburg, and Potomac railroad from Grimes's men, beginning the line of First Corps brigades that stretched northwest all the way to Ox Ford. Following their now-usual practice, the Confederates placed their sharpshooter battalions in the dense woods well in advance of their main line. Unlike the jagged main line, the skirmish line ran due east more than a mile to Doswell House. Rodes's four sharpshooter battalions—one-sixth of his division—covered the sector east of the railroad to the river.

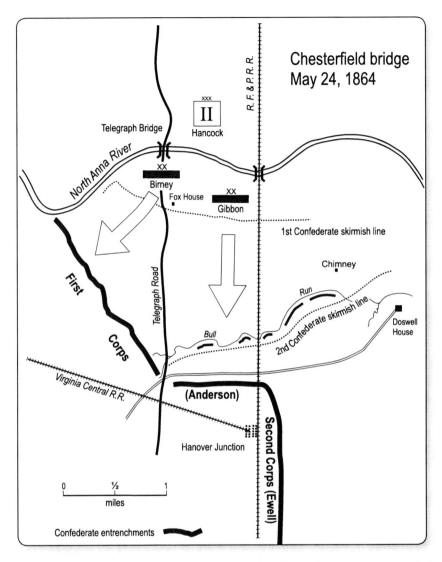

In mid-morning Hancock sent two brigades forward to clear away Rebel skirmishers and make contact with their rear guard, but this was to be a much tougher proposition than he had anticipated. A brigade under Colonel Nelson Miles moved through the woods with three regiments up and two back, "advancing into the woods where we soon met the rebel skirmish line, but drove it and advanced till we found a strong line of breastworks, strongly manned, and well protected by artillery." This was the upper leg of the "hog snout," manned by Anderson's First Corps. Miles's men knew well enough they could not carry works like this but nevertheless provoked an indecisive firefight that lasted the rest of the morning. The marksmen among them amused themselves by shooting at the wagons passing behind

Confederate breastworks, where they "annoyed the rebels by disabling the teams." Around noon the Yankees' ammunition started to run low. While Miles's aide-de-camp, Lieutenant Robert Robertson, brought forward pack mules to re-supply them, the Rebels launched an attack on the brigade's left flank that was beaten off only with some difficulty.[15]

Doswell House

Hancock's other brigade, under Colonel Thomas Smyth, a thirty-two-year-old Irish immigrant, advanced down the railroad into the woods. Their first encounter began near "a large and dilapidated mansion known as Fox's house," just west of the railroad, from which the Rebel sharpshooters harassed them. A detachment of forty men from the 1st U.S.S.S. rushed through a field past the house "under a close and heavy fire from the enemy," captured the house, and drove the graybacks from the slave shacks and outbuildings some distance away. "Sharp exchanges took place at distances varying from 300 to 1,000 yards, resulting in close shooting on both sides." The action continued all afternoon.[16]

Meanwhile Colonel Smyth sent forward the 1st Delaware and 108th New York in skirmish formation. After about a half mile they ran into the sharp-shooters of Cox's North Carolina brigade. Crossing an open field, the Federals "encountered so heavy a fire that they came back quite as fast as they went." Smyth brought up the 14th Connecticut to support his outgunned skirmishers, but the Tarheel farm boys, crouched in rifle pits at the edge of the woods, refused to budge until a fourth regiment, the 12th New Jersey, charged them. The ragged blue lines swept forward, following the wraith-like men in butternut as they melted back into the forest. Colonel Bryan Grimes's North Carolina sharpshooters came up to reinforce Cox's men, while the sharpshooter battalion of Evander Law's Alabama brigade capped their rifles across the railroad grade from them. About five hundred yards farther into the forest Smyth's men ran into Confederate breastworks that had been built by Rodes's men the night before. Second Corps, however, had pulled back closer to Hanover Junction, leaving only the Division Sharp-shooters to hold them. Protected by this formidable barrier, their heavy, accurate fire once again stopped the Yankees cold.[17]

Smyth sent in two more regiments and called for reinforcements. His division commander, Brigadier General John Gibbon, moved up two brigades in support, but nevertheless Smyth's advance remained stalled. Gibbon sent the 19th Maine to cover Smyth's exposed left flank, but the nervous staff officer sent to guide them waved them off in the general direction of Doswell Plantation then "disappeared from sight." The Mainers charged up a hill and found themselves in the open, with no support on either flank and the Confederate sharpshooters crouching at the edge of the wood "no more than twenty rods away." Amid "a storm of shot and shell" they tumbled back down the slope. So fierce was the Rebel fire that they were unable to recover their wounded.[18]

The Rebels at the forest's edge were probably Battle's Sharpshooters—Eugene Blackford's men—who held the eastern end of the Confederate skirmish line. Rodes had sent out two guns from the Richmond Howitzers to back his skirmish line, and these, placed at the extreme end of it near the Doswell house, were well positioned to enfilade the entire Union line, as the Mainers had just learned. A good road ran right along the Confederate front, making it easy for them to shift men and guns laterally, while the Federals could do it only with great difficulty through the dense woods.[19]

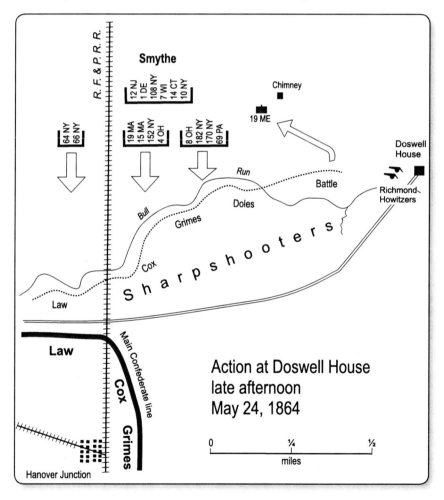

By late afternoon the Rebel skirmish line—which amounted to no more than eight hundred riflemen backed by two artillery pieces—held firm. Meanwhile the men of the 1st U.S.S.S. who had taken over the Fox House had shot up nearly all their ammunition. Finally, "after repeated signals for aid," another detachment relieved them. With the Rebels "liable at any time to crowd them out from the behind the rude huts," the sharpshooters fell back to the safety of their regiment, where everyone who could was scratching out a hole as fast as possible. From their position in the grove behind the Fox House, they could see General Hancock conferring with three of his generals. Although Hancock still assumed he faced only a line of rifle pits, some of the news his generals brought disturbed him: the prisoners Miles's men had captured nearby were from the Confederate First Corps and those taken by Gibbon's division were from Ewell's Second Corps. Hancock's Union II Corps was now south of the North Anna, but most of the army was six miles away at Jericho Mills. Only a single division north of the river at Ox Ford connected the two wings of the Army of the Potomac. So far Lee's plan had worked perfectly. Grant, at Jericho Mills, still thought he faced only a rear guard action, but Hancock was beginning to realize that something larger was afoot. By now the Southerners had added artillery to their Minié balls, and the shells screamed over the Union position "as if hunting for somebody." Hancock's conference broke up, and as he entered the house a shell tore through a sharpshooter's knapsack and exploded "with terrific force" where the generals had stood but a moment before. Fortunately the knapsack's owner, Sergeant Richard Tyler, was not wearing it at the time.[20]

With more reinforcements Smyth finally got his attack rolling late in the afternoon. His men took a section of the North Carolina rifle pits, believing they had captured the main Confederate line. Smyth ordered them to hold it, but at 5:30 the Tarheels counterattacked, driving the Yankees back and retaking part of their works. The fighting in the forest degenerated into a series of brutal close-range fights by small groups of increasingly desperate men. Given the volume of powder smoke, the density of the woods, and the darkness from the storm clouds, it was nearly impossible for either side to maintain any kind of alignment or tactical plan. Smyth tried to push on, but Rodes began to feed men up from his main line, sending part of the Fourteenth North Carolina to aid Cox and the Fifty-third North Carolina and part of the Forty-third to backstop Grimes.

The detachment from the Forty-third North Carolina—two companies of about seventy men—lost their way and walked right into the 170th New York. Both groups, perhaps letting their wishes get the better of their common sense, assumed that the other side meant to surrender. The two units mingled in friendly fashion, and one pair actually shook hands, until a Confederate lieutenant tried to take a Union soldier's rifle away, whereupon the man threatened to "blow his damn brains out." The Southern officer quickly jumped back and yelled "Fire!" as his men let loose a volley. After a short struggle, some of it hand to hand, the Yankees (who had little ammunition left) broke for the rear, leaving thirty-nine men on the field.[21]

Meanwhile Colonel John Brooke's brigade of Barlow's division had pushed forward on Smyth's right, feeling for the Confederate flank. Brooke's men drove General Evander Law's Alabamians out of their rifle pits and reached the main Confederate line, only to be thrown back abruptly after trying an attack. As Brooke retreated, Law counterattacked with reinforcements from his line regiments, supported by a 12-pounder Napoleon dragged up on the railroad grade so that it could fire down the tracks, and retook his rifle pits. During the action General Law himself fought a duel with a Yankee sharpshooter. As he walked behind the parapet along which his men had leaned their loaded muskets, someone yelled "Stoop!" He did, and a moment later a bullet whizzed past his head. "Turning quickly, I caught a glimpse of something blue disappearing behind a pile of earth that had been thrown out from the railroad cut some distance in front. Taking one of the muskets leaning against the works I waited for the reappearance of my friend in blue, who had taken such an unfair advantage of me. He soon appeared, rising cautiously behind his earth-work, and we both fired at the same moment, neither shot taking effect." Instead of ducking, the Yankee rifleman began to reload, evidently assuming that Law would do the same. The general snatched up another musket and immediately shot at his opponent. "He was found there, wounded, when my skirmishers were pushed forward," Law noted with satisfaction.[22]

Despite committing his entire division, Gibbon had not even reached Lee's main line in force. As the storm clouds gathered, the furious struggle for the center of the Confederate picket line continued. In a savage seesaw battle, fought at times with bayonets and clubbed muskets, the 4th and 8th Ohio slugged it out with Grimes's sharpshooters. The Tarheel commander, Captain R. L. Hill, was killed, and as the fight continued the Ohio boys "would summon up all our courage, and occasionally without any orders would charge with a cheer, compelling the enemy to give way for a few more yards. Then the Confederates would rally and in turn force us back over the ground we had just won." With his leading regiments exhausted and almost out of ammunition, Smyth managed to bring up a fresh brigade to relieve them—no easy task under the circumstances. The Rebels were alert for this, however, and fired into the 152nd New York as the regiment approached over the heads of the troops they were replacing. Although stung by the volley, the veteran New Yorkers charged past the West Virginians in front of them. They made scant progress, fired off their ammunition, and soon found themselves defending their position with bayonets.[23]

Rebel pressure began to increase on the Union left flank as Battle's Alabamians—Blackford's men—began pressing the Irishmen of the 170th and 182nd New York. The butternut sharpshooters seemed to be everywhere—infiltrating in small groups into the gaps between the Federal units, lapping around their flanks, and sniping at them from behind every bush and tree.

When the Irish troops used up all their cartridges, one of their number, Sergeant Major Joseph Keele, ran through a gauntlet of rifle fire to carry word of their plight to General Hancock, who sent ammunition and another Irish regiment, the 69th Pennsylvania, to reinforce them. Even so, the inexperienced 170th New York, completely out of ammunition, had only their bayonets for protection against the Rebels, who shot them down where they stood. With Grimes's Tarheels in front and Battle's Alabamians on their flank and rear, the left end of the Union line began to unravel. Panic laid hold of the sons of Erin, sending them into an undignified rout from which they were rallied with only great difficulty.[24]

Skirmish line. *B&L*

Now on the defensive, Smyth was determined to hold on to what he thought was the main Confederate line. Near sunset the same drenching thunderstorm that soaked Ledlie's men covered the forest, temporarily suspending hostilities. "There we stood," said an Ohio officer, "our line and that of the enemy, poised for another deadly blow and looking at each other without firing, fearful that our ammunition would be soaked by the rain." As soon as the downpour abated the battle began anew with redoubled fury, "and lasted as long as there was light."[25]

On the right end of the Federal line the 19th Massachusetts was also having a hard time of it. As the rain slacked off, the Rebels came at them through the dripping woods, yelling like demons. The Bay Staters fired a volley as they closed but then saw that they had been flanked. One soldier's quip to his comrade summed it up for the regiment: "What is it, Jack? Richmond or legs?"

"Legs!" answered his comrade as the Massachusetts men scrambled back into a creek bed, which they held until help arrived. The fighting began to taper off as night fell, with the Yankees retaining a tenuous hold on the center of the Confederate skirmish line.[26]

May 24 at the North Anna had been quite a battle. Far from being brushed aside, Rodes's "skirmishers" had stopped a reinforced Federal division pretty much on their own. "Yankees still continue obstinate and still continue to rush on to their doom, as more of them did yesterday when they came on my line," wrote Colonel Grimes the next day, who assured his wife that his brigade had done most of the fighting. "We drove them with considerable slaughter," he exulted, "losing but few." A lieutenant in Battle's brigade was not so optimistic: writing his fiancée that "the enemy, I thought, would never stop last night."[27]

At Union headquarters, where "the obstinacy of their skirmishers was regarded as very remarkable," Grant was only beginning to fully understand his predicament. His II Corps was nearly isolated and facing the bulk of Lee's army. To make matters worse, the afternoon's storms had flooded the North Anna, making either reinforcement or retreat difficult. Burnside's IX Corps was similarly backed against the river at Quarles's Ford, six miles away, and only a single division held his center. But just at Lee's moment of opportunity, a bout of dysentery laid him low. That night, as Hancock dug in and brought up his artillery, Lee's chance for a decisive counterstroke faded with each passing hour. By the next morning formidable breastworks protected the Federal positions all along the line, and their engineers set three pontoon bridges across the flooded river.[28]

On May 25 the Federal commander attempted to probe the Confederate lines and investigate their defenses. On the right Warren pushed his V Corps eastward to link up Crawford and Crittenden's men, still isolated at Quarles's Mill, then advanced as close as he dared to A. P. Hill's fortified line, touching off intense firefights on a "terribly hot skirmish line." Cutler's division attempted to brush aside the butternut sharpshooters but had to give up the attempt and dig in. One soldier in Mahone's brigade described the fighting as "one continuous roar of musketry. We used 5 boxes of cartridges and slayed many Yankees." Warren correctly concluded that Hill's position was impregnable.[29]

On the left flank Hancock's men found the Rebel skirmish line even stronger than the day before. Private Will Greene and his mates in four companies of the 2nd U.S.S.S. "went to the front & after crawling about half a mile on our hands and knees with shovels, laid on our bellys under fire of their S. S. & threw up some breast works. ... After we had got fortified we opened our *battery* on them & kept at them until after dark." Greene wrote his brother that their Sharps rifles, which could be loaded and fired from the prone position, had given them a decided advantage in the fight: "we would fire into them & then lay low & it was impossible for them to get a bullet through our breast works." The greencoats added verbal harassment as well. "We would hallow at them once in awhile & ask them how they like

Hail Columbia, Yankee Doodle, etc." During the day Greene and his comrades fired some fifty rounds each at their southern counterparts. In some spots the battle raged with a deadly fury all day long, with no quarter asked or given by either side, even for recovering the (mostly Union) wounded. In other sectors, however, the soldiers established an informal truce, began trading personal items, and promised to warn each other of an impending attack. Among the more unusual prisoners taken that day was a female Confederate sharpshooter.[30]

Meanwhile at Ox Ford, the Federals brought up a half-dozen brass Coehorn mortars and at dawn began to pound the Confederate positions across the North Anna. These high-angle weapons, "dropping shells with frightful precision," caused considerable damage to the Rebels. "The effect was magical," said the Union artillery commander, Colonel John Tidball. "Even the fire of the sharpshooters was stopped." The men on the receiving end agreed. "Our works gave us no protection," said one. "We scampered out and begged our artillery to blow up the infernal 'coehorns.'" Direct artillery fire could not reach the mortars, however, so the Confederates resorted to a more immediate solution, sending the sharpshooters of Bryan's Georgia brigade back across the river. "We got little relief till Strickland's sharpshooters made it so hot for the men manning the mortars that they had to fall back over the hill," wrote one.[31]

Union Coehorn mortars in action. *B&L*

Grant now finally grasped the layout of Lee's position, "appearing so different from what I expected," and had the good sense to realize that he was effectively checked. Rather than attacking, the Federals contented themselves for the rest of the 25th and 26th with more skirmishing and tearing up the railroad tracks, and that night they began withdrawing across the river on another flank move.[32]

The backtracking Yankees tapped the 1st U.S.S.S. as rear guard, and the sharpshooters covered the trench lines in a "black, lonely wood" until midnight. The night was a rainy one and "the darkness … so intense [that] it was with great difficulty they found their way out." Captain Wilson and Lieutenant Stevens led the way, stumbling through the gloom and "almost running on to the rebel lines, made manifest by a low but determined 'halt!'" The Federal sharpshooters quickly reversed course and "left the puzzled Johnny to discover nothing in his front but fast retreating steps." Finally, near daylight, they made their way across the pontoon bridge over the swollen river to rejoin the army.[33]

The next morning Confederate scouts found nothing but empty trenches and burned bridges where the Yankees had been. "Soon after, the rifle pits on the south bank were filled with rebel sharpshooters," said one Union officer. "We had left a skirmish line on the north bank, and the men had to lie close in their holes and behind trees to protect themselves. I had to carry orders to the picket line several times and each time narrowly escaped the sharpshooter's bullets."[34]

For the Confederates the North Anna was a great might have been. "General Lee," observed one Union soldier, "never had a better chance to inflict terrible punishment on his antagonist than on the North Anna." After failing to stop Grant from crossing the river, Lee had neatly turned the tables on his opponent and put him at a decisive disadvantage that almost cost him a substantial part of his army. One of the distinctive features of the battle was the way the Confederates had used terrain, light infantry, and field fortifications to build a winning tactical and strategic combination. Lee, trained as a military engineer, had been quick to spot the commanding ground running from Ox Ford and to recognize the possibilities it offered. The plan would not have worked, however, if Lee's army had simply withdrawn into the salient. Instead, it was necessary to keep the Federals from finding out the exact nature of the position for as long as possible, until a counterstroke could be mounted. The army's sharpshooters had a vital role in the plan, keeping back the enemy's scouts and skirmishers and making them fight for every glimpse at their main entrenchments. The heavily wooded terrain—where the southern infantryman was very much at home—made their job that much easier. "The Confederate in his faded uniform was almost invincible in the woods," remarked one Federal officer, "and his skill as a marksman, his knowledge of bushcraft, certainly compensated largely for a considerable inequality of numbers."[35]

The training, marksmanship, and élan of the Confederate sharpshooters had given them a decisive edge over the ad hoc skirmish formations of the Army of the Potomac. Further, they had given the elite Federal sharpshooter regiments, the 1st and 2nd U.S.S.S., as much action as they could handle. On the left the sharpshooters covered Hill's retreat after the debacle at Jericho Mills, surrounded Crawford's division and pinned it to the river at Quarles's Ford, and contributed significantly to Ledlie's humiliating defeat at Ox Ford. It had been well into the afternoon of the twenty-fifth before Warren's men got a close look at the Confederate line. On the other flank Rodes's men had not only slowed Gibbon's advance but had counterattacked and put him on the defensive, even though his troops considerably outnumbered them. The dense woods broke up the Union lines of battle while offering cover and concealment to their opponents, who made the most of it, combining local attacks with infiltration, fighting in semi-independent groups that sought out gaps and weak points in the Union line.

The Union response had been uninspiring. Hancock was one of the best generals in the Army of the Potomac, and though he had been quick to size up the situation, even he had been outgeneraled at the tactical level. Like most of his peers Hancock seems to have had little appreciation of the value of light infantry, and he failed to effectively deploy his most obvious asset to handle the obstinate Rebel skirmishers—his two sharpshooter regiments. They remained with Birney's division, where they were split into small groups of approximately forty men.

On the Confederate side in Hancock's sector, Grimes's brigade lost about 150 men killed and wounded, and Cox's brigade lost about fifty. The losses in Battle's and Doles's brigades were probably somewhat less. Allowing for some casualties in Law's brigade and the other units of First Corps, the total Confederate losses probably did not much exceed three hundred men killed and wounded, and their accounts make it clear that due to the nature of the battle, there was a higher proportion of wounded than usual.[36]

In addition to the battle itself, Federal casualty returns included both preliminary actions from May 22, such as the storming of Henagan's Redoubt, and subsequent but relatively minor engagements on the Pamunkey and Totopotomoy up until June 1. Some comparisons can still be useful, however. Smyth's brigade, which bore the brunt of the fighting, listed only seventy-three casualties for the entire period. Three regiments—the 14th Connecticut, 7th West Virginia, and 12th New Jersey—accounted for more than half the brigade's total casualties, losing fifteen, seventeen, and twenty-two men respectively. The 4th and 8th Ohio, which had also been hotly engaged on the 24th, lost only ten men between them (and only two of these were killed). General Smyth would have another rendezvous with a Confederate sharpshooter the following year: on April 7, two days before Lee's surrender, a marksman put a bullet through his neck. Paralyzed, Smyth died two days later.

The 19th Maine, from McKeen's brigade, lost thirty men (twenty-one of whom fell May 23-6) after being caught out on the left flank, and the 19th Massachusetts, which held the right of the line, lost eleven. In Owen's brigade the 152nd New York, which had relieved the 7th West Virginia, lost sixteen men, showing that this was a fairly hot sector. The green 170th New York had the dubious distinction of being the battle's hard-luck regiment, losing a staggering ninety-nine men—twenty-two killed, fifty-five wounded, and twenty-two missing. Part of the Corcoran Legion, the 170th New York had been in service for two years, mainly on the coast or in garrison, and their lack of experience on the battlefield may be the cause of the high casualties. The two regiments supporting the 170th, the 182nd New York and the 69th Pennsylvania, lost only six men each. Some inexperienced outfits thought it unmanly to lie down or hide behind trees—an attitude that cost them heavily.

Especially considering their declining strength, the Federal sharpshooter regiments also suffered significant losses: the 1st U.S.S.S lost twenty-five men and the 2nd regiment twenty-two. An educated guess for Federal losses in the skirmish fighting of May 24 would probably be between four and six hundred men. Overall battle casualties for both sides were about the same, approximately two thousand each.[37]

Cold Harbor

Within a week the two armies faced each other again, this time at Cold Harbor—just ten miles from Richmond. On May 31 Major General Philip Sheridan's Union cavalry seized the important crossroads at Old Cold Harbor, and the next day Kershaw's brigade, which had just been strengthened by the addition of the large Twentieth South Carolina, was sent to retake it. The Twentieth, fresh from garrison duty on the coast, was inexperienced in the brutal realities of Virginia warfare, and unfortunately for the Rebels its commander, Colonel Lawrence Keitt, was the senior man in the brigade and thus commander of the attack. Keitt dressed his lines with parade-ground precision and led the advance on his fine gray charger, scornfully dismissing suggestions that he dismount. As the South Carolinians neared the hasty breastworks, Sheridan's veteran cavalrymen let loose with their Spencer "seven shooters." Keitt fell in the first volley, and his regiment broke and carried the rest of the brigade back with it. It was a textbook case of how *not* to employ the sharpshooters. "A few skirmishers thrown out would have accomplished the object of a reconnaissance and would have saved the lives of many brave men," Colonel William Wallace of the Second South Carolina wrote bitterly.[38]

Kershaw's troops redeemed themselves that evening by repulsing a Federal infantry assault. As both sides brought up reinforcements, the lengthening lines began to settle down even closer than they had been at Spotsylvania. "We who were there," wrote one Union soldier, "well remember those ten or twelve long days that we lay hugging our breastworks, when it was almost sure death to show a head. ... There was no time during the war, probably, when the sharpshooters got in their deadly—I might say murderous—work, more successfully." The relatively static situation allowed the Union sharpshooters plenty of time to bring up their heavy target rifles from the trains, and one of their first victims was Confederate general George Doles, who fell on June 2 near Bethesda Church.[39]

Concluding that Lee's army was near collapse, Grant ordered a grand assault on June 3. It was a bloody failure, the worst Union defeat since Fredericksburg. Under the watchful gaze of the sharpshooters large numbers of wounded soldiers (almost all of them Yankees) died miserably between the lines in the stifling heat while the two commanders negotiated a cease-fire. The situation between the trenches was horrific:

> Men lay in places like hogs in a pen—some side by side, across each other, some two deep, while others with their legs lying across the head and body of their dead comrades. Calls all night long could be heard coming from the wounded and dying, and one could not sleep for the sickening sound "W-a-t-e-r" ever sounding and echoing in his ears. Ever and anon a heartrending wail as coming from some lost spirit disturbed the hushed stillness of the night. ... The sharpshooters with globe-sighted rifles would watch through the brush in front of their rifle pits and as soon as a head was thoughtlessly raised either from our pits, which were now not more than fifty yards apart, or our breastwork, "crack!" went a rifle, a dull thud, and one of our men lay dead.[40]

Confederate soldiers began "burrowing like rabbits" and could soon move about in a network of connected trenches without exposing themselves, "crawling along the tunnels all dug with bayonets, knives, and a few worn-out shovels." One Yankee sharpshooter was so good, however, that he could anticipate a man's movement by seeing his shadow darken a gap in the works—and have a bullet waiting for him when he got there. A lieutenant of the Fifteenth South Carolina led a detail of riflemen after him, while other soldiers in the works tried to distract the shooter and draw his fire by waving blankets in the openings. They found the Northerner "in the top of a tall gum tree, his rifle resting in the fork of a limb," and the South Carolinians sighted in on the man and waited for his next shot. The moment he fired, they loosed a volley on him and he fell from the tree, "beating the air with his hands and feet, grasping at everything within sight or reach, his body rolling and tumbling among the limbs of the tree, his head at times up, at others down, till at last he strikes the earth." The southerners scrambled back to their lines without checking to see if their man was dead, confident that "one Yankee, at least, had been given a long ride in midair."[41]

One of the Confederates who fell that day was Lieutenant Thomas Taylor of the Sixth Alabama. In April Taylor had proudly written his family that "I have today sicceded in getting a position in the Army that I have been working for some time to get. I have now commissioned a Company of Sharpshooters. This is not a Bomb proof department by any means but I think I will like it very much. There is some little honor attached to it but honor is nothing more than a puff of wind. There are some advantages to be derived from it in times of battle." He quickly established a name for himself in the Overland campaign: "if there ever was a man heedless of danger it was Lieut. Taylor at the head of his corps of sharpshooters." But on June 3 his luck ran out. A bullet struck him "in the chin and passed through his head and as he fell over and another passed through his breast," killing him instantly.[42]

The artillery also suffered heavily, since their batteries were special targets. In the argot of the day, commanders often complained of sharpshooters "annoying" them. This, explained Lieutenant Colonel Theodore Lyman, "is another military eccentricity. When half the men are killed or wounded by the enemy's riflemen, an officer will ride pleasantly in to the chief of artillery, and state that the battery is a good deal 'annoyed' by sharpshooters, giving to the novice the impression that the sharpshooters complained of have been using provoking and impertinent language to the battery." Similarly, Union general W. F. Smith complained that "the sharpshooters trouble my batteries very much," but Confederate gunner Robert Stiles penned an eloquent portrait of what it was actually like to experience that kind of fire.[43]

I remember counting ninety odd bullet holes through a "dog tent," which was stretched immediately back of [Captain Morgan] Calloway's guns, and he walked backward and forward between this tent and his pieces during the great attack. Though he did not leave the field, he was wounded in several places, and his clothes looked as if he had been drawn through a briar patch. His field glasses were smashed by a bullet and the guard of his revolver shot away....

When we left Cold Harbor, all our bronze guns looked is if they had had smallpox, from the striking and splaying of leaden balls against them. Even the narrow lips of the pieces, about their muzzles, were indented in this way. One of the guns ... was actually cut down by musketry fire, every spoke of both wheels being cut. Indeed, I had an extra wheel brought and substituted for that which first became useless, and this also shared the same fate. ... Much of the other wood work of this and other guns was badly split and splintered by musket balls, and some of the lighter iron parts and attachments were shot away.

The particular gun referred to was finally rendered absolutely useless for the rest of the fight. The men had worked it, for the most part, upon their hands and knees.[44]

When the fight was finally over someone tipped the gun's muzzle forward, and a handful of lead shot fell out of it.

The armies confronted each other for another week until June 14, when Grant crossed the James River to invest Petersburg. For most of the Army of Northern Virginia this signaled the end of the war of maneuver and the beginning of trench warfare, which presaged the European struggle fifty years in the future. After the Yankees pulled out of Cold Harbor, Mahone's sharpshooters had to approach their trenches to see if they were indeed empty. Given recent events, this was not a job anyone looked forward to. In fact, they considered themselves a "'forlorn-hope' attacking party," and they wondered if any of them would survive the mission. Nevertheless they charged over the works where, to their immense relief, they received "only a few scattering shots" from some cavalry pickets. "Too much credit cannot be given them for their daring," wrote their chronicler, "as the information obtained was of great value at the moment."[45]

Not everyone in the army moved into Petersburg trenches, however. The Army of Northern Virginia's Second Corps, including Rodes's division, was on the march toward the Shenandoah.

15

Monocacy and Fort Stevens

"A Pretty Stiff Picket Line"

The war in Virginia in the second half of 1864 presented a tactical paradox. On the one hand, at Petersburg, the two armies embraced each other in an extended trench stalemate. Across the Blue Ridge Mountains in the Shenandoah Valley, however, smaller forces sparred in a fluid war of feint and maneuver that had few equals during the war. The Valley was, quipped one Yankee, "a queer place, and it will not submit to the ordinary rules of military tactics. Operations are carried on here that Caesar or Napoleon never dreamed of. Either army can surround the other, and I believe they can both do it at the same time."[1]

Always considerably outnumbered, Confederate general Jubal Early and his army substituted bluff and movement for numbers. In part because of the poor quality of Early's cavalry, the sharpshooters played an even more prominent role in the campaign than usual. In a hundred different skirmishes up and down the Valley they repeatedly demonstrated their grit and tenacity. "During the summer," said Sergeant Marcus Herring, "most of the fighting was done by regularly organized sharpshooters." During the campaign Robert Rodes continued to refine the sharpshooters' tactical doctrine and organization. His Division Sharpshooters—the four combined sharpshooter battalions in his division—often acted as advance and rear guard, and at times operated for extended periods as an independent unit.[2]

In the wee hours of June 13 the Second Corps, now commanded by Early, departed the trenches of Cold Harbor and hustled toward the vital city of Lynchburg, which was in danger of falling to a Federal army under Major General David "Black Dave" Hunter. After an eighty-mile forced march Early's leading troops reached the city on the evening of June 17, just in time to forestall a Federal attack. Although both Robert Rodes and Eugene Blackford had served in Alabama units, they were natives of Lynchburg, where many of their family members still resided. Both men would be literally fighting for their homes. Rodes's division, much to their commander's chagrin, did not reach the city until the next morning. When they arrived, however, Rodes quickly sent Blackford and his men forward. As the sharpshooter commander glanced into the crowd, he saw his sister-in-law, Susan Leigh Blackford, and when he established his skirmish line on the outskirts of town, he made his headquarters in a cemetery "within 50 yards of my Father's grave." Susan Blackford and the other civilians (including Blackford's elderly mother, Mary) watched the day's maneuvers and skirmishing, "fascinating beyond description," unfold before them. Everyone expected a major battle the next day, but when the sun rose on June 19 Hunter and his Yankee minions had vanished. "Then commenced the race," said Blackford, "which I shall remember to my death as being the most miserable two days of my existence." The race was ultimately in vain: Hunter handled his rear guards skillfully and Early could not bring him to bay.[3]

Early now added to his Second Corps those Valley units that had been defending Lynchburg, forming the Army of the Valley. With four infantry divisions (Rodes's, Gordon's, Ramseur's and Breckinridge's), three battalions of artillery, and an ersatz cavalry division made up of four local brigades, on a good day Early's little army might just top 16,000 men. The cavalry—inadequately armed, poorly mounted, and indifferently disciplined—was the army's weakest arm, and one whose normal missions often fell to the sharpshooters.[4]

Monocacy

With Lynchburg safe and Hunter retreating into West Virginia, Early boldly headed north. Sidestepping Federal forces at Harpers Ferry, he crossed the Potomac on July 5 and headed for Washington, causing panic in the city. With the Confederacy supposedly near defeat at Petersburg, Early's appearance outside the nation's capital would be a major embarrassment for the Lincoln Administration—especially in an election year. To make matters worse, U. S. Grant's need for infantry had stripped the forts surrounding the city of their garrisons that summer, leaving Washington almost undefended. Frantic Federal authorities dragooned war department clerks, "hospital rats,"* and most anyone else capable of shouldering a musket into long-dormant units. The only other available force in the city was a scratch brigade of national guard and home defense troops under Brigadier General Erastus Tyler. Slow to appreciate the situation, perhaps because his intelligence service still placed Early in Petersburg until virtually the moment he crossed the Potomac, Grant had providentially dispatched Brigadier Gen-

---

* Men who spent an inordinate amount of time in the hospital, often for minor or imaginary illnesses.

eral James Ricketts' division (part of the U.S. VI Corps) to Baltimore by sea to handle the perceived threat to Harpers Ferry. Major General Lew Wallace combined Tyler's and Ricketts' units into an improvised army, not quite six thousand strong, to meet the Confederates near Frederick, Maryland. Skirmishing began west of the town on July 8, as Wallace withdrew toward Monocacy Junction, a position east of the city that would allow him to block the roads to both Baltimore and Washington.

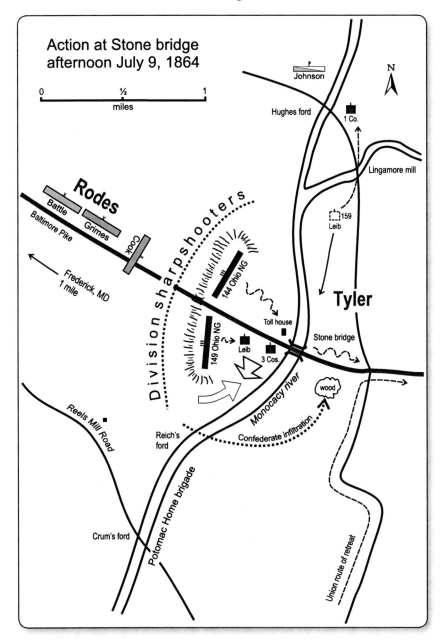

Action at Stone bridge afternoon July 9, 1864

The next day, while three of Early's divisions advanced southeast on the Georgetown Pike toward Washington, Rodes engaged Tyler's makeshift brigade on the National Road leading east to Baltimore. Rather than launching a full-scale attack, Rodes sent forward his division sharpshooters, who at the time probably numbered between five hundred and six hundred men. Although no detailed Southern account of the action survives, the Federal reports give—perhaps inadvertently—an excellent flavor of the action. Tyler placed the 149th and 144th Ohio National Guard regiments, totaling ten companies of about 660 men, across the Baltimore Pike on high ground just west of a stone bridge over the Monocacy River. These hundred-days men, under the command of Colonel Allison L. Brown, had been in service since May but had yet to see action. The rest of Tyler's line, three Maryland militia regiments of the Potomac Home Brigade, stretched southwest in a thin line covering two fords across the Monocacy to where the bend of the river met the Baltimore and Ohio Railroad. Brown also had at his disposal a hundred-man detachment of mounted infantry from the 159th Ohio National Guard under Captain Edward Leib, a regular cavalry officer who had been hastily summoned from mustering duty in Baltimore. Altogether, Brown's force at the stone bridge, also called the Jug bridge, probably numbered about 750 men.[5]

Rodes's advance guard arrived mid-morning and began peppering Brown's line with musketry, while Rebel cavalry (probably some of Bradley Johnson's men) attempted to turn his right by crossing the fords upstream of his position. Brown sent Leib's horsemen and an infantry company up to drive them off, then tried to guess the location of the main Confederate thrust. Around 11:30 he found out: Blackford's sharpshooters had lapped around his left flank, "under cover of the ground, which at that point was very favorable to the enemy for that purpose," and enfiladed his position. His men fell back in confusion, and Brown attempted to restore his line by having a reserve company launch a bayonet attack. This move probably brought some guffaws from the grizzled Southern veterans, who hunkered down behind a fence and shot them to pieces. The Rebels then surged forward to within a hundred yards of the bridge, scattering the hundred-days men. Fortunately for the Federals, the intrepid Captain Leib and his mounties had just returned from their mission on the right flank. Gathering up the reserve Ohio guardsmen near the bridge, Leib launched a counterattack, driving back the Southerners, killing a few and capturing two. "I then assisted Colonel Brown to establish the line," he wrote, "and he threw his whole force over. The position was a very good one. The enemy tried hard to take it, but at every point were driven back." Next Leib pulled his men back to the bridge to act as a reserve, but it was now mid-afternoon and Wallace's entire position was caving in fast.[6]

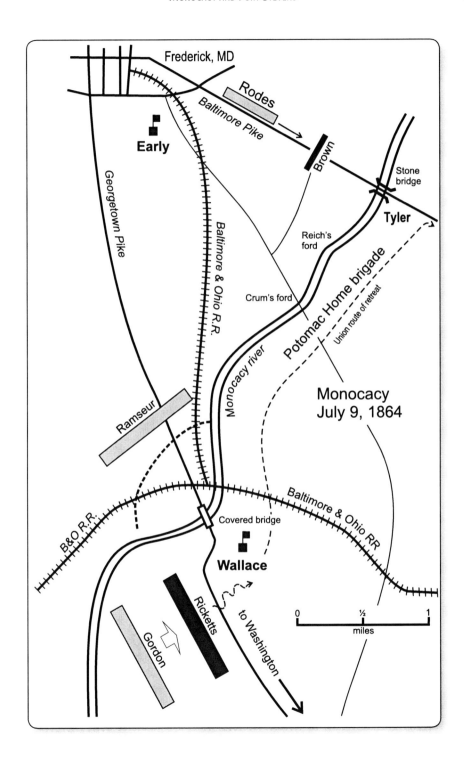

Frederick, MD

Rodes

Early

Baltimore Pike

Brown

Stone bridge

Tyler

Georgetown Pike

Reich's ford

Baltimore & Ohio R.R.

Crum's ford

Potomac Home brigade

Union route of retreat

Monocacy river

Monocacy
July 9, 1864

Ramseur

B&O R.R.

Baltimore & Ohio RR

Covered bridge

Wallace

Ricketts

to Washington

Gordon

0   ½   1
miles

Early, however, was more interested in the road to Washington. Unwilling to assault directly across the Monocacy against Ricketts' VI Corps veterans, Old Jube demonstrated in front with Ramseur's division and sent John Gordon's division farther down to cross the river and turn Wallace's left flank. By four o'clock Gordon was in position and engaged Ricketts in a bitter and costly standup fight, the heaviest of the day. Within an hour the bluecoats were in full retreat and the Confederates stood astride the road to Washington. Wallace began withdrawing north to the Baltimore Pike, his only remaining escape route. He ordered Brown to hold the Jug bridge against Rodes "to the last extremity."[7]

Keeping hold of the bridge was easier said than done. Rebel pressure on Brown's bridgehead increased by the minute, and around six o'clock Brown reported that "a heavy attack was made along my entire front, and at the same time my left flank was turned." Further, he learned that another group of Rodes's sharpshooters had infiltrated across the river and into the woods, where they prepared to assault the bridge from the rear, "thus cutting off my retreat entirely." This development unmanned Brown's command, which, he admitted, "was withdrawn in confusion" across the bridge. Meanwhile Rodes sent forward a battery that dropped a shell on the bridge just as Brown's men crossed, adding to the panic. Company E of the 149th Ohio National Guard tried to form a rear guard, and "held them for a few minutes until most of the regiment had crossed the bridge and passed us, and then we started on the double quick, the rebs still pouring it into us from every point." Brown rallied some of his men on the other side in an orchard and got them to fire a few volleys at their pursuers, but Blackford's sharpshooters "opened fire on my flank ... on the east side of the river, which added to the confusion." One man confessed that "when the reb crew charged us we broke for a wheat field, where I laid until dark." Word began to spread among the Yankees that the rest of their army had departed, leaving them surrounded and about to be captured. This was enough for the hundred-days men—most simply threw down their arms and skedaddled for Baltimore. "Every one must save themselves," scribbled one man. "The Rebs are following us, throwing shells." Nevertheless Brown claimed to have rallied three hundred of his men that evening.[8]

At last Tyler gave the order to pull back. Leib tried to cover the withdrawal, but by now "the rebels were coming in [our] rear and on all our flanks" and were in possession of the ford and the bridge. The captain "was compelled to ride my horse down a very steep bluff into the river." Swimming his horse across, he found a company of the 149th Ohio who took off even as he tried to direct them, so he galloped back toward the bridge to look for his own men. By then "all had gone, and the rebels [were] in possession of the ground." The Southern cavalry appeared again and almost captured Tyler and Leib, who escaped with a handful of their men. As the smoke cleared, Tyler's men streamed eastward, leaving their dead behind. The battle at the stone bridge had not been particularly lethal. The 149th and 144th Ohio, who had done the most fighting, reported only six killed and twenty-one wounded but listed 235 men as missing (many of whom had simply taken to the bush and would turn up in the next few days). Rodes's losses were light. According to Robert Park, who spent the day in the ranks of Battle's brigade waiting on the pike, only one sharpshooter from the Twelfth Alabama was killed in the action, which if averaged across the Division Sharpshooters would mean total casualties of twenty to twenty-five men. Wallace withdrew toward Baltimore. He had lost the battle but saved the capital, and reinforcements were on the way.[9]

The sharpshooters had performed in exemplary fashion by whipping Tyler's brigade, but the question remains: why did Rodes not smash through Brown's position with his infantry brigades, which he could easily have done, and cut off Wallace's retreat? Old Jube had an unfortunate habit of fighting his battles piecemeal, and apparently he saw Rodes's role as only a holding action. Considering that Early's headquarters lay closest to Rodes's division, it seems unlikely that the lack of follow-through was due to excessive caution on Rodes's part. Whatever the reason (he would later say that he "did not desire prisoners"), Early called off the pursuit that evening and concentrated on his move toward Washington. In his postwar memoir Lew Wallace lavished praise on Brown and his men who, "attacked by a largely superior force … were behaving splendidly." Erastus Tyler also wrote glowingly about the "unequal combat" they faced with such "determined spirit." In reality, though Brown and his men had done all that could have reasonably been expected of inexperienced troops in their situation and had—barely—accomplished their mission, they had faced only Rodes's Division Sharpshooters and some of Johnson's cavalry, whom they almost certainly outnumbered. Had Rodes attacked with his full force, the result would have been swift and sanguinary.[10]

Fort Stevens

Jubal Early, riding just behind his cavalry, reached the outskirts of Washington about 1 p.m. on July 11. Just in front of him he could hear the rifles of Lieutenant Colonel David Lang's Sixty-second Virginia Mounted Infantry popping as the men moved forward on both sides of the Seventh Street Pike in a dismounted skirmish line. Although a nearby farmer told Early that "nothing but earth works" lay before him, the Confederate commander saw forbidding defenses through his field glasses. Meanwhile "flour barrels" and "nail kegs"—huge shells from the heavy siege guns in the forts ringing the city—roared harmlessly overhead as the amalgam of hospital rats, clerks, home guards, "military riff-raff" and hundred-days men in the forts tried to find the range. "For some of us," admitted one Yank, "it was the first powder we had seen burned in battle." The dismounted Virginians, who probably numbered no more than two hundred after deducting their horse holders,* pressed toward the nearest work, Fort Stevens. It was a formidable bastion, protected by ditches and abatis, whose 375-yard perimeter enclosed seventeen heavy guns and mortars. To the east of Fort Stevens lay Fort Slocum, west of it loomed Fort DeRussy, which sported among its copious armaments a 100-pound Parrot rifle, and the intervening space was connected by batteries, rifle pits, and trenches. Had the Confederates but known it, however, only a company of seventy-eight green hundred-days men from the Ohio National Guard, some fifty-two convalescents, and a seventy-nine-man battery of Michigan artillerymen held Fort Stevens just then. "There had been talk among us about a chance to go to the front," quipped one guardsman, "but now the front had come to us." As the fight freshened four men pushed a carriage loaded with small arms ammunition out to the picket line, returning a short time later with whole skins but a "riddled" buggy.[11]

The defenses of Washington, 1864. *B&L*

---

* Mounted infantry units like the Sixty-second Virginia typically detailed one soldier in four to hold the unit's horses just behind the line, and this reduced their front-line strength accordingly.

Lang's Virginians pushed the pickets and skirmishers of the 150th Ohio National Guard and Veteran Reserves[†] (most of whom were armed with obsolete smoothbore muskets) down the pike, and by 1:30 the commander of the fort, Lieutenant Colonel John Frazee, reported that they were "within a distance of 150 yards of our immediate front and 50 yards of our right." The Federals responded by sending out their own dismounted horsemen, the 25th New York Cavalry, which had arrived late the night before and camped behind the fort. This still-unmounted unit, raised in January and not yet complete, had spent most of its time doing guard and provost duty for Grant's army at City Point, Virginia. So far the only combat these men had seen was a brush with Rebel cavalry in late June, but the four hundred New Yorkers seemed willing enough as they filed out in front of Fort Stevens and deployed in skirmish formation. "Hardly had it taken position," wrote one trooper, "when the Rebels were coming down the opposite hill, a perfect cloud of skirmishers," whereupon the Empire Staters began exchanging shots from their breech-loading Burnside carbines with the Virginians' long Enfields. These men were obviously not "melish,"[‡] and their appearance was enough to give the Confederate chiefs pause. "They are no hundred-day's men, General," said Rodes, who had just arrived. "They are veterans."[12]

At some point—the exact sequence of events is unclear—a scratch outfit of five hundred to six hundred horseless troopers, who had been awaiting remounts at Camp Stoneman, arrived to join the New Yorkers. These men hailed from assorted cavalry commands of the Army of the Potomac, and though not a cohesive unit, they had seen the elephant and many wielded fast-firing Sharps, Colt, and Spencer carbines. Their arms and numbers gave them a decided edge over Lang's men, who began falling back toward Silver Spring, site of the prosperous farms and elegant mansions of the Blair family.[§] It also happened to be where Rodes's division, straggling badly in the stifling ninety-degree heat, was starting to concentrate after a fifteen-mile march undertaken at four that morning. "We arrived near the outer defenses of Washington about 12 or 1 pm," scrawled a Tarheel officer from Grimes's brigade in his diary. "Sharpshooters immediately sent to the front." From the rising ground near the Blair house the ragged men in gray could see the unfinished capitol dome, but they would get no closer under arms. After the war men of the Sixty-second Virginia would claim that their flag had come the closest to the White House, and they were probably right.[13]

---

† The Veteran Reserve Corps (formerly the Invalid Corps) consisted of men who had been wounded or otherwise disabled in the service but who could still perform light duties including acting as guards.

‡ Militia

§ Near the grounds of present-day Walter Reed Army Medical Center. Some of Blackford's sharpshooters are said to have fired from a tulip tree that stood there until recently.

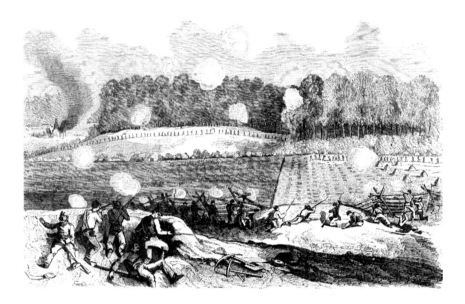

Confederate assault on the works near Washington repulsed by dismounted
cavalry and militia, July 11, 1864. *The Soldier in Our Civil War*

Rodes dispatched Blackford and his veteran Division Sharpshooters to deal
with the horse soldiers. The New Yorkers had advanced far enough to burn
some houses capable of concealing Confederate marksmen, but Blackford's
men drove them back toward their line of rifle pits in front of the forts in
"sharp fighting" that cost the Empire State troopers five men killed and
thirteen wounded. Meanwhile Early's exhausted soldiers continued to
dribble up. Later he would estimate that no more than a third of his men
were available that afternoon. Through his field glasses Early saw the dust
clouds in the south that heralded the arrival of Union reinforcements. The
race was over.[14]

Getty's division of VI Corps, recently arrived from Petersburg, began
disembarking at Alexandria just after noon, joined by the first regiments of
XIX Corps from Louisiana. Major General Henry Halleck, the Union Chief
of Staff, sent Brigadier General Frank Wheaton, the division's acting commander[*] and his two brigades out to the far left of the line near the Potomac,
but countermanded the order as the Rebels began to press Fort Stevens.
Wheaton's men reversed course and marched out Seventh Street, arriving
around four, then had to wait in a wood half a mile away while Union chiefs
tried to sort out the Byzantine Federal command structure.

---

[*]   The division's commander, Major General George Getty, was recuperating from a wound.

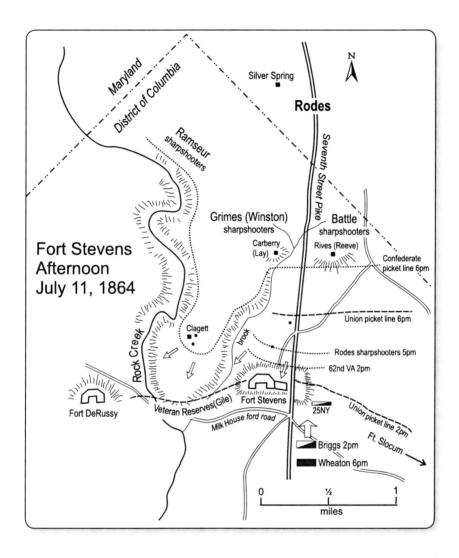

Fort Stevens
Afternoon
July 11, 1864

By 5 o'clock, however, the situation was again becoming critical. Blackford's sharpshooters were "annoying … very considerably" the Union skirmish line, effectively using houses and trees as sniping posts and infiltrating down the ravine between Forts DeRussy and Stevens. The Federals had blocked the gulch with abatis, but this failed to keep small groups of Rebel riflemen from using it to approach their picket line. Another dust-up developed on a knoll just to the west of the ravine, as the Confederates sent "a considerable body of skirmishers to re-enforce their skirmishers, who had worked down in close proximity to this fort [DeRussy]." There the Rebels faced a brigade of Veteran Reserves under Colonel George Gile, who repulsed them with the help of the fort's heavy guns. Confederate sharpshooters, probably from Ramseur's division, pulled back to a group of houses near the crest and continued to snipe at the Federals, their Enfields easily outranging their opponents' smoothbore weapons.[15]

Major General Horatio Wright, the recently arrived VI Corps commander, thought only a light skirmish line faced him and wanted to "clean it out," but the Union chiefs dithered. If Early were to launch a serious attack, they preferred to keep Wheaton in reserve for a counterstroke. "The rebels were said to be 'just out thar,'" remarked one VI Corps man, "and the skirmish line within five hundred yards of Fort Stevens, the yip! of rebel bullets into, and over the Fort, and the wounded going back, showed that they were indeed 'that.'" Rodes's sharpshooters peppered the fort's parapets with Miniè balls from a nearby peach orchard, driving the gunners from their pieces. "The sharpshooters advanced to within 200 yards of the fort," claimed one Tarheel commander, "but retired to a position about 300 yards to the rear, where they halted and dug rifle pits." To relieve the pressure, around five p.m. Wheaton sent out three regiments from his own brigade in skirmish formation. A serious fight developed when Rodes, in turn, backstopped his sharpshooters with Grimes's brigade, which had been the first to arrive, and the Fifth Alabama from Battle's brigade. Wheaton brought up two more regiments and after an hour or so of hard fighting the Federal picket line stood about where it had been that morning. By seven o'clock things settled down somewhat, but the popping of muskets continued all evening.[16]

One of Ft. Totten's heavy Parrot rifles. Guns mounted "en barbette" had a wide field of fire but were vulnerable to sharpshooters. *B&L*

How close had they come to actually capturing the city? "We could have gone into Washington with a loss of a thousand or two men from their Artillery," wrote Blackford. "What then? The men would have sacked the

City—and have been drunk and unmanageable in an hour. ... No private in our ranks ever had any idea that 'Old Jubilee' really intended to attack the place. Forts were as thick as blackberries around the town,—with plenty of artillery, but no men." That evening Early and his generals raided Mr. Blair's wine cellar and held a council of war. All were reluctant to quit after coming so far, but the risks of remaining grew hourly. Early decided to attack the next morning, but only after another look at the defenses.[17]

At sunup on July 12 Blackford's men probed the forts, which they found fully manned, and Old Jube called off the offensive. Feigning an attack, Early sent his skirmishers up front, and his light field pieces barked like popguns against the heavy cannon in the forts. The sharpshooters moved forward once again, saturating the Federal positions with rifle fire from their skirmish line, which ran through heavy brush just behind a small brook at the base of a low knoll.

During the day Lucius Chittenden, a civilian Treasury official who had wrangled a pass to the front to do a little sightseeing, made his way to Fort Stevens. By the time he arrived in early afternoon the VI Corps was in place and Blackford's men had fallen back, but several soldiers assured Chittenden that the Rebels "had intended to storm the forts ... had occupied the opposite hill, and had filled the clusters of buildings" in front of the forts earlier that day. "There had been a sharp-shooter behind every stump and log and boulder, up to within a hundred yards of our lines." A Vermont captain, whom Chittenden knew from home, told him that "before the Sixth Corps came their fire had been effective, and the loss on our side heavy." The firing had slacked off, and Chittenden could see Union skirmishers spread out in front of the fort in a cornfield and peach orchard. A few Yankees fired from earthworks in front of the trench that cut across the pike, connecting Forts Stevens and Slocum, dropping down to reload after each shot. Yet on the enemy's skirmish line, some hundreds of yards distant, "not a man was visible, but from every square rod of it as it seemed to me we could see the smoke and hear the report of the musketry." One of the men near him, who was using a heavy target rifle and a field glass, caught his attention. "He was as deliberate as firing at a mark," wrote Chittenden. "After one discharge he continued looking through his glass for a long time. He then dropped back into the ditch and quietly remarked, 'I winged him that time!' He pointed to a fallen tree, behind which, he said, a particularly dexterous sharp-shooter had been firing all morning, killing two men and wounding others. He had borrowed the target-rifle to stop him, and thought he had done it, 'for he didn't show up any more!'"[18]

Several local houses just behind their skirmish line provided excellent cover for Confederate sharpshooters, as did "two strong wooded hills in our front, the possession of which gave the enemy great advantage of position near our intrenched line." On a knoll west of Silver Spring road stood an ideal lair for sharpshooters, "a fine wooden mansion two stories in height, with a cupola," which belonged to Mr. Lay, a post office official. Just across the pike lay another spacious dwelling, "surrounded by an orchard and large shade trees," which also gave a fine view of the Yankee lines. Houses on the other knoll, across the ravine and northwest of Fort DeRussy, provided a haven for another troublesome lot of marksmen. As usual the sharpshooters made themselves at home. "All the houses in our vicinity were vacated by their inmates on our approach, and the skirmishers in front were soon in them," wrote Robert Park, who also noticed that "many articles of male and female attire were strewn over the ground." Although Park deplored the looting, he allowed himself to read some "very disreputable letters, received and written by young ladies which had been found in the houses, and which exhibited the decadence of moral sentiment in the masses of the North." The Federals had strangely neglected to clear out the dwellings near the forts in the three years prior to the battle, a circumstance that now worked against them. Where possible they quickly made up for lost time, razing or burning a dozen nearby houses "because they obstructed the range of our guns; one situated directly across the pike from the Fort, and the residence of a widow of strong southern proclivities," who was allowed only twenty minutes to pack her belongings. This, thought the writer, "served to give the semi-rebels in that vicinity a practical taste of the horrors of war."[19]

Robert Park, standing in the ranks of Battle's brigade near the Blair house, could see that "some of the enemy were dressed in citizens' clothes, and a few had on linen coats." Indeed, battlefield tourists had become, in spite of the efforts of the provost marshal, a sizable problem for the Federals. In addition to well-connected bureaucrats like Chittenden, these included congressmen, cabinet officials, and even President Abraham Lincoln and his wife, who visited Fort Stevens on both days of the battle. As one soldier put it:

> It is a wonder that more men were not wounded or killed there, as the grounds in and near the fort were crowded with citizens, whose curiosity had induced them to be so venturesome. I was much amused to see the "cits," as the boys call them, duck their heads and even go through the very undignified performance of hugging mother earth as an occasional bullet came whizzing by. The "rebs" could have picked off very many of them had they chosen as their white summer costumes formed a good, conspicuous mark, but they humanely refrained, and when a "stray" bullet did come over it seemed always to pick out some poor soldier as its victim.

Observers on the Union side of the line noted that the chief executive wore a linen duster, so it may have been Lincoln himself whom Park saw rubbernecking from the ramparts. Given the skill of the Southern riflemen and the range of their weapons, the president was in great danger, which became very clear when the presidential party drew a fusillade of shots from Rebel sharpshooters, one of whom wounded a surgeon standing near Lincoln—the only U.S. chief executive to come under enemy fire while in office. Legend has it that a young Massachusetts officer, Captain Oliver Wendell Holmes, then gave his commander-in-chief a preemptory order to "get down, you fool." Other stories have General Wright plucking at the president's sleeve to get him out of the line of fire. Lincoln removed himself to safety, but dozens of other sightseers remained. The soldiers were unimpressed by the gawkers—"every hill top that could be reached by the citizens was crowded," scoffed one. "I suppose they think it was a splendid sight, but we poor fellows could not see much fun in it."[20]

President Lincoln visited the battlefield on both days of the battle, and narrowly escaped being hit on July 12. *The Soldier in Our Civil War*

The artillerymen in the forts replied to the sharpshooters' fire by lobbing shells at the offending houses, but even the heavy artillery seemed powerless to stop the bullets. The overall Union sector commander, Major General Alexander McCook, complained that "from these two points our skirmish line was very much annoyed by the enemy, they killing and wounding about 30 of our skirmishers during the day." He ordered the hills carried and the houses burned. To this end a company of Veteran Reserves under a certain Captain Clark sallied out from Fort DeRussy, but Rodes's men were waiting for them. As the Yankees approached one of the buildings, "they were opened on by the enemy from behind a breast-work of logs and brush" and driven back, with Clark and four others being wounded. To destroy the postal mansion McCook sent out a force from Fort Stevens, "a company of about seventy-five who were selected from the various regiments of the Divisions and attached to General Getty's [division] headquarters as sharp-shooters, under command of Captain Alexander M. Beattie of the Third Vermont." Captain Beattie and his Federal sharpshooters fared no better than had the Veteran Reserves. They "lost quite severely" and failed to take the house.[21]

Union strength grew as the second division of VI Corps began arriving around mid-morning, and Federal commanders shifted the 25th New York cavalry over to Fort DeRussy to bolster the Veteran Reserves. Thrown out in a skirmish line, they "had ... hardly taken position when the music opened again in lively style." One trooper praised "the effectiveness of our Burnside rifles," which, he wrote, "began to be apparent in the number of stretchers which the Rebs began to bring into requisition on their side of the field."[22]

Though Washington was now secure, Federal commanders seemed locked in a defensive mindset, unable to decide what to do next. Colonel N. P. Chipman, an aide to the Secretary of War, scribbled out a report sometime that afternoon at Fort Stevens, detailing the Union strength (a mixed bag of just under eight thousand men on the northern sector facing Early, not counting VI Corps), the command problems (Generals McCook, Wright, Augur, and Meigs all shared some responsibility), and his estimate of Early's strength. Two helpful Georgia sharpshooters from Cook's brigade, captured that morning near Fort Stevens, had volunteered their army's numbers at fifty thousand men. An anxious Chipman reduced this to thirty thousand—still more than twice the actual number of Rebels who stood in Old Jube's ranks. "The enemy maintain a pretty stiff picketline," he conceded, "and are not easily driven." A moment later he noted that "a rebel sharpshooter just wounded severely a soldier standing on the parapet of Fort Stevens." At the Union command level it was a classic case of too many chiefs. "Stars and ea-gles were at a discount," cracked one man, "Brigadiers without number and Colonels by the dozens. A private was a rarity." One group wanted to launch an all-out attack, while another faction—which eventually prevailed—fa-vored advancing a strong skirmish line to develop the situation.[23]

Late that afternoon, after spending most of the day arguing strategy and sorting out the niceties of protocol, Federal commanders—their minds concentrated by the near-miss of President Lincoln—readied a force to drive off the pesky Confederate sharpshooters. General Wheaton still had his skirmish line in place from the previous day, and he ordered Colonel Daniel Bidwell, commanding the division's Third brigade, to select his three "very best regiments" to join him in an assault on the two Confederate-held knolls. Bidwell quietly moved the 7th Maine, plus the 43rd and 49th New York, up at trail arms just behind Wheaton's skirmish line. "The pseudo-soldiers who filled the trenches around the Fort," sneered one VI Corps soldier, "were astounded at the temerity displayed by these war-worn veterans in going out before the breast-works, and benevolently volunteered most earnest words of caution. The enemy's skirmishers were at this time within six hundred yards of the Fort in strong force, and their bullets, which were plenty, were assisted by shells from artillery planted behind them."[24]

When all was ready, about five o'clock, the guns of Forts Stevens and Slocum opened up on the Confederates. After thirty-six shots—one for each star on the national flag—Wheaton began his attack. His own brigade surged ahead in skirmish order while Bidwell's three regiments "dashed forward, surprising and hotly engaging the enemy." About that time the gunners in the forts got lucky and put several heavy shells into the Lay mansion, setting it alight. Through their field glasses the Yankee gunners could see Rebel riflemen bailing out of the upper stories just ahead of the flames, as well as "the forces of the enemy massed behind it ... scattering in disorder into the open field beyond." Waiting in reserve, the commander of the 122nd New York, Lieutenant Colonel Augustus Dwight, who had until now assumed that his brigade was going to relieve the picket line, watched as the 7th Maine, one of Bidwell's handpicked regiments, stacked their knapsacks, formed a skirmish line, and started up the knoll east of the road "in splendid order." They surprised the Rebel pickets, who "skedaddled as fast as they could, leaving everything in their pits." The Mainers took the hill and the Rives house, but there the Yankee advance ran into trouble. The Rebels, though caught off guard, were "found to be much stronger than had been supposed."[25]

Captain Cary Whitaker, a company commander with the Forty-third North Carolina, heard the firing increase on the picket line and went forward to investigate. Standing at a fence line with Colonel John R. Winston (acting commander of Grimes's brigade in that general's absence), he watched the Confederate sharpshooters pull back. "Some of the 53rd NC stayed in the cellar of a barn," Whitaker later wrote, "and Col. Winston was desirous of getting someone to go and order them to fall back. Ordered a man to deliver the message, but he seeming unwilling and afraid to go. I volunteered to carry the message. He availed himself of my services. I ran forward to near the skirmish line, hallowed to an officer to tell them, he gave them the order and turned and told me they could come if they wished." Whitaker started back with some of the sharpshooters, only to find his own regiment and the Forty-fifth North Carolina coming forward in skirmish order. "They went up beautifully," reported Colonel David Cowand, "and the men of the Fifty-third North Carolina Troops and the sharpshooters joined in."[26]

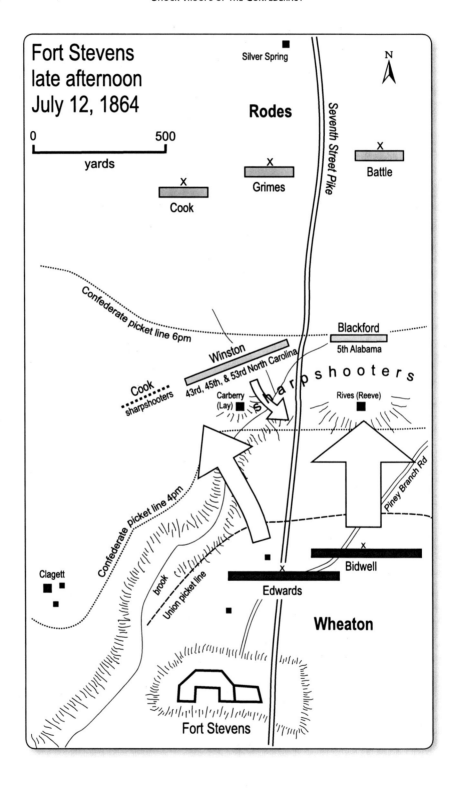

In response Colonel Bidwell brought forward his three reserve regiments, the 150-man picket reserve of the 102nd Pennsylvania, and Captain Beattie's sharpshooters. The boys of the 122nd New York hustled up the slope at a double-quick, deploying in a double skirmish line across the pike to cover their brigade's left flank. At the top of the hill the "Twosters," along with the 43rd New York and 61st Pennsylvania, ran into "a strong force of the enemy ... behind a board fence." The Confederates, whose fire was "well directed," put up a stout resistance. "Our line was getting thinned," recalled one Yankee, "but the men protected themselves as best they could and poured such an incessant fire on the prostrate enemy that it compelled them to retreat in disorder." The Confederates allowed the leading companies of the 122nd to advance almost unopposed then slid around their left flank, enfilading them and forcing them to fall back. Union private Belas North and his comrades "were having it all our way when, presto, they halted, rallied, turned and under sharp fire advanced to gobble us."[27]

"We got over a fence and soon found out we were trying to take back where the sharpshooters had lost," remembered Whitaker, back in command of the Forty-third North Carolina. He led his men forward in a charge: "In front of my Regt. was a house on fire in our front. Yankees behind them firing at us, we charged them from behind these houses. Found it a pretty hot place." When Whitaker looked back, he found he was missing the three right companies of his regiment, who had joined the sharpshooters of Cook's Georgia brigade. He pulled both forward to cover his right flank. Across the pike the Yankees pushed Battle's sharpshooters back past the burning Rives mansion, and General Rodes again sent up the Fifth Alabama to backstop Blackford and his men.[28]

Winston's counterattack forced the Federals on the defensive. They crouched behind the fence, from where they poured "a destructive fire" on Whitaker and his Tarheels. "In a short time the Rebs formed in two lines of battle and charged us, but it was 'no go'; such destructive vollies were poured into them, they could not stand it." The Southerners broke, reformed, and came on again. By now the New Yorkers were down to their last few cartridges; even so, Colonel Dwight claimed that his Onondagas "held their ground for twenty minutes ... then fell back, rallied again, charged them without ammunition and drove them back again." One of his rifleman lay down with a comrade behind some cedar posts "at a point where the enemy's lines were in easy range ... and directed our fire on the heads of the enemy as they raised up to take aim." Five men from the 61st Pennsylvania soon joined the two, despite their protests that so many men were sure to draw fire. "They fought well for a time," he recalled, "and in the darkness that gradually settled down on the contest like a funeral pall, we did not notice that their guns were silent and the five lay as if asleep. Placing my hand on the head of the man to my right, I found the brain and

blood oozing from the wound of the deadly minié bullet." The other four
Pennsylvanians lay in a similar state. The soldier (probably Private Thomas
Scott of Company B) beat a hasty retreat but received "a disabling wound in
the arm" as he departed.[29]

Faced with such stubborn resistance, Wheaton and Bidwell called for
more reinforcements. "In no other engagement of our three year's service
did we witness so many acts of individual valor and daring," remembered
another soldier, who termed it "a desperate engagement." One of those who
fell was the "gallant, but hasty" commander of the 43rd New York, Lieutenant
Colonel James D. Visscher, who "lost his life by his own imprudence."[30]

At Silver Spring Robert Park and the men of Battle's Alabama brigade
waited next to the pike. "It was a day of conjecture and considerable excitement, in our momentary expectation of being ordered 'forward,'" he wrote
in his diary, but the moment never came. Major Henry Kyd Douglas, one
of Early's staff officers, watched nervously as the Yankee attack developed:
"I saw it coming and thought we were 'gone up,'" he later confessed. An
Ohio National Guardsman, captured at Monocacy, claimed that "the whole
rebel army came pell-mell, almost a stampede," to the rear. Rodes's division stood athwart the road and did most of the fighting, and he appears
to have handled the battle much as he had at the North Anna, feeding infantry reinforcements to the skirmish line as they were needed to shore up
threatened points. A sizable ravine behind the postal mansion and some
defiladed ground behind the knolls allowed him to bring up troops unseen
by the Federals and protected from their fire. By this time the gunners in
the forts had improved their artillery practice enough to cause "some little
damage" to Grimes's men, wounding five or six of his sharpshooters. Lucius
Chittenden waxed eloquent as he watched the shells in flight: "They rose
in long, graceful curves, screaming like demons of the pit, then descending
with like curves into the crowds of running men. The men swayed outward
with the explosion, but many fell and did not rise again."[31]

The fighting on the knolls surged back and forth, with each side claiming to have repulsed three attacks by the other. Colonel David Cowand
wrote that his Tarheels "soon established their line again on the right of the
road, but the troops on the left could not succeed in going quite as far as
their original line. The troops fought remarkably well indeed, being under
very heavy artillery fire, and we had none replying, and besides, the enemy
had decidedly the advantage in position, but our men went up cheerfully
and confidently." The experiences of the Alabamians west of the pike were
similar. One soldier tersely noted: "we had to fight hard until night." Blackford, who doubled as the commander of the Fifth Alabama and the division
sharpshooters, wrote his sister that his regiment had "distinguished itself"
in the engagement.[32]

Finally around six p.m. Wheaton received the command to halt his attack and hold what he had gained. The fighting on July 12 was at last over, and both sides believed they had won the day. The Yankees congratulated themselves on having captured both knolls, driving away the enemy, and saving the capital, and the Confederates thought they had successfully covered their withdrawal with "but slight loss." Old Jube thought he had accomplished his larger goal as well. "Major, we haven't taken Washington," he told Douglas as they left the city, "but we've scared Abe Lincoln like hell!" That night, covered by a two-hundred-man rear guard under Major Douglas, the Army of the Valley decamped for parts south without interference. Their Washington campaign was, thought one Federal, "the most impudent thing the rebels ever attempted."[33]

Scene of the fight between detachments of the Sixth Corps, General Wright, and Rodes's and Gordon's divisions at Fort Stevens, Washington, D.C., July 12, 1864. *The Soldier in Our Civil War*

That evening Lucius Chittenden, the sightseeing treasury bureaucrat, roamed the battlefield, viewing with horrified fascination the "sickening spectacle" of Rebel sharpshooters burned—some while still alive—in the houses near the battle line, where the odor of charred flesh still lingered. Chittenden penned some of the best descriptions of Southern sharpshooters in the field. "Near a large fallen tree lay one in the uniform of an officer. His sword was by his side, but his hand grasped a rifle. What could have sent an officer here to act as a sharp-shooter?" he wondered. Chittenden put his hand on the man's chest to see if he was still alive, and was surprised to find that he was wearing "a sheet of boiler-iron, moulded to fit the anterior portion of his body, and fastened at the back by straps and buckles." The armor had failed in its purpose, however, since "directly over his heart, through the shield and through the body, was a hole large enough to permit the escape of a score of human lives." A wound that large was probably caused by artillery fire. Next Chittenden found the man who had been "winged" by the soldier with the target rifle.

> There, behind the log, he lay, on his back, his open eyes gazing upwards, with a peaceful expression on his rugged face. In the middle of his fore-head was the small wound which had ended his career. A single crimson line led from it, along his face, to where the blood dropped upon the ground. A minié-rifle, discharged, was grasped in his right hand; a box, with a single remaining cartridge, was fast to his side. The rifle and cartridge-box were of English make, and the only things about him which did not indicate extreme destitution. His feet, wrapped in rags, had coarse shoes upon them, so worn and full of holes that they were only held together by many pieces of thick twine. Ragged trousers, a jacket, and a shirt of what used to be called "tow-cloth," a straw hat, which had lost a large portion of both crown and rim, completed his attire. His hair was a mat of dust and grime; his face and body were thickly coated with dust and dirt, which gave him the color of the red Virginia clay.
>
> A haversack hung from his shoulder. Its contents were a jack-knife, a plug of twisted tobacco, a tin cup, and about two quarts of coarsely cracked corn, with, perhaps, an ounce of salt, tied in a rag. My notes, made the next day, say that this corn had been ground upon the cob, making the provender which the Western farmer feeds to his cattle. This was a complete inventory of the belongings of one Confederate soldier.
>
> How long he had been defending Richmond I do not know. But it was apparent that he, with Early's army, during the past six weeks had entered the valley at Staunton, and had marched more than three hundred miles, ready to fight every day, until now, when in the front, he was acting as a sharp-shooter before Washington. He was evidently from the poorest class of Southern whites.[34]

Fort Stevens had been the largest open-order battle of the war, and in contrast with many relatively bloodless skirmish actions, one of the deadliest. Most fell during Wheaton's attack on the afternoon of July 12, in which the losses of the Federals were "very severe." Indeed, the sharpshooting Confederates killed or wounded all of Bidwell's regimental commanders along with many of his other officers, and the action cost his command roughly a third of its men. One unfortunate outfit, the understrength 49th New York, lost twenty-six of its eighty-five men. Moreover, observed a veteran of the 122nd New York (which itself lost five killed and twenty wounded), the proportion of dead to wounded was unusually high, with more than a third of the wounds being fatal as opposed to the normal sixteen to twenty percent for a major action—another tribute to Southern marksmanship. Given the much smaller number of men engaged (two thousand to twenty-five hundred men on both sides), the percentage of dead and wounded for those units actually in the fray compares favorably with the battle of Monocacy fought only a few days before.[35]

Southern losses, as always, are harder to tally. Cary Whitaker gave the losses in his Forty-third North Carolina at five killed and fifteen wounded, and a modern count puts the losses of the Fifty-third regiment at four killed, six wounded, and twenty-two captured. Present-day estimates put overall casualties at about five hundred Rebels and six hundred Yankees over the two days.[36]

Although the overall casualties did not approach those of major battles, they were real enough to the soldiers involved. That evening James Laird, orderly sergeant of the national guard company that had held Fort Stevens that day, helped a man hobble from an ambulance into the hospital behind the fort. "As we came into better light," he wrote, "I noted that his uniform was gray." The soldier, almost certainly one of Grimes's sharpshooters, "begged that I would not allow his leg to be taken off," saying that he had "a wife and six children in Carolina." "No help for you," replied the surgeon, long since hardened to his work. "If it were one of our own soldiers we should do the same. The knee is shattered." Together they lifted the man on the boards. Laird held the chloroformed sponge over man's face, and the leg came off. "The tables," he remembered, "were filled with mangled men under the surgeon's hands."[37]

16

Charles Town, Winchester, and Fisher's Hill

"Take charge of the boys, do the best you can and give the Yanks Hell."

The "Mimic War"

Laden with plunder acquired on his march through Maryland, Early recrossed the Potomac on July 16 and continued south, easily outdistancing a tepid Union pursuit. After sharp actions at Snicker's Gap and Rutherford's Farm he withdrew to Fisher's Hill near Strasburg. The Union commander, Major General Horatio Wright, assumed that Early was on his way to rejoin Lee at Petersburg, and so began pulling the VI and XIX Corps back to Washington. Old Jube proved him mistaken, however, and on July 24 he whipped a Union army under Major General George Crook at Kernstown. The Federals retreated to Harpers Ferry as Early sent his cavalry into Pennsylvania to burn Chambersburg and once again watered his horses in the Potomac—entirely too close for official Washington's comfort.

These repeated disasters finally caused Grant to replace a number of marginal commanders and consolidate all the Union forces in the Valley under the command of Major General Philip Sheridan. In addition to the Army of West Virginia (Hunter's old force, now informally renamed VIII Corps), Sheridan now commanded VI Corps and both divisions of XIX Corps[*], newly arrived from Louisiana. Grant also released to him two cavalry divisions from Petersburg, which, when added to the one present, gave the Yankees an overwhelming superiority in that arm. Sheridan's new Army of the Shenandoah numbered forty-five thousand soldiers, and for the first time in the war they all served under one general. Still, the new Union chief faced major constraints. Early's raid had thoroughly rattled Washington, and with the presidential elections only a few months away, "Little Phil"

---

[*]   The second division of XIX Corps did not join the army until August 1.

was under pressure not to lose a battle. The Union high command also retained inflated ideas of Early's strength; some reports put his numbers at more than forty thousand men.

Lieutenant General Jubal A. Early, CSA. (left)
Major General Philip Sheridan, USA. *B&L* (right)

Old Jube, of course, did what he could to encourage this sort of thinking, staying in motion to give the impression of greater numbers. For the next six weeks the cantankerous Virginian marched and countermarched his men across the area between Strasburg and Harpers Ferry in a campaign the troops quickly dubbed "the Mimic War," in the process tying down three times his number of Federals. The two armies skirmished on an almost daily basis. The sharpshooters, acting as "foot cavalry" to compensate for the Confederate weakness in the mounted arm, fought most of these nameless engagements. An example of this type of fight took place on September 2 near Bunker Hill, Virginia. Early was withdrawing toward Winchester, with Battle's brigade acting as his rear guard. When the Rebels were about six miles north of the town, the Federal horsemen routed Brigadier General John Vaughn's cavalry brigade, who then passed through Rodes's division in "a perfect stampede." Battle's men first tried to stop the flying horse soldiers with cheers, "but it was of no avail, & they turned in to abuse them by calling them cowards, etc." The pursuing Yankees had nabbed Vaughn's trains and a herd of cattle his men had been driving. Battle sent out his brigade sharpshooters, who soon drove off the Federals and recaptured their booty, but instead of returning it to the cavalry they kept it for themselves. Rodes turned his division around and drove the Federals back to Bunker Hill.[1]

During the retreat from Washington Early placed Colonel Hamilton A. Brown in command of Rodes's Division Sharpshooters, presumably with Rodes's acquiescence. Though a stout fighter and a highly regarded regimental commander, Brown had the personal idiosyncrasy of stuttering badly under the stress of combat. Almost all of Brown's regiment, the First

North Carolina, had been killed or captured in Hancock's May 12 attack at Spotsylvania. The remnants (less than fifty men) had been consolidated with another regiment and transferred to Brigadier General William Cox's North Carolina brigade of Rodes's division, leaving Brown, his remaining officers, and the senior NCOs without jobs. Most ended up in the division sharpshooters. Naming Brown the sharpshooter commander does not seem to be a reflection on Blackford, who had been the acting regimental commander of the Fifth Alabama since Spotsylvania as well as its only field officer. Blackford, who continued to command Battle's brigade sharpshooters, was increasingly troubled with varicose veins in his leg, the result of his 1862 bout with typhoid fever, and the discomfort was beginning to place major limitations on his activities.[2]

Sheridan made the first move on August 10, advancing on Berryville and, after some brisk cavalry skirmishes, forcing Early to fall back past Strasburg to Fisher's Hill. There the irascible Virginian took up a position too strong to assault, while Sheridan settled behind nearby Cedar Creek. The looming bulk of nearby Massanutten mountain dominated the area, and Early had established a signal station on a spur from which his men could observe the entire area. A detachment of Yankees climbed the mountain on August 14 and captured the station, but Early sent Captain Benjamin Keller and a hundred sharpshooters from Gordon's division to retake it. After "several small but severe fights," in which Keller and his men killed two Federals and captured three, the sharpshooters succeeded. Early's signal station was vital to his communications with a reinforcing column under Lieutenant General Richard Anderson as it approached from Front Royal. Anderson brought with him Kershaw's division, an artillery battery, and two brigades of cavalry under Fitz Lee. Sheridan fell back, mindful of his orders, unsure if this new force on his flank was the entire Confederate First Corps.[3]

Early trailed Little Phil past Winchester and nearly caught him out near Charles Town, where the Yankee general had withdrawn to protect the Baltimore & Ohio Railroad and his supply hub at Harpers Ferry, a persistent Confederate target. During this phase of the campaign the dominant terrain feature was Opequon Creek, whose steep banks neatly bisected the ground north to south between Harpers Ferry and Winchester. To get at the other, each army's first task was to cross this "very formidable barrier." Old Jube moved first, in the early hours of August 21, traversing the Opequon at Smithfield Crossing with Rodes's division in the lead. Anderson advanced on a converging movement through Summit Point to the south, and Fitzhugh Lee drove up from Berryville. With luck they would unite that morning at Cameron's Station, about two miles outside Charles Town.[4]

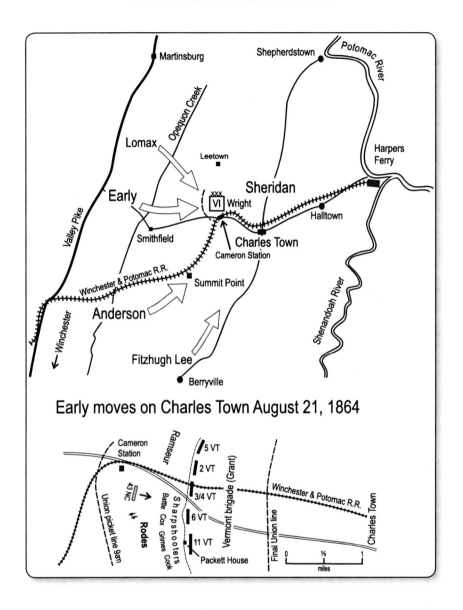

Early moves on Charles Town August 21, 1864

Charles Town

Cameron's Station happened to be where the soldiers of the Vermont brigade, part of Getty's division of the VI Corps, were preparing for Sunday inspection, relishing their first break in the nearly uninterrupted marching since they had arrived at Washington more than a month ago. No one there worried much about Old Jubilee and his Rebs: the brigade was, after all, protected by a picket line, "which described a grand curve around our left flank as it covered the army front perhaps half a mile from our camp" through the gently rolling terrain. Aldace Walker, newly promoted major of the 11th Vermont, still slept, having skipped breakfast after a bout of dysentery the night before. The first hint of trouble came at 9:30, when the entirely unexpected sounds of heavy firing rolled in from the picket line. To their amazement the pickets "in confusion were seen making rapidly for camp across the fields," and then commenced an affair Walker would describe as "only a skirmish, to the army at large, but which was inscribed upon the flags of The Vermont Brigade as the Battle of Charlestown."[5]

The uninvited Sunday callers were Rodes's Division Sharpshooters, fighting that day under Colonel Hamilton Brown. Eugene Blackford took part also, leading the sharpshooters of Battle's Alabama brigade. Screened by Brigadier General "Tiger John" McCausland's cavalry, they had achieved almost complete surprise. The Rebels quickly deployed, staking out a skirmish line that covered almost the entire Federal front, and soon some of them were approaching the Yankee camps. Ramseur's division moved up beside Rodes, adding its sharpshooters to the fight. But the Vermonters, who enjoyed a reputation as one of the toughest outfits in the Army of the Potomac, were veteran soldiers and not prone to panic. As General Getty and his staff trotted through camp, the men scrambled for their arms and equipment, struck their tents, and fell into ranks. Getty ordered Brigadier General Lewis Grant, the brigade's commander, to re-establish his picket line. "The order was simple," explained Walker, "but its execution seemed likely to be difficult, for the line had been driven in for nearly or quite a mile in extent along the semi-circle of which our position was the centre, and whether by a line of battle or a skirmish line was entirely unknown, as well as in what direction we were to expect the strongest hostile force."[6]

Grant put the 3rd, 4th, and a portion of the 6th Vermont into skirmish formation and sent them out to where the firing seemed heaviest. The rest of the brigade followed in support, "more deliberately on various radii of the curve assumed by the skirmishers." Directly in front of the Vermonters lay a hill covered with corn "of so high a growth that a man passing through it could not be seen; it soon appeared that it concealed a uniform line of rebel skirmishers." After giving them a volley the Green Mountain men "plunged recklessly into the corn" and pursued the retreating Southerners to a fence line. The rest of the brigade took off after them. Regiments on the right stopped after seeing a Confederate line on the next hill, but the ones on the left—who had not heard about stopping when they re-established the picket line—kept going "a half mile beyond it" before General Getty and his chief of staff could rein them in. Among those injured in the initial confusion was Walker's commander, Lieutenant Colonel George Chamberlain, who fell with a mortal wound.[7]

Getty's caution was well justified. Rodes's sharpshooters fell back a piece while Colonel Brown requested reinforcements. Rodes sent a courier galloping to General Grimes, who sent up the Forty-third North Carolina. Their commander, Captain Cary Whitaker, arrayed his men in skirmish order and used them to extend the left end of Brown's line. The Confederates now suddenly about faced and counterattacked, touching off "a general musketry battle" all along the line. "By this time," recalled Walker, "all the Brigade had reached the front line, and, becoming deployed, covered the whole mile as skirmishers. The enemy attacked us from behind trees, ridges, fences, and walls with a force that could not clearly be made out, and with a vigor that expressed their disappointment at finding themselves no better off than in the early morning." Captain Whitaker found the enemy's fire "pretty severe" and had to fall back a bit himself. The Vermonters, who vowed to "make a day of it," scraped together makeshift shelters from fence rails and whatever else they could find. Walker readily conceded that they were "pressed most dangerously." The 6th Vermont in the line's center suffered the most severely, while those posted on the right of the line lost only a few men.[8]

Walker's battalion of the 11th Vermont fell back to a large brick house on the left of the line owned by the Packett family, "in a position entirely exposed to the enemy's fire … while the rebels from behind a stone wall at short range were annoying them terribly." They quickly lost their color bearer and a number of other men, and Getty's favorite horse was killed as the general inspected their lines. Now on foot, Getty authorized Walker to station sharpshooters in the house. As he spoke to another officer of the 11th, a bullet whistled between the two of them.[9]

Walker and his men occupied the dwelling, which he quickly realized was the key to the position. "All the windows that faced the enemy," he reported, "were opened and filled with picked marksmen." Filling the house with Yankees immediately drew almost all the Rebel fire toward it, with the happy effect of giving relief to the hard-pressed men outside. To complicate matters, the pro-Southern family who lived there flatly refused to leave, taking refuge in the basement instead. Even though there was "a constant rattle of bullets against the walls of the mansion," the Vermonters seemed safe enough. Shortly after noon, however, the Confederates upped the ante with a field piece, throwing a shot over the building that "was intended as a warning for us to withdraw." The Vermonters stood fast, even when another shot took down the chimney, showering them with bricks. The Rebel gunners cranked down their piece and kept shooting. "Shell after shell plowed through its walls and exploded in its rooms," recalled Walker. "One hole torn in its side was used as a loophole by some brave fellow, not a half a minute after the shell had entered"—an act of bravado that rated a cheer from both sides. Some shells hit the basement, causing the homeowners to bolt to the rear, "weeping and shrieking." Miraculously, neither the family members nor the soldiers had yet been hurt, though Walker's men twice had to extinguish fires started by the shells. Walker stepped out of the room moments before a "death-bearing missile" entered it, killing one man and wounding several others. At this point the major thought it prudent to retire. As they decamped, "the musketry re-opened all along the line with renewed vigor, and the battle continued until the evening fell."[10]

All day Old Jube held off his attack, scanning the roads south with his field glasses for the telltale dust clouds that would herald Anderson's approach. Unfortunately for the Confederates, however, both Anderson and Fitzhugh Lee had been held up by Yankee cavalry, and Sheridan quickly brought up reinforcements. With its fast-firing Spencer repeaters, the Federal cavalry had become a serious threat in its own right, as the Confederates would shortly learn. Thus did Early's best opportunity of the campaign to strike a crippling blow at Sheridan's army pass away as the shadows lengthened.[11]

The firing tapered off in the late afternoon, allowing Walker and some other officers the chance to take a break on the back porch of the brick mansion, where they were fed by the "thoroughly subdued" owner. About six o'clock Federal reinforcements arrived in the form of an outfit from another of the corps's divisions passed by on its way to the left of the line, and the men guyed the exhausted Vermonters about "fighting a phantom" all day. The fresh regiment marched forward, "preserving a capital front, until they approached the stone-wall mentioned above, when suddenly a gray line of rebels rose up" and let them have it. "Saluted by a thousand rifles," the newcomers broke and legged it to the rear without firing a shot, followed by the jeers and catcalls of the Green Mountain boys.[12]

That evening they totaled up the day's losses, figuring that the day had cost the Vermont brigade twenty-three killed, ninety-eight wounded, and two missing, for a total of 123 men. The exposed 6th Vermont accounted for thirty-nine casualties, including all its field officers, and Walker placed his own losses at ten killed and forty wounded. By comparison their casualties at the hard-fought battle of Cedar Creek that October would be 284, so the engagement can hardly be dismissed as trivial. The sharpshooting Confederates had also taken many of their best officers. Overall Union casualties for the day ran to about 275 men killed and wounded—making it a "brisk" action on a par with Fort Stevens. "Two mules were employed all day bringing up ammunition," recalled Walker. "The Brigade consumed 56,000 cartridges. So steady and constantly severe a fire has rarely been known." He claimed his own battalion had fired seven thousand rounds from around the house, and swore that he had been fighting off "a full line of battle with artillery to boot, and had held our ground with a skirmish-line."[13]

Confederate accounts of the day's fighting are few, but Early and his topographer Jed Hotchkiss make clear that it was a skirmish action only. Colonel David Cowand, commanding the Thirty-second North Carolina, reported that the sharpshooters of Grimes's brigade had "quite a severe fight." This action certainly fits the general pattern of Rodes's tactics since the North Anna for him to put in his Division Sharpshooters with an infantry regiment in open order and a few pieces of artillery. Confederate inspection reports of August 20 show thirty-three hundred men in Rodes's division and about two thousand in Ramseur's. Assuming the one man in six ratio for sharpshooters, this would mean that their combined division sharpshooters probably numbered somewhere between eight hundred and nine hundred men, plus whatever infantry reinforcements Rodes gave them.[14]

Although not broken down by brigade, Federal returns list the overall infantry strength of VI Corps on September 10 at 12,674 men, which would mean that individual brigade strengths were between fourteen hundred and two thousand men. Wilbur Fisk gives the strength of the Vermont brigade on October 4 (after the battle of Winchester) as being about sixteen hundred men, which means that six weeks earlier it was probably nearer two thousand. Captain James Garnett, Rodes's ordnance officer, estimated that on August 21 Rodes's division fired sixty thousand rounds—even more than the Yankees shot—even without including Ramseur's men. As for casualties, Cowand says that the sharpshooters and their supporting regiment "suffered a good deal," and Garnett calculated the day's casualties for Rodes's division at 160 men. Cook's Georgia brigade, on the other hand, does not seem to have been as heavily engaged as Grimes's Tarheels. In an August 27 letter, Jack Felder, a sharpshooter with Co. K, Fourth Georgia, gave the losses in his company as two slightly wounded on August 21 and none on August 24. All told, though, Colonel Brown's sharpshooters had given an excellent account of themselves at Charles Town.[15]

A few days after the battle Private Wilbur Fisk of the 2nd Vermont mused on what it took to soldier on the skirmish line:

> Almost any man had rather stand in the open field and fight, when he knows where the enemy are, and knows that he has an equal chance with them, than to pick his way along an advancing skirmish line, without knowing when he may receive a whole volley from the enemy, and liable all the time to run upon a line of concealed sharpshooters, or an ambush of lurking foes. Skirmishers have to feel out the enemy's position, and are the first the receive their fire. … It requires peculiar courage in the men, and particular sagacity and courage in the officers, to do good skirmishing. I always feel uneasy when I am on the skirmish line, in front of the enemy, unless I am being handled by skillful hands. We must not advance upon a superior force of the enemy and expose ourselves needlessly; and we must not

break our connection with those on our right and left, or lose our directions and get lost or captured. ...

With a good General to lead, we can string the whole brigade of us, in a line five feet apart, or ten if they want; and advance straight ahead without pulling apart here, or crowding together there, keeping a straight line and going straight ahead, until we come upon the enemy's works, and find out all we wish to know, and then we can turn about and go back again without having a man captured, and if it is in the night, without letting the enemy know when it is done, or getting lost ourselves.[16]

Fisk also pondered why the Vermonters seemed to draw the duty so often. One reason was that "we all know that it requires nerve and reckless daring, to make a good skirmisher," qualities the Green Mountain boys naturally had in abundance. Another, he thought, was that the brigade's commander, Brigadier General Lewis Grant, was "the best General in the corps to manage a skirmish line." In short the Vermonters got the job because they were good at it, "everywhere and all the time." Still, Fisk thought that perhaps his commanders favored them a bit *too* much—"it seems to me to be a poor return for valor, that the best troops should *always* have the hardest work to do."[17]

Sheridan, still unwilling to risk a general engagement, retreated the night of the twenty-first to his fortifications at Halltown, near Harpers Ferry. Although Yankee cavalry blocked their crossing, Old Jube's weary infantry once again washed their feet in the Potomac. The Confederates followed Sheridan's army through Charles Town and took up positions outside his lines. After a quiet day there was some more fighting on the twenty-fourth, and Robert Park described watching the sharpshooters at work:

A sharp skirmish took place in front of our camp, which we could see very plainly. It was a deeply interesting sight to watch them advancing and retreating, firing from behind trees and rocks and clumps of bushes, falling down to load their discharged muskets, and rising quickly, moving forward, aiming and firing again—the whole line occasionally running rapidly forward, firing as they ran, with loud "Rebel yells," and the Yankee hirelings retreating as rapidly and firing as they fell back. It is so seldom we have an opportunity to look on, being generally interested combatants ourselves, that the exciting scene was very enjoyable.[18]

Park's regiment relieved the sharpshooters on picket that night, then swapped places with Kershaw's men the next day under fire. Early held Sheridan's attention with Anderson's force—a daring move, considering that it was only one division—and maneuvered his own army north to Shepherdstown while Fitz Lee demonstrated at Williamsport, "as if to cross into Maryland, in order to keep up the fear of an invasion of Maryland and Pennsylvania." Early and Anderson then pulled back across the Opequon, fighting a running battle with Sheridan's horsemen on August 28 and 29, camping that night at Bunker Hill, just north of Winchester. On the morning of the thirty-first Rodes marched to Martinsburg to run off some Yankee cavalry. Battle's Alabama brigade led Rodes's advance, and according to Robert Park they were "shelled severely" by Yankee horse artillery just outside Martinsburg. With their mission accomplished the sharpshooters marched back to Bunker Hill, having covered twenty-two miles that day. "These reconnaissances may be very important and very interesting to general and field officers, who ride," groused Park, "but those of the line, and the fighting privates, wish they were less frequent, or less tiresome this sultry weather. We have walked this pike road so often, that we know not only every house, fence, spring and shade tree, but very many of the citizens, their wives and children."[19]

Another brisk action erupted on September 3 when Kershaw's division bumped into the part of the Union VIII Corps under Colonel Joseph Thoburn near Berryville. Kershaw routed part of Thoburn's force, but the Yankees dug in that night. When Old Jube arrived the next morning he found himself facing most of Sheridan's army, now protected with strong entrenchments. Early sensibly declined battle and again fell back behind the Opequon. The weather deteriorated, soaking the Valley with heavy rain and confining both sides to their camps for the next two weeks. On September 15 Kershaw's division and Cutshaw's artillery started back toward Petersburg, as Sheridan quickly learned through his spies. Unfortunately Early chose that moment to split his forces, sending Rodes and Gordon back to Martinsburg on a "wild goose chase" to tear up the rail yards and leaving only Ramseur's small division at Winchester.[20]

Winchester

On the morning of September 19 Sheridan made his move. His cavalry splashed across the Opequon at first light, driving back Ramseur's pickets, while his infantry filed through Berryville Canyon toward Winchester. Only the combination of a massive traffic jam in the narrow defile and Ramseur's dogged defense outside the town slowed the Federals long enough for Rodes and Gordon to return. After spending most of the morning positioning his men, Sheridan kicked off his offensive just before noon. Rodes held the center of Early's line with three brigades, keeping Battle's Alabama brigade in reserve in a ravine behind him. His sharpshooters, as always, screened his front. "We moved forward at a run to a piece of woods a few hundred yards in advance," said one, "when we ran into a strong line of battle of Yankees."[21]

Gordon's division, still arriving, filed into position on Rodes's left behind a small rise. He sent his "old reliable sharpshooters," who had been marching off to the left of the line as a flank guard, up on it to cover his front. Almost immediately they came running back in disorder, which drew some snickers from the rank and file. "What's up?" yelled one. "You'll soon see," replied the sharpshooter.[22]

The quick-thinking commander of the Thirty-First Georgia, Colonel John Lowe, could see what was happening from his mounted perch and ordered the brigade up on the high ground. There they found themselves literally eyeball to eyeball with the Yankees. "The entire brigade brought down their guns," said one soldier, "and a flame of fire flashed along its entire length; at the same time a dreadful yell arose that stampeded the enemy the length of our line." The Georgians drove the Yankees back to a skirt of woods but were outflanked in turn and driven back in confusion, disordering one of Rodes's brigades as well. With Ramseur under intense pressure on the right, the Confederate line began buckling on both ends, and it looked as though their entire position might collapse. Rodes and Gordon conducted a hurried conference on horseback and decided that a counterattack might allow enough time for an orderly withdrawal.[23]

As Colonel Tom Carter's artillery fired canister into the "long lines of splendid infantry advancing," Rodes brought up his only reserve: Battle's Alabama brigade, men who had served him fearlessly on every field since Seven Pines and never yet failed him. From his vantage point on horseback Rodes could see that as the Federals advanced a space opened between VI Corps, which was battling Ramseur, and XIX Corps, which was focused on Gordon. As Carter's artillery fire disordered their advance, he launched Battle's brigade straight into the advancing wall of blue. The ragged Alabama boys hit the Yankee line like a thunderbolt, shattering Colonel Warren Kiefer's brigade. Gordon Bradwell, a Georgian from Evans's brigade who had fallen in with Battle's men, described the fight: "These brave Alabamians rushed at the enemy like tigers, and for a time the two lines were so near each other that the paper of their cartridges flew into our faces. At one point to my left the lines came together, and I saw the ensign of one regiment snatch the colors out of the hands of a Federal soldier and drag them along on the ground, while he held his own standard aloft." Robert Park, commanding the brigade's right-hand company, described the result of this exchange: "The enemy soon ran precipitately before us, and officers and men were in the utmost confusion. We raised the well known 'rebel yell,' and continued our onward run, for we actually ran, at our greatest speed, after the disordered host in our front." The sharpshooters joined the line of battle as it came up, "and drove the yanks about half a mile."[24]

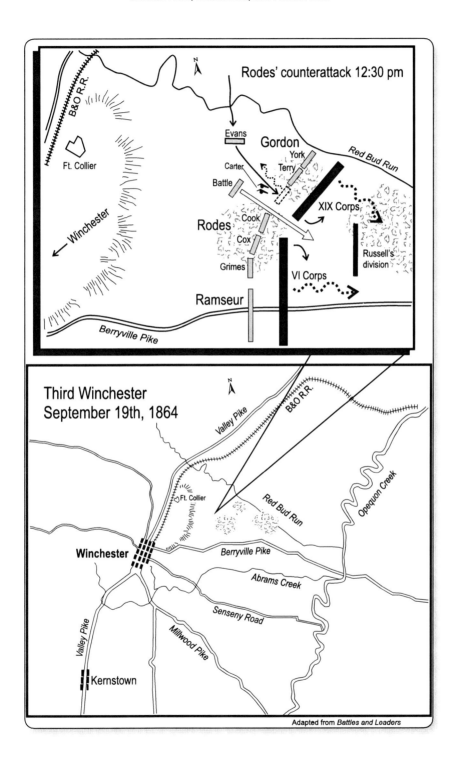

Rodes' counterattack 12:30 pm

Third Winchester
September 19th, 1864

Adapted from *Battles and Leaders*

Another Georgian, G. W. Nichols, a member of Gordon's division who had been caught between the lines, watched the battle. The Yankees, who "seemed resolute" at first, stopped at the top of a hill. He heard one of their officers shout, "the Rebs are flanking us on the left." He looked about and "could see our men swinging around them in excellent order ... their guns shining in the morning sun like silver." Nichols, who had been playing possum to escape capture, watched as Battle's men topped a hill "in full view of the retreating Yankees. And I have never seen such a deadly volley fired as those noble Alabamians fired at the retreating enemy," he said. "It was so terrible that it really looked sickening. It seemed that the first volley cut down half their line." About the same time a XIX Corps brigade commander looked to his left and saw to his horror "a line of butternut sweeping past our flank and into our rear."[25]

Rodes now ordered his whole division forward, joined by Gordon's reorganized men. The tall Virginian, mounted on his "splendid black mare," followed Cox's North Carolina brigade, moving it up on Battle's left. One of Cox's sharpshooters, Sergeant Marcus Herring, led his men in front of the brigade at the double-quick. Herring, like many others in the Corps of Sharpshooters, had come over with Colonel Brown from the First North Carolina, and up until a few minutes before had been marching along assuming this was just another Yankee chase. "Every one was in fine spirits when we were lined up on a high ridge overlooking a valley," he said, "but all of this jubilation stopped suddenly when the regiment halted and General Cox rode to the front and gave the sharp command: 'Sharpshooters, forward!'"[26]

Herring and his men flushed some Yankee skirmishers from a strip of woods and drove them back. As they reached an area about a hundred and fifty yards in front of the brigade, he heard Cox order the brigade up behind them. "The troops came on with a rush," remembered Herring. "We stopped, and they went for the blue line. At the same time the artillery came in on the run, took position, and gave them a taste of grape and canister. When the battle line passed, the sharpshooters were at liberty to join their regiments." The disorganized Union lines retreated before them as they moved through a skirt of woods, but the covering Yankee shell fire was brisk and accurate. "They had good range," remarked another soldier, "and every shell burst in our faces." Herring, who was on his way to rejoin his regiment, saw a group of senior officers, including Rodes, just behind them. The general was struggling to control his horse, a gift from the citizens of Lynchburg, amid the hail of shells. Seeing the Union line, he yelled "Charge them, boys! Charge them!" A moment later a shell burst over him. The major general slumped in his saddle, then fell headlong to the ground. Robert Rodes, hit behind the ear by a shell fragment, died a few minutes later.[27]

His men pressed on, but confusion developed over the succession of command, and the advance halted while it was straightened out. Meanwhile Sheridan, watching with General Horatio Wright from his headquarters on a nearby hill, could hardly believe his eyes. His battle of annihilation, begun only six hours before, was starting to look like a disastrous defeat. Little Phil threw in two fresh brigades from Brigadier General David Russell's division, who slugged it out with Rodes's men, neither side willing to give way. The Confederates pumped out volleys at three rounds a minute with machinelike precision, scything down their opponents—some of whom were armed with repeaters—but losing heavily themselves as they pushed the two Yankee brigades off the low rise they were defending. In this fluid battle the veteran butternuts had the advantage over the bookish maneuvering of their opponents. "They aimed better than our men," admitted a Federal officer, Captain John De Forest. "They covered themselves (in case of need) more effectively, they could move in a swarm, without much care for alignment and touch of elbows. In short, they fought more like redskins, or like hunters, than we. The result was that they lost far fewer men, though they were far inferior in numbers."[28]

A few minutes into the battle Russell, like Rodes, fell victim to a shell burst. Just as it looked as though even the two reserve brigades would not be enough to stop Battle's rampaging Alabamians, Brigadier General Emory Upton launched Russell's third brigade into the Confederate flank, scattering Cook's Georgians and pummeling Cox's Tarheels. Chastened, Rodes's men pulled back under cover of their artillery, and by one o'clock the attacks and counterattacks had settled down into a fitful firefight. "Victory appeared to be ours," observed a North Carolinian.[29]

Unfortunately for the weary soldiers in gray, the battle was far from over. George Crook's fresh VIII Corps moved up from its position near the Opequon, joining the battle against Gordon's division. By three o'clock and after a bloody fight Crook drove Gordon's men out of the woods. The cavalry battle was also going badly for the Confederates. Yankee cavalry had progressively driven back Early's hillbilly horse soldiers along the Valley Pike, and by mid-afternoon they were just outside the Collier Redoubt, a tumbledown old fort on the northern outskirts of Winchester. Jubal Early was running out of men. He pulled Wharton's division back from its role of stiffening his outnumbered horsemen and flung it into the infantry battle. Two of Wharton's brigades covered the gap between his cavalry and Gordon's flank, while the other, under Colonel George S. Patton,[*] remained on the Pike. Meanwhile Gordon, under intense pressure from Crook's VIII Corps, wheeled his division round to face north, at a right angle to Rodes

---

[*]   Grandfather and namesake of the WWII general.

and Ramseur, linking up with Wharton's men and refusing his flank—an extremely difficult maneuver under fire. Digging in their heels, Gordon's and Wharton's men put up "a vivid sheet of flame," and stopped the advancing Yankees with heavy casualties.[30]

Alfred Waud's sketch of Ricketts' division advancing
against Rodes's men outside Winchester. LC

On the firing line Gordon's Georgians and Louisianans had pinned down De Forest and his men, "though not a Rebel was visible." The Connecticut captain watched as one of his men, lying prone, took a shot "exactly through the top of his head," while another was wounded by a shot that struck just in front of him. "The only signs of battle," he said, "were long stretches of smoke from musketry, and graceful, rolling masses of smoke from the batteries." Even though they were taking cover as best they could, seventy of the 350 men of the 12th Connecticut fell in a few hours that afternoon, mostly from rifle fire. "It seemed impossible that the enemy could hit so many of us," he said, "unless they had some vantage spot from which to make out our exact distance and position. Probably every man of us occasionally glanced at the branches of the trees in our front with the expectation of discovering sharpshooters aloft there. But our adversaries were no doubt good shots, and besides they fired more continuously than we did. They must have had reserve ammunition at hand, while we were at a considerable distance from ours, and moreover the ground behind us was swept by hostile musketry."

Down to five rounds per man, De Forest's men stopped firing at their invisible opponents and awaited the command to charge.[31]

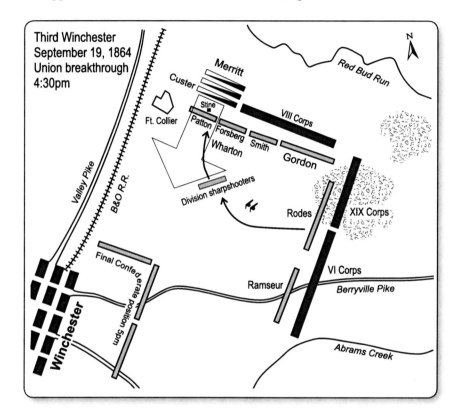

Gradually, under intense pressure, the Rebel line assumed the shape of an upside-down L, with Ramseur and Rodes's men on one leg and Gordon's and Wharton's on the other. At about five o'clock some seven thousand "splendidly equipped and admirably disciplined" Federal horsemen struck the Confederate left flank in a hell-for-leather charge. The Rebel cavalry collapsed, fleeing through the streets of Winchester and leaving Patton's brigade in a death struggle with the Yankee horsemen and a division of VIII Corps. With all his other units committed, Early called for Rodes's Division Sharpshooters. Sergeant Sam Collier, a Tarheel from the Second North Carolina, described what happened next: "Col. Brown ... carried us at a double-quick to where our cavalry were fighting both Yankee infantry and cavalry." Brown strung out his sharpshooters and tried to make a stand behind a stone fence to aid Patton's men, but Brigadier General George Custer's Michigan brigade slammed into them "like a thousand bricks." Lieutenant Jason Patton, commanding the Twelfth Alabama sharpshooters, took a bullet that shattered his arm. As he staggered back to the rear, he turned to Sergeant Oscar Whitaker and said, "Whitaker, they have got me at last. I must go—take charge of the boys, do the best you can and give the yanks Hell." Another ball struck Brown in the thigh, knocking him down. It smashed his silver watch and made an ugly wound, but did no permanent damage. A Federal horse soldier ordered him to the rear as a prisoner, but the colonel protested that he was too badly hurt to move. Artillery fire now began landing among them, disorganizing the bluecoats, and a moment later a Rebel counterattack swept over the fence. Brown then "mounted his horse, waved his hat to cheer his men, and with them was on the heels of the fleeing horsemen." At this point the Yankees were just about as "badly scattered" as their opponents. "The cavalry fell back behind the crest of the hill to reform," said Colonel James Kidd of the 6th Michigan, "for the infantry fire was exceedingly hot."[32]

Custer regrouped and awaited his chance. Just as the Southerners abandoned their fence line and began moving rearward, the Wolverines topped the hill at a gallop and "charged down upon them with a yell that could be heard above the din of battle." The sloping ground added to the momentum of their attack, and the effect was catastrophic: after firing a scattering of shots the Confederates broke, some running while others surrendered. Colonel Patton fell with a mortal wound while trying to rally them.[33]

Union cavalry charge at Winchester, Virginia. *Harper's Weekly*

"We fell back when every thing at this moment began to run, wagons, ambulances and every thing mixed up together," recalled Collier. "The whole face of the earth was literally alive with rebels running for their lives." Wharton's and Gordon's infantry divisions dissolved, and soon the entire left wing of the army was "whirling through Winchester" in disorder. The blue-jacketed horsemen hacked their way through the evaporating gray formations, capturing seven flags. Collier and the rest of the sharpshooters joined the rout: "I would run a while and stop and laugh at others and think what fools we were making for ourselves—then some shell would come tearing among us and every thing would start off again, I would be among them. I never ran so fast in all my life." Collier confessed in a letter that he had legged it all the way to Newtown, ten miles away, "and I can assure you I had company from Brig. Gen'l down to privates."[34]

Brigadier General Cullen Battle, who had taken over Rodes's division, tried to change front to deal with the masses of Yankee cavalry bearing down on his flank. His outnumbered infantrymen took position on a low rise just outside town and in some 1862 entrenchments. There, running short on ammunition, they could fall back no further. They were almost in the streets of Winchester, fighting under the very muzzles of their guns. Accounts are few, but Dodson Ramseur wrote that Rodes's division "came off in tolerable order," so Battle seems to have kept at least part of it together as it withdrew through town. Ramseur's division, first on the field, came off last and formed the rear guard. Old Jube had taken a beating, but had escaped with his army intact. He withdrew to Fisher's Hill, the traditional refuge for the Confederates.[35]

Fisher's Hill

Two days later, on September 21, Sheridan and Early again faced each other at Fisher's Hill, near Strasburg. Blocking the Valley Pike, Fisher's Hill rose from just past a small stream called Tumbling Run to a high ridge abutting the North Fork of the Shenandoah River. The position was extremely strong—"hills high and commanding, crowned with earthworks and artillery, separated by rugged ravines which were blocked up with slashed and fallen timber, every rod of hill and hollow well guarded by rifle pits and abattis and bayonets"—but after their losses at Winchester, the Confederates did not have enough men to hold it.[36]

As the Federals approached, Early's sharpshooters fell back slowly from Strasburg, skirmishing with the advancing bluecoats as they closed with his position. When Sheridan's men arrived they found that Old Jube's sharpshooters had staked out a claim on Flint Hill, a knoll about a mile from the pike that blocked both sight and access to the vulnerable left end of the Confederate line. Sheridan wanted the hill so that he would have an "unobstructed view" of Early's position, but the Rebels "evinced an unexpected determination to remain in possession of it."[37]

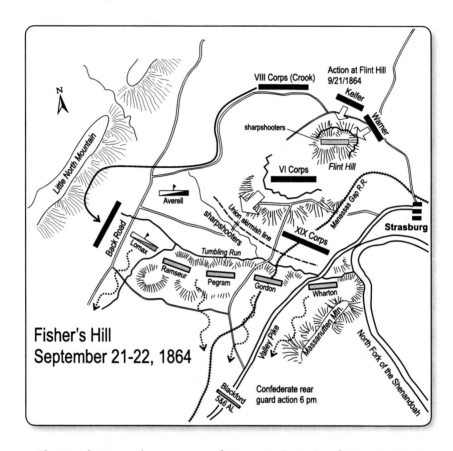

Fisher's Hill
September 21-22, 1864

The 139th Pennsylvania, part of Warner's brigade of Getty's division, drew the job of clearing the knoll. These men were veterans of the skirmish line and had been among the outfits that had tangled with Rodes's men at Fort Stevens. Their commander, Major Robert Munroe, led them forward to empty a houseful of sharpshooters, but soon ran into butternut riflemen dug into a line of rifle pits "on a prominent crest in front." The Rebels had set up their position for enfilading fire and dropped twenty men in five minutes, including Major Munroe, leaving the regiment "in great confusion" as it fell back. A second regiment, the 126th Ohio, came in support, but ran into the same "galling fire" that had stopped the Pennsylvanians. The ranks of the Buckeye Staters included a number of inexperienced conscripts, who made the mistake of halting to deliver a volley just after they left the protection of a skirt of woods. Then, "being much exposed and suffering terribly without the ability to inflict much loss on the enemy," they scurried rearward after losing four killed and seventeen wounded. At this point the Confederates apparently counterattacked, because a third regiment, the 6th Maryland, took credit for "driving the enemy to a line of works he had constructed of rails," likely "bull pens," or three-sided enclosures of rails with earth heaped up around them.[38]

Tiring of piecemeal attacks, General Getty brought up the rest of Warner's brigade and sent it up the hill with fixed bayonets, which decided the issue in short order: the Rebels abandoned the knoll, leaving four prisoners, and Sheridan had his view. Warner lost thirty-eight men in the attack, and the overall toll to the Federals for this little affair was eighty-six men killed and wounded. Other than the four prisoners, Confederate losses are unknown. "A ball cut my gun strap into," wrote one Georgia sharpshooter, "and struck me centrally on the left nipple, nearly knocking me down, but being too nearly spent to enter the skin or disable me. It being the first ball that ever hit me, I was pretty smartly scared but not enough to fail to do my duty." That night the swearing soldiers of VI Corps stumbled through the darkness to occupy the hill, and by daybreak the next morning, they had dug "a solid entrenchment, traced boldly on the front of Flint's Hill, curving gracefully to the rear as the ground fell away on our right, and overlooking a beautiful field sloping down to the brook. The rebels were in plain view before us, scarcely half a mile distant across the stream, occupying a long entrenchment similar to our own."[39]

The Federals began emplacing their artillery on the knoll, and Sheridan himself made an appearance, scanning the Rebel line with a telescope while muttering "I'll get a twist on 'em, d—n 'em!" He quickly made his plans. General Ricketts's division of VI Corps would advance from the knoll to make a noisy demonstration, while General George Crook and the two divisions of his VIII Corps made a flank march across the lower slopes of Little North Mountain, nearly three miles away. Meanwhile General William Averell's cavalry would picket Ricketts's right flank as if it were the end of the line. Sheridan also needed Ricketts to deal with the aggressive Confederate skirmishers and their supporting artillery. Although driven off Flint Hill, they continued to harass the Federals so effectively that General Horatio Wright conceded "they almost turned our right." Three VI Corps batteries added to the din with counter-battery fire as Ricketts's men stepped off toward the low ground around Tumbling Run, "firing not only on the enemy's batteries bearing upon Ricketts, but upon a battery farther to our right which was being used with much effect on Crook's advancing column." They found other targets, too, like the big tree across the way from which "puff after puff of smoke" arose. Captain Jacob Lamb, "a grey-haired Rhode Islander who commanded half a dozen ten-pound Parrotts," sent a rifled shell screaming through the branches with his first shot, and a few moments later "a dozen 'Johnnies' dropped in great haste to the ground and scampered up the hill." Covered by the guns, Ricketts and his men advanced in two lines to the run, "sweeping in grand display over the enemy's skirmishers, and finally halting at a very oblique angle to our line some distance in our front" in front of Rodes's division.[*] Wright then sent the two other divisions of VI Corps up "to within some 700 or 800 yards of the enemy's works" where he told to await orders to attack.[40]

Meanwhile Crook's five-thousand-man column laboriously worked its way around Old Jube's left flank. Although many noted seeing the column, including General Bryan Grimes, whose brigade held the left of the line, no one did anything about it. Unfortunately, Early's weakest units—his unreliable Valley cavalry, who had been dismounted for the occasion—held the far left flank. The sharpshooters, who would have been ideal for dealing with such a flanking force, were fully occupied with Ricketts, and the cavalry seems to have made no effort to scout or screen the ground in front of them. Therefore when Crook lit into them about 5 p.m., the troopers broke and fled almost immediately. At the same time both VI and XIX Corps attacked Early's front, and the Confederate position collapsed. The Rebel army once again dissolved into a rout, but Eugene Blackford cobbled together a scratch force made up of sharpshooters and two Alabama regiments from Battle's brigade. He managed to form enough of a rear guard to keep the Yankee cavalry at bay and allow Early's little army to escape southward. Thus covered, Early retreated to Waynesboro to lick his wounds while Sheridan devastated the Valley. The Union commander considered the matter to be at an end. Old Jubilee and his army had been whipped beyond redemption.[41]

---

[*]   Following Rodes's death at Winchester, Dodson Ramseur took command of his division, and turned his division over to one of his brigade commanders, Brigadier General John Pegram.

17

Cedar Creek

"It must be confessed that we bought our victory at a dear rate."

Despite having been badly whipped, Old Jube was not ready to concede the Shenandoah to the Yankees. Lee returned Kershaw's division to the Valley, and after sorting out his army, Early trailed Sheridan northward to his camp near Strasburg, Virginia. On October 13 he picked a fight with some of George Crook's men at nearby Hupp's Hill and routed them. Early then pulled back to Fisher's Hill, hoping Sheridan would either attack him there or give him an opening to strike. Little Phil did neither, leaving Early with few options in this devastated country. With the weather worsening he would have to either retreat or attack an army nearly three times his size in a strong position that had just badly beaten him twice in the past month.

After three days of pondering his options Early sent John Gordon and the Second Corps on a perilous night march past Massanutten Mountain around the Union flank. Kershaw's division was slated to attack the Federals head-on across Cedar Creek, while Wharton's division and the artillery advanced up the Valley Pike. Kershaw's task was in many ways the most difficult. In the preceding week Sheridan's men had transformed the line along Cedar Creek, according to one South Carolinian, into "the most completely fortified position by nature, as well as by hand, of any line occupied during the war." Kershaw's men began marching just after midnight on October 19, under strict orders to make no noise. The columns of gray and butternut got within sight of the Yankee campfires without being detected, then silently filed into position. "When near the river [Cedar Creek] the brigade was halted," wrote a soldier from Connor's (formerly Kershaw's) brigade, "and scouting parties sent ahead to see how the land lay." The division's leading unit, Colonel James P. Simms's 520-man Georgia brigade, deployed and began moving forward "steadily and firmly" about 4:30 a.m., ignoring the pickets firing into their shadowy line, until they closed with the Federal position. They crested the barricades in a sudden rush. "No daybreak rush of moccasined Shawnees or Wayandots was ever more dexterous and triumphant than this charge," admitted one New England officer in its path.[1]

Crook's Federals struggle to resist Gordon's men at Cedar Creek. *B&L*

"The enemy made a stubborn resistance," recalled Simms. "Some of them were shot down while firing upon our men at the distance of a few feet." Accompanying the Georgians was the Third South Carolina Battalion which, "having some months before been organized into brigade sharpshooters ... preceded the [Connor's] brigade and was to charge the fords and capture the pickets." While the rest of the division waited silently in the darkness, "a charge was made—a flash, a report or two, and the enemy's outpost at this point was ours." South Carolinian Jim Milling agreed that "we surprised completely the first line of works," while conceding that there were "some Georgians ... in front." The sharpshooters caught many of the Yankees still undressed and rousted them from their formidable entrenchments with a loss of only two men. Perhaps it was one of these unfortunates who passed Captain Augustus Dickert on a litter. "Nothing but a low, deep groan was heard," he remembered, "which told too plainly that his last battle had been fought."[2]

Connor's South Carolinians crossed Cedar Creek and formed a line of battle beside Simms's men, the sharpshooters strung out in front as skirmishers. A hundred yards away the second line of Federal entrenchments faced them at "a considerable elevation." Milling and his comrades began to draw fire, at which point "We lay down to let the brigade come up, they advancing in as pretty a line as if on drill." As the brigade approached, the sharpshooters joined them, and together they assaulted the breastworks, scattering the defenders "like chaff before the wind." The Confederates took the Federal camp just beyond, including nearly the entire 5th New

York Heavy Artillery—more than three hundred gunners fighting as infantry—and seven guns.[3]

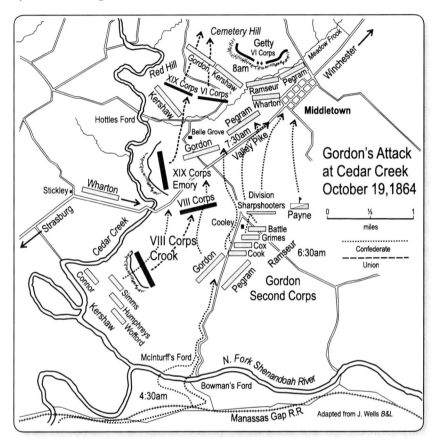

At almost the same time John Gordon, who had successfully completed his daring night march around the Union flank, launched his own attack on the Federal left with Second Corps. The ragged Southerners scored a stunning surprise, and in the foggy half-light quickly overran and dispersed the Union VIII Corps, then took on the XIX Corps. Union captain John De Forest, now a staff officer, had a panoramic view of the battle. As he watched, his old brigade was driven out of a patch of woods onto a hill, where they were "severely raked" by Confederate fire: "A semicircle of dropping musketry converged on the new position, for Early's reserve under Wharton had just got within range, and its skirmishers were raking us from the south. Our men were apparently bewildered, and did not know which way to face, and could not be brought to fire." The brigade withdrew north in some confusion, and once again De Forest marveled at the Confederates' invisibility: "We were being peppered and demoralized and beaten (like Braddock's and St. Clair's regulars) by an undiscoverable enemy." The attack

on XIX Corps drew the Confederates west of the Valley Pike, which led
from Strasburg through Middletown to Winchester, and thus from control
of the routes of advance and retreat. Young Major General Dodson Ramseur,
now commanding Rodes's division, sent his Division Sharpshooters north
to cover the corps' right flank and occupy Middletown. Because of the presence of the formidable Union cavalry north of the town and the paucity of
Confederate horsemen on the field, a strong flank guard was an absolute
necessity.[4]

By mid-morning Old Jube's veterans had whipped XIX Corps also, driving it past Belle Grove and off Red Hill. Meanwhile VI Corps, which had not
yet been engaged, had formed up and taken a position on the high ground
behind Belle Grove Mansion, where it began a disjointed fight with Early's
Confederates in the mist. In spite of fierce resistance the butternut fighters
drove them back as well. The focus of the battle now shifted to Cemetery Hill,
a low rise just west of Middletown, where Major General George Getty's VI
Corps division held a semicircular position near the summit. The Confederates, disorganized by their rapid advance and hampered by poor visibility
on the fog-shrouded battlefield, launched a series of piecemeal attacks on
Getty's position. After two attacks were beaten back with heavy casualties,
Early launched a fresh brigade—Brigadier General Bryan Grimes's North
Carolina brigade of Ramseur's (formerly Rodes's) division—at the hill.

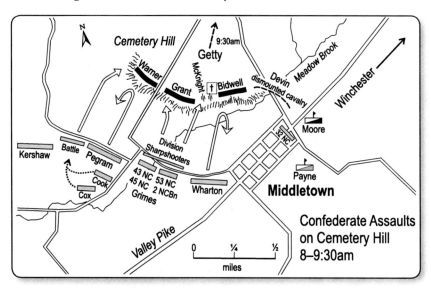

During the engagement two brigades of Federal cavalry had fortuitously
showed up, a small one under Colonel Alpheus Moore and a much stronger
one under Brigadier General Thomas Devin. While Moore's men picketed
the road out of Middletown, Devin's troopers dismounted to cover Getty's
left flank (nearest the town) with their fast-firing Spencers. On the Confed-

erate side, the combination of Ramseur's sharpshooters and Colonel William Payne's small cavalry brigade had cleared Middletown but were unable to push beyond it because of the Federal cavalry. The fog still lay so thickly that it hid the positions of both attacker and defender. From the pike Grimes swung left toward Cemetery Hill, sending the Thirty-second North Carolina up to Middletown and getting the Division Sharpshooters in return. As the brigade approached the hill it became separated into two parts. The Forty-third and Forty-fifth North Carolina regiments drifted left in the fog, while the Fifty-third North Carolina and the Second North Carolina battalion aimed straight up the hill toward the cemetery.

Thus Grimes's main assault force—the Fifty-third regiment and Second battalion, plus the Division Sharpshooters—attacked directly into the cemetery with the sharpshooters leading in open formation and the tough Tarheel infantry just behind. The sharpshooters did not stop to wait for the line to catch up. "I could not believe they were actually going to close with us," said one of the gunners of Captain James McKnight's battery, "until the men on the remaining gun of the left section abandoned it and retreated toward the old graveyard wall. Their front line was not in order, but there was an officer leading them, and I distinctly heard him shout: 'Rally on the Battery! Rally on the Battery!'" The officer in question may have been Colonel Hamilton Brown, the commander of Ramseur's sharpshooters. Union gunners, who realized "there was no stopping them," managed to send off a last shot of double canister, but "as the Rebel veterans understood this kind of business they 'opened out' so that the charge did not hit any of them." In a moment the Southerners were among them, "amid smoke, fog, wreck, yells, clash and confusion … man to man, hand to hand, with bayonet and musket butt on their side and revolvers, rammers, and hand spikes on ours!" A vicious close-quarters fight raged for several long minutes before a counterattack by the Vermonters drove the Rebels out. The assault by the brigade's other two regiments also ended in failure, as did a subsequent attack by Wharton's division.[5]

The Confederates now brought up Colonel Tom Carter's artillery and blasted the hill, driving the Yankee infantry to ground. Most of the ordnance went high, however, and Getty's men held their position. Finally Battle's Alabama brigade, having broken through the line of the XIX Corps on Red Hill, launched an attack on the southeastern end of Cemetery Hill. Joined by two other brigades of Ramseur's division, they finally convinced the stubborn defenders to quit the hill. Getty, ever the consummate professional, retreated north in good order, and the exhausted Southerners did not molest him. Early then halted—a decision that would forever haunt him—to rest and reorganize his scattered and winded army, then slowly trailed the Federals to a position about a mile north of Middletown. Meanwhile Phil Sheridan, who had been absent at Winchester, arrived on the field and began reinvigorating his beaten force. Around one o'clock General John Gordon advanced toward the Union line, half-hidden in the woods. Although accounts are scarce, Gordon seems to have used his sharpshooters to feel out Sheridan's position. What he found—a revitalized and reorganized Yankee army—was not encouraging, and he quickly withdrew under cover of his artillery. Early pulled back his line and hunkered down just north of Middletown.

Confederates in the ranks, however, considered the day to have been won, and fairly so. They had marched all night, fought all morning, and had not eaten since the day before. Some plundered the rich Yankee camps while others slept. One group relaxing that afternoon was the Third South Carolina battalion of sharpshooters, who had been sent out as a picket "in a cornfield several hundred yards in our front." The men lounged behind a stone fence in the cornfield, "without a dream of the enemy ever being able to rally and make an advance." Phil Sheridan, having rallied his army and prepared a counterstroke, would soon destroy their repose. At 4:30 p.m. he attacked, catching them unawares. The advancing Yankees quickly overran the sharpshooters' position, capturing most of the battalion and killing its commander, Captain Benjamin Whitener. Lieutenant U. B. Whites, who commanded one of the companies, got away with a handful of men and rallied them behind the brigade. The men in the main line, also behind a stone fence, barely had time to pick up their rifles before the Federals were upon them. Nevertheless, they repulsed the first assault. The division commander, General Joseph Kershaw, arrived and sent Whites and his band hustling off to cover the left flank, where John Gordon's thinly spread division was already starting to waver. "When I arrived at the point designated," related the unfortunate officer, "to my horror I found the place literally alive with Yankees. I had double-quicked right into the midst of the 'blue bellies.'" A Northern voice from the woods demanded, "Surrender!" Whites and his men headed rearward with the rest of the battalion. Jim Milling and a few other men escaped.[6]

Next in line was Ramseur's division, which held the Confederate center near Miller's Mill. The terrain here, light woods broken up by farmsteads with stone walls, was excellent for defense. Ramseur's sharpshooters were as usual well forward, and—unlike the South Carolinians—they were ready. Supported by Carter's artillery, their accurate rifle fire began to extract a heavy toll on the advancing bluecoats. Their old enemies, the veterans of the VI Corps, gradually pushed the sharpshooters back, only to run up against the formidable Confederate main line. Despite a sharp jog in the line where it crossed the Valley Pike, the sharpshooters, backed by Grimes's brigade, prevented the Federals from outflanking it. Early's men disastrously repulsed the first Union attack, scything down their opponents, knocking down their colors, and sending them streaming rearward in disorder. A spontaneous cheer sounded, but hardly had it died when Early's left flank began to collapse. Gordon's division disintegrated, followed shortly afterward by part of Kershaw's.

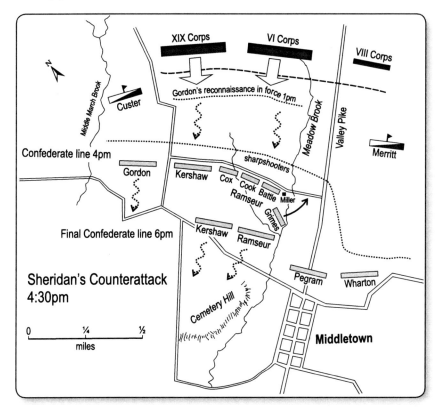

By late afternoon the Southern line, pressed front and flank, was near breaking. As more and more fugitives materialized from the left, they disordered the regiments of Kershaw's and Ramseur's divisions which still held the VI Corps at bay. Seeing this, and in spite of the best efforts of their officers, some of their men began to leak rearward also. General Dodson Ramseur's magnetic personal leadership held them together for a time. Heedless of danger, he galloped from one threatened point to another, encouraging his men, whacking laggards, and keeping the remaining men in line by the sheer force of his personality. If they could hold until dark on this short fall day, they might yet make an orderly retreat. The wavering gray line retreated, stopped, then retreated again, steadily hemorrhaging men but still retaining its cohesion. As one of the few men on horseback, Ramseur attracted a storm of bullets. Colonel Brown and his sharpshooters, "under the immediate command of General Ramseur," anchored the defense until a bullet hit the young general, penetrating both lungs. With Ramseur gone, even the grizzled veterans of Stonewall Jackson's famed Second Corps began to lose heart. Nevertheless a few stalwarts, including the sharpshooters, Battle's Alabamians, Grimes's Tarheels, and some of Kershaw's Mississippians, continued to hold out.[7]

Twenty-seven-year-old Major General Stephen Dodson Ramseur was mortally wounded near dusk on October 19, 1864. Captured that evening, he died the next morning at Belle Grove mansion. *B&L*

General George Custer's cavalry delivered the final blow at dusk, slamming into the disintegrating Confederate left and scattering the remnants of Kershaw's division, which in turn swept away Ramseur's men in their frantic attempts to escape. The Rebel army fell apart, each man quitting the field on his own. Yankee cavalry hammered the flanks, hacking at fugitives. A broken bridge on the outskirts of Strasburg completed the Southern misfortunes, causing them to lose most of their trains and artillery. Thus ended one of the most remarkable battles ever fought on American soil. "It must be confessed," wrote Captain De Forest, "that we bought our victory at a dear rate." He pointed out that the Federals had lost four thousand men killed and wounded to eighteen hundred for the Confederates, "although we were fully double their number, and presumably used twice as many cartridges." He readily admitted that "they were obviously the best shots, and their open-order style of fighting was an economical one. Moreover, when they retreated, they went in a swarm and at full speed, thus presenting a poor mark for musketry. We, on the contrary, sought to retire in regular order, and suffered heavily for it."[8]

Although Cedar Creek broke Confederate power in the Shenandoah, most of Old Jube's men escaped to the hills to avoid the dreaded Yankee prison camps. The amazingly resilient Army of the Valley reformed and again dogged Sheridan's footsteps, preventing him from transferring the bulk of his army back to Petersburg. The remaining sharpshooters would continue their scouting, screening, and skirmishing duties for the rest of the fall.

Repercussions followed the disastrous battle. Determined to both restore discipline to his defeated army and find scapegoats for its misfortunes, Jubal Early worked his courts-martial overtime. "Charges will be preferred," he snarled, "especially against officers." One of those caught in the vortex of blame was Eugene Blackford, who was charged with alleged misconduct before the enemy. After the battle of Fisher's Hill Blackford had gone home briefly for further treatment on his leg, which continued to trouble him. He returned just before Cedar Creek with little improvement, unable to walk any distance. Yet, characteristically, he had refused to stay in camp during the battle, instead joining the march around the Union flank with Gordon's men. Following standing orders he had dismounted when the attack began, but the brigade's advance had been so rapid that he was unable to keep pace. Although he eventually rejoined his regiment north of Middletown, Blackford was caught up in the army's general collapse and spent the night on the field evading Yankee patrols. In truth the court-martial owed more to personal animus against him by other officers in the regiment (some of whom stood to be promoted in his stead) than to any lack of courage on Blackford's part. The charges were brought by Lieutenant Colonel Edwin Hobson, acting commander of the Fifth Alabama and of Battle's brigade, whom Blackford characterized as "a bitter personal enemy." With Hobson in line for promotion to colonel after the medical retirement of the regiment's commander, the two senior captains, Thomas Riley and Thad Belcher, stood to be promoted to lieutenant colonel and major respectively. Blackford's friend and patron, Robert Rodes, was dead, and the new division commander, North Carolinian Bryan Grimes, believed that "the only salvation for this army will be to inflict severe punishment on all who fail to discharge their duty." Given their commander's vengeful mood, the court-martial no doubt felt bound to render strict justice, and on November 4 it convicted Blackford of misconduct and sentenced him to be dismissed from the service.[9]

Following the conviction a round of petitions, letters, and appeals went all the way to President Jefferson Davis. The men of Battle's brigade petitioned on Blackford's behalf in January 1865 (by which time the brigade was back at Petersburg), and the document is a valuable snapshot of the unit at that time. That month's inspection report gave the present-for-duty strength of Battle's brigade as 667 men, and in the petition Sergeant Major Shelby Chadwick carefully noted the strength of the Fifth Alabama as 166 men. Yet the brigade sharpshooters numbered 145 men—nearly a quarter of those present, showing their continuing importance to the Confederate command.[10]

The Shenandoah campaign of 1864 and the battles of Winchester, Fisher's Hill, and Cedar Creek (as well as many of the minor battles and skirmishes in between) have been covered in more detail than previous battles because they give a good picture of the Southern sharpshooters in action and the differences in the way that they fought as compared to the line of battle. Indeed the 1864 Valley campaign, like Stonewall Jackson's in 1862, stands out for its exceptional hard marching and rapid maneuvering. In such a campaign the sharpshooters performed many roles, exacerbating the problem of assessing exactly what they did.

At Winchester sharpshooters served as flank guards for marching columns (since no cavalry was available for the job) and then went forward to cover the division's deployment and develop the enemy position. When the line of battle advanced, the sharpshooters rejoined their regiments, but later in the battle they were pulled out again and sent to the left flank as a demi-brigade in a forlorn attempt to stop the onrushing Union cavalry. At Fisher's Hill the sharpshooters attempted to screen Early's line, particularly his left flank, giving Sheridan's men a very hard time at Flint's Hill. Even when driven off the hill, they continued to contest the flank until swept away by Ricketts's men. The unaccountable failure of both Early and Ramseur to react to Crook's flanking column, and the utter rout of Early's cavalry, led to disaster.

The battle of Cedar Creek shows the mature evolution of the sharpshooters, particularly those of Rodes's division, in their various roles. Unfortunately the man who commanded the division that day, General Dodson Ramseur, did not survive to write a report. The man who did describe the action, General Bryan Grimes, commanded a brigade and thus did not personally see much of what happened. Ramseur initially used the sharpshooters to screen the division's front and flank. Grimes in his report noted that "Major-General Ramseur had skirmishers thrown to the front and to the right, driving the sharpshooters of the enemy from Middletown," but given the way the division sharpshooters had been used all summer, it seems highly unlikely that Ramseur (who had previously used his own sharpshooters quite effectively) would suddenly have reverted to the old system. Grimes, or whoever transcribed the report, may also have inadvertently switched nouns when writing, having meant to say that Ramseur "had *sharpshooters* thrown to the front ... driving the *skirmishers* of the enemy from Middletown." No Confederate accounts early in the battle mention sniper fire coming from Middletown, although the Confederates were rightly worried about Federal cavalry on their flank.[11]

Between that point and the time Getty made his stand on Cemetery Hill, the sharpshooters drop from the account. Ramseur's division became separated during its rapid advance that morning, with Cook and Cox's brigades attacking straight ahead with Gordon's men, while Battle and Grimes angled north, ending up on the Pike just south of Middletown. Battle then attacked west with Pegram's division, eventually swinging north and outflanking Getty on Cemetery Hill, while Grimes drew the task of assaulting Getty frontally. And yet Grimes detached a regiment to cover Middletown, a move that reduced his fighting strength by twenty percent—even though Ramseur's "skirmishers" had already cleared the area and Payne's cavalry brigade was also in the town. Why? The most likely explanation is that Ramseur had assigned the Division Sharpshooters (who probably numbered about five hundred men at this point) to cover his flank, then gave them to Grimes for the assault on Getty's position. For this to happen, however, Grimes would have had to replace them with one of his regiments, but this would still have given him a net increase in strength. Union accounts describe Grimes's men going up the hill in two lines, the sharpshooters in front and his infantry just behind them. The "skirmishers," still in their open order, did not halt but instead closed with the artillery in a hand-to-hand fight, marking the use of the sharpshooters as assault troops. It also helps to explain why the assault was so successful when it was supposedly made only with one regiment and a battalion of infantry.

There is still one more problem to consider, however. The man who wrote the "eyewitness" account of the storming of Cemetery Hill, Augustus Buell, was almost certainly not there. In fact, there is no evidence that he ever personally participated in any of the actions he describes in his 1890 book *The Cannoneer*, or that he ever served in the army at all. After the war Buell became a writer of popular histories in which he liberally mixed fact and fiction. His account is used here without mentioning Buell by name, because most of the incidents in his book are accurate insofar as they can be verified from other sources. Historian Robert K. Krick suggests that Buell might have begun the project as a unit history and interviewed surviving gunners, but was unable to resist injecting himself into the story. Like the sharpshooters, no official source mentions McKnight's battery being on Cemetery Hill, but author Theodore Mahr was able to independently confirm it to his satisfaction. In addition to the fact that it closely fits the emerging tactical doctrine, one more piece of evidence shows that the sharpshooters led the assault. After the war Colonel Hamilton Brown wrote the history of his regiment, the First North Carolina, but also included some information about his service as commander of Rodes's sharpshooters. Brown, a man not given to exaggeration, mentions "the sharpshooters capturing twelve pieces of artillery before the main body arrived" at Cedar Creek. Given that the sharpshooters stayed on the division's flank near Middletown, this would preclude their participation in any of the other artillery captures except on Cemetery Hill. Though is somewhat speculative, this reconstruction fits both the available evidence and the way Confederate commanders used the sharpshooters.[12]

The sharpshooters' performance in smaller battles like Charles Town and
Fort Stevens also shows their versatility. Robert Rodes seems to have perfected the tactical use of the sharpshooters at the North Anna, resulting in a
system that was about as close as anyone in the Civil War came to the open
order of the late-nineteenth century. Rodes's technique was to establish a
thick, active skirmish line with his four battalions of division sharpshooters,
first under Eugene Blackford and later under Hamilton Brown. These expert
marksmen made effective use of cover and concealment and were capable of
doing most of the work of a line of battle. However, given the slow rate of fire
for muzzle-loading arms, they could not match the concentrated firepower
of men standing elbow to elbow. It is interesting to speculate, however, what
Rodes might have come up with if he had had access to significant numbers
of Sharps, Spencers, or Henry rifles and plenty of ammunition. Nevertheless
the line of battle was loosening up, at least on the Confederate side, and
Captain De Forest's comments, quoted above, are illuminating. He saw his
opponents fighting as "a swarm" without the need for a formal alignment,
using the ground to reduce their own casualties and their marksmanship
to increase those of their opponents. A Federal staff officer remarked that
he had been in two big battles "yet I had *scarcely seen a Rebel* save killed,
wounded, or prisoners! I remember even line officers, who were at the battle
of Chancellorsville, said: 'Why, we never saw any Rebels where we were;
only smoke and bushes, and lots of our men tumbling about.'" Years later
Berry Benson tried to describe what it had been like on the Southern line of
battle, and his description, which follows, fleshes out that of De Forest's.[13]

> A battlefield is not a drillroom, nor is battle an occasion for drill,
> and there is the merest semblance of order maintained. I say
> *semblance* of order, for there is an undercurrent of order in tried
> troops that surpasses that of the drillroom;—it is that order that
> springs from the confidence comrades have in each other, from
> the knowledge that these messmates of yours, whether they stand
> or lie upon the ground, close together or scattered apart, in front
> of you three paces, or in rear of you six, in the open or behind a
> tree or a rock,—that these, though they do not "touch elbows to
> the right," are nevertheless keeping dressed upon the colors in
> some rough fashion, and that the line will not move forward and
> leave them there, nor will they move back and leave the line.
>
> A battle is entered into, mostly, in as good order and with as
> close a drill front as the nature of the ground will permit, but at
> the first "pop! pop!" of the rifles there comes a sudden loosening
> of the ranks, a freeing of selves from the impediment of contact,
> and every man goes to fighting on his own hook; firing as, and
> when he likes, and reloading as fast as he fires. He takes shelter

wherever he can find it, so he does not get too far away from
his Co., and his officers will call his attention to this should he
move too far. He may stand up, he may kneel down, he may lie
down, it is all right;—tho' mostly the men keep standing, except
when silent under fire—then they lie down. And it is not officers
alone who give orders, the command to charge may come from
a private in the line whose quick eye sees the opportunity, and
whose order brooks then no delay. Springing forward, he shouts
"charge, boys, charge!" The line catches his enthusiasm, answers
with yells and follows him in the charge. Generally it is a wild
and spontaneous cry from many throats along the line, readily
evoked by the least sign of wavering in the enemy. A battle is too
busy a time, and too absorbing, to admit of a great deal of talk,
still you will hear such remarks and questions as "How many
cartridges you got?"—"My gun's getting mighty dirty."—"What's
become of Jones?"—"Looky here, Butler, mind how you shoot;
that ball didn't miss my head two inches." "Just keep cool, will
you; I've got better sense than to shoot anybody." "Well, I don't
like your standing so close behind me, nohow." —"I say, look
at Lieut. Dyson behind that tree."—"Purty rough fight; ain't it
Cap'n?" "Cap'n, don't you think we better move up a little, just
along that knoll?"—all this mixed and mingled with fearful
yells, and maybe curses too, at the enemy. And a charge looks
just as disorderly. With a burst of yells, a long, wavering, loose
jointed line sweeps rapidly forward.[14]

By 1864 the Confederate line of battle had loosened considerably. *B&L*

In other words, by 1864 (at least in some units) the line of battle looked a
lot like the skirmish line, except for the intervals. As mentioned previously,
Sergeant Benson had been captured behind enemy lines at Spotsylvania,
narrowly escaped being shot as a spy, and sent to the Union lockup at Point

Lookout, Maryland. Once there he had escaped but had been recaptured, and was then forwarded to the infamous Yankee prison camp at Elmira, New York. Never one to give up, Benson tunneled out of Elmira with a few other fearless souls and made good his escape, walking all the way back to Virginia where after many adventures he finally made contact with Confederate cavalry pickets in the Shenandoah on October 27.

Before returning to Petersburg it is worthwhile to compare casualties on the skirmish line versus those on the line of battle. The most frequent battle scenario was when large numbers of men concentrated and shot it out at close range. By 1864 this typically occurred when one side or the other assaulted a strongly entrenched position. Winchester, however, was an exception. Not since Antietam had the two sides slugged it out so bloodily in the open, and the casualty figures for Rodes's division (686 men killed or wounded, including Rodes himself) reflect this. One soldier observed the deadly effect of this close-range marksmanship, watching Battle's Alabamians "cut down half their line" with a single volley. A Federal soldier graphically described the aftermath of the battle of Winchester: "The two lines of battle must have stood for some time, steadily firing at each other. Between two thickets, probably twenty rods apart, there was a row of blue clad dead lying close together, and fairly touching each other; and only a few yards in front of them a similar windrow of gray clad dead, lying as closely and straightly aligned as were their opponents of a few hours before."[15]

Casualties on that scale simply did not happen on the skirmish line, in part because the men stayed behind cover, but also because they simply could not load and fire their muzzle-loaders fast enough to cause the same losses. Thus the battles outside Fort Stevens cost about five hundred men on each side—not trivial, but certainly not on the same level as the casualties at Winchester, where Battle's brigade suffered about 40 percent casualties. One of the bigger skirmish fights of the war was at Charles Town, when Rodes's Division Sharpshooters tangled with the Vermont brigade. Although the amount of ammunition fired off by both sides was astounding by Civil War standards—more than 116,000 rounds—much of it went wide of the mark. Once again the casualties, about five hundred for both sides, were significant but did not compare with those of major battles where large bodies of troops in close order faced each other.

(Top row) Major Eugene Blackford, Fifth Alabama (l) and his patron and mentor Major General Robert Rodes (r). Blackford organized the first sharpshooter battalion in the Army of Northern Virginia in January, 1863. Rodes was killed at Winchester on September 19, 1864.

(Bottom row) Private Ben Powell (l) Co. A, McGowan's Sharpshooters. Powell is a strong candidate for the shooting Union major general John Sedgwick at Spotsylvania on May 9, 1864. (*courtesy John Everett*). Captain Wiliam Dunlop (r). Co. B, Twelfth South Carolina. Commanded McGowan's sharpshooters 1864-65.

(Top row) Sergeant Marion Hill Fitzpatrick (l) Company K, Forty-fifth Georgia. Served with the sharpshooters of Thomas's brigade, Wilcox's division. Later appointed sergeant major, he was wounded on April 2, 1865 and died on April 6. *Courtesy Marion Hodges.* Sergeant Berry Benson (r). Co. A, McGowan's Sharpshooters. Benson was captured on a scout at Spotsylvania in May, 1864 and sent to Elmira prison in New York. He escaped and returned to his regiment, serving until the end of the war.

(Bottom row) Brothers Lewis (r) and James Branscomb (l), both of Company D, Third Alabama, served with Blackford's sharpshooters. Lewis was killed at Harris Farm, May 19, 1864; James at Harper's Ferry on July 4, 1864. *Both courtesy Frank Chappell*

(Top row) Colonel Hamilton A. Brown (l) and Captain Thomas Boone (r) both First North Carolina. Brown commanded the First North Carolina until most of his regiment was killed or captured at Spotsylvania on May 12, 1864. In August 1864 he took over command of Rodes's Division Sharpshooters, a post he held until his capture at Ft. Stedman on March 25, 1865. Boone also escaped and joined Rodes's Division Sharpshooters, as did many of the surviving officers and senior NCO's of the First North Carolina.

(Bottom row) Major Edwin A. Osborne (l). Fourth North Carolina. Osborne commanded the sharpshooters of Ramseur's brigade at the Wilderness. Later promoted to Colonel. Captain William E. Stitt (r) Company B, Forty-third North Carolina. Stitt commanded the sharpshooters of Grimes's brigade, Rodes division.

(Top row) Captain Alexander Beattie (l), 3rd Vermont, commanded the sharpshooters of Getty's division at Petersburg and Ft. Stevens, and Major Aldace Walker (r), 11th Vermont, who thought the skirmish line was "the favorite position of the experienced soldier." (both courtesy *Vermont Historical Society*)

(Bottom row) Colonel Samuel Carroll (l), 8th Ohio, LC. Captain Jerry Brown (r), 148th Pennsylvania, led a daring raid on Confederate lines on October 27, 1864.

Flamboyant self-promoting inventor and businessman Hiram Berdan organized the 1st United States Sharpshooters in 1861 and commanded them until 1863 when he left the army. Although his sharpshooters performed well, Colonel Berdan's field leadership left much to be desired. LC

Major General John Sedgwick was fatally hit by a Confederate sharpshooter on May 9th, 1864 shortly after saying, "They couldn't hit an elephant at this distance." LC

Lieutenant Colonel Homer Stoughton, 2nd U.S.Sharpshooters. Stoughton commanded the 2nd U.S.S.S. at Gettysburg and in the 1864 Overland campaign. Wounded at Spotsylvania on May 9, he returned to the regiment at Petersburg on June 21st only to be captured. LC

Brigadier General Napoleon McLaughlen was captured in Fort Stedman by Confederate sharpshooter Lieutenant Billy Gwyn of the Fourth Georgia on the morning of March 25, 1865.

The interior of Fort Stevens, August, 1865. LC

Fraises protecting Union Ft. Sedgwick, near Petersburg. LC

Two French Zouaves in the Crimea, 1853. These colorful soldiers invented modern infantry tactics. LC

Berry Benson's unsurrendered .577 caliber Enfield, a short
P60 "two-band" model favored by the sharpshooters.
Augusta Museum of History

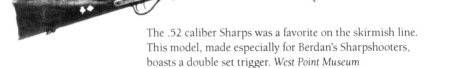

Each sharpshooter battalion got one or two of the deadly
.451 caliber Whitworth rifles. *West Point Museum*

The .52 caliber Sharps was a favorite on the skirmish line.
This model, made especially for Berdan's Sharpshooters,
boasts a double set trigger. *West Point Museum*

This heavy Morgan James target rifle is typical of those
used by Union sharpshooters. *West Point Museum*

Sharpshooter's badge worn by Henry A. Wise,
Second Maryland Battalion, Archer's brigade. A
red quatrefoil on a black background, it is the only
example of sharpshooter's distinctive insignia to
survive. *Dean Nelson/Maryland Historical Society*

The interior of Fort Stedman, taken after the war. LC
General John Gordon (inset) led the Confederate assault on March 25, 1865.

An advanced picket post
at Petersburg, April 1865.
LC

The Confederates
protected their works
at Petersburg with
these formidable
chevaux-de-frise. LC

18

Petersburg

"They done the thing up brown and deserve credit for it."

While Jubal Early and his hard-marching Army of the Valley had been conducting one of the most mobile campaigns of the war, the rest of the Army of Northern Virginia remained tied down at Petersburg in a war of position that presaged the trench warfare fifty years hence. By summer 1864 the troops no longer considered it unmanly to fight from behind cover. They had learned to set up hasty breastworks whenever they halted on the battlefield and to rapidly improve them to the point of being virtually impregnable. "The great feature of this campaign," observed a Union staff officer, "is the extraordinary use made of earthworks." He reckoned "it is a rule that, when the Rebels halt, the first day gives them a good rifle pit; the second, a regular infantry parapet with artillery in position; and the third a parapet with an abatis in front and entrenched batteries behind. Sometimes they put this three days' work into the first twenty-four hours." Assaults against these fortified positions became increasingly bloody, and both sides became wary of attempting them.[1]

After the initial Federal attempt to take Petersburg failed in June, both sides quickly dug themselves into increasingly formidable defensive positions, protected first by ditches and abatis, then by more elaborate obstacles like *fraises* and *chevaux-de-frise*. On the firing line the soldiers put "head logs" up on the parapets and dug protected bunkers called "bombproofs" for themselves and magazines for their ammunition behind them. As the siege continued into the fall, the trench lines crept steadily westward as Grant continued his outflanking attempts, leading to a series of bitter battles for the rail lines to the city. The sharpshooters found ready employment in this harsh new environment. Trench warfare put a premium on small unit tactics, since a nearly constant *petite guerre* went on between major engagements.

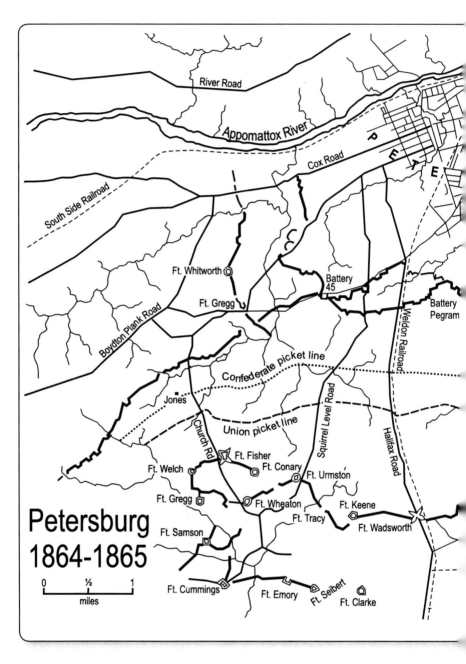

Picket lines had to be maintained and sometimes reestablished, enemy positions scouted and mapped, and prisoners captured and questioned.

The distance between the opposing trenches varied greatly from one sector to another. At Colquitt's salient, near the eastern Petersburg suburb of Blandford, they stood only 150 yards apart, but as the lines bent west past the Jerusalem Plank Road, the distance between them increased to more

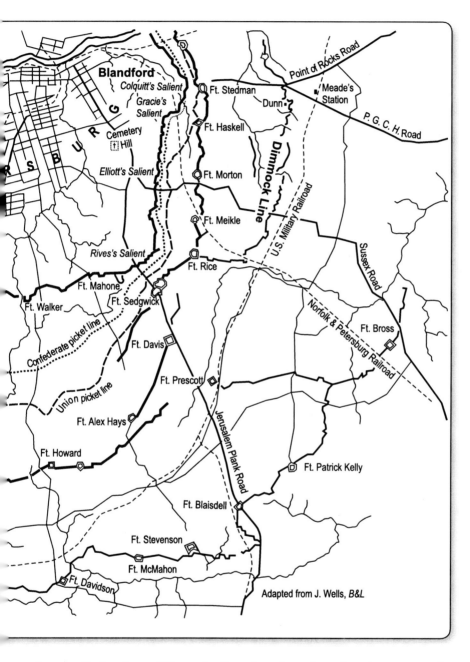

Adapted from J. Wells, *B&L*

than a mile in places. Where the lines lay close sharpshooting was nearly constant, but in more distant sectors the action revolved around patrols, picket fights, and trench raids. Where possible, each side threw out a picket line tied to a series of rifle pits two hundred to five hundred yards in advance of their main position. Soldiers in the advance rifle pits screened the main line, protecting it from enemy reconnaissance and surprise attack. In areas where the lines were far apart, commanders placed their pickets still further out and generally backed them with a body of infantry. The Confederates usually occupied advanced positions only during the night, while the Union picket line stayed manned around the clock.[2]

At Colquitt's salient and other locations where the lines were close together, sharpshooters on both sides continued their constant harassment:

> As the pickets could not look over the works without exposing themselves to certain destruction, small loopholes were provided at intervals of fifteen or twenty feet, large enough to admit the barrel of a musket and enable the owner of the weapon to see the enemy's works over its sights. From these little openings on either side a desultory fire was kept up, each side firing at the only vulnerable spots, which were these loopholes. They were easily located by the smoke from the muskets, and their exact situation became known to all. So accurate was the marksmanship that the wood around the openings was worn away by the bullets, and in many places soldiers replaced it with iron rails from the railroad track. Once in a while a man would be killed by a musket ball coming through these openings."[3]

Still, the Confederate sharpshooters mostly did what they had been initially formed to do—picket duty—which remained a difficult, dangerous task. "We were never safe one minute of the time from the missiles that continually sizzled and buzzed in the air around and about us," remembered one soldier, "striking in the ground and tearing out great craters large enough to bury an ox, while their riflemen were ever on the alert with their long-range guns to pick off any of our men who exposed themselves to view." A Georgian, Gordon Bradwell, gives us an idea of what it was like in the Blandford sector. Although not a sharpshooter himself, he volunteered for picket duty one night because his regiment's company was shorthanded. At dusk Bradwell met a sharpshooter who was supposed to conduct him to his post. The man quickly inspected his gun and said, "Are you ready?" The two bounded over the parapet to be greeted by "a shower of balls," then ran forward to the line of rifle pits. His companion pointed right, said "That's your picket," and disappeared. Bradwell caught his canteen strap on a stake, which brought him up short as the bullets whistled by. He got loose and jumped into the rifle pit, landing in the "stinking, cold mud" up to his knees. "In this miserable hole I sat and shivered until midnight," he remembered, "when I was relieved by a comrade who brought with him a plank which reached from one side of the pit to the other and afforded us a good seat thereafter." The commander of Thirty-first Georgia's regimental sharpshooters, Lieutenant Billy Gwyn, came around periodically to check on them. He ordered the pickets to fire off a round every fifteen minutes to stay awake. Whether or not there were still two "corps" of sharpshooters, Gwyn divided the pickets into two reliefs during the night, then alternated them nightly so that the first relief became the second on the next night. The only consolation was that they got the next the day off and were exempt from camp details.

Union sharpshooters at Petersburg. "A common plan of protection was that shown in the sketch, by a wooden tube widening outwards like a miniature embrasure buried in the crest of the rifle pit and protected by sandbags." Alfred Waud, LC.

Despite the toil and dangers of the picket line, soldiers found ways to amuse themselves. One was to hollow out a Minié ball with a pocket knife until only a shell remained, then fill it with powder that the rifleman had moistened with his own saliva. He would ram the shell upside down on a full charge of dry powder, then fire it off at the enemy lines. Especially after dark, the "squib" looked like a lit mortar shell and thus caused "great confusion" wherever it landed. "Friend and foe alike enjoyed the joke, and after a while the enemy caught on to the trick."

One night Bradwell was waiting in the darkness when he heard a hoarse whisper saying, "Don't shoot, don't shoot; I'm coming in." A few moments later a Yank, "gun in hand and fully equipped," rolled into the pit with him and surrendered. There were six more men with him, he said, and asked Bradwell to pass the word down the line not to fire on them. "This class of men," explained Bradwell, "was not to be feared," as they were Union bounty jumpers who wanted only to desert after collecting their money.

On another occasion "bedlam broke loose" after some overenthusiastic picket firing touched off a sizable firefight between the trenches, making the rifle pits an extremely dangerous place to be. The Yankee videttes, thinking it was a full-scale attack, ran back to their forts in a panic. Out in the rifle pits Bradwell could hear the rest of the garrison turning out and manning their guns. They soon put them to use, and he watched in awe as "the heavens and the surrounding scene were lit up by their artillery. Screeching mortar shells, with a tail of fire following them a yard long, were ascending toward the blue dome of heaven, while shells from the mouths of their rifle cannon were sweeping over our heads and bursting in the rear." The show turned deadly, however, when the mortar shells began falling on the shallow pits that sheltered Bradwell and his comrades, their explosions covering them with dirt while the Federal infantry cut loose with their muskets from the parapets. "The fort," he wrote, "was a veritable volcano in eruption, and every minute I expected one of those big shells to drop in on me and tear me into atoms." Terrified and feeling totally alone, Bradwell wondered if his last moments on earth had arrived. "How long I remained in this state of uncertainty I cannot say; but when I could stand it no longer, I jumped up, determined to find some one to die with me or to advise me." He ran through the zigzag trench to the adjacent post, but found it empty, then bolted further along the ditch until he tripped over a musket and landed in a heap. At first all he could do was rub his injured ankle, but in the fitful light of the gun flashes and explosions he saw the man whose picket post it was slumped against the side of the ditch "awaiting his fate and crying like a child." Together they decided to return to the main line by the connecting trench. When they finally made it back they found, much to their surprise, everyone in their regiment standing calmly at arms, awaiting developments. No attack developed, and eventually the firing slackened. As terrifying as it had been for Bradwell and his fellow pickets, the action was more or less routine and probably did not rate a special mention at headquarters.[4]

In addition to their picket duties, the sharpshooters increasingly conducted what would now be called special operations missions for such tasks as capturing prisoners to obtain information. Major Thomas J. Wooten of the Eighteenth North Carolina, a man "cool and brave, but modest as a girl," was especially good at it. Wooten had succeeded Captain Nicholson in command of Lane's Brigade Sharpshooters. "He was a terror to the enemy's picket lines," remarked one of his fellow Tar Heels, "and had a reputation in both armies." In his sector of the Petersburg trenches where the lines were widely separated, Wooten became known for his technique of "seine-hauling" Yankee prisoners. His brigade commander, Brigadier General James Lane, explained how it worked: "With the whole of a part of his command, he would move by the flank in double ranks toward the enemy's line, taking advantage of all natural features; and sometimes the command would crawl until within running distance. Then they would quietly rush forward. Wooten would halt on the line of pits, and when the rear of his command reached him, he would order both ranks to face outward and wheel. Wheeling on Wooten as the pivot they would return at a run in single rank, empty every pit before them, and never fire a gun." Another soldier swore that "in all of his dashes he [Wooten] never lost a man, killed, wounded or captured." On one occasion Wooten captured an entire Yankee picket line and their reserves, a feat that earned him the personal congratulations of his corps commander, General A. P. Hill.

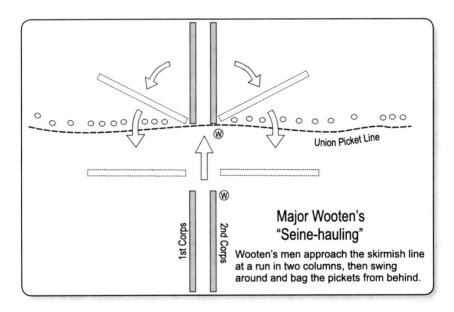

Major Wooten's
"Seine-hauling"

Wooten's men approach the skirmish line
at a run in two columns, then swing
around and bag the pickets from behind.

His regimental historian characterized Wooten's exploits as "proverbial," adding that "he was liberally used by division, corps and army headquarters for ascertaining the enemy's lines or movements." On another occasion General Lee asked that General Lane "catch a Yankee" for information on their movements, and Lane passed the assignment to Wooten. "After sitting a while with his head between his hands, he [Wooten] looked up with a bright face, and said: 'I can get him.' Early next morning, followed by a crowd of laughing, ragged Rebels, he marched seven prisoners to headquarters, and with a merry good morning, reported: 'I couldn't get that promised Yankee for General Lee, but I caught seven Dutchmen.'" Wooten became so notorious that Yankee pickets often anxiously inquired across the lines as to whether "Major Hooten" was about, and on other occasions Union officers asked to be introduced to him during truces.[5]

The Crater

The siege of Petersburg dragged on all summer, and on July 30 the Federals literally tried to blow the stalemate open with a mine. While a regiment of Pennsylvania coal miners dug the shaft and packed it with powder, the Union chiefs made their plans for the assault. The man chosen to lead the attack was General James Ledlie, the hero of Ox Ford. The mine went off just before 5 a.m., obliterating a section of earthworks along with the battery of artillery holding it and killing nearly three hundred South Carolina infantrymen. The white soldiers of Ledlie's division and the black troops of Ferrero's division crowded into the crater, where they became inextricably mixed up and, held back by a thin line of Confederate reserves, lost their momentum. The Confederates hastily brought up reinforcements, including Colonel David Weisiger's (formerly Mahone's) Virginia brigade. Weisiger's sharpshooters, under the command of Captain William Wallace Broadbent, "a man of gigantic strength and stature," marched with them. Broadbent's sharpshooters were essentially a sixth regiment, nearly as strong as the line outfits. Their presence was more or less an accident, as they were just preparing to go out on picket duty that morning.

They soon found themselves embroiled in one of their most desperate fights of the war. "We had no order to charge that I ever heard," wrote one Rebel, "but, seeing a column of Negro soldiers being pushed over the breast-works and lodged in a ditch, we, one and all, said that if we did not go now we would all fall later, and we started in zig-zag shape. Soon all minor officers said forward, and we rushed up to the Crater."[6]

"The line was about one hundred and fifty yards in length when it started forward," recalled another, "but with the men moving at slightly different paces and lengthening out a little on the right as the right regiments and sharp-shooters obliqued to the right towards the crater, before we were half across the field, the line had probably lengthened a hundred or two feet, and widened to twenty feet or more, and the men thus moving forward with open ranks ... every man of whom appreciated the vital importance of getting to the works and closing with the enemy in the quickest possible time." The sharpshooters's position in this "splendid" charge was on the far right of the brigade, which exposed them to a severe enfilading fire from the Federal lines. When they reached the Crater, the fight quickly degenerated into a hand-to-hand struggle. The sharpshooters's commander, Captain Broadbent, fell with "twelve or fifteen bayonet wounds through his body." Weisiger's brigade provided the winning edge for the Confederates at the Crater, but the cost was high. "The proportion of wounded and killed in the sharpshooters," recalled a survivor, "was exceedingly large, probably without a parallel. The battalion went into the fight with 104 men and officers, and of these ninety-four men and officers were killed and wounded; of the nine officers present eight were shot through the breast."[7]

The Confederate assault at The Crater. *B&L*

In spite of high casualties, however, the sharpshooters generally had little trouble keeping their ranks filled. "There was a generous rivalry among the regiments of the brigade, in keeping their quota of this corps to the highest efficiency and it was deemed an honor to secure a detail to fill a vacancy in it," wrote a chronicler of Lane's North Carolina brigade. "Several of its members refused to accept promotion to lieutenant, and return to their companies to command them."[8]

Having botched perhaps his best chance to end it quickly, Grant had little choice but to continue the siege. Captain John Young, the commander of Scales's sharpshooters, recalled that at Petersburg "the sharpshooters were in greater demand than ever before. It was a common thing for a general officer to request their assistance in the establishment of his picket lines." They also made raids for reasons of their own, continuing to rely on the Federal commissariat for much of their material needs. Scales's brigade was part of Wilcox's division, which also included McGowan's South Carolina brigade (and Captain Dunlop's sharpshooter battalion) and Lane's Tarheel brigade, home of the notorious Major Wooten. Wilcox's men occupied a sector near the Boydton Plank road several miles west of Petersburg. Nearly a mile separated the lines there, which made for a relatively quiet sector. The Confederate picket line was about five hundred yards forward of the works. "In some places, this line had regular entrenchments, but, as a rule, we had only strong rifle pits. The pits were about ten paces apart. The picket of the brigade generally consisted of two hundred privates." The distance to the Federal pickets varied, but some were as close as 250 yards away. According to Lieutenant J. F. J. Caldwell the sharpshooters, whose strength he estimated at this stage of the war at about 125 men, pulled picket duty "every third or fourth day" and "performed the only active service on the picket line."[9]

A Union soldier, William Phillips, wrote a harrowing description of some of their activities on the last day of December 1864.

Phillips's tale begins before dark with eight "Johnnie" deserters coming in. These troopers warned the boys of the 5th Wisconsin that there would be an attack that night, "and seemed to be in a great hurry to get to the rear," but the Yankees dismissed it "as we had heard so many such stories." Since the lines were far apart, Phillips ended up early that morning on an advanced picket "in a little belt of timber, while to the right and left in front was an open field and in the rear of the line there was a heavy wood." He had just begun to walk his post when he heard an owl hoot nearby. "I thought it did not sound natural but did not pay any attention to it," he wrote, "then I heard a noise in the field right clost by the edge of the woods like quails." This was not unusual either: "there is lots of quails here and they always whistle just before day light."

A moment later, however, a Rebel yell split the air. "There was the darndest yelling that was ever heard in bedlam—the Johnnies had crawled up along the edge of the wood to the right and left of us." Philips belatedly realized that the bird calls had been the signal for their attack, and in only a few moments more the Rebs reached the picket post some fifty yards behind him and fired a volley at the men there, most of whom took off "without their guns or hats or gear into the woods" or toward camp.[10]

The culprits were McGowan's and Scales's sharpshooters, who were due to go into winter quarters and had requested permission "to make a requisition on their blue coated neighbors ... for such articles of camp equipment as might be necessary to render them comfortable during the winter." Their commanders, Captains Dunlop and Young, had gone out just after dark for a reconnaissance, returning later that evening to make their preparations. "About 4 o'clock the following morning," reported Dunlop, "some two hours before daybreak, the two battalions met at the point designated—which was between the lines, some distance east of the Weldon railroad—and formed at right angles with the line to be attacked, about twenty paces apart, back to back. Eight men of superior courage and activity were selected from each battalion and formed at intervals of five paces across the forward flanks of the two battalions, facing the enemy." With sixteen chosen men acting as the "spike head," the Confederates crept forward. They soon ran across a ditch about a hundred yards in front of the Union picket line, "into which every man fell as his turn came." Unfortunately the last soldier in Dunlop's battalion fired his musket as he stumbled, wounding the man in front of him and alerting a section of the Yankee picket line, which responded by firing "a harmless volley" at them. "At the same instant," wrote Dunlop, "the battalions charged and drove their spike head squarely through the Federal lines, capturing half a dozen rifle pits with their occupants. When the battalions had moved half their length through the gap, the right battalion faced to the right, the left battalion to the left, and throwing forward their wings so as to form a sack, and swept the lines." The ditch, evidently missed in the evening's reconnaissance, disoriented Dunlop's command somewhat. One of his men who had fallen into it, Sergeant Robert Plexico, "rubbed the mud and water from his eyes, he discovered that he had lost his bearings, as well as his connection with the spike head, but made for a rifle pit—which he supposed to be the right one—some distance to the left of the point on which his comrades were bearing, and charged it single handed and alone, capturing a corporal and four other prisoners, whom he marched off to the rear."[11]

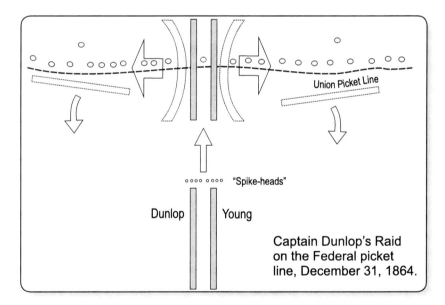

Captain Dunlop's Raid on the Federal picket line, December 31, 1864.

Private Phillips now stood isolated at his post. The Rebels were behind him, and he could hear them ordering his comrades to surrender. "Not very anxious to spend the winter at Libby prison," he started back for his own lines, and in spite of calls to come in "if I did not want my head shot off," he kept running, figuring that "they was 3 or 4 rods [fifteen to twenty yards] from me and it was so dark that they couldn't see me very well." He was right—three raiders fired at him as he passed a pine tree, one ball showering him with bark and sap as it glanced off the tree. Phillips replied with a shot of his own and heard curses behind him as he took "leg bail" for the picket reserve post. He arrived to find it empty except for one man in a blue overcoat who was "gathering our things up." He asked the fellow if he was headed for camp, only to find that he was a Reb. The Johnny grabbed his gun and ordered Phillips to surrender, but the plucky Wisconsin soldier ran off a short distance and began hastily reloading his own piece. He was just in the process of capping his Springfield when his enemy, whom he could see by the firelight, took his leave "with our blankets and all he could carry." Phillips reckoned that if he'd had ten more seconds, "he would never have had the pleasure of sleeping on his stolen blankets." As it was the Reb dropped some of his loot, and a few minutes later Phillips heard the Confederates retreating to their own lines, followed by scattered shots from his comrades in the woods. Phillips and his fellow pickets, determined to regain their honor, returned to one of their picket posts, but "we went back and was standing by the fire when crack! crack! two sharpshooter's balls went whizzing by us we went back in the dark and stayed till it began to get light." When daylight finally arrived, the rest of the men began drifting in from their hiding places as Phillips and one of his comrades gathered up their scattered gear. Overall Private Phillips was lucky—the Rebels had overlooked most of his own belongings and he had escaped wounds or capture. He blamed his own officers for the failure—instead of sending reinforcements to the picket posts under attack, "they heard the Rebs yell and they thought that they was rite on them, the long roll was beat and the men stumbled out to the breastworks." He predicted that "there will be some stripes and shoulder straps drop off to pay for the scrape."[12]

Indeed, Union headquarters was not happy about the affair, but the commanders tried to put the best face on the debacle. The 1st division commander, General Frank Wheaton, admitted to "some confusion" in the darkness but claimed that Captain Thurber, the division officer of the day, had warned the picket line, "which was prepared for the attack." The enemy assault, he said, had taken only five of his twenty posts and had lasted only two minutes. "I believe all the troops concerned behaved well, and thwarted a well-formed plan of the rebels to accomplish very much more than they succeeded in doing." Still, he admitted losing sixteen prisoners and three men wounded. The corps commander, General Horatio Wright, listed his overall casualties as two killed, three wounded, and thirty-seven missing from his 1st and 3rd divisions. Private Phillips, however, gave the casualties in his own (1st) division as seventeen prisoners, two killed and one wounded, and those in adjacent division as twenty-seven prisoners, four killed, and one wounded. On the other side Captain Dunlop, always prone to exaggerate, claimed "not less than three hundred" Yankee casualties. Phillips thought the raid was no mystery. "The main object of the Rebs," he said, "was to get warm clothes and blankets and prisoners." In his opinion, "they done the thing up brown and deserve credit for it."[13]

Young and Dunlop had attacked at a vulnerable point, the boundary between two Federal divisions. Even though the picket posts of the two divisions stood next to each other, their chain of command rapidly diverged to two separate division headquarters located far apart, making any coordinated action along this "seam" exceedingly difficult. The sharpshooters had achieved complete surprise, and according to Dunlop their only casualty was the one man wounded by the accidental musket fire when crossing the ditch. "We secured all the supplies necessary to our comfort for the winter," he reported, "and returned to camp about sunrise, a happy command."[14]

William Morse, a soldier in the 1st Maine Veteran Volunteers (part of Getty's 2nd division), described another such action on January 9, 1865 in his diary: "About 5 a.m. we were aroused by a volley of musketry on the picket line directly in front of us. A few random shots followed, then all was quiet." It was Captain Dunlop and his men again, this time in search of a prisoner for their corps commander, General A. P. Hill. The sharpshooters had orders to get their man only "if it can be done without risking too much," so earlier that night Blackwood Benson—Berry Benson's brother, who had taken his place—had stolen up to the Yankee picket line with a comrade for a look. After the December 31 fiasco the Federals had drawn their sentries closer to their reserve posts, and the two returned about 4 a.m. empty-handed. "It now became necessary," recalled Captain Dunlop, "to extract the information desired by force." Putting two of his sharpshooter companies in column five paces apart, "we advanced slowly and cautiously until we reached a point not exceeding thirty yards from the Federal lines, when a vidette discovered our approach and fired. Instantly we sprang forward and measured our full length on their rifle pits, routed their line for some distance on either flank, captured fourteen prisoners and returned to our position before daylight without losing a man. The prisoners were promptly sent under guard to brigade headquarters for examination."

"At noon we received information that about 75 rebs," Morse continued, "under cover of night and secreted by their old breastworks, which run at right angles with, and across two picket lines, crawled up to within a few yards of our videttes, arose, gave a volley, and charged our line. The most of our pickets fled panic-stricken leaving guns, blankets, haversacks and all, which the Rebs hastily gathered up and hurried back to their own lines, taking with their plunder twenty or more prisoners. Our regiment lost eight men in the deal." A Federal officer complained that "the videttes and sentinels were being relieved at the time of the attack, and the enemy being clothed in the Light Blue Uniform of our troops it was impossible to distinguish them from our own men, which prevented most of the men on the posts from firing as they supposed them to be the videttes and sentinels falling back, and were surrounded by the enemy who captured fourteen men and wounded one." Once again Dunlop had struck "at the point where the 2nd and 3rd Division line connects." As Morse summed it up, "Towards night the Rebs and our boys had a jolly time joking about it, but I think the Johnnies had the best of it." By the fourth year of the war both sides considered this sort of thing to be nothing more than good clean fun.[15]

Soldiers coming out of their respective rifle-pits on cessation of firing, and exchanging civilities and "Yankee notions," during the investment of Petersburg.
The Soldier in Our Civil War

Not all raids went so well. Corporal Sam Pickens of the Fifth Alabama described one bungled sortie on the night of February 1. Colonel John Winston took his regiment, the Forty-fifth North Carolina, along with detachments from the Cook's Georgia brigade and the Fifth Alabama (all of whom were stationed on the eastern end of the line in the Blandford area), on an ambitious expedition to roll up the entire Federal picket line all the way to the Appomattox river. The mission, however, "proved a complete failure," when, according to Pickens, Winston's Tarheels "broke and ran" at the first shots from the Yankee pickets, only two or three of whom they captured for their trouble. In spite of this unpleasantness, by the time the sun came up "the pickets in our front were on good terms again, talking the thing over, & swapping papers, knives, tobacco, etc."[16]

On the 21 of that chilly month the sharpshooters had a pleasant surprise. Pickens recorded in his diary that "Maj. Blackford who has been reinstated, arrived in Camp to-night & as soon as it was known the majority of the Regt. turned out & cheered him heartily." After a long bureaucratic battle Blackford had finally won back his sword and was now in line to be promoted to the vacant lieutenant colonelcy of the Fifth Alabama. His leg continued to trouble him, however, and he was also up for transfer to the Invalid Corps.[17]

That winter desertion had become a major problem for both armies, but it was especially hard on the thin Confederate ranks. Here again the sharpshooters provided a partial solution—when used as pickets at night they were less likely to desert themselves, and they kept others from going over the hill as well. "There is some deserters comes in every night," reported William Phillips. "There would more come in if they had a chance but their videttes have to stand close to the fire of the relief posts if they start to leave the whole post would know it and if any one is caught trying to desert they are shot. They keep scouts out in the night to catch any one that is trying to leave and watch our movements, but with all their caution there is lots gets away." One such was a supposedly faithful Rebel private chosen by his captain to trade tobacco for soap. "When he was half way," chortled Phillips, "the Reb captain told him to stop but he kept on and come in to our lines." Some of his comrades fired "but did not come within a rod of him." Later Phillips and his messmates had a grand time guying the Rebel captain about it across the way: "We would holler 'how is your soap' and he would jump up and down and swear."

Incidents like this led, predictably, to some hard feelings against the sharpshooters. Confederate deserters had warned William Phillips and his fellow pickets about the impending raid, and while they were ignored, such was not always the case. On another occasion a defector "who had it in for those blockheads and wanted to see them annihilated," revealed an upcoming foray that allowed the Vermonters of Colonel William Truex's brigade to set a trap in which a number of sharpshooters were captured. Desertions by North Carolina troops became so serious that Lee sent Robert Johnston's Tarheel brigade to put up a cordon along the Roanoke River to stop them. The brigade sharpshooters, as usual, drew the toughest job—going to the hills of western North Carolina to deal with the "recalcitrant mountaineers" there.[18]

Having been burned on the picket line, the Federals took to patrolling the open space between the lines of their VI Corps and the Confederate Third Corps. These small light infantry formations, not in any book of tactics, seem to have evolved in the latter part of 1864 for the same reasons we use them today—to prevent surprise, gather information, and dominate the space between the lines. Yankee William Phillips left some excellent descriptions of patrolling, including the tale of how one of his comrades was captured: "he went up too clost to the Rebs and one of their patrols took him. The wind blew so hard that they did not hear each other they both fired their muskets and did not hit each other." At this point one of the Rebels bluffed by claiming to have a revolver, and Phillips's friend surrendered. He was escorted to their picket post but managed to escape. "I guess some friendly Reb helped him get away."

"I have been on patrol twice," wrote Phillips, "and once the other fellow went within 10 rods of the Rebs. The night was still and we could hear all they said." He and his companion were well armed, however, and he boasted that "it would have taken several Rebs to have taken us for the other fellow had a dispenser [Spencer] 7-shooter rifle and I had a musket and a revolver that would take a man at 40 rods. I can hit a 3 inch ring 10 rods every time … it carys copper cartridges and can be loaded in 15 seconds."[19]

During the siege the Federals had come to appreciate the advantages of the fast-firing Spencers. The day after Christmas Phillips wrote, "A and B Companies are going to draw Sharps 6 shooters they are skirmishers. They need good rifles." Phillips almost certainly means Spencers here, a weapon that the entire 37th Massachusetts had been armed with since July. The 37th, in fact, drew a lot of patrol and skirmish duty, as its men could put out nearly as much lead as a line of battle. On another occasion Phillips describes "quite a lively time": he was on picket, with three patrols from the 37th Massachusetts out in no man's land. According to Phillips the Confederates allowed themselves to be silhouetted by their own camp fires. The Massachusetts men "stayed down and waited till the Rebs got clost to them, [then] they jumped up and give them 7 shots as fast as they could pull the trigger. They did not stop to see what damage they did." The Southerners returned fire but failed to hit any of their tormentors. "In less than 30 minutes the Rebs had a line of battle formed," wrote Phillips, "we could hear them giving their commands. They expected to be attacked."[20]

The war of raids and sharpshooting continued all winter, punctuated by a series of battles as the lines gradually extended farther west. In general the Confederates tended to dominate the picket line. Sharpshooter commanders, such as Dunlop, Young, and Wooten, epitomized qualities needed for trench warfare: courage, initiative, and a willingness to innovate. Together they developed a set of tactics that, allowing for the differences in technology, would have stood them in good stead in 1916 and were far more advanced than Hardee's *Tactics*. Their technique, in essence, was to quickly penetrate the picket line and then sweep right and left, scooping up the enemy's pickets before they were able to react. And, as Phillips and his comrades found out, they often seem to have left a few riflemen behind to make sure that no one followed them. "I never heard of a single casualty among them," said a staff officer in McGowan's brigade.[21]

19

Assault on Hare's Hill

"Knock down and drag out."

By March 1865 the Confederate lines around Petersburg were gossamer thin, and Lee realized he would have to abandon Richmond and join General Joseph Johnston's army in the Carolinas. Before leaving Virginia, however, he decided to strike one last blow against the Yankees. The plan, hatched by General John B. Gordon, now commander of the Second Corps, envisioned a daring thrust toward the main Union supply depot at City Point, only ten miles northeast of Petersburg. If the Confederates could capture or severely damage the Yankees' primary logistical center, they might cause enough confusion to allow the Army of Northern Virginia to disengage and withdraw unmolested.

For his offensive Gordon selected a spot about a mile south of the Appomattox river, where the Union defenses were somewhat weaker and the lines only 150 yards apart. Here Colquitt's salient jutted out of the Confederate line toward Fort Stedman and Battery X, which in turn stood where the Union line bulged outward, their pickets standing at one point only 435 feet from the butternut sentries. Just south of Colquitt's salient lay Gracie's salient, another small bulge in the Confederate line. Gordon planned the operation with his usual thoroughness, carefully scouting the lines for a week beforehand, questioning prisoners and deserters, looking for weak spots. He and his staff estimated how long it would take to remove the obstacles in front of the Union forts and how long it would take to cross the open ground to reach them. They also needed to know if any ditches might slow or stop the attack and the best spot to rush across without waking their foe. Gordon's own Second Corps, reduced to around seventy-five hundred men, would deliver the main assault. Two additional brigades from Major General Bushrod Johnson's division under Brigadier General Robert Ransom would bring his total force to between 9,500 and 10,500. In addition, he had another four brigades from A. P. Hill's Third Corps on call.[1]

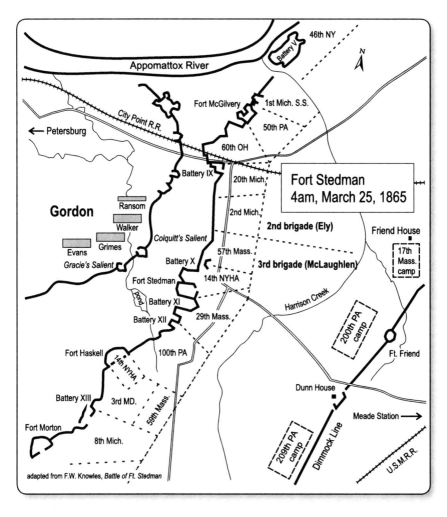

Fort Stedman
4am, March 25, 1865

adapted from F.W. Knowles, *Battle of Ft. Stedman*

The 2nd and 3rd brigades of Major General Orlando Willcox's 1st division, part of the eighteen-thousand-man Union IX Corps, held the sector across from Gordon, their defenses anchored on three forts. These were General Ledlie's men, used so badly at Ox Ford and the Crater, who had finally been freed of their old leaders (including corps commander Ambrose Burnside) after the latter debacle. At the north end of the line, near the Appomattox river, lay Fort McGilvery. From there the ground sloped down through a marshy bottom past Batteries VIII and IX about three-quarters of a mile to Fort Stedman, which stood on a low rise called Hare's Hill. Fort Stedman covered about three-quarters of an acre and even included a grove of shade trees, but a Union engineer had assessed it not long before as "one of the weakest and ill-constructed forts of the line." Its proximity to the Confederate line and the close attentions of Rebel sharpshooters prevented construction of the usual in-depth defenses and kept repairs to a minimum.

Still, enclosed by a earthen rampart pierced for its four 12-pounder cannon that "had greatly settled during the winter," the fort boasted an infantry parapet, a ditch, *abatis*, and *fraises*[*] for protection. To add to an attacker's difficulties the Federals had wrapped telegraph wire across the stakes, making it virtually impossible to climb over them unaided. Protected by similar obstacles, Batteries X and XI—smaller works open at the rear—flanked the fort on either side. One of Fort Stedman's defensive flaws was that the open rear of Battery X, which held two 3-inch rifled cannon and seven mortars, opened directly on to, and at the same level with, the adjacent northern parapet of Fort Stedman. Battery XII, with six more mortars, lay just past Battery XI, and from there the ground declined into another swampy area through which two watercourses ran. Three-eighths of a mile from Fort Stedman stood Fort Haskell, a fortification "about the size of a steamer's deck" holding six "light twelves" (12-pounder Napoleons) and a battery of Coehorn mortars. Only on the higher and more solid ground around Hare's Hill could an attacker hope to move large bodies of troops quickly, but those bare slopes were also fearfully exposed to the fire of the flanking forts.

A breast-high infantry parapet ran much of the way along the Federal lines, giving the soldiers some protection from the ever-vigilant grayback sharpshooters. In addition to Willcox's two infantry brigades each fort had its own garrison. The 14th New York Heavy Artillery, fighting as infantry, provided eight companies to Fort Stedman and Battery X and four to Fort Haskell. Several artillery detachments in the forts worked the various guns and mortars. A bit less than a mile behind the first line of Union defenses, on a low north-south rise, lay the old Confederate Dimmock line, which had been captured during the Union attack the previous June. It had never been improved or maintained since its capture by the Federals, who had no plans to defend it. The only active work on it was Fort Friend on Dunn Hill, a small enclosure just off the road to Meade's Station, which held a single six-gun battery without an infantry garrison. A quarter of a mile behind that lay Meade's Station, which housed the hospitals, supply dumps, and reserve artillery of the IX Corps. Just then, however, the reserve artillery consisted of only four guns in two sections. Of more consequence was the 3rd division of IX Corps. Commanded by Brigadier General John Hartranft, this outfit consisted of six brand-new, full-strength Pennsylvania regiments. Two regiments of its 1st brigade, the 200th and 209th Pennsylvania, camped less than a mile to the rear of Fort Stedman near the Dimmock line, and the rest were within an hour's marching distance.[2]

Gordon optimistically envisioned a "tremendous possibility" for the attack—nothing less than "the disintegration of the whole left wing of the

---

[*] Sharpened logs at the base of the parapet, set about eight inches apart and sticking out at a slight upward angle.

Federal army." Still, in the face of such formidable fortifications and the weakness of his own army, he would have to use both force and guile to quickly seize Fort Stedman and the three supporting forts. The sharpshooters were the obvious choice to lead the assault, and it would be they who would precede each of the three assaulting columns, one from each of the corps' three divisions[†], in a pre-dawn attack on March 25. Colonel Hamilton Brown and the Division Sharpshooters of Grimes's division would take Fort Stedman, while the sharpshooters of Walker's division were to assault Battery X just north of it and Evans's division secured Battery XI to the south. Ransom's brigade would join Walker's division in the assault, and Wallace's brigade would be a follow-on unit.[3]

Major General John B. Gordon, CSA. *B&L*

To clear the obstacles protecting the Union positions, Gordon assigned each column a fifty-man pioneer detachment armed with axes. Hard on the heels of the pioneers came a storming party of sharpshooters, about a hundred strong, and just behind them would march the infantry brigades. A company of artillerymen, led by Lieutenant Colonel Robert Stribling, was to accompany the assault troops and turn the Yankee guns on their owners. Once Fort Stedman had fallen, Gordon planned to take the supporting forts by a *ruse de guerre* as the Second Corps infantry approached. Three hundred-man "Trojan horse" companies would pass though both the Confederate assault forces and the Union defenders to seize the supporting forts.

---

† Second Corps now consisted of Grimes's division (Robert Rodes's old division, now commanded by Major General Bryan Grimes) and Walker's division (Ramseur's old division, which had then become Pegram's division and was now commanded by Brigadier General James A. Walker). Brigadier General Clement Evans commanded Gordon's division, since the latter was acting as corps commander.

Because they would be operating in the darkness, and since the last year's campaign had drastically altered the terrain, Gordon assigned men from the area to each company as guides and saw to it that their commanders knew the names of Union officers in their sector. Although his soldiers wore Confederate uniforms, Gordon figured that in the semi-darkness these detachments would be able to pass either as retreating Union infantry or Confederate deserters. Since the Federals paid a cash bonus for each weapon a line-crosser brought in, it was not unusual to see armed Confederate deserters, or even whole groups of them, at the picket line. Once the supporting forts had fallen, another wave of infantry would move forward and begin rolling up the Union line from north to south while a cavalry detachment galloped through to cut telegraph lines, burn the pontoon bridges over the James river, and generally sow confusion. Although this was an audacious and well-thought-out plan, it was also an intricate one that depended on a great many things going right at exactly the same time. Could the Confederate army, weak and exhausted after the long siege, pull it off?[4]

During the frosty early morning hours of March 25 the shivering Confederates began moving into their assembly areas in Colquitt's and Gracie's salients. The weather was perfect—a clear, starry night with fog starting to gather in the hollows. The preparation was complex. Gordon needed to bring up Johnston's brigade from the Roanoke river, where it was corralling deserters, and fetch Cox's brigade of Grimes's division from across the Appomattox river. Unfortunately the courier got lost and the order was fatally delayed, depriving Grimes of a quarter of his strength. At the last minute Gordon requested Pickett's division from First Corps, but given the chronically uncertain state of Confederate military railroads, it was a tossup whether the division would arrive in time. The Second Corps held the line from the Appomattox river to the vicinity of the Crater, so the men first had to march back out of the trenches far enough to form up, mass into columns, and finally move to the line of departure—all without the Yanks figuring out what they were up to. "No commands were given," remembered Brigadier General James Walker, "but the words were passed in low tones from man to man." Some confusion was inevitable, and at one point in the darkness another column moved across that of the Louisiana brigade, cutting it in two.[5]

Around 3 a.m. Gordon gathered all the sharpshooters for a pep talk. Oscar Whitaker, a sharpshooter from the Twelfth Alabama, recalled:

> General Gordon got us to close up around him that night, while he stood on a stump and told us how Lee was situated, what a long line we were having to keep up and the Yanks might break our lines at any time. In front of us he said was Ft. Stedman he

told us if we would take it he would have our names in every paper in the South, of course we being old soldiers told him we would do it. He told us for not a man to load his gun, and at a signal from him to rush over to the fort—knock down and drag out, and he would have 50,000 troops in behind us.

The general also passed out white strips of cloth that his own wife had prepared, worn "drawn over the right shoulder to the left side, passed around the body and tied" so that the men could recognize each other in the darkness. Captain Joseph P. Carson, who commanded the sharpshooters of Cook's Georgia brigade, remembered that Gordon had also promised them a silver medal and a thirty-day furlough if they succeeded. "It was a stirring and impressive speech," he recalled, "standing there in the night with the awful task and eternity staring us in the face."[6]

Within an hour the sharpshooters, nerves on edge, moved up as close to the picket line as they dared and lay down. The pioneer detachments began to pull aside the triple line of *chevaux-de-frise* protecting the Confederate lines. Before the days of barbed wire, these spiked wooden horses, chained end to end, presented an unbroken breast-high hedge of sharpened stakes that had to be parted before an attacker could advance. This was the most delicate part of the whole operation: if the Union sentries alerted their line, the assaulting columns would be slaughtered. The Confederates kept a line of pickets in rifle pits just forward of this obstacle belt at night, which put them only about fifty yards from their counterparts. Although sharpshooters ruled the days, opposing pickets often got quite chummy during the night, chatting away the lonely hours. On this chilly morning, however, the boys in gray seemed much more friendly than usual.[7]

Generals Gordon and Walker went up to the picket line to watch the preparations across from Battery X, the closest work to their lines. In front of them the pioneers were working out in an old cornfield between the lines, making the dry stalks rattle. "I say, Johnny, what are you doing in that corn?" shouted a Union picket. "All right, Yank, I am just gathering me a little corn to parch!" "All right Johnny, I won't shoot!" A bit later the Federal asked, "I say, Johnny, isn't it almost daylight? I think it is time they were relieving us." "Keep cool, Yank; you'll be relieved in a few minutes."[8]

When the way was open, a group of Walker's sharpshooters moved toward the Federal picket line as if to desert. To complete the illusion, their commander, a Tarheel lieutenant named Jim Edmonson, jumped up behind them and shouted "O boys, come back! Don't go!" The Southerners quickly overpowered the sentinel, who still managed to bayonet one of them before being knocked senseless, and captured most of his compatriots. At least one escaped, however, firing off his rifle and yelling "The Rebels are coming! The Rebels are coming!" as he headed back to the fort. The sharpshooters followed the fleeing picket, who unwittingly led them back through his own obstacles. Gordon drew his revolver and fired three pistol shots—the signal for the attack.[9]

Now it was up to the sharpshooters. Captain Joseph Anderson, the Virginian who commanded Walker's sharpshooters, ordered "Forward! Double-quick!" The soldiers rose and moved swiftly at trail arms, the only sound that of their feet crunching on the frosty ground. Colonel Hamilton Brown and the sharpshooters of Grimes's division took the center route directly toward Fort Stedman, while Walker's men moved left toward Battery X and Evans's sharpshooters angled south from Gracie's salient toward Batteries XI and XII. With the shortest distance to go, Walker's men, joined by the sharpshooters of Ransom's brigade, reached their objective first. Ransom's pioneers, under Lieutenant Wood Flemming, "a beardless boy not more than 19 years old," began hacking through the abatis and fraises protecting the forts, while another assault group under Lieutenant Thomas Roulhac moved up to support it. In a few moments they were inside the works, swinging their Enfields like clubs and overrunning the New England artillerymen in Battery X and its adjacent mortar battery. The Federal section commander, Lieutenant Ephraim Nye, died defending his guns. Without firing a shot the attackers swiftly captured or drove off the rest of his men. Minutes later cheers echoing through the still morning air told General Walker that the fort had fallen, and he started his infantry column forward.[10]

Inside Fort Stedman Major George Randall, commander of the 14th New York Heavy Artillery, which made up the fort's infantry garrison, tried desperately to organize a defense, but the Rebels had by now passed through Battery X, come out behind it, and stood on top of Fort Stedman's parapet. Captain Edward Rogers, the fort's artillery commander, complained that "the first intimation my men in Fort Stedman had of the approach of the enemy was the rush and the cheer with which they carried Battery No. 10." Rogers's men (two sections of the 19th New York Battery) fired their guns— he claimed to have gotten off ten or twelve rounds of canister—but "by that time the force of the enemy that had taken Battery No. 10 had ... rushed into the fort without opposition." Yankee gunners tried to manhandle one of their four Napoleons around to bear on the sally port, but ran out of time. Others received a surprise as well. An all-night card game, liberally lubricated with spirits, was suddenly interrupted when "a strange face looked in at the poker players' hut, and the gamblers dropped their cards and cups and reached for weapons." Private "Hence" Proctor, a sharpshooter with the Forty-fifth North Carolina, poked his head into another bombproof. "Come out of there," he demanded. "I know you are in there." The Yankee officer inside, still in his night clothes, grabbed his sword with one hand and Proctor's long hair with the other, and proceeded to belabor the unfortunate sharpshooter about the head and shoulders with it. "Hence's fixed bayonet on the end of his gun while thus held by the hair," wrote an observer, "was no match for the saber in the hands of his adversary, and but for the timely aid from one of his comrades, he would have been quickly overcome." Even so Proctor left the encounter "with many gashes to his head and face." A "straggling free fight" broke out in the darkness at the rear of the fort, during which Captain Anderson got a mortal wound. His second in command, Lieutenant Hugh Powell, also died in the melee.[11]

While Anderson's men rampaged through Battery X, Colonel Hamilton Brown and his sharpshooters stealthily approached Fort Stedman's front by means of a drainage ditch. Blackford appears to have been hospitalized at the time, leaving command of Battle's Alabama sharpshooters to Lieutenant P. H. Larey of the Sixth Alabama. The men crept forward undetected nearly to the fort, but when waved up to take out a sentinel they lost their composure, "yelled like a bunch of Comanche Indians," and rushed the parapet.[12]

Meanwhile another column of sharpshooters from Grimes's division under Captain Joseph Carson made its way forward after hearing Gordon's signal. Carson, a Georgian, had slept fitfully that night, not so much from pre-attack jitters as for worrying about his younger brother Bob. The high-spirited eighteen-year-old, who normally had a safer job as a courier, had insisted on joining him for the attack. Having lost two brothers already, Carson could not shake off the feeling that Bob would not survive the day. Nevertheless he pressed forward, leading his men across a creek between the lines and then through "three lines of obstructions as perfect as human ingenuity ... could make them." They had not gone twenty-five yards, however, when the fort's guns opened up. Carson was nonplussed. "We were not visible and made no noise, but they knew we were coming and our direction," he said, not knowing that Walker's men had reached the fort before him. Now the sharpshooters had to cross two hundred yards of ground that the gun flashes made "light as day." Running at top speed, they managed to get under the gun's line of fire without anyone being hit. "We were still going on the run as hard as we could when we crossed the branch and started up the hill," recalled Carson. "How we got past the first line of obstructions I could never remember. I was very fleet of foot, but when I reached the line Bob was there ahead of me. I saw him for an instant in the flash of the cannon tearing down and dragging aside the wire and logs. He was very strong, and had broken the wire when I got up. We went through the gap together. How the others crossed I do not know. The next minute we struck the middle line of brush, climbing and rolling over it into the open ground beyond." They were now so close to the forts that the cannon blasts blew off their hats, their roar overwhelming everything else. Hats in one hand and guns in the other they reached the fraises protecting the parapet, hacking and dragging them out of the way "with the strength of desperation." Now they began to attract rifle fire as well as rounds from the flanking artillery. "It was every man for himself," Carson allowed.

The men jumped into the ditch that surrounded the fort and tried to scramble up the slippery thirteen-foot slope as the defending infantrymen fired at them from the top. Another Georgian, Lieutenant John Gay, was hit and slumped back into the ditch, "and would have drowned had we not lifted him back upon the bank, where he died." Unable to ascend the parapet, Carson ordered his men to load their rifles and "shoot every Yankee who showed himself." While this kept the defender's heads down, they continued to stick their rifles over the parapet and fire blindly into Carson's men. "It was a critical moment," he recalled, for "we could neither advance nor retreat." Some of the men wanted to fall back, but others passed down the word that they had found a low spot in the parapet. Carson and his men were soon inside, where he formed his line and began moving forward. The Yankees began to surrender, first individually and then in groups.[13]

The southern column consisted of Colonel Eugene Waggaman's Louisiana brigade, which Brigadier General Clement Evans had selected to lead the assault "on account of the valor of your troops," plus the Division Sharpshooters under Captain William Kaigler and an assault group from the Thirteenth and Thirty-first Georgia regiments under Colonel John Lowe. The Tenth Louisiana's commander, Lieutenant Colonel Henry Monier, noted in his diary: "corps of sharpshooters, Louisiana brigade, head of attacking column." Waggaman's brigade, which after four years of war numbered only some four hundred men, suffered considerable disorganization as its soldiers stumbled through the darkness, "and at one time the column seemed in danger of being entirely cut up, in the general mixing up of regiments, and in the treacherous character of the ground." Waggaman became mired in the muddy ditch surrounding the fort, most likely Battery XI, and had to be dragged out by a private. The first men over the parapet were a detachment of eight sharpshooters (two four-man sections) led by Lieutenant Benjamin Smith of the Second Louisiana. Hard pressed by the defenders, they held out "with remarkable coolness ... until reinforcements arrived." When the rest of the Louisiana Tigers in the supporting column entered the fort, they found the garrison "fully awake and stirring," and subdued the men only after "rough and tumble fighting" with bayonets and rifle butts, "the opposing soldiers being locked together like serpents."[14]

Inside Fort Stedman the free-for-all continued. Although Major Randall would later claim to have repulsed three attacks on the rear of the fort, Captain Rogers, "seeing that any further attempts at resistance were useless, ordered the men to take care of themselves. The enemy at this time were on three sides of the fort, as well as in it." Rogers escaped in the confusion, as did about half of his artillerymen. Three of his gunners had enough presence of mind to bring their guns' breech sights with them, thus complicating the job of Colonel Stribling's men, who were even then turning the guns around. As his men surrendered, Major Randall grabbed his colors and tried to escape but was captured. Captain Carson quickly sent the prisoners, which he estimated at more than five hundred, hustling to the rear. Fort Stedman was now firmly in Confederate hands, or so it appeared.[15]

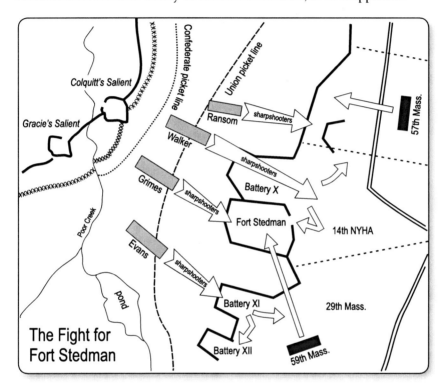

Just behind the forts lay the camps of the two supporting infantry regiments, the 57th and 29th Massachusetts. Incredibly, no one had yet given a general alarm. The men of the 29th had been roused after hearing a few shots, but this in itself was not unusual, and they relaxed when the sentry standing on the Battery XI parapet called down "no attack." One observer noted that "the pickets of this regiment could be seen standing quietly by their fires in the ravine below." More shots rang out—this time closer—leading the guard commander to rather testily pass the word to cease firing lest they hit their own men. "The latter order had hardly been given when Gordon's troops suddenly appeared in the rear." The sharpshooters swept into the camp, scattering the drowsy Federals out of their tents in as wild a confusion as they had had at Cedar Creek. "Before our men had time to man the works," wrote the commander of the 29th Massachusetts, "the enemy entered our camp at the north front. They fired no shots, but used the butts of their muskets. The three companies on that front were captured, and the enemy then advanced to the west front ... a desperate encounter ensued, in which most of our men were taken prisoners." Color Sergeant Conrad Homan, however, managed to spirit the regiment's flag to safety despite being surrounded by Confederates. When a Rebel seized Private Edward Carney by the throat and ordered him to surrender, he said "I don't see it" and fought his way free of his captors, in the process receiving "several severe blows upon the back with a musket and a slight gunshot wound in the head." Several other men made similar narrow escapes. Some survivors collected outside the forts, while others made their way south toward Fort Haskell.[16]

The camp of the 57th Massachusetts, a 217-man outfit that was about to cement its place as one of the army's hard-luck regiments, lay immediately behind Battery X. Alerted by one of their number who had escaped the picket line, the Bay Staters had just time enough to form up and rush to the infantry parapets north of the battery, only to find that the Confederates were now behind them. Order collapsed, and many men were captured in the darkness. Still, Major James Doherty, the regiment's acting commander, rallied a determined few east of the camps, and as at Cedar Creek many of the starving Southerners stopped to loot the luxurious tents of their opponents, further disorganizing their attack. But something was missing. "Sergeant-major, where in hell are the colors?" shouted Doherty. Sergeant Major Charles Pinkham, who belatedly remembered that the color sergeant was on furlough, sprinted back to his tent to get them. The 57th had lost its colors at the Crater, and he was not about to let their flag be captured again. Pinkham retrieved the colors and, "though half frightened to death by the bullets whizzing around my ears," regained the regiment without injury. It was forty-five minutes until daylight.[17]

The sector commander, Brevet Brigadier General Napoleon McLaughlen, had learned of the disturbance at Fort Stedman, but assumed it was a raid. He formed his reserve regiment, the 59th Massachusetts, which was camped behind Fort Haskell, and double-quicked it north. Passing through Battery XII, McLaughlen ran into the commander of the 29th Massachusetts, Major Charles Richardson, who told him that he had just been driven out of Battery XI. Ordering the mortars in Battery XII to open up on Richardson's former position, McLaughlen sent in the 59th Massachusetts and what he could find of the 57th and 29th with fixed bayonets to retake the battery. The Massachusetts men went with a will, carrying Battery XI and part of Fort Stedman as well, where they captured many surprised sharpshooters, including Colonel Hamilton Brown and a number of his men.

By now, however, the infantry columns of Grimes, Evans, and Walker began to arrive, lending their weight to the attack. General Grimes followed his division across the parapet but could not convince his horse to join him. Finally he found another one—most likely the unfortunate Major Randall's—and continued. "It would have done your heart good," he wrote his wife, "to hear the men cheer as I rode up and down the line urging them to do their duty." Meanwhile General McLaughlen "crossed the parapet into Fort Stedman on the right, and meeting some men coming over the curtains, whom in the darkness I supposed to be a part of the picket, I established them inside the work, giving directions with regard to position and firing, all of which were instantly obeyed." A slight problem of protocol arose, however, when it became clear that the general was giving orders to the wrong army. Lieutenant Billy Gwyn, commanding the sharpshooters of the Thirty-first Georgia, appeared out of the darkness, informed the general of his error and demanded his surrender. When McLaughlen asked if he was an officer, Gwyn replied "It does not matter, sir, whether I am or not, surrender or I will blow out your brains." McLaughlen surrendered.[18]

The Southern counterattacks had retaken Fort Stedman and Battery XI. It had been no walkover: the Federals characterized the fighting at that point as "desperate … in which the works were carried back and forth several times," while Confederate accounts called it "a tug of war." Hamilton Brown recalled that "a portion of the assaulting column, including its commander, was captured by the enemy, under the command of General McLaughlen, but was shortly afterwards recaptured, and in turn captured General McLaughlen and his command." Individuals continued to change hands as well. Major Randall escaped with his colors, but Major Richardson of the 29th was captured, and Major Doherty of the 57th mortally wounded. John Gordon entered Fort Stedman, where, as he put it, he "relieved" General McLaughlen of his command as well as his sword. "While standing by General Gordon," wrote the Yankee general, "four brigades moved forward toward our works, their commanders reporting to him." Joining the Union general were one of his aides and one of his staff officers, Captain Henry Swords, who had been bagged by Captain Carson. Gordon was pleased. "Up to this point," he wrote, "the success had exceeded my most sanguine expectations." Long after the fact he claimed that his losses to that point had been only eleven men.[19]

Gordon's next task was to widen the breach by capturing Forts McGilvery and Haskell, and to this end some of the assaulting columns turned north and south. Captain Carson recalled that after taking the fort, and hearing nothing from Gordon, he advanced on his own initiative some three-quarters of a mile. His memory seems questionable, however, since Gordon was in the fort and Carson had just delivered Major Swords to him. Carson most likely moved forward with the Division Sharpshooters to cover the flank of Grimes's division, and seems to have taken no part in the attacks that followed. South of Fort Stedman Brigadier General William Terry's Virginia brigade crossed immediately behind the assaulting column, and was in turn followed by the rest of Evans's Georgia brigade. With these fresh troops in play Evans quickly overran Battery XII and began pressing toward Fort Haskell.[20]

On the Union side, following the failure of McLaughlen's counterattack, the 59th and remnants of the 29th Massachusetts retreated south toward Fort Haskell. The 100th Pennsylvania, whose men styled themselves the "Roundheads" after the Parliamentary forces in the English Civil War, was next to receive a call from Waggaman's Louisianans and Terry's Virginians. "The first thing the boys knew," wrote one soldier, "they were firing down our line from the right to the left of the regiment. The boys were asleep in their bunks at the first volley, but grabbed guns and cartridge-boxes, not even stopping to dress. Some were barefooted; some only with shirts and pants on, so that the uniforms were not fully up to the Government standard, but the fighting qualities were above par. The regiment had been practically cut in two. The right took shelter in the rear in some old rifle-pits, while Cos. B and G ran into Fort Haskell." Among those mortally wounded in the retreat was the regiment's commander, Lieutenant Colonel Joseph H. Pentecost. The Confederates continued to press their attack, their sharpshooters mingling with the retreating Pennsylvanians and calling out Pentecost's name.[21]

Still, in spite of the shock and confusion of the attack, there was remarkably little panic in the Federal ranks—certainly not the "disintegration" Gordon had hoped for. The remaining men of the battered 57th Massachusetts retreated east along the road toward the Dunn house. Three times they stopped to make a stand, but each time were flanked by the advancing Confederates.[22]

Fortunately for the Federals, however, the garrison of Fort Haskell—four companies of the 14th New York Heavy Artillery, a six-gun artillery battery, and a mortar detachment—had been alerted by the sounds of fighting coming from up the line. As sentry Sylvester Hough looked toward Fort Stedman, he first saw a series of blue lights, which he later realized was the signal for the taking of the fort, then heard the sounds of men approaching. "The party was in two ranks," wrote one man, "and had filed into our lines through the gap in front of Stedman, and was moving upon us unopposed, for they were between us and our pickets. These Confederates supposed that they were approaching the rear of the little fort, and were moving very confidently, expecting an easy triumph." Recognizing the enemy, Hough hustled back to give the alarm. The fort's gunners double-shot three of their guns with canister, trained them where they expected the column to appear, and waited. Captain Charles Houghton, the garrison's commander, ordered the gunners to wait until they could see the raiders. Soon they heard the whispered voices of the approaching men, "Steady! We'll have their works. Steady, my men!" A moment later Houghton gave the command, "Now!" and the guns' deafening reports rent the air. "Not a word was spoken," wrote one soldier, "but in perfect concert the cannon belched forth grape and our muskets were discharged upon the hapless band." The man who led the burial detail the next day, George Kilmer, claimed to have counted fifty dead Rebels in front of the fort. Still, the Confederates, whoever they were, did not give up easily. The cannon blasts had taken off the head of the column, which was moving at nearly right angles to the fort, but the survivors "split into squads and moved on the flanks, keeping up the by-play until there were none left." Gordon had just lost his best chance of taking Fort Haskell, a failure that would have dire consequences.[23]

In the northern sector Walker's and Ransom's troops pushed toward Battery IX using the same infiltration tactics that had proved so successful elsewhere, but it was hard to hide from the next regiment in line, the 2nd Michigan. Lieutenant John Hardy, in charge of the brigade's picket line, could hear scattered shots and see shadowy figures coming out of Battery X, and a short time later two breathless Massachusetts men arrived to tell him that their regiment had been overrun and captured. Hardy sent word to his commander, Captain John Boughton, who ordered him to arrest the fugitives to stop them from talking. "A few minutes later," noted Boughton, "a crowd of men came running down the trench. Supposing they were of one of our regiments, and running from the enemy, I stepped out and ordered them to halt, saying that it was useless to run away." One of the men put his hand on Boughton's shoulder, saying "Come with me," while another told his men, "it's of no use now; it's all over; you might as well throw down your guns." The Yankee captain realized he had just been captured. "In a minute," he said. "Stepping hastily backward, I ordered the men to fire, which they obeyed immediately with good effect." The Rebels captured fifteen of Boughton's men, but he and the rest escaped to Battery IX. There he reformed his unit and sent out a company to block a Rebel force that was attempting to take the battery from the rear. Alerted by the energetic Lieutenant Hardy, the brigade commander, Colonel Ralph Ely, arrived to take stock of the situation. It was obvious now that communication with the division was cut off, and he would have to fend for himself.[24]

The Rebels, meanwhile, had given up any pretense of stealth and commenced shelling the Federal positions from Fort Stedman. Colonel Ely ordered Major Ed Buckbee of the 1st Michigan Sharpshooters, who held the far right of the line near the river, to take two companies out of line and move them up to cover his flank. These were the same men whom Ramseur's Tarheels had thrashed so badly in the Wilderness. They still

maintained their specialty as light infantry, and a hard year in the line had
honed their combat skills to perfection. Buckbee mounted his horse, John
the Baptist, and turned over tactical command to one of the company commanders, Captain Jim DeLand. One of the companies was the Indian outfit,
Company K, whose members voiced some memorable sentiments as they
moved along. "Me shoot-um damn Johnnie," said one. "Me kill-um much,"
agreed another. "It would have pleased you," Buckbee wrote his mother, "to
hear their remarks."[25]

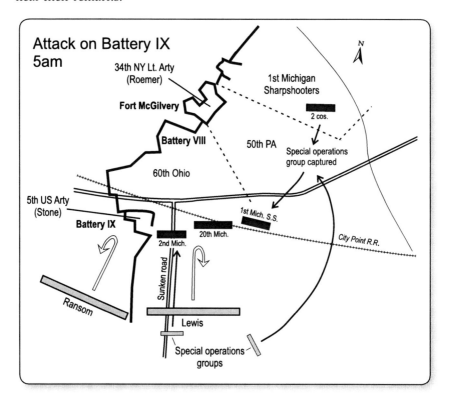

On his way forward Buckbee literally stumbled over one of Gordon's special operation groups, whom he mistook for prisoners. "See! See!" shouted
one of the Rebels, "Shoot that *cuss* on that horse—surrender, you damn
yank." Had they kept quiet, they might have captured or avoided Buckbee,
but as it was he spurred his horse through "more bullets in a square yard
than I had ever experienced before" and escaped unscathed back to his
men. The Indians let loose a war cry that put the Rebel yell to shame and
"went straight at the Rebs on the run." The Confederates promptly surrendered, and their leader wanted to know, "Where is that battery that I
was told was up on the hill just beyond here? I lost my *barrins* entirely and
in some way got away from my men." In their report the Michigan men
claimed to have captured four officers and fifty enlisted men. Buckbee put

his soldiers behind the grade of the City Point railroad, connecting with Boughton's troops and two companies of the 20th Michigan behind Battery IX, effectively blocking any flanking move. Once again the alert Union defenders had stymied Gordon's attempt to quickly take the flanking forts by deception.[26]

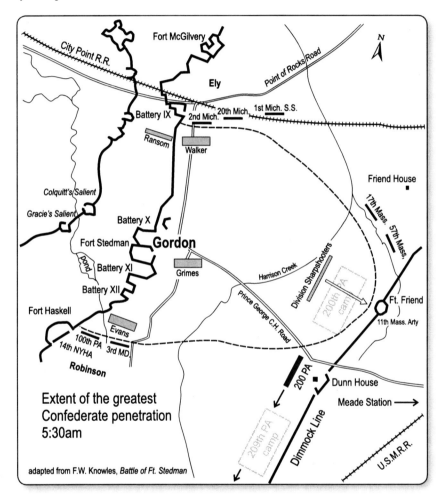

The Federal commanders struggled to sort out conflicting reports and form a plan. In the immediate area they had available the 200th Pennsylvania, which was camped nearly due east of Fort Stedman, just in front of Fort Friend; the 209th Pennsylvania, which lay about a half mile south of it; and the small hundred-man 17th Michigan, which was acting as corps engineers. Between five and five-thirty a.m. the survivors of the 57th Massachusetts joined them, bringing their overall numbers (the two Pennsylvania regiments were nearly full strength) to about two thousand men—comparable to the number of men in Grimes's division, whose sharpshooters were just then approaching the high ground on which Fort Friend lay. The headquarters of the reserve division commander, Brigadier General John Hartranft, was about two miles south, so as he rode through the darkness to join the battle, the division commander on the spot, Major General Orlando Willcox, issued orders to his regiments directly from his own headquarters at the Friend House, half a mile north of the 200th Pennsylvania's camp. Unfortunately, Willcox misjudged both the direction and extent of the Confederate offensive, and put the two Keystone regiments in motion southward. "This movement," wrote Hartranft, "uncovered the objective point of the enemy's attack, viz., Meade's station, and, although the detour of the 209th finally brought it into effective position on the extreme right, the 200th was, for the moment, the only regiment left in any position to strike the enemy."

Willcox had unwittingly swung wide the door to City Point, leaving only a few skirmishers in Grimes's way. Hartranft turned both regiments around, and when he arrived at Willcox's headquarters he found that general packed up and ready to evacuate. As the two generals conferred near the Friend House, they could see, in the dawn's half light, puffs of smoke coming from the woods just behind Fort Stedman. This, realized Hartranft, "being in the rear of our lines, disclosed unmistakably an attack in force, and not a feint. It was a skirmish line followed by an assaulting column or a line of battle." The skirmishers, likely Colonel Hamilton Brown and his sharpshooters, moved out in open order across the low ground where Harrison Creek ran, firing as they advanced. They were now within a quarter mile of the Friend House, with only a few men of the 17th Michigan and the 57th Massachusetts, who were "but feebly replying," to oppose them. Some sharpshooters crossed the creek and made their way up the hill to Fort Friend by way of a ravine. It was just now becoming light enough to see, and the fort's commander, Captain Edward Jones, began throwing shells from the 3-inch rifled guns of his 11th Massachusetts battery toward the dimly seen column moving on Fort Haskell. At nearly the same moment he noted, to his horror, shadowy figures approaching his own position. Unlike the forts on the first line Jones had no infantry with him, but he gamely cranked his guns down and blasted the attackers with canister.[27]

Gordon was now within a hairsbreadth of victory. His men stood at the gates of Fort Haskell and Battery IX, the capture of which would secure his flanks, and were knocking on the door of Fort Friend, the key to the second line. Beyond this, nothing lay between them and City Point.

20

Fort Stedman

"It was better to attack than be attacked."

What John Hartranft needed most now was time—time to bring up his own men before the Rebels could consolidate their position, time for dawn to come, and time for the Union artillery to get into position. Somehow he had to upset John Gordon's timetable. His first break came when the corps artillery commander, Brigadier General John Tidball, rolled his four reserve guns over the rise that formed the second line, "and taking position on the crest of the hill in front of the station opened fire upon the enemy's skirmish line, which by this time had advanced to the ravine between this hill and Fort Stedman." Colonel Hamilton Brown's sharpshooters, unsupported and caught in a withering crossfire, fell back. Fort Friend was safe for the moment, but ten guns and two weak infantry regiments were not enough to stop Second Corps.[1]

Hartranft's battle philosophy was brutally simple: "It was better to attack than be attacked." But thanks to Willcox's ill-advised move he had only one unit—the untried 200th Pennsylvania—within striking distance. Undeterred, he sent the Pennsylvania farm boys straight toward the Rebels. "Intending to force the fighting," he explained, "no time was lost in feeling the enemy or fighting his skirmishers, but the regiment advanced in line of battle." It was their first fight, and with the 17th Michigan and the remnants of the 57th Massachusetts advancing in open order on their right, they swept back Brown's sharpshooters and pushed all the way to the Federal camps at the rear of Fort Stedman. There "the line was strong and the enemy was in force, while the guns of Fort Stedman just captured, turned against us, were on our right." The green Pennsylvania boys kept going, "but the enemy was too strong to be pushed, and the fire from the supports and Fort Stedman was very severe." They fell back to some old works about forty yards behind the fort and took what cover they could.[2]

General Tidball, meanwhile, boldly moved up his guns to support Hartranft's attack. Seeing this, Colonel Stribling, who had run his captured guns out in the rear of Fort Stedman, let fly at them. Perhaps because of their lack of sights the fire of the Rebel cannoneers was, according to Tidball, "inaccurate and straggling and did no injury, and was soon silenced by the fire of artillery concentrated upon that point." Tidball's fire forced a direct reply from the Confederate guns, preventing them from engaging the Union infantry.[3]

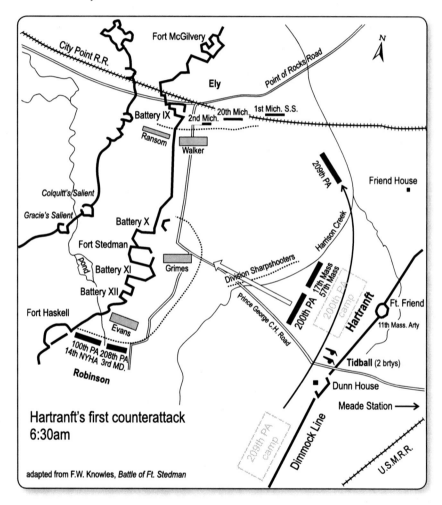

From his saddle Hartranft could see Confederate reinforcements pouring through Fort Stedman. It seemed worth another attack to disrupt this, so he sent the 200th back in. "In the face of a galling fire in front and flanks it succeeded in reaching a fairly defensible position, and for a few moments the troops struggled tenaciously to hold it. Fighting under the eye of the general, every officer and man stood up nobly, and for twenty minutes struggled desperately to hold their own in the face of supporting batteries within a hundred yards and superior forces pressing on all sides." After losing a hundred men during twenty minutes of what Hartranft called "the heaviest fighting of the day," the Pennsylvanians broke and headed rearward. Even so, the general and their officers managed to rally them near where they had started.[4]

Brigadier General John F. Hartranft was breveted to
major general for his performance at Fort Stedman. *B&L*

While the 200th Pennsylvania bled in front of Fort Stedman, Hartranft sent a staffer galloping over to the 209th Pennsylvania. Instead of ordering them to join the 200th in their attack, however, he marched the 209th past them to link up with Colonel Ely's troops near Battery IX, thus firmly barring the door to City Point. Another officer sped south to the brigade's third regiment, the 208th Pennsylvania, ordering them to link up with the troops covering Fort Haskell, extending their line and blocking any attempt to flank it. Meanwhile Hartranft's other brigade of three Pennsylvania regiments hustled into position. By this time it was getting light enough for Union heavy artillery in the surrounding forts to take effective aim.[5]

For John Gordon, on the other hand, the news turned bad. None of the Trojan Horse companies had succeeded, and his men had so far failed to take the flanking forts. Prompt Union counterattacks had disrupted his advance, leaving his plan only half-completed at daylight, and his reinforcements had not yet arrived. Although Gordon had ordered his commanders not to waste men in futile large-scale assaults, attempts to take the forts continued. Indeed, Fort Haskell was far from secure: the work was so crowded with men that not all of them could get to the parapet, so those inside loaded muskets and passed them up to the men on the ramparts. Confederate artillery from Fort Stedman and the forts across no-man's land slammed into

Fort Haskell, sharpshooters let loose "showers of miniés," and mortar shells from the adjacent captured batteries began landing inside. "The air was full of shells," recalled one of the Yankees inside, "and on glancing up one saw, as it were, a flock of blackbirds with blazing tails beating about in a gale. At first the shells did not explode. Their fuses were too long, so they fell intact, and the fires went out. Sometimes they rolled about like foot-balls, or bounded along the parapet and landed in the watery ditch. But when at last the Confederate gunners got the range, their shots became murderous." One exploding shell seriously wounded the fort's commander, Captain Charles Houghton. Major Randall, who had made his way over from Fort Stedman, took command.[6]

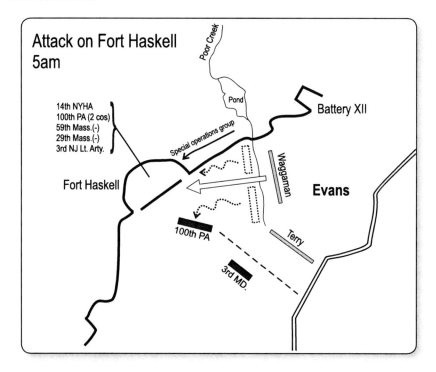

Private George Kilmer watched as "the venturesome Confederate column"—Waggaman's Louisiana Tigers—"came bounding along" toward the fort with a yell. He noted that the column "was preceded, as usual, by sharp-shooters, and these, using the block-houses of the cantonments along the trenches for shelter, succeeded in getting their bullets into the fort, and also in gaining command of our rear sally-port." The veteran Louisianans had picked an angle of attack that was difficult to cover, and although the fort's artillery commander, Captain Christian Woerner, had man-handled a piece to bear on them, Kilmer estimated that no more than fifty muskets could fire at the attackers, who now began to cross a ravine only 165 yards away. While Woerner opened up on them with canister, the infantry "blazed away" with their rifles, momentarily stopping the column. "Each check on this column by our effective firing was a spur to the Confederates at a distance to increase their fire upon us," explained Kilmer. One of Woerner's officers, Lieutenant Julius Tuerk, had an arm blown off while aiming his piece, but Woerner, whose life seemed charmed that day, stepped up and finished adjusting the sights. He left a corporal in charge of the gun while he attended to another, whereupon a sharpshooter put a bullet through the man's brain. To add to the confusion some of the other Union forts thought Haskell had fallen and began to fire at it. Major Randall sent out a plucky detachment from the fort's rear with orders to wave the colors "in the faces of the Confederates" and show the other batteries they were still holding out. Four of the eight men in the color detachment were hit and one died, but the friendly fire stopped.[7]

The climax of the battle was now at hand. "The ranks of the enemy soon broke under the fire of our muskets and Woerner's well-aimed guns," reported Kilmer, "but some of the boldest came within speaking distance and hailed us to surrender. The main body hung back beyond canister range near the ravine at the base of the slope, but within range of our bullets." To clinch the fight the Confederates sent in their elite troops, the sharpshooters. "Suddenly a great number of little parties or squads, of three to six men each, rose with a yell from their hidings down along those connecting parapets, and dashed toward us. The parapets joined on to the fort, and upon these the Confederates leaped, intending thus to scale our walls." But Captain Woerner was ready, and he fired off his other three guns, all loaded with canister. "Some of the squads were cut down, others ran off to cover, and not a few passed on beyond our right wall to the rear of the work and out of reach of the guns. With this the aggressive spirit of that famous movement melted away forever."[8]

Brevet Captain Valentine Stone, commanding a section of Union guns at Battery IX, the next work north from Fort Stedman, strained to see what was happening down the line. "I could just see in the gray of dawn (it was then about 5:15 a.m.) a line of battle drawn up, moving toward me, their right being inside of our works," he recalled. "This line extended along the ravine between Battery No. 9 and Fort Stedman, their left resting near the rebel lines." The Confederate attack, however, had by now lost all chance of surprise. Stone judged the range at about four hundred yards and sent out spherical case from his two 12-pounders to greet the newcomers. Behind him, in Fort McGilvery, another of the Army of the Potomac's doughty gunners, Brevet Major Jacob Roemer, turned around three of his four 3-inch rifles and followed suit. As soon as they did, the Confederate batteries across the lines and in Fort Stedman unleashed a storm of fire. Undeterred, the Yankee gunners pumped out round after round at the approaching line of battle, which broke and retreated. "I thought after I had fired some 100 rounds that the enemy's progress was stopped, as we saw them for a short time falling back," recalled Roemer, "but it was not long before I could see them returning and attacking with double the strength in numbers." More worrisome to Roemer was a number of shadowy figures moving up the sunken road that ran behind the line of forts in an attempt to outflank Battery IX. "To check this movement of the enemy I ran one gun on the barbette in rear of the fort, and by some eight or ten splendid shots turned the enemy's flank and they retreated." This detachment was, according to Colonel Ely, "cut off and captured." During the fight a shell burst wounded Captain Roemer, but he stayed with his guns, helping to repulse another assault.[9]

Across the lines the Fifty-seventh North Carolina, part of Walker's division, hunkered down under a "veritable inferno" of shells, while on the line's far left end the men of the Fifty-sixth North Carolina found "a peculiar use for those troublesome bayonets of which we had been complimented on the inspection of the division"—digging holes for protection against the fire of Stone's guns and Ely's Michigan troops, who "had shown no disposition to get out of our way, or to let us alone." After it was over a Confederate captain told his captors that "the column making the last assault on Battery IX was composed of two brigades, Ransom's and [Lewis's brigade of Walker's division]." He stated that the orders to the attacking party were to move upon the flank and rear of our line, clear the works to McGilvery, and take the fort by assault in the rear. As the captain expressed it, the assailants got along well enough till they "came to this rise (indicating Battery IX), where you-uns sort of discouraged us."[10]

As the sky lightened, Hartranft's second brigade came puffing up. He had a staff officer send the 205th and 207th Pennsylvania regiments to plug the gap between the 200th Pennsylvania, which had fallen back in front of Fort Stedman, and 208th Pennsylvania near Fort Haskell. The brigade's third regiment, the 211th Pennsylvania, moved around to cover the road to Meade's Station. In less than two hours Hartranft had forged a ring of steel around Gordon's men. It would soon become a ring of fire as well.[11]

Full daylight revealed the desperation of the Confederate position. Fort Stedman lay at the apex of an arc, with Forts Haskell and McGilvery at the ends. Union artillery there commanded the ground behind Fort Stedman, making any Southern withdrawal a risky business. From the high ground behind Fort Stedman the guns of IX Corps sent a hurricane of shells toward the exposed Southerners, driving them back into bombproofs or holes hastily scratched from the earth. Gordon had only the six guns captured earlier that morning to make a response. No one could fault Colonel Stribling and his men, but they were running low on ammunition and subject to intense counter-battery fire. His plan in tatters, Gordon gave the order to retreat.[12]

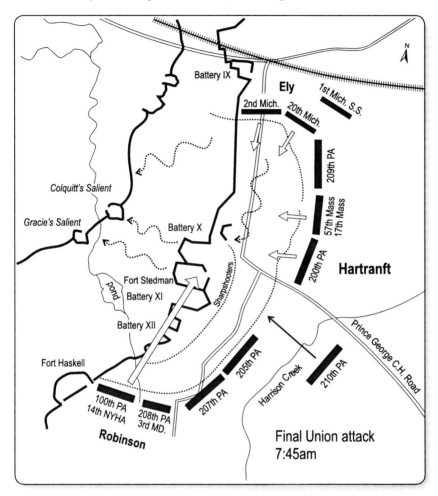

Meanwhile, the situation inside Fort Stedman grew steadily worse. Major Theodore Miller, a Union staff officer captured earlier that morning, observed that "the artillery ... had opened furiously, and their fire was most accurate and destructive. Rebel officers came and reported the effect to be terrible, and stated that their lines could not be held at any point. ... The wounded were brought in in great numbers; I noticed among them a large proportion of officers. The number of stragglers and skulkers was astonishingly large, and I saw several instances where the authority of the officers who urged them on was set at defiance."[13]

Seeing their opponents waver, the Union commanders decided to attack. Hartranft's superiors wanted him to wait for reinforcements, but the

Pennsylvania general gave the order for a general assault around 7:30. Upon hearing the order, the commander of the troops around Fort Haskell, Colonel Gilbert Robinson (who replaced the captured General McLaughlen), "seeing the demoralized condition of the enemy, and fearful that a large amount of prisoners might be lost by longer delay ... determined to dash on the enemy at once." Captain Carson watched them coming. "The whole field was blue with them," he recalled. "I think the columns must have been twenty deep. With our Whitworth rifles we began to pick off a few prominent individuals; but we could not kill a whole army, and presently we had to retire, which we did, contesting every foot of ground."[14]

Carson's comments notwithstanding, Confederate resistance collapsed under the rain of shells and a concerted infantry attack. "All order seemed to be at an end," observed Union major Miller, who talked a couple hundred of his erstwhile captors into surrendering to him. The rest of the Rebels, privates and generals alike, scrambled back across no-man's land to their trenches through a hail of shells that "screeched and screamed like fiends, plowing up the ground on all sides, exploding with a sound like thunder claps, sending their fragments on errands of death and destruction in every direction." From Fort Haskell George Kilmer watched the ground between the lines turned into "a place of fearful slaughter. My mind sickens at the memory of it—a real tragedy in war—for the victims had ceased fighting, and were now struggling between imprisonment on the one hand, and death or home on the other." A soldier from the Sixth North Carolina wrote that "some laid down and was taken prisoners, but when I thought of Point Lookout you better know I come out."[15]

General James Walker was one of the last men to quit the fort, watching the "gallant fight" of his sharpshooters as they tried to hold off the advancing Federals long enough for the rest of the division to escape. "Suddenly I heard a shout," he said, "and looking in the direction of the sound, I saw a body of Federal infantry coming over the wall of the fort on the opposite side." These were Robinson's men, led by the 100th Pennsylvania, who would always claim that their colors were first in the fort. The Roundheads' early arrival from the south meant that almost all the sharpshooters outside the fort were now cut off. Exercising his discretion the general vaulted the parapet and was soon "crossing the stormswept space between us and our works." But the rising sun had softened the frosty ground, and mud soon caked his thigh-high cavalry boots. "My speed slackened into a slow trot, then into a slow walk, and it seemed as if I were an hour making that seventy-five yards." To add his discomfiture the Union infantry now in the fort added their musketry, "thick as hail," to the cannon fire. "Every time I lifted my foot with its heavy weight of mud and boot," he remembered, "I thought my last step was taken. Out of the ten or a dozen men who started across that field with me, I saw at least half of them fall, and I do not believe more than one or two got over safely." Among the many wounded were John Gordon, lucky to have only a flesh wound, and Lieutenant Billy Gwyn, shot through both legs. "Nearly all my gallant skirmish line was captured," lamented Walker. So, apparently, was most of Grimes's. Colonel Brown and—to judge by the number of sharpshooters who later turned up at Point Lookout—most of his men went in the Federal bag. This was the most serious loss of the day for the Confederates, as they represented a great many of their best remaining soldiers. Hartranft's Pennsylvanians arrived minutes later, completing the Federal sweep.[16]

Captain Carson was one of those who made his way safely back across the killing zone, but any relief he might have felt about his escape was tempered by personal tragedy—just as he had feared, a bullet had found his brother Bob. Carson found a horse and brought back his brother's body. "As I entered our lines again, from which we had gone so hopefully in the early morning," he wrote, "I looked back on Fort Stedman. There in the sunlight floated again the Stars and Stripes."[17]

When the smoke cleared the Federals counted more than a thousand Rebels captive, while admitting the loss of just under eleven hundred men of their own men, half of them prisoners taken in the initial rush. They also prided themselves, when all was over, in losing not a single gun or color. Overall Confederate casualties probably topped twenty-six hundred men.[18]

Eventually the "long gray procession" of Confederates began shuffling toward City Point, not as victors but as prisoners. "Really these men possess a capacity for looking 'rough' beyond any people I ever saw," noted a Union staff officer who watched them. "They grew rougher and rougher. These looked brown and athletic, but had the most matted hair, tangled beards, and slouched hats, and the most astounding carpets, horse-sheets and transmogrified shelter-tents for blankets, that you ever imagined." What they saw during their trek discouraged them beyond measure. "In going to the rear I saw thousands of Yanks playing ball and in camp," wrote Alabama sharpshooter Oscar Whitaker, "and our poor boys fighting and dying against tremendous odds in front. I was taken to Grant's Headquarters there was a Yankee Corps passing in review. I saw Gen. Grant, Abe Lincoln and his son Bob." Most of them concluded then and there that the cause had "gone up." The president had come to City Point to confer with his top general, and about the only effect of Gordon's offensive had been to delay this review from mid-morning to mid-afternoon. Lincoln described it in a telegram as "a little rumpus up the line this morning, ending about where it began." When someone wanted to give him a message about it from the IX Corps commander, the commander-in-chief pointed to the prisoners and said "Ah, *there* is the best despatch you can show me from General Parke!"

Ironically, this particular batch of captives almost certainly contained some of the sharpshooters who had taken shots at him at Fort Stevens.[19]

That afternoon, when General Lee wrote Secretary of War John Breckinridge about the offensive's failure, he noted that "the conduct of the sharpshooters of Gordon's corps, who led assault, deserves the highest commendation." Two days later he dashed off an addendum to praise the conduct of Colonels Jones and Stribling, the artillerymen who "carried the enemy's breast-works with the sharpshooters of the corps, and immediately turned upon the enemy the captured guns." Among his generals, the reaction was mixed. Gaston Lewis called it "a fiery trial," while Bryan Grimes thought it was "badly managed" and wondered why Gordon did not immediately withdraw when it became clear that the operation could not succeed. Clement Evans was unhappy with the performance of his division, which showed the effects of the long siege: "Many of the troops behaved well, but in this as in former actions, I could but observe how sadly we need reorganization and discipline. It is almost impossible at times to maneuver the troops at all."[20]

Overall the offensive had left Lee's army even weaker than before and raised the morale of their opponents correspondingly. The Federal IX Corps, in particular, had come a long way since the days of Burnside and Ledlie, and many of its men thought that their victory at Fort Stedman had in some way made up for what they had suffered at the Crater.

Over time, the sharpshooters gradually dropped out of the accounts of the battle. Gordon does not specifically refer to them in his surviving postwar writings, nor did General Walker. General Lee, however, praised them in his report written the day of the battle, and numerous soldier accounts and official histories credit the sharpshooters with leading the assault. One ex-general who did not forget was William Cox (a former sharpshooter commander himself), who specifically mentions that Colonel Brown and his sharpshooters, whose outfit was "about the size of an ordinary regiment," took part in the attack, even though the rest of his brigade did not.[21]

Rather than advancing in a single line, Gordon seems to have sent the sharpshooters forward in a number of semi-independent groups that did not worry about their flanks or the progress of the units next to them. In other words, this was an example of a true nonlinear formation—something virtually unheard of in the nineteenth century. The same goes for the innovative Trojan Horse infiltration units who attempted to capture the supporting forts. Clement Evans, whose report alone survived, gives the clearest idea of what would today be called the task organization of his force into three groups—again, a revolutionary concept for the nineteenth century. Judging from the surviving accounts, these groups operated more or less independently in assaulting Batteries XI and XII. When the forts had been taken, Terry's Virginia brigade, along with the rest of Evans's Georgia brigade, joined them. The way Evans (or perhaps Waggaman) attempted to take Fort Haskell is of interest also. After failing to take it by a *ruse de guerre*, the Confederates tried an assault with "a great number of little parties or squads" rather than a mass attack, which Evans had been ordered to avoid. Other sharpshooters provided suppressive fire—again, a modern concept—while their comrades went forward. They very nearly succeeded.[22]

Many questions about the battle of Fort Stedman remain that are beyond the scope of this book to address. Why did Gordon not use the four brigades of infantry he did have on hand? Why did he wait so long to withdraw? Why did he not make a stronger push toward Fort Friend? In any case, whatever his failures, John Gordon stands out as a brilliant tactical innovator. Here, at almost the end of the war, we get a glimpse of things to come—nonlinear formations, the use of elite troops to infiltrate the enemy lines, and combined arms task organizations. Technical innovations that would change the face of the battlefield—land mines, hand grenades, and repeating rifles—were either not readily available or in relatively primitive form, while others, like barbed wire and fully automatic weapons, lay in the future. Nevertheless, the armies of both sides found themselves facing many of the problems that their successors would find fifty years hence: the necessity of moving through a heavily fortified zone and the difficulty of supporting an offensive across no-man's land. Gordon's attack on Fort Stedman marks the first clear break between the linear line-of-battle world of the nineteenth century and the nonlinear world of the twentieth.

21

Decision at Petersburg

"These men will fight."

Concluding that Lee had weakened the Army of Northern Virginia else-where to attack Fort Stedman, Grant ordered the rest of his army to attack the Confederate lines, and during the afternoon of March 25 the Federal II and VI Corps drove in the Rebel pickets, taking their rifle pits and pressing their main works. Their job was made easier because the Confederate sharpshooters who would normally have been on the picket line were either resting after a night of guard duty or supporting Gordon. Fortunately the pickets delayed the Yankees long enough for the four brigades General A. P. Hill had sent to aid Gordon's Second Corps time enough to return to their lines and stabilize the situation. While the Federals failed to make any real breakthroughs, they captured more than eight hundred prisoners and took some four miles of Confederate picket lines and forward positions—gains that would soon prove critical. Both sides suffered some twelve hundred to fifteen hundred casualties each, about as much as they had at Fort Stedman. Up to this point the lines at the western end of the siege had been rather widely separated, but they were now nearly as close as the lines on the eastern sector.[1]

Late in the day the Confederates, led by their sharpshooters, began a series of sharp counterattacks to regain their picket lines. Cooke's Tarheels marched directly into the fight, and according to Colonel Samuel Walkup of the Forty-eighth North Carolina, "we then sent out our Sharpshooters on their left flank & drove the Yankees out of our pickets without much loss." Supported by the Second Mississippi of Davis's brigade, Major Wooten's sharpshooters of McRae's brigade "broke through a strong line of battle, and, wheeling to the right, swept everything before them." Few of the attacks went as well, and as night fell the Federals held most of what they had gained that day.[2]

One of the day's most bitter fights took place toward the end of the lines near Battery 45, where the Federals had wrested most of the picket line away from Wilcox's division. After a seesaw battle at Jones's Farm the Confederates were finally driven back at dusk. Captain Dunlop's Sharpshooters (who had been off duty) came up "and engaged the enemy at a range of about two hundred and fifty yards, which caused them to hug their works with amusing tenacity." At dusk some of the sharpshooters moved forward and occupied the Jones House—a "commodious residence" between the new lines—and began harassing the Federals, who were fortifying their gains. This led to a sortie by the Vermont brigade, which cleared the house, then came back with three companies to burn it.[3]

Both sides spent the chilly night establishing new picket lines, this time much closer to each other. The most troublesome consequence of the Federal advance, from the Confederate point of view, was their occupation of a low knoll called McIlwaine's Hill. This overlooked their line and could cause serious problems for the Rebels if the boys in blue chose to place artillery there.

The next day passed without any major combat, but in spite of a short truce to recover the dead and wounded, both Union and Confederate sharpshooters remained active. Dunlop claimed that his men "with merciless accuracy were peeling the topknots from every Federal head that peered above their rifle pits in McGowan's front; for be it remembered, 'they never touched a trigger without drawing blood.'" Sergeant Berry Benson described the fight: "Our Battalion of Sharpshooters had been inside the main breastworks when the attack occurred. We were now thrown out front, Co. C going first, then Co's A and B to connect with it, to sharpshoot. As we became immediately exposed to after leaving the breastworks, we had to hide the best we could, by creeping along gullies and depressed ground, taking every advantage of that kind possible." A hot picket fight continued the rest of that day and into the next, with the Rebel sharpshooters digging another line of rifle pits about eighty yards in front of the picket line. "As the slightest exposure of a man was certain to call forth a number of shots, some of the boys concluded to try the time-honored dodge of holding up a dummy," recalled Benson. He and his mates constructed a crude mannequin made of a coat tied to a stick or a ramrod with a hat on top. "Pop, went the rifles! Dummy was dropped, and a shout went up from the enemy. One more 'rebel' killed!" The ruse continued until the Yankees caught on, but "even then we could sometimes fool them by moving the dummy along as though it were a man walking."[4]

McIlwaine's Hill

At 10 o'clock p.m. on March 26 Dunlop met with his brigade commander, General Samuel McGowan, who told him that McIlwaine's Hill had to be retaken "at all hazards" and promised the men a thirty-day furlough as an incentive. About 1:30 a.m. Dunlop conferred with the other sharpshooter battalion commanders, including Major Wooten and Captain Young, and together they laid their plans. After some deliberation they decided to assault "in solid order of battle" (i.e. elbow to elbow) and take the hill by storm. They would use a variation of Wooten's "seine-hauling": Dunlop's and Wooten's battalions would advance first in column, with Young's battalion and the sharpshooters of Thomas's brigade just behind them. Upon breaking through the Federal line the two leading battalions would wheel—Dunlop to the left and Wooten to the right—and the other two battalions would pass between them to take the crest of the hill. Their total force amounted to about four hundred men. As the leaders prepared for the attack, the soldiers on the line put out their fires a few at a time so as not to arouse suspicion, and their commander ensured that "every precaution [was] taken so that our movements might not be discovered." Just before dawn—Dunlop thought it was about 5 a.m.—they began crossing their breastworks. "We were bound on an adventure," recalled Benson, "in which each Brigade's Battalion determined to outdo every other Battalion." [5]

The Federals had some inkling of the danger. VI Corps commander Horatio Wright ordered a "stand-to" at 4 a.m. and sent a column of reinforcements toward the hill. Still, after two days of hard fighting the bluecoats were exhausted and their guard was down. While they slumbered the sharpshooters crept forward a hundred yards or so then silently crossed a ditch. "With but a moment's delay to adjust the lines and see that none stuck in the ditch," remembered Dunlop, "the advance was continued." Sergeant Benson could not believe their luck—"the snapping of sticks, the rustlings of brush seemed to me so loud that I could not understand how we went so far undiscovered." Finally there came a challenge, a shot, and "in the same instant a wild Confederate yell split the air." The sharpshooters rushed forward, overrunning the Union line and then quickly wheeling right and left, clearing the works while the following column pushed past them. Surprise was so complete that the Yankees, who belonged to Getty's division, fled after firing only "a few scattering shots." The Vermont brigade lost forty-nine men (about half captured), and the other defending brigade (Hyde's) about as many. As dawn approached a Union relief column hove into view, only to be driven off by long-range rifle fire and a lone artillery piece. Dunlop put his losses at ten or fifteen men and boasted that the storming of the hill had been "unquestionably one of the most daring and successful engagements ... ever witnessed." While Dunlop's immodest assessment might have been

true, victory at McIlwaine's Hill did little to change the overall situation the
Army of Northern Virginia now found itself in—overstretched in an ever-
lengthening defense line under close and constant pressure.[6]

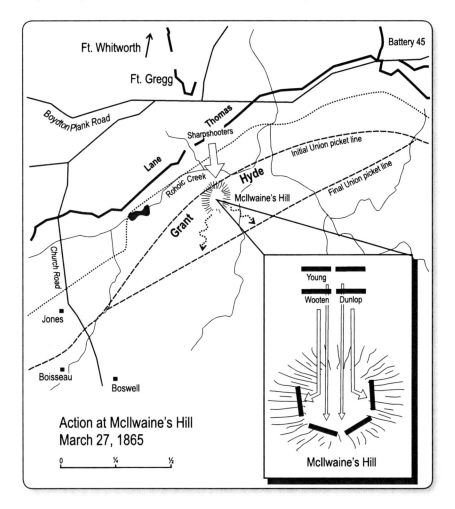

Action at McIlwaine's Hill
March 27, 1865

On March 29 McGowan's brigade, sharpshooters in the lead, shifted
westward to Burgess's Mill, near the end of the Confederate line. The sharpshooters went on picket, exchanging long-range fire with Yankee sentries
that caused little damage to either side. "The rain was pouring down," recalled Major Dunlop, "and the roads were heavy with deep mud." Two days
later Lee attacked at nearby White Oak Road, attempting to take advantage
of the open Union flank there. Initially the attack went well. Berry Benson,
still on the picket line, listened as the sounds of skirmishing swelled into
those of a full-blown battle. Soon he saw "a beautiful sight": his brigade
advancing though the woods, driving the Federals before them in disorder.

The line passed and sounds of battle faded into the forest but picked up again a short time later. McGowan's men appeared again, this time retreating as Yankee reinforcements pressed them. The sharpshooters, whose position ran obliquely along the flank of the battle line, began enfilading the enemy lines as they came into range. Having driven the main part of McGowan's brigade into its entrenchments, the Yankees now turned their attention to Benson and his comrades.

"In solid double line of battle they formed," he recalled, "and out from the woods into the field they marched, flags flying. We at once opened up on them ... and did good execution." Benson shouldered a captured Spencer "seven-shooter" and fired his forty available rounds, stopping once to let his piece cool off. The sharpshooters knocked down the Federal colors three times, and most of the Yankees dropped to the ground to avoid the hot Rebel fire. "How we did keep pouring bullets into them, [using] the flags for a mark!" Benson remembered. Finally the Federal officers got their men back on their feet and into a charge. The sharpshooters waited until the Yankees closed, then fired a last volley and beat it back to their breastworks. "It was a dear fight for them; their losses had been heavy, while ours had been astonishingly light." No one in Benson's outfit had been killed, and only a few wounded.[7]

Early the next morning General McGowan summoned Benson for a scouting expedition. The brigade moved westward to meet a Union threat near Dabney House on White Oak Road, and no one knew exactly where the Yankees were. Benson's description of the advance shows how sharpshooters were used in such a fluid situation: "I was ordered to proceed with two or three men as scouts, while at a distance behind us should follow the Sharpshooters, and behind them the brigade in line-of-battle. I took Ben Powell and Shade Thomas, and posting one to the right of me, one to the left at a distance of between 50 and 100 yards, we moved forward through the forest." Benson and his scouts spotted the Yankee entrenchments across White Oak Road, and seeing no one in them, climbed over "with fast beating hearts." Their luck held. Not only were the Federals gone, they had left behind a huge amount of "knapsacks, guns, and provisions of all kinds" for the taking.[8]

Breakthrough at Petersburg

On April 1 General Philip Sheridan crushed the Confederate forces under George Pickett and Fitzhugh Lee at Five Forks, and that afternoon Grant ordered a "general assault along the lines" for the next morning. The men in blue spent the rest of the day and night preparing for this momentous event, which might decide the campaign. Some thought the order an April

Fool's joke, while others, perhaps more realistically, began scribbling their names and units on slips of paper to be pinned to their uniforms. The Union commanders had learned a great deal about trench warfare in the last year, much of it from their opponents.

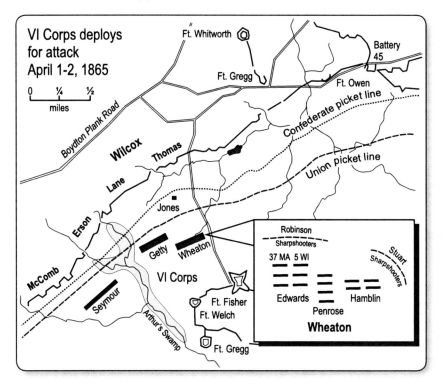

General Horatio Wright had organized his VI Corps into a giant fly-ing wedge. Getty's division would form the point of the advance, with his brigades in columns of regiments. The corps other two divisions, organized similarly, were echeloned back on either side. The center of the blow would fall at Jones's Farm, site of the extended picket fight the week before. Com-manders cautioned their men to speak in low tones during the advance to the picket line and ordered them to leave their canteens and packs behind. They would make the assault without firing, so the leading ranks would go in with their rifles unloaded and bayonets fixed. As had Gordon's men the week before, each column would include a pioneer detachment armed with axes to cut through the abatis and four lines of *chevaux-de-frise*. Wright attached a battery of artillery to each division with two more in general sup-port and also sent along a volunteer detachment of cannoneers equipped to make use of captured enemy guns. Retaining their tactical innovation of the previous year, each of VI Corps's divisions fielded a company of sharpshoot-ers drawn from across the unit. General Getty assigned his own division

sharpshooter company, under Brevet Major William H. Terrell of the 43rd
New York, to bolster his picket line, which was under the overall command
of Colonel Charles A. Milliken of the same regiment.[9]

The ball opened at ten o'clock that night with a stunning artillery bom-
bardment along the lines. "It is probable," boasted one Union gunner, "that
never since the invention of gunpowder has such a cannonade taken place."
While the guns fired, the Federal troops groped their way through the mist
and smoke to their assembly positions, just shy of the Federal picket line.
There they waited, some lying and some standing, on the rising ground
behind the line. The cannonade tapered off around 1 a.m., but an hour later
a "severe and galling" picket fight broke out. Unlike the afternoon of the
twenty-fifth, this time the Confederates had their elite sharpshooters standing guard. One of these was J. S. Kimbrough, a sharpshooter with Thomas's
Georgia brigade who had been sent out two hundred yards in front of his
picket line to see what was going on. "I could hear distinctly the enemy in
my front preparing for the charge," he remembered, "when suddenly to my
right, perhaps a mile below, our skirmish line began a rapid firing which
came steadily up the line until our men behind me caught the infection and
began pouring a fusillade into the woods behind me." Kimbrough hurriedly
crawled back to his own lines, whereupon he "gave my excited comrades
a piece of my mind in not very complimentary terms." Even though these
men had no clear idea of what lay beyond the Yankee picket line, their fire
began to take a toll on the packed ranks of the waiting assault columns, who
suffered in silence as one man after another dropped into the muck with
a muffled groan. The commander of the Vermont brigade, General Lewis
Grant, was carried from the field with a minor but painful head wound,
while the less fortunate commanders of the 49th New York and 61st Pennsylvania sustained mortal injuries. Eventually the firing tapered off, and
someone shouted "April Fool, Johnnies!" There was nothing to do now but
wait in the freezing mud until 4 a.m., the time scheduled for the attack.[10]

The rumble of IX Corps artillery up the line that morning masked the sound
of the VI Corps signal gun, and thus it was nearly a quarter of five before
Wright's three divisions jumped off. On Getty's right the men of Brigadier
General Frank Wheaton's division—the veterans of Fort Stevens—slogged
forward in the darkness. On his left, next to Getty's division, marched Colonel Oliver Edwards's brigade, his narrow front consisting of the 37th Massachusetts and the 5th Wisconsin. A line of seventy-five men "picked men"
from the 37th Massachusetts under Captain John Robinson screened the
brigade's front with their fast-firing Spencer repeaters, as well as covering a
twenty-man pioneer detachment equipped with axes. Edwards also saw to
it that extra axes went to the men in the first line, "in case the axmen had

trouble." Sharpshooting Rebel pickets in the rifle pits before them "severely harassed" Edward's skirmish line as it formed up in the darkness.[11]

Colonel Joseph Hamblin's brigade stood on the right of Wheaton's division and VI Corps. Wheaton had placed his own division sharpshooters, commanded by Captain James Stuart of the 49th Pennsylvania, in a flank guard role similar to long-established Confederate practice. This unit probably looked like that of Getty's division, with about a hundred men drawn from the units across the division. Some three-quarters of Stuart's men carried Spencer "seven-shooters," and it was these soldiers who were strung out in a skirmish line on Hamblin's flank. The rest, armed with "telescope and globe rifles," remained behind in support.[12]

Once in motion, the Federal juggernaut quickly swamped the Confederate pickets and closed with their main line. The avalanche fell mainly on Lane's North Carolina brigade, but even considering his supports (there were no reserves), the fight pitted some fourteen thousand Yanks against less than three thousand Confederates, who in their own estimation presented only a "cob-web force" to stop them. Nevertheless, the Rebels resisted gamely. General Wheaton admitted that while "it was known that the works we were ordered to storm were well protected by lines of abatis, all were astonished to find these obstructions such serious obstacles and so difficult to remove; openings were made in them, however, under a severe canister and musketry fire." Even though his commanders considered Captain Robinson and his sharpshooters a "forlorn hope," they performed excellent service in covering the axmen. Robinson was severely wounded, but soon the blue columns reached the breastworks, overwhelming the defenders in stiff fighting that was at times hand to hand. After a brief resistance the defense collapsed, leaving great gaps in the lines of the Confederate Third Corps. Its commander, General A. P. Hill, was killed in the ensuing confusion when he ran into a Union detachment. Wright's men surged forward, crossing the Boydton Plank Road and splitting the Army of Northern Virginia in two.[13]

On the line's right end Captain Stuart's division sharpshooters had moved forward with the attack, screening Hamblin's flank. Once the brigade reached the works, however, Stuart remained outside them and wheeled right—"my line conforming to their movements put me on the flank of the picket-line of the enemy, the most of which I captured for the distance of about half a mile." In the process Stuart scooped up about sixty-five Rebel pickets. As soon as Lieutenant House, who had been left behind with the marksmen armed with target rifles, saw that the works had been captured, he brought them forward and put them to work on the enemy's artillery. Having penetrated the Confederate position (whose defenders, conceded one Yank, "showed the greatest obstinacy"), a detachment from Hamblin's brigade under Lieutenant Colonel Henry Fisk of the 65th New

York and Lieutenant Colonel John Harper of the 95th Pennsylvania also
wheeled right and began rolling up the Southern line, while Stuart's men
paced them on the outside of the works. Meanwhile Colonel Milliken's skirmishers, who had crossed the lines with Getty's division, also turned right
and moved up in front of Hamblin's men, who continued northeast against
disorganized resistance for nearly two miles. Most of the rest of VI Corps,
including Getty's division, stopped for reorganization on the Boydton Plank
Road then reoriented on a line facing southwest. Only part of Hamblin's
brigade and the two picket/sharpshooter outfits continued pushing east
toward Petersburg. Colonel Hamblin had task-organized his command in a
very modern sense, sending detachments north to cut the telegraph and the
South Side Railroad as well as the one moving east.[14]

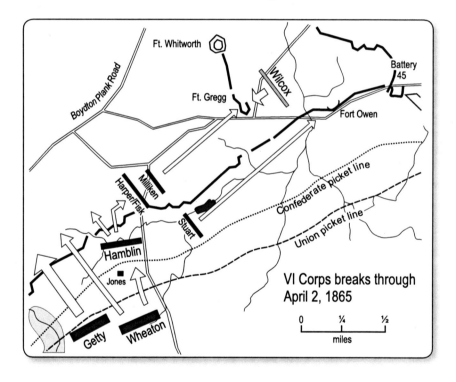

Ahead of them lay Lee's last bastion—the west-facing inner line defending Petersburg itself, which ran north from Battery 45. About a quarter
mile in front of it stood two unfinished earthworks, Forts Whitworth and
Gregg. Just south of Fort Gregg, on the main line, lay another redoubt, Fort
Owen, which the Confederates had hastily constructed after the Federal
offensive of March 25. Just now they were both lightly defended: only a
couple of guns of the Washington Artillery and a score of men under Lieutenant Henry Battles garrisoned Fort Owen, and a few artillerymen armed
with rifles protected Fort Gregg. Scattered in and around the forts were the

jumbled remnants of Lane's and Thomas's brigades, among them sharp-shooter J. S. Kimbrough. "We left our position on the skirmish line and fell back to the works," he said, "only to find them deserted and the enemy, line after line with colors flying, close in pursuit of our decimated and now scattered column. Our skirmish line commander no longer tried to keep us in ranks, and each man constituted himself a committee of one to look out for his own safety." Along with an officer and a few men from his company, Kimbrough stopped at Fort Owen long enough to see "one defiant fellow, who seemed to be in command, walking the parapets around his gun with hat off and hurling anathemas loud and deep at the advancing foe, while the air was vocal with the hiss of their bullets." The officer, probably Lieuten-ant Battles, implored the Georgians to help him defend his battery from the Yankees, who were now within two hundred yards of them. Seeing no chance of success they continued on toward Fort Gregg, only to see a squad of Federals advancing a hundred yards ahead of them, intent on cutting them off. Kimbrough knelt, laid his Enfield on the berm, and squeezed off a shot at the bluecoat officer leading them. "At the crack of my gun I saw his sword thrown into the air above his head and the brave fellow fall forward upon his face. The men gathered around him and made no further effort to cut us off." It was Kimbrough's last shot in the war.[15]

Meanwhile the Federals closed on the inner defenses. "Having met with success so far," reported Colonel Milliken, "I ordered the line forward again and about seventy-five men, pickets and sharpshooters, entered a work known as Fort McGraw and captured three guns." As Milliken and his men did so, Captain Stuart wheeled left and overran another work, which he also thought was Fort McGraw, capturing by his count "3 guns, 3 commissioned officers, and 25 men." Since there was no work by that name on the Confed-erate line, however, what they almost certainly occupied were Forts Gregg and Owen respectively—the keys to the city of Petersburg. Their triumph was brief, however: a Confederate counterattack was brewing and Federal ammunition was running low. As the graybacks approached, the Yankee sharpshooters, who probably numbered no more than two hundred men, fell back after exchanging a few long-range shots. Milliken blamed Stuart for the loss: "This work [Gregg] could have been held had the picket-line of the First Division advanced and kept up the connection between the two divisions." It was an unfortunate retreat. Recapturing Fort Gregg later that day would require a bloody assault.[16]

While Hamblin probed Petersburg's defenses, the bulk of VI Corps began moving westward toward Hatcher's Run, quickly overrunning Fort Alexan-der, a four-gun battery that stood in their way. A quarter of a mile further lay another work, Fort Davis. Flushed by their success, a mixture of units from Brigadier General Truman Seymour's division swept over it, capturing its two guns. Instead of running, however, the defenders—Brigadier General William McComb's Tennessee brigade—withdrew to a swampy patch of woods nearby, keeping up a brisk fire at the invaders. As McComb tried to reorganize his brigade for a counterattack, "telling his men of their many glorious deeds and that he was prepared to sacrifice his own life if necessary," reinforcements arrived from an unexpected quarter. McComb's Brigade Sharpshooters, under Lieutenant Fergus Harris, had been caught out on the picket line when VI Corps broke though. "Each minute was worth a million of dollars," explained Sergeant Henry Manson. "If we remained a little longer the whole command would be surrounded and captured. Besides, our brigade needed our help." Manson ran back to the main lines, dodging more than a few friendly bullets before he convinced his comrades to cease firing. The sharpshooters obliqued back into position, "in such perfect order that it seemed as if keeping step." Captain John Allen, a staff officer who had been "making the air blue" rousting shirkers, met him. "Harris, the men are badly demoralized," he said. "I don't believe we can retake the battery. Can you lead them?" "These men will fight," replied Harris. "Let me lead them with my sharpshooters."[17]

Harris then "jerked off his hat, waved it in the air, and struck up a brisk trot toward the enemy, hurrahing at the top of his voice," and led the brigade toward the fort, his men bounding over the parapet into what Sergeant Manson called "a regular devil's picnic." Manson soon met "a tall, angular Federal" on the breastworks who loosed a shot at him "at a point blank range of less than forty steps." Manson ducked behind the corner of a log hut as bark spattered on his face. Then, "with a prayer for the soul of the bravest Yankee I ever saw," he brought his own Sharps rifle up and put a ball squarely into the man's chest. The remaining Federals withdrew back across the swamp. General McComb was pleased: "I never saw our boys make a more gallant charge." He promoted Harris to captain on the spot.[18]

The Yankees refused to give up their prize so easily. They fired into Fort Davis with the guns captured at Fort Alexander while they prepared to renew their offensive. Sometime around 7 a.m. they came forward again, this time reinforced by the Vermont brigade, which moved on their flank. As McComb's sharpshooters pumped bullets into the approaching ranks, Captain Arch Norris ordered Manson to take some men and try to block the flanking column. "At the rally call a handful of seven responded—seven men that would try anything—and they charged that column." Manson fell almost immediately to a bullet that broke his leg. His men attempted to carry him off the field, but "by this time the line was broken and the enemy had it all their own way." The Tennesseans lost the fort and would not regain it.[19]

The advancing Federals captured Manson and relieved him of his valuables, but "a big, red-faced, thick-set Major" ordered them to return the items then made sure that the Tennessee sergeant was put on an ambulance and sent to a certain surgeon the major trusted. Manson lost his leg but survived. Two days later, much to his surprise, the soldier he had shot at Fort Davis walked into the hospital. Oddly, however, his wound was in his jaw. "Calling him to my bed, I found that he was the same man, and his wounds were explained by himself thus: 'I shot at a feller at the corner of a cabin, and missed him, when he shot me in the breast here,' pulling open his shirt, 'the ball hitting in front on the collar-bone and knocking me off the works. Some of our own cowardly fellows shot me in the jaw after I got up.'" Manson told him that he was "the feller that drew a bead on him," and attributed his opponent's survival to the poor quality of the cartridges he had been using. The two became fast friends.[20]

After losing Fort Davis McComb's men retreated "in a demoralized condition" until they ran into a company of McGowan's Sharpshooters under Captain William Brunson, who had been detached to retake the picket line near Hatcher's Run. Brunson's men had already thrashed a Yankee cavalry outfit that morning, and many of his sharpshooters were now clomping around in oversized cavalry boots as a result. Sending out a screen of sharpshooters, Brunson helped cover McComb's retreat while the latter tried to rally his troops. The South Carolinians played "a game of bluff" with the horsemen in blue, pretending to attack and then retreating, which worked well enough for the Rebels to escape westwards. Meanwhile Berry Benson and his men also fell back, after first breaking up some abandoned rifles to keep them out of Union hands, and then "making a stand at any favorable point" as the enemy began to press them.[21]

Sutherland's Station

The attacks on the far western end of Lee's line began later that morning, with the Federal II Corps overwhelming the Confederate picket line about 7:30 a.m. and driving them from their main line near Hatcher's Run a half hour later. The defenders were a polyglot mix of understrength brigades—Scales's and McGowan's from Wilcox's division, plus Cooke's and McRae's from Heth's division—under the command of Major General Henry Heth (the same man who in 1858 had translated the manual on target practice). Heth, still mindful of his mission to protect the South Side Railroad, withdrew in good order toward Sutherland's Station and there took a strong position on a bare ridge running a half mile parallel to the tracks. While the Southern infantrymen hastily dug in with bayonets and tin cups, Captain Dunlop's sharpshooters, who had joined Heth's command as it pulled back, conducted a stubborn delaying action with some of Cooke's Tarheels. The Confederates had one minor bit of good fortune on their side: due to a

Federal command foul-up, only one of II Corps's divisions, that of Brigadier General Nelson Miles, was actually pursuing them. Even so, Miles deployed some eight thousand men, considerably outnumbering Heth, whose strength was between twelve hundred and four thousand soldiers. General Heth was soon called away to take the place of his fallen corps commander, A. P. Hill, leaving Brigadier General John R. Cooke in command. As the Union soldiers approached, the Confederate sharpshooters fell back and took their positions some two hundred yards in front of the line. McRae's brigade, which had been mauled during VI Corps's breakthrough, had only three of its five regiments present. Nevertheless the Tarheel general increased his sharpshooters to one hundred men by detailing soldiers from the line regiments, showing the emphasis the Confederates still placed on maintaining a thick, aggressive skirmish line. Dunlop's sharpshooter battalion of McGowan's brigade, "deployed several hundred yards in front," could hardly have been much stronger.[22]

The leading Union unit, Colonel Henry Madill's New York brigade, pushed forward into a hasty attack without bothering to form. After an all-night march, the Yanks were weary but spoiling for a fight. Thinking that the Rebels were on the verge of collapse after their easy victories of the morning, they went in with a cheer. "The sharpshooters opened fire at once," reported Dunlop. Men began to fall as the New Yorkers closed with the skirmish line. As Dunlop described,

> The sharpshooters continued their fire with spirit and effect as the Federals advanced, opening in the center and assembling on the flanks upon the high grounds on either side ... facing inward. When within easy range of the main line the brigade rose and delivered volley after volley into the face of the assailants, while the two wings of the sharpshooters closed upon each flank, driving home with fearful accuracy every discharge of their deadly rifles. The enemy hesitated, then broke and fled the field, pursued by the merciless sharpshooters and a perfect stream of lead from the brigade, which piled the ground with killed and wounded. The conflict was short, sharp and deadly.[23]

Colonel Madill fell wounded. As his men pulled back, the Rebel sharpshooters hung on their flanks, dropping man after man until the bluecoats reached the safety of the woods. After bringing up his artillery and another brigade under Colonel Robert Nugent, General Miles sent his men in again. "They fell upon our sharpshooters," recalled one officer, "who skirmished in front. ... The skirmish line fired with remarkable precision, and held their position with a tenacity worthy of their reputation; but they were forced back upon the main body." The infantry on the ridge opened fire at long range—"three or four hundred yards"—tearing holes in their advancing lines. "The enemy fought with the desperation of veterans with minds made up to succeed," noted Dunlop. "But … when they saw their ranks writhing under the storm of lead which crashed through them from front and flank … they broke in wild confusion and yielded the field again to the Confederates, with a large number of prisoners, which the sharpshooters gathered up as they swept down the face of the hill in pursuit." The sight literally moved Captain Dunlop to tears: "I never saw finer fighting anywhere."[24]

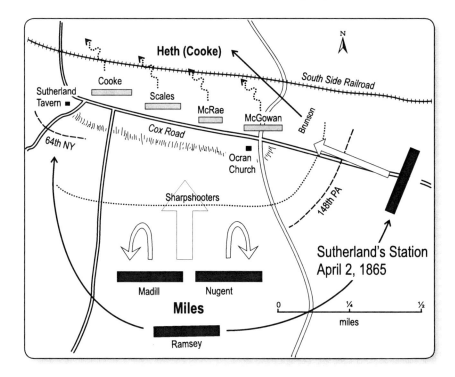

The battle now settled down to long-range exchanges between artillery and sharpshooters. Far from ready to concede defeat, General Miles sent another of his brigades on a wide flanking move around the Confederate left, its movement screened by the Spencer-armed 148th Pennsylvania. At the same time he dispatched another regiment in skirmish order to lap around Cooke's right, drawing his attention and preventing him from reinforcing his other flank. While Miles made his dispositions, Berry Benson and his fellow sharpshooters traded shots with their Federal counterparts, who had moved forward to cover Miles's line and were now hunkered down in a road about four hundred yards away. "I had reluctantly thrown away my Spencer, for which I could find no ammunition," wrote Benson, "and had taken up an Enfield." In the course of "some right lively sharpshooting" he saw something he'd never seen in front of him before: "a little black spot." By the time he realized it was a bullet, "whiz it went, close to my ear."[25]

Anticipating Miles's move, General McGowan shifted most of Dunlop's sharpshooter battalion over to cover his left flank. By midafternoon the Federals were ready. After a short artillery barrage the men of Colonel John Ramsey's brigade surged forward, swamping Dunlop's position, while Nugent's and Madill's brigades (the latter now under its third commander of the day) renewed their attack on Cooke's front. Dunlop gave the attack a melodramatic coda: "Our lines opened fire in full chorus at long range, and as the enemy closed upon us the vigor of our defense increased, until the entire line was enveloped in one living cloud of blue coats, whose muskets spurted fire and smoke and death." Outflanked, the Confederate position abruptly collapsed. "Now," lamented Lieutenant Caldwell, "was the most disorderly movement I ever saw among Confederate troops." Benson, who had remained on the main line, watched as "the break kept coming down the line till it reached us." Then he, his brother, and one other man ran as "a shower of bullets whizzed past us."[26]

Ramsey's flank attack quickly rolled up the Confederate line from left to right. His rapid advance cut off many of McRae's sharpshooters still on the skirmish line, leaving them no option but surrender. One of their captors noted that the sharpshooters had a red cross on their sleeves. Captain Brunson's company of Dunlop's battalion, at the far left end of the Confederate line, fell back in fair order across the railroad over a deep ravine and there made a short stand. When the Yankees charged across the bridge, Brunson's men sent them a volley and "feeling lonesome, departed." Dunlop had instructed his men that if their position was overrun they were to head west and rejoin the army. He made his own way north, hoping to swim the Appomattox river, but found it swollen from recent rains and impassible. One sharpshooter drowned trying to cross. Dunlop and a number of his men spent the rest of the day and night hiding in the thickets along the river, but they were flushed out and captured the next morning.[27]

The battle of Sutherland's Station effectively ended organized resistance south of the Appomattox river. Miles took about six hundred prisoners, but fortunately for the remaining Confederates he did not pursue them, turning instead back toward Petersburg. The remnants of Third Corps drifted west, the men—generals and privates alike—crossing the river when they could to rejoin the army. Berry Benson, having once been in the hellhole of Elmira prison, was determined not to be captured again. He found General McGowan, who told him that no one knew exactly where the crossings were. "It became plain," he reported, "that if the enemy did come, even in a very small force, our men were so badly demoralized that they would make no fight." Benson decided to strike out on his own and asked for volunteers to join him. Fifteen stalwarts, including his brother, responded, and they marched upstream all night, taking only a short rest. Early the next morning they found a boat to ferry them across, and shortly afterwards found the headquarters of General Heth. Meanwhile, Captain Brunson and General McGowan had narrowly escaped capture by swimming across a tributary, Deep Run. "Brunson was so exhausted when he crawled out on the opposite bank," said Dunlop, "that he was compelled to lie down and rest under a sharp fire from the Federal cavalry." Some of McGowan's brigade did rally at Goode's bridge on April 4, where they joined Longstreet's corps. Captains Brunson and Hasell (who had just returned from leave) took over the sharpshooter battalion, "now but a skeleton of its former self." According to Benson it numbered only forty men.[28]

"With the beginning of the retreat began also the most arduous labors of the sharpshooters," remembered Captain John Young, the commander of Scales's Sharpshooters. "We rested at odd and uncertain intervals," recalled Benson, "sleeping as we lay down with gun in hand, bundled up with whatever baggage we carried. ... Harassed on all sides by the enemy's cavalry, we of the Sharpshooters were often thrown out on the flank, and had more or less skirmishing to do."[29]

The Road to Appomattox

At Petersburg, thanks to hard fighting by Gordon's Second Corps and the heroic defense of Forts Gregg and Whitworth, the Army of Northern Virginia retreated across the Appomattox river on the night of April 2. As they did J. S. Kimbrough and two fellow sharpshooters slumbered peacefully in a grape arbor only fifty yards from the road. The three waked the next morning to the victorious shouts of the Federals entering Petersburg. "We sprang from our sleeping place, snatched our guns, and in double-quick time made our way to the bridge across the now swollen Appomattox. Yankees were visible everywhere when we arrived at the river. Our rear guard had passed over and fired the bridge, and nothing but the charred, smoking abutments were left to show where it stood." Cornered, Kimbrough smashed his Enfield on a rock and flung it into the river as he surrendered to a squad of bluecoats.[30]

On April 6 Grant caught up with the Confederates at Sailor's Creek, cutting off and capturing almost a quarter of the army. Lee reformed and continued west, the Federals pressing him at every opportunity. "The succeeding days passed with little variation," wrote a Georgian of Evans's division, "the sharpshooters marching on the side of the column at a distance of several hundred yards to prevent surprise, and forming a line of battle about noon each day to allow the wagon trains to pass. Thus the troops moved by day and a greater portion of the night."[31]

Since no rations had arrived from Richmond, this particular soldier went on a foraging expedition one night with a man he called "the Irrepressible Alabamian." His comrade, a commissary who had been wounded earlier in the war, proved quite adept at the game, and soon the two had scrounged enough flour for bread and had talked a local family into baking it. At daylight on the ninth Union cavalry interrupted their labors, so the pair quickly divided their booty and split up. "Guided by instinct, a soldier's judgment, or perhaps nothing at all, I ran full tilt into the sharpshooters of my brigade. The corps had deployed and was ready for battle." Distributing his bounty among the sharpshooters, the soldier hastily returned to his post at the ordnance train. These men were division sharpshooters of Evans's division, under Captain William Kaigler, who were just then moving to the south of Appomattox Court House to protect the flank of Second Corps. Well before dawn on April 9 the exhausted infantrymen of Grimes's division had tramped through the village and formed up just to the west, their mission to break through Union cavalry blocking the way to Lynchburg. The remnants of his division sharpshooters, including a few of Blackford's remaining veterans, led the way. The men raised the Rebel yell and went forward, taking a battery of guns and scattering the cavalry, only to find Federal infantry behind them. Reluctantly, under orders from General Gordon, Grimes pulled back as the Tarheels of Cox's brigade fired a last volley to cover his retreat.[32]

Just south of them, at about the same time, General Evans moved forward also "nearly a mile ... most of this in open field." A Federal line of battle materialized out of the mist, forcing him to move his front to meet them. Kaigler's Sharpshooters, "thrown out on the flank and front," covered the maneuver and "made captures that surprised us all." With the sharpshooters still screening their front, Evans's men fell back also. The firing stopped, and soon Brigadier General George Custer rode through the lines with a flag of truce. He approached General Evans and told him that surrender negotiations were in progress. The war in Virginia was over.[33]

On the other side of the village Berry Benson and his remaining men filed toward the front for yet another skirmishing assignment. He recognized a Yankee prisoner he had taken at Petersburg. "I wished him good treatment and in prison and an early exchange and he thanked me in all seriousness, neither recognizing the absurdity of it," remembered Benson. The sharpshooters started out across a field but were abruptly recalled. As they returned they could see a Yankee field piece coming in—with the Union gun crew still in place. A few minutes later a Federal officer rode through with a white flag, and the word filtered down to the ranks: General Lee had surrendered. Rather than taking a chance on going back to prison, Benson again decided to strike out on his own. He found General McGowan in the woods by himself, crying and changing into his dress uniform. After getting his permission, Benson and his brother Blackwood departed, "carrying our rifles, skulking through thick bushes and behind trees, now crawling along a ditch to conceal ourselves, now hiding in a fence corner, we at last eluded the vigilance of the enemy's pickets and made good our way out of his lines." Catching a train to Greensboro, North Carolina, the brothers attempted to join Joseph Johnston's army, but it too had surrendered. Still under arms, they made their way home to Augusta.[34]

22

Weapons and Uniforms

The Minié revolution

The quest for a self-sealing bullet began in 1818 when a British officer in India, Captain John Norton, observed native blow guns with a flexible seal around the base that maximized the shooter's lung power. Thinking this might work in a rifle, Norton designed a conical bullet with a hollow base that would expand to grip the rifling when the weapon was fired. It worked, but the expansion was uneven and not reliable enough for military use. Norton's design lay fallow until 1836, when London gunsmith William Greener placed a wooden plug underneath the ball, ensuring an even expansion of the skirt. The conservative British Army rejected it.

Across the channel the French were also working on the problem, and in 1826 Captain Henri-Gustave Delvigne designed a rifle with a small chamber at the breech end of the gun into which the powder fell when the piece was loaded. The soldier then rapped the round ball against the base of the chamber three or four times with a heavy ramrod, deforming it enough to grip the rifling. The sub-chamber prevented the rammer from crushing the powder grains, and the ball's deformation eliminated the need for a greased patch to seal the barrel. Delvigne's system represented an advance over previous systems, but if the soldier rammed the ball too hard, the bullet would fly erratically; if he did not ram it hard enough, the bullet would not grip the rifling properly. A steady touch was difficult under the stress of combat. The system worked well enough, however, to give the French an edge in Algeria in the 1840s.

French colonel Louis-Etienne de Thouvenin made the next major advance by inserting a narrow steel rod called a *tige* into the base of the chamber. This served both to keep the bullet from crushing the powder grains and to expand it from the inside, making the amount of force less critical. Thouvenin's conical projectile was also far more aerodynamic than Delvigne's round ball, improving range and accuracy. But the rifle was difficult to clean with the *tige* in place, it sometimes broke, and the soldier still had to tap the bullet with the ramrod. Nevertheless, cost-conscious governments across the continent adopted the *tige* system because it could easily be retrofitted to existing weapons.

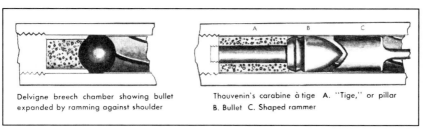

Delvigne breech chamber showing bullet expanded by ramming against shoulder

Thouvenin's carabine à tige A. "Tige," or pillar B. Bullet C. Shaped rammer

Jack Coggins. *Arms & Equipment of the Civil War*

In 1849 Captain Claude Minié took the next logical step. He moved Thouvenin's *tige* to the bullet itself by inserting a steel cup into the bullet's hollow base. This kept the chamber clean and expanded the skirt automatically, but sometimes the steel cup blew right through the lead bullet. The French Army rejected Minié's brainchild, but the British recognized its effectiveness. The British Army paid the fortunate captain a handsome sum for his invention, belatedly recognized Greener's contribution as well, and incorporated Minié's system into the new Enfield rifle. The British called their version of the Minié projectile, a long, smooth-sided swaged (rather than cast) bullet, the Pritchett (or Metford-Pritchett). The cartridge featured a built-in paper patch that helped to seal the bore and a boxwood plug, later replaced by one of burnt clay, that was less likely to damage the bullet. The system worked quite well, making the Enfield one of the most accurate arms in the world in the late 1850s.

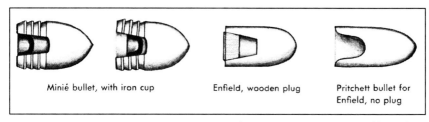

Minié bullet, with iron cup   Enfield, wooden plug   Pritchett bullet for Enfield, no plug

Jack Coggins. *Arms & Equipment of the Civil War*

Somewhat later American arms designer James Burton thinned the sides of the skirt so that the combustion gasses could expand the bullet without the need for a plug. Now the rifle ball could be made slightly smaller than the bore for faster loading while actually improving accuracy. At long last there was no appreciable difference in the time it took to load a smoothbore musket or a rifle.

A Sharpshooter's Weapons

Enfield Rifles

Confederate ordnance chief Josiah Gorgas called the Enfield, or British Pattern 53 Long Rifle-Musket, named for the year of its adoption, "the finest arm in the world." Sturdy, reliable, and extremely accurate even at extended ranges, it consistently outshot everything but the Whitworth and quickly became a favorite on both sides. This nine and a half pound, single shot, muzzle loading, .577 caliber rifle was as close to a standard infantry weapon as the Confederacy ever got and was also used in large numbers by the Union.

Three metal bands held the P53s three-groove, 39-inch barrel (which sported a 1:78 twist) to the stock, and as such the weapon was often referred to as the "three-band" model. Sixty-eight grains of black powder pushed a 530-grain Prichett ball (or a Burton-Minié ball) along at about 850-900 feet per second. The Enfield's adjustable ladder rear sight had steps for 100 (the default or "battle sight" range), 200, 300, and 400 yards. For distances beyond that an adjustable flip-up blade sight was graduated (depending on the model and date of manufacture) from 900 to 1250 yards. With practice a good marksman could hit a man-sized target at about half that distance. Including the 17-inch blade on its triangular socket bayonet, the Enfield rifle-musket measured just over six feet long. The term "rifle-musket" meant that the rifle was the same length as the musket it replaced. The long rifle was thought necessary so that the muzzles of the second rank of soldiers would project beyond the faces of the men in front, and so that the weapon would be sufficiently long for a bayonet fight.

In the years following Enfield introduced several models of the Short Rifle-Musket. All had 33-inch barrels and an overall length of 48½ inches and were often called "two-band" Enfields after the number of bands securing the barrel. The Pattern 56 and 58 rifles had a light three-groove barrel, while the Pattern 60 Army rifle and the Pattern 58 Navy rifle both featured a heavier five-groove barrel with progressive depth rifling and a faster 1:48 twist, giving them superior accuracy. Because of the desire to have a weapon of equal length in a bayonet fight, the two-band Enfields featured long sword (or in the case of the naval model, a cutlass) bayonets.. The army sword bayonet, made to a forward-curved Turkish pattern known as the *yataghan*, boasted a 23-inch blade and attached via a lug on the side of the barrel.[1]

The two-band Enfield quickly became the top choice for Confederate sharpshooters (who, so far as I am aware, never used the sword bayonet). "Every short Enfield which came into possession of any of our men was taken away and given to these men," said a Georgian in Gordon's brigade, "but there were not enough, and some of them had the common long Enfield.

Both kinds had a long range and were very effective. The short guns were given them, as they were lighter and handier." A soldier in Mahone's brigade reported that the sharpshooters used "a long English-made cartridge. We never used any ammunition made by the Confederate Government." He may be referring to the Pritchett cartridge, which gave superior results in the Enfield and was slightly longer than the Burton-Minié cartridges issued by the Confederacy.[2]

Neither side used "real" Enfields (export of actual British service arms was forbidden) but rather copies manufactured by a host of private contractors. Due to a coup by purchasing agent Caleb Huse, most Confederate Enfields were of superior quality. Many of the two-band Enfields were actually Volunteer rifles; that is, they had been privately purchased by members of the British Volunteers, "a self-uniformed, self-armed combination militia and target shooting organization." When Whitehall rearmed these units in 1862 with service Enfields, many of the men sold their old arms to Southern buyers. In all, approximately 281,612 Enfield rifles of all types reached the Confederate army through the naval blockade. The Confederacy captured many Enfields on the battlefield, and Cook & Brother in Athens, Georgia, manufactured copies.[3]

U.S. Model 1861 Springfield Rifle-Muskets

The Federal infantry arm was functionally identical to the British Enfield but had a fractionally different .58 caliber bore size. Weighing ten pounds and four ounces, it fired the standard Minié ball through a 40-inch barrel. Measuring fifty-six inches overall, it, like the Enfield, took a triangular socket bayonet with an 18-inch blade. Line infantry on both sides used this sturdy rifle in greater numbers than any other, but although sighted to 500 yards it lacked the pinpoint accuracy of the Enfield and Whitworth rifles, making it second choice for the skirmish line. Eventually over twenty contractors produced more than a million of these weapons.

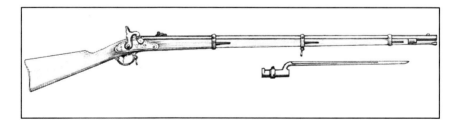

The Springfield rifle and its functionally identical twin the Enfield equipped the bulk of American armies in the 1860s. Jack Coggins, *Arms & Equipment of the Civil War*

Whitworth Rifles

Sir Joseph Whitworth, one of the premier inventors and firearms designers of his era, manufactured his singular rifle in Manchester, England. It fired a unique, hard metal, hexagonal-sided bullet with a very long aspect ratio (.445 inches by 1.45 inches, or 2½ times its diameter) that gave it superior ballistic performance at extended ranges. In order to give his long bullet the same 530-grain weight as that of the Enfield, Sir Joseph reduced the caliber to .451. Seventy to eight-five grains of British-manufactured powder launched the bullet at twelve hundred to fourteen hundred feet per second, considerably faster than the Enfield. In the field the sharp crack of the Whitworth distinguished it from the dull boom of the service muskets. The best Birmingham gunsmiths were able to hold tolerances to 1/350th of an inch, while Whitworth's high-tech facility maintained a then-incredible 1/5,000th of an inch. His special investment-cast, pre-stressed steel barrel combined light weight with extreme rigidity, allowing him to tame barrel whip, one of the major bugbears associated with long-range shooting. When fired with a heavy charge, a rifle barrel tended to move up and down slightly as the bullet passed through it, causing dispersion at longer ranges. The conventional solution was to use a massive "bull" barrel to resist flexing, but this made for a heavy, cumbersome rifle. Whitworth, however, was able to obtain the same accuracy with a rifle that weighed just under ten pounds. The light weight meant that while a soldier could easily carry the Whitworth around the battlefield, he could count on it giving him a heavy kick when he pulled the trigger.[4]

The Whitworth was a popular sporting arm as well, and in 1858 the company produced a "trials" version with a 39-inch barrel. Although the British Army briefly equipped their rifle corps with Whitworths, the arm had the disadvantages of a high cost and a tendency to foul the bore under field conditions. Overall, the Enfield made a better all-purpose infantry weapon, and equaled the Whitworth's accuracy to five hundred yards.

The rifle was produced in a number of variations, including half-stocked sporting versions and hybrid guns with both civilian and military characteristics. All Whitworths had an extremely high level of fit and finish, and many came with fine checkered stocks more appropriate for expensive civilian sporting pieces. They were available with and without bayonet attachments and came with a 36-inch or a 33-inch barrel, which made for an overall length of 49 to 52½ inches. All had a hexagonal bore and a fast 1:20 twist. "Typical 'Confederate Whitworths' featured a 33-inch barrel, two Enfield pattern barrel bands, iron mounts of the military target rifle pattern, and Enfield-type lock with no safety bolt and an Enfield-style hammer; open sights, with a blade front being adjustable for windage allowance, and a stock which extends to within a short distance of the muzzle, giving the rifle a snub-nosed appearance."[5]

Sighting arrangements varied also. Some Whitworths had Enfield-type sights graduated to twelve hundred yards, and others had a sophisticated sliding blade sight with a vernier screw adjustment for windage; some had simple front sights, and others boasted an adjustable post-and-globe front sight. A few rifles sported a four-power telescopic sight, fitted in an adjustable mount on the gun's left side. Although the technology was not new, the Whitworth's patented telescopic sight, designed by British officer Lieutenant Colonel D. Davidson, addressed many of the shortcomings of earlier models. A scope mounted on top of the barrel had limited movement and could not depress far enough for exceptionally long shots. Davidson's side-saddle mounting allowed the scope to drop as far as needed, independently of the barrel, without requiring the shooter to raise his head from the buttstock. It included a hand wheel running through the stock that adjusted for bullet drift and windage as well. A rifleman could easily detach Davidson's scope if need be, and it did not interfere with his iron sights. On one occasion General Patrick Cleburne borrowed a Whitworth sharpshooter's scope to view the enemy's lines before an attack. While the skinny 14⅝-inch by ¹⁵⁄₁₆-inch brass telescope was primitive by today's standards—one modern firearms expert described using it as "a little like peering into a dark tunnel"—and while it was a state-of-the-art system in 1864 it did have its drawbacks. "After a fight those who used them had black eyes," remembered one sharpshooter, "as the end of the tube rested against the eye while taking aim, and the 'kick,' being pretty hard, bruised the eye."[6]

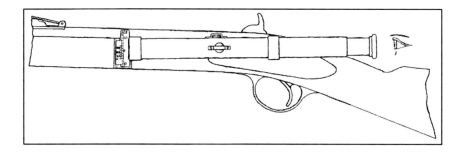

The four-power telescope mounted on the left side of the Whitworth could be independently adjusted for long-range shooting. *Journal of the Royal Service Institution.*

Although records are scarce, the Confederacy appears to have imported around 250 Whitworth rifles of all types. Most of the men in the Sharpshooter battalions used Enfields, and only one or two men per battalion bore them. Of the two in Gordon Bradwell's brigade, "one of these was given to Irvin Spivey, a noted rifleman of the 26th [Georgia]. His duty was to watch his opportunity and pick off Federal officers." Thus in the approximately thirty-six infantry brigades of the Army of Northern Virginia, there were most likely between thirty-six and seventy-two of these rifles in service. The Army of Tennessee utilized its Whitworths differently, and a report dated June 24th, 1864 shows 32 of them on hand, along with 3,400 rounds of ammunition. Though Union authorities were well aware the Whitworth's capabilities, apparently they never seriously considered it for their own sharpshooters, depending instead on a combination of heavy target rifles, Sharps, and service muskets.[7]

The small number of Whitworths used during the war reflected their high cost, which ranged from $100 for a bare rifle to $1,000 for one equipped with a telescope, a full kit, and a thousand rounds of ammunition. Enfields, by contrast, cost $12 to $25 each. The ammunition was pricey as well. While sharpshooters preferred to use British-made cartridges for Enfields and Whitworths, each Whitworth came with a bullet mold to cast a cylindrical lead bullet that formed itself to the bore when fired. The swaging process needed to manufacture the hard metal hexagonal bullets was quite beyond the capabilities of Southern industry. "Accuracy appears to have been roughly equal with either slug," observed period firearms expert Joe Bilby, "and both types have been recovered ... although the cylindrical are far more common."[8]

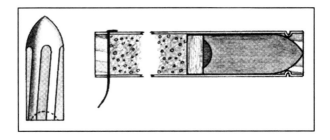

The Whitworth rifle used a unique hexagonal bullet, which came from the factory in a cardboard case. To load, the rifleman pulled out the slip of paper, then rammed the bullet and powder down the barrel. Jack Coggins, *Arms & Equipment of the Civil War*

Whitworths appear on blockade runner manifests as early as December 1862, but the first references to field use are in 1863, when Colonel Josiah Gorgas dispatched "20 Whitworth (Telescopic) Rifles" to the Army of Tennessee on May 29. "These arms are reported to be very effective at 1200 yards," wrote the Confederate ordnance chief. "I have the honor to request that they may be placed in the hands of careful and reliable men only as they are very costly, so costly indeed that it is not deemed expedient to increase the number already brought in. Ammunition and a copy of the instructions will accompany the arms." An equivalent number also seem to have gone to the Army of Northern Virginia. Ben Powell, a sharpshooter in McGowan's brigade, received his Whitworth just before the battle of Gettysburg. Major General Patrick Cleburne, a division commander in the Army of Tennessee, wrote of his retreat from Wartrace, Tennessee, in late June 1863: "I had no ammunition to spare, and did not reply to the continual fire of the enemy except with five Whitworth rifles, which appeared to do good service. Mounted men were struck at distances ranging from 700 to 1,300 yards."[9]

The issue of how far the black powder Whitworth could effectively shoot has divided pundits since the war ended. Ex-Confederate sharpshooters were prone to exaggerate their claims, especially as they grew older. In 1896 Captain Fergus S. Harris, a Tennessean who had served in Virginia, claimed that he witnessed a Union general picked off his horse at 2,250 yards by a Whitworth sharpshooter. In 1907 Isaac Shannon, a sharpshooter with Cleburne's division, recalled an instance in which he and fellow marksmen hamstrung a Yankee wagon train: "So great was the distance that we put our sights up to twenty-two hundred, and then aimed at the tops of the pine trees in the rear of the field." After a trial shot to estimate the windage, he and his mates opened fire, "and in less than thirty minutes there was not a wagon or team left." Despite veterans' tendency toward exaggeration—for one thing, the rifle's blade sight only adjusted to twelve hundred yards—the fact remains that the Whitworth could and did strike at a thousand yards and beyond. Sharpshooters often employed their Whitworths in an area fire mode; that is, rather than singling out an individual at long range, they would aim at the center of a larger target, such as a mounted man, an artillery battery and their horses, and a column of troops or wagons. Although actual casualties might be few, the number of bullets whizzing about would frequently convince the Federals to seek a safer place.[10]

"The least exposure above the crest of the parapet will draw the fire of his telescopic Whitworths," complained a Union engineer outside Charleston at the time, "which cannot be dodged. Several of our men were wounded by these rifles at a distance of 1,300 yards from [Fort] Wagner." The official report states that Federal casualties averaged ten men a day, and modern testing tends to confirm some of the stories. "The claim of 'fatal results at 1,500 yards,'" concluded one modern expert, "was no foolish boast."[11]

Although some of the Whitworth rifle's exploits are undoubtedly exaggerated, it was a deadly weapon that, in the right hands, repaid its high cost many times over. "I do not believe a harder-shooting, harder-kicking, longer-range gun was ever made than the Whitworth rifle," asserted sharpshooter veteran Isaac Shannon.[12]

English Match Rifles

In the mid-1850s match rifle shooting at long ranges—in some cases up to a thousand yards—became quite popular in Britain, and a number of manufacturers (e.g. Turner, Rigby, Henry, Nuthall) produced high-quality rifles to fill the need. These included civilian versions of the Whitworth, such as the Beasley, as well as other rifles using licensed copies of Whitworth's patented hexagonal bore. Other innovative designs were used as well, and unlike the heavy target rifles common in the United States, the British match rifles weighed no more than a service musket. A number of these rifles made their way across the Atlantic and into the hands of Confederate soldiers. The most widely used was the Kerr, made by the London Armoury Company. This finely crafted rifle outwardly resembled the Enfield—just about all the parts were interchangeable—but fired a .446 caliber bullet through a 37-inch barrel that featured a patented, six-groove progressive rifling system. While extremely accurate its shorter, somewhat lighter bullet lacked the carrying power of the Whitworth at very long ranges. The ten-pound Kerr used a rear sight similar to the standard Enfield ladder and an adjustable globe sight on the front.

Most Civil War Kerrs were used in the western theater by the Army of Tennessee. The Kentucky brigade received eleven from "an English admirer," and Cleburne's division at one time deployed a forty-six-man sharpshooter corps that boasted thirty Whitworth and sixteen Kerr rifles. Many of the Kerr sharpshooters appear to have shot the cylindrical Whitworth round in battle, likely improving its long-range performance.[13]

Another sharpshooter's match rifle, the Turner, was imported in small numbers. Manufactured by Thomas Turner of Birmingham, these hand-crafted, .451 caliber rifles resembled the Kerr. Some versions used Turner's patented five-groove rifling, and others came with the Whitworth hexagonal bore. Some Confederate sharpshooters also used the Nuthall, which also looked much like the P53 Enfield, the Daw, the Jacob's, and the Lancaster. Just how many of these rifles came into the South is impossible to say, but they were few.[14]

Model 1859 Sharps Rifles

The Sharps, a light (eight pounds, eight ounces), breech-loading, single-shot, .52 caliber rifle, combined a high rate of fire with excellent long-range accuracy. By releasing a catch a soldier could pull down the trigger guard, which dropped the breech and allowed him to insert a combustible cased linen cartridge. Returning the trigger guard closed the breech and sheared open the cartridge. A trained rifleman could put ten 370-grain slugs a minute down the 30-inch barrel in the same time it took a soldier with a muzzle loader to get off three, and the breech-loading feature allowed him to easily reload while prone—an awkward operation with a muzzle-loader. Sighted to eight hundred yards, the Sharps was quite accurate and could reliably hit a man-sized target at about half that range. It came with a Lawrence pellet primer system, but the soldiers preferred to use conventional primers except during cold weather, as the pellet primer worked better with numb fingers.

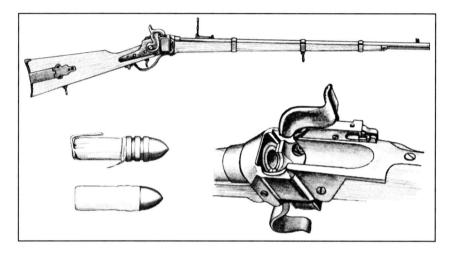

Pulling the trigger guard of a Sharps forward dropped the sliding breech block, allowing the insertion of a paper (top) or linen (bottom) cartridge. When the block rose it sheared off the end of the cartridge to insure ignition.
Jack Coggins, *Arms & Equipment of the Civil War*

Although the Sharps sometimes leaked combustion gasses through the breech seal, overall it was a sturdy and effective design that held up well in the field. The company also made a carbine version with a 22-inch barrel for cavalry use. Undoubtedly the company's most famous rifles, however, were the two thousand made expressly for Colonel Hiram Berdan's 1st and 2nd U.S. Sharpshooter regiments, which sported a double "set" trigger. Pulling the rear trigger would "set" the front one, which would then fire the weapon at the slightest touch. Berdan's rifles also had a more practical angular socket bayonet rather than the usual sword bayonet.[15]

As a skirmisher's rifle, the Sharps was hard to beat. Some Southerners like Eugene Blackford swore by it:

Yesterday I went to Gen. Rodes' Hd. Qrs. to make some experiments with breech loading firearms, together with the Ordinance officer of the Division. I carried with me my Sharps rifle—the Gen. seeing a pig 700 yards off on a hill side and asked me how near I could come to him if I were a Yankee skirmisher. I told him to look and see—& fired. The ball passed just over the animal's back causing it to squeal at a great rate—so you see I am quite proud of my skill and actually regard it as a most useful accomplishment at this time.[16]

Unfortunately the Confederacy was never able to field more than a few captured weapons, and although they produced some five thousand copies themselves at Richmond, they never had enough to make a difference. The conservative Federal ordnance establishment distrusted breechloaders and was appalled by their cost: at about $42 each, they cost roughly twice as much as an Enfield or Springfield rifle-musket. Throughout the war the Union followed a very inconsistent arming pattern—with politics playing as much a part as policy—in issuing these rifles to various selected regiments. The 5th New York, for example, received two hundred Sharps rifles to arm its flank companies in 1862. The 42nd Pennsylvania/13th Reserves, the famous "Bucktails," were issued 180, which they used to good effect at South Mountain and elsewhere. Connecticut armed a number of its regiments with Sharps rifles purchased with state funds.[17]

Sharps also made a line of target rifles, the precursor to its famed buffalo guns, similar to its military models but of varying barrel lengths and calibers, using the same drop-breech loading mechanism. One such, a .52 caliber Model 1853 target rifle, resides today the museum at Gettysburg National Military Park. It has set triggers, a heavy 34-inch octagonal barrel, and weighs about fifteen pounds. Found after the battle, the rifle's origins are unknown.[18]

Spencer Rifles

Introduced midwar, the .52 caliber Spencer was an effective repeating rifle that held seven shots in a tubular magazine in the stock. Pulling down the trigger guard rotated the breech block, ejecting the spent case and allowing the magazine spring to push one of the metallic rimfire cartridges forward. As the shooter returned the trigger guard, the breech block pushed the bullet home. The hammer had to be manually cocked for each shot. To reload, a soldier opened the buttstock, dropped in seven rounds, and replaced the spring-loaded follower. With its modern one-piece metal cartridges, the Spencer was virtually immune to moisture and required no separate primer. The handy Blakeslee cartridge box, introduced late in the war, allowed a soldier to keep a number of loaded "magazines," which were actually tubes from which he dumped the cartridges into the buttstock. The Spencer came in two versions: a 47-inch model for the infantry and a 39-inch version for mounted use. If a ready supply of pre-loaded magazines was available, a soldier could fire fifteen aimed shots a minute. As one modern firearms expert put it, "a Spencer can be emptied in under ten seconds and reloaded in well under a minute."[19]

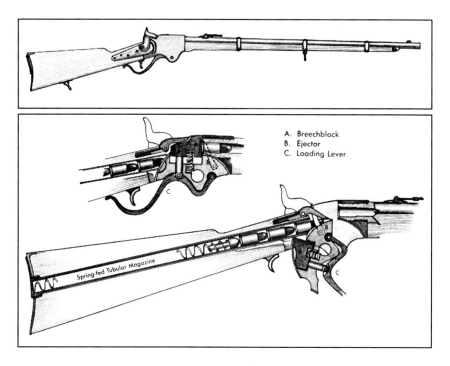

A. Breechblock
B. Ejector
C. Loading Lever

Spring-fed Tubular Magazine

The Spencer rifle fed seven metallic cartridges through a tubular magazine
in the stock. Jack Coggins, *Arms & Equipment of the Civil War*

Still, this wonder weapon had some shortcomings. It occasionally jammed, and at ten pounds it was rather heavy. The ammunition was even heavier. The 37th Massachusetts, for instance, found that because of the higher rate of fire they now had to carry a hundred rounds as a basic load instead of the forty to sixty needed for the Springfield (and even so, they still ran out of ammunition at Third Winchester in September 1864). The Spencer's blunt-nosed 285-grain bullet, driven by only forty-eight grains of powder, had poor aerodynamics and consequently a rather short range. Coupled with an indifferent short-radius sighting system, especially on the carbine, its effective range was not much over two hundred yards, and it was not as accurate as a sharpshooter would prefer. Given its firepower, however, and the closeness of most Civil War engagements, this was not as disadvantageous as it might seem. "I consider a skirmish line armed with them fully equal to a line of battle armed with the Springfield," asserted the 37th Massachusetts's commander, Colonel Oliver Edwards. Certainly the Spencer rifle was the choice weapon for trench warfare. Late in the war the Federals armed their division-level sharpshooter companies with Spencers, distributing them to the flank companies of regiments like the 5th Wisconsin and using Spencer-armed regiments like the 37th Massachusetts for skirmishing duties. It was, in effect, the assault rifle of its day.[20]

The Confederate sharpshooters with their short Enfields could outshoot the Spencer-armed Yankees at longer ranges, but the Rebels could not match their close-in firepower. Although the Confederacy captured large numbers of the weapons, they were unable use them effectively because they could not manufacture the necessary rimfire metallic cartridges. Ultimately the Spencer made its greatest contribution to the Northern war effort as a carbine where, issued to Union cavalry, it was a major factor in the dominance of that arm in 1864-65. Overall, the U.S. Army took delivery of almost fifty-eight thousand Spencers during the war.[21]

Colt Revolving Rifles

The Model 1855 .56 caliber Colt Revolving Rifle was the rifle version of Colt's pistol, complete with a five-shot revolving cylinder. A prewar design, it was issued to a few eastern Federal units like Berdan's but was generally not considered a success. Although quite accurate with a high rate of fire, it also had the nasty habit of occasionally mangling the shooter's fingers if it malfunctioned. Since it used a cap and ball system like the revolvers of the time, loading was a cumbersome process. The Federal government purchased more than forty-six hundred rifles, most of which saw service in the West.

Henry Rifles

Several western outfits, such as Birge's Sharpshooters (66th Illinois), bought and used the $42 Henry repeating rifle, which might have made an effective skirmisher's weapon if it had been more widely issued. The 43½-inch-long rifle could hold fifteen .44 caliber rimfire metallic cartridges, plus a sixteenth in the chamber, in a spring-loaded magazine tucked under the 24-inch barrel, and could fire all of them in less than a minute. A lever underneath the brass receiver activated a toggle-link mechanism that extracted the spent cartridge, cocked the action, and loaded another round. The Henry cartridge, in which twenty-five grains of powder drove a 216-grain bullet, had about the same power as today's .44 Special pistol cartridge—rather anemic by Civil War standards. Like the Spencer, the 9¼-pound Henry was a short-range weapon, but extremely effective nonetheless. Only a few Henrys saw action in the eastern theater.

American Target Rifles

For sniping duties the Federals fielded a wide variety of civilian target rifles, most of which were heavy and not very mobile. One soldier, reviewing the sharpshooter's weapons in his unit, observed that "each rifle has a telescope running the entire length of the barrel. The average weight is about 35 lbs., the lightest weighing 17 lbs. and heaviest 50 lbs." While their accuracy was excellent, loading was a slow and cumbersome process. Many of these rifles used a "false muzzle," a protective metal cone that slipped over the muzzle to protect the lands when loading—and rendered the weapon nearly useless if lost. Though quite effective in a static situation, these rifles were unsuitable for a mobile campaign. Indeed, two companies of Yankee sharpshooters suffered heavily at Antietam when caught in an open field, and one soldier bitterly remembered that the expensive target rifles had been "little better … than clubs." If the tactical situation allowed the Yankees to use their scoped target rifles, they soon proved the worth of their weapons. South Carolina sharpshooter Berry Benson described a meeting with his friend Ben Powell, who was the battalion's Whitworth marksman. "I remember Powell coming up one day with a hole in his hat. He had been dueling with one of the enemy's sharpshooters who proved himself an excellent shot, that Powell though it prudent to retire."[22]

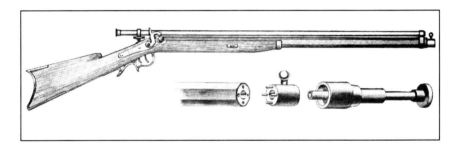

Union sharpshooters often used civilian target rifles.
Most featured a false muzzle and a special bullet starter for loading.
Jack Coggins, *Arms & Equipment of the Civil War*

Yankee sharpshooter Wyman White, who often used his company's "thirty pounder" target rifle, describes an incident in which he was called to engage a group of Rebels beyond the range of his men's Sharps rifles. White sent five shots whizzing in among the Southerners, who scattered.

This performance proved beyond a doubt that the big muzzle loader was a longer range gun than the Sharps rifle, and there was a reason. The charge in loading it was four inches of powder, a good flannel wad, a bullet that weighed more than an ounce that was wedged into the grooves of the rifling inside by use of a false muzzle. So that when the fire from the percussion cap touched the four inches of powder it would send a bullet more than a mile and do good execution. I have no doubt the working party of rebels was more than a mile away and I had no trouble in driving them away. I also have no doubt that if I hit any of them they received an awful wound.[23]

Eventually the Federal authorities issued service rifles to most sharp-shooter outfits, who placed their target rifles in company wagons until the situation settled down enough to move them forward. Some sharpshooter units retained quite a number of their heavy rifles until the end, while others kept only two or three per company. Ordinary infantry regiments occasionally fielded one or two privately-owned target rifles as well. Late in the war the Federal division sharpshooter companies were armed with both fast-firing Spencers and heavy target rifles.

Uniforms and Insignia

The Confederates, more or less by accident, stumbled on a very effective camouflage uniform. Wearing a butternut brown or gray uniform and a slouch hat, the Confederate sharpshooter was very difficult to spot in the woods. The British army, which had concluded that "good marksmen make considerable havoc," spent a great deal of time and effort to reach the same conclusion. In 1800 the British conducted an experiment with various uniform colors to determine which was most suitable for the skirmish line. The testers limited the experiment to three colors: red, green, and gray. Accordingly, five marksmen from the 5/60th Rifles fired at a target of each color at 125 yards, each man taking as much time as he needed. They repeated this the following day. On the third day, they increased the range to 150 yards, but the red target had by now been so damaged that it was near falling to pieces, and the green target was also severely injured. Even after 108 shots, however, "the gray remained sound, and was afterwards used again." Their colonel, Charles Hamilton-Smith, recommended that riflemen wear "some gray unostentatious uniform, leaving the parade dress for peace and garrison duty." The British Army, however, ignored his findings and continued to use green uniforms for light infantry (as did the Americans) and red for the line infantry until the turn of the next century. Further testing later in the century confirmed Hamilton-Smith's findings.[24]

In 1915 Major Hesketh Hesketh-Pritchard, who was then organizing a sniping program for the British Army, commented on how hard it was to pick out German soldiers in their feldgrau. German snipers, on the other hand, had no problems finding British officers in their distinctive uniforms. Hesketh-Prichard also noted that their round hats, whose artificial shape stuck out in a natural environment, gave the British away. German soldiers, who wore soft caps, were much harder to see. "The ideal army, could I clothe it," noted the major, "would wear a very curious shape of cap, with certainly an uneven outline."[25]

The Confederate sharpshooter's uniform, well adapted to the needs of its wearer, differed from the uniform of a regular infantryman in only a few minor ways. Major Eugene Blackford authorized his men to wear "a little red trefoil shaped piece of flannel" on their breast as an identifying badge. North Carolina sharpshooters under General William McRae sewed a gold cross on their left sleeve along with the names of the battles in which each had fought; other Tarheel units wore a red cross on their sleeves. One of Mc-Gowan's men, William McGill, described the sharpshooters as "privileged characters," and noted that they were identified by "a red band running diagonally across the left elbow with a red star just above the band." This badge, he claimed, "would pass the sharpshooter anywhere." The only such insignia to actually survive is that of Private Henry A. Wise of Company B, Second Maryland Battalion (part of Archer's brigade). It consists of a black octagonal wool patch about 1½ inches across, evidently worn on the pocket, overlaid with an irregular red wool quatrefoil insignia.[26]

The Confederate practice differed from that of the British, who allowed their best shots to wear identifying insignia. The Confederate badge signified not a soldier's ability to shoot so much as his membership in an elite unit, similar to modern badges like ranger tabs, airborne wings, and shoulder patches.

23

Confederate Sharpshooters in the West

Although this book concerns itself primarily with the Army of Northern Virginia's sharpshooter battalions, it is worthwhile to compare them to those of the other major Confederate field army, the Army of Tennessee. One outfit, Lieutenant General James Longstreet's First Corps, served in both theaters and had organizations common to both.

Major General Patrick Cleburne. *B&L*

Major General Patrick Cleburne, an immigrant Irishman who served in the Army of Tennessee, was one of the few commanders to run a regular marksmanship program, and in spring 1862 he detailed five of the best men per company to form a sharpshooter company. Having served with the British Army, Cleburne understood the value of accurate fire. In late May 1863 Confederate ordnance chief Colonel Josiah Gorgas dispatched twenty Whitworths to the Army of Tennessee, and after receiving five of them Cleburne formed a "Corps of Whitworth Sharpshooters." Rather than distributing the weapons down to his brigades, Cleburne used them in a unit that reported directly to division headquarters. This proved so successful that "a corps comprising all the Whitworth rifles in Bragg's army was organized near Chattanooga, and did grand service till the end of the war." One sharpshooter reported that "the Whitworth men on the Confederate side were of a class quite to themselves." Like Blackford's men, they drilled extensively in range estimation, although they were used more like modern snipers than as skirmishers. The Irish general's sharpshooting corps continued to grow, and by mid-1864 numbered forty-six men armed with Kerr and Whitworth rifles.[1]

Other units formed similar companies as more rifles became available. Private Sam Watkins of the First Tennessee (Maney's brigade, Cheatham's division) described how the Whitworths—"the finest long range guns in the world"—were distributed. Soldiers who wanted the guns shot three rounds at a mark five hundred yards away. "Every shot that was fired hit the board," recalled Watkins, "but there was one man who came a little closer to the spot than any other one, and the Whitworth was awarded to him."[2]

An English observer of the war, FitzGerald Ross, visited the Army of Tennessee's camps in winter 1863 and wrote that "attached to each corps were some picked sharpshooters, armed with a telescopic Whitworth rifle, with which they did great execution." Accounts of the war in the west often describe a group of Whitworth sharpshooters. One such company of "a dozen marksmen" was reported to have killed Union Major General William Lytle at Chickamauga.[3]

Another group of Confederate sharpshooters who won fame were the men of the Kentucky "Orphan" brigade. In April 1864 the two best shots from each regiment went into a sharpshooter company commanded by Lieutenant George Burton of the Fourth Kentucky, whom a contemporary thought "took more pleasure in a fight than any other man I ever saw." The brigade's commander, General John Breckinridge, supplied eleven Kerr rifles that had been donated to him. Burton ordered his men to stay well back from the line of battle, at least four hundred yards, in order to maximize the superior range and accuracy of their weapons against enemy targets, especially artillery batteries. A modern chronicler claimed that "probably no more elite band of marksmen served anywhere else in the Confederate Army." Like their counterparts in Virginia, the Orphan sharpshooters were exempt from camp duties, and in spite of heavy casualties (nearly 50 percent at Resaca in May), volunteers were eager to join.[4]

The Western armies also successfully used their long-range rifles in an anti-matériel role, which may have been more due to the higher, more open terrain than to any tactical doctrine. For example, during the siege of Chattanooga Confederate sharpshooters turned back wagon trains attempting to supply the Federal army. Captain William McElwee, a Tennessean, set up a long-range ambush where "the road narrowed to barely the width of a wagon on account of a steep bluff on one side and the Tennessee river on the other." Whitworth marksman Henry Green "shot the four mules pulling the leading wagon, and then the others as fast as they came up." A long column like this was an ideal target for the Whitworth, since its plunging fire was almost sure to hit something. McElwee's men soon blocked the road, forcing the train to retrace its steps and find another route. *The Illustrated London News* correspondent Frank Vizetelly, who traveled with FitzGerald Ross, described another incident that involved "a small force of picked men from General Longstreet's corps, armed with Whitworth telescopic rifles." The ambush took place on the Tennessee River twelve miles behind Union lines, with the Rebels firing from "the crags of Raccoon Mountain" into a Federal wagon train across the river, leaving the road "choked with dead and dying men and mules, and overturned wagons."[5]

Longstreet's Whitworth sharpshooters engage a Union wagon train on the Tennessee River near Chattanooga. *The Illustrated London News*

While Longstreet's corps was in Tennessee Georgia cavalryman J. W. Minnich met up with some of its Whitworth sharpshooters on two occasions. The first was on November 16, 1863, at the battle of Campbell's Station. As Minnich screened the Confederate advance, he spied the butt of a rifle sticking out of a bunch of briars. Picking it up, he found it "heavy ... more deeply grooved than any gun I had ever seen, of smaller caliber than any of our guns, and it was sighted for 2,200 [more likely twelve hundred] yards." As the Federals began falling back, a fellow Rebel appeared and demanded the return of his gun. The man told Minnich he was a sharpshooter and he had stashed his rifle during the Yankee advance to keep it safe. Upon further questioning, the scout explained that the weapon was "a 'Whitworth Rifle,' English make, and that they cost $1,200 each, and 'that there were only twenty of them in Longstreet's Corps's in the hands of the sharpshooters only ... and that every man of them acted on his own free will ... subject only to orders from the division commander or Longstreet himself."[6]

A few months later, in mid-January, Minnich encountered another of Longstreet's scouts, "a tall, bewhiskered Alabamian or Mississippian," in a barn near Dandridge, Tennessee. After a brief introduction the man told the same story about the cost of the Whitworth and Longstreet's group of twenty sharpshooters. Minnich tagged along on a sniping expedition, and presently the two spied a cavalryman in the distance. Together they estimated the range at about eight hundred yards, which Minnich thought was too long a shot for his Enfield. The sharpshooter adjusted his sights, then "raised his rifle slowly and deliberately 'off hand' as if aiming for some inanimate target and pulled the trigger." Minnich thought it was "one of the prettiest shots I have ever seen." But the lucky horseman moved forward just as the bullet reached him, and the shot struck his mount's rump. Both man and horse escaped without further injury, and Minnich and his new friend parted ways.[7]

After Longstreet moved back to the eastern theater, there is some evidence that he may have continued to use his corps of Whitworth sharpshooters in Virginia. Jim Milling, in his description of the storming of Henagan's Redoubt on the North Anna, mentions being joined by "one of Longstreet's scouts," who was armed with "a globe-sighted Whitworth rifle." Milling was a sharpshooter himself, and the fact that he did not know the man in question and refers to him as one of the corps commander's scouts is significant, as is the fact that he never mentions any Whitworths in his own battalion. Similarly, a soldier in the Tenth Georgia also mentions "a band of sharpshooters composed of the best shots in the corps" but gives no other details.[8]

The Army of Tennessee's Corps of Whitworth Sharpshooters rendered invaluable service during the ensuing battles in Georgia and Tennessee.

Due to the high casualty rate they had to reorganize again at Meridian, Mississippi, after Hood's disastrous Tennessee campaign, but continued to serve until General Joseph Johnson's surrender in the Carolinas. The Kerr sharpshooters of the Orphan brigade disbanded in September 1864, after the battle of Jonesboro had reduced the brigade to a mere remnant, and those who remained became mounted infantry.

There are some accounts of sharpshooter battalions in the Army of Tennessee being used in a light infantry role like those in the Army of Northern Virginia. For example, the Second Battalion Georgia Sharpshooters (part of Brigadier General States Rights Gist's brigade) led the way as skirmishers on the march to Spring Hill, Tennessee, in November 1864 and continued to do so at Franklin and Nashville. Whether this was the battalion's normal role or whether General Gist simply assigned it to them is not clear. The state of Georgia fielded two more sharpshooter battalions in the West. The First Battalion Georgia Sharpshooters was formed in the summer of 1862 by Major Robert Anderson from the infantry regiments then stationed in Savannah, in accordance with the authorizing legislation passed by the Confederate Congress in May. Recruiting went slowly, but the battalion eventually enrolled some 361 officers and men into four companies. Although its men were said to be proficient in skirmish drill and were armed with "long Enfield rifles," there is no evidence that they had any special marksmanship training. After the participating in the defense of Fort McAllister in 1862, the battalion went to the Army of Tennessee in time for the battle of Chickamauga, where it suffered heavily. The First Sharpshooters participated in the Atlanta and Nashville campaigns, acting as skirmishers, line infantry, and provost guard. The battalion effectively ceased to exist at the battle of Nashville on December 16, 1864. In addition, there are brief mentions of the Fourth Battalion Georgia Sharpshooters, also part of the Army of Tennessee, being used as division skirmishers.[9]

In an action west of Atlanta on July 28, 1864, Second Lieutenant J. B. Downing commanded an outfit consisting of the Ninth Mississippi Sharpshooters, a three-company outfit of about 150 men, plus a company each from the Tenth and Forty-first Mississippi regiments of Sharp's brigade. Although junior to two other officers, Downing commanded the five companies on the skirmish line and "drove the enemy from their rail piles back upon their line of battle ... and held the position they had occupied until our line of battle advanced and charged their works. I was then ordered to remain in rear and keep up stragglers." It was a classic sharpshooter action.[10]

Other small battalions were formed and disbanded. The First Mississippi Battalion Sharpshooters consisted of three companies that served as light infantry in the Vicksburg campaign and later as part of Featherston's brigade of Loring's division in the Atlanta campaign. Unlike some of the other sharpshooter units, it retained its distinct organization until the end of the war. In late 1862 General Patrick Cleburne formed the small (two companies, seventy-eight men) Fifteenth Battalion Sharpshooters from men detailed from Wood's (Lowery's) brigade of his division, which consisted of both Mississippi and Alabama units. The battalion served at the beginning of the Atlanta campaign but seems to have been disbanded in early 1864. Another small, short-lived sharpshooter unit was Pound's Battalion of Mississippi Sharpshooters, organized from the detached companies of the Forty-third and Thirty-eighth Mississippi (and perhaps some others) after their parent regiments had been cut off in Vicksburg. The battalion, attached to Ector's Brigade of Walker's Division, served at Jackson and Chickamauga.[11]

Although the Army of Tennessee appears not to have had an army-wide organization of sharpshooter battalions, they fielded at least a few units based on the Army of Northern Virginia pattern. Colonel Edward O'Neal and his Twenty-sixth Alabama regiment left the Army of Northern Virginia in winter 1864 after a political tiff and ended up in Georgia for the Atlanta campaign, where O'Neal took command of Cantey's brigade. He organized a sharpshooter battalion like the one in Rodes's brigade (which he had temporarily commanded), complete with a First and Second Corps of Sharpshooters. Although personally courageous, O'Neal's limited tactical skills eventually cost him his command, whereupon the sharpshooters appear to have fallen into disuse. Another unit appears about the same time, however, in Walthall's brigade: "a battalion of sharpshooters, 22 officers and 180 men, detailed from the various regiments of the brigade, under the command of Capt. J. W. Ward." According to a very brief postwar history, it "was engaged with Sherman's sharpshooters and skirmishers almost every day, sometimes many times in one day, until disbanded at Atlanta, July 22, 1864, when there remained on duty the Major commanding, two Lieutenants and 19 privates." Neither organization appears to have survived the reorganization of the army after the Atlanta campaign.[12]

In June 1862 Rapley's Sharpshooters was formed in the Confederate Army of the West at Priceville, Mississippi, by order of Major General Earl Van Dorn, who had commanded a division in Virginia before being sent west. The idea was not new; after all, Cadmus Wilcox had recommended in his prewar book that fully one-fourth of each brigade should be "light troops ... thoroughly instructed at target practice and at the skirmish drill." Van Dorn's order similarly mandated that a battalion of sharpshooters be formed for each brigade. They were, he said, to be "chosen men, all of whom must be able-bodied, active and good rifle shots and of tried courage," and officers were to be "selected and thoroughly examined" before appointment. Van Dorn wanted the sharpshooter battalion to be 750 strong, and he specified that "no pains will be spared to make the Battalions the elite of the Army of the West. ... An opportunity is therefore now afforded to young men of spirit to enroll themselves in a corps which is unquestionably to become the most distinguished in our Army." The general wanted each company to be from the same state but was open to the idea of a mixed-state battalion, which he wanted equipped "with long range guns, and if possible that the guns of each company are of uniform calibre."[13]

Major General Earl Van Dorn; *B&L*

Three days later Colonel Thomas Dockery appointed Captain Griff Bayne to form a sharpshooter battalion in his Arkansas brigade. Evidently even at this early date it become obvious that the 750-man figure was unattainable, and Dockery tasked each regiment to send between twenty-nine and fifty men. Unlike the later units formed in Virginia, the resulting 200-man Twelfth Arkansas Battalion was constituted on a permanent basis. Major William F. Rapley soon took over the four-company battalion, which adopted his name. It "underwent rigorous training, quite unusual for a typical Confederate unit, and became an efficient, professional, and deadly force. ... The Sharpshooters were the army's 'fire brigade,' specializing in rear-guard actions, holding off superior Union forces while the Confederate army tried to maneuver through Mississippi. They were tenacious fighters and suffered correspondingly heavy casualties at Corinth, Hatchie Bridge, Big Black River and Port Gibson."[14]

As part of Brigadier General Martin Green's brigade, Rapley's sharp-shooters were eventually penned up in Vicksburg with the rest of the Confederate army, where they put their marksmanship skills to good use. Captain John S. Bell, the commander of Company A, described a duel with a Yankee sharpshooter, who harassed their position from "a solitary pine tree on a knoll probably five hundred yards away." The Federal was evidently armed with a target rifle, and though Bell had his best shots take a crack at the man, none was able to hit him. Finally one of his men, Tom White, volunteered to crawl through the Union lines that night and wait for the Yankee sharpshooter. Bell approved the mission, and that night the young Southerner left his post about 3 a.m. and shinnied through the abatis. "At daylight," reported Bell, "I saw a puff of smoke rise from the brush about fifty yards from the tree." As the Yankee tumbled from the tree, Bell and his men opened fire to cover White, who managed to evade Union patrols and return safely.[15]

Rapley's Sharpshooters surrendered with the rest of Pemberton's army on July 4, 1863. After its men were exchanged, at least part of the Twelfth Arkansas Battalion reconstituted and next appeared as part of Kirby Smith's Trans-Mississippi command as part of Fagan's cavalry division. The unit appears to have disbanded late in the war.[16]

24

The Opposition

Skirmishers and Sharpshooters of the Army of the Potomac

The Federals began the Civil War with some very effective light infantry units, but their existence owed more to accident than design. Among the hundreds of volunteer companies formed in 1861 were various specialist units that billed themselves as sharpshooters. Some established strict entrance exams requiring that applicants shoot to a certain standard. Although the South produced many natural marksmen, the Union boasted "a great number of men who had made rifle shooting a study, and who, by practice on the target ground and at the country shooting matches, had gained a skill equal to that of the men of the South in any kind of shooting, and in long range practice a much greater degree of excellency." In heavily German-populated areas, for instance, the *shutzenfest* was an established social institution. Many Union riflemen, like their Southern counterparts, were eager to prove their mettle.[1]

Berdan's Sharpshooters

The volunteer riflemen quickly found a champion in Hiram Berdan, a wealthy inventor and businessman with extensive political connections and a reputation as the best rifle shot in the country. He began advocating a plan to organize the newly enlisted sharpshooter companies into a separate corps, which would be unique in several ways. Unlike the rest of the volunteer army, the sharpshooter companies hailed from throughout the Union (initially four from New York and three from Michigan) rather than from a single state. Each man had to shoot a satisfactory "string" before being accepted, and as an added incentive Berdan promised each man a $60 bounty for providing his own rifle. A born promoter, he moved easily in the circles of official Washington and quickly won over General-in-Chief Winfield Scott, Secretary of War Simon Cameron, and President Abraham Lincoln.

Berdan began recruiting in mid-June 1861 and on August 2 he received his commission as colonel of the 1st United States Sharpshooters. So many men responded to his call, however, that another regiment of eight companies, the 2nd U.S.S.S., was formed as well. Berdan established a training camp near Washington where he regularly staged rifle matches and demonstrations for the press and dignitaries, including the president. On one occasion Berdan placed a 600-yard offhand shot into the eye of a target (said to be the likeness of Jefferson Davis) after President Lincoln himself had called it.[2]

Berdan outfitted his corps in a manner very similar to the British rifle regiments or the old U.S. Rifle Regiment. Each soldier wore a rifleman's distinctive green blouse in contrast to the regulation blue, a small touch that provided better camouflage, built *esprit de corps*, and attracted the press. Indeed, turned out in their green jackets, sky blue (later green) pants, leather leggings, and kepis with an ostrich feather plume, the sharpshooters cut dashing figures on the parade ground. The regiment's training proceeded along the lines of European light infantry, including the use of terrain for cover and bugle calls for maneuver. Like their opponents they used Hardee's drill manual, itself a translation of the Zouave manual from Vincennes. Since Hardee was now a Confederate general, his name disappeared from the Federal volume.

It became obvious early on that heavy target rifles were not suitable for a field campaign, so Berdan looked for a substitute. He settled on the Sharps rifle and made the mistake of promising it to the men, who were already unhappy that he had not honored his pledge to pay them for their own rifles. In fact, Hiram Berdan rubbed just about everyone in the regiment the wrong way. He feuded with his officers. The regular army man sent to shape up the outfit, Lieutenant Colonel Fredrick Mears, resigned after a dustup with Berdan, and his relations with his men were not much better. Almost everyone found him arrogant and overbearing.

Still, his political skills shone when he made an end run around the Chief of Ordnance, Brigadier General James Ripley, to get expensive breechloading Sharps rifles instead of standard-issue Springfields. Not satisfied with the standard Sharps, Berdan specified a custom-made rifle with special sights, a double "set" trigger, and an angular bayonet. Procuring these custom arms required time and left some of Berdan's companies temporarily unarmed. The government issued them Colt Revolving Rifles until the Sharps arrived, which provoked an outright mutiny. Berdan's sharpshooters, always an unruly, high-spirited lot, flatly refused to take the Colts and at one point besieged their colonel in his own headquarters. Eager to get into the field and somewhat mollified with the promise of the Sharps, the sharpshooters accepted their Colts, though two companies elected to retain their own target rifles.

Berdan's Sharpshooters at practice with their target rifles early in the war.
The Soldier in Our Civil War

Berdan's Sharpshooters joined the Army of the Potomac for the Peninsular campaign and quickly proved their effectiveness. Although they disliked the Colt, it proved quite accurate and provided excellent firepower on the picket line against the poorly armed Confederates. The sharpshooters soon dominated the skirmish line, made life miserable for Rebel artillerymen, and prompted urgent calls in the Confederacy for more rifle-armed troops. Doubts soon surfaced about Berdan's leadership and gallantry in action, however. He was not a man who led from the front; rather, he was usually to be found in the rear attending to administrative tasks. This did not prevent him from making exaggerated boasts about his role in various battles and ensuring that he and his men got an inordinate amount of press coverage.

For the campaign the commanders split the 1st and 2nd U.S.S.S. into company-sized units and distributed them across the army, where they served as pickets, scouts, skirmishers, and marksmen. They did not always have things their own way. In one case "a particularly obnoxious and skillful" Southern rifleman began exchanging shots with Private John Ide, "one of the few men who still carried his telescopic target rifle." Ide, firing from behind an outhouse, continued the duel, which "began to take the form of a personal affair." The Confederate proved the better shot, however, and put a ball through Ide's head just as he raised his rifle.[3]

Constantly exposed on the skirmish line, the sharpshooters suffered heavily during the Peninsular campaign, losing almost a third of their numbers to death, wounds, and sickness. The promised Sharps rifles arrived at last in late May 1862, and by early June both regiments were fully outfitted.

They were, said one man, "all that we could have wished for." They served with distinction at both Second Manassas and Antietam, leaving many of their brothers on both fields. By late 1862, after a season of campaigning, both regiments stood at half strength and looked pretty rough—"black and dirty" said one man—in a mix of uniforms, their bayonets long since discarded. In March their Swiss-born lieutenant colonel, Caspar Trepp, even proposed that the two regiments be consolidated. Berdan, meanwhile, continued his imperious ways, court-martialing Trepp on trumped-up charges. He was acquitted.[4]

In spite of Berdan's influence, Army politics continued to dog the sharpshooters. In June Berdan lost an entire company to the 1st Minnesota. Two companies of Massachusetts sharpshooters, originally slated to join the 2nd U.S.S.S., were kept out by Governor John A. Andrews of Massachusetts. Instead, the 1st and 2nd Companies Massachusetts Volunteer Sharpshooters, who called themselves "Andrews's Sharpshooters" in the governor's honor, spent the war attached to various Bay State infantry regiments. Although they, like most others, started with heavy target rifles, they were quite willing to draw the Sharps, especially after being caught on the field at Antietam without a decent infantry rifle. Other outfits raided the supply of Berdan's Sharps rifles at the Washington arsenal, causing him a great deal of heartburn.[5]

Berdan lost two key political allies when General Winfield Scott retired as general-in-chief in late 1861, and Edwin Stanton took over from Simon Cameron as Secretary of War early in 1862. Scott's replacement was Major General George McClellan, creator of the Army of the Potomac. While Little Mac worked wonders organizing and drilling the army after its demoralizing defeat at First Manassas, he had scant use for any concept outside the narrow confines of the drill manuals. The abrasive Major General Henry Halleck, who replaced McClellan in June, had his own ideas about the organization and employment of sharpshooters. That fall Stanton wrote Rhode Island governor William Sprague that "there has been some delay and difficulty in determining the best organization of sharpshooters," but that Halleck had decreed "that the organization should be by separate companies, to be under the disposition of the commanding general in the field, and employed as circumstances shall require." Thus Stanton authorized Sprague to raise "as many separate companies of sharpshooters as may be in your power."[6]

The problem was that most field commanders had little idea of how to use these specialized units effectively, and Halleck's dictates virtually precluded using them in a body. Still, when Major General Ambrose Burnside took command of the Army of the Potomac in winter 1862 he bestowed a signal honor on Berdan by appointing him "Chief of Sharpshooters." Burnside designated the 1st and 2nd U.S.S.S. regiments a separate brigade of sharpshooters, to be considered "a distinct arm of the service," with

Berdan elevated to the job of brigade commander—albeit without a brevet to brigadier.[7]

Thus organized, the U.S. Sharpshooters shone at Chancellorsville in May 1863. There, as part of Major General Daniel Sickles' III Corps, they led the advance toward Catherine Furnace to attack the rear guard of Stonewall Jackson's flanking column. Advancing in open order, they smothered the outnumbered Twenty-third Georgia with their sheer volume of accurate rifle fire, capturing most of them. Although the battle was a clear tactical win for the sharpshooters, it actually contributed to the Union defeat. Berdan's men had overwhelmed Jackson's rear guard, but they had not seriously interfered with his flanking movement or even properly detected it. Sickles and Berdan, in fact, convinced themselves that they had won a great victory and that the Confederates were retreating, news that helped lull the Union command into a fatal state of complacency. They would have done well to pay attention to the captured Georgian who predicted, "you'll catch hell before night."[8]

The battle at Chancellorsville was the only time Berdan's sharpshooters saw use as a light brigade, which was unfortunate, since they had the potential to win against the Southern sharpshooters. Berdan's brigade numbered some fifteen hundred handpicked men, more than a match for the combined sharpshooter battalions of a Confederate division. Nonetheless, when Jackson's flank attack had driven Hooker's army up against the Rappahannock, Berdan's regiments were again split into company-sized units and sent into the woods as skirmishers to meet the newly organized Confederate sharpshooter battalions. In his battle report Major George Hastings of the 1st U.S.S.S. described how a skirmish line of his men turned back a line of battle unaided, which he attributed to "the superior skill of these skirmishers as marksmen," as well as "the rapidity with which their Sharps rifles can be loaded and fired," and of course "the remarkable coolness and steadiness of the men themselves." Hastings also wrote a letter to Trepp with his report (neither of which were ever forwarded through channels) telling how during the battle he had seen Berdan "in the field but out of sight of the enemy." Although he conceded that this did not necessarily prove anything, he authorized Trepp to use his name on "any proper paper … recommending against Hiram Berdan's promotion or against his having control of more sharpshooters."[9]

In spite of Berdan's indifferent leadership, his sharpshooters continued to excel in the field, earning the respect of their enemies. They always seemed to have more than their share of characters, men with names like California Joe, Swearing Bob, Buckshot, and Snap Shot, not to mention their "fighting parson," Chaplain Lorenzo Barber, whose favorite weapon was the heavy target rifle. Nor did they gladly suffer fools or martinets. When General

Hobart Ward threatened to summarily shoot sharpshooter Bill Sweet, the sound of the rest of the company's cocking hammers was enough to induce him seek a quick change of scenery.

At Gettysburg on July 2 the sharpshooters were positioned on the Union army's left flank, where they helped to foil Longstreet's attempt to turn their line. That morning the situation was still uncertain, and General David Birney placed Berdan in command of a detachment of four companies (about a hundred men) of the 1st U.S.S.S., backed by the 3rd Maine. The sharpshooters ran into some Alabamians from Cadmus Wilcox's brigade near Spangler's Woods, at what was just then the far right flank of Lee's army. Berdan as usual handled his men inexpertly, "marching and halting in plain view of the enemy," according to Caspar Trepp, who commanded the detachment. A sharp skirmish action soon broke out in Pitzer's Woods with the Tenth and Eleventh Alabama. Apparently Wilcox had not yet formed a sharpshooter battalion. The sharpshooters pushed the outnumbered Alabamians back across an open field, where they dropped to the ground and returned fire. Berdan quickly called up the 3rd Maine, and a hot firefight continued for about twenty minutes, after which the Alabamians charged and drove back Berdan and his men. In all, the sharpshooters lost two officers and sixteen men (nearly 20 percent of their force), plus forty-eight men of the 3rd Maine. Wilcox's two Confederate regiments, on the other hand, reported losing fifty-six men, of whom eleven were killed. While this hard-fought action, fought in open order at fairly long ranges, had little overall effect on the battle, it seems to have been part of what encouraged General Dan Sickles, commander of the Union III Corps, to make his famous and ill-advised advance to the Emmitsburg Road.[10]

Later Berdan would inflate this little fracas to mythic proportions, claiming that he had discovered Longstreet's flanking column—which actually arrived some time later—and had single-handedly held off thirty thousand men for twenty minutes, long enough for reinforcements to arrive and save Little Round Top. Thus in his own mind Hiram Berdan had saved the army at Gettysburg and, by extension, the Union itself. The story fit well into the larger Sickles-Meade controversy, which continued well after the war.

After the defeat of Sickles's III Corps, the sharpshooters fell back toward the Round Tops. As historian Wiley Sword puts it, "despite the prominence given to their reconnaissance to Pitzer's Woods, the sharpshooter's greatest contribution at Gettysburg was their effort during the furious fighting with Longstreet's men in the Emmitsburg Road and Little Round Top sectors. A consideration often not mentioned by historians is the devastating effect their breechloaders had in helping to throw back attack after attack." It is interesting, however, to compare Berdan's expenditure of ammunition to that of Eugene Blackford's sharpshooter battalion at Oak Hill. Berdan reported that his 450 men fired an average of thirty-two rounds per man for all three days of the battle, while Blackford claimed that each man in his battalion, which numbered less than half as many, fired "not less than 200" on July 3 alone.[11]

After the battle at Gettysburg the army command again split the two sharp-shooter regiments, assigning each to a brigade in Birney's division of III Corps. Hiram Berdan went on an extended leave of absence in August and eventually resigned in January 1864. Caspar Trepp, whom many credited with originating the idea of a sharpshooter regiment, died that December at Mine Run.

Berdan's sharpshooters continued to earn a distinguished service re-cord in the 1864 Overland Campaign. As was their policy the Union brass repeatedly parceled them out in small units along the front, a much less efficient way of using them than the Confederate method of having an in-tegral sharpshooter battalion for each brigade. The sharpshooters marched together but had to be dispersed along the line when the army halted, then reconcentrated and moved separately when the battle shifted. In the nearly continuous combat of the summer of 1864, this took a great deal of time, especially with a Federal command not attuned to the sharpshooters' op-erational necessities.

In June the sharpshooters participated in Grant's attempt to take Peters-burg. After the Confederates stopped the initial Yankee thrust, the line settled down with "sharp shooting constantly going on." There were times, however, when the troops agreed to an informal truce, "generally for the purpose of boiling coffee or preparing food. Half an hour perhaps would be the limit of time agreed upon; but whatever it was, the truce was scrupu-lously observed. When some one called 'time,' however, it behooved every man to take cover instantly."[12]

In one case a Rebel soldier was slow to get the word. "While all others hurried to their posts he alone sat quietly blowing his hot coffee and munch-ing his hard-tack." Declining to shoot him on the spot, one of the Yankee sharpshooters, "less bloodthirsty than some others," called out to him "I say, Johnny, time is up, get into your hole." The Southerner, not appreciat-ing the danger he was in, simply responded "All right." "Just hold that cup still," replied the Yank, "and I will show you whether it is all right or not." A moment later a bullet smashed the cup out of the man's hand, "and left it in such a condition that it could never serve a useful purpose again." The Reb dived for cover, followed by jeers and catcalls from both sides of the lines. "Thus men played practical jokes on each other at one moment, and the next were seeking to do each other mortal harm."[13]

Soldiers hurriedly resuming their positions on hearing the first gun announcing the reopening of hostilities. *The Soldier in Our Civil War.*

Colonel William Ripley, of Company F, 1st U.S.S.S., summed up the nature of the sharpshooter's life, which might have applied to either side:

> Service of this independent nature had a peculiar fascination for these men. In fact, sharp shooting is the squirrel hunting of war; it is wonderful to see how self-forgetful the marksman grows—to see with what sportsmanlike eyes he seeks out the grander game, and with what coolness and accuracy he brings it down. At the moment he grows utterly indifferent to human life or human suffering, and seems intent only on cruelty and destruction; to make a good shot and hit his man, brings for the time being a feeling of intense satisfaction. Few, however, care to recall afterwards the look of the dying enemy, and there are none who would not risk as much to aid the wounded victim of their skill as they did to inflict the wound. War is brutalizing, but the heat of the actual conflict passed, soldiers are humane and merciful, even to their foes.[14]

The sharpshooters spent the rest of the war in the trenches, where they acquitted themselves with distinction. It simply underscored the high command's lack of appreciation of their capabilities that they were not sent to the Shenandoah in 1864, which, with the rapid movement and constant skirmishing, would have been an ideal venue for a light brigade in the British fashion. Part of this reluctance to employ the sharpshooters as a unit, however, may have been a result of questions about suitable leadership.

Casualties and sickness gradually chipped away at the Sharpshooters' strength, and many of the men's three-year enlistments expired in late 1864.

By September the 1st U.S.S.S had shrunk to a battalion, which was finally disbanded in December. A number of the remaining men transferred to the 2nd U.S.S.S., which lasted until February 1865 when it, too, was broken up. Thus ended the Army of the Potomac's rifle regiments—at a time when they might have been most useful. The high command apparently never considered the idea of using the sharpshooters as shock troops on the German pattern at Petersburg.

The Army of the Potomac made one other brief experiment with a light unit in early 1863, shortly after Major General Joseph Hooker took command. Hooker, at the behest of the War Department, tried out the French idea of the "flying column" by forming a light division that spring. Consisting of just five regiments, the name referred mostly to logistics rather than any special weapons or light infantry skills. The idea was for the soldiers to discontinue using wagons and to rely on pack mules and the soldiers' backs for transporting weapons and personal items, thus freeing themselves from the roads and gaining the capability for quick, decisive movements. The concept, which might have held promise, foundered against the twin shoals of army conservatism and bureaucracy. The men refused to travel light, the mules proved unruly and unsuitable for transport, and Hooker left his "flying column" with its parent VI Corps, which drew a diversionary mission at Fredericksburg in the Chancellorsville campaign. Thus, ironically, the light division's only combat assignment ended up being a frontal assault against the Confederate position at Marye's Heights, which they carried at heavy cost. The army disbanded the unit shortly afterwards, and the regiments returned to their brigades.[15]

Berdan's former division commander in III Corps, Major General David Birney, tried to raise another sharpshooter regiment late in the war. Birney, a political general who nevertheless seems to have developed an appreciation for light infantry, recruited the 203rd Pennsylvania in late 1864 specifically as a sharpshooter outfit on the pattern of Berdan's regiments. Unfortunately he died of malaria shortly after the 203rd arrived in Virginia, and his successors treated it as an ordinary infantry regiment. Such was the fate of many outfits recruited as sharpshooter regiments, such as the 9th New Jersey, when their wishes ran counter the rules of a conservative military establishment.[16]

Ambitious men often recruited sharpshooter companies on their own, sometimes by promising that they would be special units exempt from normal soldier duties, and then presented them to the government, which usually had little idea of what to do with them. Other outfits, like the 57th Massachusetts, a "Veteran" unit formed in 1864, recruited one of their ten companies (Company K) as a sharpshooter company, although this practice was by no means universal. The sharpshooters of the 57th initially drew Springfields, and not until mid-July did they receive their promised Spencer seven-shooters, purchased for them by their home state. By that time the sharpshooter company was considerably understrength, and thus the balance of the rifles eventually went to the line companies, each of which received seven or eight that fall.[17]

Politics often trumped military necessity, and state officials frequently intervened to keep troops from their state together, as had Governor Andrews of Massachusetts. New York had four sharpshooter companies that had been intermittently recruited during the spring of 1863, and formed them into a battalion, the 1st Battalion New York Sharpshooters, for three years' service. Initially armed with target rifles, the battalion first saw service during the siege of Suffolk that spring, and ended up with the V Corps of the Army of the Potomac at Petersburg. Serving throughout the war, they retained their independent status as a battalion serving at brigade level, and they were listed in late June 1864 as having eighty-one Sharps rifles on hand. In 1864 the state of Maine also formed a sharpshooter battalion, the 1st Battalion Maine Sharpshooters. Recruiting went slowly, and the eight-company battalion did not enter combat service at Petersburg until January 5, 1865.[18]

Michigan Sharpshooters

The state of Michigan raised several sharpshooter companies early in the war, four of which went into Berdan's two regiments. Another, Brady's sharpshooters (sometimes called Dygert's sharpshooters after its commander, Captain K. S. Dygert) was raised in early 1862 from Detroit. This independent company was assigned to the 16th Michigan Infantry and remained with them for the rest of the war. In 1863 Captain George Jardine recruited another independent sharpshooter company (Jardine's sharpshooters) in the same area, which was also attached that June to the 16th Michigan as a second company. At about the same time twenty-seven Sharps rifles appear on the regiment's list of ordnance. It is not clear who carried the Sharps rifles, but most likely it was one of the sharpshooter companies. The 16th was not the only one of that state's regiments, however, to have two attached sharpshooter companies. The 27th Michigan served as a normal infantry regiment with IX Corps until its return from the western theater in April 1863, when it received two Michigan sharpshooter companies—Perrin's and Vosper's—both of which carried Spencer repeaters. The rest of the men were so taken with these new weapons that they petitioned to have themselves all armed with them to act as a sharpshooter regiment. Their entreaties unheeded, they finished the war with Springfields.[19]

The best-known light infantry outfit from the Wolverine state was the 1st Michigan Sharpshooters. Recruited in late 1862 by Charles V. DeLand—newspaper editor, politician, and ardent abolitionist—the Michigan riflemen expected to be employed much as Berdan's men had been. However, though Colonel DeLand was quite well-connected in Michigan, he lacked the sheer political mojo of Hiram Berdan and was unable to convince the army brass to issue him Sharps (or later, Henry) rifles. Instead, he and his men had to settle for standard-issue Springfields. Since most of the willing men had been skimmed off in summer 1862, recruiting went slowly. By June 1863 DeLand had raised only six companies, which forced him to lower his standards somewhat and give up any idea of enforcing an entry standard of marksmanship. The shortage of volunteers also led him to accept American Indians, who had been refused enlistment in 1861. Therefore, the regiment included a company of Ottawa and Ojibwa (Chippewa) Indians, many of whom were excellent shots and masters of field camouflage.

For the rest of 1863 the sharpshooters guarded the Dearborn arsenal and chased General John Morgan's raiders in Ohio. That winter they drew the thoroughly unglamorous job of guarding Confederate prisoners at Camp Douglas, near Chicago. Still expecting specialized duty as skirmishers, they trained extensively in that discipline, even detailing a bugler to each company to facilitate controlling an extended skirmish line. To their chagrin they remained far from the fighting, but this gave them time to recruit to full strength, drill, and institute a comprehensive marksmanship program—an unusual luxury for most infantry regiments.[20]

Not until April 1864 did the 1st Michigan draw a combat assignment with the Army of the Potomac, participating as part of Burnside's IX Corps in the Overland campaign. Their reception at the Wilderness was a rough one, but they soon recovered their equilibrium and gained a reputation as a first-class unit, participating in heavy action at Spotsylvania (where Colonel DeLand was wounded), Cold Harbor, and Petersburg. The regiment had departed Michigan that spring with seven hundred men, but after the battle of the Crater in mid-July only sixty-one were left unhurt.[21]

That July one of DeLand's company commanders, Captain Andrew Hall, resigned to raise his own sharpshooter unit, which he envisioned as being an independent battalion armed with target rifles. Although Governor Austin Blair's official policy was to discourage the formation of new units in favor of keeping the old ones up to strength, he nevertheless approved Hall's efforts. By August "Hall's Independent Sharpshooters" had recruited 108 Michigan men and formed them into two companies. Hall then made the unfortunate blunder of charging his officers for their commissions, and soon found himself under arrest. The small battalion headed for Virginia without him in November 1864 and served briefly as part of City Point's garrison before being sent to a relatively safe area of the Petersburg front. On March 12, however, the army summarily incorporated Hall's Sharp-shooters into the 1st Michigan Sharpshooters, which increased its strength by ninety-seven badly needed men.[22]

Although they served mostly as a line regiment, the sharpshooters frequently drew skirmishing and picketing duties, but not as much as their name and training had led them to expect. Like Berdan, Colonel DeLand had a tense relationship with his officers. Though courageous enough, DeLand was a lackluster field commander who tended to be haughty and opinionated. Some of his officers intrigued against him, and as Hall recruited his regiment in July, DeLand's political enemies in Michigan produced a letter supposedly written by Captain Levant Rhines—who had just been killed while commanding the regiment at Petersburg—implying that DeLand had acted in a cowardly manner. The Democratic press in Michigan, many of whom had old scores to settle, convicted DeLand (who was in the hospital) in print and cost him his reputation. The embattled colonel managed to fight off an attempt by Governor Blair to disband the Sharpshooters, but in September he was severely wounded and captured. Although swiftly paroled, he was effectively out of a job and the army discharged him for disability in February 1865.

DeLand's sharpshooters went on to play a vital part in the repulse of the Confederate attack on Fort Stedman in March 1865, and they made an important diversionary attack on the morning of April 2, capturing a section of enemy works near the Appomattox River before being thrown back. That evening, as the Army of Northern Virginia withdrew, the 1st Michigan Sharpshooters were the first Union troops to enter Petersburg, and the next morning it was their flag that flew from the court house of the fallen city.[23]

The Pennsylvania Bucktails

The famed Pennsylvania Bucktails regiment was a sharpshooter outfit, at least in the sense of being a first-class light infantry unit. The Bucktails, so called for their habit of wearing a deer's tail attached to their caps, were one of thirteen volunteer regiments mustered in 1861 from men who were excess to the Federal government's troop requirements. Although initially refused, Governor Andrew Curtin formed these men into the Pennsylvania Reserve Corps and eventually had them accepted into Federal service. Together the Reserves served in the only Federal division made up of men from a single state. Thomas Kane, a prominent lawyer, had begun recruiting a rifle regiment in western Pennsylvania shortly after the war broke out. The men who joined were outdoorsmen—hunters, loggers, and the like—and excellent shots. "Kane's Rifles" soon gained a reputation as an unruly bunch, ever prone to brawling, drinking, and all the other vices associated with the lumber camps. Initially the 1st Pennsylvania Rifles, they became the 13th Reserves after their incorporation into Curtin's reserve corps and eventually were officially designated as the 42nd Pennsylvania Volunteer Infantry (and unofficially as the "Wildcats"). Their first commander was Colonel Thomas Biddle, a regular officer. Kane, in a display of humility all too rare in the volunteers, assumed the office of lieutenant colonel under Biddle because he felt he lacked military experience.

The Bucktails trained specifically as light infantry in the British tradition, and their commanders often used them on the skirmish line. One former officer, Captain John Bard, described their training as follows:

> When exposed to heavy fire the Bucktails were instructed to scatter, and at all times were required to take advantage of whatever cover the ground afforded. If any part of the line was better protected than another, the men in that location would push forward and vigorously engage the enemy, under cover of their fire the more exposed part of the line would rush forward. Great responsibility was thrown upon the individual soldier. They were taught to take care of themselves and to take advantage of every opportunity for an advance of the line. In many instances the men had, of their own accord, without orders, rushed forward when under heavy fire and gained important advantage. They were taught to estimate distances on various formations, the estimates being proven by actual measurements, and, except when in general line of battle, to fire only when they had an object fairly in the sights of their rifle. In addition they were skilled marksmen and were constantly practicing at long range, from two hundred to one thousand yards. To their peculiar tactics, constant practice, individual responsibility and good marksmanship, can be credited the fearful punishment inflicted upon the enemy in every action in which they were engaged, without a proportionate loss to them.[24]

Like other sharpshooter outfits, the Bucktails had problems obtaining good arms. They initially drew obsolescent smoothbore muskets but later purloined 180 Sharps rifles from Hiram Berdan's stash. The regiment split for its first campaign, with four companies going to the Shenandoah under Colonel Kane, who would be captured there, while the rest went to the Peninsula with McClellan's army. At Second Manassas under Colonel Hugh McNeil the Bucktails lost heavily as they formed part of the army's rear guard.

The famed Pennsylvania Bucktails distinguished themselves by wearing
a deer's tail on their caps. *The Soldier in Our Civil War*

The Bucktails' finest moment as light infantry came at South Mountain
on September 14, 1862, when they faced Robert Rodes's Alabama brigade
on the steep, wooded slopes near Turner's Gap. The Alabamians detailed
groups of handpicked riflemen—the precursors of the sharpshooter battalions—to oppose them. Pushing uphill "in single line at intervals of from
two to twenty feet" and backed by the 11th Reserves, the Bucktails seeped
between the Confederate positions and nearly brought about the collapse
of Rodes's position. Few other regiments in the Army of the Potomac could
have done as well: "Quickly taking shelter behind trees and rocks, the
Bucktails brought into play their accuracy of marksmanship. Having in
their hands Sharps rifles, they were enabled to pick off many a Confederate,
who, attempting to reload his inferior weapon, was compelled to partially
expose his person."[25]

Still, the Rebel fire was intense and did "terrible execution." The colors
of the 11th Reserves went down, and the fire was so hot that no one could
pick them up. Finally Captain Edward Irvin got the men moving again, but
he fell with a severe head wound. The Reserves continued uphill through
what their division commander called "the most rugged country I almost
ever saw." At one point Colonel McNeil himself took up a rifle and bagged
two Rebels with one shot, using the incident to draw their attention in order
to cover a flanking movement that captured the entire Confederate detachment. Finally, near dusk, they faced Rodes's men across a cornfield, and
the Alabamians poured volleys at them from behind a stone wall. Brigadier
General Truman Seymour, the brigade commander, ordered Colonel Joseph
Fisher of the 5th Reserves to "put your regiment into that corn-field and
hurt somebody!" "I will, general, and I'll catch one alive for you," replied

Fisher. Backed by the 1st and 6th Reserves, Seymour's men swept over the wall then "delivered a murderous volley into the ranks of the panic-stricken enemy, who retreated in hot haste down the western slope of the mountain." A wild cheer broke out "that was heard along the entire line, and was taken up by brigade after brigade" all along the mountain top. Night and a last stand by the Rodes's men near Turner's Gap put an end to the day's fighting, and by the morning the Confederates were gone.[26]

Meade's Reserves division lost 95 killed and 296 wounded. The Bucktails, who had gone into the battle with about 275 men, lost 16 killed and 34 wounded—nearly 20 percent of those engaged, and having one killed for every two wounded said a lot about their opponents' shooting. Rodes, however, lost far more heavily and left a third of his brigade on the slopes: 61 killed, 157 wounded, and 204 captured. Even given that the Alabamians had been badly outnumbered and thinly spread along the ridges, they had clearly been outfought on the skirmish line.[27]

Three days later the Pennsylvanians fought at Antietam, where they lost their commander. Leading the way in skirmish order to clear a fence line, Colonel McNeil fell victim to a Confederate rifleman. The next year the Bucktails fought with the rest of the Reserves division at Chancellorsville and Gettysburg, where they figured prominently in defending Devil's Den against the advancing Confederates. Yet for all their light infantry expertise, they fought as often in line of battle as in extended order, and along with the rest of the Reserves gradually declined in strength. A Yankee correspondent described them later in the war as

> a regiment of Pennsylvania backwoodsmen, whose efficiency as skirmishers has been adverted to by all chroniclers of the Civil War. They wore the common blue blouse and breeches, but were distinguished by squirrel tails fastened to their caps. They were reputed to be the best marksmen in the service, and were generally allowed, in action, to take their own positions and fire at will. Crawling through thick woods, or trailing serpentlike through the tangled grass, these mountaineers were, for a time the terror of the Confederates. But when their mode of fighting had been understood their adversaries improved upon it to such a degree that at the date of this writing there is scarcely a corporal's guard of the original regiment remaining. Slaughtered on the field, perishing in prison, disabled or paroled, they have lost both their prestige and their strength. I remarked among these worthies a partiality for fisticuffs, and a dislike for the manual of arms. They drilled badly, and were reported to be adepts at thieving and unlicensed foraging.[28]

The Pennsylvania Reserves went into the 1864 Overland campaign with barely a month left on their three-year enlistments, which understandably dampened their ardor somewhat. Over the winter the Bucktails drew some Spencer repeaters, presumably to replace their Springfields and supplement their Sharps rifles. On May 8 at Spotsylvania they ran up against their old enemies from Rodes's Alabama brigade, now under Battle's command. Spearheaded by Blackford's sharpshooter battalion, the Alabamians badly whipped the Reserves in the dark pine forests, capturing one of their brigade commanders, Colonel William Talley. The Bucktails, along with the rest of the Pennsylvania Reserves, ended their enlistment at the end of May 1864 and were mustered out. Veterans who opted to re-enlist and recruits with time still left transferred to 190th and 191st Pennsylvania on June 1. Some of these men appear to have kept their Sharps rifles, because the 190th is listed as having ninety-eight at the end of the month.[29]

Although the Bucktails and their skirmish tactics had little effect overall effect on the way the Army of the Potomac fought, they did, ironically, have a great deal to do with the Army of Northern Virginia's adoption of light infantry tactics and the organization of their sharpshooters: three months after Robert Rodes's pummeling at South Mountain, he was organizing the first of the Army of Northern Virginia's sharpshooter battalions.

Late War Union Sharpshooters

The Army of the Potomac continued to employ various sharpshooter units throughout the war, but always on an improvised basis. In 1862 the Army of the Potomac had been far ahead of its Confederate opponents in sharpshooting and light infantry, but by 1864 the Southern army had, with its sharpshooter battalions, effectively reversed the situation. To add to Federal discomfiture in that area, many of their elite light infantry units like the Bucktails and the 1st and 2nd U.S.S.S. were fading away from attrition and expired enlistments. During the Overland campaign the Federals had been regularly outshot on the picket line, and in the winter of 1864-65 they did make some effort to arm the flank companies of many veteran regiments, such as the 5th Wisconsin and 5th Michigan, with either Sharps or Spencer rifles and to give better rifles to regiments who specialized in skirmish duty. But the distribution of rifles, by itself, was not enough to fix the problem.

Since the Army of the Potomac never adopted any sort of formal tactical doctrine for light infantry or sharpshooters, individual commanders had to improvise. Some formed their own organic sharpshooter units as early as April of 1864. "The regiment's best shots were invited to try out for a regimental sharpshooter detachment," writes a modern historian of the 15th New Jersey, part of VI Corps. "Targets were shot at 300 yards over a three day period and those who qualified were expected to demonstrate 'coolness under fire and undaunted courage' in the coming campaign. The sharpshooters were placed under the command of Sergeant Elias H. Carlile of Company H, the best shot in the regiment." Just whose idea this was, whether they were part of a larger unit, or whether it was in any way related to Confederate practice is unclear.[30]

In any case, General George Getty first mentions a division sharpshooter company in his VI Corps division during the fighting around Petersburg in 1864. Numbering about ninety men under Captain Alexander M. Beattie of the 3rd Vermont, the division sharpshooters "pushed forward on a scout" in the direction of the Weldon Railroad on June 23. While Beattie and his sharpshooters stood guard, a group of pioneers tore up the tracks for one of Petersburg's main supply arteries. Getty ordered Brigadier General Lewis Grant, commanding the Vermont brigade, to send two hundred men from the 11th Vermont to further protect the working party on the north side. That afternoon, however, a large force of Confederates arrived and began pressing Grant's men.

What followed was a classic picket line fiasco. Beattie and his men, along with the pioneers, retreated in good order, skirmishing as they went. But the officer commanding the 11th Vermont's battalion, Major C. K. Fleming, decided to make a stand—even though he was three-quarters of a mile from the rest of the brigade—and threw up a makeshift breastwork of rails. The man in charge of the picket line, Lieutenant Colonel Samuel Pingree (the corps Officer of the Day, also from the Vermont brigade), then did exactly the wrong thing and sent up the 4th Vermont in support. Instead of attacking Fleming frontally as he expected, the Rebels flanked him on the left, striking at the vulnerable joint between commands. The connecting pickets of Ricketts's division pulled back abruptly, leaving Fleming's men and nearly all of the 4th Vermont surrounded. Lewis Grant, out of the chain of command, could only watch helplessly as over four hundred of his men were marched off to Southern prisons. Four days later Beattie and twelve of his sharpshooters again scouted to the Weldon Railroad, driving off some Rebel cavalry and cutting the telegraph wires, reporting upon their return that the tracks had not been repaired.[31]

Beattie's sharpshooters put in an appearance again three weeks later at Fort Stevens as "a company of about seventy-five who were selected from the various regiments of the Division attached to General Getty's headquarters as sharpshooters." They took part in an unsuccessful attempt to storm a house full of Confederate sharpshooters on July 12 and fought later that day in the larger battle before Fort Stevens. Getty's division sharpshooters continued their service in the subsequent Shenandoah Valley campaign under Captain Charles Terrell of the 43rd New York. Getty thought Terrell "deserving of especial mention" for his services at the battle of Fisher's Hill on September 22, 1864: "He held the extreme left with his detachment, and after rendering most efficient service was seriously wounded." Terrell recovered and continued to lead the 2nd division's sharpshooters until the end of the war. The VI Corps returned to Petersburg that winter, and the sharpshooters remain unmentioned until the Union breakthrough of April 2, 1865. In an order issued the day before, General Horatio Wright, the corps commander, directed that "division sharpshooters will be so disposed as to be rendered most effective," implying that each of his three divisions had a company of them.[32]

General Frank Wheaton's division (1st division, VI Corps) had such an outfit. Captain James Stuart of the 49th Pennsylvania commanded a company composed of both light infantry armed with Spencer seven-shooters and sharpshooters armed with long-range target rifles, likely composed of seventy-five light infantrymen and twenty-five long-range sharpshooters, the best shots and most daring men drawn from across the division. At Petersburg Wheaton employed his division sharpshooters as a flank guard, leaving the long-range sharpshooters with their target rifles back at the forts until he had secured his objective, whereupon they joined the company to fire at the Rebel artillery. Stuart acted independently, wheeling right before entering the enemy works to scoop up the Confederate picket line.[33]

Stuart's men were not Wheaton's only light infantry, however. Of the two regiments leading his attack, the 37th Massachusetts was wholly armed with Spencer repeaters and the 5th Wisconsin had them in its flank companies. Screening the narrow front of the advance were seventy-five "picked men and volunteers" from the Spencer-armed 37th Massachusetts under Captain J. C. Robinson. Not just skirmishers, these men led the assault, covering a group of twenty pioneers armed with axes to clear the obstacles.[34]

Late in the war the 37th Massachusetts had found increasing employment on the skirmish line to oppose the Confederate sharpshooter battalions, whose trench raids had proved greatly embarrassing. There is also some evidence of an informal Union effort to arm one regiment per division with Spencer repeaters, and to use this outfit for skirmishing duties. One such was the 148th Pennsylvania (Miles's division, II Corps), which launched a raid of its own in the early evening of October 27, 1864, on the Confederate works across from Fort Morton. Led by Captain Jerry Brown, a hundred picked men hacked their way through the abatis, stormed the fort and captured four officers and eleven men. The Confederate response was immediate, however, and Brown soon found himself fending off a vicious counterattack that cost him several men and obliged him to withdraw before his supports could come up. Nevertheless, his superiors were pleased with the action and awarded him a brevet to major.[35]

The 148th Pennsylvania assaults a Rebel fort at Petersburg, October 27, 1864.
A.W. Warren, *Harper's Weekly*

Three nights later the Confederates returned the favor by capturing most of Brigadier General Nelson Miles's picket line, manned by 387 men of the 69th and 111th New York. The Irish 69th New York had just absorbed a large number of new recruits, many of doubtful quality who were on the picket line for the first time. Ten of them deserted a day or two prior and seem to have revealed the details of the Federal position and picket schedule. The raiders infiltrated between the two regiments (who were from different brigades) at the time of the guard change and then turned left and right. Wearing Union overcoats and caps, they marched down the line as if they were relieving the picket, capturing 246 men and withdrawing without loss. Although the identity of the Confederates remains unknown, one of the Federal officers who avoided capture estimated their numbers at 150-200 men, or about the size of a sharpshooter battalion.[36]

The XVIII Corps, part of the Army of the James, also employed division sharpshooter companies. In a congratulatory order on October 11, 1864, corps commander Major General Benjamin Butler praised Capt. Phillip Weinmann of the 6th U.S. Colored Troops, "commanding division of sharpshooters," for his "excellent conduct in managing his line of assault on the 29th of September." The division commander of Butler's all-Black 3rd division, Colonel Alonzo Draper, again mentions Weinmann (now a major) and his sharpshooters "deployed as skirmishers on the right" in an October 27 report.[37]

Reports from the corps's 1st division also mention hearing from "the officer commanding the division sharpshooters" on August 18. Their commander, Brigadier General Gilman Marston, describes an action in a report submitted on October 30: "I ordered the division sharpshooters' corps, Captain Goss, and the One hundred and eighteenth New York Volunteers, Major Dominy commanding, to be deployed as skirmishers, Captain Goss, with the sharpshooters, being on the right, and Major Dominy, with the One hundred and eighteenth New York Volunteers, stretching about 200 yards to the left of the Williamsburg pike."[38]

Although these reports suggest that sharpshooter companies were part of all the corps's divisions, this is the last mention of them. On December 3, 1864, the Army of the James reorganized into the all-Black XXV Corps and the all-White XXIV Corps, and the sharpshooters disappear from the records.

As for the other corps of the Armies of the Potomac and the James, a few late-war sharpshooter units rated a mention in the *Official Records*. A dispatch by Colonel Fred Locke, assistant adjutant general of the V Corps, mentions how "three men of the First Division sharpshooters, Major [R. William] Jacklin commanding," captured fourteen Confederate cavalrymen on April 1, 1865. Jacklin's men, "all of the Sixteenth Michigan Veteran Volunteers detailed as sharpshooters," took the prisoners while out on patrol.[38]

Another fairly typical ad-hoc unit appears in the report of Lieutenant Colonel Gilbert Robinson of the 3rd Maryland (U.S.) battalion, a veteran four-company outfit belonging to the 2nd brigade of the IX Corps's 1st division. In the aftermath of the mine explosion at the Crater, the brigade advanced under the command of Colonel E. G. Marshall but was quickly stalled by the confusion in command and prompt Confederate counterattacks. Robinson had organized some of his men (he does not say how many) into a sharpshooter unit armed with Spencer repeaters under the command of Captain David Weaver. Robinson, who held the far right of the Federal position, positioned his sharpshooters to fend off the Rebel counterattacks. "The Spencer rifles in that regiment did great execution upon the enemy," said Robinson, "and demonstrated the advantages of an organized corps of sharpshooters." Robinson commended both Captain Weaver and Sergeant Barnard Strasbaugh, who, "in charge of a squad of sharpshooters, armed with Spencer rifles, greatly distinguished himself. Taking a favorable position, he single handed captured 8 prisoners in one squad, wounding 2 of them, and 3 more in another. The effectiveness of the Spencer rifle in good hands was abundantly demonstrated during the day." Robinson went on to brigade command, and did not mention this unit again, even though the 3rd Maryland played a prominent role in the battle of Fort Stedman. Nor does any other mention of such a unit, or of division sharpshooter companies, appear in the official papers of the IX Corps. Like their Confederate counterparts, the Union division sharpshooters seldom appeared on strength or casualty reports, since these were tabulated for their parent units.[39]

Overall the Federal armies in Virginia obviously appreciated the services of both light infantry and sharpshooter-snipers but never made any sort of concerted effort to field them. The higher command seems to have remained oblivious to the problem, leaving local commanders to solve it on their own. Union and Confederate efforts inversely mirror each other, with the Federals entering the war with excellent light infantry units that they allowed to atrophy, while the Southerners started with none but finished the war with excellent sharpshooter units throughout the Army of Northern Virginia.

25

The Open Order

The Boer War to World War I

The slow rate of fire of their muzzle-loading muskets, as well as the difficulty of loading them in the prone position, hampered the overall effectiveness of the Confederate light infantry sharpshooters. Despite extensive training in range estimation, long-range shooting was always somewhat problematic with the low muzzle velocities of black powder weapons, and the ever-present smoke quickly obscured both targets and shooters. The introduction of breech-loaders and repeaters late in the war not only did not solve these problems; in some ways they made them worse by increasing the amount of smoke on the battlefield.

After the American Civil War, however, technological progress in rifle design was extremely rapid. In 1866 the British Army transformed its service P53 Enfields into breech loaders with the Snider-Enfield conversion, which allowed it to fire a center-fire brass cartridge. The United States, swamped with millions of surplus rifles, converted many Springfields to a .50 caliber breech-loading "trapdoor" model, replaced in 1873 by the .45-70 Springfield that saw extensive service in the American West. Beginning in 1871 the British began replacing the venerable Enfield with the Martini-Henry rifle, a single shot .45 caliber weapon that had the distinction of being the first British service rifle designed from scratch as a breech loader. Both Britain and America had by now settled on a .45 caliber, center-fire, metallic case cartridge as their service standard. Hiram Berdan remained active as a firearms designer, and his patented center-fire primer remains in use today. The caliber of the service rifles, however, continued to decrease. The British .303 Lee-Metford, one of the first truly modern rifles with a bolt action and an eight (later ten) round box magazine, began phasing out the Martini-Henry in 1888. Although the Lee-Metford Mk I first appeared as a black powder weapon, it was soon converted to use the newly available smokeless powder ammunition. In 1907 the British rolled out the classic SMLE, or

Short Magazine Lee-Enfield, which their infantry used through World War II. About the same time Mauser in Germany fielded a rifle that matched and even exceeded these rifles, so that by the time of the Boer War a line rifleman shouldered a weapon superior to even the vaunted Whitworth. Spain adopted Mausers in 1893, which their infantry used to good effect against the Americans in Cuba in 1898.[1]

Smokeless powder changed everything. The muzzle velocity of a service rifle doubled to well over two thousand feet per second. This increased velocity, combined with denser, more streamlined metal-jacketed "spitzer" bullets, gave these rifles vastly superior performance at long ranges and left no telltale cloud of smoke to mark the shooter's position. They also virtually eliminated bore fouling, allowing tighter tolerances and thus greater accuracy. A "stripper" clip allowed a soldier to load five rounds into the box magazine very quickly with a push of his thumb.[2]

It was ironic that the British, who had done much to usher in this technological revolution in riflery, were among the first to feel its deadly sting.

The Boer War

In the last year of the nineteenth century the British found themselves at war with an opponent in Southern Africa much like the Confederates they had supported and admired during the American Civil War. Like the Southerners (or the old Balkan *grenzers*), the Boers were small farmers with a tradition of independence, self-reliance, and marksmanship from an early age. Their "army," a loosely organized collection of local militia units called *kommandos*, was essentially composed of mounted sharpshooter battalions. Though difficult to discipline, they knew the veldt intimately and were superb small-unit fighters. Unlike the Rebels, however, they had modern Mauser repeating rifles using smokeless powder ammunition, a factor that greatly complicated attempts to subdue them.

The British Army, although it had keenly observed the Americans in their Civil War, seemed to miss the lessons of its last year. They might have done well to consult an 1878 article in a Philadelphia newspaper by former Confederate sharpshooter Captain John Young. By mid-war, said Young, both sides had adopted "the system of fighting from behind earthworks. So universal had this become that intrenching tools formed part of the soldier's regular equipment as much as did his arms of offense, and the spade and mattock were ranked almost equal in importance with the sabre and rifle.... Thus it came to pass that whenever a line was formed or a position occupied where there was any likelihood of attack, trenches were dug at once and earthworks thrown up, which were elaborated and extended as the approach of the enemy increased the chances of an action."[3]

The generals of the British Empire, who had of late mostly fought unsophisticated foes over whom they had a vast technological superiority, now came squarely up against one who was as well-armed as they, understood European tactics, and had little use for the fripperies and outdated glories of Continental warfare. The result was a series of humiliating defeats that would have seemed inevitable to anyone who had studied the campaigns at Petersburg and Atlanta rather than the battles of Waterloo and Austerlitz.

The Boers moved first. In November 1899 they laid siege to Ladysmith and badly defeated a series of British attempts to relieve it. The first was at Spioenkop, where the British, seventeen hundred strong, stormed the hill in a dawn bayonet attack, but then came under withering rifle fire from a Boer counterattacking party when the fog cleared later that morning. Pinned under the relentless bullets of the Boer marksmen, the Englishmen suffered heavily. Some two hundred surrendered while others fled. Fighting off a fierce assault, the survivors barely hung on until dark, then retreated. The British lost 332 men killed, 563 wounded, and 189 taken prisoner, while the badly outnumbered Boers lost 58 killed and 140 wounded.

On the second attempt at Colenso the British commander, General Sir Redvers Buller, tried to flank the Boer position rather than assault it directly, but the Dutchmen, though outnumbered three to one, caught his flanking column on broken ground, savaged it with accurate rifle fire and forced it to retreat with heavy casualties. Boer sharpshooters picked off English gun crews and officers alike with impunity. The result was another bloody British reverse to the tune of a thousand men and eleven guns. Boer losses were light.

Another British column under General Lord Paul Methuen marching to relieve Kimberly also paid a high price when crossing the Modder River in late November, but perhaps the classic reckoning came at Magersfontein that same month, when Methuen sent his troops forward in close order against a Boer trench system (protected by yet another modern innovation, barbed wire) on a rocky height. The British artillery preparation was largely ineffective, although it accounted for most of the Boer casualties. The Highland brigade that bore the brunt of the dawn assault lost over seven hundred men, including their brigadier, all from rifle fire. "Never," wrote Sir Arthur Conan Doyle, "has Scotland had a more grievous day than this." Overall British casualties exceeded a thousand men, while those of their opponents probably did not top two hundred.[4]

In the other battles around Ladysmith the Boers continued to hold the advantage, and General Buller, even though he greatly outnumbered the besiegers, did not break through until his third try at Thukela Heights, and then only at great cost. The discrepancy in both strength and casualties is striking: the British, with 28,000 men and 85 guns, suffered some 5,000 casualties, while the Boers, who had only 5,000 men and 11 guns, lost 232 men and withdrew unmolested.

Finally the overwhelming resources of the empire began to tell, and the Boers (who had little expertise at the operational level of war) made a number of critical mistakes. More reinforcements arrived, and with better commanders in place the British in short order raised the sieges of Mafeking, Kimberly, and Ladysmith, then advanced into the Transvaal to capture Johannesburg and Pretoria. Organized Boer resistance ceased in July 1900, but they continued to fight a guerrilla war for nearly two more years, provoking harsh British countermeasures. When the war finally ended in May 1902 the British had had to commit some half million troops from all over the empire to subdue a foe who never put more than forty thousand men in the field.

"What happened," explained one historian, "was that the British Army, for the first time since the War of 1812, met hostile mounted riflemen and aimed small arms fire. The experience of some 85 years of formal and little wars in Europe and around the world went into the discard, and an entire new system of tactics and techniques had to be evolved on the battlefield." This pronouncement, however, proved a bit premature.[5]

Developments in Europe Prior to World War I

Armies all over the world slowly began to change in response to the newly available firepower, exchanging their colorful uniforms for better camouflage resembling what Eugene Blackford's men had worn: dun brown and field gray. The Germans, who had informally supported the Boers in much the same way that the British had supported the Confederates, intensively studied the battles in South Africa. Noting the heavy British casualties, they began experimenting with a more open order. In war games held in 1902 German officers tried replacing the attacking battalion columns with a heavy skirmish line and allowing their men to use available cover.

This approach had its own problems, and the biggest was command and control. Although firearms technology had progressed a long way since the American Civil War, battlefield communications had not. Grant had used the telegraph to send orders to his corps commanders in 1864, and by 1915 field telephones went down to battalion level, but they were useless in controlling a mobile formation in the attack. Officers on the battle line still directed their men with bugles, whistles, hand signals, and couriers. In at least one respect the problem was worse than it had been a hundred years earlier—officers and couriers no longer dared to ride horses on the battlefield.

Another problem, perhaps more perceived than real, was shirking. Many senior officers firmly believed that any soldier not actually under the eye of his officers would find a protected place and stay there, as had happened with some reserve units during the 1870-71 Franco-Prussian War. The Germans solved both problems by entrusting their non-commissioned officers with greater leadership and tactical responsibilities on the battlefield, to be where the officers could not.

The open-order debate continued for the rest of the decade in the Imperial German Army, with neither side able to have their ideas definitively adopted. Many senior officers wanted to refight the Franco-Prussian War and attack in dense columns of platoons. To back their position they cited Japanese success with mass attacks in the Russo-Japanese War while downplaying the heavy casualties. The more progressive elements wanted to use the looser "Boer tactics" and pointed to the enormous losses both sides had suffered when taking fortified positions in Manchuria. The controversy was still far from settled in 1914 when the guns of August cut short the debate.[6]

The Great War

France, still obsessed by its humiliating defeat in 1870, had adopted philosophy in preference to tactics, eschewing the defense almost entirely for the attack. This was based at least partly on philosopher Henri Bergson's concept of the *elan vital* (sometimes called vitalism), translated through Colonel Louzeau de Grandmaison into the "School of Attack." The *elan* of the soldier in the attack was all-important and could not be resisted, so the theory went, even by modern arms. In practice this meant that the French Army attacked in dense columns reminiscent of the first Napoleon and suffered enormous losses.

In Britain tradition swiftly overcame the lessons of the Boer War, at least as far as the offensive was concerned, and generals continued to send the Tommies forward in columns of platoons, much as they had in South Africa. In the defense, however, the English readily recognized the importance of trenches protected by barbed wire. They also rigorously trained their regular army (the famous "Contemptibles") in rapid aimed fire using their .303 Lee-Enfield rifles, which could fire fifteen aimed shots a minute. In their first contest at Mons, the Tommy riflemen mowed down their opponents, who advanced in dense lines. So heavy and accurate was the British fire that the Germans convinced themselves the British were using machine gun battalions.[7]

On the German side, the field regulations left enough room for an enterprising commander to use open order tactics, and many of the more forward-thinking officers did so. Many others did not, however, and the eagerness of German commanders for a quick knockout blow in the early months of the war led them to concentrate more men in a sector than they might have otherwise. The result was that "time after time the infantry was sent in, advancing in thick skirmish lines reminiscent of those of the American Civil War." Casualties soared, and after the initial German offensives failed, both sides dug in. The "race to the sea" began a short time later, and soon a continuous line of trenches running from the Swiss border to the North Sea defined the Western front.[8]

The last German attempt to break through the line at Ypres in November 1914 incurred such heavy losses that it was dubbed the Slaughter of the Innocents. German reservists, including a number of students, advanced to their deaths shoulder to shoulder, singing patriotic songs. The war of maneuver in the West had ended and the days of trench warfare had begun.[9]

Of the three main armies involved, only the Germans took immediate steps to fix the tactical deficiencies that had cost them so many men in the opening stages of the war. "The tactical debate of the last decade or so was over," observed historian Bruce Gudmundsson. "Boer tactics had been vindicated. The dense column had given way to the skirmish line. ... A similar thinning out of formations and a replacement of columns with skirmish lines occurred in all German armies fighting on the western front. The two assumptions upon which the tactics ... had been based—the need for officers to maintain personal control over their units and the need to mass rifle fire to achieve fire superiority—had been proved both false and costly."[10]

Since the Germans had gone over to the strategic defensive in the West, this change had little immediate effect. A more pressing need was for the development of tactics appropriate for trench warfare.

Storm Troops East and West

There remained in the German Army a few units directly descended from the old *jäger* units of Frederick the Great's day. One such was the Guard Rifle Battalion, which had actually been organized and trained as a *jäger* outfit. In December 1914 this outfit stormed a section of French trenches using the same methods that Captain Dunlop's sharpshooters had used at Petersburg. Advancing silently through the dark across no man's land, they overran the trenches in a sudden rush, then pushed left and right in a technique they called *aufrollen*. One of the men who distinguished himself in the action was a company commander, Captain Willy Rohr.

After the battles of 1914 Germany's attentions shifted east, and with the exception of a few major offensives like Verdun, most operations on the Western Front for the next two years would be attacks with limited objectives intended to take a section of the line but with no expectation of a general advance. Although their open order tactics allowed the Germans to cross no man's land with far less loss than their opponents, they came up against the same problem the Confederates had encountered at Fort Stedman: cracking the fortifications once there was a difficult and costly task. Rohr and his superiors set themselves to solve this tactical problem.[11]

Two methods suggested themselves. One was improved weapons. Hand grenades, heretofore limited to pioneers (combat engineers), provided an excellent way to clear trenches and bunkers, and so the Germans began issuing them to ordinary infantrymen. Another effective and terrifying weapon was the man-portable flamethrower, carried into action by special pioneer detachments. They also began experimenting with portable trench mortars and a 3.7cm cannon light enough to be manhandled in the trenches.

The second approach was to organize special assault detachments (*sturmabteilungen*) to be especially trained and equipped with these weapons. In March 1915 the German War Ministry formed a makeshift battalion of two pioneer companies and a battery of twenty light 3.7cm infantry guns. Initially the experiment went poorly, but in August the commander was relieved and the energetic Captain Rohr put in charge. From then on progress was rapid, and Rohr's outfit began to make a name for itself. Rohr found a patron in his army commander, General Hans Gaede, who also gave him a machinegun platoon of two Maxim guns, a trench mortar platoon of four guns, and a flamethrower detachment. Rohr discarded the puny 3.7cm guns and instead used cut-down Russian 76.2cm field guns for direct fire against strong points. He stripped his Maxim machineguns of their heavy carriages and configured them so that they could be more easily carried across broken ground in the attack. Rohr exchanged the heavy hobnailed infantry boots for lighter alpine models, put leather patches on the men's knees and elbows to aid them in crawling, and adopted the steel helmet well in advance of the rest of the army. Each of his men received a bag of grenades and a carbine version of the Mauser 98 service rifle.[12]

Rohr, like Blackford, proved to be a tactical innovator as well. He devolved even more authority on his NCOs, making them combat leaders rather than "file closers" for the first time. He dropped the skirmish line altogether and had his men advance independently by squads, giving their leaders considerable leeway to accomplish their missions. Rohr also saw to it that his artillery support was carefully coordinated and insisted on conducting elaborate rehearsals prior to the attack using full-scale models of the objective. Like Blackford, he emphasized marksmanship and instituted a rigorous training program. When time permitted, Rohr conducted training sessions in his new tactics for other units.[13]

The first big test came in the battle of Verdun, which began in February 1916. Unfortunately for the Germans, their commander, General Erich von

Falkenhayn, designed this battle from the outset as an artillery battle of attrition rather than an infantry offensive. Local infantry commanders also had little idea of how to employ Rohr's new *stosstruppen* (shock troops), as they had come to be known, and often split them into small, ineffective groups. Although successful in the initial attacks, Rohr and his men were eventually withdrawn after the battle degenerated into a slugging match. Even though the experiment had proved less than totally successful, von Falkenhayn was pleased, and in April he approved the permanent establishment of *Sturmbatallion Rohr*, to which he added two more pioneer infantry companies (for a total of four) and upped the machinegun platoon to a company. Rohr also got a light artillery battery equipped with 7.5cm mountain guns.[14]

The War Ministry also ordered that the existing *jäger* battalions be converted to assault battalions modeled on Rohr's unit. These units, whose ranks still included many hunters, gamekeepers, and other outdoorsmen, preserved much of the traditional independent spirit that had always characterized the *jägers*. For the rest of the war the high command would keep a certain number of elite assault battalions, including Rohr's, in reserve, usually at army level, to be thrown in where they would be most effective. The *stosstruppen* were now elite units with a corresponding esprit. They were, recalled one German officer, "like football [soccer] stars. They lived in comfortable quarters, they traveled to the 'playing ground' in busses, they did their jobs and disappeared again, and left it to the poor foot sloggers to dig in, to deal with counter attacks and to endure the avenging artillery fire of the enemy."[15]

Still, it was obvious that these few battalions, however good, would not be enough to win the war. Von Falkenhayn therefore ordered Rohr to teach his new tactics to the rest of the army, and the captain began a "train the trainer" program for officers and NCOs at his base at Beauville, France. These men were expected to go back to their units and organize company-sized assault units intended mainly for trench raiding. As more and more men went through Rohr's two-week school, the number of *stosstrupp* units throughout the army increased accordingly. By the end of 1916 almost all divisions on the western front—even those composed mostly of reservists—had some sort of special assault detachments. Since there was no standard unit establishment, their organization varied widely, and some commanders were more enthusiastic about the concept than others. A common arrangement was for each regiment to have a company-sized assault unit that could be grouped together at division level into an ad hoc battalion. Other divisions, however, organized a permanent assault company or battalion at division level.

These assault companies were formed out of existing units by an across the board draft, much like the Confederates had used, instead of by designating a certain company as an elite unit. Commanders had to be constantly on guard that units did not dump their worst men into the new company just to be rid of them. Rohr himself had this problem initially and spent considerable time and effort weeding out the undesirables. As with Blackford's sharpshooter battalion, the *stosstruppen* marched and messed with their parent unit until formed for a mission, and were exempt from guard and fatigue duty as well.

The Germans did not neglect other aspects of trench warfare. They also emphasized sniping and established an early lead. Their snipers, who operated in two-man teams, first used sporting weapons but later fielded the telescoped version of the standard service rifle, the *Scharfschüzen Gewehr 98*. The British in particular suffered heavily since their officers insisted on wearing distinctive "long tunics, riding breeches, trench boots and Sam Browne belts." This was, averred a junior officer, "one reason why the officer's casualties were so high. The Germans had a further advantage in their sniping. With them it was done by their *jäger* battalions, picked sharpshooters who in peacetime had been gamekeepers and guides. They wore green uniforms instead of gray and were permanently stationed in one sector, so they knew every blade of grass." In 1914 the German Army had available some twenty thousand telescopic sights (six went to each infantry company), and had an established training program.[16]

The German Army also continued to develop lighter and more specialized weapons suitable for the type of warfare practiced by the new *sturmbatallione*. They designed a lighter version of the standard MG 08 machinegun, the MG 08/15, which featured a wooden shoulder stock, bipod, and a 100-round drum magazine. At 44 pounds it was still quite heavy and, while not the equal of the Lewis gun, was still much more mobile than the standard models. Unfortunately, it did not become widely available until well into 1917. The Germans also reworked captured Lewis guns to fire their standard 8mm service cartridge, resulting in a superior assault weapon that the soldiers preferred, although there were never enough to go around. Combat engineers continued to refine the portable flamethrower, the support companies received a new version of the 7.6cm light trench mortar with a wheeled carriage, and the artillery provided a specially lightened version of the 7.7cm field gun that could be dragged forward for direct fire support, much as artillery pieces had been used in the American Civil War. These early assault guns, the brainchild of artillery Colonel Georg Bruckmüller, were grouped together into "close-combat batteries."[17]

Still, the individual storm trooper needed more firepower. The rifle, even in carbine form, was awkward and slow to fire in the close confines of the trenches. They first tried the long-barreled "artillery" Luger pistol that had been developed for protecting gun crews. With a shoulder stock and a drum magazine it was reasonably handy but rather delicate and not capable of automatic fire. Eventually the Germans produced the first real "machine pistol"—the Bergmann MP 18. Looking like a sawed-off rifle, the fully automatic Bergmann spat out 9mm pistol bullets at a rate of 450 rounds per minute and used the same 32-round "snail" magazine as the Luger. This weapon revolutionized trench warfare, giving a storm trooper a marked advantage over a rifle-armed opponent at close quarters. German industry was not able to supply the Bergmann until mid-1917, and then only in relatively small numbers.[18]

After Verdun the Germans remained on the strategic defensive in the West. The Kaiser removed von Falkenhayn and replaced him with General Erich von Ludendorff, who quickly became an enthusiastic advocate of the *stosstruppen*. "Storm battalions," he noted, "had proved their high value both intrinsically and for the improvement of the infantry generally. They were examples to be imitated by other men." The general formally ordered each army on the western front to form its own assault battalion, and by February 1917 the German Army boasted fifteen new *sturmbatallionen* and two assault companies in addition to the two already existing ones. To facilitate the process Captain Rohr wrote a short tactical manual that was widely disseminated. Ludendorff's initial plan was an extremely ambitious one—nothing less than to train the entire German Army as *stosstruppen*, at which point the assault battalions could be reabsorbed. However, he soon realized that this just was not possible. The average infantryman simply could not meet the high standards set by Rohr, and in any case Germany did not have the requisite time or equipment.[19]

Nevertheless, Ludendorff came to see the *stosstruppen* as a way of overcoming the stasis of trench warfare, restoring mobility to the battlefield, and perhaps even ending the war. Two events in late 1917 lent weight to this conclusion. The first was the smashing German victory at Caporetto (October 24 to November 12) that virtually knocked Italy out of the war. Their success was due in large part to the use of *stosstruppen* and *jäger* battalions to infiltrate the Italian position and bring about a general collapse of their lines. The "non-linear" tactics perfected by Rohr—small groups of storm troopers moving forward independently without regard to their flanks, bypassing strong points and making for the rear areas—had worked to perfection in their first large-scale test.[20]

The second event was the successful German counteroffensive at Cambrai. On November 21 the British launched the first major tank offensive of the war, overrunning a section of the Hindenburg Line and advancing over five miles against disorganized resistance. The Germans quickly recovered, however, and organized a counteroffensive using their new storm troop tactics on the thirtieth. In spite of having no tanks themselves, they not only retook the ground they had lost but also captured some held by the Allies since the beginning of the war, and narrowly missed cutting off a substantial part of the British Army.

Taking advantage of the post-Cambrai lull, Ludendorff began a massive training program for the German Army, organizing and training a quarter of his best infantry divisions on the storm troop pattern. These he designated "attack" divisions as opposed to the second-rate "trench" divisions. Even the second-line divisions, however, had the now-normal *stosstruppen* units of varying strengths.[21]

Time was running out, however. Although Germany had defeated Russia and emasculated the Italians, allowing them to bring the bulk of their armies west, the United States had joined the Allies. Ludendorff had to act before their full weight could be brought to bear in France. He decided to strike the British in an attempt to split them from the French and cripple them as he had the Italians, thus forcing a peace settlement. The *Kaiserschlacht* offensive kicked off on March 21, 1918, on the old Somme battlefield. The *stosstruppen* swiftly moved forward behind a short but intense creeping barrage, bypassing British strong points and leaving them for the following infantry to reduce. German commanders had organized the army assault battalions into *sturmblocks*, self-contained task forces that were attached down to regimental level to lead the attacks. These elite units supplemented the organic storm troops of the attacking divisions. The initial German gains were impressive: they took several thousand prisoners and a number of guns on the first day, and by the third day Ludendorff had torn open an eighty-kilometer wide hole in the British line and was pressing forward well beyond the trench zone. There had been no advance like this in the West since 1914.

The British, in disarray, found an unexpected benefit from their supply dumps. The hungry German soldiers often stopped to plunder the dumps, as the Confederates had, slowing and disorganizing their advance. Eventually Ludendorff's advance ground to a halt from sheer exhaustion and the inability of the Germans to resupply their forward troops. There were just not enough storm troopers to keep the offensive going. Nevertheless, the "Peace Offensive" pressed the Allies to the limit and nearly caused a general retreat to Paris. Ultimately, however, the series of subsequent German offensives (at Lys on April 9, Aisne on May 27, Noyon-Montdidier on June 8, and the Marne on July 15) all fell short of their objectives.[22]

While the storm troop tactics had proven devastatingly effective in ripping open the Allied front, they did not restore a war of maneuver. Military historian Bruce Gudmundsson concluded that the weapon that kept the German Army from winning ... was not the machine gun but the railroad. ... No tactical system ... could solve the fundamental operational problem ... that the enemy's railroads and motor transport could always bring up more fresh troops. The means of dealing with this problem would have to wait until the next war. Beginning in 1939, the fully motorized ... *Panzer* division gave the German Army the means to move troops ... around the battlefield faster than Germany's enemies could move troops behind it. The innovation wasn't the tank ... rather, it was the mobility of complete formations. ... In the absence of suitable transport, the storm trooper and his victories remained Germany's forlorn hope.[23]

The other European armies experimented with similar tactics as well. The Austro-Hungarians copied the German model directly. In 1917, just before their collapse, the Russians began using "shock battalions" at division level. The Italians formed the *Arditti* (*Reparti d'assalto*), who were armed and trained in a fashion similar to the German Army *sturmbatallione*. Like the Germans, the Italians also formed platoon-sized shock troops at regimental level drawn from across the unit.[24]

The British, on the other hand, remained blissfully ignorant of the havoc their weapons had wrought on the dense German ranks at Ypres, and walked straight into the German guns at the Somme in the summer of 1916 in the same close order formations that had proven suicidal in the Boer War. On July 1 more than fifty-seven thousand British troops fell before the sun set, many before they left their own trenches. This debacle finally forced the British to change their offensive tactical doctrine. By 1918 they used tactics very similar to those developed by the Germans, with the additional advantages of having ever-larger numbers of tanks and fresh American troops.

The British also began using snipers more effectively as well. The driving force behind the change was Major Hesketh Hesketh-Prichard, a big game hunter and expert rifle shot. Like Captain Rohr he proved to be an excellent organizer, successfully navigating the shoals of army bureaucracy and tradition to establish a first-class school for snipers. "It is difficult now to give exact figures of our losses," he wrote of the early days, "but suffice to say that in early 1915 we lost eighteen men in a single battalion in a single day to enemy snipers." Hesketh-Prichard taught not only marksmanship but the techniques of stalking and scouting derived from his years as a hunter, including the adoption of the camouflage "ghillie suit" long used by Scottish gamekeepers. His object, he said, was to instill "the hunter spirit" in each man. As the Confederates had learned, he found that hunters usually made the best snipers. After all, he said, "sniping was really ... a very high class form of big game shooting, in which the quarry shot back."[25]

British snipers in World War I used the .303 caliber Pattern 1914 Enfield rifle. This excellent weapon, originally designed as an improved version of the SMLE, ended up being produced in the United States by Remington and Winchester. Winchester produced a sniper variant with a fine-adjusting micrometer back sight adjustable for elevation and windage, as well as a version with a side-mounted telescope (which Hesketh-Prichard disliked). Simple, sturdy, and highly accurate, it proved a great success.

Hesketh-Prichard also organized his snipers into two-man teams, one a rifleman and the other a scout equipped with either a telescope or field glasses. In addition to picking targets, the scout observer brought back invaluable information about enemy positions. Some of his best "glassmen" were the Scots of the Lovats Scouts Sharpshooters, many of whom had been gamekeepers at home. By the end of war, graduates of Hesketh-Prichard's "School of Sniping, Observation and Scouting" had spread throughout the army, giving the British a marked advantage in that particular tactical specialty.[26]

The French Army, shocked by the bloodbaths of 1914 and 1915, never managed to make the necessary changes, even though it, too, produced tactical innovators. Captains Andre Laffargue and Charles Baux both wrote treatises advocating a tactical system similar to that developed by Rohr, but the French Army, although it gave lip service to the concept, proved institutionally incapable of adopting it in practice. By 1918 both the French and Italians were making their offensives with artillery, leaving to the infantry the task of occupying the pulverized objectives. The losses of these years left a scar on the French national psyche, later given physical form in the Maginot Line.[27]

26

Evaluating the Sharpshooters

"Sharpshooters, like fiddlers, are born and not made."

— General Ambrose Powell Hill, C.S.A.[1]

Killers and Fillers

The Confederate sharpshooter battalions should be seen as part of a continuum of light infantry that began in the 1700s and continues today. While the concept was one of great tactical value that gave the Army of Northern Virginia a superior degree of tactical flexibility, it was not a war-winning innovation, nor, given the relative strength of the Confederacy, could it have been. The sharpshooter concept made good use of the unique strengths of many Confederate soldiers, especially their innate spirit of independence, self-reliance, and initiative—qualities not always readily available in the armies of nineteenth century. The tactical concept put the best and bravest men where they would do the most good, separating them from the mass of line infantry.

In 1982 U.S. Army colonel Thomas Horner studied the combat effectiveness of fighter pilots with an eye to predicting the battlefield performance of tank commanders. Horner concluded that the men in ordinary combat units could generally be divided into three categories that he called "killers, fillers, and fodder." A relatively small percentage of "real *killers*" would inflict the majority of the enemy casualties. Most of the rest would be *"fillers,"* who moved with the unit but whose main concern was to stay alive and unharmed, and some would be *"fodder,"* the men who "were certain to be defeated within their first few encounters with the enemy." He cited figures from World War II and Korea to show that in each war roughly 5 percent of the fighter pilots made about 40 percent of the aerial kills (the killers) while another small group were shot down almost immediately (the fodder). The bulk of the pilots either scored only a few kills or none at all (the fillers).[2]

Although extrapolating from fighter pilots to Confederate infantry may seem to be stretching the point, Horner buttressed his work with material from army leadership laboratories showing that the same general principles applied to ground units as well. Both the Confederates and later the Germans found that by concentrating their "killers" into special units they could get superior performance beyond what numbers might indicate. A battalion of sharpshooters or *stosstruppen* in the right place might be worth a brigade or more of ordinary infantry. Indeed, it is reasonable to assume that the sharpshooters of both sides inflicted a disproportionate number of casualties relative to their numbers. At Spotsylvania, for instance, one Rebel marksman "was said to have taken twenty lives."[3]

The sharpshooter concept did have some disadvantages, however. Unless a commander was careful when assigning the sharpshooter battalion a separate mission like flank guard, he could end up denuding his line regiments of their scouts and skirmishers. This was exactly what happened in the disastrous attacks of Iverson's and O'Neal's Confederate brigades at Oak Hill on July 1, 1863, the failures of which were due in large part to lack of proper reconnaissance. The sharpshooters of both brigades were fully occupied, along with Doles's brigade, in holding off the advancing Union XI Corps. As a result many of the regiments seem to have reverted to using the old style of skirmishers, with all its attendant problems.

The other obvious drawback was that the sharpshooter battalions siphoned the best men away from the line units, thereby reducing their effectiveness. This problem became especially acute in late 1864 and into 1865 as the regiments began to fill up with conscripts, substitutes, and bounty men whose devotion to the cause was questionable. Southern commanders placed a high priority on keeping the sharpshooter units up to strength, which required a progressively larger percentage of men from the line. By late 1864 the sharpshooter battalions were often as strong as any of the regiments of the brigade, showing the weakness of the Rebel line. The combination of officer attrition and detailing the best men to the sharpshooters greatly reduced the effectiveness of many Confederate line units late in the war and contributed directly to fiascos like Fisher's Hill. Near the end of the 1864 Valley campaign Jubal Early complained that "we have very few field or company officers worth anything, almost all our good officers of that kind having been killed, wounded, or captured, and it is impossible to preserve discipline without good field and company officers."[4]

If the elite units did most of the fighting, it also meant that they suffered the most casualties. Both the Confederates in late 1864 and early 1865 and the Germans in 1918 found that most of their "killers" had become casualties, leaving their armies short of aggressive leadership at all levels.

In the end, attrition acted most heavily in this respect: it was not enough to put a certain number of men in the ranks if their main concern was self-preservation. Over the course of the war attrition gradually replaced the enthusiastic, ideologically motivated volunteers of 1861 and 1914 with men who simply wanted to keep themselves in one piece until the war was over. Fear of disgrace or the provost marshal might hold them in the ranks, but it could not make them aggressive fighters, especially on the skirmish line. Others, initially resolute, grew weary of the apparently endless slaughter and lost their motivation. Because of their smaller numbers, this loss of quality affected the Confederacy and the Central Powers the most. The Union and the Allies, with their larger pool of manpower, were better able to prevent this by putting a steady stream of new men in their units, but even so they suffered from the same problems on a lesser scale.

Weapons

The quality and variety of weapons available to the light infantryman improved steadily from 1700 on, yet some items remained remarkably constant. For example, in the late seventeenth century each French infantry company included a four-man squad of grenadiers, later increased to one company per battalion. Each man had "a sabre, a hatchet, and grenade pouch containing between 12 and 15 grenades." Theirs was a dangerous job, as they were a cross between pioneers and assault troops. Commanders selected only the largest and strongest men for the job, and they soon gained a reputation as elite soldiers. Two hundred and fifty years later the German *stosstruppen* carried bags of grenades to use in the trenches, and in 1917 they were given the honorary title of grenadiers.[5]

The biggest improvement for the infantryman, however, was in the rifle he carried. In 1700 only specialist troops carried the rather primitive rifles available, but by the end of the nineteenth century these had steadily improved into a weapon whose effective range was limited only by how far a soldier could see. When paired with barbed wire and the machinegun, the rifle made defensive positions nearly impregnable. Starting with the Boer War, this led to the gradual loosening of the close order that had dominated the European battlefield since Classical times, yet armies did not universally adopt the open order until 1916. Eugene Blackford's men did not have repeaters, so they simply did not have the firepower to make their open order work without a line of battle to back it.

At the turn of the century the Boers showed what could be done with long-range repeating rifles, and the German storm troopers bettered this with the addition of light automatic weapons, mortars, flame throwers, and the like. Almost all the weapons adopted by the World War I *stosstruppen*—

hand grenades, trench mortars, cannon, and even machineguns—existed in primitive form in 1865. The only real exceptions were the flame thrower and the machine pistol. All were, however, too large and heavy to accompany the assault troops.

Both in the trenches and on the skirmish line the Germans, Boers, and Confederates all quickly stripped down to the bare essentials for fighting and demanded shorter, handier weapons. The Germans adopted the Mauser 98K, the Rebels the two-band Enfield, and the U.S. Army the Spencer rifle. This need eventually led to specialized weapons like the Bergmann machine pistol and eventually the modern assault rifle. And in a final twist, both the U.S. Army and Marines are now beginning the put "designated marksmen" armed with long-range rifles back into the line units.

Leadership and Tactical Innovation

The last ingredient for the success of the sharpshooters and storm troopers was a command environment that encouraged and rewarded tactical innovation. The Imperial German Army, for instance was a "decentralized, mission-oriented organization that placed a great deal of trust in its officers." The same could be said for the Army of Northern Virginia. When Colonel Bristor Gayle wanted to reorganize his skirmishers, his brigade commander, Robert Rodes, let him and then adapted his innovations to the entire brigade. The leaders of the Army of Northern Virginia—D. H. Hill, Stonewall Jackson, and Robert E. Lee—gave Rodes permission to set up his experimental sharpshooter battalion then adopted its organization for the entire army, as they did Rodes's further innovation of the division sharpshooters. It proved to be a very successful experiment.[6]

This sort of bottom-up innovation was characteristic of the Army of Northern Virginia and was one reason that it was an effective organization. Lee decentralized command when possible at all levels, and gave his commanders quite a bit of latitude in organizing their sharpshooter battalions: some had three companies, some four, and some five. On the other hand, the Army of the Potomac, like the British Army, was a relentlessly by-the-book, top-down organization where, thanks to George McClellan, any initiative and innovation in the ranks was viewed with great suspicion. Tactical innovators in the Army of the Potomac such as Emory Upton and Philip Sheridan fought an uphill battle and succeeded only after being backed by Grant. Even so, while the western general might be in command, it was still very much Little Mac's army. A staff officer identified "one weakness, the lack of springy formation, and audacious, self-reliant initiative," and even Grant never appreciated the importance of light infantry.[7]

John Gordon proved to be another tactical innovator of the first order in the later stages of the war. Since there was little precedent for the attack on Fort Stedman, Gordon had to devise tactics as he went along. For this last Confederate offensive he came up with an organization very similar to that organized by Willy Rohr. Both, for example, used mixed groups of pioneers and "storming parties" of elite light infantry to first clear the obstacles and then attack the fortifications. Armies of the nineteenth century generally observed a fairly rigid segregation of the three combat arms (infantry, cavalry, and artillery), but at Fort Stedman the Confederates fought using mixed assault groups much like the German *sturmblocks* of 1917. The Confederate army was just beginning to form separate combat engineer units at the end of the war, and if it had lasted longer they might have integrated them into the assault forces. Gordon, with his ideas of the Trojan horse companies and sharpshooter assault troops, was just beginning to use non-linear tactics, and it would have been interesting to see how far this trend would have gone with the weapons available to them. The Federals VI Corps used a mixed force of pioneers and Spencer-armed sharpshooters for the final assault on Petersburg, with excellent results.

The similarities also apply to trench raiding. Captain Wooten's "seine-hauling" looked a lot like the German technique of *aufrollen*, where the assault troops turned right and left to capture the trench lines on either side of them. Captain Dunlop's assault at McIlwaine's Hill follows the same pattern, with the assault troops first penetrating the line and then swinging to both sides.

After the Civil War Confederate sharpshooters were virtually forgotten, and later their proud battle flag was hijacked by racists. In Nazi Germany street thugs made the once-honorable term "storm trooper" a synonym for political repression. Hollywood producer George Lucas even used it as such in his *Star Wars* movies. The Russians, on the other hand, made extensive use of the term "shock" to connote an elite unit. In World War II the Soviets fielded entire Shock Armies, and even designated some outstanding industrial cadres as "shock workers."

Although light infantry fell into disuse in Europe, the concept remained viable elsewhere. In Korea the Chinese used light infantry infiltration tactics brilliantly against the road-bound Americans in their 1950 offensive, and during the Vietnam War the Viet Cong and North Vietnamese used special light pioneer troops called sappers. Like the sharpshooters and storm troopers before them, the sappers were elite units, and like the grenadiers of old they often entered battle with little more than a bag of satchel charges. Trained in stealth and able to crawl through barbed wire entanglements without being detected, these daring men inflicted considerable damage on the better-equipped American troops.

From the 1970s through the end of the century most armies switched from using long-range semiautomatic or bolt action rifles to shorter-range assault rifles capable of automatic fire. Lately, however, many armies have rediscovered both the sniper and the light infantry rifleman. The U.S. Army, for example, has found snipers quite useful in both Iraq and Afghanistan, especially for warfare in built-up areas, where the ability to pick targets greatly reduces civilian casualties and collateral damage. Army force development specialists are now considering a designated marksman with a specially adapted rifle in every squad, and a sniper squad in every battalion. If they were to group these men into a specialized unit, the Americans would have a unit very similar to what the Confederates organized in 1863.

Appendix A

Testing the Sharpshooters' Weapons

Accuracy

Anyone today attempting to establish the accuracy of Civil War-era rifles, much less compare them with modern rifles, quickly runs into problems. For starters, marksmanship standards were different in the old days. Many military tests used rather large targets—some were six feet high and fifty feet long, intended to simulate an artillery battery or an infantry column. Even standard musketry targets were oversize by today's standards. Henry Heth's riflery manual specified four types of targets for various ranges: all were six feet high and varied in width from 22 to 110 inches. Even conventional shooting matches usually used the "string" system, which measured the distance of each shot from the bull's eye rather than the overall size of the shot group. Thus a relatively large shot group centered around the bull's eye would beat a much smaller shot group some distance away.[1]

What rifles should we be testing? Will a 140-year-old weapon, which has an unknown history of use, equal the performance of a newly manufactured one? If we use reproductions, how can we be sure that they are accurately made and equivalent to the originals? What about ammunition, lubricants, and gunpowder? All present problems and may introduce major variations in performance, not to mention the experience and abilities of the shooter. Taking all this into account, however, we can still come up with some valid conclusions.

Probably the most thorough modern tests were conducted by Jac Weller in 1954 and again in 1971, using original Civil War-era rifles and muskets. While there were problems, Weller did an good job of documenting his testing, and his results are reasonably consistent. Therefore we can make a rough comparison with data from the nineteenth century. Weller initially tested (among others) the .54 caliber Austrian Lorenz rifle, the .58 caliber Springfield, and .577 caliber Enfield rifle muskets; and the short Enfield musketoon (the 24-inch artillery carbine, not the two-band "short" rifle favored by the sharpshooters). At one hundred yards both Enfields shot an approximately 7½-inch group, while that of the Springfield (and the Remington "Zouave" copy) measured 10¼ inches, and the Lorenz lagged behind with a 13-inch group. He then made fifteen shots at a 72-inch by 72-inch target at four hundred yards. The Lorenz hit at this range only three times, while the Springfield scored seven hits and the Remington six. On the other hand the long Enfield, with its three-groove barrel, scored thirteen hits while the diminutive carbine, with a five-groove barrel, made a respectable eleven hits. The little musketoon, said Weller, "turned in the tightest five-shot group at 100 yards of any of the Civil War guns—3¼-inch vertical by only .62-inch horizontal. Considering its short barrel and large bore, its excellent accuracy at all ranges was surprising." It is certainly reasonable to assume that the two-band Enfield, which featured the same five-groove, progressive-depth rifling and a slightly longer barrel, would show similar or better results. "Even the cal. .54 Austrian rifle, the least accurate of the lot, would put rounds into an area occupied by a field gun and its crew at 1,000 yards," said Weller. He attributed the Enfield's superiority to two factors: "more tightly fitting bullets and superior craftsmanship ... even old, beat-up Enfields show remnants of fine craftsmanship and both ... had grooves considerably deeper at the breech than at the muzzle, a difficult production task a century ago."[2]

Weller then tested two original 1862 Whitworths, which posted 5.25-inch and 4.75-inch groups respectively at one hundred yards. Both Whitworths hit the 400-yard target a convincing fifteen out of fifteen times and rated "first class plus" at one thousand yards. According to firearms expert W. B. Edwards, "at short ranges the Enfield and Whitworth were nearly equal. It was at ranges beyond 500 yards ... that the long Whitworth hex slug showed its value." At five hundred yards the mean deviation from the aim point was 2.25 feet for the Enfield and .37 inches for the Whitworth, but at eleven hundred yards the Whitworth still held 2.62 feet, and at fourteen hundred yards it held 4.62 feet. Even at the incredible range of eighteen hundred yards a shot would still fall within 11.62 feet. By contrast, the Enfield would not group at all much beyond one thousand yards. Cadmus Wilcox, writing in the late 1850s, cites a study from the British School of Musketry at Hythe in which the Whitworth repeatedly hit a 32-foot by 2-foot target at 1,880 yards, while the Enfield scored no hits at 1,440 yards. "Shooting with period long range arms is a science due less to the trajectory than to the drift," cautions Bill Adams. "A Whitworth bullet drifts approximately two feet to the right in 500 yards, and the drift and trajectory is different for cylindrical bullets than it is with hexagonal bullets." The rifle's blade sight was marked "C" on one side and "H" on the other to allow for this.[3]

For an interesting comparison Weller also tested a "new," unfired Spencer repeater that was found still crated in a New York warehouse. It shot a 10-inch group at one hundred yards (slightly better than the Springfield), but beyond that accuracy fell off badly—it registered only two hits out of fifteen on the 400-yard target and barely eked out a "poor" rating at one thousand yards. A Sharps rifle also registered a 10-inch group at one hundred yards but rated "very good" at four hundred yards.[4]

In short, Weller roughly validated what Captain Dunlop and the other sharpshooters had found in their own tests: the Enfield was the most accurate rifle available in large numbers to the Confederates. Later in the war many Southern sharpshooters used Sharps and Spencer rifles when they could get them, in an attempt to match the firepower of their Union counterparts, and had either rifle been available in large numbers there might have been an earlier transition to the open order. The Enfield, while quite accurate, was still hampered by a slow rate of fire and the difficulty of loading a muzzle-loader while in the prone position.

Beginning in the Civil War another phenomenon emerged that would become quite common: service rifles would accurately shoot far in excess of any normal engagement ranges. Because of terrain and tactical considerations engagements still tended to be rather close, and few if any firefights took place at extended ranges of three hundred to four hundred yards. Later in the war, however, trench warfare showed the need for another type of weapon, one with a lot of firepower at close ranges. Had the war continued for another year, the Spencer and Henry rifles would likely have been increasingly used by light infantry units, just as World War I gave birth to the submachine gun and World War II the assault rifle. Military authorities often demanded long-range firepower far in excess of any realistic requirements. For instance, until the adoption of the M16 rifle in 1967, both the U.S. Army and Marines insisted that a rifle have an effective range of one thousand yards, even though historically almost no actual engagements had taken place at these longer ranges.

Modern Sniping

As far as sharpshooting goes, it is interesting to compare the guns and men of the 1860s with modern snipers and their weapons. ("Sniper" is a British term that came into general use in the late nineteenth century). Modern military parlance distinguishes between a sniper, who operates semi-independently and shoots at ranges of five hundred to fifteen hundred yards, and a designated marksman (DM), who uses an "accurized" service rifle, such as an M-16, and engages targets with more rapid fire at closer ranges of one hundred to six hundred yards. The designated marksman, unlike the sniper, stays with his unit and uses no special camouflage. Thus the Whitworth riflemen correspond with today's snipers, while the Enfield-bearing battalion sharpshooters are more like modern designated marksmen.[5]

What about the rifles? The accuracy standard today for sniper rifles is expressed in Minutes of Angle, or MOA, which is the angle formed with the apex on the gun's muzzle and the sides on each side of the cone formed by the circle made by the shot group. A good rifle should shoot at least 1 MOA, which means that a group shot at one hundred yards will fall roughly within a 1-inch circle, at four hundred yards within four inches, and so on. Many will shoot even tighter groups with the right ammunition. Typical of today's sniper rifles are the U.S. Army M24 and the Marine Corps M40A1/A3. Both .308 caliber (7.62mm) weapons are based on the commercial Remington M700 bolt action and have heavy 24-inch match barrels with a 1:11.2 twist. Each weighs about fourteen to sixteen pounds with its ten-power scope and will shoot 1 MOA or better. The Army rates their rifle effective to eight hundred yards, while the Marines figure theirs will do the job out to a thousand. Today the U.S. Army estimates that a soldier armed with an M16 assault rifle will hit a man-sized target at three hundred yards 10 percent of the time, while a trained sniper with his specialized weapon has a 90 percent chance of getting a first round hit at six hundred yards.[6]

The best Weller was able to do with his two Whitworths was a 4¾-inch group at one hundred yards, which is considerably outside the standard. Both Enfields turned in a slightly better performance but neither approached the magic one-inch circle. However, tests from the mid-1850s record better results for a Whitworth when fired from a mechanical rest. William Edwards cites a mean deviation of .37 feet (4.4 inches) from the point of aim at five hundred yards, and since the mean deviation amounts to half the group size (e.g., a 1-inch mean deviation from the point of aim gives a 2-inch group), this would give a group size of 8.8 inches, somewhat outside 1 MOA but still quite good for a 140-year-old rifle.[7]

Even if the Whitworth has the required accuracy for the job, its field effectiveness versus modern weapons has to be considered in light of three major changes on the battlefield, two technical and one tactical. The first technical change is the vast improvement in sighting. Today's light-gathering ten-power telescopes are several orders of magnitude ahead of the primitive four-power optic of the Whitworth, especially in less than optimal lighting conditions, and have internal adjustments for elevation and windage.[8]

Secondly, muzzle velocity has increased due to the use of smokeless powder. A bullet leaving a modern rifle has over double the speed of even a black powder match rifle, giving it a much flatter trajectory. This makes range estimation less critical, and in any case with a hand-held laser range finder a shooter can find the distance almost instantly. Shooters of the

1860s, however, had to estimate the range (a critical skill) with their eyes, assisted only by a crude brass stadia.

The third major change, however, works against the modern sniper. At the beginning of the Civil War armies operated in the open in Napoleonic fashion, which provided the sharpshooter with large, clearly defined targets such as groups of men, artillery batteries, and mounted troops. He could engage these at extended ranges, considerably beyond that which he could expect to hit an individual. By 1864 breastworks had become the rule, however, and when the lines settled down at Petersburg and elsewhere the targets became smaller still. By then, a sharpshooter was lucky to get a fleeting shot at a man's head—a condition that continues to this day. By 1917 British sniper experts discouraged shots at over four hundred yards to avoid wasting ammunition and prematurely wearing out the rifle's barrel. Major H. Hesketh-Prichard claimed, however, that with a few days' instruction his snipers made seventeen hits out of twenty-one shots on head-sized targets at 430 yards. So much had the rifles improved over the intervening fifty years, however, that distance estimation, the core of the 1860s sharpshooter curriculum, was of secondary importance in World War I.[9]

Today the U.S. Army's forthcoming Squad Designated Marksman weapon will give one soldier in each infantry squad the capability to deliver precision fire out to 500 meters. Their weapon is a modified M4 .223 caliber rifle (a variant of the venerable M16) with a heavier barrel, a bipod, and a telescopic sight. The Marines use a similarly modified rifle, the M16A3, and are considering creating a permanent squad position for a designated marksman using a modified .308 cal./7.62mm M-14 rifle.[10]

Appendix B

Orders Issued by the Confederacy Pertaining to Sharpshooters

WAR DEPARTMENT
Adjutant and Inspector General's Office

Richmond, May 3, 1862

General Orders No. 34.

I. The following act of Congress, and accompanying regulations, are published for the information of all concerned:

An act to organize battalions of Sharp-shooters.

Sec. 1. *The Congress of the Confederate States of America do enact,* That the Secretary of War may cause to be organized a battalion of sharp-shooters for each brigade, consisting of not less than three nor more than six companies, to be composed of men selected from the brigade, or otherwise, and armed with long-range muskets or rifles; said companies to be organized, and the commissioned officers therefor appointed by the President, by and with the advice and consent of the Senate. Such battalions shall constitute parts of the brigades to which they belong, and shall have such field and staff officers as are authorized by law for similar battalions, to be appointed by the President, by and with the advice and consent of the Senate.

Sec. 2 *Be it further enacted* That, for the purpose of arming said battalions, the long-range muskets and rifles in the hands of the troops may be taken for that purpose *provided*; the government has not at its command a sufficient number of approved long-range rifles or muskets wherewith to arm said corps. [Approved April 21, 1862.]

II. Generals commanding military departments may cause to be organized within their commands battalions of sharp-shooters, as provided in this act, in such numbers as they may deem necessary, not exceeding one such battalion for each brigade, and will report to the department the organization of such corps, recommending for appointment the commissioned officers allowed by law.

III. In organizing such battalions, Generals commanding may cause such details or transfers to be made as will not reduce any company or corps below the minimum number required by law, taking the men for each such battalion, so far as possible, from the particular brigade of which it is to form part.

IV. Requisitions will be made upon the Ordnance department for the arms for such battalions; and, until the said requisitions can be filled, the Generals commanding may cause such exchanges and transfers of long-range muskets and rifles to be made as may be necessary to arm the said battalion, returning surplus arms, when such requisitions are filled, to the Ordnance department:

V. – *Supplementary to General Order, No. 30, section VI.*
The commissions of the staff officers of reorganized regiments and battalions of twelve months volunteers are not affected by such reorganization, except that of the adjutant, whose commission expires with that of the commanding officer, if the said officer be not re-elected.

By command of the Secretary Of War.

S. COOPER,
Adjutant *and Inspector-General*

Head Quarters 3rd Div
April 2nd, 1862

General Orders

No. 7

In each brigade of this Division, there will be detailed a battalion of which will more than the other troops be instructed in the duties of Light Infantry.

Two companies in each Regt. will be selected by the Brigade Commander for this purpose, selecting as far as possible, rifled arms, either Minnie Muskets or Mississippi Rifles. No especial selection for this purpose will be made, in case the Regt. by so doing will have less than eight (8) companies in line.

In each Brigade for five (5) or more companies there will be two field officers selected to command this force, & one for a less number. When acting with their respective Regiments this force will constitute the skirmishers when in line, the reserve in square. A report of the number & designation of companies and names of officers, Company as well as Field, made in compliance with this order, is required as early as possible.

It is not intended that these companies shall be separated from their Regiments more than other skirmishers, nor will the field officers have other jurisdiction than the instruction &, when especially directed, the command in action.

By order of Genl Ewell

Official

   Wm. Carrus A.A. Genl

UNC-SHC
CSA Army 21st NC Order Book
#5090-z
Page 131

Organization of the Sharpshooters

These orders, transcribed by Rob Wynstra, were found in the Order Book of the 23rd North Carolina (Record Group #109, NA). They are some of the few that survive describing the organization of the sharpshooters. Rodes prescribes the number of the corps to be 1/12th of the men of the brigade, which at the time would have been about twelve hundred men. This would have given a battalion of one hundred men. This was later increased to 1/6th and later accounts confirm a two-hundred-man battalion.

Headqtrs [Rodes] Division
Jan. 28, 1863

Genl Order
No. 6

A corps of sharpshooters will be at once organized for each Brigade in the following manner.

Each corps will number one twelfth of the men now present for duty in its Brig. It will be composed of picked men, who may volunteer for the service & armed with long range pieces.

An officer not below the rank of Captain selected for his gallantry & experience will be detailed by the Brigade commander to command the corps & each regimental detail will be commanded by a Subaltern volunteering for the duty.

The corps of Sharpshooters thus formed will be constantly drilled as Skirmishers by its commander but is not to be considered a separate command except in the immediate presence of the enemy when it will cover the front of the brigade. At all other times the officers and men belonging to it will remain & do duty with their respective Regts.

If practicable it is recommended that the corps be drilled under the superintentance of the Brig.

By Command of Brig. Gen. Rodes
Archer Anderson
AAGen

—————————————————————————————

Headquarters Iverson's Brigade
Jan. 28, 1863

Circular

Regimental Comdrs will organize their respective quotas of this corps according to the provisions of Gen. order No. 6 without any delay & make their reports as soon as the organization is complete.

By Order of Brig. Gen. Iverson
D. P. Halsey
A.A. Genl.

Hd. Qtrs. Iverson's Brig.
May 25, 1863

Special Order
No. 10

In accordance with Special Order #60 ANV Hdqrs a second battalion of sharpshooters will at once be organized in this Brigade containing the same number of men as the first one twelfth (1/12) of the whole number of men present for duty in each of Regts. Volunteers for this duty to the number required will alone be incentive. An officer Lieut. (also a volunteer for duty) will be placed in command of the corps from each regiment. The whole battalion to be commanded by a captain hereinafter appointed.

Head Qrs. Iverson's Brigade
June 2, 1863

Special Order
No. 79

The officers and men of the two corps of sharpshooters are excused from guard duty and also all fatigue duties that will keep them from drilling. It is not however to be understood that they are excused from the regular police. When their Regiments go on Picket there will be no drill for the sharpshooters.

Each corps of Sharpshooters will be drilled three days in each week. The first corps on Mondays, Tuesdays & Wednesdays. The second corps on Thursdays, Fridays and Saturdays.

Brigade drill taking place in the evening will be attended by them.

Commanding officers of the corps of sharpshooters will arrange their hours of drill and report them to this officer for confirmation. The corps will be drilled by the bugle.

By order of Genl Iverson
D. P. Halsey
AAG

These orders, found in the papers of James A. Englehard (AC No. 00-272, GDAH) specify the training of the sharpshooters of Wilcox's division in early 1864.

Hd. Qtrs. Wilcox's Lt. Div.
April 2nd, 1864

Gen.,

The orders (printed) are to be distributed to the officers in charge of your Corps [of] Sharp Shooters. You will direct them however that they will not begin the target practice until further orders. Judging distance drill will commence at once and reports made to these Hd. Qrts. in compliance with the order on that subject.

I am Gen. Very Resp.
Your obt. Servt.

(signed) Jas. A. Englehard
A.A.G.

Hd. Qtrs. Wilcox's Lt. Div.
April 9th, 1864

General,

The Major Gen'd commanding directs me to call your attention to the printed order from these Hd. Qtrs. March 20th, 1864, for instruction of the Corps [of] Sharp Shooters. He desires them to be instructed in accordance thereto, and particularly in *judging distance drill*. The reports called for will be regularly made to these Hd. Qrts.

Ammunition for target practice will soon be issued by the proper officer, but the men will not be practiced in this drill until some proficiency is made in judging distances.

I am, Gen., very respectfully
        Your obt. Servt.
(signed) Jas. A. Englehard
        A.A.G.

Hd. Qtrs. Wilcox's Lt. Div.
April 19th, 1864

Circular

The Corps of Sharp Shooters will be upon the receipt of this order commence the target practice drill with ball cartridges. Twenty-two rounds will be issued to each man, and drill will be in accordance with the following schedule:

At 100 yards	3 cartridges
At 300 yards	5 cartridges
At 600 yards	10 cartridges
At 900 yards	4 cartridges

The men will be permitted to fire with a rest, and much care should be taken to ascertain the accuracy with which each Rifle shoots.

The practices at 100 yards will require but *one* day; at 300 yds., *two*; at 600 yds., *three*; and at 900 yards two days. At the different distances every shot will be measured and the average of the *five* best marksmen of each Brigade will be reported to these Hd. Qrts. in the order of their merit. In reporting the average of each man, the report should state whether the fire was to the right or left, above or below, the object aimed at.

Arms should be carefully inspected before each drill, and at 600 and 900 yards the practice should not take place on a windy day.

While the target practice drill is going on, those not so engaged will be exercised in judging distance drill and the reports heretofore required in this drill will continue to be sent into Division Hd. Qrtrs.

By command of Maj. Gen. Wilcox
(signed) Jas. A. Englehard
A.A.G.

Appendix C

The Assault on Fort Stedman:
Numbers and organization

During the postwar years John Gordon—war hero, governor of Georgia, and U.S. Senator—made a number of statements about the battle of Fort Stedman, many of them contradictory. "As to the battle of Hare's hill," he wrote former Confederate general Gaston Lewis in 1886, "I fear I can't be of much service in giving you the details which you wish—I have kept no memoranda & of course had no time from that date to the 9th of April to write a formal report. I can give you only the most general facts connected with that attack. I have now no recollection as to the locality in the movement of the different commands." Like many old soldiers he relied on a gradually fading memory and sometimes embellished his stories, which makes present day sorting of fact from fiction difficult. Therefore, rather than clutter the body of the book with my own deductions and speculations on the battle of Fort Stedman, I have chosen to treat them here in a separate appendix. Gordon's most familiar account of the battle appears in Chapter XXVII of his 1904 book *Reminiscences of the Civil War*, but he had also described the battle in an 1880 letter to Jefferson Davis that appeared in Davis's 1881 book *The Rise and Fall of the Confederate Government*, and in various public and private statements. Two more sources—his letter to Gaston Lewis and his post-Appomattox report—have come become available in recent years, which allow us to address some of the questions and ambiguities surrounding the battle.

What were the numbers of Gordon's attacking force?

Gordon had his own Second Corps, as well as two brigades from Bushrod Johnson's division under Brigadier General Robert Ransom. Ransom's force, about 3,000 men, consisted of his own North Carolina brigade (Twenty-fourth, Twenty-fifth, Thirty-fifth, Forty-ninth, and Fifty-sixth

North Carolina) and a South Carolina brigade under Brigadier General William H. Wallace (Seventeenth, Eighteenth, Twenty-second, Twenty-third, Twenty-sixth South Carolina and the Holcombe Legion). In his post-Appomattox report Gordon also lists four Third Corps brigades—two from Wilcox's division and two from Heth's—as being available, and we know from other sources that they were actually moved into staging areas at Petersburg but not used. Why, Gordon never explained. Pickett's 6,500-man division appears to have been a last-minute addition, and Gordon does not mention it in his report, in which he gives the strength of Second Corps at Hare's Hill (Fort Stedman) as seventy-five hundred men, which tallies well with surviving returns and inspection reports. However, one needs to deduct roughly a thousand men from Second Corps for the attack, since Cox's brigade of Grimes's division did not make it into the fight, nor did at least part of Johnston's brigade of Walker's division, which had to be brought up from duty on the Roanoke River. Thus Gordon would have had 9,500 to 10,500 men available for the attack, plus another 4-5,000 in support. Adding Pickett's division would have increased the total to some 20,000 men.[1]

How were the assault columns organized?

In his 1904 book Gordon describes what sounds like a single column of three 100-man "Trojan Horse" companies, preceded by a group of fifty ax-wielding pioneers, followed by a column of infantry. The three special operations companies were to pass through Fort Stedman and attempt to take the supporting forts by a *ruse de guerre*.[2]

In his 1880 letter to Jefferson Davis (quoted in *Rise and Fall*), however, Gordon simply says "three separate bodies of men" formed the special operations groups, to follow an assault detachment of "three hundred men, armed with bayonets fixed and empty muskets, who were to mount and enter the fort as the axemen cut away the obstruction of sharpened rails." Then, he says, a division of infantry was to cross, face right (south) and begin rolling up Grant's line. At this point, the rest of the force would advance and widen the breach in both directions. He still seems to refer to a single assault column.[3]

In his 1886 letter to General Lewis he says "three separate details of 100 men each were selected & organized to make the rush across with the first assault, which three bodies with chosen guides were to attempt by the *"ruse"* referred to pass beyond Fort Steadman." This could mean either that there were three assault elements of 100 men each, or that the special operations companies were 100 men each and were expected to both take Fort Stedman and the supporting forts—a tall order.[4]

Gordon's most contemporary descriptions were a brief report written on March 27th, in which he credits "the sharpshooters of this corps" with the assault, and a longer one written on April 11th, two days after Lee's surrender and eighteen days after the battle of Fort Stedman. In it he describes "a select order of men from the Second Corps, consisting principally of 100 sharpshooters of the [illegible] divisions commanded by chosen officers and accompanied by a company of artillery from Colonel [Hilary Pollard] Jones' command, assaulted the enemy's front." Again, Gordon could mean one hundred sharpshooters or one hundred from each division, and he does not specifically mention any special companies, nor does he specify how many assaulting columns there were. General Lee also specifically credits "the sharpshooters of Gordon's corps" for leading the assault in a report filed the day of the battle.[5]

It is difficult to see how any group of 100 (or even 300) men could be expected to take Fort Stedman and the supporting forts as well, especially in view of the sustained fighting that took place inside the fort during the initial assault, although it may explain why Colonel Brown and his men were so easily captured in General McLaughlen's counterattack. We also know from other accounts that there were at least three assaulting columns and maybe as many as six, and from both Union and Confederate sources that the Sharpshooters led the way. I have assumed, therefore, that Gordon meant that each divisional column had, in round numbers, an assault force of between one hundred and three hundred sharpshooters leading it, and that each was preceded by a pioneer detachment (who were probably sharpshooters as well) of fifty men with axes. The Trojan Horse companies would have followed just behind the Sharpshooters, with the infantry brigades of Second Corps coming next.

Of the three division commanders, General Bryan Grimes wrote his wife about the battle shortly after the battle but did not give the details of the attack. Almost no information exists about the composition of his assault force, other than it was organized around the Division sharpshooters under Colonel Brown. General James Walker did not pen a description of the battle until 1903, in which he wrote that "a storming party consisting of fifty picked men carrying axes to clear away the *chevaux-de-frise,* and one hundred picked infantry men armed with muskets, commanded by a captain and one lieutenant" was to take Fort Stedman. Although Walker does not identify him as such, his Sharpshooter commander, Captain Joseph Anderson, led the storming party. He makes no mention of any sort of special operations group, but merely notes that "a strong skirmish line of Confederates was at once thrown forward towards the second line of the enemy's works, and got within easy musket range, but though they were guarded by a small force it was too large to be dislodged by skirmishers." He does not mention the bloody battle for Battery IX by Lewis's brigade of his own division and Ransom's brigade, which had its own sharpshooter assault force under Lieutenants Roulhac and Flemming, "each at the head of one hundred men, half of Flemming's men with axes, the others with guns, Roulhac's all with unloaded guns." [6]

The only actual division commander's report to survive is that of Clement Evans. In it Evans gives a much more complex version of his attack and task organization than did either Gordon or Walker subsequently. His division, he said, advanced in three groups: "one by the division sharpshooters [Captain William Kaigler], one by the 31st and 13th Georgia regiments, Col. J. H. Lowe commanding, and one by the Louisiana troops, Col. Waggaman commanding." The Louisiana brigade kept its own sharpshooters, which would have reduced Kaigler's numbers accordingly. Waggaman's men turned south toward Fort Haskell, followed by Terry's Virginia brigade. [7]

While it is possible that the whole idea of a separate special operations or Trojan Horse company was confabulated by John Gordon well after the fact, it is more plausible that that each division's sharpshooter demi-brigade, of whatever strength, was assigned the task of actually taking Fort Stedman and its adjacent batteries, and each was task-organized into two groups —one to take the fort and another to move through and take the supporting forts. A late February return gives the strength of Second Corps' divisions as 3300 men for Grimes's, 2400 for Walker's, and 2300 for Gordon's (Evans's) for a total of just under 8000 men. Even if we reduce this slightly to match John Gordon's figure of 7500 men a month later, assuming the sharpshooters to be one man in six gives us sharpshooter strengths of just over 500 men for Grimes, 375 for Walker, and 360 for Gordon (Evans), or a total of just over 1200 sharpshooters for Second Corps. Adding in around 250 sharpshooters from Ransom's brigade gives us around 1500 men for the initial assault force—enough for both assault and follow-on units. If so it may be that a smaller group of three hundred sharpshooters, the "select of the select" made the initial assault, with the rest following for subsequent attacks. Thus, although the evidence solidly supports the Sharpshooters' taking of Fort Stedman and leading the assault on Fort Haskell, we will probably never know their exact organization and numbers. [8]

Where were the supporting forts, and what happened to the special operations groups?

What were the objectives of the special operations groups? Gordon is vague in his post-Appomattox report, saying only that "The original intention was to seize by a rapid movement the strong enclosed works of the enemy [in] rear of his main line. … The capture of the forts depended [upon] the success of the movement. That effort failed for want of a proper guide and a knowledge of the ground." In his 1880 letter to Jefferson Davis he says it was to "surprise and capture, by a stratagem, the commanding forts in the rear," and in his letter to Gaston Lewis he says "the 3 Forts in rear" and in his book "the three other forts in the rear which command Fort Stedman." Most analysts have interpreted this as a failure of military intelligence: that Gordon mistook the old Confederate Dimmock line, captured the previous summer, as a Union second line of defense with three bristling forts on it. It is hard to believe, however, that a commander as astute as Gordon would make a mistake of this magnitude, or that he would by implication ignore the flanking forts, whose retention by the Yankees would have (and did) make any further advance impossible.[9]

My conclusion is that the three forts Gordon meant, and to which he sent his Trojan Horse companies, were Fort Haskell in the south, Fort Friend on the second line, and the complex of Batteries VIII, IX and Fort McGilvery in the north. Only this would have made sense militarily, and would have allowed him to capture these forts from the rear without costly frontal assaults and thus secure his flanks. General Evans confirms in his report that he was "not to assault a line of breastworks and a fort directly in front, especially if protected by abatis or other obstructions." In his letter to General Lewis Gordon specifically mentions a "Lt. Col. Pendergrass" as being one of the officers whose name was part of the ruse. This is almost certainly Lieutenant Colonel Joseph H. Pentecost of the 100th Pennsylvania, whose regiment was south of Fort Stedman (not behind it on a second line) protecting Fort Haskell. Union sources describe Confederate sharpshooters mingling with the retreating Yankees, just as Gordon said.[10]

Assuming they existed, what happened to these three groups? Gordon was wildly inconsistent in his postwar statements about their fates. In his own book he states: "Soon I received a message from one of these three officers, I believe General Lewis of North Carolina, that he had passed the line of Federal infantry without trouble by representing himself as Colonel - - - - - of the Hundredth Pennsylvania, but that he could not find his fort, as the guide had been lost in the rush upon Stedman. I soon received a similar message from the other two, and so notified General Lee." Yet Lewis's brigade was north of Fort Stedman near Battery IX and the 100th Pennsylvania south of it near Fort Haskell. Waggaman's Louisianans took the Roundheads on, but were never able to "pass" the Pennsylvanians and seem to have had no trouble finding Fort Haskell. After the war, however, General John Hartranft stated that "General Gordon has since told me that he never heard from these detachments; not one of them returned to report."[11]

According to George Kilmer, a group of Confederates attempted to take Fort Haskell by stealth but were detected and repulsed with loss. Another account from the 1st Michigan Sharpshooters details the capture of a fairly large group of Rebels behind Battery VIII. Considering that both these groups were attempting to take these pivotal works from the rear, these may have been two of the special operations companies. As for the third, General Hartranft thought that the "skirmishers" who approached Fort Friend were from another of these groups. "They must have been the ones who cut the telegraph lines to City Point," he said, "and I must have ridden on my way to General Willcox's headquarters, between them and the enemy in the forts. What the 200th [Pennsylvania] attacked was, in my judgment, a heavy line and groups of skirmishers." While it is more likely that the skirmishers were Grimes's Division Sharpshooters, the men who approached Fort Friend through the ravine may well have been a special operations group. In no case does it appear that the entire group was killed or captured, so some may have survived to report to Gordon. There also may well have been more than three groups.[12]

What was the signal for the attack?

Just exactly what the signal was for the attack remains in doubt—Gordon says a rifle shot, Walker three rifle or pistol shots "fired in quick succession," and Captain Carson a bugle. All wrote long after the event. Given the fact that picket firing was normal during the night and that a bugle would have been rather obvious, three pistol shots—which would have stood out from the ordinary musket fire—seems the most likely.[13]

Pickett's division

In his postwar writings John Gordon made much of the non-arrival of Pickett's division, attributing it in at least one case to divine intervention. Gordon describes a council of war on the night of March 23 in which he and General Lee made the final arrangements for the attack. There, he says, Lee informed him that he had found local guides for the Trojan Horse companies, and had "selected different troops to send me...from Longstreet's and A. P. Hill's corps." A few paragraphs later, however, Gordon (who had previously told Gaston Lewis that he had no memoranda of the event) gives the contents of a note from his commander dated 4:30 on the afternoon of the 25th in which Lee says "I have received yours of 2:30 P.M. and telegraphed for Pickett's Division, but I do not think it will reach here in time." If so this would date the request for Pickett's division (then commanded by Brigadier General George Steuart) to sometime in the mid-afternoon of March 24th, and makes it look like it was done at Gordon's request.[14]

A flurry of telegrams, which unfortunately do not have the times noted, went back and forth to First Corps on the 24th, directing Pickett to move to Petersburg by rail. The resulting schedule was that "1,200 men can be shipped at 9 o'clock, about 2,000 at 1 or 2 o'clock in the morning [of March 25], about the same number at 7 o'clock in the morning." The last brigade could not get rail transportation until 11 a. m. Considering that the attack was to start at four, this would mean that if everything went exactly right, one brigade *might* have gotten into position to support the attack. Two of Pickett's other brigades do not appear to have actually gotten the order to move until sometime on the 25th. The orders moving Pickett were cancelled later that day, and there is no mention of any mechanical difficulties on the railroad.[15]

Later Gordon would strongly imply that if Pickett's division had not been delayed, the battle would have turned out differently, but this is difficult to credit given the initial failure to take the flanking forts and the reluctance of the Confederates to expend men in frontal attacks on them. My conclusion is that Pickett's failure to arrive was due mostly to bad staff work, and it did not make a great deal of difference in the battle's outcome.[16]

What were the Confederate casualties at Fort Stedman?

Many accounts of the battle number Confederate casualties in excess of 4,000 men. The Federals claimed nineteen hundred prisoners, but a report from General Grant submitted that summer makes it clear that 834 of these were captured by the II and VI Corps elsewhere along the line.

In his unpublished report General Clement Evans gives his overall casualties as 531 men, General Bryan Grimes in a letter to his wife assesses his as 478. Walker's were probably similar. General Richard Anderson assessed the losses of Ransom and Wallace as "above 1,200 in the two brigades." In his post-Appomattox report Gordon gives Second Corps' strength as seventy-five hundred men on March 24 and five thousand on March 29, but picket line fighting continued pretty much unabated between the two dates. In a postwar analysis Frederick Phisterer estimated Confederate casualties at 2,681 men, although the actual number may have pushed three thousand.[17]

BIBLIOGRAPHY

Manuscript Sources

Alabama Department of Archives and History
    Battalion History Files
        Gracie's Special Battalion
        Seventeenth Alabama Battalion, Sharpshooters
        Twenty-third Alabama Battalion, Sharpshooters
    Regimental History Files
        Third Alabama Infantry
        Fifth Alabama Infantry
        Sixth Alabama Infantry
        Twelfth Alabama Infantry
        Twenty-sixth Alabama Infantry
        Sixty-first Alabama Infantry

Fredericksburg and Spotsylvania National Military Park, Fredericksburg, Virginia
    Ben Powell Letter
    Stuart Vogt, "The Death of Major-general John Sedgwick U.S.A. May 9th, 1864"

Georgia Department of Archives and History, Atlanta, Georgia
    Confederate Reminiscences and Letters 1861-1865 14 vols. Georgia Division
        UDC, 1992-1998.
    James A. Englehard Papers
    Reminiscences of Confederate Soldiers and Stories of the War 1861-1865. 19 vols.
        Georgia Division UDC, 1940-1955.

Gilder Lehrman Institute of American History, New York, NY
    Jeremiah M. Tate Collection

Huntington Library, San Marino, California
    Civil War Collection

Brock Collection

James Eldridge Collection

Maryland Historical Society, Baltimore, Maryland
    Eugene Blackford letters, Gordon-Blackford Papers

National Archives, Washington, D.C.
> Record Group 94, Records of Confederate Soldiers Who Served During the Civil War
>> Compiled Service Records
>>> Major Eugene Blackford, Fifth Alabama Infantry
> Record Group 109, War Department Collection of Confederate Records
>> Order Book of the Twenty-third North Carolina Regiment

Navarro College, Corsicana, Texas
> Pearce Civil War Collection
>> Robert Rodes letter

North Carolina Department of Archives and History, Raleigh, North Carolina
> J. D. Barnwell Reminiscence
> J. D. Barrier Reminiscence
> Sam Collier Papers
> James B. Gordon Papers
> Newsom E. Jenkins Memoir
> Lowery Shuford Collection
>> John W. Bone Memoir

Petersburg National Military Park
> Edward Steere, "A Study of The Battle of Fort Stedman March 25, 1865"

South Carolina Department of Archives and History
> *Recollections and Reminiscences 1861-1865*. 12 Vols. South Carolina Division UDC, 1990-2002.

Troup County Archive, LaGrange, Georgia
> Julius L. Schaub, "Confederate War Record"

University of North Carolina, Southern Historical Collection, Chapel Hill, North Carolina
> Bryan Grimes Papers
> W. G. Lewis Papers
> Perry Family Papers
> Thatch Family Papers
>> Otis Smith, "Reminiscences"
> Cary Whitaker Papers
>> Diary

University of Virginia, Alderman Library, Charlottesville, Virginia
> William H. Blackford Diary
> Blackford Family Papers

U.S. Army Military History Institute, Carlisle Barracks, Pennsylvania
> Eugene Blackford Diary/Memoir
> Eugene Blackford Letters
> *National Tribune Scrap Book*

Virginia Historical Society
> Greene Family Papers

Wisconsin Historical Society
> William Phillips Letters

Newspapers and Periodicals

America's Civil War, 2000, 2002-2004
America's First Freedom, 2002
American Rifleman, 1954, 1971
Arms Gazette, August 1975
Atlanta Journal 1901
Blue and Gray, 2004
Century Magazine, 1887
Chambers's Journal 1859
Chatham (North Carolina) Record, 1912
Civil War Times Illustrated, 1967
Confederate Veteran (Nashville, TN), 1893-1932
Fayetteville (New York) Weekly Recorder 1888-1893
Gettysburg Commemorative Issue, 2003
Gettysburg Magazine, 1990
Greensboro (Alabama) Record 1903
The Gun Digest, 1977
Gun Review, 1970
Journal of the Royal United Service Institution, 1865
The Illustrated London News, 1863
Mobile (Alabama) Advertiser and Register 1864, 1910
Muzzle Blasts, 2003
North and South, 2001-2004
Old Fort News, 1965
Parameters: Journal of the U.S. Army War College, 1982
Philadelphia Weekly Times, 1878, 1885
Quarterly Journal of Military History, 1998
Quarterly Periodical of the Florida Historical Society, 1932
Rifle Magazine, 1977
Salisbury (North) Carolina Watchman 1863
South Carolina Historical Magazine, 1962
Southern Historical Society Papers, 1876-1959
Susquehanna University Studies, 1983
Transactions of the Huguenot Society of South Carolina, 1974
Turnwold Plantation (Georgia) Countryman 1862

Official Publications

Center of Military History. *American Military History*. Washington: U.S. Government Printing Office, 1988. Also available online at http://www.army.mil/cmh-pg/books/amh/AMH-09.htm/.

C.S. War Department. *General Orders from Adjutant and Inspector-General's Office, Confederate States Army, from January, 1862 to December, 1863*. Columbia, SC: Evans and Cogswell, 1864.

C.S. War Department. *A System of Musketry Instruction: Prepared and Ordered by the Order of General Bragg for the Army of Tennessee.* Richmond, 1863.

A Digest of the Military and Naval Laws of the Confederate States, From the Commencement of the Provisional Congress to the End of the First Congress Under the Permanent Constitution, Columbia, SC: Evans & Cogswell, 1864.

Hewett, Janet B., ed. *North Carolina Confederate Soldiers, 1861-1865.* Wilmington, NC: Broadfoot Publishing, 1999.

Hewett, Janet B., ed. *Supplement to the Official Records of the Union and Confederate Armies.* 100 vols. Wilmington, NC: Broadfoot Publishing, 1997.

Jordan, Weymouth T., ed. *North Carolina Troops, 1861-1865: A Roster.* 17 vols. Raleigh: North Carolina Office of Archives and History, 1966-.

U.S. War Department. *A System of Target Practice for Use of the Troops When Armed with the Musket, Rifle-Musket, or Carbine.* Washington, DC: Government Printing Office, 1862.

U.S. War Department. *War of the Rebellion: A Compilation of the Official Records of the Union and Confederate Armies.* 128 vols. Washington, DC: Government Printing Office, 1880-1901.

Primary Sources

Adams, Charles R., ed. *A Post of Honor: The Pryor Letters, 1861-1863; Letters From Capt. S. G. Pryor, Twelfth Georgia Regiment and His Wife, Penelope Tyson Pryor.* Fort Valley, GA: Garret Publications, 1989.

Agassiz, George R., ed. *With Grant and Meade from the Wilderness to Appomattox.* Lincoln: University of Nebraska Press, 1994.

Barber, Captain. *Instructions for the Formation and Exercise of Volunteer Sharp-shooters.* 1804. Reprint, Ottawa: Museum Restoration Service, 1968.

Beck, Henry. *Memoirs of Henry Beck 1864-65, Battle's Brigade, Rodes' Division, 2nd Corps, Army of Northern Virginia.* Birmingham, AL: Birmingham Public Library, 1940.

Benson, Susan, ed. *Berry Benson's Civil War Book: Memoirs of a Confederate Scout and Sharpshooter.* Athens: University of Georgia Press, 1992.

Berkeley, Henry Robinson. *Four Years in the Confederate Artillery: The Diary of Private Henry Robinson Berkeley.* Edited by William H. Runge. Richmond: Virginia Historical Society, 1991.

Bernard, George S., ed. *War Talks of the Confederate Veterans.* Petersburg, VA: Fenn and Owen, 1892.

Blackford, Susan Leigh. *Letters from Lee's Army, or, Memoirs of Life In and Out of the Army in Virginia During the War Between the States.* 2 vols. 1896. Reprint, Lynchburg, VA: Warwick House, 1996.

Blackford, W. W. *War Years with Jeb Stuart.* New York: Charles Scribner's Sons, 1945.

Blight, David W., ed. *When This Cruel War is Over: The Civil War Letters of Charles Harvey Brewster.* Amherst: University of Massachusetts Press, 1992.

Bryan, Mary Givens, ed. *Letters of a Private in the Confederate Army: Jack Felder.* Bound volume in Georgia Dept. of Archives and History, July 1951.

Buell, Augustus. *The Cannoneer: Recollections of Service in the Army of the Potomac.* Washington, DC: National Tribune, 1890.

Buel, Clarence C., and Robert U. Johnson, eds. *Battles and Leaders of the Civil War.* 4 vols. New York: Century, 1887-1888. Reprint, New York: Thomas Yoseloff, 1956.

Busk, Hans. *Rifle Volunteers: How to Organize and Drill Them in Accordance With the Latest Regulations.* 8th ed. London: Routledge, Warne, and Routledge, 1861.

Carter, Robert Goldthwaithe. *Four Brothers in Blue, or Sunshine and Shadows of the War of the Rebellion: A Story of the Great Civil War from Bull Run To Appomattox.* 1913. Reprint, Austin: University of Texas Press, 1978.

Chappell, Frank Anderson, ed. *Dear Sister: Civil War Letters to a Sister in Alabama.* Huntsville, AL: Branch Springs, 2002.

Chittenden, L. E. *Recollections of President Lincoln and His Administration.* New York: Harper and Brothers, 1891.

Couture, Richard T. *Charlie's Letters: The Correspondence of Charles E. DeNoon.* N.p.: Privately published, 1982.

Cowper, Pulaski, ed. *Extracts of Letters of Major-Gen'l Bryan Grimes, to His Wife: Written While in Active Service in the Army of Northern Virginia. Together with Some Personal Recollections of the War, Written by Him after its Close, etc.* Raleigh, NC: E. Broughton, 1883.

Dana, Charles A. *Recollections of the Civil War.* New York: D. Appleton, 1898. Reprint, Lincoln, NE: University of Nebraska Press 1996.

Davis, Jefferson. *The Rise and Fall of the Confederate Government.* 2 vols. New York: D. Appleton, 1881.

De Forest, John William. *A Volunteer's Adventures: A Union Captain's Record of the Civil War.* New Haven: Yale University Press, 1946.

Douglas, Henry Kyd. *I Rode with Stonewall.* Chapel Hill: University of North Carolina Press, 1960.

Early, Jubal A. *Autobiographical Sketch and Narrative of the War Between the States.* Philadelphia: J. B. Lippincott, 1912.

Elliott, James Carson. *The Southern Soldier Boy: A Thousand Shots for the Confederacy.* Raleigh, NC: Edwards and Broughton, 1907.

Gordon, John. *Reminiscences of the Civil War.* New York: Charles Scribner's Sons, 1904.

Govan, Gilbert E. and James W. Livingood, eds. *The Haskell Memoirs.* New York: G. P. Putnam, 1960.

Grossman, Julian. *The Civil War: Battlefields and Campgrounds in the Art of Winslow Homer.* New York: Abradale Press/Harry N. Abrams, Inc. 1991.

Hale, Laura Virginia. *Four Valiant Years in the Lower Shenandoah Valley, 1861-1865.* Front Royal, VA: Hathaway Publishing, 1968.

Hastings, William H., ed. *Letters from a Sharpshooter: The Civil War Letters of William B. Greene, Co. G, Berdan's Sharpshooters.* Belleville, WI: Historic Publications, 1993.

Heth, Henry. *A System of Target Practice: For the Use of Troops When Armed with the Musket, Rifle-Musket, Rifle, or Carbine.* Philadelphia: H. C. Baird, 1858.

Hesketh-Prichard, H. *Sniping in France: With Notes on the Scientific Training of Scouts, Observers, and Snipers.* New York: E. P. Dutton, 1920. Reprint, Mt. Ida, Arkansas: Lancer Militaria, 1993.

Hodgkins, William H. *The Battle of Fort Stedman, March 25th 1865.* Boston: Privately published, 1889.

Hotchkiss, Jedediah. *Make Me a Map of the Valley: The Civil War Journal of Stonewall Jackson's Topographer.* Edited by Archie P. McDonald. Dallas: Southern Methodist University Press, 1973.

Hubbs, G. Ward, ed. *Voices from Company D: Diaries by the Greensboro Guards, Fifth Alabama Infantry Regiment, Army of Northern Virginia.* Athens, GA: University of Georgia Press, 2003.

Humphreys, Andrew A. *The Virginia Campaign of 1864 and 1865.* New York: Charles Scribner's Sons, 1883.

Huse, Caleb. *The Supplies for the Confederate Army: How They were Obtained in Europe and How Paid For.* Boston: Marvin Bean, 1904.

Jones, Melvin, ed. *Give God the Glory: Memoirs of a Civil War Soldier.* 1979. Rev. ed., Eagle River, MI: Privately published, 1997.

Johnson, Pharris Deloach, ed. *Under the Southern Cross: Soldier Life with Gordon Bradwell and the Army of Northern Virginia.* Macon, GA: Mercer University Press, 1999.

Kidd, J. H. *Riding with Custer: Recollections of a Cavalryman in the Civil War.* 1908. Reprint, Lincoln: University of Nebraska Press, 1997.

Ledoux, Tom, ed. *Quite Ready to be Sent Somewhere: The Civil War Letters of Aldace Freeman Walker.* Victoria, BC: Trafford, 2003.

Leon, Louis. *Diary of a Tarheel Confederate Soldier.* Charlotte, NC: Stone Publishing, 1913.

Lowe, Jeffrey C. and Sam Hodges, eds. *Letters to Amanda: The Civil War Letters of Marion Hill Fitzpatrick, Army of Northern Virginia.* Macon, GA: Mercer University Press, 1998.

Menge, W. Springer and J. August Shimrak, eds. *The Civil War Notebook of Daniel Chisholm: A Chronicle of Daily Life in the Union Army 1864-1865.* New York: Orion Books, 1989.

Montgomery, George F. Jr., ed. *Georgia Sharpshooter: The Civil War Diary and Letters of William Rhadamanthus Montgomery, 1839-1906.* Macon, GA: Mercer University Press, 1997.

Moore, Frank, ed. *Anecdotes, Poetry, and Incidents of the War: North and South, 1860-1865.* New York: Bible House, 1867.

Murphy, Kevin C. *The Civil War Letters of Joseph K. Taylor of the Thirty-seventh Massachusetts Volunteer Infantry.* Lewiston, NY: Edward Mellen Press, 1998.

Nevins, Alan, ed. *A Diary of Battle: The Personal Journals of Colonel Charles S. Wainwright, 1861-1865.* New York: Harcourt and Brace, 1962.

Parker, Eddie R., ed. *Touched by Fire: Letters from Company D, 5th Texas Infantry, Hood's Brigade, Army of Northern Virginia, 1862-1865.* Hillsboro, TX: Hill College Press, 2000.

Parramore, Thomas and F. Roy Johnson. *Before the Rebel Flag Fell.* Murfreesboro, NC: Johnson Publishing, 1965.

Pearce, T. H., ed. *Diary of Captain Henry A. Chambers.* Wendell, NC: Broadfoot's Bookmark, 1983.

Rommel, Erwin. *Infantry Attacks.* 1937. Reprint, Wren's Park Publishing, 2002.

Rosenblatt, Emil and Ruth, eds. *Hard Marching Every Day: The Civil War Letters of Private Wilbur Fisk, 1861-1865.* Lawrence: University Press of Kansas, 1983.

Ross, FitzGerald. *Cities and Camps of the Confederate States.* Edited by Richard Barksdale Harwell. Chicago: University of Illinois Press, 1997.

Schön, J. *Rifled Musketry Arms: A Brief Description of the Modern System of Small Arms as Adopted in the Various European Armies. Translated by J. Gorgas.* 1855. Reprint, Springfield, MA: Privately published, 1986.

Silliker, Ruth, ed. *The Rebel Yell and the Yankee Hurrah: The Civil War Journal of a Maine Volunteer, Private John W. Haley, 17th Maine Regiment.* Camden, ME: Down East Books, 1985.

Sheridan, Philip H. *Personal Memoirs of P. H. Sheridan: General United States Army.* 2 vols. New York: Charles L. Webster, 1888.

Stephens, Robert Griffin Jr., ed. *Intrepid Warrior: Clement Anselm Evans.* Dayton, OH: Morningside House, 1992.

Stiles, Robert. *Four Years under Marse Robert.* New York: Neale Publishing, 1904.

Styple, William B., ed. *Writing and Fighting from the Army of Northern Virginia: A Collection of Soldier Correspondence.* Kearny, NJ: Bell Grove, 2003.

--------. *Writing and Fighting the Civil War: Soldier Correspondence to the New York Sunday Mercury.* Kearny, NJ: Bell Grove, 2000.

--------. *Writing and Fighting the Confederate War: The Letters of Peter Wellington Alexander, Confederate War Correspondent.* Kearny, NJ: Bell Grove, 2002.

Townsend, George Alfred. *Rustics in Rebellion: A Yankee Reporter on the Road to Richmond, 1861-1865.* Chapel Hill: University of North Carolina Press, 1950.

White, Russell C., ed. *The Civil War Diary of Wyman S. White, First Sergeant of Company F, 2nd United States Sharpshooter Regiment, 1861-1865.* Baltimore: Butternut and Blue, 1993.

Wilcox, C. M. *Rifles and Rifle Practice: An Elementary Treatise upon the Theory of Rifle Firing, Explaining the Causes of Inaccuracy of Fire, and the Manner of Correcting It, with Descriptions of the Infantry Rifles of Europe and the United States, Their Balls and Cartridges.* New York: D. Van Nostrand, 1859.

Worsham, John H. *One of Jackson's Foot Cavalry: His Experience and What He Saw during the War 1861-1865, Including a History of "F Company," Richmond, Va., 21st Regiment*

Virginia Infantry, Second Brigade, Jackson's Division, Second Corps, A. N. Va. New York: Neale Publishing, 1912.

Secondary Sources

Allen, T. Harrell. *Lee's Last Major General: Bryan Grimes of North Carolina.* Savas Publishing Company, 1999.

Baldwin, James J. *The Struck Eagle: A Biography of General Micah Jenkins and a History of the Fifth South Carolina Volunteers and the Palmetto Sharpshooters.* Shippensburg, PA: Burd Street Press, 1996.

Bilby, Joseph G. *Civil War Firearms: Their Historical Background, Tactical Use and Modern Collecting and Shooting.* Combined Books, 1997.

Blackford, L. Minor. *Mine Eyes Have Seen the Glory: The Story of a Virginia Lady, Mary Berkeley Minor Blackford, 1802-1896, Who Taught Her Sons to Hate Slavery and to Love the Union.* Cambridge, MA: Harvard University Press, 1954.

Bull, Stephen. *Stormtrooper: Elite German Assault Soldiers.* London: Publishing News, 1999.

Coates, Earl J., and John D. McAulay. *Civil War Sharps Carbines and Rifles.* Gettysburg, PA: Thomas Publications, 1996.

Coates, Earl J., and Dean S. Thomas. *An Introduction to Civil War Small Arms.* Gettysburg, PA: Thomas Publications, 1990.

Coco, Gregory A. *The Civil War Infantryman: In Camp, on the March, and in Battle.* Gettysburg, PA: Thomas Publications, 1996.

Cooling, B. Franklin. *Jubal Early's Raid on Washington, 1864.* Baltimore, MD: Nautical & Aviation Publishing, 1989.

--------.*Monocacy: The Battle That Saved Washington.* 1997. Reprint, Shippensburg, PA: White Mane Publishing, 2000.

Cooling, B. Franklin, and Walton H. Owen. *Mr. Lincoln's Forts: A Guide to the Civil War Defenses of Washington.* Shippensburg, PA: White Mane Publishing, 1988.

Cross, Davis Faris *A Melancholy Affair at the Weldon Railroad: The Vermont Brigade, June 23, 1864.* White Mane Publishing, 2003.

Doyle, Arthur Conan. *The Great Boer War.* London: Smith, Elder, 1902. Also available online at http://www.classicbookshelf.com/library/arthur_conan_doyle/the_great_boar_war.

Dupuy, R. Ernest, and Trevor N. Dupuy, *Encyclopedia of Military History from 3500 B. C. to the Present.* New York: Harper & Row, 1970.

Dyer, Frederick H. *A Compendium of the War of the Rebellion.* Des Moines, IA: Dyer Publishing, 1908.

Edwards, William B. *Civil War Guns.* Gettysburg, PA: Thomas Publications, 1962.

Elliott-Wright, Philip. *Rifleman: Elite Soldiers of the Wars against Napoleon.* London: Publishing News, 2000.

Encyclopedia of Military History from 3500 B.C. to the Present. Harper & Rowe, 1970.

Fies, William B. *Grant's Secret Service: The Intelligence War from Belmont to Appomattox.* Lincoln: University of Nebraska Press, 2002.

Fox, William F. *Regimental Losses in the Civil War.* Albany, NY: Albany Publishing, 1889.

Fredricksen, John C. *Green Coats and Glory: The United States Regiment of Riflemen, 1808-1821.* Youngstown, NY: Old Fort Niagara Association, 2000.

Fuller, Claud E., and Richard D. Steuart. *Firearms of the Confederacy.* Lawrence, MA: Quartermain Publications, 1944.

Gallagher, Gary W., ed. *The Antietam Campaign.* Chapel Hill: University of North Carolina Press, 1999.

--------, ed. *Chancellorsville: The Battle and Its Aftermath.* Chapel Hill: University of North Carolina Press, 1996.

--------, ed. *The First Day at Gettysburg: Essays on Confederate and Union Leadership.* Kent, OH: Kent State University Press, 1992.

--------. *Stephen Dodson Ramseur: Lee's Gallant General.* Chapel Hill: University of North Carolina Press, 1985.

--------, ed. *Struggle for the Shenandoah: Essays on the 1864 Valley Campaign.* Kent, OH: Kent State University Press, 1991.

Greene, A. Wilson. *Breaking the Backbone of the Rebellion: The Final Battles of the Petersburg Campaign.* Mason City, IA: Savas Publishing, 2000.

Griffith, Paddy. *Battle Tactics of the Civil War.* New Haven: Yale University Press, 1989.

Gudmundsson, Bruce I. *Stormtroop Tactics: Innovation in the German Army, 1914-1918.* Westport ,CT: Praeger Publishers, 1995.

A Guide to the Fortifications and Battlefields Around Petersburg. 1866. Reprint, Ft. Washington, PA: Eastern National, 2003.

Hartzler, Daniel D. *A Band of Brothers: Photographic Epilogue to Marylanders in the Confederacy.* Belleville, MD: Privately published, 1992.

Hauptman, Laurence M. *Between Two Fires: American Indians in the Civil War.* New York: Free Press, 1996.

Holmes, Clay W. *The Elmira Prison Camp: A History of the Military Prison at Elmira, N.Y. July 6, 1864, to July 10, 1865.* G. P. Putnam's Sons, 1912.

Judge, Joseph. *Season of Fire: The Confederate Strike on Washington.* Berryville, VA: Rockbridge Publishing, 1994.

Katcher, Philip. *Sharpshooters of the American Civil War.* Osprey Publishing, 2002.

Kenan, Thomas S. *Sketch of the Forty-third Regiment of North Carolina Troops (Infantry).* 1895. Reprint on CD-ROM, Clearwater, SC: Eastern Digital Resources, 2003.

Kennedy, Francis M., ed. *The Civil War Battlefield Guide.* 2nd ed. Boston: Houghton Mifflin, 1998.

Krick, Robert K. *Lee's Colonels: A Biographical Register of the Field Officers of the Army of Northern Virginia.* Dayton, OH: Press of the Morningside Bookshop, 1979.

--------. *The Smoothbore Volley That Doomed the Confederacy: The Death of Stonewall Jackson and Other Chapters on the Army of Northern Virginia.* Baton Rouge: Louisiana State University Press, 2002.

Lewis, Thomas A. *The Guns of Cedar Creek.* New York: Harper and Row, 1988.

Mahr, Theodore C. *The Battle of Cedar Creek: Showdown in the Shenandoah, October 1-13, 1864.* Lynchburg, VA: H. E. Howard, 1992.

McChristian, Douglas C. *An Army of Marksmen: Development of the United States Army Marksmanship in the 19th Century.* Fort Collins, CO: Old Army Press, 1981.

Miller, Michael J. *The North Anna Campaign: "Even to Hell Itself."* Lynchburg, VA: H. E. Howard, 1989.

Morrow, John Anderson. *The Confederate Whitworth Sharpshooters.* 1989. 2nd edition. N.p.: Privately published, 2002.

Mottelay, Paul F., and T. Campbell-Copeland. *The Soldier in Our Civil War: A Pictorial History of the Conflict, 1861-1865.* 2 vols. New York: Stanley Bradley Publishing, 1890.

Newton, Steven E. *Lost for the Cause: The Confederate Army in 1864.* Mason City, IA: Savas Publishing, 2000.

Nosworthy, Brent. *The Bloody Crucible of Courage: Fighting Methods and Combat Experience of the Civil War.* New York: Carroll & Graf, 2003.

Patterson, Gerard A. *From Blue to Gray: The Life of Confederate General Cadmus M. Wilcox.* Mechanicsburg, PA: Stackpole Books, 2001.

Phisterer, Frederick. *Statistical Record of the Armies of the United States.* 1883. Reprint, Edison, NJ: Castle Books, 2002.

Pond, George E. *The Shenandoah Valley in 1864.* New York: Charles Scribner's Sons, 1889.

Roads, C. H. *The British Soldier's Firearm, 1850-1864.* London: Herbert Jenkins, 1964.

Rhea, Gordon. *The Battle of the Wilderness, May 5-6, 1864.* Baton Rouge: Louisiana State University Press, 1994.

--------. *The Battles for Spotsylvania Court House and the Road to Yellow Tavern, May 7-12, 1864.* Baton Rouge: Louisiana State University Press, 1997.

--------. *To the North Anna River: Grant and Lee, May 13-25, 1864.* Baton Rouge: Louisiana State University Press, 2000.

Rodenbough, Theophilus Francis, and William L. Haskin, eds. *The Army of the United States: Historical Sketches of Staff and Line with Portraits of Generals-in-Chief.* New York: Maynard, Merrill, 1896. Also available online at http://www.army. mil/cmh-pg/books/R&H/R&H-FM.htm/.

Satterlee, L. D., ed. *Ten Old Gun Catalogs for the Collector Vol. 1.* Privately published, 1940. Reprint, Chicago: Follett Publishing, n.d.

Sears, Stephen W. *Chancellorsville.* Boston: Houghton Mifflin, 1996.

--------. *Landscape Turned Red: The Battle of Antietam.* New Haven: Ticknor & Fields, 1983.

--------. *To the Gates of Richmond: The Peninsula Campaign.* New York: Ticknor & Fields 1992.

Sword, Wiley. *Firepower from Abroad: The Confederate Enfield and the Lemat Revolver.* Lincoln, RI: Andrew Mowbray, 1986.

--------. *Sharpshooter: Hiram Berdan, His Famous Sharpshooters and Their Sharps Rifles.* Lincoln, RI: Andrew Mowbray, 1988.

Tagg, Larry. *The Generals of Gettysburg: The Leaders of America's Greatest Battle.* New York: DaCapo, 1998.

Trudeau, Noah Andre. *The Last Citadel: Petersburg, Virginia, June 1864-April 1865.* Boston: Little, Brown, 1991.

--------. *Out of the Storm: The End of the Civil War, April-June 1865.* Boston: Little, Brown, 1994.

Vandiver, Frank. *Jubal's Raid: General Early's Famous Raid on Washington in 1864.* New York: McGraw-Hill, 1960.

Wellman, Manly Wade. *Rebel Boast: First at Bethel—Last at Appomattox.* New York: Henry Holt, 1956.

Wert, Jeffry D. *From Winchester to Cedar Creek: The Shenandoah Campaign of 1864.* Carlisle, PA: South Mountain Press, 1987. Reprint, Mechanicsburg, PA: Stackpole Books, 1997.

Whitehorne, Joseph W. A. *The Battle of Cedar Creek: Self-Guided Tour.* Washington DC: Center of Military History, 1992.

Unit Histories

Adams, John G. B. *Reminiscences of the Nineteenth Massachusetts Regiment.* Boston: Wright, Potter Printing, 1899. Also available online at http://sunsite.utk.edu/civil-war/Mass19.html/.

Anderson, John. *The Fifty-Seventh Regiment of Massachusetts Volunteers in the War of the Rebellion.* Boston: E. B. Stillings, 1896.

Barker, Lorenzo A. *Birge's Western Sharpshooters in the Civil War, 1861-1865.* 1905. Reprint, Huntington, WV: Blue Acorn Press, 1994.

Bartlett, Napier. *Military Record of Louisiana, Including Biographical and Historical Papers Relating to the Military Organizations of the State.* 1875. Reprints, Baton Rouge: Louisiana State University Press, 1964.

Best, Isaac O. *History of the 121st New York State Infantry.* Chicago: Lieut. Jas. H. Smith, 1921.

Bilby, Joseph G. *Three Rousing Cheers: A History of the Fifteenth New Jersey from Flemington to Appomattox.* Revised edition. Hightstown, NJ: Longstreet House, 2001.

Brown, Russell K. *Our Connection with Savannah: A History of the 1st Battalion Georgia Sharpshooters*. Macon, GA: Mercer University Press, 2004.

Bowen, James L. *History of the Thirty-seventh Regiment Mass. Volunteers in the Civil War of 1861-1865*. Holyoke, MA: Clark W. Bryan, 1884.

Brewer, Willis. *Brief Historical Sketches of Military Organizations Raised in Alabama During the Civil War*. Montgomery: Alabama Civil War Centennial Commission, 1962.

Caldwell, J. F. J. *The History of a Brigade of South Carolinians First Known as "Gregg's" and Subsequently as "McGowan's Brigade."* 1886. Reprint, Dayton, OH: Morningside Press, 1992.

Clark, Walter, ed. *Histories of the Several Regiments and Battalions from North Carolina, in the Great War 1861-65*. 5 vols. Raleigh, NC: E. M. Uzzel, 1901.

Cutcheon, Byron M. *The Story of the Twentieth Michigan Infantry*. Lansing, MI: Privately published, 1904.

Davis, William C. *The Orphan Brigade: The Kentucky Confederates Who Couldn't Go Home*. Doubleday, 1980.

Day, W. A. *A True History of Company I, 49th Regiment North Carolina Troops in the Great Civil War between North and South*. Newton, NC: Privately published, 1893. Reprint, Baltimore: Butternut and Blue, 1997.

Delauter, Roger U. *62nd Virginia Infantry*. Lynchburg, VA: H. E. Howard, 1988.

Dickert, D. Augustus. *History of Kershaw's Brigade, with Complete Roll of Companies, Biographical Sketches, Incidents, Anecdotes, Etc.* 1899. Reprint, Dayton, OH: Morningside Press, 1976.

Dunlop, W. S. *Lee's Sharpshooters; or, the Forefront of Battle: A Story of Southern Valor That Never Has Been Told*. 1899. Dayton, OH: Morningside Press, 1988.

Gannon, James P. *Irish Rebels, Confederate Tigers: A History of the 6th Louisiana Volunteers, 1861-1865*. Mason City, IA: Savas Publishing, 1998.

Gavin, George C. *Campaigning with the Roundheads: The History of the Hundredth Pennsylvania Veteran Volunteer Infantry Regiment in the American Civil War, 1861-1865*. Dayton, OH: Morningside Press, 1989.

Haines, Alanson A. *History of the Fifteenth Regiment New Jersey Volunteers*. New York: Privately published, 1883.

Herek, Raymond J. *These Men Have Seen Hard Service: The First Michigan Sharpshooters in the Civil War*. Detroit: Wayne State University Press, 1998.

Hess, Earl J. *Lee's Tar Heels: The Pettigrew–Kirkland–McRae Brigade*. Chapel Hill: University of North Carolina Press, 2002.

Howard, O. R., and William H. Rauch. *History of the "Bucktails," Kane Rifle Regiment of the Pennsylvania Reserve Corps (13th Pennsylvania Reserves, 42nd of the Line)*. Philadelphia: Regimental Association, 1906.

Howerton, Bryan R. *Rapley's Sharpshooters (12th Arkansas Battalion, CSA)*. Available online at http://www.couchgenweb.com/civilwar/rapley1.html.

Hubbs, G. Ward. *Guarding Greensboro: A Confederate Company in the Making of a Southern Community.* Athens: University of Georgia Press, 2003.

Iobst, Richard W. *The Bloody Sixth: The Sixth North Carolina Regiment, Confederate States of America.* Raleigh: NC Confederate Centennial Commission, 1965.

Leeke, Jim, ed. *A Hundred Days to Richmond: Ohio's "Hundred Days" Men in the Civil War.* Bloomington: Indiana University Press, 1999.

Mahon, John K., and Romana Danysh. *Army Lineage Series: Infantry, Part I: Regular Army.* Washington, DC: Office of Chief of Military History, 1972. Also available online at http://www.army.mil/cmh-pg/books/Lineage/in/infantry.htm/.

Nichols, G. W. *A Soldier's Story of His Regiment and Incidentally of the Lawton–Gordon–Evans Brigade.* Kennesaw, GA: Continental Book, 1961.

Park, Robert Emory. *Sketch of the Twelfth Alabama Infantry of Battle's Brigade, Rodes Division, Early's Corps of the Army of Northern Virginia.* 1906. Reprint, Clearwater, SC: Eastern Digital Resources, 1998.

Ripley, William Y. W. *A History of Company F, First United States Sharp Shooters.* Rutland, VT: Tuttle & Co., Printers, 1883. Also available online at *http://www.vermontcivilwar.org/units/ss/ripley.php.*

Rowland, Dunbar. *Military History of Mississippi, 1803-1898.* 1908. Reprint, Spartanburg, SC: Reprint Company, 1978.

Smith, John Day. *The History of the Nineteenth Regiment of Maine Volunteer Infantry, 1862-1865.* Minneapolis, MN: Privately published, 1909.

Smith, W. A. *The Anson Guards: Company "C," Fourteenth Regiment North Carolina Volunteers, 1861-1865.* Charlotte, NC: Stone Publishing, 1914.

Stevens, C. A. *Berdan's U.S. Sharpshooters in the Army of the Potomac, 1861-1865.* St. Paul, MN: Price-McGill, 1892.

Stone, DeWitt Boyd Jr., ed. *Wandering to Glory: Confederate Veterans Remember Evans's Brigade.* Columbia: University of South Carolina Press, 2002.

Swinfen, David B. *Ruggles' Regiment: The 122nd New York Volunteers in the American Civil War.* Hanover, NH: University Press of New England, 1982.

Sypher, Josiah R. *History of the Pennsylvania Reserve Corps.* Lancaster, PA: Elias Barr, 1865.

Thomas, Henry W. *History of the Doles-Cook Brigade, Army of Northern Virginia.* Atlanta, GA: Franklin Publishing, 1903.

Thompson, J. M. "Reminiscences of the Autauga Rifles, Read Before the Historical Association Dec. 19th 1879 at Autaugaville, Alabama," Sixth Alabama regimental file ADAH.

Walker, Aldace F. *The Vermont Brigade in the Shenandoah Valley, 1864.* Burlington, VT: Free Press Association, 1869.

White, Gregory C. *A History of the 31st Georgia Volunteer Infantry: Lawton–Gordon–Evans Brigade, Army of Northern Virginia 1861-1865.* Baltimore: Butternut and Blue, 1997.

Wilkinson, Warren. *Mother, May You Never See the Sights I Have Seen: The Fifty-seventh Massachusetts in the Last Year of the Civil War, 1864-1865.* New York: Harper & Row, 1990.

Woodward, E. M. *Our Campaigns: The Second Pennsylvania Reserves Volunteers.* Philadelphia: J. E. Porter, 1865. Reprint, Shippensburg, PA: Burd Street Press, 1995.

Internet Articles

Gourley, Scott. "United States Marines Antiterrorism Force: Special Weapons and Tactics of This New Elite Brigade." Available online at http://www.popularmechanics.com/science/defense/1281481.html.

Robert Henderson, "Canadian Fencible Light Company at the Battle of the Chateauguay, 1813." Available online at http://www.warof1812.ca/chatgy.htm.

Popenker, Max. "Modern Sniper Rifles." Available online at http://world.guns.ru/sniper/sn00-e.htm/.

Simonowicz, Vincent J. "History of the 20th South Carolina Volunteer Infantry." Available online at http://www.geocities.com/Heartland/Hills/9908/20hist.html/.

LIST OF ABBREVIATIONS

ADAH	Alabama Department of Archives and History
BD/M	Eugene Blackford Diary/Memoir, U.S. Army Military History Institute, Carlisle Barracks, Pennsylvania
B&L	Buel, Clarence C., and Robert U. Johnson, eds. *Battles and Leaders of the Civil War.* 4 vols. New York: Century, 1887-1888. Reprint, New York: Thomas Yoseloff, 1956
CV	*Confederate Veteran*
CSR	Soldier's Compiled Service Record at the National Archives
FSNMP	Fredericksburg and Spotsylvania National Military Park
GDAH	Georgia Department of Archives and History
GLI	Gilder Lehrman Institute of American History, New York, New York
LC	Library of Congress
MHS	Maryland Historical Society
NA	National Archives
NCDAH	North Carolina Division of Archives and History
OR	U.S. War Department. *War of the Rebellion: A Compilation of the Official Records of the Union and Confederate Armies.* 128 vols. Washington, DC: Government Printing Office, 1880-1901.
OR Supp.	Hewett, Janet B., ed. *Supplement to the Official Records of the Union and Confederate Armies.* 100 vols. Wilmington, NC: Broadfoot Publishing, 1997. All cites are to Part 1.
SHC	Southern Historical Collection at the University of North Carolina Chapel Hill.
SHSP	*Southern Historical Society Papers*
USAMHI	U.S. Army Military History Institute, Carlisle Barracks, Pennsylvania
VHS	Virginia Historical Society
WHS	Wisconsin Historical Society

NOTES

Chapter 1 – Antecedents

1. The information in this section is drawn primarily from Philip Elliott-Wright's *Rifleman: Elite Soldiers of the Wars against Napoleon* (London: Publishing News, 2000). Ferguson designed a unique and effective breech-loading rifle that the conservative British army never saw fit to adopt in sufficient numbers to realize its full potential. His unit performed well but was eventually disbanded, and Ferguson himself fell later in the war at King's Mountain.

2. Henry Beaufoy, *Scloppeteria* (Repr., Surrey, UK: Richmond, 1971), 22-23, quoted in Gary Yee, "The Lone Marksman Revisited," *Muzzle Blasts* 64 (August 2003): 74.

3. Elliott-Wright, *Rifleman*, 93. See pp. 70-80 for more detailed information on the Baker rifle.

4. Ibid., Captain Barber *Instructions for the Formation and Exercise of Volunteer Sharp-Shooters* (1804. Reprint, Ottawa: Museum Restoration Service, 1968), 1-5, 14-19. Captain Barber's book of instruction for volunteer riflemen is one of the few period training texts that have survived.

Chapter 2 – American Riflemen

1. John C. Fredricksen, *Green Coats and Glory: The United States Regiment of Riflemen, 1808-1821* (Old Fort Niagara Association, 2000), 7.

2. Joseph G. Bilby, *Civil War Firearms: Their Historical Background, Tactical Use and Modern Collecting and Shooting* (Combined Books, 1997), 41. An American rifleman habitually carried a tomahawk in his belt for close quarters fighting, but this more primitive weapon was no match for a British soldier with a Brown Bess and a bayonet.

3. John K. Mahon and Romana Danysh. *Army Lineage Series: Infantry, Part I: Regular Army* (Washington, DC: Office of Chief of Military History, 1972), 7-9.

4. Fredriksen, *Green Coats and Glory*, 9-11. Fredriksen's slim volume remains virtually the only in-depth study of this important and sadly neglected unit. An exhibit at the National Firearms Museum in Fairfax, VA, says that the Model 1803 rifle is "considered by many to be the most elegant military arm ever produced in the United States of America."

5. Ibid., 28-30.

6. Ibid.

7. Ibid., 31-37, 50-51.

8. Ibid., 56-60.

9. In the argot of the British Empire the term "fencible" meant a home defense unit much like the American National Guard. Unlike a militia unit, which had elected officers, a fencible officer held a Crown commission. However, a fencible unit could not be deployed out of the area where it was raised or sent overseas. See Robert Henderson, "Canadian Fencible Light Company at the Battle of the Chateauguay, 1813," available online at http://www.warof1812.ca/chatgy.htm/

10. Gary Yee, "The Longest Shots Ever (April-May 1813)…and Walter Cline's Attempt to Validate the Feat," *Muzzle Blasts* 65 (November 2003): 33.

11. Gary Yee, "The Lone Marksman Revisited," *Muzzle Blasts* 64 (August 2003): 70, 76.

12. Mahon and Danysh, *Regular Army,* 17-19. The army did not officially drop the appellations of "light" and "grenadier" for flank companies until 1855.

13. Theophilus Francis Rodenbough and William L. Haskin, eds., *The Army of the United States: Historical Sketches of Staff and Line with Portraits of Generals-in-Chief* (New York: Maynard, Merrill, 1896), 194; Mahon and Danysh, *Regular Army,* 17.

14. Mahon and Danysh, *Regular Army,* 19-20; Fredriksen, *Green Coats and Glory,* 7-8.

Chapter 3 – Zouaves

1. William B. Edwards, *Civil War Guns* (Gettysburg, PA: Thomas Publications, 1962), 8-10; Brent Nosworthy, *The Bloody Crucible of Courage: Fighting Methods and Combat Experience of the Civil War* (New York: Carroll & Graf, 2003), 23-28. In particular, the *carabine à tige* was difficult to clean.

2. Nosworthy, *Bloody Crucible,* 53-58.

3. Ibid., 57-8, 79. The French manual was titled *Ordonnance du Roi sur l'exercise et les manoeuvres des bataillons de chasseurs à pied,* or "Instructions for the Evolutions and Maneuvers of the Foot Chasseurs."

4. Nosworthy, *Bloody Crucible,* 34-5; C. M. Wilcox, *Rifles and Rifle Practice: An Elementary Treatise upon the Theory of Rifle Firing, Explaining the Causes of Inaccuracy of Fire, and the Manner of Correcting It, with Descriptions of the Infantry Rifles of Europe and the United States, Their Balls and Cartridges* (New York: D. Van Nostrand, 1859), 239-41. The full title of the French manual was *Instruction provisoire sur le tir, à l'usage des bataillons de chasseurs à pied;* Heth's was *A System of Target Practice: For the Use of Troops When Armed with the Musket, Rifle-Musket, Rifle, or Carbine / Prepared Principally from the French.* Heth was careful to note that he did "not claim the credit of presenting to the army any thing new, but only a digest of what has already been practised, with great success, by the English and the French."

5. Nosworthy, *Bloody Crucible,* 41-5, 49.

6. Nosworthy, *Bloody Crucible,* 87-90; Gerard A. Patterson, *From Blue to Gray: The Life of Confederate General Cadmus M. Wilcox* (Mechanicsburg, PA: Stackpole Books, 2001), 10-11. Upon publication the War Department promptly ordered a thousand copies of Wilcox's book, almost enough for each officer in the service to have one. "R.E.C.," most likely Raleigh Edward Colston, an instructor at Virginia Military Institute, published "Modern Tactics" in the *Southern Literary Messenger* in 1858. Both Colston and Wilcox would wear general's wreaths in the Army of Northern Virginia.

7. Wilcox, *Rifles and Rifle Practice,* 204, 174-7, 243-7.

8. Ibid., 243-4, 174-5.

9. Ibid., 245-6.

10. Rodenbough, *Army of the United States,* 532-4.

11. Ibid., 533.

12. Douglas C. McChristian, *An Army of Marksmen: Development of the United States Army Marksmanship in the 19th Century* (Fort Collins, CO: Old Army Press, 1981), 15-16; Heth, *System of Target Practice,* 41-2; For the British system of the time, see Wilcox, *Rifles and Rifle Practice,* 259. In England the best shots of the battalion received a handsome badge and extra pay for their efforts, while the penny-pinching Americans required the winner of a brass stadia to turn it in before he could receive a silver one.

13. Rodenbough, *Army of the United States,* 534, 536.

14. *Scientific American,* January 19, 1861, 48; *Military Gazette,* July 15, 1859, 214; "Rifled Guns" *The Atlantic Monthly,* October 1859, 444-453; all quoted in Nosworthy, *Bloody Crucible,* 93-4, 97, 152, 373.

Chapter 4 – Beginnings

1. Center of Military History, *American Military History* (Washington, DC: U.S. Government Printing Office, 1988), 185.

2. Richard D. Steuart, "How Johnny Got His Gun," *Confederate Veteran* 32 (1924); Gamma [George William Bagby], "Letter from Virginia," *Mobile Advertiser and Register,* February 12, 1864.

3. Thomas Caffey, "Letters from the Front," *Confederate Veteran* 26 (1918).

4. D. Augustus Dickert, *History of Kershaw's Brigade, with Complete Roll of Companies, Biographical Sketches, Incidents, Anecdotes, Etc.* (1899. Reprint, Dayton, OH: Morningside Press, 1976), 421-2; Aldace F. Walker, *The Vermont Brigade in the Shenandoah Valley, 1864* (Burlington, VT: Free Press Association, 1869), 56-7.

5. John D. Young, "A Campaign with the Sharpshooters: The Organization of the Riflemen in the Confederate Service. Their Work in the Wilderness and at Petersburg. Personal Reminiscences of Some Distinguished

Officers," *Philadelphia Weekly Times, January 26, 1878; George R. Agassiz, ed., With Grant and Meade from the Wilderness to Appomattox* (Lincoln: University of Nebraska Press, 1994), 301.

6. Agassiz, *Grant and Meade,* 300, 301.

7. William Y. W. Ripley, *A History of Company F, 1st United States Sharp Shooters* (Rutland: Tuttle & Co., Printers, 1883), 4-5. Also available online at http://www.vermontcivilwar.org/units/ss/ripley.php.

8. C. S. Army, *21st NC Infantry Order Book, #5090-z,* SHC, 131. Because of the fragmentary state of the Confederate records it is not clear if Ewell was implementing an order from his superior, Joseph Johnston, or whether he issued the order himself.

9. James J. Baldwin, *The Struck Eagle: A Biography of General Micah Jenkins and a History of the Fifth South Carolina Volunteers and the Palmetto Sharpshooters* (Shippensburg, PA: Burd Street Press, 1996), 87.

10. Young, "Campaign with the Sharpshooters."

11. Archibald Gracie, "Major Gracie's Battalion at Yorktown and Williamsburg in 1862" n.d. Gracie's Special Battalion file, ADAH.

12. James M. Rudulph to Father, April 13, 1862, http://rootsweb.com/~alhenry/6th/letters/rudulph1.htm; Robert Rodes to Jubal Early, n.d., Pearce Civil War Collection, Navarro College, Texas. Rodes's letter appears to have been written the same day as Rudulph's.

13. *OR* Ser. 1, XIV: 472-3.

14. Ripley, *History of Company F,* 35-6.

15. *A Digest of the Military and Naval Laws of the Confederate States, From the Commencement of the Provisional Congress to the End of the First Congress Under the Permanent Constitution,* (Columbia, SC: Evans & Cogswell, 1864) 24:38; C. S. War Department, General Orders 34, May 3, 1862, in *General Orders from Adjutant and Inspector-General's Office, Confederate States Army, from January, 1862 to December, 1863* (Columbia, SC: Evans and Cogswell, 1864).

16. R. W. Wharton, "First Battalion (Sharpshooters)" in Clark, Walter, ed. *Histories of the Several Regiments and Battalions from North Carolina, in the Great War 1861-65.* (Raleigh, NC: E. M. Uzzel, 1901) 4:27-28; S.O. 32, Trimble's Brigade, May 21, 1862, Perry Family Papers #906-2, SHC; "Our Soldier Boys," *Turnwold Plantation Countryman,* June 3, 1862. The Forty-fourth Georgia ended up in Doles's Georgia brigade, part of Rodes's division, which in due time formed a sharpshooter battalion. About the same time Col. J. D. Waddell of the Twentieth Georgia wrote that "Col. Jones is trying to get off home to raise a battalion of sharp shooters to be incorporated with our Brigade," but no record survives of any such unit actually being formed. Robert K. Krick, e-mail message to the author, July 10, 2004.

17. Bryan R. Howerton, *Rapley's Sharpshooters (12th Arkansas Battalion, CSA),* available online at http://www.couchgenweb.com/civilwar/rapley1.html. One Lieutenant John A. Jones attempted to recruit a similar battalion in Georgia about the same time, apparently without success. Russell K. Brown, *Our Connection with Savannah: A History of the 1st Battalion Georgia Sharpshooters.* (Macon, GA: Mercer University Press, 2004), 12.

18. Since of the three only Blackford survived the war, reconstructing the development of the sharpshooter units necessarily involves some speculation. Rodes, unfortunately, left little behind other than his official reports, which do not discuss the matter in any detail. Just before her death Rodes' widow burned all his letters and personal papers.

19. Robert E. Park, "Diary of Robert E. Park, Macon, Georgia, Late Captain Twelfth Alabama Regiment, CSA," *SHSP* 1 Nos. 5, 6 (1876); *SHSP* 2, Nos. 1, 4, 5, 6 (1876); *SHSP* 3, Nos. 1, 2, 3, 4, 5, 6 (1877); *SHSP* 26 (1898).

Chapter 5 – Seven Pines, Gaines's Mill, and South Mountain

1. Robert E. Park, "The Twelfth Alabama Infantry, Confederate States Army," *SHSP* 33 (1905) 218-229.

2. Ibid.

3. Ibid.

4. Ibid.

5. Daniel Harvey Hill, "The Battle of South Mountain, or Boonsboro," *B&L* II: 564.

6. Park, "The Twelfth Alabama Infantry," 278-9.

7. *OR,* Ser. I, XIX/1: 1020-23, 1034.

8. Josiah R. Sypher, *History of the Pennsylvania Reserves Corps* (Lancaster, PA: Elias Barr, 1865), 368-9; and generally D. Scott Hartwig, "It Looked Like a Task to Storm: The Pennsylvania Reserves Assault South Mountain, September 14th, 1862," *North and South* (October 2002);

9. Park, "The Twelfth Alabama Infantry," 279; Otis Smith, "Reminiscences," Thatch Papers, SHC; Cullen Battle, "The Third Alabama Regiment," Third Alabama Regimental file, ADAH, 50. No accounts have come to light

about the fate of the skirmishers of the Twenty-sixth Alabama, but it is doubtful that they fared any better than the rest of the brigade.

10. J. W. Williams, "Company D Captured at the Battle of South Mountain," *Greensboro Record*, December 24, 1903; J. W. Williams, "A Search for a Sword," *Greensboro Record*, September 3, 1903.

11. Smith, "Reminiscences," 8-9.

12. "The Sharpshooter," *Mobile Advertiser and Register*, April 28, 1910.

13. Thomas S. Taylor letter to Thomas C. Taylor, September 1862, Alabama Volume #3, Richmond National Battlefield Park, Richmond, VA; Battle, "Third Alabama," 51; *OR*, Ser. 1, XIX/1: 1035-6.

14. Sypher, *Pennsylvania Reserve Corps*, 369-70.

15. Park, "The Twelfth Alabama Infantry," 279; Priest, *Before Antietam*, 244; *OR*, Ser. I, XIX/1: 261.

16. *OR*, Ser. 1, XIX/1: 1036. Admittedly, the numbers do not add up. Williams states in his account that he surrendered with three companies totaling 150 men, and Captain Ready is supposed to have accounted for another 50. Robert Park and a number of his men were captured also [and Otis Smith & Co.], which puts us far over the 204 missing, at least some of which had to have been from the main line. Still, assuming most of the 204 were captured on the skirmish line, this amounts to 17 percent of Rodes's force of 1200 men, or about the percentage of the force tactically necessary for skirmishers.

17. *OR*, Ser. I , XIX/1: 1034-6.

18. See generally Robert K. Krick, "It Appeared As Though Mutual Extermination Would Put a Stop to the Awful Carnage," in Gary Gallagher, ed., *The Antietam Campaign* (Chapel Hill: University of North Carolina Press, 1999).

19. Records do not indicate exactly which riflemen were in the farm's buildings, but the main bodies of Rodes's and Anderson's divisions were about five to six hundred yards away in and behind the sunken road, or about the right distance away for an advanced picket line.

Chapter 6 – Winter at Fredericksburg

1. L. Minor Blackford, *Mine Eyes Have Seen the Glory: The Story of a Virginia Lady, Mary Berkeley Minor Blackford, 1802-1896, Who Taught Her Sons to Hate Slavery and to Love the Union* (Cambridge, MA: Harvard University Press, 1954), 210.

2. Ibid., 211, 212.

3. Ibid., 212, 213. Emphasis in original.

4. Ibid., 213; BD/M, 196.

5. BD/M, 198-9.

6. BD/M, 201-2. Blackford's statements on the strength of the sharpshooters are somewhat confusing. Initially the corps was one man in twelve, which gave a battalion of about one hundred men. Later a second corps was formed, also of one man in twelve, which gave an overall strength of about two hundred men.

7. Young, "A Campaign with the Sharpshooters"; Frank Anderson Chappell, ed., *Dear Sister: Civil War Letters to a Sister in Alabama* (Huntsville, AL: Branch Springs Publishing, 2002), 128; BD/M, 201-2.

8. Eugene Blackford to his mother, January 15, 1863, Gordon-Blackford Papers, MHS.

9. BD/M, 202; W. S. Dunlop, *Lee's Sharpshooters; or, the Forefront of Battle: A Story of Southern Valor That Never Has Been Told* (1899. Dayton, OH: Morningside Press, 1988), 22; Sam Pickens diary entry, December 28, 1862, in G. Ward Hubbs, ed., *Voices from Company D: Diaries by the Greensboro Guards, Fifth Alabama Infantry Regiment, Army of Northern Virginia* (Athens, GA: University of Georgia Press, 2003), 128.

10. BD/M, 202-4.

11. Ibid.; C.S. War Department, *A System of Musketry Instruction: Prepared and Ordered by the Order of General Bragg for the Army of Tennessee* (Richmond, 1863), emphasis in the original.

12. BD/M, 202-4.

13. BD/M, 204-5. Blackford claims credit for inventing the system, but the British had used a similar if not quite so sophisticated system to train their riflemen. Blackford's basic program, with some refinements, would be adopted by the U.S. Army and used until the early 1960s, when pop-up targets replaced it. The author remembers using this system at a ROTC range in the 1960s.

14. BD/M, 205-6; Eugene Blackford to My Dear Mary, August 4, 1863, Eugene Blackford Letters, USAMHI.

15. Pickens diary entry, December 28, 1862, in Hubbs, ed., *Voices from Company D,* 128.

16. Eugene Blackford to his mother, January 25, 1863 Gordon-Blackford Papers, MHS.

17. Ibid.

18. Army of Northern Virginia General Order 6, January 28, 1863. Order Book of the Twenty-third NC Regiment (Iverson's brigade), Record Group 109, National Archives. Transcribed by Rob Wynstra. See also Matt. Manly "Second Regiment" in Clark, ed., *Histories of the Several Regiments and Battalions From North Carolina:* 169, for a mention of a sharpshooter battalion in Ramseur's brigade.

19. Eugene Blackford to his mother, March 1, 1863, Gordon-Blackford Papers, MHS.

20. Ibid.

21. Ibid.; BD/M, 199, 206-7. This is probably the first example of a skill badge used by an American army.

22. George F. Montgomery, Jr., ed., *Georgia Sharpshooter: The Civil War Diary and Letters of William Rhadamanthus Montgomery, 1839-1906* (Macon, GA: Mercer University Press, 1997), 84. The letter is dated May 7. Montgomery wrote this just after Chancellorsville, but it is evident from the letter that the battalion must have existed for some time before that since he describes its exploits during the battle.

Wofford's brigade consisted of the 16th, 18th, and 24th Georgia, plus Cobb's and Phillips's Georgia Legions.

23. Dunlop, *Lee's Sharpshooters,* 11, 17; J. M. Smither to "My Dear Uncle," July 24, 1864, in Eddie R. Parker, ed., *Touched by Fire: Letters from Company D, 5th Texas Infantry, Hood's Brigade, Army of Northern Virginia, 1862-1865* (Hillsboro, TX: Hill College Press, 2000), 94. Although Smither states that the year the battalion was formed was 1862, he ties it to the Suffolk campaign, which was in April-May 1863, and this seems more likely.

Chapter 7 – Chancellorsville

1. BD/M, 209-10; Eugene Blackford to My Dear Mary, May 21, 1863, Gordon-Blackford Papers, MHS.

2. Eugene Blackford to My Dear Mary, May 21, 1863, Gordon-Blackford Papers, MHS.

3. Eugene Blackford to My Dear Mary, May 21, 1863, Gordon-Blackford Papers, MHS; BD/M, 210.

4. BD/M, 211.

5. James Power Smith, "Stonewall Jackson's Last Battle," in *Battles and Leaders of the Civil War* (1894. Reprint, New York: Thomas Yoseloff, 1956), 3:205; BD/M, 211; Rodes, *OR,* Ser. I, XXV/1: 943.

6. Blackford to My Dear Mary, May 21, 1863, Gordon-Blackford Papers, MHS.

7. Blackford to My Dear Mary, May 8 and 21, 1863, Gordon-Blackford Papers, MHS; BD/M, 212-3.

8. BD/M, 213; Rodes, *OR,* Ser. I, Vol. XXV/1: 944-5. In a letter to his family Blackford gave the casualties in the Fifth Alabama as "more than 278 out of 500," although he noted that about a hundred of these were prisoners who would soon be exchanged. Blackford to My Dear Mary, May 21, 1863, Gordon-Blackford Papers, MHS.

9. Montgomery, ed., *Georgia Sharpshooter,* 84-8. For a more complete account of the action see Stephen W. Sears, *Chancellorsville* (Boston: Houghton Mifflin, 1996), 364.

10. Montgomery, ed., *Georgia Sharpshooter,* 85.

11. Ibid.

12. See Sears, *Chancellorsville,* 403 and Chapter 15.

13. John W. Bone, "Civil War Reminiscences" (1904), Lowery Shuford Collection, NCDAH.

14. Blackford to his father, May 7, 1863, Blackford Letters, USAMHI; Blackford to My Dear Mary, May 8, and 21, 1863, Gordon-Blackford Papers, MHS; BD/M, 212-13, 215-16.

15. Bone, "Civil War Reminiscences" (1904), Lowery Shuford Collection, NCDAH.

16. BD/M, 215.

17. BD/M, 216; Chappell, ed., *Dear Sister,* 144.

18. S. G. Pryor to Penelope May 22, 1863, in Adams, Charles R., ed. *A Post of Honor: The Pryor Letters, 1861-1863; Letters From Capt. S. G. Pryor, Twelfth Georgia Regiment and His Wife, Penelope Tyson Pryor* (Fort Valley, GA: Garret Publications, 1989), 358.

19. Army of Northern Virginia Special Order 79, June 2, 1863. Order Book of the Twenty-third NC Regiment (Iverson's brigade), Record Group 109, National Archives. See appendix B for full text. Blackford (BD/M, 201-2) first gives the one in twelve figure but then states that his battalion's strength is two hundred men, which simply does not work out for a twelve-hundred-man brigade.

20. Louis Leon, *Diary of a Tarheel Confederate Soldier* (Charlotte, NC: Stone Publishing Company, 1913), 30.

21. Montgomery, ed., *Georgia Sharpshooter,* 88, 91.

22. J. F. J. Caldwell, *The History of a Brigade of South Carolinians First Known as "Gregg's" and Subsequently as "McGowan's Brigade"* (1886. Reprint, Dayton, OH: Morningside Press, 1992), 129-130.

Chapter 8 – Gettysburg

1. Blackford to his father, June 22, 1863, Blackford Letters, USAMHI; Blackford, *Mine Eyes Have Seen the Glory,* 217; Blackford to Mary Blackford, June 28, 1863, Blackford Letters, USAMHI.

2. DB/M, 238.

3. The XI Corps, now under Major General Carl Schurz, advanced with two divisions totaling five thousand to six thousand men against Rodes while leaving one division in reserve on Cemetery Hill. Against this Doles's brigade probably numbered 1200-1300 men plus 150-200 of Blackford's sharpshooters. For the Federal forces I have generally followed D. Scott Hartwig's excellent article "The 11th Army Corps on July 1, 1863," *Gettysburg Magazine* 2 (January 1990): 33-49, available online at http://www.gdg.org/11tha.html, and for the Confederates Robert K. Krick, "Three Confederate Disasters on Oak Ridge," in Gary Gallagher, ed., *The First Day at Gettysburg: Essays on Confederate and Union Leadership* (Kent, OH: Kent State University Press, 1992), 132-3.

4. DB/M, 238.

5. Blackford, *Mine Eyes Have Seen the Glory,* 218; DB/M, 239; Chappell, ed., *Dear Sister,* 160.

6. Pickens diary entry, July 1, 1863, in Hubbs, ed., *Voices from Company D,* 182.

7. John D. Vautier, "At Gettysburg," *Philadelphia Press,* November 10, 1886 quoted in Krick, "Three Confederate Disasters on Oak Ridge," in Gallagher, ed., *The First Day at Gettysburg,* 132-3.

8. Pickens diary entry, July 1, 1863, in Hubbs, ed., *Voices from Company D,* 182; "Historical Sketch of the Forty-fifth," in New York Monuments Commission for the Battlefields of Gettysburg and Chattanooga, *Final Report on the Battlefield of Gettysburg (New York at Gettysburg)* (Albany, NY: J. B. Lyon Company, 1902). Also available online at http://www.dmna.state.ny.us/historic/reghist/civil/infantry/45thInf/45thInfHistSketch.htm. Iverson was relieved from command for his negligence, and O'Neal's commission to brigadier general canceled. He and his regiment eventually transferred out of the army.

9. Noah Andre Trudeau, "5th Alabama Sharpshooters: Taking Aim at Cemetery Hill," *America's Civil War* July 2001, also available on line at http://www.historynet.com/acw/blsharpshooters/.

10. Robert Rodes, "General R. E. Rodes' Report Of The Battle Of Gettysburg" *SHSP* 2 (1876): 148.

11. Trudeau, "5th Alabama Sharpshooters."

12. Irsch eventually received the Medal of Honor for his exploits that day, but spent the rest of the war in Libby Prison.

13. Blackford, *Mine Eyes Have Seen the Glory,* 218.

14. See generally Krick, "Three Confederate Disasters on Oak Ridge," in Gallagher, ed., *The First Day at Gettysburg,* 124-35. One Federal account mentions O'Neal's "line of battle, covered by a cloud of busy skirmishers," advancing across Mummasburg Road; see Vautier, "At Gettysburg," *Philadelphia Press,* November 10, 1886.

15. Trudeau, "5th Alabama Sharpshooters"; Blackford, *Mine Eyes Have Seen the Glory,* 218.

16. Trudeau, "5th Alabama Sharpshooters."

17. Ibid.; Blackford, *Mine Eyes Have Seen the Glory,* 218.

18. "Historical Sketch of the Forty-fifth"; Trudeau, "5th Alabama Sharpshooters."

19. Trudeau, "5th Alabama Sharpshooters"; Blackford, *Mine Eyes Have Seen the Glory,* 218; "Historical Sketch of the Forty-fifth."

20. Blackford, *Mine Eyes Have Seen the Glory,* 218.

21. Trudeau, "5th Alabama Sharpshooters."

22. Ibid.

23. Ibid.

24. Ibid.

25. Ibid.

26. Ibid.

Chapter 9 – Manassas Gap

1. Blackford, *Mine Eyes Have Seen the Glory,* 221-2; Krick, "Three Confederate Disasters on Oak Ridge," in Gallagher, *The First Day at Gettysburg,* 137-8.

2. Blackford, *Mine Eyes Have Seen the Glory,* 221-2; Krick, "Three Confederate Disasters on Oak Ridge," in Gallagher, *The First Day at Gettysburg,* 137-8.

3. BD/M, 258-9.

4. *OR*, Ser. I, XXVII/2: 560.

5. BD/M, 260-2.

6. Ruth Silliker, ed., *The Rebel Yell and the Yankee Hurrah: The Civil War Journal of a Maine Volunteer, Private John W. Haley, 17th Maine Regiment* (Camden, ME: Down East Books, 1985), 112; *OR*, Ser. I, XXVII/1: 496.

7. *OR*, Ser. I, XXVII/2: 560-1.

8. Silliker, *Rebel Yell and Yankee Hurrah*, 114-5; *OR*, Ser. I, XXVII/2: 490. The Excelsior Brigade consisted of the 70th, 71st, 72nd, 73rd, and 74th New York.

9. *OR*, Ser. I, XXVII/2: 626; Blackford to My Dear Mary [Blackford], August 4, 1863, Blackford letters, USAMHI.

10. *OR*, Ser. I, XXVII/2: 449, 598.

11. For Confederate casualties see Rodes and Andrews reports at *OR*, Ser. I, XXVII/2: 560-1, 627; for Union casualties see *OR*, Ser. I, XXVII/1: 192; C. Russell White, ed., *The Civil War Diary of Wyman S. White, First Sergeant of Company F, 2nd United States Sharpshooter Regiment, 1861-1865* (Baltimore: Butternut and Blue, 1993), 337; Ripley, *A History of Company F*, 128-9.

12. *OR*, Ser. I, XXVII/2: 626; For Union casualties at Wapping Heights see *OR*, Ser. I, XXVII/1: 192; Silliker, *Rebel Yell and Yankee Hurrah*, 115.

13. BD/M, 263-5. In Blackford to My Dear Mary, August 4, 1863, Blackford Letters, USAMHI, Blackford gives a slightly less dramatic account, saying that he ran into a friendly cavalry vidette who told him of the Yankees in the gap.

14. BD/M, 265.

Chapter 10 – Winter 1863-64

1. BD/M, 268-9.

2. BD/M, 270-1.

3. BD/M, 272-3.

4. BD/M, 268-69.

5. BD/M, 274-5; Jeremiah Tate to sister, November 1, 1863, Jeremiah Tate letters, GLI.

6. BD/M, 274-5.

7. *OR*, Ser. I, XXIX/1: 365, 367.

8. BD/M, 277-9.

9. Ibid.

10. Ibid.

11. BD/M, 280; Eugene Blackford to mother, October 15, 1863, Gordon-Blackford Papers, MHS.

12. Thomas Francis Galwey, *The Valiant Hours: A Narrative of "Captain Brevet," an Irish-American in the Army of the Potomac* (Harrisburg, PA: Stackpole Books, 1961), 170; *OR*, Ser. I, XXIX/1: 731-3.

13. *OR*, Ser. I, XXIX/1: 876-7, 879, 887-8; Nat [Jacob Nathaniel Raymer, pseud.], "From the 4th North Carolina," *Salisbury Carolina Watchman*, December 5, 1863; Jeremiah Tate to sister, December 10, 1863, Jeremiah Tate letters, GLI.

14. Park, "Diary," November 6-7, 1864.

15. *OR*, Ser. I, XXIX/1: 730-1; Galwey, *Valiant Hours*, 171.

16. Chappell, ed., *Dear Sister*, 177.

17. Galwey, *Valiant Hours*, 171-2.

18. Jeremiah Tate to sister, December 10, 1863, Jeremiah Tate letters, GLI.

19. Nat, "From the 4th North Carolina"; Ripley, *History of Company F*, 135. The division commander, General David Birney, also included the 3rd Maine and the 124th Pennsylvania in his extended skirmish line under the 3rd Maine's commander, Col. B. R. Pierce. *OR*, Ser. I, XXIX/1: 750.

20. Ripley *History of Company F*, 139-140.

21. Jeremiah Tate to sister, December 10, 1863, Jeremiah Tate letters, GLI.

22. Nat, "From the 4th North Carolina."

23. Ibid.

24. Jeremiah Tate to sister, December 10, 1863, Jeremiah Tate letters, GLI; Ripley, *History of Company F*, 140.

25. *OR*, Ser. I, XXIX/1: 680, 731-5, 876, 884.

26. Larry Tagg, *The Generals of Gettysburg: The Leaders of America's Greatest Battle* (New York: DaCapo, 1998). See excerpt online at http://www.rocemabra.com/~roger/tagg/generals/general13.html. Carroll lost an arm at Spotsylvania, which kept him out of the field for the rest of the war but won him a promotion to brigadier general.

Chapter 11 – Preparing for 1864

1. Dunlop, *Lee's Sharpshooters*, 11, 17. Despite diligent searching I have not been able to locate a copy of Lee's 1864 order. Although several writers refer to it no one actually quoted it or cited its number.

2. Dunlop, *Lee's Sharpshooters*, 17-8, 20-22. Although Dunlop represented himself as a major in his 1899 book, his service record does not reflect any promotions beyond the grade of captain. Lieutenant Caldwell gave slightly different numbers: "A detail of six commissioned officers, ten non-commissioned officers, and one hundred and sixty privates constituted the [sharpshooter] corps." Caldwell, *History of a Brigade of South Carolinians*, 172.

3. Jeffrey C. Lowe and Sam Hodges, eds., *Letters to Amanda: The Civil War Letters of Marion Hill Fitzpatrick, Army of Northern Virginia* (Macon, GA: Mercer University Press, 1998), 128-9.

4. Wilcox's April 2 order and a circular dated April 19, 1864, can be found in James A. Englehard Papers, AC No. 00-272, Georgia Dept. of Archives and History; Lowe and Hodges, eds., *Letters to Amanda*, 141.

5. Chappell, ed., *Dear Sister*, 193, Jeremiah Tate to sister, April 17, 1864, GLI.

6. The Third Georgia Sharpshooters have been discussed in Chapter 7. Dickert, *History of Kershaw's Brigade*, 225, says that the Third South Carolina battalion had been augmented "by one man from each company in the brigade."

7. Young, "A Campaign with the Sharpshooters"; Dunlop, *Lee's Sharpshooters*, 11-12; John E. Laughton, "The Sharpshooters of Mahone's Brigade," *SHSP* 22 (1894); James Alexander Milling (1846-1916), 3rd South Carolina Infantry Battalion "Jim Milling and the War" mss. in possession of the author, 4 .

8. Jeremiah Tate to sister, January 1, 1864, GLI.

9. Russell C. White, ed., *The Civil War Diary of Wyman S. White, First Sergeant of Company F, 2nd United States Sharpshooter Regiment, 1861-1865* (Baltimore: Butternut and Blue, 1993), 24-5.

10. Ibid.

11. BD/M, 281-2.

12. Jeremiah Tate to sister, April 17, 1864, GLI. See also Paddy Griffith, *Battle Tactics of the Civil War* (New Haven: Yale University Press, 1989). The average figure is based on three army corps of three divisions, with each division having four infantry brigades. If each sharpshooter battalion numbered around 200 men, this would equal 7,200 men, or between 10 and 15 percent of the army's strength. The composition of the army varied somewhat during the course of the campaign, and it is not entirely clear whether units that joined it in the later stages of the campaign (e.g. Breckinridge's division) had such organizations.

Chapter 12 – The Wilderness

1. BD/M, 283-4; Battle, "The Third Alabama Regiment," 98-9; J. W. Williams, "Company D at the Battle of the Wilderness," *Greensboro Record*, July 2, 1903.

2. BD/M, 284.

3. Ibid. Some North Carolinians from Steuart's brigade eventually recovered them early the next morning.

4. Ibid.

5. Dunlop, *Lee's Sharpshooters*, 28-30.

6. Susan Benson, ed., *Berry Benson's Civil War Book: Memoirs of a Confederate Scout and Sharpshooter* (Athens: University of Georgia Press, 1992), 61-2. Captain Dunlop, on the other hand, says that the sharpshooters "went into action on the left" (Dunlop, *Lee's Sharpshooters*, 30), so it is possible that the sharpshooters were divided into two "corps" with one on the left and one on the right. White, ed., *The Civil War Diary of Wyman S. White*, 227.

7. Benson, ed., *Berry Benson's Civil War Book*, 63; Gordon Rhea, *The Battle of the Wilderness, May 5-6, 1864* (Baton Rouge: Louisiana State University Press, 1994), 238.

8. Benson, ed., *Berry Benson's Civil War Book*, 63-4.

9. Ibid.

10. White, ed., *Civil War Diary of Wyman S. White*, 228-30.

11. Ibid.

12. IX Corps had four divisions, one of which (Ferrero's) had been left to guard the baggage train, and another (Stevenson's) had been left near Wilderness Tavern on Grant's orders. Thus for this operation Burnside had two divisions, those of Generals Robert Potter and Orlando Willcox, available to him.

13. Raymond J. Herek, *These Men Have Seen Hard Service: The First Michigan Sharpshooters in the Civil War* (Detroit: Wayne State University Press, 1998), 118-9.

14. Ibid.; White, ed., *Civil War Diary of Wyman S. White*, 250.

15. Herek, *These Men Have Seen Hard Service*, 118; Leon, *Diary of a Tarheel*, 73.

16. *OR*, Ser. I, XXXVI/1: 906, 907, 1081.

17. Newsom E. Jenkins memoir, NCDAH; Jenkins was sergeant major of the Fourteenth North Carolina; *OR*, Ser. I, XXXVI/1: 965, 966, 972, 1081.

18. Jenkins memoir, NCDAH; Herek, *These Men Have Seen Hard Service*, 121-2; W. A. Smith, *The Anson Guards: Company "C," Fourteenth Regiment North Carolina Volunteers, 1861-1865* (Charlotte, NC: Stone Publishing, 1914), 235; R. T. Bennett, "Fourteenth Regiment," in Clark, ed., *Histories of the Several Regiments and Battalions from North Carolina, in the Great War 1861-65*, 1:46.

19. Herek, *These Men Have Seen Hard Service*, 121-2; *OR*, Ser. I, XXXVI/1: 972, 973.

20. Young, "A Campaign with the Sharpshooters," *Philadelphia Weekly Times*, January 26, 1878.

21. Benson, ed., *Berry Benson's Civil War Book*, 67.

Chapter 13 – Spotsylvania

1. Gregory A. Mertz, "General Gouverneur K. Warren and the Fighting at Laurel Hill During the Battle of Spotsylvania Court House, May 1864," *Blue and Gray* (Summer 2004): 16.

2. Milling, "Jim Milling and the War," 5.

3. Dickert, *History of Kershaw's Brigade*, 357-8; John Coxe, "Last Struggles and Successes of Lee," *Confederate Veteran* 22 (1914): 357; Mertz, "General Gouverneur K. Warren," 17, 19.

4. Mertz, "General Gouverneur K. Warren," 17, 19; Milling, "Jim Milling and the War," 5; John C. Haskell, *The Haskell Memoirs* (New York: G. P. Putnam, 1960), 67-8. Potts, along with half his men, perished in the engagement.

5. Dickert, *History of Kershaw's Brigade*, 357-8.

6. Milling, "Jim Milling and the War," 5.

7. Ibid.

8. Mertz, "General Gouverneur K. Warren," 17, 19; *OR*, Ser. 1, XXXVI/1: 581, 594, 597, 602. See also Gordon Rhea, *The Battles for Spotsylvania Court House and the Road to Yellow Tavern, May 7-12, 1864* (Baton Rouge: Louisiana State University Press, 1997), 53-64. Robinson's division was so badly mauled that it was broken up.

9. Milling, "Jim Milling and the War," 5-6; Frank Williams Jr., ed., "From Sumter to the Wilderness: Letters of Sgt. James Butler Suddath, Co. E, 7th Regiment, S.C.V." *South Carolina Historical Magazine* LXIII (1962), 77; Rhea, *Battles for Spotsylvania Court House*, 64, 70-1; Alan Nevins, ed., *A Diary of Battle: The Personal Journals of Colonel Charles S. Wainwright, 1861-1865* (New York: Harcourt and Brace, 1962), 357, 359.

10. Rhea, *Battles for Spotsylvania Court House*, 66, n 57.

11. James W. Roberts, "The Wilderness and Spotsylvania, May 4-12, 1864," *Quarterly Periodical of the Florida Historical Society* 11 (October 1932): 65-6; J. M. Thompson, "Reminiscences of the Autauga Rifles" Sixth Alabama regimental file, ADAH, 9; J. W. Williams, "Battles around the Bloody Angle," *Greensboro Record*, July 30, 1903.

12. Williams, "Battles around the Bloody Angle."

13. Ibid.

14. Ibid.; Roberts, "The Wilderness and Spotsylvania, May 4-12, 1864," 65-6.

15. Young, "A Campaign with the Sharpshooters."

16. Benson, ed., *Berry Benson's Civil War Book*, 68.

17. Young, "A Campaign with the Sharpshooters"; Dickert, *History of Kershaw's Brigade*, 358.

18. Young, "A Campaign with the Sharpshooters."

19. Dickert, *History of Kershaw's Brigade*, 375-6.

20. Dunlop, *Lee's Sharpshooters*, 45.

21. Robert Stiles, *Four Years under Marse Robert* (New York: Neale Publishing, 1904), 301.

22. "Sharpshooting in Lee's Army," *Confederate Veteran* 3, No. 4 (1895): 98.

23. Rhea, *Battles for Spotsylvania Court House*, 213; Ruth Silliker, ed., *The Rebel Yell and the Yankee Hurrah: The Civil War Journal of a Maine Volunteer, Private John W. Haley, 17th Maine Regiment* (Camden, ME: Down East Books, 1985), 153.

24. Berry Benson, "How General Sedgwick Was Killed," *Confederate Veteran* 26 (1918): 115-116. No one knows exactly how many Whitworths the ANV had. Berry Benson states that his battalion had two; others claim two or four was the usual number, and some more. A good estimate for the army is probably sixty to seventy-five guns, based on a distribution of one to two per sharpshooter battalion. For more on the Whitworth's accuracy, see Appendix A.

25. Alanson A. Haines, *History of the Fifteenth Regiment New Jersey Volunteers,* (New York: Privately published, 1883) 161; Martin McMahon, "The Death of General John Sedgwick," *B&L* 4:175; Stuart Vogt, "The Death of Major General John Sedgwick, U.S.A., May 9th 1864," FSNMP.

26. Martin McMahon, "The Death of General John Sedgwick."

27. Martin McMahon, "The Death of General John Sedgwick."

28. Melvin Jones, ed., *Give God the Glory: Memoirs of a Civil War Soldier* (Rev. ed., Eagle River, MI: privately published, 1997), 68-9. In his diary (cited above) Private Simon Cummins of the 151st New York confirms the circumstances of Sedgwick's death, including the use of the phrase "could not hit an elephant."

29. Benson, "How General Sedgwick Was Killed," 115-116; Henry W. Thomas, *History of the Doles-Cook Brigade, Army of Northern Virginia* (Atlanta: Franklin Publishing, 1903), 76; V. M. Fleming, "How General Sedgwick Was Killed," *Confederate Veteran* 16 (1908): 347; Thomas A. Prideaux, "The Killing of General Sedgwick," *Confederate Veteran* 26 (1918): 197. See generally Rhea, *Battles for Spotsylvania Court House*, 96 n. 21, and the monograph by NPS historian Stuart Vogt, "The Death of Major General John Sedgwick, U.S.A., May 9th 1864," FSNMP. Powell also claimed to have killed Sedgwick in a 1907 letter to his wife (Ben Powell to his wife, November 21, 1907, BV 200, FSNMP). Another obvious candidate was Oscar Cheatham, although he never made a claim to that effect. Given the distinctive "shrill whistle" of the round, it most likely came from a Whitworth, although at five hundred yards it was well within the range of the less powerful Enfield. One last aspirant is "Kansas Tom" Johnson, of Company E, Tenth Georgia, who was described as being one of "a band of sharpshooters composed of the best shots in the [First] corps." Johnson was killed a few days later, leaving no account of his exploit. However, since the incident occurred in the First Corps area, he remains a possibility. A. J. McBride, "Tenth Georgia at Spotsylvania," *Atlanta Journal*, July 20, 1901.

30. Rhea, *Battles for Spotsylvania Court House*, 96; Dunlop, *Lee's Sharpshooters*, 54.

31. Dunlop, *Lee's Sharpshooters*, 54; Dickert, *Kershaw's Brigade*, 358; John W. Bone, "Civil War Reminiscences," 50, Lowery Shuford Collection, NCDAH.

32. Dunlop, *Lee's Sharpshooters*, 54; Young, "Campaign with the Sharpshooters,"; Laughton, "The Sharpshooters of Mahone's Brigade," 101.

33. Captain Watkins Phelan of the Third Alabama, who had previously commanded the sharpshooters when Blackford was on furlough, had also been wounded.

34. William H. Hastings, ed., *Letters from a Sharpshooter: The Civil War Letters of William B. Greene, Co. G, Berdan's Sharpshooters* (Belleville, WI: Historic Publications, 1993), 207.

35. Bone, "Civil War Reminiscences," 19. Bone survived his wound and was back in the ranks by fall.

36. "Our Army Correspondence," *Mobile Advertiser & Register*, June 1, 1864; Dunlop, *Lee's Sharpshooters*, 64, 70.

37. John H. Worsham, *One of Jackson's Foot Cavalry: His Experience and What He Saw during the War 1861-1865, Including a History of "F Company," Richmond, Va., 21st Regiment Virginia Infantry, Second Brigade, Jackson's Division, Second Corps, A. N. Va.* (New York: Neale Publishing, 1912), 215. It is also possible that the sharpshooter in question was from Perrin's Alabama brigade, which was also in the vicinity.

38. "Lane's Corps of Sharpshooters," *SHSP* 28 (1900): 27.

39. White, ed., *Civil War Diary of Wyman S. White*, 248.

40. Dunlop, *Lee's Sharpshooters*, 71; Benson, ed., *Berry Benson's Civil War Book*, 71-4.

41. Lowe and Hodges, eds., *Letters to Amanda*, 144-6.

42. Benson, ed., *Berry Benson's Civil War Book*, 78-80. Although Benson mistakenly states that Sweitzer had actually lived in the South, his biographical sketch (*Biographical Encyclopaedia of Pennsylvania of the 19th Century* (1874), 646, 647.) gives the details of his capture and incarceration at Libby prison.

43. For a general account of the action at Harris's Farm see Gordon Rhea, *To the North Anna River: Grant and Lee, May 13-25, 1864* (Baton Rouge: Louisiana State University Press, 2000), 170-86.

Chapter 14 – The North Anna and Cold Harbor

1. Patrick McDonald, *Opportunities Lost, The Battle of Cold Harbor,* unpublished but available online at http://www.civilwarhome.com/coldharborsummary.htm; William H. Hastings, ed., *Letters from a Sharpshooter: The Civil War Letters of William B. Greene, Co. G, Berdan's Sharpshooters* (Belleville, WI: Historical Publications, 1993), 207. The former division commander, General Hobart Ward, had been relieved at Spotsylvania for drunkenness and was eventually cashiered.

2. Ripley, *A History of Company F,* 168.

3. Ibid., 169; Milling, "Jim Milling and the War," 7. The term "globe sight" here is an indefinite one. Technically it refers to a globe and post sight, i.e. a hooded iron sight mounted near the muzzle. However, a speaker of the day may have been referring to the four power Davidson telescopic sight mounted on the Whitworth. Longstreet may have had a separate corps of sharpshooters at corps level armed with Whitworth or similar rifles; see chapter 22.

4. Hastings, ed., *Letters from a Sharpshooter,* 210-1.

5. Dunlop, *Lee's Sharpshooters,* 81.

6. Lowe and Hodges, eds., *Letters to Amanda,* 147

7. Ibid., 148.

8. Dunlop, *Lee's Sharpshooters,* 82.

9. John Laughton, "The Sharpshooters of Mahone's Brigade," *SHSP* 22 (1894): 102-103; Sypher, *History of the Pennsylvania Reserve Corps,* 542. British rifle regiments in the Napoleonic wars had used a similar procedure with two-man sections.

10. Laughton, "The Sharpshooters of Mahone's Brigade," *SHSP* 22 (1894): 103.

11. Laughton, "The Sharpshooters of Mahone's Brigade," *SHSP* 22 (1894): 103; Sypher, *History of the Pennsylvania Reserve Corps,* 542.

12. C. A. Stevens, *Berdan's U.S. Sharpshooters in the Army of the Potomac, 1861-1865* (St. Paul, MN: Price-McGill, 1892), 434.

13. Michael J. Miller, *The North Anna Campaign: "Even to Hell Itself"* (Lynchburg, VA: H. E. Howard, 1989), 101-103

14. See generally Gordon Rhea, *To the North Anna River: Grant and Lee, May 13-25, 1864* (Baton Rouge: Louisiana State University Press, 2000), 338-41.

15. Rhea, *To the North Anna,* 338-41; Charles N. Walker and Rosemary Walker, eds., "Diary of the War by Rob't S. Robertson," *Old Fort News* Vol. 28, No. 4 (October-December 1965), 195.

16. Stevens, *Berdan's U.S. Sharpshooters,* 434-7.

17. Miller, *The North Anna Campaign,* 111-3; Walker and Walker, eds., "Diary of the War by Rob't S. Robertson," 195. Thomas S. Kenan, *Sketch of the Forty-third Regiment of North Carolina Troops (Infantry),* (CD-ROM, Clearwater, SC: Eastern Digital Resources, 2003), 23.

18. John Day Smith, *The History of the Nineteenth Regiment of Maine Volunteer Infantry, 1862-1865* (Minneapolis, MN: Great Western Printing, 1909), 177-8.

19. Whether Blackford, who had assumed command of the Fifth Alabama at Spotsylvania, was with Battle's sharpshooters is unknown, since few Confederate accounts of the action have survived.

20. Stevens, *Berdan's U.S. Sharpshooters,* 435-6; and generally Miller, *North Anna Campaign,* 111-3.

21. Cary Whitaker diary entry, May 24, 1864, Cary Whitaker Papers, 767-z, SHC; Kenan, *Sketch of the Forty-third North Carolina,* 24; Miller, *North Anna Campaign,* 114-5.

22. Evander Law, "From the Wilderness to Cold Harbor," *B&L* IV:136-37.

23. Galwey, *Valiant Hours,* 225.

24. Miller, *North Anna Campaign,* 116-8; Keele got a Medal of Honor for his deeds that day, as did Lieutenant Colonel Michael Murphy, commander of the 170th New York.

25. Galwey, *Valiant Hours,* 225.

26. John G. B. Adams, *Reminiscences of the Nineteenth Massachusetts Regiment* (Boston: Wright, Potter Printing, 1899), 96.

27. Pulaski Cowper, ed., *Extracts of Letters of Major-Gen'l Bryan Grimes, to His Wife: Written While in Active Service in the Army of Northern Virginia. Together with Some Personal Recollections of the War, Written by Him after its Close, etc.* (Raleigh, NC: E. Broughton, 1883), 56; T. T. Greene to Eliza Skinner, May 25, 1864, Greene family papers, VHS.

28. Charles A. Dana, *Recollections of the Civil War* (Lincoln, NE: University of Nebraska Press 1996), 203; *OR*, Ser. I, XXXVI/1: 67.

29. D. P. Marshall, *Company K, 155th Pa Volunteer Zouaves* (N.p., 1888), 164, quoted in Rhea, *To the North Anna*, 355; Richard Coutre, ed. *Charlie's Letters: The Correspondence of Charles E. DeNoon*, (N.p.: Privately published, 1982), 222.

30. Hastings, ed., *Letters from a Sharpshooter*, 213; Miller, *North Anna Campaign*, 126, 132, 133.

31. A. J. McBride, "Tenth Georgia at Spottsylvania," *Atlanta Journal*, July 20, 1901; Miller, *North Anna Campaign*, 126.

32. *OR*, Ser. I, XXXVI/3: 68; Miller, *North Anna Campaign*, 136.

33. Stevens, *Berdan's U.S. Sharpshooters*, 438-9.

34. Walker and Walker, eds., "Diary of the War by Rob't S. Robertson," 196.

35. Smith, *History of the Nineteenth Regiment of Maine Volunteer Infantry*, 179; Union colonel Augustus C. Hamlin quoted in Henry W. Thomas, *History of the Doles-Cook Brigade, Army of Northern Virginia* (Atlanta: Franklin Publishing, 1903), 4.

36. Rhea, *To the North Anna*, 443 n. 65.

37. *OR*, Ser. I, XXXVI/1: 67; Miller, *North Anna Campaign*, 138. See also William F. Fox, *Regimental Losses in the Civil War* (Albany, NY: Albany Publishing, 1889).

38. *OR Supp.*, Vol. 36 (Ser. 67-68): 661. Jim Milling says that the sharpshooters of the Third South Carolina battalion were placed on the flank. See Milling, "Jim Milling and the War," 8.

39. A. Du Bois, "Cold Harbor Salient," *SHSP* 30 (1902): 278. Du Bois was in the 7th New York Heavy Artillery serving as infantry.

40. Dickert, *History of Kershaw's Brigade*, 377, 378.

41. Ibid.

42. Thomas Taylor to his sister, April 7, 1864, letter in possession of the author, available online at http://rootsweb.com/~alhenry/6th/letters/taylor10.htm; J. M. Thompson, "Reminiscences of the Autauga Rifles," Sixth Alabama regimental file, 9.

43. Agassiz, ed., *With Grant and Meade*, 247; *OR Supp.*, Vol. 36 (Ser. 67-68): 647.

44. Robert Stiles, *Four Years under Marse Robert* (New York: Neale Publishing, 1904), 302-3.

45. Laughton, "The Sharpshooters of Mahone's Brigade" 103.

Chapter 15 – Monocacy and Fort Stevens

1. Emil and Ruth Rosenblatt, eds., *Hard Marching Every Day: The Civil War Letters of Private Wilbur Fisk, 1861-1865* (Lawrence: University Press of Kansas, 1983), 250. Fisk was a member of the 2nd Vermont.

2. Marcus Herring "General Rodes at Winchester" *Confederate Veteran* 38: 184.

3. Blackford, *Mine Eyes Have Seen the Glory*, 236; Susan Leigh Blackford, *Letters from Lee's Army, or, Memoirs of Life In and Out of the Army in Virginia During the War Between the States* (1896. Reprint, Lynchburg, VA: Warwick House Publishing, 1996) II 256, 263.

4. For a detailed study of the strength of Jubal Early's Army of the Valley, see the appendices in Theodore C. Mahr, *The Battle of Cedar Creek: Showdown in the Shenandoah, October 1-13, 1864* (Lynchburg, VA: H. E. Howard, 1992). For a closer look at Early's cavalry and its problems, see Robert K. Krick, "The Cause of All My Disasters," in *The Smoothbore Volley that Doomed the Confederacy: The Death of Stonewall Jackson and Other Chapters on the Army of Northern* Virginia (Baton Rouge: Louisiana State University Press, 2002), 185-213. After consulting many unpublished sources, ranger Gloria Swift and volunteer researcher Gail Stephens at Monocacy National Battlefield estimated Early's overall strength just prior to the battle at slightly more than sixteen thousand men of all arms (personal communication with Swift and Stephens).

5. Colonel Allison "Ally" L. Brown had previously served as an NCO in the 73rd Ohio and as a captain in the 89th Ohio, according to Jim Leeke, ed., *A Hundred Days to Richmond: Ohio's "Hundred Days" Men in the Civil War* (Bloomington: Indiana University Press, 1999), 119. Brown's numbers are from his official report, *OR*, Ser. I, XXXVII/1: 216; Leib's are in Leeke, ed., *Hundred Days*, 240 n. 28.

6. *OR*, Ser. I, XXXVII/1: 216, 221.

7. B. Franklin Cooling, *Monocacy: The Battle That Saved Washington* (Shippensburg, PA: White Mane Publishing, 2000) 157-8

8. *OR*, Ser. I XXXVII/1: 216-9; Leeke, ed., *Hundred Days*, 125, 126.

9. *OR*, Ser. I, XXXVII/1: 191, 200, 213, 214, 216, 221; Frances H. Kennedy, ed., *The Civil War Battlefield Guide*, 2nd ed. (Boston: Houghton Mifflin, 1998), 505-8; Park, "The Twelfth Alabama Infantry," 265. See also generally B. Franklin Cooling, *Monocacy: The Battle That Saved Washington* chaps. 4, 5, and B. Franklin Cooling, *Jubal Early's Raid on Washington, 1864* (Baltimore, MD: Nautical & Aviation Publishing, 1989), chap. 3.

10. Leeke, ed., *Hundred Days*, 238 n 14, 239 n 17; Jubal A. Early, *Autobiographical Sketch and Narrative of the War Between the States* (Philadelphia: J. B. Lippincott, 1912), 387-8. Early merely notes that Rodes's division was "covering the roads from Baltimore and the crossings of the Monocacy above the Junction."

11. J. A. Early, "The Advance on Washington in 1864" *SHSP* 9 (1881) 306. Leeke, ed., *Hundred Days*, 130, 131. The Sixty-second Virginia Mounted Infantry was part of Brigadier General John Imboden's brigade, which at the time (Imboden being ill) was commanded by Colonel George Smith. A June 23 report lists its strength as 207 effectives (277 aggregate), and in an 1881 letter Early put their numbers at "about two hundred strong." A reasonable estimate of its strength at Ft. Stevens would be 200 to 250 men, of which a quarter would have been detailed to hold the horses during the advance. Having been on a raid, Imboden-Smith's brigade had missed Monocacy and so was relatively fresh. See James Eldridge, *Field Return of the Regiments, Battalions &c of the different Brigades of the 1st & 2nd Divisions*, June 23, 1864, Box #7, James Eldridge Collection, Huntington Library; Roger U. Delauter, *62nd Virginia Infantry* (Lynchburg, VA: H. E. Howard, 1988), 37-8

12. *OR*, Ser. I, XXXVII/1: 231, 245; William B. Styple, ed., *Writing and Fighting the Civil War: Soldier Correspondence to the New York Sunday Mercury* (Kearny, NJ: Bell Grove Publishing, 2000), 270-1; J. C. Featherston, "Gen. Jubal Anderson Early," *Confederate Veteran* 26 (1899) p. 431. The 25th New York Cavalry (Sickles Cavalry) had been slowly raised, company by company, from January through October 1864, and in July still fielded only 7 companies. Frederick H. Dyer, *A Compendium of the War of the Rebellion* (Des Moines, IA: Dyer Publishing, 1908), part 3, p. 1, 382; According to a report made June 20, the command numbered twenty officers and 386 men, but another filed just five days later gave its strength as eighteen officers and 293 men. One of their officers, Captain S. E. Chamberlain, estimated in a postwar article that the regiment had five hundred men present on July 11. *OR*, Ser. I XXXVI/3: 783, 793; Smith D. Fry, "Two Critical Periods: The Capture of Washington in 1861 or 1864 Would Have Resulted in Foreign Recognition of the Southern Confederacy," *National Tribune Scrap Book*, n.d., USAMHI

13. Early, "The Advance on Washington in 1864" *SHSP* 9 (1881) 306; Cary Whitaker diary entry, July 11, 1864, SHC. Whitaker noted "during the day saw the dome of the Capital"; Francis Marion Calhoun obituary, *Confederate Veteran* 37 (1929) 307.

14. Kennedy, *Civil War Battlefield Guide*, 505-8; Fry, "Two Critical Periods"; Early, *Autobiographical Sketch*, 390-5 and "The Advance on Washington in 1864" *SHSP* 9 (1881) 306; *OR*, Ser. I, XXXVII/1: 348-9; *OR*, Ser. I, XXXVII/1: 231; Early's estimation of his effective strength that afternoon was probably reasonably close. An NCO in Ramseur's division wrote home that his men were "worn out," and that out of seventy-eight men in his company, only thirty-seven were present that afternoon. Weymouth T. Jordan, ed., *North Carolina Troops, 1861-1865: A Roster* (Raleigh: North Carolina Office of Archives and History, 1966-), 13:219 n 219. Just who made those clouds of dust has been the subject of some speculation. The VI Corps was just then debarking at Alexandria and did not arrive until around 4 p.m. Cooling suggests that the dustmakers were the dismounted cavalry detachment under Major George Briggs, which arrived after the New Yorkers. In a July 18 article in the *New York Sunday Mercury*, "B.O.B." gives the 25th New York Cavalry casualties for both days as nine killed and seventeen wounded. Styple, *Writing and Fighting the Civil War*, 270-1.

15. *OR*, Ser. I, XXXVII/1: 241, 242, 344. Colonel George Gile had been the commander of the 88th Pennsylvania until he was severely wounded at Antietam and transferred to the Veteran Reserve Corps. His brigade consisted of four Veteran Reserve regiments totaling probably one thousand to twelve hundred men, scattered between the Rockville Pike and Fort Stevens. Gile's report is both self-serving and difficult to decipher. He makes incredible claims of advances made by his men, but these are hard to credit considering that he suffered only a dozen casualties.

16. *OR*, Ser. I, XXXVII/1: 231, 265, 272-3, 275-6, 602; David B. Swinfen, *Ruggles' Regiment: The 122nd New York Volunteers in the American Civil War* (Hanover, NH: University Press of New England, 1982), 50; Cooling, *Jubal Early's Raid*, 124-5; Thomas Kenan, "Forty-third Regiment," in Clark, *Histories of the Several Regiments*, 3:13; Hubbs, *Voices from Company D*, 299. Colonel Thomas Kenan of the Forty-third North Carolina stated that the sharpshooters advanced to within two hundred yards and then pulled back three hundred, which tallies very well with Federal estimates of the skirmish lines being five hundred to six hundred yards from the fort, where it remained until the next afternoon. The Federals claimed to have driven the regiment back, but Kenan makes claim for a voluntary movement, adding that "in the afternoon the enemy threw forward a heavy line of skirmishers, who attacked vigorously, but were repulsed with some loss" (Clark, ibid.). Two hundred yards was rather close to the big guns of the forts, and even when considerably further back Kenan says they were "subjected to a severe shelling."

17. Blackford, *Mine Eyes Have Seen the Glory*, 257. There would be plenty of second-guessing both then and later as to whether Old Jube could have taken Washington. For a roundup of opinions pro and con, see Cooling, *Jubal Early's Raid*, chap. 9. Two recently discovered letters reveal that Lee and Early had indeed discussed

the capture of Washington, and that Early was to take it "if I find an opportunity"; Jubal Early to R. E. Lee, June 28, 1864, Civil War Collection, Huntington Library.

18. L. E. Chittenden, *Recollections of President Lincoln and His Administration* (New York: Harper and Brothers, 1891), 414-5; Lucius Chittenden ms. in the author's possession.

19. OR, Ser. I, XXXVII/1: 232, 242, 275; Frank Vandiver, *Jubal's Raid: General Early's Famous Raid on Washington in 1864* (New York: McGraw-Hill, 1960), 169; Park, "The Twelfth Alabama Infantry," 266; Walker, *Vermont Brigade,* 27-31. The two prominent dwellings referred to in the OR and elsewhere are marked on the map as the Rives (or Reeve) and Carberry houses. Mr. Lay resided in the Carberry house. The other "knoll" appears to be the rise west of Rock Creek northwest of Fort DeRussy on which sat the Titman and Pilling houses.

20. Park, "The Twelfth Alabama Infantry," 266-7; Cooling, *Jubal Early's Raid,* 125-6, 140-5; "The Fort Stephens Fight – The Sixth Corps Comes to the Relief of Washington" *Fayetteville (New York) Weekly Recorder,* July 19, 1888; Swinfen, *Ruggles' Regiment,* 51. According to the precise survey conducted by Fort Stevens artillerymen, the Lay mansion stood 1,078 yards from the parapet—a long shot, but certainly possible for a Whitworth rifle with a telescopic sight (OR, Ser. I, XXXVII/1: 246). Just who said what to Lincoln, as well as what his exact words and actions were and who in his party, are the subject of much speculation and postwar memory. For details see Cooling, *Jubal Early's Raid,* chap. 5.

21. OR, Ser. I, XXXVII/1 p. 232, 242, 275; Walker, *Vermont Brigade,* 27-31. Captain Beattie's unit first appears in official reports just after Cold Harbor, where some writers called it "division sharpshooters" and others simply a "detachment." Getty continued to use this sharpshooter company throughout the war, as did some other Union divisions. See Chapter 24 for more information on these units.

22. Styple, *Writing and Fighting the Civil War,* 270-1.

23. OR, Ser. I, XXXVII/1: 234; Walker, *Vermont Brigade,* 27-33; Leeke, ed., *Hundred Days,* 242 n. 18. Given the straggling, his losses on the campaign and at Monocacy, and the fact that a considerable portion of his cavalry (some fifteen hundred men under General Bradley Johnson) was detached on a raid, Early's army at Washington probably numbered around thirteen thousand men, of which between ten thousand and eleven thousand were infantry. The Federals now had two divisions of VI Corps (the third, Ricketts's, had retreated to Baltimore with Wallace) and parts of one division of XIX Corps on hand, plus some twenty thousand second-line garrison troops of various descriptions. This does not count the armies of Hunter and Sigel (twenty-eight thousand) still in the Valley. In a letter to Grant on July 26, Major General Henry Halleck estimated the strength of VI Corps at "a little over 11,000" and the combined strength of VI Corps, XIX Corps (one division), and attached cavalry at nineteen thousand men. (OR, Ser. I, XL/3: 457) Subtracting Ricketts's division, but adding the eleven hundred dismounted cavalry (the 25th New York cavalry plus the "scratch" brigade under Maj. George Briggs, both of which were available July 11-12), and allowing that the XIX Corps troops then on hand probably numbered no more than a thousand, the total number of Union soldiers available on July 12 in Washington would have been around thirty thousand men, or almost 2½ to Early's 1. For a detailed look at the strength of the Washington garrison, see Cooling, *Jubal Early's Raid,* 275-9.

24. OR, Ser. I, XXXVII/1: 275; Walker, *Vermont Brigade,* 27-33

25. Cooling, *Jubal Early's Raid,* 145-50; Leeke, ed., *Hundred Days,* 136; Swinfen, *Ruggles' Regiment,* 51; OR, Ser. I, XXXVII/1: 276. Colonel Dwight often signed his columns as "D." See, for example, an 1864 letter printed in "Veteran's Column," *Fayetteville (New York) Weekly Recorder,* April 12, 1888.

26. Cary Whitaker diary entry, July 12, 1864, SHC; OR, Ser. I, XLIII/1: 602, 603. The Fifty-third North Carolina lost twenty-two men captured that day, most likely the ones in the cellar. Jordan, *NC Troops,* 13:37.

27. Swinfen, *Ruggles' Regiment,* 51; "War Reminiscences: Narrow Escape of Washington from Capture," July 3, 1890, and "Veteran's Column," February 12, 1891, *Fayetteville (New York) Weekly Recorder.*

28. Cary Whitaker diary entry, July 12, 1864, SHC; Hubbs, *Voices from Company D,* 300.

29. Swinfen, *Ruggles' Regiment,* 51; "War Reminiscences: Narrow Escape of Washington from Capture," *Fayetteville (New York) Weekly Recorder,* July 3, 1890. Scott is listed as having received a "slight contusion of right elbow" at Ft. Stevens, the only wound that fits with the description of the anonymous writer. In later years he was a prolific contributor to the *Weekly Recorder's* "Veteran's Column," in which this account appears.

30. OR, Ser. I, XXXVII/1: 275; "War Reminiscences: Narrow Escape of Washington from Capture," *Fayetteville (New York) Weekly Recorder,* July 3, 1890.

31. Park, "The Twelfth Alabama Infantry," 266-7; Henry Kyd Douglas, *I Rode with Stonewall* (Chapel Hill: University of North Carolina Press, 1960), 295; Leeke, ed., *Hundred Days,* 135; OR, Ser. I, XXXVII/1: 232, 349; Chittenden, *Recollections,* 417.

32. OR, Ser. I, XLIII/1: 602, 603; Hubbs, *Voices from Company D,* 300; Eugene Blackford to Mary Blackford Cooke, July 23, 1865, Gordon-Blackford papers, MHS. Colonel David Cowand's report, written in early March 1865, is one of the few contemporary tactical accounts of the action from the Southern side. It differs somewhat from John Winston's much later account in the *Philadelphia Weekly Times,* wherein Winston states that the

entire brigade charged the Federal line and drove it back. Winston, "A Spirited Campaign at Cedar Creek," *Philadelphia Weekly Times,* July 25, 1885.

33. Early, *Autobiographical Sketch,* 394; Douglas, *I Rode with Stonewall,* 295-6; "The Fort Stephens Fight: The Sixth Corps Comes to the Relief of Washington," *Fayetteville (New York) Weekly Recorder,* July 19, 1888.

34. Chittenden, *Recollections,* 419-21.

35. OR, Ser. I, XXXVII/1: 232; Cooling, *Jubal Early's Raid,* 151-4, "The Fort Stephens Fight: The Sixth Corps Comes to the Relief of Washington," *Fayetteville (New York) Weekly Recorder,* July 19, 1888, and "Veteran's Column," *Fayetteville (New York) Weekly Recorder,* April 12, 1888.

36. OR, Ser. I, XXXVII/1: 277; Cooling, *Jubal Early's Raid,* 149-50; Cary Whitaker diary entry, July 12, 1864, SHC; Jordan, *NC Troops* 13:37; Kennedy, *Civil War Battlefield Guide,* 506-8.

37. Leeke, ed., *Hundred Days,* 137.

Chapter 16 – Charles Town, Winchester, and Fisher's Hill

1. Joel McDiarmid diary entry, September 2, 1864, in Hubbs, ed., *Voices from Company D,* 310.

2. Hamilton A. Brown, "First Regiment," in Clark, ed., *Histories of the Several Regiments and Battalions From North Carolina,* 1:154; Thomas Parramore and F. Roy Johnson, *Before the Rebel Flag Fell* (Murfreesboro, NC: Johnson Publishing, 1965), 87. For a detailed, impartial look at Jubal Early's numbers, see Mahr, *Battle of Cedar Creek* Appendix II. Mahr estimates that for most of the campaign Early never had a force larger than fourteen thousand men, of which no more than ten thousand were infantry. The only exception was a brief period in late August and early September when he was reinforced with elements of First Corps (Kershaw's infantry division, Fitz Lee's cavalry division, and Cutshaw's artillery), which brought the Army of the Valley up to about twenty-one thousand men. For another look at the strength figures for the Army of the Valley, see Steven E. Newton, *Lost for the Cause: The Confederate Army in 1864* (Mason City, IA: Savas Publishing, 2000), 81-3. Swift and Stephens estimate Early's pre-Monocacy numbers at about sixteen thousand men, so allowing for his casualties at Monocacy and Fort Stevens (fifteen hundred to eighteen hundred men), as well as in the almost daily skirmishes, this tracks fairly well with Mahr's estimate. "Army of the Valley strength figures," report by Gail Stephens, Monocacy National Battlefield.

3. Early, *Autobiographical Sketch,* 407; Jedediah Hotchkiss, *Make Me a Map of the Valley: The Civil War Journal of Stonewall Jackson's Topographer,* ed. Archie P. McDonald (Dallas: Southern Methodist University Press, 1973), 222. Captain Benjamin Keller, "a handsome and daring young officer" of the Sixty-first Georgia, commanded Gordon's Sharpshooters until he was captured at Winchester on September 19. Pharris Deloach Johnson, ed., *Under the Southern Cross: Soldier Life with Gordon Bradwell and the Army of Northern Virginia* (Macon, GA: Mercer University Press, 1999) 233.

4. OR, Ser. 1, XLIII/1: 69; Early, *Autobiographical Sketch,* 407.

5. Walker, *Vermont Brigade,* 59; Tom Ledoux, ed., *Quite Ready to be Sent Somewhere: The Civil War Letters of Aldace Freeman Walker* (Victoria, BC: Trafford, 2003), 291.

6. Park, "The Twelfth Alabama Infantry," 274; Hotchkiss, *Make Me a Map,* 223-4; Walker, *Vermont Brigade,* 60-9.

7. Walker, *Vermont Brigade,* 60-9.

8. Cary Whitaker diary entry, August 21, 1864, SHC; OR, Ser. 1, XLIII/1: 604; Walker, *Vermont Brigade,* 60-9.

9. Walker, *Vermont Brigade,* 60-9; Hotchkiss, *Make Me a Map,* 224, OR Ser. 1,XLIII/1: 1025. The 11th Vermont, a heavy artillery unit serving as infantry, had been previously stationed at Fort Stevens. It was variously referred to as the First Artillery, the First Vermont Heavy Artillery, or simply as "the Heavies." At this point in the war it consisted of two large battalions (in effect, regiments), of which Walker commanded one.

10. Ibid.; Ledoux, *Quite Ready to be Sent Somewhere,* 291-2.

11. Early, *Autobiographical Sketch,* 409. Reinforced by Kershaw's infantry division and Cutshaw's artillery, Early fielded almost twenty-one thousand men—the strongest the Army of the Valley would ever be, but still just half the size of Sheridan's army.

12. Walker, *Vermont Brigade,* 60-9.

13. OR, Ser. 1, XLIII/1: 19-20; Walker, ibid. Ledoux, *Quite Ready to be Sent Somewhere,* 292.

14. Early, *Autobiographical Sketch,* 409; Hotchkiss, *Make Me a Map,* 223-4; OR, Ser. 1, XLIII/1: 603, 1002

15. OR, Ser. 1, XLIII/1: 61, 603; Rosenblatt and Rosenblatt, eds., *Hard Marching Every Day,* 263; James M. Garnett, "Diary of Captain James M. Garnett, Ordnance Officer, Rodes's Division, 2nd Corps, Army of Northern Virginia," *SHSP* 27 (1899), 2; Mary Givens Bryan, ed., *Letters of a Private in the Confederate Army: Jack Felder,* 128. By this time Bryan Grimes was back in command of his brigade, but left no report of the action. Colonel

David Cowand included a short description in his 1865 report. Grimes mentioned in a letter home that "I have had today a good many killed and wounded, we being in advance, but have not had all my command engaged." Cowper, ed., *Extracts of Letters of Major-Gen'l Bryan Grimes*, 62.

16. Rosenblatt and Rosenblatt, eds., *Hard Marching Every Day*, 254-5.

17. Ibid.

18. Park, "Diary," August 21-24, 1864.

19. Early, *Autobiographical Sketch*, 409; Park, "Diary," August 31, 1864.

20. Johnson, ed., *Under the Southern Cross*, 194.

21. Sam Collier to his parents, September 9-21, 1864, Sam Collier Papers, Folder #416, NCDAH; Jeffry D. Wert, *From Winchester to Cedar Creek: The Shenandoah Campaign of 1864* (Carlisle, PA: South Mountain Press, 1987; Mechanicsburg, PA: Stackpole Books, 1997), 55.

22. I. G. Bradwell, "Early's Valley Campaign, 1864," *Confederate Veteran* 28 (1920), 218-219.

23. Ibid.; John Gordon, *Reminiscences of the Civil War* (New York: Charles Scribner's Sons, 1904), 322.

24. Bradwell, "Early's Valley Campaign," 218-219; Park, "Diary," September 19, 1864; Collier to his parents, September 21, 1864, Sam Collier Papers, Folder #416, NCDAH.

25. G. W. Nichols, *A Soldier's Story of His Regiment and Incidentally of the Lawton–Gordon–Evans Brigade* (Kennesaw, GA: Continental Book, 1961), 185; John William De Forest, *A Volunteer's Adventures: A Union Captain's Record of the Civil War* (New Haven: Yale University Press, 1946), 177.

26. Marcus Herring, "General Rodes at Winchester," *Confederate Veteran* 38 (1920): 184.

27. Ibid.; J. L. Schaub, "Gen. Robert E. Rodes," *Confederate Veteran* 18 (1908): 269.

28. De Forest, *Volunteer's Adventures*, 190.

29. John Cowand and J. I. Metts, "Third Regiment," in Clark, ed., *Histories of the Several Regiments and Battalions From North Carolina*, 1:207.

30. Wert, *From Winchester to Cedar Creek*, 86, and generally 75-99. In general I have followed Wert in describing the battles of the 1864 Valley Campaign.

31. De Forest, *Volunteer's Adventures*, 180-1, 185-6.

32. Parramore and Johnson, *Before the Rebel Flag Fell*, 87; Collier to his parents, September 21, 1864, Sam Collier Papers, Folder #416, NCDAH; H. A. Brown to his mother, September 30, 1864, James B. Gordon papers, NCDAH; O. C. Whitaker to Robert Park, April 17, 1904, Twelfth Alabama regimental history file, ADAH; J. H. Kidd, *Riding with Custer: Recollections of a Cavalryman in the Civil War* (1908. Reprint, Lincoln: University of Nebraska Press, 1997), 391-3.

33. Kidd, *Riding with Custer*, 391-3. Accounts differ of when and where Patton was wounded. Family stories place it in the streets of Winchester.

34. Kidd, *Riding with Custer*, 391-3; Collier to his parents, September 21, 1864, Sam Collier Papers, Folder #416, NCDAH; *OR*, Ser. 1, XLIII/1: 124.

35. Gary W. Gallagher, *Stephen Dodson Ramseur: Lee's Gallant General* (Chapel Hill: University of North Carolina Press, 1985), 201 n. 103.

36. Walker, *Vermont Brigade*, 109-23.

37. Philip H. Sheridan, *Personal Memoirs of P. H. Sheridan: General United States Army* (New York: Charles L. Webster, 1888), 2:36. Few Confederate accounts of the fight at Flint Hill have survived, but the men there were almost certainly from one or more of Early's sharpshooter demi-brigades, and given the history of the campaign, it was most likely Rodes's Division Sharpshooters. Indeed, the one sharpshooter account of the action is that of Sergeant Joseph J. "Jack" Felder, Co. K, Fourth Georgia, which was part of Cook's brigade, Rodes's division (Bryan, ed., *Letters of a Private in the Confederate Army*, 130).

38. *OR*, Ser. 1, XLIII/1: 205, 248, 253-4, 263; Wert, *From Winchester to Cedar Creek*, 118.

39. *OR*, Ser. 1, XLIII/1: 152, 199; Bryan, ed., *Letters of a Private in the Confederate Army*, 130; Wert, *From Winchester to Cedar Creek*, 114; Walker, *Vermont Brigade*, 109-23.

40. Walker, *Vermont Brigade*, 109-23; *OR*, Ser. 1, XLIII/1: 152, 199.

41. Wert, *From Winchester to Cedar Creek*, 111-5; *OR*, Ser. 1, XLIII/1: 605. Brigadier General Bryan Grimes, who commanded the left hand infantry brigade on Early's line, spotted the flanking column but could not get his superiors to take action; Cowper, ed., *Extracts of Letters of Major-Gen'l Bryan Grimes*, 71. Artillerist Henry Robinson Berkeley also noted the column in his diary; Henry Robinson Berkeley, *Four Years in the Confederate Artillery: The Diary of Private Henry Robinson Berkeley*, ed. William H. Runge (Richmond: Virginia Historical Society, 1991), 99-100. Blackford's role in the rear guard is described by Captain Rinaldo Green, who commanded the

Sixth Alabama at Fisher's Hill, in the transcript of Blackford's court martial; Eugene Blackford CSR (M374 roll 4, p. 41). Colonel John Winston, commanding the Forty-fifth North Carolina of Grimes's brigade, stated in a postwar article that there were some sharpshooters with the cavalry, but no other source supports this. John Winston, "A Spirited Campaign at Cedar Creek," *Philadelphia Weekly Times*, July 25, 1885.

Chapter 17 – Cedar Creek

1. Dickert, *History of Kershaw's Brigade*, 446-7; *OR*, Ser. 1, XLIII/1: 591, 593; De Forest, *Volunteer's Adventures*, 209. Major General Joseph Kershaw now commanded the division, but his old South Carolina brigade, nominally under the command of Brigadier General James Connor (who had himself been wounded at Hupp's Hill a few days earlier), went into the battle of Cedar Creek under the command of Major James Goggin. Thus it was officially called Connor's brigade, but many continued to call it Kershaw's brigade.

2. *OR*, Ser. 1, XLIII/1: 591, 593; Milling, "Jim Milling and the War," 17-8; Dickert, *History of Kershaw's Brigade*, 446-7. What part the Third Georgia Sharpshooter Battalion of Wofford's brigade had in this action is unknown. Simms's brigade also had a sharpshooter unit, but he makes no mention of it in his report.

3. Milling, "Jim Milling and the War," 17-8; *OR*, Ser. 1, XLIII/1: 591; Wert, *From Winchester to Cedar Creek*, 178-9.

4. De Forest, *A Volunteer's Adventures*, 212-3. It is more likely that the two units opposing him were Gordon's division, which had just come up, and the sharpshooters of Kershaw's division. *OR*, Ser. 1, XLIII/1: 599. For a detailed description of the engagement see Mahr, *Battle of Cedar Creek*, 162-75.

5. Augustus Buell, *The Cannoneer: Recollections of Service in the Army of the Potomac* (Washington, DC: National Tribune, 1890), 288; Mahr, *Battle of Cedar Creek*, 219-31.

6. Dickert, *History of Kershaw's Brigade*, 450-1, 458-9; Milling, "Jim Milling and the War," 19.

7. Hamilton A. Brown, "First Regiment," in Clark, ed., *Histories of the Several Regiments and Battalions From North Carolina*, 1:155.

8. De Forest, *A Volunteer's Adventures*, 231. Early was outnumbered even more than De Forest realized—nearly three to one. In addition to the killed and wounded the Confederates lost twelve hundred men captured, and the Federals fourteen hundred.

9. *OR Supp.*, Vol. 43 (Ser. 90): 575; Cowper, *Extracts of Letters of Major-Gen'l Bryan Grimes*, 217; The sudden emphasis on discipline struck a lieutenant of the Sixty-first Alabama as a case of "the stable door is to be locked, after the horse is stolen." He also observed that "many officers are 'quaking in their boots' for fear." T. T. Greene to Elise, October 28, 1864, Greene Family Papers, VHS.

10. It also shows the sad state of the Confederate army in late 1864, since at full strength a regiment numbered just over 1,000 men. The petition is in Eugene Blackford's CSR (M374, roll 4, NA); the inspection report of Rodes's division is in the Reports of the Inspector General of the Army of Northern Virginia, M935, roll 14, frames 783-5, NA. Blackford was eventually reinstated by Jefferson Davis.

11. *OR*, Ser 1, XLIII/1: 599.

12. Mahr, *Battle of Cedar Creek*, 218 n. 7; Brown, "First Regiment," in Clark, ed., *Histories of the Several Regiments and Battalions From North Carolina*, 1:154.

13. Agassiz, ed., *With Grant and Meade*, 101; De Forest, *Volunteer's Adventures*, 177.

14. Benson, ed., *Berry Benson's Civil War*, 22, 23.

15. Nichols, *A Soldier's Story of His Regiment*, 185; Isaac O. Best, *History of the 121st New York State Infantry* (Chicago: Lieut. Jas. H. Smith, 1921), 184.

Chapter 18 – Petersburg

1. Agassiz, ed., *With Grant and Meade*, 100.

2. Johnson, ed., *Under the Southern Cross*, 223; A. Wilson Greene, *Breaking the Backbone of the Rebellion: The Final Battles of the Petersburg Campaign* (Mason City, IA: Savas Publishing, 2000), 65-9.

3. James A. Walker, "Gordon's Assault on Fort Stedman, March 25th, 1865: A Brilliant Achievement," *SHSP* 31 (1903): 22.

4. Johnson, ed., *Under the Southern Cross*, 226-8.

5. James Lane, "Brief War Record of Major T. J. Wooten," *Selections from War Correspondence by James Lane*, available online at http://www.rootsweb.com/~sckersha/records/majorwooten.htm; "Lane's Corps of Sharpshooters," *SHSP* 28 (1900): 5; *OR*, Ser. III, Vol. II: 1039; William H. McLaurin, "Eighteenth Regiment," in Clark, ed., *Histories of the Several Regiments and Battalions From North Carolina*, 2:59.

6. W.R.S. "The Sharpshooters Of Mahone's Old Brigade At The Crater" *SHSP* 28 (1900): 307-308

7. George S. Bernard "The Battle Of The Crater, July 30, 1864" *SHSP* 18 (1890): 9; W.R.S. "The Sharpshooters Of Mahone's Old Brigade At The Crater" *SHSP* 28 (1900): 307-308; John E. Laughton "The Sharpshooters Of Mahone's Brigade" *SHSP* 22 (1894): 103-104; Young "A Campaign with the Sharpshooters" *Philadelphia Weekly Times* July 26th, 1878.

8. William H. McLaurin, "Eighteenth Regiment," in Clark, *NC Regiments* 2:59.

9. Young, "A Campaign with the Sharpshooters"; Caldwell, *History of a Brigade of South Carolinians,* 252-3, 260.

10. William Phillips to his parents, January 1, 1865, William Phillips letters, WHS.

11. Dunlop, *Lee's Sharpshooters,* 224-7.

12. Phillips to his parents, January 1, 1865, William Phillips letters, WHS.

13. *OR,* Ser. I, XLII/3: 1106, 1107, 1111-2; Phillips to his parents, n.d., William Phillips letters, WHS; Dunlop, *Lee's Sharpshooters,* 227; The Bureau of Military Information report of December 31 concluded that "all that can be learned of the affair last evening is that a part of McGowan's brigade, about a regiment or less, relieved Young's battalion of sharpshooters, of Scales's brigade, and the latter made a dash upon our picket-line early this a.m.; no other reason is given for the attack than that it was expected a sufficient number of overcoats, shoes, and blankets would be captured to pay for the undertaking; of these articles they were sadly in need; some of them were barefooted." It also reports twenty-three deserters from Lee's army that day. Phillips's second letter, though undated, clearly refers to the events of December 31 and was probably written a day or two later.

14. Dunlop, *Lee's Sharpshooters,* 228. It is striking how many accounts tell of Confederate raids on the division boundaries. The Federals may have inadvertently aided them with their practice of using colored cap badges to distinguish the different divisions in a corps (red for the first division, white for second division, and blue for the third division). It would have been an easy enough matter for a scout to determine where one color badge changed to another.

15. Morse, "The 'Rebellion Record' of an Enlisted Man," *National Tribune Scrap Book,* n.d., USAMHI; Dunlop, *Lee's Sharpshooters,* 233; Greene, *Breaking the Backbone of the Rebellion,* 68. Morse served with the 5th Maine, which along with the 6th and 7th Maine had been consolidated into the 1st Maine Veteran Volunteers in August 1864. The Federal officer in question, Lieutenant Colonel Charles Milliken of the 43rd New York, figures prominently in a number of skirmish actions.

16. Sam Pickens diary entry, February 2, 1865, in Hubbs, ed., *Voices from Company D,* 355.

17. Sam Pickens diary entries, February 2 and 21, 1865, in Hubbs, ed., *Voices from Company D,* 355. Blackford claimed to be a lieutenant colonel after the war, but no record of the promotion survives, though it may have been lost in the final days of the Confederacy.

18. Phillips to his parents, March 25, 1865, William Phillips letters, WHS; Greene, *Breaking the Backbone of the Rebellion,* 68, 115-30; V.E. Turner and H. C. Wall, "Twenty-third Regiment" Clark, *NC Regiments* 2:263.

19. Phillips to his parents, March 17, 1865, William Phillips letters, WHS. Phillips's pistol was probably a Smith & Wesson Model 2 revolver, which fired six .32 caliber copper rimfire cartridges through a six-inch barrel. The Model 2, though never officially adopted by the military, was nicknamed the "Army" or "Old Army" because of its popularity with the soldiers. His estimate of its accuracy appears somewhat exaggerated.

20. Phillips to his parents, March 24, 1865, William Phillips letters, WHS.

21. Caldwell *History of a Brigade of South Carolinians* p. 254.

Chapter 19 – Assault on Hare's Hill

1. *OR,* Ser. I, XLVI/1: 388-9; *OR Supp.,* Vol. 46, (Ser. 95): 794-5; William R. Cox, "The Anderson–Ramseur–Cox Brigade," in Clark, ed., *Histories of the Several Regiments and Battalions From North Carolina,* 4:450-1. Gordon's numbers are discussed more fully in Appendix C.

2. *OR,* Ser. I, XLVI/1: 173; William H. Hodgkins, *The Battle of Fort Stedman, March 25th 1865* (Boston, 1889), 9-15; George L. Kilmer, "Assault and Repulse at Fort Stedman," *Century Magazine* (September 1887), 791; and George L. Kilmer, "Gordon's Attack at Fort Stedman," *B&L* 4: 579-80. The artillery at Fort Friend consisted of the six 3-inch rifled cannon of the 11th Massachusetts Battery; the reserve artillery was two sections of 12-pounder Napoleons.

3. John Gordon, *Reminiscences of the Civil War* (New York: Charles Scribner's Sons, 1904), 400-3. Considering Brown's rank (full colonel), experience, and the fact that the other division sharpshooter commanders were captains, he may have commanded the entire sharpshooter force of Second Corps. There is, however, no direct evidence of this.

4. Ibid., 400-3, 406-10; Jefferson Davis, *The Rise and Fall of the Confederate Government* (New York: D. Appleton, 1881) 2:652. The artillery party consisted of volunteers from Dearing's artillery battalion, which had served in the area for some time with Johnson's division prior to the arrival of Second Corps. Colonel Hilary P. Jones

exercised overall command of the Confederate artillery during the offensive. See http://www.alexandersbattalion.org/fauquier_artillery.htm. Confederate Organization is discussed in more detail in Appendix C.

5. *OR Supp.*, Vol. 46, (Ser. 95): 794-5; William R. Cox, "The Anderson–Ramseur–Cox Brigade," in Clark, ed., *Histories of the Several Regiments and Battalions From North Carolina*, 4:450-1. OR, Ser. 1, XLVI/3: 1341; Gordon, *Reminiscences*, 407. The Louisiana brigade, and most likely the rest of Evans's division as well, jumped off from Gracie's rather than Colquitt's salient. Napier Bartlett, *Military Record of Louisiana, Including Biographical and Historical Papers Relating to the Military Organizations of the State* (Baton Rouge: Louisiana State University Press, 1964): 39; James A. Walker, "Gordon's Assault on Fort Stedman, March 25th, 1865: A Brilliant Achievement," *SHSP* 31 (1903): 24. Gordon's request for Pickett is discussed more fully in Appendix C.

6. O. C. Whitaker to Robert Park, April 17, 1904, Twelfth Alabama regimental file, ADAH; "Fort Steadman's Fall" *Confederate Veteran* 22 (1914): 461; Carson commanded Company I, Fourth Georgia. He also states that he was "captain of the sharpshooters, about one hundred in number."

7. Walker, "Gordon's Assault," 21.

8. Ibid., 24-5.

9. Ibid.; Gordon, *Reminiscences,* 408-409; J. D. Barrier reminiscence, 2-3 (1923) Civil War Misc. Box 70, NCDAH; J. D. Barnwell reminiscence, 2-4, Lowery Shuford Collection, NCDAH. See also Kilmer, "Gordon's Attack at Fort Stedman," 581, who confirms that "on this occasion Confederates claiming to be deserters came in in large numbers, and very soon overpowered the pickets and passed on to the first line of works." Exactly what the signal was for the attack is discussed in Appendix C.

10. A section of the 14th Massachusetts Light Artillery manned Battery X, and a detachment from Company K, 1st Connecticut Heavy Artillery held the mortar battery. Walker, "Gordon's Assault," 24; Kilmer, "Gordon's Attack," 580; Thomas R. Roulhac, "The Forty-ninth N.C. Infantry, C.S.A.," *SHSP* 23 (1895): 74; Hamilton R. Jones, "Fifty-seventh Regiment," in Clark, ed., *Histories of the Several Regiments and Battalions From North Carolina*, 3:423; W. A. Day, "Life Among Bullets—in the Rifle Pits," *Confederate Veteran* 29 (1921): 218. Flemming was with the Sixth North Carolina and Roulhac with the Forty-ninth.

11. OR, Ser. I, Vol. XLVI/1: 341-2, 361-2; Kilmer, "Assault and Repulse"; Cyrus B. Watson, "Forty-fifth Regiment," in Clark, ed., *Histories of the Several Regiments and Battalions From North Carolina*, 3:57.

12. William Henry Philpot, "Capture of Fort Stedman," Sixty-first Alabama Regimental file, ADAH; P. H. Larey letters to Robert Park September to October 1910, Twelfth Alabama Regimental file, ADAH; Eugene Blackford CSR M374 roll 4.

13. "Fort Steadman's Fall," *Confederate Veteran* 22: 461-462; Thomas, *History of the Doles–Cook Brigade*, 37-41.

14. Stephens, ed., *Intrepid Warrior*, 535-536; Bartlett, *Military Record of Louisiana*, 39-40, 55; James P. Gannon, *Irish Rebels, Confederate Tigers: A History of the 6th Louisiana Volunteers, 1861-1865* (Mason City, IA: Savas Publishing Co., 1998), 307. Colonel W. R. Peck, the then-commander of the Louisiana brigade, confirms in a February 10 report that Lieutenant Smith commanded the Brigade Sharpshooters. OR, Ser. I, Vol. XLVI/1: 391.

15. OR, Ser. I, Vol. XLVI/1: 361-62. Union General John Hartranft put the actual number of men captured from the 14th NYHA at 201 (John Hartranft, "Recapture of Fort Stedman," B&L 4: 589). This does not count those captured from McLaughlen's brigade, nor presumably from the other artillery units in the forts.

16. Hodgkins, *Battle of Fort Stedman*, 25; OR, Ser. I, Vol. XLVI/1: 317-8, 332-4, 338.

17. OR, Ser. I, Vol. XLVI/1: 339-340; Warren Wilkinson, *Mother, May You Never See the Sights I Have Seen: The Fifty-seventh Massachusetts in the Last Year of the Civil War, 1864-1865* (New York: Harper & Row, 1990), 330, 364. Doherty was in command because the regiment's commander, Lieutenant Colonel Julius M. Tucker, was the division officer of the day. Though the 57th Massachusetts was in service slightly less than a year, its casualties were some of the highest of any unit in the war: 213 men killed plus 49 who died in Confederate prisons, an astonishing 20.5 percent, plus 370 wounded and 137 captured.

18. OR, Ser. I, Vol. XLVI/1: 331-2; Cowper, ed., *Extracts of Letters of Major-Gen'l Bryan Grimes*, 101; Johnson, ed., *Under the Southern Cross*, 234-5; I. G. Bradwell, "Holding the Lines at Petersburg," *Confederate Veteran* 28 (1920): 457-8.

19. OR, Ser. I, Vol. XLVI/1: 332-4; H. A. Brown, "First Regiment," in Clark, ed., *Histories of the Several Regiments and Battalions from North Carolina* 1: 155; Parramore and Johnson, *Before the Rebel Flag Fell*, 92; "Fort Steadman's Fall," *Confederate Veteran* 22 (1914): 462; Gordon, *Reminiscences,* 410. In view of the intense fighting in the fort, this loss figure is questionable.

20. Stephens, ed., *Intrepid Warrior*, 535-535; "Fort Steadman's Fall," *Confederate Veteran* 22 (1914): 462. Carson's reminiscence originally appeared in the *Macon Telegraph* in 1882 and was written down by an unnamed reporter after an interview, and contains some obvious errors. A slightly different version appears in Thomas, *History of the Doles–Cook Brigade*, 36-42. Evans's Georgia brigade was commanded by Col. John H. Baker, with Colonel John Lowe commanding an assault detachment from the Thirteenth and Thirty-first Georgia.

21. J. R. Holibaugh, "Battle Days of the Roundheads: The Civil War Experiences of the Famous 100th Pa., a Fighting Regiment. Part II," unknown newspaper, ca. 1897, available online at http://www.100thpenn.com/battledays.htm; OR, Ser. I, Vol. XLVI/1: 332-3, 342-3; John B. Gordon to W. G. Lewis, August 21, 1886, W. G. Lewis papers #23142, Folder 4, SHC. In his letter Gordon specifically mentions a "Lt. Col. Pendergrass" as being one of the officers whose name was to be included in the ruse.

22. OR, Ser. I, Vol. XLVI/1: 332-3.

23. Kilmer, "Assault and Repulse at Fort Stedman," *Century Magazine* (September 1887): 785-6; Kilmer, "Gordon's Attack on Fort Stedman," *B&L* 4: 581-2. Even though the *B&L* article is reprinted from *Century Magazine*, there are significant differences between the two, such as the number of Confederates said to have been killed by artillery.

24. OR, Ser. I, Vol. XLVI/1: 326, 327.

25. Herek, *These Men Have Seen Hard Service*, 306-7; OR, Ser. I, Vol. XLVI/1: 327. Buckbee was technically still a lieutenant, since his majority had not yet been officially approved.

26. Herek, *These Men Have Seen Hard Service*, 306-7.

27. Hartranft, "The Recapture of Fort Stedman," *B&L* 4: 589; OR, Ser. I, Vol. XLVI/1: 322-5, 357.

Chapter 20 – Fort Stedman

1. OR, Ser. I, Vol. XLVI/1: 357.

2. Hartranft, "The Recapture of Fort Stedman," *B&L* 4: 586.

3. OR, Ser. I, Vol. XLVI/1: 357.

4. Hartranft, "The Recapture of Fort Stedman," *B&L* 4: 587-9.

5. Ibid.

6. Kilmer, "Gordon's Attack at Fort Stedman," *B&L* 4: 582-3; Gordon, *Reminiscences*, 411; Stephens, ed., *Intrepid Warrior*, 535-536.

7. Kilmer, "Gordon's Attack at Fort Stedman," *B&L* 4: 582-3

8. Kilmer, ibid. In his report Woerner says he fired 117 rounds of canister that day. Considering that canister was not of much use beyond a hundred yards, this shows the sustained closeness of the fighting. OR, Ser. I, Vol. XLVI/1: 188.

9. OR, Ser. I, Vol. XLVI/1: 190-1, 326, 363-4. This may have been the group captured by the 1st Michigan Sharpshooters.

10. J. D. Barrier reminiscence, 2-3, Lowery Shuford Collection, NCDAH; J. D. Barrier, "Breaking Grant's Lines," *Confederate Veteran* 33 (1925): 417; Robert D. Graham, "Fifty-sixth Regiment," in

Clark, ed., *Histories of the Several Regiments and Battalions from North Carolina* 3:391; Kilmer, "Gordon's Attack at Fort Stedman," *B&L* 4: 582

11. Hartranft, "The Recapture of Fort Stedman," *B&L* 4: 587-9.

12. Gordon, *Reminiscences*, 411.

13. OR, Ser. I, Vol. XLVI/1: 359.

14. Hartranft, "The Recapture of Fort Stedman," *B&L* 4: 587-9; "Fort Steadman's Fall," *Confederate Veteran* 22 (1914): 462.

15. OR, Ser. I, Vol. XLVI/1: 333, 359; Walker, "Gordon's Assault on Fort Stedman," *SHSP* 31 (1903): 28; Kilmer, "Gordon's Attack at Fort Stedman," *B&L* 4: 583; Richard W. Iobst, *The Bloody Sixth: The Sixth North Carolina Regiment, Confederate States of America* (Raleigh: NC Confederate Centennial Commission, 1965), 252.

16. Walker, "Gordon's Assault on Fort Stedman," *SHSP* 31 (1903): 29. For whatever reason, the losses among the sharpshooters of Evans's division seem to have been considerably less. After the war there was considerable controversy about who entered the fort first. Walker's description lends credence to the long-standing claim by the 100th Pennsylvania and 14th N.Y.H.A. Holibaugh, "Battle Days of the Roundheads," unknown newspaper, 1897? http://www.100thpenn.com/battledays.htm.

17. "Fort Steadman's Fall," *Confederate Veteran* 22 (1914): 462.

18. OR, Ser. I, Vol. XLVI/1: 70-71. Confederate casualties are discussed in more detail in Appendix C.

19. OR, Ser. I, Vol. XLVI/1: 109; OR Ser. I Vol. XXXVI/1: 53-54; Frederick Phisterer, *Statistical Record of the Armies of the United States* (1883. Reprint, Edison, NJ: Castle Books, 2002), 218. Confederate casualties are discussed more fully in Appendix C. Agassiz, ed., *With Grant and Meade*, 324; Oscar Whitaker to Robert Park, April 17, 1904, Twelfth Alabama regimental file, ADAH.

20. *OR*, Ser. I, XLVI/1: 382-3; Gaston Lewis to Mittie, March 27, 1865, W. G. Lewis papers #23142, Folder 4 (1865-1911), SHC; Bryan Grimes to wife, March 29, 1865, Bryan Grimes Papers #292, SHC; Stephens, ed., *Intrepid Warrior*, 535-6.

21. *OR*, Ser. I, Vol. XLVI/1: 382-3, 391; H. A. Brown, "First Regiment," in Clark, ed., *Histories of the Several Regiments and Battalions from North Carolina* 1:155; Thomas S. Kenan, "Forty-third Regiment," in Clark, ed., *Histories of the Several Regiments and Battalions from North Carolina* 3: 15-16; Henry London, "Thirty-second Regiment," in Clark, ed., *Histories of the Several Regiments and Battalions from North Carolina* 2: 534-5; Parramore and Johnson, *Before the Rebel Flag Fell*, 92; William R. Cox, "The Anderson–Ramseur–Cox brigade" in Clark, ed., *Histories of the Several Regiments and Battalions from North Carolina* 4: 450-1.

22. Stephens, ed., *Intrepid Warrior*, 534-6; Kilmer, "Gordon's Attack at Fort Stedman," *B&L* 4: 582. Confederate organization and some of the other questions are treated more fully in Appendix C.

Chapter 21 – Decision at Petersburg

1. For a more detailed look at the capture of Lee's picket line see A. Wilson Greene, *Breaking the Backbone of the Rebellion: The Final Battles of the Petersburg Campaign* (Mason City, IA: Savas Publishing, 2000), 161-83.

2. Ibid., 178-9.

3. Ibid., 179-81; Dunlop, *Lee's Sharpshooters*, 249.

4. Dunlop, *Lee's Sharpshooters*, 249; Benson, ed., *Berry Benson's Civil War Book*, 178-9.

5. Dunlop, *Lee's Sharpshooters*, 252-3; Benson, ed., *Berry Benson's Civil War Book*, 179. As senior officer, Major Wooten was in command.

6. Greene, *Breaking the Backbone of the Rebellion*, 202-5; Dunlop, *Lee's Sharpshooters*, 254-5; Benson ed., *Berry Benson's Civil War Book*, 179; Caldwell, *History of a Brigade of South Carolinians*, 266-76.

7. Dunlop, *Lee's Sharpshooters*, 258; Benson, ed., *Berry Benson's Civil War Book*, 183-4; Greene, *Breaking the Backbone of the Rebellion*, 225-9. Benson reported that the Federal force had three colors, which would indicate a brigade-size force attacking the hundred or so men of the sharpshooters.

8. Benson, ed., *Berry Benson's Civil War Book*, 185.

9. Greene, *Breaking the Backbone of the Rebellion*, 266-7; *OR*, Ser. I, XLVI/1: 901-4, 953-6, 962. The 43rd New York was a veteran but depleted unit consisting of only five companies, and usually referred to as a battalion at this stage of the war. Many of its men appear to have been on the skirmish line with Milliken and Terrell, and the rest went forward with the third line of Hyde's brigade. In Federal practice the officer of the day (at both division and corps) was responsible for the conduct of the skirmish line.

10. *OR*, Ser. I, XLVI/1: 1072; Greene, *Breaking the Backbone of the Rebellion*, 273-5, 283; J. S. Kimbrough, "From Petersburg to Hart's Island Prison," *Confederate Veteran* 22 (1914): 499; Best, *History of the 121st New York*, 210. About 150 sharpshooters from McGowan's brigade, which had been sent west, remained to stiffen the picket line.

11. *OR*, Ser. I, XLVI/1: 941.

12. *OR*, Ser. I, XLVI/1: 910-1, 940, 941, 953-6; Greene, *Breaking the Backbone of the Rebellion*, 277. There is little information about Stuart's unit other than that mentioned in the *Official Record*.

13. Greene, *Breaking the Backbone of the Rebellion*, 266, 282-283, 305; *OR*, Ser. I, XLVI/1: 910; Bowen *History of the Thirty-seventh Regiment Mass. Volunteers* p. 410-411. I have relied on Greene's comparative numbers for the assault, which I believe are the best available.

14. Greene, *Breaking the Backbone of the Rebellion*, 364-5; *OR*, Ser. I, XLVI/1: 909-12, 931-2, 941, 953, 962. Both Getty and Milliken are vague about the exact movements of Second Division's sharpshooters/skirmishers. Getty merely puts them "on the right of the main attack," while Milliken places his passage of the lines as "near the Jones House."

15. William Miller Owen, "The Artillery Defenders of Fort Gregg," *SHSP* 19 (1891): 68-69; J. S. Kimbrough, "From Petersburg to Hart's Island Prison," *Confederate Veteran* 22 (1914): 499; Greene, *Breaking the Backbone of the Rebellion*, 364-5. Fort Whitworth was actually Fort Baldwin, but was so called because of the nearby Whitworth house.

16. *OR*, Ser. I, XLVI/1: 962. Milliken reported losing 1 killed, 5 wounded, and 4 captured; Stuart listed 3 men wounded. Since Stuart was outside the works, and Fort Owen lay directly south of Gregg on the main line and had a battery of guns inside it (sources differ as to whether there were two or three), it is difficult to see how he could have taken any work other than Fort Owen. By the same token, Milliken (who was moving inside the lines), obviously did not capture the same work as Stuart, whom he blamed for failure to keep up a connection between the two. This makes sense considering the two works were quite close together. Hamblin, on the other hand, fails to mention either sharpshooter company and says that a detachment from his brigade under colonels Fisk and Harper captured the forts. Especially in light of Hamblin's low casualties (1 killed, 48 wounded,

1 missing) I find this unlikely, although they may have been in the area. Finally, General Getty is specific in his report that two forts were captured, although he says that only one was abandoned. Against this interpretation one must consider Confederate Colonel William Owens's report (cited above). According to him Fort Owens was lost but not Gregg, and Owens was quickly recaptured by a detachment from Fort Gregg. I believe that both Forts were captured by the Federals, but held only briefly. Hamblin's division commander, General Frank Wheaton, gives the number involved as "some 80 men," but this evidently does not include Milliken's detachment, which was from the Second Division. Thus the number would have been around double that, or between 150 and 200 men. (*OR*, Ser. I, XLVI/1: 909-12, 931-2, 941, 953, 962.)

17. H. W. Manson, "Story from the Ranks," *Confederate Veteran* 1 (1893): 68; "Last Charge of Lee's Army," *Confederate Veteran* 5 (1897): 565; Greene, *Breaking the Backbone of the Rebellion*, 352-60. McComb's command, often still called Archer's brigade after a former commander, consisted of eight understrength Tennessee regiments and the Second Maryland battalion.

18. H. W. Manson, "Story from the Ranks," *Confederate Veteran* 1 (1893): 68; "Last Charge of Lee's Army," *Confederate Veteran* 5 (1897): 565.

19. H. W. Manson, "Story from the Ranks," *Confederate Veteran* 1 (1893): 68.

20. ibid.

21. Dunlop, *Lee's Sharpshooters*, 268-70; Benson, ed., *Berry Benson's Civil War Book*, 188-9.

22. Greene, *Breaking the Backbone of the Rebellion*, 432-7; Earl J. Hess, *Lee's Tar Heels: The Pettigrew–Kirkland–McRae Brigade* (Chapel Hill: University of North Carolina Press, 2002), 294-5; Caldwell, *History of a Brigade of South Carolinians*, 282. Greene estimates the Confederate strength at four thousand; Hess at twelve hundred. Caldwell, who was there, says "we certainly had not four thousand troops, and probably not that many." He estimates the strength of his own brigade (McGowan's), which had not been engaged, at about a thousand men. Considering that some of the other brigades, especially McRae's, had been badly hurt, a fair estimation of Confederate numbers would probably be between two and three thousand.

23. Dunlop, *Lee's Sharpshooters*, 274-5.

24. Caldwell, *History of a Brigade of South Carolinians*, 283-4; Dunlop, *Lee's Sharpshooters*, 275-6.

25. *OR*, Ser. I, XLVI/1: 711-12, 175, 746-48, 792; Benson, ed., *Berry Benson's Civil War Book*, 189-90

26. Greene, *Breaking the Backbone of the Rebellion*, 439-40; Dunlop, *Lee's Sharpshooters*, 276; Caldwell, *History of a Brigade of South Carolinians*, 286; Benson, ed., *Berry Benson's Civil War Book*, 189-90.

27. Hess, *Lee's Tarheels*, 296; W. Springer Menge and J. August Shimrak, eds., *The Civil War Notebook of Daniel Chisholm: A Chronicle of Daily Life in the Union Army 1864-1865*. (New York: Orion Books, 1989), 74; Dunlop, *Lee's Sharpshooters*, 278-9, 312-3.

28. Dunlop, *Lee's Sharpshooters*, 279-80; Benson, ed., *Berry Benson's Civil War Book*, 191-5.

29. Young, "A Campaign with the Sharpshooters," *Philadelphia Weekly Times*, January 26, 1878; Benson, ed., *Berry Benson's Civil War Book*, 195-6.

30. J. S. Kimbrough, "From Petersburg to Hart's Island Prison," *Confederate Veteran* 22 (1914): 500.

31. "The Night before the Surrender with the Irrepressible Alabamian," *Confederate Reminiscences & Letters 1861-1865*, 3: 34-6, GDAH.

32. ibid.

33. William Kaigler, "Concerning Last Charge at Appomattox," *Confederate Veteran* 6 (1898): 524. After the war both Cox and Kaigler would claim the honor of firing the last shot at Appomattox.

34. Sergeant Benson's unsurrendered rifle—a two-band P60 Enfield favored by the sharpshooters—may be viewed today at the Augusta Museum of History in Augusta, GA. Blackwood Benson took home a Whitworth rifle, but it was later destroyed in a fire.

Chapter 22 – Weapons and Uniforms

1. Bill Adams, "Introduction to the Enfield," ms. in possession of the author. According to Enfield expert Bill Adams, "The P56 and P58 sabre bayonets are 28.2-inch long overall with a 22.8-inch blade. The P60 bayonet is 28-inch overall with a 22.75-inch blade. Some Volunteer models may have a slightly longer or shorter blade as they weren't made to regulation specs. The grips and mounts can vary considerably." Adams e-mail message to author, April 21, 2004.

2. Gordon Bradwell, *Under the Southern Cross: Soldier Life with Gordon Bradwell and the 31st Georgia*, compiled and edited by Pharris Deloach Johnson (Macon, GA: Mercer University Press, 1999), 232-3; John E. Laughton, "The Sharpshooters of Mahone's Brigade," *SHSP* 22 (1894): 99.

3. Wiley Sword, *Firepower from Abroad: The Confederate Enfield and the Lemat Revolver* (Lincoln, RI: Andrew Mowbray, 1986), 67; *OR*, Ser. IV, Vol. II: 383; Richard D. Steuart, "How Johnny Got His Gun," *Confederate Veteran* 32 (1924): 167-169. See generally Edwards, *Civil War Guns*, 249-63, and Bilby, *Civil War Firearms*, 58-9. According to Enfield authority Bill Adams, "The commonly encountered Volunteer Rifle is a 2-band rifle in either P56, P58 Army, or P60 configuration. Some of the rifles have heavy barrels; many have chequered stocks. The two band rifles were purchased by the Volunteers and used for muster as well as for target shooting. Some of the rifles were in .451 and other calibres." Adams e-mail message to author, April 21, 2004. Steuart's figures from 1863 show eight 3-band Enfields for every 2-band imported. However, General William T. Sherman's Chief of Ordnance, Colonel T. G. Baylor, records in his report during the Carolinas campaign that Union forces captured nineteen hundred Enfield rifle muskets (3-band) and two thousand Enfield rifles (2-band), which suggests that more of the short rifles were imported late in the war. *OR*, Ser I., XLVII: 181.

4. Wilcox, *Rifles and Rifle Practice*, 211-2. The actual weight of the rifle varied between 8.95 and 10.5 pounds, according to configuration, sighting, etc. John Anderson Morrow, *The Confederate Whitworth Sharpshooters*, 2nd ed. (N.p., 2002), 9-13. Period firearms expert Bill Adams clocked the rounds from a reproduction Whitworth at 1300 feet per second using a modern chronograph. Adams e-mail message to author, May 13, 2005.

5. Morrow, *Confederate Whitworth Sharpshooters*, 12-3, 24.

6. Edwards, *Civil War Guns*, 219-20; D. Davidson, "Lieut. Col. Davidson's Patent Telescopic Rifle Sight," *Journal of the Royal United Service Institution* 8 (1865): 426-429; Morrow, *Confederate Whitworth Sharpshooters*, 51, 83; Isaac N. Shannon, "Sharpshooters with Hood's Army," *Confederate Veteran* 15 (1907): 124-125. Stan C. Harley, Reminiscence, *Confederate Veteran* 7 (1899): 307.

7. W. S. Curtis, e-mail message to author, November 2, 2003; Bradwell, *Under the Southern Cross*, 233; "W.R.S." in "The Sharpshooters of Mahone's Brigade," *SHSP* 22 (1894): 98 says: "There were, besides, two globe-sighted rifles for use on special occasions, which were valuable additions to our armament," but he does not specify their type. Berry Benson says that McGowan's brigade received two (Benson, ed., *Berry Benson's Civil War Book*, 68-70). Captain Young of Scales's brigade says four, but this seems unlikely (Young, "A Campaign with the Sharpshooters," *Philadelphia Weekly Times*, January 26, 1878). *OR*, Ser 1, XXXVIII/4: 792. The total for the Army of Tennessee may also have included Kerr sharpshooter rifles reported as "Whitworths," since they were known to have these weapons, yet they are not mentioned as such in the reports.

8. Bilby, *Civil War Firearms*, 120-1; Morrow, *Confederate Whitworth Sharpshooters*, 19-23, 27-28. Bilby points out that the British government paid about $50 U.S. each for their Whitworths, bare, and over $100 U.S. additional to have a Davidson telescope fitted, and that the higher Confederate cost (if true; no written records survive) may have been a reflection of their depreciated currency.

9. Morrow, *Confederate Whitworth Sharpshooters*, 30, 88, 55; Ben Powell to wife, November 21, 1907, BV 200, FSNMP; *OR*, Ser 1 XXIII/1: 586.

10. Fergus S. Harris, "Fine Shots in the Virginia Army," *Confederate Veteran* 4 (1896): 73; Isaac N. Shannon, "Sharpshooters with Hood's Army," *Confederate Veteran* 15 (1907): 126; Morrow, *Confederate Whitworth Sharpshooters*, 8. Harris was also the commander of the Brigade Sharpshooters of Archer's brigade.

11. *OR*, Ser. 1 XXVIII/1: 277; Morrow, *Confederate Whitworth Sharpshooters*, 24; Edwards, *Civil War Guns*, 220.

12. Isaac N. Shannon, "Sharpshooters with Hood's Army," *Confederate Veteran* 15 (1907): 127.

13. Morrow, *Confederate Whitworth Sharpshooters*, 37, 77.

14. C. H. Roads, *The British Soldier's Firearm, 1850-1864.* (London: Herbert Jenkins, 1964), 134-8; D. W. Bailey and J. B. Bell, "The London Armoury Company Kerr Rifle," *Guns Review*, April 1970. Some manufacturers, like Kerr, made their small-bore barrels interchangeable with that of the service .577 Enfield, allowing Volunteer shooters to order their rifles with both barrels so that they could drill and shoot matches with the same weapon. Some of these "small-bore Enfields" may have seen Confederate service, but because soldier accounts habitually refer to sharpshooter rifles simply as "small-bore," "globe-sighted," or in similarly vague terms, it is impossible to tell exactly what make of rifle they mean. Thanks to Bill Adams for helping me to sort out British match rifles.

15. See generally Wiley Sword, *Sharpshooter: Hiram Berdan, His Famous Sharpshooters and Their Sharps Rifles* (Lincoln, RI: Andrew Mowbray, 1988), 63 et. seq., and Bilby, *Civil War Firearms*, 105-14.

16. Eugene Blackford to Mary Blackford, August 4, 1863, Gordon-Blackford Papers, MHS.

17. Earl J. Coates and John D. McAulay, *Civil War Sharps Carbines and Rifles* (Gettysburg, PA: Thomas Publications, 1996), 13-23.

18. Information from museum display, Visitor's Center, Gettysburg NMP.

19. Bilby, *Civil War Firearms*, 206.

20. Greene, *Breaking the Backbone of the Rebellion*, 305.

21. Bilby, *Civil War Firearms*, 197-206.

22. Gregory A. Coco, *The Civil War Infantryman: In Camp, on the March, and in Battle* (Gettysburg, PA: Thomas Publications, 1996), 66; Bilby, *Civil War Firearms*, 113; Benson, ed., *Berry Benson's Civil War Book*, 77.

23. White, ed., *Diary of Wyman S. White*, 258-9.

24. Keith Raynor, ed., "C. Hamilton Smith's Experiment with the Colour of Uniforms," available online at http://www.warof1812.ca/hamilton.htm. Raynor transcribed Hamilton-Smith's article from "Aide-Memoire to the Military Sciences, volume 1," London: N.p., 1853; A British Volunteer officer cited a French study and advised in 1861 that "light regiments…should be habited in gray." Hans Busk, *Rifle Volunteers: How to Organize and Drill Them in Accordance With the Latest Regulations.* (London: Routledge, Warne, and Routledge, 1861).

25. Hesketh-Prichard, *Sniping in France,* 110-1.

26. Blackford D/M, 206-7; Hess, *Lee's Tarheels,* 237-8; Menge and Shimrak, eds., *Civil War Notebook of Daniel Chisholm,* 74; W.T. McGill, "Sketch of Moses Allen Terrell," *Confederate Recollections and Reminiscences 1861-1865,* 3:17-18, South Carolina Department of Archives and History; Katcher, *Sharpshooters of the American Civil War,* 51-52; Hartzler, *Band of Brothers,* 187. Wise's badge is at the Maryland Historical Society.

Chapter 23 –Confederate Sharpshooters in the West

1. Morrow, *Confederate Whitworth Sharpshooters,* 26-8; Chas. F Vanderford, "Attention, Whitworth Sharpshooters," *Confederate Veteran* 1 (1893): 117; "Whitworth Rifle Sharpshooters," *Confederate Veteran* 16 (1908): 172.

2. Sam Watkins, *Company Aytch, A Side Show of the Big Show* (Nashville, TN 1882) quoted in Morrow, *Confederate Whitworth Sharpshooters,* 35. Since Watkins did not join the sharpshooters, he mentions the outfit only in passing. Documenting these units is difficult, but there was at least one more was in Cockrell's Missouri brigade: one of its marksman, Private Charles Ingram of the Third Missouri, never surrendered and took his Whitworth home with him. Gary Lantz, "The Whitworth Rifle," *America's First Freedom,* May 2002, 51-55.

3. FitzGerald Ross, *Cities and Camps of the Confederate States.* Ed. Richard Barksdale Harwell. (Chicago: University of Illinois Press, 1997), 132; John Edwards, "The Death of General Lytle," *Confederate Veteran* 26 (1918): 248.

4. William C. Davis, *The Orphan Brigade: The Kentucky Confederates Who Couldn't Go Home* (Doubleday, 1980), 215-6.

5. "Whitworth Rifle with a History," *Confederate Veteran* 30 (1922): 45; Frank Vizetelly, "The War in America; Confederate Sharpshooters Firing on a Federal Supply-Train on the Tennessee River," *The Illustrated London News,* December 5, 1863. It is quite possible that these accounts refer to the same incident.

6. Ross, *Cities and Camps of the Confederate States,* 97 n. 4; J. W. Minnich, "Famous Rifles," *Confederate Veteran* 30 (1922): 247. Like Viztelly, Ross refers to a corps of Whitworth sharpshooters under Longstreet, so it appears that General Longstreet organized a sharpshooter outfit similar to those of the Army of Tennessee. The most detailed accounts of this corps are Minnich's. Given his description of a "deeply grooved" barrel, not a hexagonal bore, it is possible that the sharpshooter's rifle was a Kerr or another English match rifle.

7. J. W. Minnich, "That Affair at Dandridge, Tenn.," *Confederate Veteran* 30 (1922): 295-296.

8. Milling, "Jim Milling and the War," 7; A. J. McBride, "Tenth Georgia at Spottsylvania," *Atlanta Journal,* July 20, 1901. The Tenth Georgia was with the Semmes-Bryan-Simms brigade. Both it and Milling's outfit (the Third South Carolina Battalion) belonged to Kershaw's division, First Corps. Perhaps some further research will be able to definitively confirm Longstreet's continued use of a corps of sharpshooters.

9. Frank Roberts, "Spring Hill—Franklin—Nashville, 1864," *Confederate Veteran* 27 (1919): 58-59; Russell K. Brown, *Our Connection with Savannah: A History of the 1st Battalion Georgia Sharpshooters.* (Macon, GA: Mercer University Press, 2004), 19-24, 135. Unfortunately no full-length accounts like those of Dunlop, Blackford, and Benson remain to shed light on the experiences of western sharpshooters, and Roberts description of his unit's role in the campaigns of 1864 is brief.

10. OR, Ser. 1, XXXVIII/3: 789-90, 792-3.

11. Dunbar Rowland, *Military History of Mississippi, 1803-1898* (1908. Reprint, Spartanburg, SC: Reprint Company, 1978), 145-6, 227-8, 353-4. Rowland describes the Fifteenth Battalion Sharpshooters being "deployed as skirmishers," but they may be the same unit that Cleburne equipped with Whitworth and Kerr rifles. They are not mentioned after February 1864.

12. Ibid., 274.

13. Wilcox *Rifles and Rifle Practice* p. 245-46; Brian Howerton "Rapley's Sharpshooters: 12th Arkansas Battalion, CSA," available online at http://www.couchgenweb.com/civilwar/rapley1.html. Among Van Dorn's subordinates in the Confederate Army of the Potomac were Richard Ewell, Robert Rodes, and Eugene Blackford.

14. Howerton "Rapley's Sharpshooters".

15. John Bell, "Arkansas Sharpshooters at Vicksburg," *Confederate Veteran* 12 (1904): 446-447.

16. Howerton, "Rapley's Sharpshooters".

Chapter 24 – The Opposition

1. Ripley, *A History of Company F,* 3-4.

2. Sword, *Sharpshooter,* 10-15.

3. Sword, *Sharpshooter,* 33-39; Ripley, *A History of Company F,* 5.

4. Sword, *Sharpshooter,* 54, 79.

5. Ibid., 84.

6. *OR,* Ser. 3, II: 575; Halleck remained general-in-chief until March 1864, when he was redesignated chief of staff. Translator of several French military treatises and author of a number of his own, "Old Brains," was considered the army's premier military intellectual.

7. Sword, *Sharpshooter,* 22.

8. Sears, *Chancellorsville,* 254-7.

9. Sword, *Sharpshooter,* 120-2.

10. Sword, *Sharpshooter,* 25.

11. Sword, *Sharpshooter,* 26-8, 57; *OR,* Ser. 1, XXVII/1: 516; *OR,* Ser. 1, XXVII/2: 598. Sword has thoroughly debunked Berdan's overblown claims about his prowess at Gettysburg.

12. Ripley, *A History of Company F,* 188.

13. Ibid., 189.

14. Ibid., 179.

15. Sears, *Chancellorsville,* 104-5, 141, 441.

16. "203rd Regiment Pennsylvania Volunteers" http://www.pa-roots.com/~pacw/203dorg.html; Bilby, *Civil War Guns,* 55. Joe Bilby comments that "the Ninth NJ was used as skirmishers often, but not always. The regiment was originally organized into three battalions, totaling 12 companies, and each company was assigned a bugler. After a while in the field, they were consolidated into ten companies." Email message to the author, October 18, 2004.

17. Wilkinson, *Mother, May You Never See,* 222-3, 305; e-mail message from Joe Bilby, September 4, 2004.

18. Union ordnance reports for 1863 list fifty-six Sharps rifles for "Massachusetts Sharpshooters." It is not entirely clear whether this refers to one company or both of the Andrews's sharpshooters, or whether the men not armed with the Sharps had issue Springfields or retained their target rifles. By mid-1864 the number had dropped to fifteen. Coates and McAulay, *Civil War Sharps Carbines and Rifles,* 22, 23; Sword, *Sharpshooter,* 84 (on page 39 Sword reproduces a photo of a soldier with the 1st N.Y.S.S. with his target rifle); Dyer, *Compendium of the War of the Rebellion,* Pt. 3: 1219, 1405.

19. "16th Regiment Michigan Volunteer Infantry 1861-1865," available online at http://www.michiganinthewar.org/infantry/16thinf.htm; "27th Regiment Michigan Volunteer Infantry 1863-1865," available online at http://www.michiganinthewar.org/infantry/27thinf.htm. The 16th Michigan drew some three hundred Sharps rifles in August 1862 from Berdan's trove but evidently had to give them back. Coates and McAulay, *Sharps Carbines and Rifles,* 20.

20. Herek, *These Men Have Seen Hard Service,* 98.

21. Ibid., 187. See chapter 12 for a detailed examination of the 1st Michigan's experience at the Wilderness.

22. Ibid., 291-5.

23. Ibid., 322-5.

24. *Pennsylvania at Gettysburg* (Harrisburg, 1904), 1:305 qtd. in William J. Miller, "Life on the Skirmish Line: Through the War with the Pennsylvania Bucktails," *Civil War Regiments* Vol. 1, No. 3, available online at http://www.pabucktail.com/Reference/Miller/Miller-Life%20on%20Skirmish.htm.

25. O. R. Howard and William H. Rauch, *History of the "Bucktails," Kane Rifle Regiment of the Pennsylvania Reserve Corps* (Philadelphia: Regimental Association, 1906), 204-5; Coates and McAulay in *Civil War Sharps Carbines and Rifles* (p. 91-92) estimate that the Bucktails fielded fourteen to twenty-five Sharps rifles per company.

26. Howard and Rauch, *History of the "Bucktails,"* 206; Frank Moore, ed., *Anecdotes, Poetry, and Incidents of the War: North and South, 1860-1865* (New York: Bible House, 1867), 339, 373; Sypher, *History of the Pennsylvania Reserve Corps,* 369-70.

27. D. Scott Hartwig, "It Looked Like a Task to Storm," *North and South,* October 2002, 38-49; Sypher, *History of the Pennsylvania Reserve Corps,* 374-5.

28. George Alfred Townsend, *Rustics in Rebellion: A Yankee Reporter on the Road to Richmond, 1861-1865* (Chapel Hill: University of North Carolina Press, 1950), 15-16.

29. Coates and McAulay, *Sharps Carbines and Rifles*, 23, 91-2. The Bucktails never had enough Sharps rifles to completely outfit the regiment; the balance were Springfields and later Spencers. The 190th and 191st Pennsylvania were consolidated late in the war.

30. Bilby, Joseph G. *Three Rousing Cheers: A History of the Fifteenth New Jersey from Flemington to Appomattox*. (Revised edition. Hightstown, NJ: Longstreet House, 2001), 114. Virtually nothing has so far been written about these units. Indeed, it is only with the aid of computer searching that references scattered throughout the OR and in private accounts have come to light.

31. *OR*, Ser. 1, XL/1: 415, 470, 495, 501-3. For a full account of the engagement see Davis Faris Cross, *A Melancholy Affair at the Weldon Railroad: The Vermont Brigade, June 23, 1864*. (White Mane Publishing, 2003).

32. Walker, *The Vermont Brigade*, 27-28; *OR*, Ser. 1, XLIII/1: 193.

33. *OR*, Ser. 1, XLVI/1: 940, 941, 945. The first official mention of Wheaton's division sharpshooters comes at Petersburg. However, since at least one of the division's regiments (the 15th New Jersey, see note 30 above) was training a sharpshooter detachment that spring, it may well have existed earlier.

34. Ibid. Although no table of organization survives, a typical division sharpshooter company for the VI Corps probably consisted seventy-five light infantrymen, armed (at least late in the war) with Spencer repeaters, and twenty-five men armed with long-range target rifles. This gave them a much smaller number of specialized light infantrymen compared to a Confederate division (meaning that the infantry brigades would have to provide most of their own skirmishers), but a much larger number of snipers in the modern sense (twenty-five versus six to eight in a Confederate division). No soldier accounts or histories of these elite units have yet come to light, and references to individuals in them are few. A postwar newspaper column dealing with veterans of the 122nd New York, for instance, mentions in passing that one soldier, Thomas Crampton of Company B, "was assigned to the special sharp shooters corps" but offers no further details. "Sketches of Old Comrades," *Weekly Recorder*, December 16, 1889.

35. *OR*, Ser. 1, XLII/1: 254-55, 412. The prisoners belonged to Wise's brigade of Johnson's division.

36. *OR*, Ser. 1, XLII/1: 255-59. The raiders were most likely from Major General Bushrod Johnson's division, which held that sector of the line.

37. *OR*, Ser. 1, XLII/3: 168; XLII/1: 815.

38. *OR*, Ser. 1, XLII/1: 802; XLII/2 p. 290

39. *OR*, Ser. 1, XLVI/3: 419; XLVI/1: 827.

40. *OR*, Ser. 1, XL/1: 541-3.

Chapter 25 – The Open Order

1. The Germans adopted the famous Model 1898 Mauser in that year and continued to use it in slightly modified form through the end of World War II. Various Afghan militias continue to use the Lee-Enfield over a hundred years after its first manufacture, and it played a fairly prominent part in their war against the Soviets in the 1980s, where it was supplied to them by the CIA. In the rugged Afghan terrain *Muhajiddin* sharpshooters armed with Enfields often outranged and outshot the Soviet forces armed with AK-47 and AK-74 assault rifles.

2. The first clip-loading magazine rifle was the American 6mm Lee Navy rifle, adopted in 1895. The designer was James Paris Lee, who also designed the Lee-Enfield.

3. Young, "A Campaign with the Sharpshooters," *Philadelphia Weekly Times*, January 26, 1878.

4. Arthur Conan Doyle, *The Great Boer War* (London: Smith, Elder, 1902), chap. VII. Also available online at http://www.pinetreeweb.com/conan-doyle-chapter-09.htm.

5. R. Ernest Dupuy and Trevor N. Dupuy, *Encyclopedia of Military History from 3500 B. C. to the Present*, (New York: Harper & Rowe, 1970), 855. The details of this section come primarily from pp. 852-855, as well as from Doyle op. cit.; Battlefields.co.za Historical Library available online at http://www.battlefields.co.za/history/index.htm; "The Tactics of the Boer War" available online at *http://www.edenpr.k12.mn.us/ephs/Conrad/ Tactics_of_the_Boer_War.html*; and Dylan Craig, "The Weapons and Battles of the Second Anglo-Boer War (1899-1902)," available online at http://www.heliograph.com/trmgs/trmgs4/boer.shtml.

6. Bruce I. Gudmundsson, *Stormtroop Tactics: Innovation in the German Army, 1914-1918* (Westport, CT: Praeger Publishers, 1995), 20-5.

7. Some accounts even claimed that the best Enfield riflemen could get off close to thirty aimed shots a minute.

8. Gudmundsson, *Stormtroop Tactics*, 6.

9. Ibid., 17-26. For a detailed description of the German attacks at Ypres see Robert Cowley, "World War I: Massacre of the Innocents," *The Quarterly Journal of Military History* (Spring 1998), available online at http://history1900s.about.com/library/prm/blmassacre1.htm?terms=kindermord.

10. Gudmundsson, *Stormtroop Tactics,* 24.

11. Ibid., 33-4.

12. Ibid., 47-52. The carbine version of the Mauser 98 (designated Gewehr 98K for Kurz, or short) reduced the barrel length from 29.1 inches to 23.6 inches. A somewhat modified version would eventually become the standard German service rifle in World War II. General of the Infantry Hans Emil Alexander Gaede had a reputation as an innovator. Alarmed by the prevalence of head wounds in the early part of the war, he designed and introduced the first steel helmets in the German Army at his own expense, then pushed for the adoption of the *stahlhelm* army-wide.

13. Gudmundsson points out that "from the day of Frederick the Great the post of the German NCO had been behind the firing line, his chief duty being to ensure that no left the firing line without authorization. ...When the squad became a tactical unit, however, the post of the squad leader changed ... he was now in front and in command." Gudmundsson, *Stormtroop Tactics,* 50.

14. For a detailed account of the battle of Verdun and Rohr's part in it, see Gudmundsson, *Stormtroop Tactics,* 55-75; for details on the organization of *Sturmbatallion* Rohr see pages 77-8. The Erhardt m/11 mountain gun could be broken down into six loads if necessary for cross-country transportation. Weighing 600kg, it fired a 6.5kg shell to a maximum range of 6000m. An image is online at http://hem.fyristorg.com/robertm/norge/Norw_weapons.html.

15. Stephen Bull, *Stormtrooper: Elite German Assault Soldiers* (London: Publishing News, 1999), 29-30.

16. Ibid., 43; H. Hesketh-Prichard, *Sniping in France: With Notes on the Scientific Training of Scouts, Observers, and Snipers* (New York: E. P. Dutton, 1920. Reprint, Mt. Ida, Arkansas: Lancer Militaria, 1993), 15-7.

17. The original version of the 7.6cm light trench mortar threw a 4.75kg bomb out to 1000m and weighed 100 kg (220 lbs); in 1916 an improved version was introduced that weighed 142 kg (312 lbs) and had a greater range of 1300m. Both were normally fitted with a small two-wheeled field carriage that enabled the crew of six to haul it, with some difficulty, across broken terrain with ropes.

18. The "artillery" model Luger pistol had an 203mm (8 in.) barrel and a leaf sight graduated (somewhat optimistically) to 800m. It came with a shoulder stock that converted it into a short carbine. The 32-round "snail" magazine proved unreliable and was eventually replaced on the Bergmann with a box magazine holding 20 or 30 rounds. Although German industry delivered less than 10,000 Bergmanns by war's end, the gun remained the standard Wehrmacht submachinegun until 1938 and continued to be produced by various manufacturers until 1945.

19. Bull, *Stormtrooper,* 29-31. Although there was never a standard army-wide organization, most *sturmbatallione* fielded four or five pioneer/infantry companies of 250 men, one or two machinegun companies, and a headquarters of 50-70 men. Normal practice was to attach a flamethrower platoon, a light mortar company, and a battery of the cut-down Russian guns for organic fire support.

20. General Oskar von Hutier is often given credit for inventing the "infiltration tactics" in the East and first using them at Riga in 1917. However, subsequent and more in-depth investigations such as that by Bruce Gudmundsson have shown that the stormtroop tactics actually originated on the western front.

21. This included even the *Landwehr* (reserve) formations.

22. The cost was high — the British lost over 300,000 men (90,000 of them captured) and 1300 guns; the Germans some 240,000 men. Unfortunately for the Germans, these were some of their best men and thus irreplaceable. Gudmundsson, *Stormtroop Tactics,* 168.

23. Ibid., 155-169, 178.

24. For an excellent capsule summary of the *Arditi* see John Farina's website online at http://www.worldwar1.com/itafront/arditi.htm.

25. Hesketh-Prichard, *Sniping in France,* 1, 21.

26. Hesketh-Prichard, *Sniping in France,* 62-63, 100-104, 202. The U.S. Army also used large numbers of these "American Enfields" as the Model 1917, rebarreled for the standard U.S. .30-06 service cartridge.

27. The French did form special assault troops called *grenadiers d'elite* for trench raiding, but these never played a major part in French offensive doctrine; Gudmundsson, *Stormtroop Tactics,* 88. Captain Laffargue has been credited with "inventing" storm troop tactics, and in fact his treatise on the matter, *The Attack in Trench Warfare,* written in late 1915, was widely disseminated in the French Army. The Germans captured copies, translated them, and passed them out to their troops as well. Bruce Gudmundsson, however, reviewed the matter and concluded that Laffargue's book had "little bearing on the question of how and why the German infantry changed its way of fighting" *Stormtroop Tactics,* 193-6.

Chapter 26 – Evaluating the Sharpshooters

1. The epigraphs in this chapter is drawn from "Sharpshooting in Lee's Army," *Confederate Veteran* 3 (1895): 98.

2. Thomas Horner, "Killers, Fillers, and Fodder," *Parameters*, September 1982, 27-34.

3. Alanson A. Haines *History of the Fifteenth Regiment New Jersey Volunteers* (New York: Privately published, 1883), 161.

4. *OR*, Ser. I, XLIII/1: 563.

5. David Cookman, "In Search of the French Grenadiers During the Seven Years War," *Seven Years War Association Journal*, available online at http://www.magweb.com/sample/s7yw/s7y91fr.htm; Gudmundsson, *Stormtroop Tactics*, 87. The German assault battalions also got double rations, "a not inconsiderable privilege in the last two years of the war."

6. Gudmundsson, *Stormtroop Tactics*, 172.

7. Andrew A. Humphreys, *The Virginia Campaign of '64 and '65* (New York: Charles Scribner's Sons, 1883), 33.

Appendix A – Testing the Sharpshooters' Weapons

1. Heth, *A System of Target Practice*, 87.

2. Jac Weller, "Civil War Minié Rifles Prove Quite Accurate," *The American Rifleman*, July 1971, 37-39; and Jac Weller, "Shooting Confederate Infantry Arms," *The American Rifleman*, 3 parts, April-June 1954.

3. Weller, "Civil War Minié Rifles Prove Quite Accurate," *The American Rifleman*, July 1971, 37-39; Edwards, *Civil War Guns*, 220; Wilcox, *Rifles and Rifle Practice*, 212; Adams e-mail message to author, April 21, 2004.

4. Weller, "Shooting Confederate Infantry Arms," *The American Rifleman*, Pt. 3, June 1954, 11-12.

5. Scott Gourley, "United States Marines Antiterrorism Force, Special Weapons and Tactics of This New Elite Brigade," *Popular Mechanics*, January 2003, also available online at http://www.popularmechanics.com/science/defense/1281481.html; U.S. Army FM 23-9 *Rifle Marksmanship M16A1, M16A2/3, M16A4 and M4 Carbine*, Section 7-29, 30; "Designated marksman" *Wikipedia Encyclopedia* http://en.wikipedia.org/wiki/Designated_marksman.

6. Max Popenker, "Modern Sniper Rifles," available online at http://world.guns.ru/sniper/sn00-e.htm; "Army Sniper School: One Shot, One Kill," available online at http://usmilitary.about.com/library/milinfo/blarmysniperschool.htm; "M24 Sniper Weapons System (SWS)," available online at http://usmilitary.about.com/library/milinfo/arfacts/blm24.htm; "M40A1 Sniper Rifle," available online at http://usmilitary.about.com/library/milinfo/marinefacts/blm40.htm.

7. In 1879 a Springfield Armory marksman hit a 6' bull's-eye at 2,500 yards with a specially modified ironsighted .45-70 rifle. The specifics of the gun were similar to the Whitworth: eighty grains of black powder driving a .45 caliber bullet at 1350 fps. The Whitworth's projectile, however, had considerably better aerodynamics. ".45-70 at Two Miles: The Sandy Hook Tests of 1879," W. John Farquharson, *Rifle Magazine*, November/December, 1977. Available online at http://www.researchpress.co.uk/targets/sandyhook.htm.

8. Edwards, *Civil War Guns*, 220.

9. Hesketh-Prichard, *Sniping in France*, 10, 129, 166-7.

10. U.S. Army FM 23-9 Rifle Marksmanship M16A1, M16A2/3, M16A4 and M4 Carbine, Section 7-29, 30; "Designated Marksman Rifle (DMR)," available online at http://www.defensedaily.com/progprof/usmc/4c4d1c169ea86a1f8525627a0077d489.html

Appendix B – Orders Issued by the Confederacy Pertaining to Sharpshooters

Appendix C – The Assault on Fort Stedman: Numbers and organization

1. *OR*, Ser. I, XLVI/1: 388-9; *OR Supp.*, Vol. 46 (Ser. 95): 794-5; William R. Cox, "The Anderson–Ramseur–Cox Brigade," in Clark, ed., *Histories of the Several Regiments and Battalions From North Carolina*, 4:450-1. A letter from a Georgia soldier confirms that Lane's and Thomas's brigades of Wilcox's division spent the night at Petersburg, but were not used. "Private Letter from the Trenches, Forty-fifth Georgia Infantry," in William B. Styple, ed., *Writing and Fighting from the Army of Northern Virginia: A Collection of Soldier Correspondence* (Kearny, NJ: Bell Grove, 2003), 312.

2. Gordon *Reminiscences* 400-407.

3. Jefferson Davis, *The Rise and Fall of the Confederate Government*, 2:652.

4. John Gordon to Gaston Lewis, August 21, 1886, W. G. Lewis papers #23142, Folder 4, SHC.

5. *OR*, Ser. I, XLVI/1: 391; *OR Supp.*, Vol. 46 (Ser. 95): 794-5.

6. Cowper, ed., *Extracts of Letters of Major-Gen'l Bryan Grimes*, 101; James A. Walker, "Gordon's Assault on Fort Stedman, March 25ᵗʰ, 1865: A Brilliant Achievement." *SHSP* 31 (1903): 28; Anderson is identified as the commander of Pegram's sharpshooters in Moffett, "Captain Joseph M. Anderson," *Confederate Veteran* 22 (1912): 425; William A. Day, "Life Among the Bullets," *Confederate Veteran* 29 (1921): 218.

7. Stephens, ed., *Intrepid Warrior*, 535-535.

8. *OR*, Ser. I, XLVI/1: 389, 383. A former soldier of the Thirty-second North Carolina (Grimes's division), Henry London, wrote a postwar account of the battle in which he gave the sharpshooters' numbers as "about 500 men." He does not say whether this was an overall number or just Grimes's division. H. A. London, "Battle of Fort Stedman," *Chatham Record*, March 27, 1912.

9. *OR*, Ser. I, XLVI/1: 391; *OR Supp.*, Vol. 46 (Ser. 95): 794-5; Jefferson Davis, *The Rise and Fall of the Confederate Government*, 2:652; John Gordon to Gaston Lewis, August 21, 1886, W. G. Lewis papers #23142, Folder 4, SHC; Gordon *Reminiscences* 403.

10. Stephens, ed., *Intrepid Warrior*, 534; John Gordon to Gaston Lewis, August 21, 1886, W. G. Lewis papers #23142, Folder 4, SHC.

11. Gordon, *Reminiscences*, 411; Hartranft, "The Recapture of Fort Stedman," *B&L* 4: 586.

12. Kilmer, "Assault and Repulse at Fort Stedman," *Century Magazine* (September 1887): 785-6; Kilmer, "Gordon's Attack on Fort Stedman," *B&L* 4: 581-82; Herek, *These Men Have Seen Hard Service* p. 306-307.

13. Gordon, *Reminiscences*, 409; Walker, "Gordon's Assault on Fort Stedman, *SHSP* 31 (1903): 23; "Fort Stedman's Fall" *Confederate Veteran* 22 (1914): 461.

14. For Gordon's belief in divine intervention at Fort Stedman, see Noah Andre Trudeau, *The Last Citadel: Petersburg, Virginia, June 1864-April 1865* (Boston: Little, Brown, 1991), 354; Gordon, *Reminiscences*, 406.

15. *OR*, Ser. I, XLVI/3: 1341-47. Pickett's division did move to the western end of the Confederate line, where it was overwhelmed a week later at Five Forks.

16. ibid.

17. *OR*, Ser. I, XXXVI/1: 53-4; Stephens, ed., *Intrepid Warrior*, 535-6; Cowper, ed., *Extracts of Letters*, 101; *OR Supp.*, Vol. 46 (Ser. 95): 820, 794-5; Frederick Phisterer, *Statistical Record of the Armies of the United States* (1883. Reprint, Edison, NJ: Castle Books, 2002), 218.

INDEX

A

Abatis, 32-33, 56, 156, 159, 189, 207, 226, 230, 257, 259, 293, 311, 350

Adams, Bill, 335

Afghanistan, snipers in, 333

Aisne offensive, 325

Alabama Infantry, 3rd, 33, 37-39, 44, 59, 66, 81, 88, 95, 99

Alabama Infantry, 5th, xiv, 32-33, 37-39, 42, 47, 49, 56, 64-66, 68, 89, 95, 99, 113, 121, 160, 167-68, 174, 201, 220-21

Alabama Infantry, 6th, 32-33, 37-39, 99, 113, 147, 231

Alabama Infantry, 10th, 299

Alabama Infantry, 11th, 299

Alabama Infantry, 12th, 32-34, 36, 39, 228

Alabama Infantry, 26th, 33, 37-38, 56, 61, 291

Alabama Infantry, 61st, 99

Algeria, French battles in, 14-15, 270

Allen, John, 262

Ambush, by sharpshooters, 287-88, 288 (ill.)

American Revolution, xi, 3, 6-8, 195

Ammunition, .45 cartridge, 315

Ammunition, quantity of used, 178-79, 206, 299-300

Ammunition, resupply of, 136, 156, 178

Ammunition, shortages of, 140, 167, 187, 189, 281

Ammunition, specialized, 276, 276 (ill.), 278, 280, 282

Ammunition supply, Confederate, xii

Amputation, 171

Anderson, Archer, 341-42

Anderson, George, 40

Anderson, Joseph, 230-31, 348

Anderson, Richard, 174, 178, 181, 352

Anderson, Robert, 290

Anderson's brigade (George), 40-41

Anderson's corps (CSA), 135

Anderson's division (Richard), 75, 180-81

Anderson's Station, 130-31

Andrews, John A., 297, 303

Andrews's Sharpshooters, 297

Antietam, Battle of (see also Sharpsburg, Battle of), 40, 206, 283, 297, 308

Antietam Creek, 40

Appling, Daniel, 10

Appomattox Court House, 268

Appomattox River, 224-25, 228, 266-67, 305

Archer's brigade, 285

Arditti (Reparti d'assalto), 326

Arkansas Sharpshooter Battalion, 12th (Rapley's), 30, 292-93

Army of Northern Virginia, xii-xiv, xvi, 21-22, 40, 42-43, 56-57, 131, 141, 148, 207, 224, 252, 255, 259, 267, 276, 286, 290-91, 305, 314, 328, 331; 1st Corps, 135, 138, 144, 228, 286, 351; 2nd Corps, 53, 53 (map), 54-57, 62, 105, 112, 125-26, 138, 148-50, 224, 228, 241, 252, 267-68, 346-49, 352; 3rd Corps, 62, 100, 130, 224, 259, 266, 347; reorganization of, 60-61; retreat of from Pennsylvania, 71, 73-75, 92; size of, 98; Whitworth rifles in, 275-77

Army of Tennessee, 286-87; rifles used by, 276-78; sharpshooters in, xvi, 286-91; Whitworth rifles in, 276-78

Army of the James, 312-13; 18th Corps, 312; 24th Corps, 313; 25th Corps, 313

Army of the Potomac (Confederate), 26

Army of the Potomac (Union), 43, 52-57, 92, 99, 127, 143-44, 296-97, 302, 307, 309, 331; 1st Corps, 62-63, 67; 2nd Corps, 86, 87 (ill.), 100-101, 121, 128, 131, 133, 138, 141, 252, 263-64, 311, 352; 3rd Corps, 62, 75, 87, 91, 298-300, 302; 5th Corps, 75, 104-105, 108, 112, 130-31, 141, 303, 313; 6th Corps, 57, 105, 112, 118, 154, 158, 160-61, 164-65, 172, 252, 254, 257-62, 264, 302, 309-11, 332, 352; 9th Corps, 103, 123, 131-32, 141, 225-26, 249-50, 258, 304, 313-14, 329; 11th Corps, 53-55, 55 (ill.), 62, 64-68; 19th Corps, 158, 172

Army of the Shenandoah, 172; 6th Corps, 172, 175, 179, 182, 191-92, 196, 198-99, 222; 8th Corps, 172, 181, 185, 187, 191, 195; 19th Corps, 172, 182, 184, 192, 195-97

Army of the Valley, 150, 169, 200-201, 207

Army of the West, 291-92

Army of West Virginia, 172

Artillery, xviii, 33-34, 36, 56, 58, 64-65, 68-70, 76, 89, 100, 110, 112, 118-19, 125, 137-39, 142, 147-48, 159, 161, 163, 165, 168, 177, 181, 191, 212, 226, 241-47, 250, 257-58, 265, 331; capture of, 203, 230, 232-33; in World War I, 321-23, 327; inexperienced, 155-56; recovery of, 123-24; Stuart's horse, 84; targeted by sharpshooters, 147-48, 160; Washington, 260

Atlanta campaign, 116, 290-91, 317

Attrition, effects of, 329-30

Aufrollen, 320, 332

Augur, Christopher C., 164

Austerlitz, Battle of, 317

Austria, infantry of, 2, 4, 18, 20

Austro-Hungarian Army, 1, 326

Averell, William, 191

Averell's cavalry, 191

B

Backsight, 17-18

Ball games, 50

Baltimore, Maryland, 151-52, 154-55

Baltimore and Ohio Railroad, 152, 174

Baltimore Pike, 152, 154

Bank's Ford, 57

Barbed wire, 317, 319, 330, 332

Barber, Lorenzo, 298

Barbour Greys, 42

Bard, John, 306

Barlow's division, 139

Barrel whip, 274

Bartlett, Joseph, 111

Bartlett's brigade, 111

Battalion of Embodied Militia, 3rd, 10

Battalions, 3

Battery VIII, 225, 350-51

Battery IX, 225, 237, 239-40, 243, 245-46, 350; attack on, 237-38, 238 (map), 348

Battery X, 224, 226-27, 229-31, 234, 237

Battery XI, 226-27, 230, 232-35, 250

Battery XII, 226, 230, 234, 236, 250

Battery 45, 253, 260

Battle, Cullen A., 37, 39, 81-82, 99, 113, 189, 202-203, 309

Battle's Alabama brigade, 81-84, 87, 95, 99, 112-13, 121-23, 134, 140-41, 155, 160, 162, 168, 173, 181-82, 184-85, 192, 197, 200-201, 206, 309

Battlefield, described, 204-205

Battles, Henry, 260-61

Baux, Charles, 327

Baxter, Henry, 63-66

Baxter's brigade, 63-68

Bayne, Griff, 292

Bayonets, 3, 5-8, 14, 20-21, 69, 139-40, 152, 191, 229, 232, 234, 257, 272-73, 279, 297; used for digging, 246, 263

Beattie, Alexander M., 164, 310

Beauregard, P.G.T., 31

Bee, Barnard, 19

Belcher, Thad, 201

Bell, John S., 293

Belle Grove, 196; mansion, 196

Bemis Heights, 6

Benson, Berry, 101-102, 106, 114, 117, 119, 124-25, 204-206, 219, 253-56, 263, 265-69, 283

Benson, Blackwood, 266-67, 269

Berdan, Hiram, xv, 26, 92, 104, 279, 294-300, 302-306, 315

Bergson, Henri, 319

Berry, Hiram, 57

Berryville, Virginia, 174, 181

Berryville Canyon, 181

Bethesda Church, 146

Biddle, Thomas, 306

Bidwell, Daniel, 164-65, 167-68

Bidwell's brigade, 164-65, 167, 171

Big Black River, 292

Big Sandy Creek, Battle of, 10

Bilby, Joseph, 6

Birney, David, 92, 127, 299, 302

Birney's division, 144, 300

Black troops, 214, 312-13; as sharpshooters, 312-13

Blackford, Eugene, xiv-xv, 31, 42-56, 58-75, 77-86, 92, 94-100, 113, 121, 149-50, 158, 160-61, 167-68, 174, 176, 192, 201, 204, 221, 279-80, 285, 299, 300, 318, 321, 330; assists wounded, 100; commands all Rodes's Confederate sharpshooters, 97, 158; court-martial of, 201; destruction of belongings of, 73; diary of, xv, 73; illness of, 52, 59, 86-87, 174, 201, 231; regimental command by, 121, 174; reinstated in army, 221; wounded, 70

Blackford, Mary, 150

Blackford, Susan Leigh, 150

Blackford, William, 70

Blair, Austin, 304-305

Blair house, 157, 161-62

Blakeslee cartridge box, 280

Blandford, Virginia, 208, 210, 220

Blockade, 273, 276

Bloody Angle (Spotsylvania), 121 (ill.), 122

Bloody Lane (Antietam), 40

Blow guns, 270

Blue Ridge Mountains, 149

Body armor, 170

Boer War, xvi, 316-19, 330

Boers, 316-18, 320, 330-31

Bombproofs, 207

Bone, John, 58-59, 120-21

"Bonnie Blue Flag," 62

Boonsboro, Maryland, 34, 35 (map)

Boonsboro, Battle of (1862) (or South Mountain), 34-36, 36 (map), 37-41

Boughton, John, 237, 239

Bowling Green, Virginia, 128

Boydton Plank Road, 215, 259-60

Braddock's regulars, 195

Bradwell, Gordon, 182, 210-12, 275

Bragg's army, 287

Brank, Ephraim, 11-12

Branscomb, Jim, 59, 65, 88, 95

Breckinridge, John, 250, 287

Breckinridge's division, 150

Bristoe Station, Virginia, 81

Bristoe Station, Battle of (1863), 83, 83 (map), 84-85

British Army, 315-18, 324-26, 331; attitude of toward inventions, 270-71, 319; camouflage tests by, 284

British Pattern 53 Long Rifle-Musket (Enfield), 272

British School of Musketry, 335

British Volunteers, rifles of, 273

Broadbent, William Wallace, 214-15

Brock road, 110, 118

Brooke, John, 139

Brooke's brigade, 139

Brown, Allison L., 152, 154-55

Brown, Hamilton, A., 173-74, 176-77, 179, 184, 187-88, 197-98, 203-204, 227, 230-31, 234-35, 240-41, 249-50, 348

Brown, J.N., 130

Brown, Jerry, 311

Brown's national guard regiments (Allison), 152, 154-55

Bruckmüller, Georg, 323

Brunson, William, 130-31, 263, 266-67

Bryan's Georgia brigade, 142

Buckbee, Ed, 237-39

Buckshot, 298

"Bucktails," Pennsylvania regiment, 37, 280, 305-309

Buell, Augustus, 203

Buford, John, 75

Bugle calls, 47, 49-50, 52-55, 69, 71-72, 74, 80, 96-97, 113, 295, 343

Buglers, 47-49, 70, 80, 84, 304

Buller, Redvers, 317

Bullets, Burton-Minié, 272-73

Bullets, experimental designs, 270, 271 (ill.)

Bullets, large-caliber, xi

Bullets, Medford-Pritchett, 271

Bullets, Minié (see also Minié balls), 271, 271 (ill.)

Bullets, Pritchett, 271, 271 (ill.), 272-73

Bullets, self-sealing, 270

Bullets, small-caliber, xi, 4-5

Bunker Hill, Virginia, 173, 181

Burgess, Thomas, 119

Burgess's Mill, 255

Burnside, Ambrose, 40, 43, 103, 105-106, 123, 131, 141, 225, 250, 297

Burnside's corps, 131, 141, 304

Burton, George, 287

Burton, James, 271

Butler, Benjamin, 312

Butler's corps, 312-13

C

Caesar, 149

Caldwell, J.F.J., 216, 266

California Joe, 298

Calloway, Morgan, 147

Calloway's battery, 147-48

Cambrai, 324-25

Cameron, Simon, 294, 297

Cameron's Station, 174-75

Camouflage, 104, 284, 304, 318, 326, 336

Camouflage tests, British Army, 284

Camp Douglas, 304

Camp life, 79

Camp Stoneman, 157

Campbell's Station, Battle of (1863), 289

Canada, War of 1812 in, 8-10

Canadian Fencibles, 10

Cannoneer, The (Buell), 203

Cantey's brigade, 291

Caporetto, 324

Carabine a tige, 14-15, 17

Carbines, breech-loading, 157; Burnside, 157; Colt, 157; Sharps, 157, 279; Spencer, 157, 178, 196, 204, 281-82

Carlile, Elias H., 310

Carlisle, Pennsylvania, 62

Carney, Edward, 234

Carroll, Samuel "Old Brick Top," 86, 92

Carroll's brigade, 88, 91

Carrus, William, 340-41

Carson, Bob, 231, 249

Carson, Joseph P., 229, 231-33, 235-36, 248-49, 351

Carter, Tom, 182, 197

Carter's artillery, 77, 182, 197-98

Casey, Silas, 32-33

Casey's Redoubt, 32-33

Casualties, 77, 91, 122, 124, 144-46, 155, 158, 169-71, 178-79, 191, 200, 206, 215, 218-20, 249, 252, 254, 287, 299, 301, 308; compared, 206; Confederate at Fort Stedman, 352; in Boer War, 317-18; in World War I, 323

Catherine Furnace, 298

Cavalry, 1-2, 57, 68, 73-75, 82, 82 (ill.), 83-86, 130; charge by, 188, 188 (ill.); Confederate, 152; Custer's, 187-89; defense against, 97; dismounted, 155-57, 192; Early's, 149, 185, 187; Sheridan's, 127-28, 181, 185, 187; Union, 178, 268

Cedar Creek, 174, 193-94

Cedar Creek, Battle of (1864), xviii, 178, 193-94, 194 (ill.), 195, 195 (map), 196-99, 199 (map), 200-202, 233-34; Gordon's attack at, 195, 195 (map)

Cemetery Hill (Gettysburg, Pennsylvania), 67-69

Cemetery Hill (Middletown, Virginia), 196, 196 (map), 197, 202-203

Chadwick, Shelby, 201

Chamberlain, George, 176

Chambersburg, Pennsylvania, burning of, 172

Chancellor's Hill, attack on, 56

Chancellorsville, Battle of (1863), xii, 21, 52-55, 55 (ill.), 56-59, 62, 64, 76, 92, 114, 204, 298, 308

Chancellorsville campaign, 302

Charge, described, 205

Charles Town, Virginia (West Virginia), 174, 175 (map), 180

Charles Town, Battle of (1864), 176-79, 204, 206

Chasseurs, 2, 94 (ill.)

Chasseurs à Pied, 15, 16 (ill.), 18

Chateaugay, Battle of, 10

Chattanooga, Siege of (1863), 287-88

Cheatham, Oscar, 117

Cheatham's division, 287

Chester Gap, 78

Chesterfield bridge, 131, 133, 135 (map)

Chevaux-de-frise, 207, 229, 257, 348

Chewning Farm, 103

Chickamauga, Battle of (1863), 287, 290-91

Chinese Army, 332

Chipman, N.P., 164

Chittenden, Lucius, 161-62, 168-70

Christ, Benjamin, 103-105

Christ's brigade, 103-106

City Point, Virginia, 157, 224, 240, 243, 249, 304-305, 351

Civil War, as a modern war, xi

Civil War, English, 236

Clark, Captain, 164

Cleburne, Patrick, 275, 277, 286, 286 (ill.), 287, 291

Cleburne's division, 278, 286-87, 291

Cline, Walter, 11

Clothing, ragged, 170

Coal miners, 214

Coehorn mortars, 142, 142 (ill.), 226

Cold Harbor, 145-49

Cold Harbor, assault on (1864), 146, 304; wounded at, 146

Cold weather, 89

Colenso, 317

Collier, Sam, 187-89

Collier Redoubt, 185

Color bearers, 102, 106, 110, 177, 182, 234, 245

Colquitt, Alfred, 60

Colquitt's Georgia brigade, 60

Colquitt's salient, 208, 210, 224, 228

Command problems, Union, 164

Communications, battlefield, 318

Comrades de battaille, 15, 95

Confederate Army, reorganization of, 26

Confederate troops, attitude of, 43

Confederates, fear of, 62; previous experience of with firearms, 25; ragged condition of, 249

Congress, Confederate, 290, 339-40

Congress, U.S., 7-8, 10

Conjockta Creek, Battle of, 10

Connecticut Infantry, 12th, 186-87

Connecticut Infantry, 14th, 136, 144

Connecticut Infantry, 27th, 57

Connor's brigade, 193-94

Conscription, in France, 2

Conscripts, in Civil War, 22

Contemptibles, 319

Convalescents, defending Washington, DC, 156-57

Cook and Brother, 273

Cook's Georgia brigade, 164, 167, 179, 185, 202, 220, 229

Cooke, John R., 264-66

Cooke's North Carolina brigade, 252, 263, 265-66

Cooper, Samuel, 339-40

Corcoran Legion, 145

Corinth, Mississippi, 292

Corps of Light Infantry, 7

Corps of Rangers, 6

Corps of Riflemen, 5

Corps of Whitworth Sharpshooters (Cleburne), 286-87, 289

Courts-martial, 201, 297

Cowand, David, 165, 168, 178-79

Cox, William 174, 184, 250

Cox's North Carolina brigade, 134, 136, 138, 144, 174, 184-85, 202, 228, 268, 347

Crater, 214, 228, 234

Crater, Battle of the (1864), 214-15, 215 (ill.), 225, 250, 304, 313

Crawford, Samuel, 112, 132, 141

Crawford's division, 112, 132, 141, 144

Crittenden, Thomas, 132, 134, 141

Crittenden's division, 132-33, 141

Crook, George, 172, 185, 191-92

Crook's corps, 185, 191-93, 194 (ill.), 202

Cross Keys, Battle of (1862), xii

Cuba, 316

Curtin, Andrew, 305-306

Custer, George, 187-88, 200, 268

Custer's cavalry, 200

Custer's Michigan brigade, 187-88

Cutler's division, 141

Cutshaw's artillery, 181

D

Dabney House, 256

Daniel, Junius, 60, 67, 81

Daniel's North Carolina brigade, 60-61, 64, 66, 81, 87, 113

Davidson, D., 275

Davis, Jefferson, 13, 16, 33, 201, 295, 346-47, 350

Davis's brigade, 252

Dearborn, Henry, 8

Dearborn arsenal, 304

Deep Run, 267

DeForest, John, 185-87, 195, 200, 204

DeLand, Charles, V. 106, 304-305

DeLand, Jim, 238

Delaware Infantry, 1st, 136

Delvigne, Henri-Gustave, 14-15, 270; rifle design by, 270, 271 (ill.)

Denison, Andrew, 110

Denison's Maryland brigade, 100-11

Deserters, Confederate, 216, 221, 228-29

Deserters, Union, 211-12

Devil's Den, 308

Devin, Thomas, 196

Devin's cavalry, 196

Dickert, Augustus, 194

Dimmock line, 226, 350

Distance, estimation of, 47, 47 (ill.), 48-49, 93-94, 315, 337-38, 343-445

Ditches, 207, 212, 217, 226, 231-32, 254

Dockery, Thomas, 292

Doherty, James, 234-35

Doles, George, 146

Doles's Georgia brigade, 60-61, 64, 67-68, 84, 113, 119-20, 134, 144, 329

Dominy, Major, 313

Doswell House, 134, 136-37, 137 (map)

Doubleday, Abner, 63

Douglas, Henry Kyd, 168-69

Downing, J.B., 290

Doyle, Arthur Conan, 317

Dragoons, 2nd, 12

Draper, Alonzo, 312

Drills, infantry, 22; sharp-shooter, 96-97

Drunkenness, 67, 76, 134

Dummy, as target, 253

Dunlop, William S., xvi, 46, 93-95, 100, 102, 115-16, 120, 122, 130, 215-20, 222, 253-55, 264-67, 320, 332, 336

Dunn Hill, 226

Dunn house, 236

Dwight, Augustus, 165, 167-68

Dygert, K.S., 303

E

Early, Jubal "Old Jube," 67, 73-74, 149-50, 154-55, 158, 160-61, 164, 168-69, 172-73, 173 (ill.), 174-75, 178, 180-81, 185, 187, 189, 192-93, 197-98, 200-202, 207, 329

Early's army, 149-50, 152, 158, 164, 170, 173, 175, 180-81, 192-93, 196, 198-200

Early's cavalry, 149-50, 155, 192

Early's corps, 150

Early's division, 67-68, 73, 126

Early's raid on Washington, DC, 150-52, 154-72

Earthworks, 207, 316-17

Ector's brigade, 291

Edmonson, Jim, 229

Edwards, Oliver, 258-59, 281

Edwards, William B., 335, 337

Edwards's brigade (Oliver), 258-59

Elan vital, 319

Election of 1864, 172

Elmira prison, 206, 219, 266

Ely, Ralph, 237, 243, 246

Emmitsburg Road, 299

Englehard, James A., 343-45

Entrenchments, Confederate, 133 (ill.)

Eustis's brigade, 112

Evans, Clement, 232, 236, 250-51, 268, 349-50, 352

Evans's division, 227, 234, 250, 267, 349

Evans's Georgia brigade, 182, 236, 251

Ewell, Richard "Baldy," 26, 30-31, 75, 77, 99-101, 103, 105, 126, 340-41

Ewell's corps, 125-26, 138

Experimental Corps of Riflemen, 5

F

Fagan's cavalry division, 293

Fallen Timbers, Battle of, 8

False muzzle, 283

Fear, of Confederates, 62

Featherston's brigade, 290

Felder, Jack, 179

Ferguson, Patrick, 3

Ferraro's division, 214

Field, E.M., 96

Field telephones, 318

Fighter pilots, 328-29

File closers, 22-23, 321

Fillers, 328-30

Fisher, Joseph, 307-308

Fisher's Hill, 172, 174, 189, 193

Fisher's Hill, Battle of (1864), 190, 190 (map), 191-92, 201-202, 310-11, 329

Fisk, Henry, 259-60

Fisk, Wilbur, 179-80

Fitzpatrick, Marion, 94-95, 124, 130

Five Forks, 256

Flags, regimental, 102-103, 106, 110, 113, 182, 189, 233-35, 249, 256, 307

Flamethrowers, 321, 323, 330-31

Flank Battalion, 10

Fleming, C.K., 310

Flemming, Wood, 230, 349

Flint's Hill, 189, 191, 202

Flooding, 141

Florida, military action in, 8

Flying column, 302

Fodder, 328-29

Food, 70-72, 108, 114-15, 125, 128; lack of, 89, 268

Foraging, 70, 72, 128, 268

Forsyth, Benjamin, 8-10

Fort Alexander, 261-62

Fort Davis, 261-63

Fort Delaware, 88

Fort DeRussy, 156, 159, 162, 164

Fort Erie, Battle of, 10

Fort Friend, 226, 239-41, 251, 350-51

Fort George, Battle of, 9

Fort Gregg, 260-61, 267

Fort Haskell, 226, 234-37, 240, 243-44, 244 (map), 245-46, 248, 251, 349-51; attack on, 243-45

Fort McAlister, 290

Fort McGilvery, 225, 235, 245-46, 350

Fort McGraw, 261

Fort Meigs, siege of, 11

Fort Morton, 311

Fort Owen, 260-61

Fort Slocum, 156, 161, 165

Fort Stedman, 224-37, 239-47, 249-50

Fort Stedman, attack on (1865), 225 (map), 228-33, 233 (map), 234-35, 239 (map), 241, 242 (map), 247 (map), 251-52, 305, 313, 321, 332, 346-50; number of Confederate attackers at, 346-52

Fort Stevens, 156-59, 159 (map), 160, 160 (ill.), 161-65, 166 (map)

Fort Stevens, Battle of (1864), 156-68, 169 (ill.), 170-71, 178, 190, 204, 206, 250, 258, 310

Fort Wagner, 277

Fort Whitworth, 260, 267

Fortifications, xiii, 114, 134, 141, 143, 155-56, 158, 161, 193, 207

Fox House, 136-38

Fraises, 207, 226, 230-31

France, infantry of, 2-3, 14; military theories in, 14-20

Franco-Prussian War, 319

Franctireur, 2

Franklin, Tennessee, 290

Fraser, Simon, 6

Frazee, John, 157

Frederick, Maryland, 151

Frederick the Great, 1, 320

Fredericksburg, Virginia, 44-45, 52, 125, 302

Fredericksburg, Battle of (1862), 43-47, 103, 146

Fredriksen, John, 8

French, William "Old Blinky," 40-41, 75-78, 92

French Army, 327; attitude of toward inventions, 270-71

Friend House, 240

Front Royal, Virginia, 174

G

Gaede, Hans, 321

Gaines's Mill, Battle of (1862), 33-36

Galway, Thomas, 86, 88-89, 91

Garnett, James, 179

Gay, John, 232

Gayle, Bristor B., 31, 33-35, 39-40, 331; death of, 39

Gayle, L., 35

Georgetown Pike, 152

Georgia Battalion, 2nd, 75

Georgia Infantry, 3rd, 75

Georgia Infantry, 4th, 60, 119, 179

Georgia Infantry, 10th, 289

Georgia Infantry, 12th, 60

Georgia Infantry, 13th, 232, 349

Georgia Infantry, 21st, 60

Georgia Infantry, 22nd, 75

Georgia Infantry, 23rd, 298

Georgia Infantry, 26th, 275-76

Georgia Infantry, 31st, 232, 235, 349

Georgia Infantry, 44th, 60

Georgia Infantry, 45th, 94

Georgia Infantry, 48th, 75

Georgia Sharpshooters, 1st Battalion, 290

Georgia Sharpshooters, 2nd Battalion, 290

Georgia Sharpshooters, 3rd Battalion, 51, 61, 95

Georgia Sharpshooters, 4th Battalion, 290

German Army, 319-26, 329, 331

German immigrants, as Union soldiers, 53-55, 64, 88

German states, infantry of, 3, 5

German War Ministry, 321-22

Germans, study of Boer tactics by, 318-20

Germany, Nazi, 332

Getty, George, 158, 164, 176-77, 191, 196-97, 202-203, 257-58, 310-11

Getty's division, 158, 164, 175, 190, 196-97, 219, 254, 257-60, 310

Gettysburg, Pennsylvania, 62, 67, 69, 69 (ill.), 70-71

Gettysburg, Battle of (1863), xii, 62-63, 63 (map), 64-71, 76, 92-93, 97, 114, 277, 300, 308; 1st day, 62-68; 2nd day, 68-69, 299; 3rd day, 69-71

Gettysburg National Military Park museum, 280

Ghillie suits, 326

Gibbon, John, 136, 139, 144

Gibbon's division, 136, 138-39, 144

Gile, George, 159

Gillium, Captain, 17

Gist, States Rights, 290

Gist's brigade, 290

Glengarry Light Infantry Fencibles, 9

Goode's bridge, 267

Gordon, John, 32, 37-39, 126, 154, 181-82, 185-86, 193, 195,

198, 224-27, 227 (ill.), 228-31, 235-37, 239-41, 243, 246-47, 249-52, 257, 268, 346-52; as tactical innovator, 251, 332; attack by at Cedar Creek, 195

Gordon family, 52, 59

Gordon's corps, 193, 194 (ill.), 195, 195 (map), 267

Gordon's division, 126, 150, 154, 182, 184-89, 198-99, 201-202

Gordon's flank march, 193, 195, 201

Gordon's Georgia brigade, 67, 272-73

Gorgas, Josiah, 272, 276, 286

Goss, Captain, 313

Grace, Charles, 91, 119

Gracie, Archibald, 27

Gracie's salient, 224, 228, 230

Gracie's Special Battalion, 26-27

Grandmaison, Louzeau de, 319

Grant, Lewis, 176, 180, 258, 310

Grant, Ulysses S., 98, 100, 102-103, 105, 107-108, 121, 123, 125-26, 128, 130-31, 138, 141-43, 146, 148, 150-51, 157, 172, 207, 215, 249, 252, 256, 267, 300, 318, 331, 347, 352

Great Britain, infantry of, 3-5, 10

Great Mutiny, 17

Green, Henry, 288

Green, Martin, 293

Green's brigade (Martin), 293

Greene, William, 129, 141-42

Greener, William, 270-71

Gregg, J. Irvin, 83

Grenadiers, 2 (ill.), 3, 10, 12, 30, 330, 332

Grenzers, 1-2, 316

Grimes, Bryan, 136, 141, 165, 177, 192, 196-97, 201-203, 234-35, 240, 250, 268, 348, 352

Grimes's division, 228, 234-35, 239-40, 268, 347, 349

Grimes's North Carolina brigade, 134, 138, 140-41, 144, 157, 160, 165, 168, 192, 196-98, 200

Guard duty, 80-81

Guard Rifle Battalion, 320

Gudmundsson, Bruce, 320, 325-26

Guerilla warfare, 2, 318

Gwyn, Billy, 210-11, 235, 249

H

Hagerstown, Maryland, 73

Haley, John, 76, 78, 116

Hall, Andrew, 304

Hall, Josephus, 121

Hall's Independent Sharpshooters (Andrew), 304-305

Halleck, Henry, 158, 297

Halltown, Virginia, 180

Halsey, D.P., 342-43

Hamblin, Joseph, 259-61

Hamblin's brigade, 259-60

Hamilton's Crossing, 52, 61

Hamilton-Smith, Charles, 284

Hancock, Winfield, 100, 103, 131, 133, 135-36, 138, 140-41, 144, 174

Hancock's corps, 100, 105, 123, 125, 131, 133-34, 136, 138, 141

Hand grenades, 321, 330-32

Hanover Junction, 130-31, 134, 136

Hardee, William J., 15-16, 17 (ill.), 295

Hardy, John, 237

Hare's Hill, 225-26, 346-47

Harper, John, 260

Harpers Ferry, Virginia (West Virginia), 34, 150-51, 172-74, 180

Harpers Ferry Arsenal, 8

Harris, Fergus S., 262, 277

Harris Farm, 125-26

Harris's Mississippi brigade, 106, 122

Harrisburg, Pennsylvania, 62

Harrison, William Henry, 8

Harrison Creek, 240

Hartranft, John, 226, 240-43, 243 (ill.), 246-51

Haskell, William T., 51, 61, 93, 267

Hastings, George, 298

Hatcher's Run, 261, 263

Hatchie Bridge, 292

Hayes's brigade, 70

Hays, Alexander, 86

Hays's division, 86, 88, 92

Head logs, 207

Heavy artillerymen, as infantry, 125-26

Henagan, John W., 108, 128

Henagan's brigade, 128

Henagan's Redoubt, 128-30, 144, 289

Herring, Marcus, 149, 184

Hesketh-Pritchard, Hesketh, 284, 326-27, 338

Hessians, 3-4

Heth, Henry, 16, 17 (ill.), 19, 62, 263-64, 267, 334

Heth's division, 62-63, 100, 263-64, 347

Higgerson place, 104

Hill, A.P., 55, 130, 141, 144, 213, 219, 252, 264; death of, 259

Hill's (A.P.) corps, 62, 85, 100-102, 105-106, 130, 224, 252, 351

Hill's (A.P.) division, 94, 141, 144

Hill, D.H., 32, 35-36, 45, 49, 331; transfer of to North Carolina, 49

Hill's (D.H.) division, 31-34, 39, 43, 59

Hill, R.L., 139

Hindenburg Line, 324

Hobson, Edwin, 37, 45, 201

Hog snout salient, 131, 135

Holcombe Legion, 347

Holmes, Oliver Wendell, 163

Homan, Conrad, 234

Hood, John Bell, 290

Hood's Texas brigade, 51

Hooker, Joseph, 52, 57, 298, 302

Horner, Thomas, 328-29

Hospital rats, 150, 155-56

Hospitals, 45, 171

Hotchkiss, Jed, 178

Hough, Sylvester, 236

Houghton, Charles, 236-37, 244

House, Lieutenant, 259

Houses, destruction of, 161, 163-65, 167, 253

Howe, William, 3

Hunter, David "Black Dave," 149-50, 172

Hupp's Hill, 193

Huse, Caleb, 273

Hyde's brigade, 254

I

Ide, John, 296

Illinois Infantry, 66th, 282

Illustrated London News, 288

Indiana Infantry, 14th, 86

Indians, 6, 193-94; as sharpshooters, 104-106, 238, 304; campaigns against, 8, 12-14, 19; in Union army, 104-106

Infanterie léger, 2

Infantry, 10th, 18-19

Infantry, in line of battle, 22, 22 (ill.); light, xii-xiv, xvi-xvii, 1-3, 5-7, 10, 12-13, 15, 18-19, 26-27, 104, 115, 127, 143-44, 222, 290, 294-95, 302, 305-309, 314, 328, 331-333, 336, 340-41; light, defined, xii; line, 3, 5-6, 10, 13, 26, 30, 98, 114; tactics of, 1-2, 2 (ill.), 3-5, 12, 22

Iraq, snipers in, 333

Irish immigrants, as Union soldiers, 140

Irsch, Francis, 64, 66-68

Irvin, Edward, 307

Italian Army, 326

Italian campaign, by France, 20

Iverson, Alfred, xii, 60, 65-66, 342-43

Iverson's North Carolina brigade, 60-61, 64-66, 68, 87, 329, 342-43

J

Jackass, captured, 59

Jacklin, R. William, 313

Jackson, Andrew, 11

Jackson, Thomas J. "Stonewall," xii, 26, 33-34, 40, 43, 52-54, 54 (ill.), 55, 200, 202, 298, 331; wounding of, 55

Jackson's 2nd Corps, 200; flanking march by, 53, 53 (map), 54, 56

Jägers, 1-5, 18, 320, 322-24

James River, 148

Jardine, George, 303

Jeffersonton, Virginia, 82-83, 96

Jenkins, Micah, 26

Jericho Mills, 130-31, 138, 144

Jerusalem Plank Road, 208

Johannesburg, South Africa, 318

Johnson, Bradley, 152

Johnson, Bushrod, 224

Johnson, Edward, 87, 99, 121

Johnson's cavalry (Bradley), 152, 155

Johnson's division (Bushrod), 224, 346

Johnson's division (Edward), 87, 99, 121-22

Johnston, Joseph, 33, 116, 224; surrender by, 269, 290

Johnston, Robert D., 87, 221

Johnston's army (Joseph), 224

Johnston's North Carolina brigade (Robert), 87-88, 221, 228, 347

Jokes, 211, 256-57, 300

Jomini, Antoine Henri, xiii

Jones, Colonel, 250

Jones, Edward, 240

Jones, Hilary Pollard, 348

Jones, John, 99

Jones, Robert, 33

Jones House, 253

Jones's Farm, 253, 257

Jones's Virginia brigade (John), 99-100

Jonesboro, Battle of (1864), 290

Jug bridge, 152, 154-55

K

Kabyles, Berber, 14

Kaigler, William, 232, 268, 349

Kaiser Wilhelm II, 324

Kaiserschlacht offensive, 325

Kane, Thomas, 305-306

Kane's Rifles, 305-306

Keele, Joseph, 140

Keitt, Lawrence, 145

Keitt's regiment, 145

Keller, Benjamin, 174

Kentucky brigade, 278

Kentucky Infantry, 4th, 287

Kentucky "Orphan" brigade, sharpshooters in, 287, 290

Kernstown, 172

Kershaw, Joseph, 95, 108, 181, 193, 198

Kershaw's brigade, 95, 108, 110, 115, 120, 128, 145, 193

Kershaw's division, 174, 181, 193,. 199-200

Kidd, James, 188

Kiefer, Warren, 182

Kiefer's brigade, 182

Killers, 328-29

Kilmer, George, 237, 244-45, 248, 350

Kimberly, 317-18

Kimbrough, J.S. 258, 261, 267

Kirby Smith, Edmund, 293

Kirk, Elijah, 11

Kolin, Battle of (1757), 1

Kommandos, 316

Korea, 328, 332

Krick, Robert K., xvi, 203; fore-word by, xi-xiv

L

Ladysmith, 317-18

Laffargue, Andre, 327

Laird, James, 171

Lamb, Jacob, 191

Lane, James H., 123, 213

Lane's North Carolina brigade, 61, 95, 101, 123, 215, 259, 261

Lang, David, 155

Lang's mounted infantry, 155-57

Larey, P.H., 231

Laughton, John E., 132

Laurel Hill, 108, 111 (ill.), 112

Laurel Hill, Battle of (1864), 108-109, 109 (map), 110-12

Law, Evander, 134, 139

Law's Alabama brigade, 134, 139, 144

Lay house, 162, 164-65, 168

Ledlie, James, 133-34, 144, 214, 225, 250

Ledlie's brigade, 133, 140, 144

Ledlie's division, 214, 225

Lee, Fitzhugh, 108, 174, 178, 181, 256

Lee, Robert E., xii, 33-34, 40, 53, 56, 58, 60, 73, 75, 78, 81-82, 85-86, 91, 93, 95-96, 101-102, 106-108, 121-26, 130-31, 134, 138-39, 141-43, 146, 172, 193, 213, 221, 224, 228, 250, 252, 255, 260, 263, 267, 299, 331, 348, 350-51; illness of, 141; sharpshooter order by, 93, 95; surrender by, 144, 268, 348

Lee's cavalry (Fitzhugh), 108, 174

Leib, Edward, 152, 154

Leib's cavalry, 152

Leon, Louis, 60-61, 105

Lewis, Gaston, 250, 346-47, 350-51

Lewis's brigade, 246, 348-49

Libby Prison, 125, 217

Lincoln, Abraham, 86, 150, 162-63, 163 (ill.), 169, 249, 294-95; under fire at Fort Stevens, 163-64, 250

Lincoln, Mary, 162

Lincoln, Robert, 249

Line of battle, loosening of, 204-205, 205 (ill.)

Link, Charles, 70

Little North Mountain, 191

Little Round Top, 299

Locke, Fred, 313

Locust Grove, 86-87, 87 (ill.)

London Armoury Company, 278

Longstreet, James, 34, 39, 101-103, 105, 286, 299

Longstreet's corps, 75, 101-102, 105, 267, 286, 288, 288 (ill.), 289, 351

Loopholes, 210

Loring's division, 290

Louisiana brigade, 228

Louisiana Infantry, 2nd, 232

Louisiana Infantry, 10th, 232

Lowe, John, 182, 232, 349

Lowery's brigade, 291

Lucas, George, 332

Ludendorff, Erich von, 324-25

Luray Valley, 78

Lyman, Theodore, 24-25, 147

Lynchburg, Virginia, 149-50

Lys offensive, 325

Lytle, William, 287

M

McCausland, "Tiger John," 176

McCausland's cavalry, 176

McClellan, George, 26-27, 33-35, 40, 297, 306, 331

McComb, William, 262-63

McComb's Tennessee brigade, 262-63

McCook, Alexander, 163-64

MacDonnell, "Red George," 9

McElwee, William, 287-88

MacGill, Dr., expulsion of from Hagerstown, 73

McGill, William, 285

McGowan, Samuel, 102, 122, 253-54, 256, 266-67, 269

McGowan's South Carolina brigade, 51, 61, 93, 95, 100-102, 122, 124, 130, 215, 223, 255-56, 263-64, 267

McIlwaine's Hill, 253-54

McIlwaine's Hill, attack on, 254-55, 255 (map), 332

McKeen's brigade, 144

McKnight, James, xviii, 197

McKnight's battery, xviii, 197, 203

McLaughlen, Napoleon, 234-36, 248, 348

McLaw's division, 56-57

McLean farm, 65-66

McMahon, Martin, 118-19

McNeil, Hugh, 306-308

McPherson's Ridge, 63

McRae, William, 264

McRae's brigade, 252, 263-64, 285

Machine guns, 319, 321-23, 326, 330-31, 336; Lewis, 323; Maxim, 321; MG 08, 323; MG 08/15, 323

Madill, Henry, 264

Madill's New York brigade, 264, 266

Magersfontein, 317

Maginot Line, 327

Magruder, John, 26-28

Mahan, Alfred Thayer, xi

Mahone's brigade, 95, 120, 131-32, 141, 214, 273

Mahr, Theodore, 203

Maine Infantry, 3rd, 299

Maine Infantry, 7th, 165

Maine Infantry, 16th, 67

Maine Infantry, 17th, 76, 116

Maine Infantry, 19th, 136-37, 144

Maine Sharpshooters, 1st Battalion, 303

Maine Veteran Volunteers, 1st, 219

Maisel, Butch, xv

Malvern Hill, Battle of (1862), 42

Manassas, 1st Battle of (1861), 31, 297

Manassas, 2nd Battle of (1862), 306

Manassas Gap, 75

Manassas Gap, Battle of (1863), 75, 75 (map), 76-78

Maney's brigade, 287

Manson, Henry, 262-63

Maps, confusing, 127

Marines, U.S., 336

Marksman, designated (DM), 331, 333, 336

Marksmanship competitions, 49, 309-10, 334

Marksmanship training, 15, 48-49, 93-94, 94 (ill.), 95, 97-98, 286-87, 304, 306, 321, 323, 344-45

Marne offensive, 325

Marshall, E.G., 313

Marston, Gilman, 313

Martinsburg, Virginia, 181

Marye's Heights, 43-44, 302

Maryland Infantry, 2nd Battalion, 285

Maryland Infantry, 3rd, 313

Maryland Infantry, 6th, 190-91

Maryland Infantry, 7th, 110

Massachusetts Battery, 11th, 240

Massachusetts Infantry, 19th, 140, 144

Massachusetts Infantry, 29th, 233-36

Massachusetts Infantry, 35th, 133-34

Massachusetts Infantry, 37th, 222, 258, 281, 311

Massachusetts Infantry, 56th, 134

Massachusetts Infantry, 57th, 134, 233-36, 239-41, 302-303

Massachusetts Infantry, 59th, 134, 234, 236

Massachusetts Volunteer Sharpshooters, 297

Massanutten Mountain, 174, 193

Maxims of War (Napoleon), xiii

Meade, George, 37, 75, 81, 85-86, 91, 112, 299, 308

Meade's division, 37

Meade's Station, 226, 240, 246

Mears, Fredrick, 295

Mechanicsville, Battle of (1862), 33

Meermans, Peter, 88

Meigs, Montgomery C., 164

Methuen, Paul, 317

Mexican War, 12-14

Michigan Cavalry, 6th, 188

Michigan Infantry, 2nd, 237

Michigan Infantry, 5th, 309

Michigan Infantry, 16th, 303, 313

Michigan Infantry, 17th, 239-41

Michigan Infantry, 20th, 239

Michigan Infantry, 27th, 303

Michigan sharpshooters, 303-305

Middletown, Virginia, 196, 196 (map), 197-98, 201-203

Miles, Nelson, 135-36, 264-66, 312

Miles's brigade, 135, 138

Miles's division, 264, 311

Militia, 11

Miller, Henry, 38

Miller, Theodore, 247-48

Miller's Mill, 198

Milliken, Charles A., 258, 260-61

Milling, Jim, 110-11, 128-29, 194, 198, 289

Mimic War, 173

Mine (explosive), 214, 313

Mine Run, 89, 99, 300; retreat from, 91

Mine Run Campaign (1863), 85 (map), 86-90, 90 (ill.), 91-92

Minié, Claude, 20, 271

Minié balls, xi, 20, 271, 271 (ill.), 272-73; described, 271

Ministry of War (France), 15

Minnich, J.W., 289

Minutes of Angle (MOA), 336-37

Mississippi Infantry, 2nd, 252

Mississippi Infantry, 9th, 290

Mississippi Infantry, 10th, 290

Mississippi Infantry, 12th, 32

Mississippi Infantry, 38th, 291

Mississippi Infantry, 41st, 290

Mississippi Infantry, 43rd, 291

Mississippi Rifles, 1st, 13

Mississippi Sharpshooters, 1st Battalion, 290-91

Mississippi Sharpshooters, Pound's Battalion, 291

Modder River, 317

Monier, Henry, 232

Monocacy, Battle of (1864), 153 (map), 154-55, 168, 171

Monocacy Junction, 151

Monocacy River, 152, 154

Mons, 319

Montebello, Battle of, 20

Montgomery, William, 50-51, 56-57, 61, 91

Moore, Alpheus, 196

Moore's cavalry, 196

Morale, Confederate, decline of, 73

Morgan, Daniel, 6

Morgan, John, 304

Morgan, Ludowick, 10

Morgan's raiders (John), 104, 304

Mormons, 19

Morris, William, 118-19

Morse, William, 219-20

Morton's Ford, 80-81, 86

Mule shoe (Spotsylvania), 120-24

Mules, 302

Munroe, Robert, 190

Murphy, Timothy, 6

Musgrave, Thomas, 3

Musicians, 43-44, 47-49, 62

Muskets, 3-4; rifled, xi-xiii; smoothbore, 3-4, 6, 8, 10, 14-15, 17-18, 20-21, 27, 48, 98, 157, 271, 306

Myers, Porter, 37

N

Napoleon Bonaparte, xii-xiii, 49, 319

Napoleon III, 19-20

Napoleonic Wars, xvi, 3, 5, 17, 22

Nashville, Tennessee, 290

Nashville, Battle of (1864), 290

Nashville campaign, 290

National Road, 152

New Jersey Infantry, 9th, 302

New Jersey Infantry, 12th, 136, 144

New Jersey Infantry, 15th, 309-10

New Orleans, Battle of (1815), 11-12

New York Battery, 19th, 230

New York Cavalry, 25th, 157-58, 164

New York Heavy Artillery, 5th, 194-95

New York Heavy Artillery, 14th, 226, 230, 236-37

New York Infantry, 5th, 280

New York Infantry, 43rd, 165, 167-68, 258, 310

New York Infantry, 45th, 64, 66, 70

New York Infantry, 49th, 165, 171, 258

New York Infantry, 65th, 259-60

New York Infantry, 69th, 312

New York Infantry, 108th, 136

New York Infantry, 111th, 312

New York Infantry, 118th, 313

New York Infantry, 122nd, 165, 167, 171

New York Infantry, 152nd, 139, 145

New York Infantry, 170th, 138-40, 145

New York Infantry, 182nd, 139, 145

New York Sharpshooters, 1st Battalion, 303

New York troops, xii

Nichols, G.W., 184

Nicholson, William, 123, 212

Norris, Arch, 262

North, Belas, 167

North Anna River, 126, 128, 129 (map), 130-33, 135 (map), 138, 141, 289

North Anna River, Battles at (1864), 128-45, 168, 179, 204

North Carolina, 49

North Carolina Battalion (Sharp-shooters), 1st, 30

North Carolina Infantry, 1st, 173-74, 184, 203

North Carolina Infantry, 2nd, 187, 197

North Carolina Infantry, 4th, 87, 105

North Carolina Infantry, 6th, 248

North Carolina Infantry, 14th, 106, 138

North Carolina Infantry, 18th, 212

North Carolina Infantry, 23rd, 341-42

North Carolina Infantry, 24th, 346

North Carolina Infantry, 25th, 346

North Carolina Infantry, 32nd, 178, 197

North Carolina Infantry, 35th, 346

North Carolina Infantry, 37th, 123

North Carolina Infantry, 43rd, 138, 165, 167, 171, 177, 197

North Carolina Infantry, 45th, 165, 197, 220, 230

North Carolina Infantry, 48th, 252

North Carolina Infantry, 49th, 346

North Carolina Infantry, 53rd, 104-105, 138, 165, 171, 197

North Carolina Infantry, 56th, 246, 346-47

North Carolina Infantry, 57th, 246

North Carolina troops, xii

Norton, John, 270

Noyon-Montdidier offensive, 325

Nugent, Robert, 264

Nugent's brigade, 264, 266

Nye, Ephraim, 230

O

Oak Hill, 64, 64 (map), 65, 70, 299-300, 329

Oak Ridge, 63, 68, 72

Official Records, 313

Ogdensburg, Battle of, 9

Ohio Infantry, 4th, 86, 139, 144

Ohio Infantry, 8th, 86, 88-89, 91-92, 139, 144

Ohio Infantry, 61st, 65

Ohio Infantry, 126th, 190

Ohio National Guard, 168

Ohio National Guard, 144th, 152, 155

Ohio National Guard, 149th, 152, 154-55

Ohio National Guard, 150th, 156-57

Ohio National Guard, 159th, 152

Ojibwa (Chippewa) Indians, 304

Old Cold Harbor, 145

O'Neal, Edward, 38, 54, 61, 65-66, 68, 76, 78, 81, 291

O'Neal's brigade, 64-68, 76-77, 329

Open order, 319-20

Opequon Creek, 174, 181, 185

Orange Court House, 79-80, 97

Orange Plank Road, 100-101, 103, 105

Orange Turnpike, 99

Orleans, Duc d', 15

Osborne, Edwin, 105

Ottawa Indians, 304

Overland Campaign (1864), 99-105, 116, 147, 300, 304, 309

Owens's brigade, 144-45

Ox Ford, 130-34, 138, 142-44, 214, 225

P

Packett family, 177-78

Packett house, 177-78

Pakenham, Edward, 11-12

Pamunkey River, 144

Panzer division, 326

Parapets, 226

Park, Robert, 31, 33-39, 155, 162-63, 168, 180-82

Parke, General, 249

Parker's Store, 103, 105

Parrott rifle (artillery), 156, 160 (ill.), 191

Patrols, 222

Patton, George S., 185, 188

Patton, Jason, xv, 34, 187-88

Patton's division (George), 187

Paul, Gabriel, 66

Paul's brigade, 66-67

Payne, William, 197

Payne's cavalry, 197, 203

Payne's farm, 87

Paysinger, Tom, 115

Peace Offensive, 325

Pegram's division, 203

Pemberton's army, 293

Pender, Dorsey, 61

Pender's division, 61

Pendergrass, Lieutenant Colonel, 350

Peninsular Campaign (1862), 26-28, 296, 306

Peninsular War (French), 71

Pennsylvania, Lee's march into (1863), 62

Pennsylvania Infantry, 42nd "Wildcats" ("Bucktails"), 280, 306-307, 307 (ill.)

Pennsylvania Infantry, 49th, 259, 311

Pennsylvania Infantry, 61st, 167-68, 258

Pennsylvania Infantry, 69th, 140, 145

Pennsylvania Infantry, 74th, 65

Pennsylvania Infantry, 95th, 260

Pennsylvania Infantry, 100th "Roundheads," 236, 248, 350

Pennsylvania Infantry, 102nd, 167

Pennsylvania Infantry, 139th, 190

Pennsylvania Infantry, 145th, 57

Pennsylvania Infantry, 148th, 265, 311, 312 (ill.)

Pennsylvania Infantry, 190th, 309

Pennsylvania Infantry, 191st, 309

Pennsylvania Infantry, 200th, 226, 239-43, 246, 351

Pennsylvania Infantry, 203rd, 302

Pennsylvania Infantry, 205th, 246

Pennsylvania Infantry, 207th, 246

Pennsylvania Infantry, 208th, 243, 246

Pennsylvania Infantry, 209th, 226, 239-40, 243

Pennsylvania Infantry, 211th, 246

Pennsylvania Reserves, 37-40, 112-13, 132, 305-306, 308-309

Pennsylvania Reserves, 1st, 131-32, 308

Pennsylvania Reserves, 5th, 38, 307-308

Pennsylvania Reserves, 6th, 308

Pennsylvania Reserves, 11th, 307

Pennsylvania Reserves, 13th "Bucktails," 37, 280, 305-307, 307 (ill.), 308-309

Pentecost, Joseph H., 236, 350

Perrin, Abner, 61

Perrin's brigade, 122

Petersburg, Virginia, 201, 206, 208, 215, 224, 260-61, 266-68, 300, 305, 347, 352

Petersburg, Siege of (1864-65), 148-50, 172, 207-208, 208 (map), 209, 209 (map), 210-15, 224, 252, 257 (map), 260 (map), 300, 302-305, 310-11, 317, 320, 332, 338

Petite guerre, 1, 127, 207

Phelan, Watkins, 87

Phelps, Charles, 110

Phillips, William, 216-19, 221-23

Phisterer, Frederick, 352

Physical exercise, 50

Pickens, Samuel, 39, 65-66, 98, 220-21

Pickets, xii, 1, 24, 24 (ill.), 25, 43, 57, 90-91, 104-105, 114, 208-16, 218-19, 221-24, 229-

30, 253, 255, 258-59, 310, 312; cavalry, 82 (ill.), 83; Confederate, 26, 50, 61, 82, 252; fraternization between, 89, 91, 116, 142, 220 (ill.), 221, 229; trading between armies by, 89, 91, 116; Union, 50, 124-25

Pickett, George, 256

Pickett's Charge, 71

Pickett's division, 228, 347, 351-52

Pingree, Samuel, 310

Pinkham, Charles, 234

Plexico, Robert, 217

Pioneers, 227, 229-30, 257-58, 310-11, 321-22, 332, 347-49

Piper, John, 106

Pistols, Bergmann MP 18, 324, 331; Colt revolving, 282; Luger, 323-24; machine, 324, 331

Pitzer's Woods, 299

Plattsburg, Battle of, 10

Plenderleath, Charles, 10

Plexico, Robert, 217

Plundering, 116, 126, 162, 172, 198, 219, 234; of dead soldiers, 115

Point Lookout prison, 125, 206, 248-49

Politics, army, 297; effect of on sharpshooters, 295, 297, 303-304

Poor House, county, 128

Port Gibson, 292

Potomac Home Brigade (Maryland militia), 152

Potomac River, crossing of by Confederates, 74-75, 150, 172, 180

Potter, Robert, 105

Potter's division, 105

Potts, John, 110

Potts's North Carolina battery, 110

Pound's Battalion of Mississippi Sharpshooters, 291

Powder, black, 315, 337; smokeless, 315-16, 337

Powell, Ben, 117, 119, 124, 256, 277, 283

Powell, Hugh, 231

Precis de l'Art de la Guerre (Jomini), xiii

Pretoria, 318

Primers, 279

Prisoners, captured for information, 212-13, 219; seine-hauling capture of, 213, 213 (map), 254, 332

Prisoners of war, 34, 38-39, 41, 43-44, 53-54, 56-57, 59, 66-67, 84, 86, 91, 104, 125-26, 138, 142, 198, 205-206, 248-49, 252, 263, 266-67, 304, 310, 312

Proctor, Hence, 230-31

Property, destruction of, 73

Prospect Hill, 43

Provost guard, sharpshooters as, 96

Prussia, infantry of, 4

Pryor, Shepherd G., 60

Q

Quarles's Ford, 130, 132, 134, 141, 144

Quarles's Mill, 132, 134, 141

"Quasi-War" with France, 8

R

Raccoon Ford, 86

Raccoon Mountain, 288

Railroads, cutting of, 260; in World War I, 326

Ramseur, (Stephen) Dodson, 66-67, 105-106, 125, 181-82, 186, 189, 192n, 196, 199-200, 200 (ill.), 202-203; commands Rodes's division, 192n, 196; death of, 199-200

Ramseur's division, 150, 154, 176, 179, 181, 187, 189, 202

Ramseur's (Rodes's) division, 196-99

Ramseur's North Carolina brigade, 56, 61, 66-67, 87, 105-106, 113, 120-22, 237

Ramsey, John, 266

Ramsey's brigade, 266

Randall, George, 230, 232-33, 235, 244-45

Ransom, Robert, 224, 346-47, 352

Ransom's brigade, 227, 237, 246, 346-47, 349

Rapidan River, 86, 99

Rapley, William F., 292

Rappahannock Court House, 82

Rappahannock River, 298; crossing of, 84-85

Rappahannock Station, attack at, 86

Raymer, Nat, 87

Ready, Edward, 37-38

Reconnaissance, xiii, 58, 74, 123, 181, 329

Red Hill, 196-97

Regiment of Fencible Infantry, 10

Regiment of Mounted Riflemen, 13

Regiment of Riflemen, 8-9, 9 (ill.), 10

Regiment of U.S. Voltigeurs and Foot Riflemen, xvi, 12

Reminiscences of the Civil War (Gordon), 346-47

Resaca, Battle of (1864), 287

Revenge, 119-20

Reynolds, John, 63

Rhines, Levant, 305

Richardson, Charles, 234-35

Richmond, Virginia, 224

Richmond, Fredericksburg, and Potomac Railroad, 134

Richmond Howitzers, 137

Ricketts, James, 151

Rickett's division, 151, 154, 186 (ill.), 191-92, 202, 310

Rifle and Light Infantry Tactics (Hardee), 16

Rifle-musket, defined, 272

Rifle pits, 114, 114 (ill.), 118, 120, 134, 136, 138-39, 143, 146, 156, 158, 160, 189-90, 207, 209-10, 212-13, 216-17, 253

Rifle Regiment, 95th (British), 5-6, 8, 11

Riflemen, 3-6, 7, (ill.), 9 (ill.); American, 6-9, 9 (ill.), 10-13; awards to for skill, 19; Confederate, 29 (ill.), 57; frontier, 11; mounted, 12-13; psychological effects of, 4, 27; role of exaggerated, 6; schools for, 16, 18; training for, 19

Rifles, xi, xvii, 3-6, 14, 104, 330; accuracy of, 46, 48, 128, 272-74, 278-79, 282, 334-38, 345; 1st, 10; 4th, 10; advantages of, 141; assault, 331, 333, 336-37;

Austrian, 46; Baker, 5, 8, 11; Beasley, 278; Belgian, 46; breech-loading, 3, 37, 102, 278-79, 295, 299, 315; British Pattern 53 Long Rifle-Musket (Enfield), 272; Burnside, 164; Colt Revolving, 282, 295-96; Confederate purchase of, 273, 275-76; cost of, 276, 280; Daw, 278; effects of, 27, 147-48, 248; Enfield, 17, 20, 46-47, 91, 105, 128, 157, 160, 230, 266, 271-76, 278, 280, 289-90, 315, 331, 334-37; Enfield, choice of Confederate sharpshooters, 272-73; Enfield, described, 272; Enfield, musketoon, 334-35, 337; Enfield, short, 272-73, 282, 334-35; English match, 278; experimental designs, 270-71, 271 (ill.); for sharpshooters, 339-42; globe-sighted, 146, 259, 278, 289; Harpers Ferry, 22; Henry, 204, 278, 282, 304, 336; improvements in, 315-16; Jacob's, 278; *jager*, 5, 8; Kentucky, 6, 8, 11; Kerr, 278, 287, 290; lack of, 21; ladder-sighted, 272, 278; Lancaster, 278; Lee-Enfield .303, 319; Lee-Metford .303, 315; Lee-Metford Mk I, 315; long range, 117; Lorenz, 334-35; M4, 338; M14, 338; M16, 336-38; M16A3, 338; M24, 337; M40A1/A3, 337; Martini-Henry, 315; Mauser, 316, 321, 331; Minnie, 46-47, 340-41; Mississippi, 22, 26, 46, 341; new designs, 14; number in use by Confederates, 272-73, 275-76; Nuthall, 278; P53 (Enfield), 272, 278, 315; Pattern 1914 Enfield, 327; percussion, 13; problems with, 3-4, 6, 274-75, 279, 281-82; range of, 11, 17-18, 20-22, 46-48, 128, 277, 281-83, 334-38; rapid loading of, 98, 271; Remington M700, 337; Remington "Zouave" copy, 335; Rigby, 278; *Scharfschützen Gewehr 98*, 323; Sharps, 37, 48, 102, 104, 141, 204, 222, 262, 278-79, 279 (ill.), 280, 283, 295-98, 303-304, 306-307, 309, 336; Sharps, chosen by skirmishers, 279; Sharps, Confederate-made copies of, 280; Sharps, target, 280; short, 8, 272-73; Short Magazine Lee-Enfield (SMLE), 315-16, 327; sights on, 272, 275, 275 (ill.); skirmisher's choice of, 279; SMLE, 315-16, 327; Snider-Enfield conversion of, 315; sniper (modern), 336-37; Spencer "seven-shooters,"

222, 256, 258-59, 265, 280-81, 281 (ill.), 282, 284, 303, 309, 311, 313, 331, 335-36; Spencer "seven-shooters," loading of, 280; Springfield, 20, 46-47, 273, 273 (ill.), 280-81, 295, 303-304, 309, 315, 334-35; Springfield, described, 273; Springfield .45-70, 315; Squad Designated Marksman, 338; target, 161, 259, 278, 280, 282-83, 283 (ill.), 284, 293, 295-98, 303-304, 311; telescopic-sighted, 117, 123-24, 259, 275-77; tests of, 334-37; Turner, 278; Union, 276, 280-84; Whitworth, 117, 128, 248, 272-77, 283, 286-89, 316, 325, 336-37; Whitworth, Confederate, 274-75; Whitworth, described, 274-75; Whitworth, range of, 277; Winchester manufactured, 327

Rifles and Rifle Practice (Wilcox), 17-18, 93, 291

Riley, Thomas, 201

Ripley, James, 295

Ripley, William, 301

Rise and Fall of the Confederate Government, The (Davis), 346-47

Rives house, 165, 167

Roanoke River, 221, 228, 347

Robertson, Robert, 136

Robertson's Tavern, 86, 87 (ill.), 88 (map), 89

Robinson, Gilbert, 248, 313

Robinson, John (Gen.), 110

Robinson, John C. (Capt.), 258-59, 311

Rodes, Robert E., xiv-xvi, 27, 30 (ill.), 31-33, 36-37, 39-40, 42-43, 45-46, 48-49, 52-56, 58-69, 71-72, 74, 76-78, 80-81, 84-85, 87, 92-93, 97, 105, 113, 137-38, 149-50, 152, 154-55, 157-58, 160, 167-68, 173, 176-77, 179, 181-82, 184, 201, 204, 279, 307-309, 331, 341-42; counterattack at Winchester by, 182, 183 (map), 184-85; death of, 184, 206; sharpshooters organized by, 341-42

Rodes's brigade, 32-33, 35-38, 40-41, 43, 49, 54, 61, 66, 76, 81, 95, 112, 291, 307-309

Rodes's division, 49-50, 52-53, 55-56, 59-64, 68, 71, 73-81, 85, 87, 91, 98-100, 104-105,

125, 134, 136, 144, 148, 150, 152, 155, 157, 168, 173-74, 179, 185-87, 189-90, 192, 196, 206

Roemer, Jacob, 245-46

Rogers, Edward, 230, 232

Rohr, Willy, 320-24, 326-27, 332

Ross, Fitzgerald, 287-88

Roulhac, Thomas, 230, 349

Royal Americans, 60th, 5th Battalion (5/60th) (British), 3-4, 6, 8

Rudulph, Murrie, 27-28

Ruse de guerre, 227, 251, 347

Russell, David, 185

Russell's division, 185

Russian Army, 2, 4, 326, 332

Russo-Japanese War, 319

Rutherford's Farm, 172

S

Sailor's Creek, 267

St. Clair's regulars, 195

Salem Church, 57

Sanders, John, 132

Sanders's Alabama brigade, 132

Santee plantation, 52, 59

Sappers, 332

Saratoga campaign, 6

Saunders Field, 99-100, 106

Scales, Alfred, 61

Scales's North Carolina brigade, 61, 95, 114, 214, 263

Scapegoats, 201

School of Attack, 319

Scientific American, 19-20

Scotland, 317

Scott, Thomas, 168

Scott, Winfield, 16, 294, 297

Scouts, xii-xiii, xvii, 104, 124-25, 327

Sedgwick, John, 118, 118 (ill.), 119

Sedgwick's corps, 57

Semmes, Paul, 56

Semmes's Georgia brigade, 56-57

Seven Days, Battles of (1862), 33-34, 42

Seven Pines, Battle of (1862), 32-33, 42

Seventh Street Pike, 155

Seymour, Truman, 261, 307-308

Seymour's division, 261-62

Shannon, Isaac, 277

Sharps, Christian, xvii

Sharpsburg, Maryland, 35 (map), 39-40

Sharpsburg, Battle of (1862) (see also Antietam), 40-41, 41 (map)

Sharpshooters, 18, 20, 106, 121-23, 126, 146, 294, 301, 329, 331-32, 336-38; accuracy of, 68, 72, 147-48; Alabama 12th, 187-88; Andrews's, 297; Arkansas, 292; Army of Tennessee, 286-88, 288 (ill.), 290; Army of the Potomac 5th Corps, 313; Army of the Potomac 6th Corps, 257; artillery targeted by, 147-48, 160; as demi-brigade, 97; as foot cavalry, 173; as plunderers, 115-16, 219; as provost guard, 96; as rear guard, 71-74; at Battle of Cedar Creek, summarized, 202; at Battle of Fisher's Hill, summarized, 202; at Battle of Gettysburg, summarized, 68; at Battle of Winchester (3rd), summarized, 202; authorizing legislation, 290; Battalion, 15th; Battle's, 88, 91, 95, 137, 139, 155, 173-74, 176, 201, 231; Beattie's, 164, 167; Berdan's, xv, 25-29, 57, 92, 279, 282, 294-95, 296 (ill.), 297-300, 303-304; Berdan's, organization of, 294-95; Birge's, 282; Blackford's, 52-59, 63-71, 73-87, 92-93, 95-96, 99-100, 106, 137, 139, 150, 152, 154, 159, 161, 167, 268, 287, 299-300, 309, 318, 323, 330; Blackford's, organization of, 45-51, 95; Blacks as, 313; Boer, 316-17; Brady's, 303; Brown's, 179, 240-41, 250, 348; Brunson's, 130-31; Bryan's Georgia, 142; "Bucktails," 306-307, 307 (ill.), 308; Cleburne's division, 278, 286-87; Confederate, xv-xvi, xviii, 26, 28-30, 33-34, 45-46, 49, 52, 87, 93-95, 111-17, 117 (ill.), 118-21, 123-24, 127, 131-32, 134, 139, 141, 143-44, 147, 165, 169-71, 173, 178, 189, 192, 201-204, 215-18, 225, 228-30, 245, 250-52, 258-59, 267-68,

300, 314-15, 328-29, 331-32; Confederate, organization of, 29-30, 45-47, 49-51, 59-61, 71, 93-96, 339-45; Confederate and Union compared, 91-92; Cook's Georgia brigade, 229; Corps of (Ramseur's division), xviii; Cox's, 136, 184; Daniel's 81, 87, 91, 104-105; defined, xii-xiii, xviii; Doles's, 91, 120; Dunlop's, 93-94, 119, 215, 217, 219, 253-54, 263-64, 266, 320; Dunlop's, organization of, 93-94; Dygert's, 303; Early's, 189-90; effects of, 147-48, 171; Evans's, 230, 232, 267, 349; female, 142; Georgia, 60-61, 91, 179, 290; Georgia 3rd, 91; Georgia, 31st, 210-11, 235; Getty's, 257-59, 310-11; Gordon's, 174, 182, 198, 233, 235, 250, 348-49; Goss's, 313; Grimes's, 136, 171, 179, 227, 230-31, 239-40, 249, 268, 348-49, 351; Hall's Independent, 304-305; Haskell's, 93; houses as cover for, 161-62; in Shenandoah Valley Campaign (1864), 149; in trench warfare, 207-13, 222; Indians as, 104-106, 238, 304; *jager*, 323; Jardine's, 303; Johnston's, 88; Kaigler's, 268; Kershaw's, 128, 180; Lane's, 123, 212; Law's, 136; Longstreet's corps, 286-88, 288 (ill.), 289; Louisiana, 70, 244; Lovats Scouts, 327; McComb's brigade, 262; McGowan's, 100-102, 124, 130, 216-18, 255-56, 263-64, 267, 277, 285; McRae's, 264, 266, 285; Mahone's, 95-96, 131-33, 148; Maine 1st Battalion, 303; Massachusetts, 297; Massachusetts 57th, 302-303; Michigan 1st, 104-106, 304-305, 350-51; Minnesota 1st, 237-38, 297; Mississippi 1st Battalion, 290-91; Mississippi 9th, 290; New Jersey 15th, 310; New York 1st Battalion, 303; Ohio 8th, 86, 92; O'Neal's, 76; opposition to organization of, 45, 47; orders concerning, 339-45; organized by Van Dorn, 291-92; origins of, xv-xvii; "orphan" brigade, 287, 290; Palmetto, 26, 30; Perrin's, 303; Pound's Battalion, 291; predecessors of, 1-8, 10; problems of, 66, 68-70, 81, 131, 315, 329; raid on Union picket line by, 217, 217 (map), 218-21, 223; Ramseur's, 58-59, 76, 87, 90, 125, 159-60, 176, 179, 197-98; Ramseur's (Rodes's) division,

197, 200; Ransom's, 230, 349; Rapley's, 30, 291-93; rifles for, 47, 272-84, 339-42; Robinson's (Gilbert), 313; Robinson's (John), 259; Rodes's division, 92-93, 125, 134, 136, 149, 152, 154-55, 157-58, 160, 163-64, 173-74, 176, 179, 181, 187, 189, 196-97, 202-204, 206, 291, 309, 331, 341-42; Sanders's, 132-33; Scales's, 114, 215-18, 267; Sherman's, 291; South Carolina, 108, 110, 112; South Carolina Battalion 3rd, 194, 198; Spencer rifles used by, 281, 332; Stuart's, 259-60, 311; successes of, 68, 72, 119-20; tactics of, 28-29, 60-61, 71, 78-79, 96-97, 114-17, 119-20, 123-24, 132, 144, 177, 179-80, 184, 202, 204, 256; Taylor's, 147; Thomas's, 254, 258; training of, 27, 47-50, 60, 65, 93-97, 295, 343-45; Union, 28, 28 (ill.), 29, 45, 70, 74, 92, 96-97, 120-21, 123, 127, 139, 146-48, 211 (ill.), 281, 283-84, 293-94, 296-307, 314, 329; Union, reorganization of, 127; U.S. 1st (1st U.S.S.S.), 76-77, 89, 91-92, 127-28, 136-38, 143-45, 279, 295-303, 309; U.S. 2nd (2nd U.S.S.S.), 76-77, 89, 91-92, 96, 101-102, 121, 127-29, 133, 141-45, 279, 295-98, 300, 302-303, 309; Vermont, 177-78; Vosper's, 303; Waggaman's, 232, 244; Walker's division, 227, 229-31, 248, 348-49; Walthall's, 291; Weinmann's, 312; Weisiger's, 214-15; Wheaton's, 259, 311; Whitworth rifles used by, 117-18, 277, 286-89; Wilcox's division, 94-95; Wofford's Georgia, 56-57; Wooten's, 252, 254; Young's, 120

Sheep, butchering of, 91

Shenandoah River, North Fork of, 189

Shenandoah Valley, 148-49, 193; devastated by Sheridan, 192

Shenandoah Valley Campaign (1862), 26, 202

Shenandoah Valley Campaign (1864), 174-203, 310, 329

Shepherdstown, Virginia, 181

Sheridan, Philip "Little Phil," 145, 172-73, 173 (ill.), 174, 178, 180-81, 185, 191-93, 197-98, 201, 256, 331; counterattack by at Cedar Creek, 198-99, 199 (map)

Sheridan's army, 172, 181, 189, 193, 201-202

Sheridan's cavalry, 145, 197

Shirking, 319

Shock Armies, 332

Shock troops, 321-23, 326

Shutzenfest, 294

Sick list, 50

Sickles, Daniel, 76, 298-99

Sigel's corps, 55

Sights, adjustable ladder rear, 272, 278; telescopic, 117, 123-24, 259, 275, 275 (ill.), 276-77

Signal station, on Massanutten Mountain, 174

Silver Spring, Maryland, 157, 168

Simms, James P., 193-94

Simms's Georgia brigade, 193-94

Skirmishers, xii, xvii-xviii, 1, 3, 5, 7, 13-15, 17-20, 23 (ill.), 24, 27 (ill.), 43, 45, 47, 49, 64, 68-69, 71, 76, 78 (ill.), 104, 106, 111, 140 (ill.), 145, 159-61, 163, 165, 176-77, 206, 222, 240, 264-65, 267, 290, 296, 298, 304, 306, 308, 311, 320, 329-31, 342, 348, 351; Alabama, 113; Confederate, 26, 35-38, 40, 83, 137, 144; described, 179-80; problems of, 23-24; Rodes's, 141; tactics of, 23-24, 36, 41, 58, 96-97, 104; training of, 45, 47, 49, 96-97, 304, 306; Union, 36-38, 86, 96-97, 134, 161

Skirmishes, 74, 88, 114, 141-42, 150, 173

Slaves, freed by soldiers, 128

Slocum, Henry, 57

Smith, Benjamin, 232

Smith, Otis, 38-39

Smith, W. F., 147

Smithfield Crossing, 174

Smoke, on battlefield, 315

Smoothbore Volley that Doomed the Confederacy, The (Krick), xiv

Smyth, Thomas, 136, 138-40, 144; death of, 144

Smyth's brigade, 136, 138-39, 144

Snap Shot, 298

Snicker's Gap, 172,

Snipers, xvii, 4, 284, 287, 323, 326-27, 333, 336-38; training of, 327

Somme, 325-26

Soult, Marshal (French), 71

South Africa, 316-19

South Carolina Infantry, 2nd, 109-10, 145

South Carolina Infantry, 3rd, 95, 108-10, 128

South Carolina Infantry, 8th, 108

South Carolina Infantry, 15th, 146-47

South Carolina Infantry, 17th, 347

South Carolina Infantry, 18th, 347

South Carolina Infantry, 20th, 145

South Carolina Infantry, 22nd, 347

South Carolina Infantry, 23rd, 347

South Carolina Infantry, 26th, 347

South Mountain, 34, 35 (map), 36 (map)

South Mountain, Battle of (or Boonsboro) (1862), 34-36, 36 (map), 37-40, 49, 68, 72, 112-13, 280, 307, 309

South Side Railroad, 260, 263

Spangler's Woods, 299

Spanish-American War, 316

Spindle farm, 108, 110-11, 118, 120, 125

Spinola, Francis, 77

Spinola's New York brigade, 77

Spioenkop, 317

Spivey, Irvin, 275-76

Spotsylvania, 100, 108

Spotsylvania, Battle of (1864), 114, 121, 121 (ill.), 122, 122 (map), 123-24, 127-28, 174, 205, 304, 309, 329

Spotsylvania Court House, 107-108, 111, 113

Sprague, William, 297

Spring Hill, Tennessee, 290

Stahel, Julius, xii

Stanton, Edwin, 297

Star Wars movies, 332

Steuart, George, 351

Stevens, Lieutenant, 143

Stewart, Warren, 131-32

Stewart, William, 5

Stone, Valentine, 245-46

Stone bridge, action at (Jug Bridge) (1864), 151 (map), 152, 154-55

Stonewall brigade, 56

Stony Point, 7

Storm troopers, 323-26, 330-32; training of, 322, 324-25

Stosstruppen, xviii, 321-25, 329-30

Strasbaugh, Barnard, 313

Strasburg, Virginia, 172-74, 189, 193, 196, 200

Stribling, Robert, 227, 233, 242, 246-47, 250

Stuart, James, 259-61, 311

Stuart, Jeb, 55, 57, 70, 84, 108

Stuart's cavalry (Jeb), 84, 108-109

Sturmabteilungen, 321

Sturmbatallion Rohr, 322

Sturmblocks, 325, 332

Suffolk, siege of, 303

Summit Point, 174

Sumner, Edwin, 40-41

Sunken road (Bloody Lane), 40

Sutherland's Station, 263

Sutherland's Station, Battle of (1865), 263-65, 265 (map), 266

Swearing Bob, 298

Sweet, Bill, 299

Sweitzer, Jacob, 125

Sword, Wiley, 299

Swords, Henry, 235

System of Target Practice, A (Heth), 16

T

Tactics (Hardee), 16, 18, 94 (ill.), 223, 295

Tactics, changes in, xi-xiii, xv-xvi, xviii, 16-20, 113-17, 120, 149, 222-23, 250-51, 320-22, 326, 328, 331-32, 337-38

Talley, William, 113, 309

Tanks, 324, 326

Target practice, 48, 94-95, 294-95, 296 (ill.), 343-45

Targets, marksmanship, 334-35, 337

Tate, Jerry, 89, 91, 95-96, 98

Taylor, Thomas, 147

Telegraph, 318; cutting of, 260, 351

Telegraph Road bridge, 128-29

Telescopic sights, 117, 123-24, 259, 275, 275 (ill.), 276-77, 323, 337-38

Tennessee campaign, Hood's, 290

Tennessee Infantry, 1st, 287

Tennessee River, 288

Terrell, Charles, 310-11

Terrell, William H., 258

Terry, William, 236

Terry's Virginia brigade, 236, 251, 349

Texas Rangers, 13

Theories, military, 14-22

Thoburn, Joseph, 181

Thomas, Edward, 130

Thomas, Shade, 256

Thomas's Georgia brigade (Edward), 61, 94, 130, 258, 261

Thouvenin, Louis-Etienne de, 270; rifle design by, 270-71, 271 (ill.)

Thukela Heights, 317

Thurber, Captain, 218

Tidball, John, 142, 241-42

Tige, 270-71

Tippecanoe, Battle of, 8

Tirailleurs, 2, 3, 15

Totopotomoy River, 144

Tourists, on battlefields, 162-63, 169-70

Trading, between armies, 89, 91, 116, 142, 220 (ill.), 221

Trench warfare, 148-49, 207-12, 222, 257, 281, 320, 322-24, 336

Trenches, 146, 148-49, 156, 207-208, 212, 319-21, 331

Trepp, Caspar, 89, 91-92, 127, 297-300; death of, 300

Tripod, 94 (ill.), 95

Trojan Horse companies, 227, 332, 347-51

Troops, rout of, 55, 101-102, 110-11, 140, 154-55, 168, 173, 187-89, 192, 200

Truce, informal, 142, 300, 301 (ill.); to recover casualties, 43, 253

Truex, William 221

Tuerk, Julius, 245

Tumbling Run, 189, 191

Turner, Thomas, 278

Turner's Gap, 34-35, 35 (map), 36 (map), 40, 307-308

Tyler, Erastus, 150, 152, 154-55

Tyler, Richard, 138

Tyler's brigade (Erastus), 150-52, 155

U

Uncle Tom's Cabin (Stowe), 42

Uniforms, British, 284, 323; Confederate sharpshooters, 284-85; German, 284, 321; Union sharpshooters, 295

Union troops, attitudes of, 43, 50

United States, in World War I, 325-26

U.S. Army, 8-10, 35, 333, 336; at beginning of Civil War, 21; conservatism of, 295, 297, 300-302

U.S. Cavalry Regiment, 3rd, 13

U.S. Colored Troops, 312

U.S. Rifle Regiment, xvi, 295

Upton, Emory, 120-21, 185, 331

V

Valley Pike, 185, 189, 193, 196, 198, 203

Van Dorn, Earl, 30, 291-92, 292 (ill.)

Vandalism, 44-45, 67, 70

Vaughn, John, 173

Vaughn's cavalry, 173

Verdun, 320-22, 324

Vermont brigade, 175, 177-79, 206, 221, 253-54, 258, 262, 310

Vermont Infantry, 2nd, 179-80

Vermont Infantry, 3rd, 164, 176, 310

Vermont Infantry, 4th, 176, 310

Vermont Infantry, 6th, 176-78

Vermont Infantry, 11th, 176-78, 310

Vermont troops, 197

Veteran Reserve Corps, 157, 159, 163-64

Vicksburg, Mississippi, 291

Vicksburg, siege of, 293; surrender of, 73, 293

Vicksburg campaign, 290

Viet Cong, 332

Vietnam War, 332

Vietnamese, North, 332

Virginia, 44 (map), 149; abolitionism in, 42

Virginia Central Railroad, 134

Virginia Heavy Artillery, 4th, 32

Virginia Infantry, 21st, 122

Virginia Infantry, 62nd Mounted, 155-57

Virginia Military and Collegiate Institute (Portsmouth), 33

Virginia Military Institute (Lexington), 31

Visscher, James D., 168

Vitalism, 319

Vizetelly, Frank, 288

Voltigeurs, 3, 5, 10

Volunteers, in U.S. Army, 21, 25

Von Hartung, Adolph, 65

Von Hartung's troops, 68

Von Falkenhayn, Erich, 321-22, 324

W

Waggaman, Eugene, 232, 251, 349

Waggaman's Louisiana brigade, 232, 236, 244-45, 349-50

Wainwright, Charles, 112

Walker, Aldace, 176-78

Walker, E.J., 75, 77

Walker, James, 228-30, 248-50, 348-49, 351-52

Walker's division (James), 227, 234, 237, 246, 347, 349

Walker's division, 291

Walkup, Samuel, 252

Wallace, Lew, 151-52, 154-55

Wallace, William H., 145, 347, 352

Wallace's brigade (William), 227, 347, 352

Walthall's brigade, 291

War of 1812, 8-11

Ward, Hobart, 76-77, 92, 298-99

Ward, J.W., 291

Ward's division, 102

Warner's brigade, 190-91

Warren, Gouverneur, 108, 130-32, 141

Warren, Sergeant, 115

Warren's corps (Gouverneur), 87 (ill.), 108, 110, 130-31, 141, 144

Warrenton, Virginia, 84

Warrior Guards, 31

Washington, George, 6-8

Washington, DC, 150-52, 154-56, 156 (map), 157, 160-61, 164, 169, 172, 175; attack on, 155-58, 158 (ill.), 160-65, 167-69, 171

Washington Artillery, 260

Waterloo, Battle of, 317

Watkins, Sam, 287

Waud, Alfred, sketch by, 186 (ill.), 211 (ill.)

Waynesboro, Virginia, 192

Weapons, breech-loading, xi, 3; changes in, xi-xii, 330-31; muzzle-loading, xi, 206; repeating, xi-xii; rifled, xi-xii

Weaver, David, 313

Webb's division, 88

Weinmann, Phillip, 312

Weisiger, David, 214

Weisiger's brigade, 123, 214-15

Weldon Railroad, 310

Weller, Jac, 334-37

Wellesley, Arthur (Duke of Wellington), xiii

Wellington, Duke of, 5

West Virginia, 150

West Virginia infantry, 139

West Virginia Infantry, 7th, 86, 144-45

Wharton, Gabriel, C., 195

Wharton's division, 185-89, 193, 195, 197

Wheaton, Frank, 158, 160, 164-65, 168-70, 218, 258-59, 311

Wheaton's brigade, 165

Wheaton's division, 258-59, 311

Whipple, Amiel, 57

Whiskey, 67

Whitaker, Cary, 165, 167, 171, 177

Whitaker, Oscar, 187-88, 228-29, 249

White, Tom, 293

White, Wyman, 96-97, 101-104, 123-24, 283

White Oak Road, 255-56

Whitener, Benjamin, 115, 129, 198

Whites, U.B., 198

Whitworth, Joseph, 274

Widow Tapp's farm, 105

Wilcox, Cadmus M., 17, 17 (ill.), 18, 93-95, 100-101, 106, 124, 130-31, 291, 299, 335

Wilcox's brigade, 299

Wilcox's division, 94, 100, 124, 130-31, 214, 253, 263, 343-45, 347

Wilderness, The, 53, 55, 86, 99, 106, 108, 113, 304

Wilderness Campaign (1864), xiii, 99-102, 103 (map), 104, 106, 237

Willcox, Orlando, 225, 240-41, 351

Willcox's division, 226

Williams, Jonathan W., 37-39, 49, 113

Williamsburg Pike, 313

Williamsport, Virginia, 181

Wilson, Captain, 143

Winchester, Virginia, 173-74, 181, 185, 187, 189, 196-97

Winchester, Battle of (3rd) (1864), 179, 181-82, 183 (map), 184-86, 186 (ill.), 187, 187 (map), 188 (ill.), 189, 202, 206, 281

Winston, John R., 165, 167, 220

Wisconsin Infantry, 5th, 216, 258, 281, 309, 311

Wise, Henry A., 285

Wittich, Captain, 16-17

Woerner, Christian, 244-45

Wofford, William T., 50-51

Wofford's Georgia brigade, 61, 95

Wofford's Georgia sharpshooters, organization of 50-51, 61

Wolsely, Garnet, xii

Wood's brigade, 291

Wooton, Thomas J., 212-15, 222, 252, 254, 332

World War I, xiii, xvi, xviii, 148, 207, 319-27, 330, 336, 338

World War II, xvi, 316, 326, 328, 332, 336

Worsham, John, 122-23

Wounded, at Cold Harbor, 146; burned to death, 59, 169; help for on battlefield, 100

Wright, Horatio, 160, 163-64, 172, 185, 191-92, 218, 254, 257-59, 311

Wright's Georgia brigade, 75-77

Wynstra, Rob, 341

Y

Yataghan, 272

York, Duke of, 5

Yorktown, 7

Young, John, 95-96, 113-15, 120, 215-16, 219, 222, 254, 267, 316

Ypres, 320, 326

Z

Zoan Church, 52

Zouaves, 15, 16 (ill.), 20, 295; dress of, 15

ABOUT THE AUTHOR

Fred L. Ray is the president and CEO of CFS Press, Inc., and author of several books on flood and swiftwater rescue. He is a U.S. Army veteran who spent most of his time in armored cavalry, during which he served two tours in Vietnam.

While researching the Civil War era as part of a family history project, he found that one of his great-grandfathers, Lieutenant Jason O. Patton, had commanded a Confederate sharpshooter company. This, in turn, led to an investigation of the sharpshooters themselves, and a book on the subject.

CPSIA information can be obtained at www.ICGtesting.com
Printed in the USA
BVOW010905120313

315308BV00003B/6/P

9 780964 958593